A *History of Europe*

A History of Europe

A Cultural and Political Survey

JOHN BOWLE

Secker & Warburg/Heinemann

Martin Secker & Warburg Ltd
54 Poland Street, London WIV 3DS
in association with
William Heinemann Ltd
10 Upper Grosvenor Street, London WIX 9PA

First published 1979
© John Bowle 1979
436 05906 1

Printed in Great Britain by
The Pitman Press, Bath

260920

CONTENTS

List of Maps

Preface

Now that Great Britain has joined a European Economic Community which may lead to closer ties, more of us will need to become familiar with the essentials of European history. In my *The English Experience* and *The Imperial Achievement* I have attempted to survey both our insular and colonialist past; I have now in the third part of a trilogy endeavoured to depict and analyse the record of the European civilization in which we have always participated.

Though some people would wish to do so, we can hardly, in the face of the economic, technological and military facts, revert to insularity after the abdication of empire: and if, after the eclipse of continental Europe and ourselves as world powers, we are threatened by new dangers, the threat demands not intellectual and moral abdication but all the vigour, enrichment and range of mind that we can command.

Far from mechanized neo-barbarism and current attacks on creative minorities making the past irrelevant, it remains more than ever important. If the optimism of liberal historians is over, and European history now appears grimmer than once believed, we still need to draw strength and wisdom from it. European civilization, like that of China, has survived major catastrophes; as, for example, the disastrous collapse of Graeco-Roman Antiquity in the west, the devastations of the Huns and Mongols, the loss of about a third of the population through the Black Death, as well as chronic maladministration, endemic warfare, famine, and disease. From all these disasters Europe has recovered; and with its exceptionally favourable environment and vigorous blend of racial talents, its cultural and economic strength and versatility have been unparalleled.

Unless blotted out by a nuclear holocaust, overrun since it lacks the will to resist, or wrecked internally by a failure of nerve and skill in maintaining coherence and productivity, European civilization, after an astonishing post-war comeback, seems set once more to regain its native vigour.

The revival has come mainly in the West, as part of an Atlantic world sustained by American power; but this survey, while relating the Atlantic peoples to their heirs in the New World, has extended, unlike many existing surveys, right across the board, devoting adequate space to the heirs of Byzantium in Eastern Europe. Two constructive themes are common, and both are cosmopolitan: the gradual improvement of agriculture, commerce and science leading to the Industrial Revolution and the modern population explosion, and the rich variety of art, architecture, music and literature in which each age has created its own idiom and by which it is most directly remembered.

Today Europe cannot return to full vigour, economic or cultural, in terms of absolute nationalism, nor can our own energies, which have made the greatest sea-borne empire in world history, and contributed so much to European politics, science, technology, and literature, be contained in our small island. A new generation already needs to understand continental European history. Sheer ignorance of a past from which the national characteristics familiar today derive, goes far to explain many of the blunders made by the statesmen at Versailles after the Great War, by the "appeasing" British Cabinets in the 'thirties, by Neville Chamberlain who regarded the Czechs as "a far-away people of whom we know nothing", and by the Americans at Yalta and Potsdam.

European history, here considered in what may be thought "conventional" terms, since inevitably based mainly on material left by rulers and literate minorities, does not present a pattern of ordered progress; but it does record the achievements of great artists, architects, musicians and poets, and of the scientists, doctors, inventors and technologists, who, backed or exploited by governments, entrepreneurs, navigators and adventurers, made European civilization the first to have a literally world-wide influence. The blunders and crimes of the more destructive men of action have not entirely thwarted the men of genius and constructive commonsense or the toiling peoples by whom civilization has been sustained. This is the main and heartening moral of European history, and a principal reason for studying it.

Civilization, like consciousness, is rare and precarious. It is a state of mind, nourished, as the ripple of life passes on with each generation, by the accumulated inheritance of genius, organization and hard work; and to survive it must be versatile and adaptable.

The civilization of Europe and North America has been the first to break out of the Malthusian fate of predominantly peasant societies. It still has the knowledge to create plenty as more scientific technology develops, if we do not destroy its capacity to do so. If it is worthy to survive, it will fend off attack and assimilate the fresh vitality of popular aspirations by its own vigour. In facing this challenge, pride and pleasure in our historic European civilization need not come amiss.

In writing this book I have been helped by many friends in Oxford, to whom I can here make only a general though, I hope, acceptable acknowledgement. I would also particularly like to thank my publisher, Mr David Farrer, who has added to his reputation as an outstanding editor by his comprehensive and meticulous revision of the script, and to thank Mr Quentin Davies for his advice on the original plan and upon aspects of economic and Russian history.

I have also to acknowledge permissions accorded for various quotations I have cited in my narrative, and the good work of Mrs Phillips and Mrs Templeton in typing and retyping the manuscript.

John Bowle
Oxford 1978.

Introduction

At the western extremity of Eurasia, thrusting out into the Atlantic in Galicia, the Algarve and Brittany and cut into a deeply indented peninsula by the Mediterranean, the Baltic and the Black Seas, Europe, the smallest of the continents, presents an unusual variety of structure and climate. Within a relatively small area—for even the Western U.S.S.R., though termed part of Europe, is climatically Eurasian—it contains the Atlantic climate of the Western seaboard, tempered, in contrast to similar latitudes in North America, by the Gulf Stream out of the Caribbean; the bitter continental winters and hot summers of central Europe, the Alps and the Balkans; and the mountainous or hilly Mediterranean environment of vine and olive, myrtle and oleander—at its most attractive in Tuscany and Umbria, at its harshest in Spain, and at its most brilliant in the clear light and sharp outlines of the Aegean.

Here and in North Africa Graeco-Roman civilization flourished, protected by the great barriers of the Alps, the Balkan massif and the Sahara; while the earliest European civilizations grew up spontaneously in Crete and the Peloponnese where vine and olive were native and the rudiments of maritime commerce developed. But although civilization came from the south and spread beyond the Alps, the greatest agricultural and mineral potential lay to the north of them, where, mountainous and divided along most of the Mediterranean coasts and hinterland, the country here extended into wide plateaux, undulating plains and low lying coasts.

Of all the European countries, France, facing the Channel, the Atlantic and the Mediterranean, rich in broad fertile valleys and rising in the south-east and south to the Alps and the Pyrenees, has the best balanced resources and most favourable climate, along with potentially the richest agriculture, great coal and iron deposits and the finest vineyards in the world under Atlantic rains and a hot sun. Historians trained in the classical tradition of an originally Mediterranean civilization and preoccupied with Antiquity and its medieval sequel, before the shift of political and economic power to the Atlantic states in early modern times, have tended to underrate the constant and primeval demographical importance of the North, and its peoples were written off by Graeco-Roman writers as barbarians; but their creative vigour, even in prehistoric ages, is now better understood; and even the Roman Empire now appears a blend of northern and southern peoples as the barbarians who threatened and infiltrated it were assimilated. Moreover, Northern European manpower, tamed by the Christian Church, became a bulwark against the

Nomads of Central Asia who, in spite of the incursion of the Huns in the fifth century and the Mongols in the twelfth, never subdued the West; only the Turks in Eastern Europe established an empire at all comparable to that of the Mongols or Manchus in China, and that not until the fifteenth century.

Beyond the Channel and the North Sea and on either side of the Skagarrak lay the Far West and the Far North, the British Isles and Scandinavia, only part of the first and none of the rest Romanized. And out of them would emerge the most dynamic peoples; the Goths and Burgundians and Vandals of the Völkerwanderung; the Normans who dominated England and some of the best areas of France, Portugal, Sicily and the Levant; the Swedish Vikings who created the framework of Kievan Russ; and the English who, disciplined by Norman method and in collaboration with the Scots and many of the Irish, founded the greatest maritime empire in world history. The development and expansion of Europe was not achieved only through the spread of a Mediterranean civilization; it came about through the interaction of the peoples of North and South. Hence the dynamic variety of the history of the continent which produced the first civilization to encompass the world.

The geographical structure itself made for variety but not for incoherence. Communications, though often difficult, were not blocked; the Alps were not so daunting a barrier as the Himalayas or the Rockies, the Pyrenees could be skirted at both extremities, and the Mediterranean in summer was navigable by coasting ships. North of the Alps the rivers, too, were favourable to trade; the Rhone and Saone led down to Lyons, Provence, and the sea; the Seine from the Côte d'Or down to Paris, the Loire from its headwaters in the Cevennes to Orléans, Tours and the Atlantic; the Rhine was a natural highway from Basel to the Netherlands, the Danube from Regensburg to Vienna, Belgrade and the Black Sea; the Elbe and Oder joined the Bohemian mountains to the Baltic, while the Dniepr formed the economic basis of Kievan Russ and the Volga of the expansion of Muscovy.

Moreover, although the hard climate and impenetrable forests and marshes of much of Northern Central Europe long held back its development, and the northern plains lay open to eastern attack, the defences of the core of central Europe were fairly good. The north European plain indeed extends unbroken from the Netherlands to the Baltic states of the U.S.S.R. and through North Germany to Warsaw and Poznan; while the plains of Wallachia, which extend nearly to Belgrade and continue again in Hungary, are an extension of the hinterland of Odessa and the South Russian steppe; but the Harz mountains and the forested uplands between Harz and Rhine bound the Northern plain below Hanover and Dortmund, while the Erzgebirge to the North and the Sudetenland flank the cardinal strategic fact of central Europe, the Bohemian bastion of which Napoleon said that he who was its master was master of the continent, a fact apparently unknown to the British cabinets in the nineteen 'thirties. Further, the Carpathians, curving south-east and round to the Danube at the Iron Gates, command the northern flank of the Wallachian plain, while the Bulgarian highlands bound it to the south. Western and central, if not eastern, Europe, with its frontiers fluctuating at the expense of East as well as West, have always been strategically as well as demographically well protected, and once areas of the German forests and the Bohemian massif had been civilized, the western peoples have not until our own day had to attempt the Roman expedient of the *limes* or the more impressive but equally ineffective Great Wall of China. It remained for them in the twentieth century to abandon the natural defences of Central Europe.

But by then the position of Western Europe had changed. It had become part of an Atlantic civilization, its strategic centre of gravity in North America. For by early modern times its supreme advantage in world history had become apparent. When its peoples found that they could exploit the sea routes to the Americas, and round Africa to India, the Far East and the Pacific, they established their civilization in the Americas and Australasia and briefly dominated India, Africa and even the Far East, while the Russians colonized Siberia and much of Central Asia, and even briefly Alaska. European civilization, backed by a revolutionary industrial technology, thus became the first to dominate the planet, surpassing those of the Near East, India and China, hitherto much more populous and better established. How Europeans came to develop their resources and their own original culture, technology and way of life in all their variety, and then, from being on the defensive after the decline of the Graeco-Roman civilization, became the predominant world influence will be the main theme of this study.

BOOK I

PREHISTORIC EUROPE

I

The Palaeolithic Hunters

Africa, not Europe or even Eurasia, is now thought to have been the original habitat of mankind. Over three million years ago the small hominid *Australopithicus Africanus,* upright, mobile and carnivorous, ranged the Transvaal using split pebbles for his kill; and one and a quarter million years after, another hominid in the Olduvai Gorge in Tanzania was striking flake stone chopping tools, long before they were made anywhere else. It was not until 900,000–300,000 BC, far into the Pleistocene geological epoch with its slow alterations of warmth and bitter cold, that the hominid *homo erectus,* larger than a modern pigmy, sparsely inhabited Europe and the Far East, while only by about 200,000 BC can the first fossil skull be classified as *homo* or, to be precise, *femina sapiens.* Discovered in the lower reaches of the Thames estuary at Swanscombe between Dartford and Gravesend, Swanscombe woman, like Steinheim man in Germany, can be considered directly ancestral to the varieties of modern mankind.

They lived during a warm interglacial time; but *homo sapiens* and his forerunners, the closely related Neanderthalers, had to face the last phase of the enormous iceage, misleadingly termed Würm, which set in from about 75,000–10,000 BC. During the first half of it, in a sub-Arctic climate, the Neanderthalers emerge; inbred specialized hunters of a kind found less specialized in Western Asia and North Africa, they are named after the first specimen unearthed in 1856 from a cave in the Neanderthal valley east of Düsseldorf.[1] They may not have been fully human; they were short, thick-set, with great brow ridges and receding chins, and their surprisingly large brains were set in broad low-browed skulls flattened at the back; they had wide nostrils, large teeth and massive chests, if they did not, as once believed, shuffle with lowered heads and bow legs but walked upright, *"L'on a dit bien souvent,"* says the *Larousse Histoire Universelle, "l'allure un peu bestiale de ce*

[1] Examined by a Professor Fuhlrott, they were classified, after two more had turned up in Belgium, as *Homo Neanderthalis,* a separate species, in 1864. But though they are more different from *Homo sapiens* than any modern races are from each other, the separate classification has since been challenged.

4 A History of Europe

type humain."[1] These stocky and brutish Mousterian people, so-called from a cave at Le Moustier in Périgord, had coarse hand axes, used fire, buried their dead with rudimentary provisions for an after life, and worshipped or propitiated the heaped up skulls of the bears they had killed. In Périgord they would place their dead in shallow graves with the best of their flints arranged round them, and in a cave on Monte Circeo, Italy, they ritually devoured the brain of the deceased; though the variety of these implements implies traditional skills and so language, and the hunting groups had the safety and solidarity of the fire-lit cave behind them, one can only wonder what kind of character existed behind so rude a mask?—"*que cachait une enveloppe aussi rude?*[1]"

By 35,000 BC they were being superseded: Cro-Magnon man out of Western Asia, *Homo Sapiens Sapiens*—so called because first found in 1868 at Cro-Magnon near Les Eyzies de Tayac, Dordogne[3]—was infiltrating Europe. Superior in physique to most modern men, with a large brain; over six feet tall, a broad short face and rather narrow mouth, he brought an entirely new strain into Palaeolithic Europe, though whether the Neanderthalers had already faded out in the extreme cold, were annihilated by their successors—a theory favoured and romanticized in the late nineteenth century—or adapted themselves in Europe over many generations to interbreed with modern man, as they did at Mount Carmel, are questions archaeologists and anthropologists still debate. Whatever happened, the Neanderthalers as such disappeared. But considering the evidence of European history it seems on the cards that their strain survived, though the descendants of the tall Cro-Magnons also helped to keep it lively.

Other contemporary *sapiens* people have been traced. In the *Grotte des Enfants* at Grimaldi near Menton, an elaborate inhumation has been discovered of people of negroid type, wearing crowns and bracelets of shells and daubed with red ochre, while in the *Grotto della Arena Candida* in Spain a boy had been entombed with a necklace of shells and stags' teeth and what are thought to be "sceptres" or "batons". All these people, whose earliest culture is termed Aurignacian after their flaked implements originally found at Aurignac in Haute Garonne, were far ahead of the Neanderthalers in goods and gear; the Cro-Magnons were a Caucasoid race, skilled hunters and artificers, living off the vast herds of bison, horses and reindeer; and, like their predecessors, they were very few, living and hunting usually in bands of twenty to twenty-five people, at most of fifty, dispersed over the continent from the South Russian Steppe through Bohemia into Central Europe, France and Spain. But they were versatile and intelligent: with them emerged mind.

Over millennia they developed their hunting cultures, most striking in South-Western France until the Aurignacian phase changed gradually to the Solutrean (from Solutré near Macon in Burgundy), then to the Magdalenian,

[1]*Larousse Histoire Universelle*. Direction M. Dunan. Paris, 1960. p. 9.
[2]*Larousse. op. cit.* p. 9.
[3]Where a Michelin starred hotel is called after him and offers *Pâté de foie de canard truffé*—to show the reality of progress.

named after the Grotte de la Madeleine near Les Eyzies, a culture which marked the culmination of the European Ice Age hunting societies.

These people had chisels and unlimited time, so they came to perfect a variety of javelins, spears, hafted axes, throwing sticks, harpoons, fish-hooks and tackle; they had lassoes and slings, but not the bow, and they used reindeer antlers for picks and mammoth tusks for ivory; by Solutrean times they had needles, bone pins, and even buttons to make and secure garments of leather and fur. Their fires kept them warm in caves and rock shelters and kept predatory beasts out; in a climate comparable to that of sub-Arctic Canada, their hunting bands would cut off and bring down their prey or corral the herds into palisaded enclosures or even stampede them over a cliff—a wasteful proceeding. When caves or rock shelters were not available or the summer climate relented, they would put up wind breaks or build semi-subterranean shacks.

Since the recognition of the superb Magdalenian rock paintings at Altamira on the Saja west of Santander in northern Spain, discovered in 1880 but not at first generally accepted, Palaeolithic artists have been famous; and while at Altamira the masterpieces are chaotically arranged, at Lascaux (c.13,000 BC) there is design. The best of these paintings, executed to promote good hunting and the fertility of the beasts, can compare with fine Japanese work in the same style and with aspects of that of French nineteenth-century Impressionists. Their art developed slowly over a vast time span.

The early Aurignacian designs are linear, incised in flint, or drawn in red or black ochre; one-dimensional but economically conveying the vision of the animal; then, after a phase of relatively clumsy monochrome silhouettes, the Magdalenian polychrome paintings convey both colour and mass. The artist would outline the beast in black, fill in the body in shaded red, then dash in the hoofs and tail in black as in the magnificent bisons of Altamira (c. 12,000–11,000 BC) or the delicate reindeer of Font de Gaume south of Les Eyzies, an astonishingly sensitive evocation. The charging wild boar of Altamira is five feet long, and at Font de Gaume a black wolf is depicted on a red ground, his rough pelt indicated by deliberate blurring of the paint. At Lascaux, discovered in 1940 and probably Aurignacian, so earlier than Altamira, horses and ponies form a rudimentary frieze, a couple of belligerent bison charge in opposite directions, and a stocky horse in light brown, black, and dull white is speared in his rump. The range of colour is particularly attractive; orange-yellows, reds, browns and blacks. The artists generally worked by the light of lamps with moss wicks or slow burning torches in cramped and inaccessible cave interiors; but, absorbed in their purpose and skill, they brought off an illusion that in the flickering light the beasts were alive. Developed over many generations, their patient technique was elaborate, and they had not only to paint but to find their pigments and preserve them. As M. H. Swindler writes,[1] "At the climax of Magdalenian art red, brown, and yellow pigments were put on, sometimes as paste, sometimes as liquid. These layers of colours were then toned down by scraping and washing and rubbing

[1]M. H. Swindler, Ancient Painting, Yale University Press, 1929.

... in preparing the colours, earth ochre and oxide of manganese were ground into a fine powder ... probably mixed with some grease or animal fat on an improvised palette, perhaps made from stone or from the shoulder blade of some animal. The paintings are not, therefore, true frescoes, though they are often loosely so-called. The pigments were kept in mussel shells or in tubes fashioned of hollowed bone ... In many cases color was applied by means of crayons whittled from chunks of ochre or oxide of manganese, a mineral found in the beds and streams." Occasionally the mark of a human hand may indicate that someone had participated in the magic, or registered in the numinous place that he had been there.

Some of them were also sculptors; the miniature horse's head carved in reindeer antler from Le Mas d'Azil, Ariège, and the ivory horse of Lourdes are full of life; and if, intent on sex, the creator of the "Venus of Willendorf" in Austria carved a steatopygous female whose serrated curls make her anonymous by blocking out her face, the tiny "Venus of Brassempouy", in Landes, France has a profile which, although chinless, is framed by neatly done hair poised on a relatively elegant neck. Already in the land which would become France someone had a glimmer of feeling for human style.

Of course, the artists were no more representative of their contemporaries than artists at any time, and most of these people, like all hunters, were mainly absorbed in the struggle for survival; but, as in all epochs of creative art, the artists had their place, integrated like the magicians who are depicted in animal masks and the flute players whose instruments have survived, into a society adapted to a hard world. And well adapted; these hunters survived for far longer than the five thousand years that extend from Minoan Crete, the first civilization in Europe, until today; and although, with the changing climate, the herds vanished and their Palaeolithic predators with them, the hunters' way of life went on, reflecting primeval needs and instincts, to survive in the cult of the chase, through Mesolithic and Neolithic into Bronze Age and historic times.

So the first Europeans created their sparse hunting cultures, common to most of the rest of mankind, with the nearest surviving, but no longer creative parallels among the aborigines of Australia and the South African Bushmen, to both of whom cave and rock paintings came as naturally. These hunters in their struggle for a cold and precarious living found that art, like common beliefs, was central to human experience and by it they are remembered. Thus, as has been admirably written, "After millennia of brutish life with little surviving material equipment, and a spiritual and moral equipment at which we can only guess, we find him [European man] at the end of the Ice Age not only a superb craftsman in flintwork—as witness, for example, Solutrean laurel leaves—but an artist, making beautiful spear throwers, sculpturing horses and human beings on the walls of his rock shelter houses and penetrating into the dark depths of deep caves to establish there cult-shrines, where in front of engravings and paintings and even models of animals, magico-religious rites were carried out."[1]

[1]Glyn Daniel. The Idea of Prehistory. Penguin, Harmondsworth, 1964. p. 167.

Brilliant at depicting animals, they also depicted themselves in animal guise; but it is not until much later, in Mesolithic times, that we have these vigorous drawings in an entirely different form. At Cogul and Alpera in Eastern Spain artists now depicted hunting scenes, ceremonial dances and war, as contemporary hunters in the Sahara recorded them. Men with elongated and enlarged legs, with ornamental garters below the knee as since worn by Zulus, and with well cut bushy hair, some with short trousers and bare torsos, dash flat-out after their prey or stalk it or escape from it as in the Cueva Remigia in Spain, or loose arrows at each other in running tribal fights, and skirted women sway in a ritual dance. Here we have tribal hunting and tribal warfare which the Palaeolithic hunters, preoccupied with the animals in a bitter climate, have not depicted and to which, though cannibals on occasion, they had presumably not attained. The Mesolithic frieze-like painting of eager bowmen at Remigia is brilliant both in psychological insight and design.

Such are the outstanding facts that illuminate the enormous vistas of time out of which all Europeans have emerged. They recede into the remote antiquity of the last phase of the last glaciation, peopled furthest back with Neanderthalers who may or may not be of our stock, then by Cro-Magnon man and his contemporaries; human, alert and ancestral. Only the most efficient and adaptable would have survived, but those who did fulfilled their instincts and in their youth and brief prime—for they can seldom have reached forty—had their moments of exultation and content. So long as the game was there, they had a rich diet or they would not have survived the cold; and they lived not, of course, in the depths of their caves but mainly in the entrances, often facing south. They had plenty of fish and a variety of wild berries, fruits and herbs; we know that the Mesolithic people gathered honey, and honey can mean fermented drink. Doubtless they had their enjoyments.

On the anatomical evidence they were handsome people; tall and slender, not at all the bestial "cave men" of popular fancy, and, although no doubt murderous on occasion, capable of forethought and collaboration. Had they not been so, their societies would not have lasted for over twenty thousand years of an Ice Age that by 10,000 BC was on the wane.

II

By around 8,000 BC the ice had so far receded that first grassland and birch woods and then mixed oak forest had spread over much of the continent, and the sub-arctic tundra had receded to the Far North, as in Lapland today. Bison, mammoth, aurochs and reindeer were succeeded by woodland animals; red deer, elk, wild cattle and wild pig; and the Mesolithic descendants of the Palaeolithic hunters lived no longer in caves but in rudimentary huts, often by river estuaries or lakes or by the sea shore, where, having diversified their carnivorous Palaeolithic diet, they have left piles of mussel and oyster shells from the Atlantic coasts to the Baltic. The British Isles were not yet separated from the Continent, and the North Sea had not yet been formed, so that a vaster area was open to them, and at Star Carr in Yorkshire a very early lakeside site has been discovered, occupied by four or five families who lived off hunting the red deer and off fish. By 8000 BC the Mesolithic North Europeans had domesticated the dog—the first people to have done so, the first known animal, found at Senkenberg near Frankfurt-on-Main, resembling an Australian dingo. Canine remains have also been found in Denmark; but since all northern Europe was then infested with large wolves, these relatively small domesticated dogs were probably brought in from the south. Once human settlements had been established, dogs might have hung around them, and a few pups taken on the strength, as pets became assets in the hunt.[1] As in the Canadian Far West, the people of such hunting and fishing settlements were no longer nomadic; they could settle into a routine and construct boats, and the Mesolithic way of life amplified the Palaeolithic. As Piggott puts it, "The basic traditions of these eighth millennium hunting and fishing communities were continued until at least the second millennium BC in various conservative areas of Northern Europe and Asia, where agriculture was not adopted. ... The skills of these Palaeolithic and Mesolithic peoples were not negligible: to them we owe not only all the basic crafts of the hunter with spear, bow and arrow and the fisherman with line, net or trap, but also the invention of the first boats, cut from the solid wood or skin-covered; sledges and skis, probably whistles and even pan pipes."[2]

This immensely ancient way of life, still apparent in the deep-seated predatory instincts of the sub-conscious mind, persisted and blended with the radical change which now very gradually pervaded the European continent— the Neolithic Revolution. Man and the animals he had domesticated now set about exploiting and sometimes devastating the natural environment, a process since much accelerated over the short time span since it began. For as Glyn Daniel reminds us, "Think of the face of a clock, and of a minute hand going round for an hour. Fifty-nine minutes of that hour represent man the food-gatherer, man in the stage of Palaeolithic savagery, man in the Old Stone Age. In the last minute but one we see him painting at Lascaux and Altamira ... but it is only at the beginning of the last minute that we see him gaining control over the cultivation of grain and the domestication of animals—it is only then that the Neolithic Revolution takes place, and only in the last half minute that the social, material and cultural changes we call civilization occur."[3]

[1]For a thorough discussion of the question see F. E. Zeuner. *A History of Domesticated Animals*. London, 1963. pp. 39-40 and 80-93. Primitive Mesolithic people, he writes, may have created this kind of symbiosis "in an elementary manifestation of the solidarity of life". (p. 39)
[2]Stuart Piggott. *Ancient Europe, from the Beginnings of Agriculture to Classical Antiquity*. Edinburgh, 1965 p. 35
[3]Daniel op. cit. p. 168.

II

Megalithic Cultures and the Higher Barbarism

While the rise of civilization in Europe was more spontaneous and autonomous than hitherto realized, its material basis, adapted to European conditions, originated mainly in the Near East. There, by the end of the Ice Age, wild wheat and barley had proliferated; the former in Anatolia, Lebanon and Armenia; the latter in Anatolia, Palestine, the Caucasus and northern Iran. Moreover, although wild cattle and wild pig were now roaming temperate Europe, it was only in Anatolia, the Caucasus and western Iran that the wild goat was common; and only in Iran and southern central Asia the much more important wild sheep. It was in these areas that farming and the domestication of livestock began and from them that the new way of life spread very slowly westward and then, between the Caspian and the Adriatic, dug itself in.

By 9000 BC sheep and goats were being herded in the valleys of the Zagros mountains in south-western Iran, and by 7000 BC the Natufians around their extraordinary site at Jericho, who were modelling on skulls the first likeness of the human face, had domesticated goats; while with the cultivation of cereal crops in the spacious valleys of southern Anatolia behind Antalya, where the country has an Asian scale, the Neolithic economy had been established.

This old fashioned term was devised because in the *Palaeolithic* or Old Stone Age implements were made of chipped stone, while in the *Neolithic* or New Stone Age they were polished. This purely technological distinction is far less important than the change over from hunting and gathering to farming; but the terms have caught on, sound well, and though irrelevant to the essential contrasts, are still accepted. The later Neolithic, of course, includes Megalithic which describes the great stone circles.

Gradually agriculture spread into eastern Europe or spontaneously developed, in Macedonia, then in Thessaly and on the fertile Danubian lands and the Hungarian plain. By 5500 BC a Neolithic peasantry were settling in, not, as in the Near East, in close packed communities, but in scattered villages with casually spaced one-roomed houses with gabled roofs. In Bulgaria and Romania the settlements were more compact, with houses of wattle and daub and even bright painted plaster which, after generations, formed "tells" as in Iraq. In Jugoslavia sculpted human heads and a striking figure with arms akimbo have survived from before 4000 BC; at Karanovo in Bulgaria clay models of rudimentary chairs and couches have survived, and from around 3000 BC at Cernavada, Romania, two pottery figures of a man apparently bored and pensive on a stool and a woman anxiously intent on some household chore show that, in contrast to the brisk bowmen of the Cueva Remigia, the Neolithic farmers paid the price of settling down.

Neolithic pottery is plentiful in Greece and Italy by the sixth millennium, in Central Europe early in the fifth, and by about 4000 BC in Britain; now, since 6000 BC, following the rise of the sea level after the melting of the ice, physically cut off from the Continent. For Neolithic farming had also spread to North Germany, Denmark, the Netherlands and North-Eastern France over an area still predominantly forest, but where patches of fertile soil rewarded even primitive shifting "slash and burn" hoe agriculture. So over the centuries of a time span longer than that since the beginning of our own era, Europe was being opened up, and by 4000 BC had been widely settled by peasant farmers who had got to know routine and to measure time. The greatest economic and social change before the Industrial Revolution was very gradually consolidated, and a population far greater than the sparse Palaeolithic and Mesolithic hunting bands could now survive and even increase. The Neolithic peasant farmers had made the transition from savagery to barbarism.

In the north, in contrast to the nucleated settlements in the Balkans, the people built big timber houses, sometimes as much as a hundred feet long by twenty-five broad, with ample room for man, beast and produce in the hard winters, a tradition continuing in the great barns of the Netherlands, West-phalia and Denmark. On the Mediterranean the pockets of fertile land in a predominantly mountainous or hilly terrain were of course early developed, often through contacts by sea, and fishermen were already rounding up the tunny. Northern and eastern Sicily and Apulia were already densely cultivated. In the west Neolithic cultures, probably emanating from Mediterranean Spain and Provence, now extended through Burgundy down the Seine Valley, to Brittany, southern Britain and western Ireland; in Denmark there was a blend of Mesolithic fishing and Neolithic farming, while extensive settlements known as Tripolye culture were early established in the Ukraine. In the heart of Europe the Swiss lake settlements, built, not, as we once thought, out over the water, but between the reedbeds and the mainland, were now in being. By 4000 BC over most of the more accessible areas of the continent these Neolithic peoples were raising their wheat and barley, tending their livestock, weaving textiles and making pottery. Their economy is basic to all subsequent development.

II

Until the techniques of radio-carbon and dendrochronology[1] to correct the

[1] After the first 2000 years radio-carbon dating is inaccurate, but the dates of the pieced together tree rings of the Californian bristle cone pine are accurate to 6300 BC. The radio-carbon dates, though accurate for Egypt and Minoan Crete, are not old enough for the Megalithic period; corrected, they place it much further back.

theory were devised, it was assumed that the religion and the social order that went with it were diffused, like the original Neolithic agriculture and stockbreeding, from the Near East. But it is now known that the far-flung Megalithic culture, so called from the great stone tombs and circles that distinguish it, which extends from Malta and Sardinia into the Iberian Peninsula, Brittany, the British Isles and Denmark, is most of it in fact Neolithic, older than the literate civilization of Egypt, and much older than the pyramids. The "diffusionist" orthodoxy widely accepted has now been disproved, and the European megalith builders, whose work preceded it and climaxed in the more famous monuments in northern Europe—Avebury, Carnac and Stonehenge—appear not as "natives" receptive of some eastern cult brought in by merchants or even "missionaries", but as creative barbarians who devised these monuments themselves since now, on the modern evidence, "suddenly and decisively the impressive Megalithic tombs of western Europe are set earlier than any comparable monuments in the world."[1] Even the extraordinary temples in Malta, which might be expected to have Levantine affinities, are now dated as early as 3300 BC, well over a thousand years before the full Minoan civilization in Crete, and so perhaps an independent development.

The Megalithic tombs of Brittany are even earlier—the earliest as far back as 4300 BC—and even the later ones can have had only an elementary economy behind them. On the Palaeolithic evidence, to commemorate a cult of the dead is something primeval, common even to Neanderthalers; and now, with a Neolithic way of life, we find a cult of the crops and the sun. At Locmariaquer near Carnac, a dolmen contains a huge upright slab, the *Table des Marchands*, with designs representing ripe wheat, surrounded with a border representing the sun's rays. Incised on the lower roof are representations, as at Gav'r Inis, Brittany, of the smooth votive axes found in the tombs. The dolmens, now often exposed, were originally covered, as here, by a mound: the Neolithic Bretons could not have made more permanent memorials to their dead, the only things comparable now being the indestructible remnants of the colossal forts constructed for the German Atlantic Wall, which, if nuclear catastrophe occurs, may remain among the few monuments to our own culture. Most of the Megalithic tombs are passage graves, long charnel houses with side chambers into which the dead were stowed away, as in the West Kennet long barrow in Wiltshire.

By the third millennium BC they were being built in Denmark; as at Blommeskobbel where the amber necklaces and votive greenstone ceremonial axes and maces are particularly fine, and where the Skarpskaling bowl is a masterpiece of Neolithic ceramics. At Carnac great 4000 feet long avenues of light grey menhirs culminating in a horseshoe of the biggest stones, some ten and even twelve feet high, dominate their Atlantic setting of heather, broom, and white slate-roofed cottages, beyond them the sea. Whatever their ritual significance, these huge cromlechs of granite, weathered by time and encrusted

[1]Colin Renfrew. *Before Civilization. The Radio-Carbon Revolution and Prehistoric Europe*. London, 1973. p. 120.

with grey and brown lichen, symbolize human effort to create order and design. Avebury in Wiltshire, a huge circle of standing Sarsen stones which still include a whole village, has the remnants of a similar avenue; at Carnac, there is a big tumulus which yielded grave goods, and at Avebury, Silbury Hill (c.2500 BC) which yielded nothing. Most famous of all, Stonehenge, which was begun probably about 2800 and finished by 2200–2100 BC, is the most elaborate and sophisticated of the Megalithic temples in northern Europe, representative of many stone circles and standing stones along the Atlantic seaboards and in central France. At Skara Brae in the Orkneys Neolithic houses, complete with stone fittings, were being built by 2600 BC, contemporary with Avebury and the early Stonehenge. It is extraordinary that the settlers should have got so far over such seas.

The other outstanding Neolithic temples are in Malta. Here by 3300 BC, well before the date of the earliest pyramids, the intricate subterranean *Hypogeum* (under the earth) at Hal Saflieni was being cut out of soft limestone rock. It is a catacomb connected over the centuries by halls and steps down to a depth of forty feet, and the middle levels form a shrine which probably housed an oracle. In this mysterious and still awesome place the prevalent colour is faded red ochre, the colour that since Palaeolithic times had been daubed on the dead, and in the largest room are traces of a black and white check pattern, as well as the print of an impressed hand and the outline of a bull. Here also were two terracotta statuettes of immensely stout skirted women, one reclining on her side as if asleep, perhaps dreaming as in the shrines of later Antiquity a dream sent by the God, or else a token of gratitude by a devotee whose dream had turned out well. In the so-called oracle room, its roof decorated with swirling black spirals on pale red, a priest's voice sounding through the aperture would have reverberated to the worshippers by whom donations were deposited, and in the most sacred semi-circular chamber five pillars cut out of the rock are surmounted by curved lintels which slope inwards to form a partly corbelled roof. There are also rope holes that probably secured the animals for sacrifice, and the place contained the macabre remains of about 7000 skeletons. Such is the weirdest and most complex subterranean setting for Neolithic religion.

Tarxien in Malta is above ground; here a frieze of sacrificial sheep, pigs and goats catches their likeness and posture, if the legs of the mother goddess— over life size—indicate that she was as broad as she was long. The abstract decoration is also extremely effective, mainly in horned and eye-shaped spirals and holes drilled in circular patterns, sometimes in double rows. But the biggest, trefoil shaped, temple is on Gozo: Ggantija is a hundred feet square, its only remaining wall seventeen feet high: with primitive corbelling to make the outer wall curve inwards, it probably supported a roof of timber and thatch. At that time well-wooded, Malta and Gozo had been settled from Sicily; and then, as since, a disproportionate amount of its resources must have been devoted to religion. These complex temples can hardly have had any considerable economy behind them: they commemorate a culture, not yet a civilization.

The economic background of the Atlantic megaliths is also elementary; the latest phase of Stonehenge may have been completed by new warrior and trading peoples, but the Breton, Irish, Welsh and Scots megaliths probably had no substantial economy or extensive trade routes behind them.

These archaic European cultures seem to have arisen spontaneously and locally, the cult of the dead giving a sense of identity and continuity to quite small communities, particularly if their farming was still "slash and burn" and mobile within their tribal or even extended family areas. The dolmens, which in Brittany are particularly thick on the ground, would thus be the spontaneous creation of perhaps twenty-five people in a territory reckoning twenty acres a head, conscious of a common ancestry as against their neighbours, and wanting to keep up with them. This hypothesis seems more realistic than the hitherto widely accepted belief that the cultures were spread by traders when there is not yet evidence for substantial commerce, or by missionaries from an Eastern civilization not yet fully in being. Add to the commemoration of the dead, which comes down from Palaeolithic times, the cult of fertility in mankind, beasts and crops, and sun worship—the most obvious cult—and we may be on the track of the religion which has left such impressive traces in Europe long before the dawn of civilization itself

III

All this culture is Neolithic—based on a cross between the old hunting techniques and routine farming by hoe cultivation, acclimatized over many centuries and spreading slowly across the continent. But by about 3000 BC in the Middle and Near East the prospects of Europe were being indirectly transformed. The exotic process termed "civilization" had now arisen in the archaic temple states of Sumeria in southern Iraq, and in the old Kingdom of Egypt. Both had millennia of Neolithic village life behind them, as had the later riparian civilizations of the Indus valley and the Yellow River in China; and although a Neolithic antediluvian culture was found at Ur beneath the thick clay which authenticates the Biblical flood which probably extended over only about 400 by 100 miles, the Sumerian walled city built above it was created by people who used metals and had cuneiform (wedge-shaped) writing. The Sumerians had come down from south-western Iran, exploited aboriginal settlements among the reed beds now drying out above the receding waters of the Persian Gulf and probably similar to those of the marsh Arabs today, so creating the complex irrigation on which their civilization was founded. They turned the swamps of Lower Mesopotamia into a vast acreage of wheat and barley, date palms and vines, and they built walled cities. Their civilization was literate; elaborate and rich beyond the wildest dreams of the barbarians of Europe.

The royal tombs at Ur bear witness to this urban wealth and sophistication, with their chalices of fluted gold, ceremonial chariots, exquisitely made harps, women's headdresses with flowers and petals wrought in lapis lazuli and cornelian with "golden pendants in the form of beech leaves, (and) great lunate

14   A History of Europe

ear rings of gold". And a silver boat was found; "wonderfully well preserved; some two feet long, it has high stern and prow, five seats and amidships an arched support for the awning which would protect the passenger, and the leaf-bladed oars are still set in the thwarts; it is a testimony to the conservatism of the east that a boat of identical type is in use today on the marshes of the Lower Euphrates, some fifty miles from Ur."[1] All this elaborate treasure provided the trappings of a ghastly holocaust in which their poisoned attendants accompanied their King A-bar-gi and Queen Shub-Ad to the next world; but human sacrifice was confined to the obsequies of royalty and the occasion was evidently regarded as a smooth transition from one world to another; indeed an honour for those involved.

The Sumerians were intensely practical: they created security and plenty out of the original wilderness, while this desire for order, the basis of all civilization, is apparent in their literature and religion, which, like that of Iran, reflects the conflict between order and chaos, light and darkness. The famous standard of Ur illustrates war and peace—anticipating the fourteenth-century frescoes in Siena on "good and bad government". They created the classic civilization of the Mesopotamian Near East.

The Sumerians were gradually absorbed by the native peoples but the Semitic Sargon of Akkad (2370 BC) ruled territories that extended to the Lebanon, and invaded Cyprus; while Hammurabi of Babylon (c.1792-1750 BC) has left a code of "Laws"—or rather decisions on particular questions—which shows how businesslike and wealthy this originally Sumerian civilization had become. Nor could it have flourished without extensive trade, for southern Iraq had no timber save palm wood, or stone or metals, and with this commerce Europe was by then involved.

IV

In Egypt civilization was even more massive and spectacular. The valley of the Nile of Upper Egypt extending north from Aswan to Lower Egypt and the Delta, then more extensive than today, was early united. Here again, of course, riparian civilization had not, as sometimes suggested, come suddenly; it had generations of village life behind it, going back to the seventh millennium. By 3200 BC Narmer of Upper Egypt possessed a "state palette" found at Hierakonpolis far up the Nile between the first bend of the river and the first cataract at Aswan, which depicts him on one side wearing the tall crown of Upper Egypt and on the other the more complex one of Lower. He had conquered both lands; the former essentially African, the latter facing the Mediterranean and Europe. His successor, Hor Aha or Men (the Established One) whom the Greeks called Menes, administratively united the whole country, and founded his capital at Memphis in Lower Egypt at the head of the Delta. By 2800 BC the Pharaoh Zozer was commemorated by the huge

[1]Leonard Woolley. Ur of the Chaldees. Seven Years of Excavation. Penguin, Harmondsworth, 1938. pp. 38-9.

stepped pyramid of Saqqara, with its meticulously fitted stone blocks and surrounding temple complex of finished and elegant architecture anticipating the best work of the Greeks. Then Pharaoh Khufu built the great Pyramid, the most gigantic of these memorials, at Giza, near Saqqara. It is so colossal that its square base covers over thirteen acres, thus dwarfing the greatest European cathedrals, and its original height was nearly 481 feet. Over a million and a quarter stone blocks weighing two and a half tons each went into its construction and it probably took thirty years to build. Like the burial place at Ur, it was a royal tomb, and the dimensions of the Pyramid of Pharaoh Kafre next to it are nearly as monstrous. They commemorate a civilization far more interesting than they are themselves, which had already (c.2700 BC) invented the calendar of 365 days. With minor modifications it is still accepted. Already the Egyptian civilization was wealthy, ordered and secure, if bought at a price, for the palette of Narmer depicts his enemies neatly decapitated. But "it has been estimated that Egyptian peasants of the third millennium BC may have been able to produce perhaps three times as much as their own domestic requirements. Under a harsh system of servile exploitation the surplus could be turned to impressive account, not only in public but also in the support of large noble, priestly and official classes, the leaders of which developed an increasingly elaborate court life around the person of the living Pharaoh and around the tombs of his predecessors. Political units were the final and vital stage in Egypt's amazingly rapid development from a jungle-filled, swampy valley to the scene of a complex and coherent society comprising several million people."[1]

This society worked copper and bronze; it was literate, its architecture with columns modelled on papyrus clumps, elegant and precise; its art depicting not only war and conquest but the everyday life of men and animals with perceptive sympathy and humour in an environment far more genial than that of Mesopotamia. Here was a self-confident, efficient bureaucracy, and social and political order. Intensely conservative and practical, the Old Kingdom alone lasted over seven hundred years—longer than from Magna Carta till today—and its memorials still astound us by their majesty and refinement. And although by c.2100 BC the classic Old Kingdom collapsed, the Pharaohs of the Middle Kingdom reunited the state.

Then under the New Kingdom (1570–1085 BC) Egypt became a great imperial power, at its climax from 1500 to 1200 BC, and commemorated by the gigantic temples at Luxor and Karnak near Thebes, the new capital in Upper Egypt in the bend of the Nile near Hierakonpolis, Narmer's original capital. If the classic Old Kingdom produced the grandest architecture and art, the splendours of the rulers of the New Kingdom under Akhnaton and his successor Tutankhamun are famous, since the treasures of the latter's tomb have survived; the sheer size and scale of the monuments of Egypt, extending from the earliest stepped pyramid of Saqqara to the pillared halls of the temple at Karnak and the Great Court of the temple at Luxor with its columns fifty-

[1]Roland Oliver & J. D. Fage. *A Short History of Africa*. Penguin, Harmondsworth, 1962. p. 37.

two feet high, attest the wealth and organization of a civilization in full tide. Even in its political decadence, it lasted into Graeco-Roman times and became the richest province of the Roman Empire.

So, decisively for Europe, by 3000 BC, in the Near East and in exceptionally favourable conditions, the two oldest riparian civilizations were in being, "a most abnormal and unpredictable event".[1] And during the next two millennia, while, overlapping each other, the Bronze Age and then the early Iron Age set in and spread gradually across the European continent, the existence of these massive civilizations became increasingly important for Europe, at least intermittently radiating an influence which interacted with vigorous native local developments; and it is against these great and lasting urban societies based on the fertility of southern Iraq and the Nile valley under an Asian and African sun that the prehistory of Bronze Age Europe must be considered.

V

The rise of the new Bronze technology was very gradual. But copper was early being mined in Transylvania and southern Spain, and by 3000–2500, contemporary with the earlier Old Kingdom in Egypt, a copper-using people were farming and stock breeding on the Lower Dniepr: diffused or spontaneous, by 2000 BC the new bronze weapons were changing the social order in societies hitherto in Neolithic barbarism; there was no reliable Neolithic answer to a bronze dagger. And where the archaic Neolithic peasants had probably lived in rough equality in kinship groups, age grades and fraternities, claiming common tribal descent, and their local loyalties had been enshrined in Megalithic sepulchures, now in the Bronze Age warrior chieftains and their followings established a new aristocracy, living off the peasant farmers and developing trade in metals and luxury goods. Such chieftainship would culminate in civilized Principality, at its climax at Mycenae in the Peloponnese, flourishing by 1400 BC. In Neolithic times any surplus was probably redistributed by the leaders in return for social labour, or used for gift exchange; a method in principle not unlike that of the warrior societies that now came in, and still apparent in the "heroic" age depicted in the Anglo-Saxon epic *Beowulf*, when a warrior King is judged by the splendour of the rings and weapons he bestows from hoarded wealth. But such treasures have to come from somewhere, and the surplus redistributed must have derived from trade more extensive and far-flung than the Neolithic trade in flints. The Bronze Age Chieftains in Britain, for example, probably grew relatively wealthy on the control of the tin mines, a rare asset, and the amber trade brought prosperity to Denmark. While by 2000 BC the population of Europe was still sparse, and vast areas of forest, heath, marsh and mountain remained uncolonized, the Neolithic economy and social order was here gradually being altered. Some immigrants, for obvious reasons known as the "Battle Axe"

[1]Piggott. *op. cit.* p. 20.

people, came from south Russia infiltrating between the Carpathians and the Black Sea; others are known more genially as the "Beaker Folk" from the bell-shaped drinking mugs;[1] for unlike the Neolithic peoples who had a kind of cider, these people had something stronger. They came from the Iberian peninsula.

The Battle Axe people may have been descendants of the copper-using agriculturalists of the Lower Dniepr; they buried their dead in round barrows akin to the *Kurgans* of the southern Steppe, their Chieftains with great splendour, and had probably tamed the Eurasian wild horse.[2] These pastoralists now spread north west into the Rhineland and Low Countries: it cannot be proved that they spoke an Indo-European tongue, but "philologists on the whole agree that an area west of the Urals and north of the Black Sea between the Carpathians and the Caucasus would best suit the evidence of common (Indo-European) words such as birch, beech, oak and willow; or animals such as bear, wolf, goose, pig, wasp; and salmon, or similar large river fish... a metal which is either copper or bronze was known, as were wheeled vehicles denoted by common words for wheels, axles, hubs and yokes, but not for the spokes of a wheel."[3]

The "Beaker Folk", warriors from Spain, were heavily armed with bronze slashing swords and daggers and they probably migrated through France into central Europe, where they exploited the metals of Bohemia; others are thought to have moved into Brittany and so across the Channel into the British Isles. Those established in central and north-western Europe blending with the "Battle Axe" people, also came into Britain, Ireland and even the Orkneys. "It is an astonishing migration this, astonishing that a race fostered in a Mediterranean country should be able to trek to central Europe and become familiar with the continental conditions of the Danube and the Rhine before pushing on to the most distant Atlantic shores ... and during all this time and over all this distance they maintained their own material culture so little changed that if four sherds of Beaker pottery from Spain and Bohemia, from Holland and Scotland, were ranged on the palm of one's hand it might be impossible to distinguish between them."[4]

Both these originally nomadic and pastoral peoples loved ornament; their Chieftains had gold mounted ceremonial maces, torques and bracelets of gold, and their women had fine necklaces of gold, amber and jet. As they settled down, trade developed, and populations increased. The Bronze Age rulers

[1]"Were these vessels really beakers in the sense of being primarily designed for drinking? It is very probable that they were, and it has even been suggested that they were intended for some fermented drink ... which helped the invaders to establish their mastery, rather as whisky has often opened the way for less scrupulous white settlers in Africa and the Pacific." Jacquetta & Christopher. Hawkes *Prehistoric Britain*. London, 1947. p. 52.
[2]The original Pryzewalski horse, thickset with yellowish dun coat and dark mane, legs and tail, like a large pony; those depicted at Lascaux are probably Tarpans, mouse grey and now extinct. See Zeuner, *op. cit.* pp. 299–337.
[3]Piggott. *op. cit.* p. 80.
[4]Hawkes. *op. cit.* p. 54.

became more prosperous, so that at its height they were trading extensively with the Mediterranean.

We come nearest to them in Scandinavia, where between 1500 and 400 BC a "peculiar radiance emanates from the Bronze Age in prehistoric Denmark ... Because the many cultural historical relics reveal a rich, refined culture with the economic prosperity necessary as its foundation ... Thousands of barrows, large and small, all over the country show how dense was the population," and "on rock surfaces in southern Sweden and Bornholm as well as on boulders in eastern Denmark are incised pictures mostly dating from the Bronze Age. The subjects of these rock carvings vary, from figure scenes: warriors, lur players (the lur was a long curved bronze trumpet), ploughmen, carts, ships ... to sacred symbols such as the sun cross, the sun wheel."[1]

Since these early Danes buried some of their dead in stout oak coffins, even their textile garments have survived—a long coat fastened rather unpractically at the back with bronze buttons and secured round the waist by a belt; a voluminous cloak, leather sandals and rudimentary puttees. One woman's outfit included a netting hair net, an extremely short smock with sleeves to the elbows, a tasselled belt fastened with a large circular ornament, and a short skirt that ended well above the knees. These Nordic women were not bundled up in the flowing garments of the south: nor had trousers, the garment of the Iron Age barbarians, yet come in; perhaps the better climate of the Bronze Age did not demand them.

Like other Bronze Age peoples, the Danes worshipped the sun. The famous Sun car from Trundholm Mose (c.1000 BC), a delicate six-wheeler, drawn by a horse with loops for reins and neatly docked tail, bears a gold plated disc as if moving across the sky. This model probably represents a life-sized equivalent in a ritual procession and is conclusive evidence for this sensible religion.

Such, in brief, are representative aspects of a time of great importance to Europe, when by the late Bronze Age plough shares were beginning to supersede hoe cultivation, when new immigrants, or people who had learnt their skills, exploited the metal deposits of the continent and the British Isles, and developed a metal and luxury trade with the south over the Alpine passes and through the Balkans. These people and their like added a new strain to the already thoroughly mixed ancestry of Europeans. Between 2000 and 1500 BC they had achieved the phase of Higher Barbarism, to be further developed north of the Alps by the Iron Age Celts, Teutons and Scandinavians, and to spill over in the folk wanderings during the climax of the Roman Empire and after its decline and fall.

While this gradual and uneven process was going on, something qualitatively different had also occurred and not this time in the Near East: the rise of the first European palaces in Crete and Mycenae. Both these highly original cultures were in environments entirely different from the riparian civilizations of Mesopotamia and Egypt, or the broad maritime valleys and massive hinterland of Asia Minor; they were due to European initiative, growing up

[1]Guides to the National Museum, Copenhagen. The Danish Collections. Antiquity. Copenhagen, 1955. pp. 45–48.

spontaneously on their own, for contrary to widespread opinion, "Aegean civilization was not brought ready made to the Aegean, nor transplanted either by migration or diffusion from other lands."[1] Its rise was due to a whole range of causes, environmental, economic, social, religious and political, which stimulated each other to the break through. The existence of the elaborate and sophisticated Egyptian civilization must naturally have had its cumulative effect, as did the civilizations of Asia Minor, the heirs of Sumeria, but the Minoan-Mycenaean palace culture was original. The old fashioned Marxist interpretation of Gordon Childe which depicted the spread of civilization as "the irradiation of European barbarism" in terms of the changing means of production, centred on the Near East, has long held the field; but as the greater antiquity of the western Megalithic cultures has demonstrated in a Neolithic context, it now appears inadequate. While the rise of Neolithic farming—the essential Neolithic Revolution—and the spread of basic inventions undoubtedly derived mainly from Asia, the first civilization in Europe arose out of a far more complex and subtle combination of circumstances than mere diffusion. It was due to the enterprise and intelligence of a maritime people. As might be expected, the first European initiative was original and dynamic, and took place in the most favourable environment that it could.

[1]Colin Renfrew. *The Emergence of Civilization. The Cyclades and the Aegean in the third millennium BC.* London, 1976. p. 476.

BOOK II

MEDITERRANEAN ANTIQUITY

III

Minoan Crete: Mycenae

There is a significant contrast between the mountainous and insular environment of Crete, set in wine-dark Levantine seas, and the flat alluvial plains of Mesopotamia and Lower Egypt or the desert-girt valley of the Nile where the first massive urban civilizations had emerged. The brisk maritime climate—even in August the waves white-capped under the *Meltéme* out of the north—was very different from the heavy heats of Egypt or the continental winters of Iraq. Moreover, before the ravages of timber-hungry men and crop-hungry goats, the Greek islands, Attica and the Peloponnese were all well-wooded, without the desiccated appearance that in full summer and in autumn they now present. Crete and the Peloponnese also lie in that southern and quintessentially Mediterranean area where the vine and olive grew wild, shielded from the bitter winds out of Thrace and Macedonia. Add to this a sea teeming with fish and on the mainland a heavily indented coast, with the interiors cut up into naturally self-sufficient valleys communicating best by sea, under hot sun and brilliant light, and here was a highly favourable setting for the first civilization in Europe.

Compared with the massive urban communities of the Near East, with their droves of docile peasantry and slave labour, the Minoan society, though organized round a priest-king and his deputies and officials and probably, in its final phases, militarized by Achaian Greeks, was based on small-scale agriculture and craftsmanship, in an environment which stimulated versatility and enterprise, at least among the rulers and their following. The entire population of Crete in the climax of the first insular European civilization is thought to have been no more than quarter of a million, less than half the population today; and even the great Minos who ruled Knossos may not have directly controlled the whole island.

The Mycenaean power—the first mainland civilization—was more substantial; more military, concentrated and formidable; but neither here nor in Crete were there great cities and temples, simply a small citadel and a palace when Chieftainship had been transformed into Kingship. "The use in ... Aegean archaeology of words such as 'palace' and 'city' has unfortunately resulted in their acquiring an emotive quality and an illusion of grandeur incommensurate with the sites they describe ... The middle Minoan palace at Mallia in Crete is just about the same size as the Roman Villa at Woodchester in Gloucestershire ... the built up area of a central European village of the fourth or fifth millennium BC could be about equal to that of Knossos."[1] The still massive ruins of the successive cities of Troy, looking down to the line of poplars that still mark the course of the Scamander or away to the Dardanelles, cover about the same acreage as Old Sarum in Wiltshire. Yet civilization is here: order, literacy, method and exploitation; even new ideas which set these Aegean peoples in their network of seaborne commerce and stored up wealth apart from the Neolithic villagers and princelings of the Higher Barbarism in contemporary Europe, and which, through the memory of Minos and of Mycenae, of Argos, Tiryns and Pylos, left a tradition that, after a dark time of confusion, still haunted the world of Homer.

By about 6000 BC Crete was already inhabited by a Neolithic people, probably from Anatolia or Syria, who cultivated olives, vines and figs; by 3000 BC, reinforced perhaps by refugees from Egypt after the conquests of Narmer and Menes, they had copper and bronze; by 2000 BC, when the Middle Kingdom had been established in Egypt and the "Battle Axe" and "Beaker Folk" were infiltrating Europe, they were already civilized, and by 1900 BC they were literate and flourishing. They long so continued; in about 1700 BC both Knossos and Phaestos were destroyed by earthquake and fire, yet they were rebuilt, and the most brilliant phase of Cretan civilization followed. For in their otherwise fine climate the Cretans lived under a terrible, if intermittent, threat: in about 1550 BC Knossos and eastern Crete were again badly hit by earthquakes, and in 1430 BC almost the entire island of Santorin, a Minoan colony—the modern Thera—blew up, perhaps sending immense tidal waves across the seventy miles to Crete, where most of the northern shore and the eastern part of the island appear to have been devastated. From this appalling catastrophe, or maybe an earthquake on the island itself, Minoan civilization never fully recovered; early Greek invaders from the mainland took over at Knossos (since Cretan command of the sea was late Minoan, Minos was Greek); but by about 1350 BC Knossos was finally destroyed. Save for settlements from the declining Mycenaean civilization of the mainland around 1150 BC, Crete went into eclipse, though the strong native tradition so far assimilated the Dorian Greeks who arrived there at the end of the Bronze Age as to make them very different from the mainland and Ionian Greeks in historic times.

The great age of Minoan civilization thus lasted for nearly five hundred years, from 1900 to about 1430 BC, its peak coincident with the imperialist New Kingdom in Egypt and the climax of the Bronze Age in Britain, Denmark and central Europe, and sank into decadence by the end of the second millennium. The old Cretan way of life was relatively peaceful, the palaces built for storage and comfort, not defence, and decorated with high-spirited paintings and frescoes depicting the more lyrical aspects of life. So outstandingly creative and dashing is their art, then so original in the context of the

[1] Piggott, op. cit. p. 122.

rest of Europe, that it has even been compared, on its miniature scale, with that of thirteenth-century Florence.

By contrast, Mycenaean citadels are grim; Mycenae itself, looking south over the plain of Argos from its strategically placed site commanding the routes into the Peloponnese, as the acropolis of Tiryns on the coast near modern Nauplion commands the sea, remains sinister to this day. Where Cretan civilization was originally the work of dark, clean-shaven Mediterranean peoples in its last epoch mastered by Greeks, Mycenae was made, from the first, by Indo-European conquerors from the north who adapted themselves to the world that they had overrun; bearded warriors, who used chariots and hunted lions with spears and enormous shields, the most successful of their contemporaries; for they were not exploiting Neolithic peasants but a civilization that had spread and taken root on the mainland before them from its original centre in Crete, though by now largely independent of it. The Mycenaean *Wanax*, or King, was the head of a society in which the *Lawagates* or military Commanders came next in rank; below them were the fief-holders or barons, the *Telestai*, while the outlying areas were controlled by semi-independent *Basileis* who owed allegiance to the King. This military hierarchy exploited the artisans, the peasants, the bondsmen and the slaves, and long protected the land from more barbarous invaders, until the final debacle before the Dorian Greeks at the end of the Bronze Age.

Though bureaucratically organized, the civilization was one of palaces and citadels, not of large cities; essentially rural, sea-faring and predatory. By 1400 BC the Mycenaean influence had spread far beyond the Peloponnese over Attica, Euboea; even over Thessaly, and beyond to Cyprus and Rhodes. The final Mycenaean prosperity was thus contemporary with that of the New Kingdom of Egypt, with Akhnaton and Tutankhamun in the mid-fourteenth century BC and with the rise of the Indo-European Hittites in Anatolia, who called them the *Akhai wai*, a version of *Achaioi*, the Homeric name for the Greeks. Indeed, it is now thought that the break in continuity during the age of barbarism between the Mycenaean culture and the Ionian civilization of the time of Homer has been exaggerated, the destructiveness of the Dorian invasions overdramatized, and that Mycenaean—and so Cretan—art and culture anticipate far more than has hitherto been realized the classical civilization of Hellas.

II

The original Cretan civilization was Levantine, the work of dark slender people of Anatolian stock, who assimilated settlers and refugees during the early Bronze Age and spoke a language still unintelligible to us, but which through Greek contributed characteristic words to our own vocabulary—as labyrinth, colossus, cypress and hyacinth; abyss, hymn and, oddly enough, absinthe.[1] The palaces and town were built agglutinatively without the central

[1] From *Apsinthion* = wormwood.

megaron or great hall with pillared entrance, reflecting, as at Mycenae, timbered originals in continental Europe. From Neolithic subsistence farming the Minoans, who had triaconters with fifteen rowers a side, became sea-borne traders and colonists, attracting as much as they compelled. Their princes were not particularly warlike, but their domination was made acceptable by religious prestige, strong management and splendour. The palaces were the scene of a cult, but there were no separate temples, and though the Cretans provided their dead magnates with miniature statuettes of girls and boys to entertain them in the after life, as well as with the usual finery, their interests were clearly more with life than with death and a supposed sequel: we do not find charnel houses or human sacrifice, but store rooms. The "palaces" at Knossos, Phaestos and Mallia, unlike the pyramids, were on a human scale, even the former covering no more than six acres, and since the Minoan fleets controlled the seas, they were not fortified. The surplus from farming, horticulture and metallurgy formed a reserve for gift exchange, princely redistribution and display, and later served for commerce. Minoan writing mainly records lists of stores; there are no surviving monumental inscriptions, civic or religious, and no big public monuments. "Inscriptions of the kind that contemporary Kings of Egypt and Mesopotamia delighted to cut on their temples are entirely absent from the Aegean."[1]

As the mixed economy of cereal crops, olive groves and vineyards, of sheep, goats and cattle, fisheries and game (the *agrimi* wild goat is still extant in the mountains) flourished in security, the princes encouraged craftsmanship and luxury trade with the European mainland, the Cyclades, Syria, Palestine and Egypt, whence pet monkeys, Nubian ivory and, later, mercenaries were imported. Long safe from outside attack, by 1700 BC the Cretans had the resources and time to look about them and depict life with a naturalness and *élan* which surpasses even Egyptian art. But beneath the sophisticated luxury of "perhaps the first people known who created works of art for the sheer joy of expressing the beauty they felt in their restless active lives",[2] lurked the menace symbolized by the Minotaur depicted on a thief-deterrent seal stone intently devouring a victim—the threat of earthquake. So the palace at Knossos, low-built round a centre court in a warren of staircases, corridors, state rooms, living rooms, light wells, shrines and patios, was designed to fit the contour of the ground and diminish the danger. The huddled flat-roofed houses at Gournia were intersected by cobbled streets, while the pipes and conduits for water and sanitation at Knossos depended on rainfall, sparse in summer.

With the vitality to transform what they took from Asia Minor and Egypt, the Minoans owed much to both. The cult of the double axe, of winged gryphons and an earth Goddess have an Asian provenance; the writing, seal stones, and decoration of the palaces have an Egyptian background, though the Cretan artists broke with Egyptian formalism. Their religion remains rather mysterious, though, living on Crete, they had a cult of the winds. But

[1]Sinclair Hood. *The Home of the Heroes. The Aegean before the Greeks.* London, 1967.
[2]Swindler, *op. cit.* p. 73.

their language remains even more so. Although the Linear B speech script (c.1450 BC) has been deciphered as primitive Greek, the earliest record of Indo-European, the earlier Linear A (c.1750 BC) defies interpretation, though some ideograms speak for themselves. The snake-bearing goddesses with Babylonian-style flounced skirts and tired heads seem part of the weird and archaic cult of the Double Axe, but the miniature ivories of the diademed chryselephantine Boy-God, the slender youth with his gold plated loin cloth seem more cheerfully worldly, and if "it is often assumed that Minoan bull fighting was a sacred performance ... there are no Minoan monuments to show that it was more than a popular spectacular sport."[1] A famous cup depicts merry-making harvesters, and the chattering spectators at a bull-leaping seem entirely secular. For all the sinister undertones of primitive religion, many Cretans would seem to have been eager extroverts.

Nor did they have an empire in the political sense; though they controlled Thera, where surviving the eruption, Minoan-style frescoes depict two children boxing and swallows in flight, and they sent out colonies to the Cyclades, Rhodes, Melos, mainland Greece, and even Sicily. The fleets of Minos put down piracy, tales of exacted tribute may have been based on memories of customs dues and the cultural and economic influence of Crete extended over much of the Aegean and its littoral.

So the first literate insular civilization in Europe emerges into history, with a "highly artificial social life"; its elegant men were clad in tightly girdled loin cloths, wearing their hair in long ringlets, an impression confirmed by the Egyptian painting of "the Keftiu" bearing elaborate merchandise from the tomb of Rehh-Ma-Ra and they also had orientalized robes for ritual—assimilating the dress of both sexes. The oldest nature frescoes are bands of flowers and rosettes, and the oldest (if heavily restored) figure fresco is a boy gathering saffron in a field of crocuses.[2] The artists employed by Evans after 1900 have over-restored both buildings and frescoes and given them a misleading touch of *art nouveau*, but enough of the originals remain to show their native colours, while the elegant vases range from the simplicity of the Melian vase and the Candian vase of the lilies to the baroque convolutions of the Octopus vase from Gournia. Indeed, the pre-Mycenae Cretans were "instinctively an artistic race ... with the sea-wind always in their nostrils; they knew a spur to action which the Egyptians, baked and beaten by the blinding sun, never could have felt. And so most of Cretan art shows a passion for movement and action, a passion as restless as the waves that washed their shores."[3]

Their main exports were olive oil, textiles, vases, cypress-wood and wine. Though they mined copper, they imported it from Cyprus; tin they obtained from Anatolia and perhaps Etruria and Southern Spain, and the gold work of the well-known "Wasp pendant" of Chrysolakkos near Mallia (c.1650 BC) can compare with anything from Sumeria or Egypt. Bronze was widely used for

[1]Renfrew. *The Emergence of Civilization. op. cit.* p. 419.
[2]Probably the same kinds of crocus afterwards cultivated by the Venetians in Crete for the same purpose.
[3]Swindler. *op. cit.* p. 73.

lamps, cauldrons and libation jugs, and serpentine stone, crystal, silver and gold for goblets; indeed "In the art of metal working as in those of engraving, vase-making and fresco painting, the Aegean, under Cretan influence probably led the civilized world at that time."[1] This Aegean culture, emanating from Crete, is a precursor to the civilization of Hellas, for though it went down in ruin through combined natural disasters and barbarian invasions, and since the last phase at Knossos was dominated by Achaian Greeks, perhaps before native Cretan revolts, its way of life and basic economy were never destroyed. It forms a brisk, maritime prelude to the dynamic civilization of Europe.

III

The martial rulers of Mycenae, as of Tiryns, Pylos and the contemporary strongholds in mainland Greece, who had assimilated and exploited Minoan culture, were part of the continental Higher Barbarism. These bearded warrior lords of the Bronze Age lived in massively fortified citadels; they were very heavily armed, with long and short swords, a heavy knife or cleaver carried inside their shields, and an axe; and they had horned or crested helmets, some decorated with boars' tusks. The Cyclopean masonry of the Lion Gate at Mycenae and at Tiryns are still formidable, and the skill of the architects of the so-called treasury of Atreus far surpasses anything on Crete. Built about 1350 BC, "It is among the most astonishing architectural masterpieces of its time anywhere in the world, and the largest vault that has survived from Antiquity until the Pantheon, rebuilt as we know it by the Emperor Hadrian some 1500 years later."[2] It remains singularly intact, with a corbelled vault over forty feet high and a high entrance under huge lintel blocks weighing more than a hundred tons. The builders of this mighty tomb challenge comparison with the Egyptians and commemorate a ruler of far-flung power: when in 1876 Schliemann discovered a gold-plated mask among the treasures of Mycenae he thought he had "looked upon the face of Agamemnon"; but the grim, contemptuous warrior who bore it had lived in much earlier times. Tiryns, also, with its Cyclopean galleries, is as old, and both sites include even older foundations.

Minoan civilization had long established itself at least superficially on the mainland before these Indo-European-speaking infiltrators and invaders came out of the north and exploited it, creating a forceful blend of barbaric and civilized cultures as the final and military phase of Cretan civilization saw a takeover by Greek-speaking invaders of Mycenaean type. Nor was their expansion confined to Crete; their influence extended over Attica and Thessaly, to Delphi and Boeotia, and south into Laconia in the Peloponnese. Mycenaean relics have been found in the Cyclades, in Rhodes, in Cyprus, and along the coast of Asia Minor, and although no trace of currency has been discovered, the original Minoan trade with Syria, Palestine, Egypt and Sicily

[1]Hood. *op. cit.* p. 104.
[2]Hood. *op. cit.* p. 115.

expanded in Mycenaean times. Indeed, it is likely that a Mycenaean expedition raided Egypt and burnt Thebes, while Mycenaean cups and jewellery have been found in central Europe, Britain and Denmark.

The economy was thus highly organized. The records of equipment and personnel found at Pylos and deciphered by Ventris reveal a bureaucratic society more akin to that of the Near East, more complex and elaborate than anything before it in Europe. We know a good deal about it; for the Minoan Linear B has been deciphered and interpreted, though, devised originally for a Minoan language, it clumsily fits the archaic Greek. Used in Crete only during the final phase, it is the only Mycenaean script, and, combining ideograms with syllables, it gives a full if not too attractive picture of the stratified and rationed labour force fulfilling its quotas of production behind the luxury and art.[1] The clay tablets which have survived, baked in the final conflagrations, record lists of farm workers, bath attendants, corn-grinders, weavers, flax-workers, bakers, armourers, and smiths (who were allowed slaves), along with their rations of wheat and figs. Rather after the manner of Doomsday book, the tablets form a census and a survey of land tenure, including lists of girls and boys being trained, and of court attendants, as "at Pylos: six (sons) of the head-band makers, and the musicians and the sweepers, six boys"; or "nine sons of the supernumerary women and of the wage earners and casual workers"; or at Knossos, "nine female slaves ... two older women under instruction, seven older girls, ten younger girls, two older boys, ten younger boys". Female slaves served the priestess at Pylos, and shepherds and goatherds were on the palace strength. Among the individuals listed are the headmen of villages, minor chiefs (*basilewes*), officers of the feudal hierarchy and landown-ers or "shareholders". Military and naval personnel are also listed; at Pylos, for example, rowers were drafted for expeditions and soldiers posted to guard the coast, probably from attack from the north-west. Even names are listed, after the name of the commander: "Command of Medius at *O-wi-to-no*, Ampelita-won, Orestos, Etewas, Kokkion";[2] "ten men of Oikhalia, thirty men of A-ka-akron ... and with them a follower".

The sustenance of the *Wanax* and his barons came from the supervised raising of wheat and barley, of beans and pulses from which a kind of porridge was made, from the herding of large flocks of sheep and goats and lesser ones of cattle, from cheese and wool, meat and hides, rather than milk and butter in a land of olive oil and wine stored in great *pithoi* impervious to damp and rats. There were many oxen—the ploughmen had names for them—but few horses: "wars and raids augmented the slave population, distinguished from serfs because not bound to the land, but mobilized in the 'palaces' and lesser households."

[1]*Documents in Mycenaean Greek. Three Hundred Selected Tablets from Knossos, Pylos and Mycenae, with comments and vocabulary* by the late Michael Ventris and John Chadwick. Cambridge, 1956. This fine work of scholarship gives the background and history of the discoveries and is superbly illustrated with ample examples of the ideograms and scripts. The claim that the language is archaic Greek has been generally, though not universally, accepted.
[2]Ventris and Chadwick. *op. cit.* p. 56.

Here is a warlike, aristocratic society, in which competition, display and military prowess are the main concern of the rulers, with hunting, a highly organized aristocratic sport employing nets and beaters and hunting dogs. Chariots of rare woods ornamented with ivory were more for show than combat, so that women are shown driving out in them. Perfumed oils and elaborate finery—in Crete plumed head-dresses and in Mycenae showy helmets—were the fashion, and where most of the people lived mainly on cereals, fruit, lentils, garlic, onions and what fish they could catch, the Mycenaean rulers and aristocracy in the manner of their kind over all Europe devoured roast meat. Evans thought that, like the Philistines in Palestine, they were beer drinkers, but none of the strainers and other accoutrements of brewing beer have been found, and if they enjoyed mead from honey, clearly what they most cared about was wine. Indeed, as well observed, in the Higher Barbarism of Bronze Age Europe, the "festive potential of wine" had long led "to the institution of social drinking",[1] and the treasures of the Early Bronze Age Aegean already show the fascination with these two topics which preoccupied the prehistoric princelings from Troy to Mycenae, from Etruria to the Celtic lands—warfare and wine.[2]

The insatiable competition for honour rendered this society unstable and wasted its resources in war: civilization was precarious, for in spite of a formidable military power, it depended on the palaces; and once their organization was disrupted, the structure collapsed. The progressive degradation of late Mycenaean art—always distinctive from that of Crete—is significant, and "as we survey the field of Mycenaean painting, we see little that commends itself as original."[3] Yet the dark age between the Mycenaean world and the rise of classical Hellenic civilization in the eighth century BC was not as dark as hitherto accepted, but only appears so since the evidence of literacy has been lost. If it is only by chance that the Minoan/Mycenaean tablets have been preserved, it seems unlikely that any people so clever as even archaic Greeks could have entirely lost the art of writing, and then, after three centuries, suddenly adopted the Phoenician alphabet. As in early medieval Christendom, the Kings and barons, both in the Bronze Age and in its aftermath, were probably illiterate.

IV

During the final years of their power the rulers of Mycenae fortified the isthmus of Corinth against invaders from the north. These people have usually been considered Dorian Greeks, though where they originally came from is unknown. Before their incursions the palace hegemonies abruptly collapsed. So that by about 1100 BC most of the strongholds had been destroyed; Tiryns was burnt, though Mycenae, diminished, survived into historic times. So also

---

[1]Renfrew. *The Emergence of Civilization. op. cit.* p. 488.
[2]Renfrew. *The Emergence of Civilization. op. cit.* pp. 284–5.
[3]Swindler. *op. cit.* p. 107.

did the polyculture of cereal crops, pulses, vines and olives which sustained the old Mediterranean way of life among the population, relieved at least of bureaucratically organized service to their overlords. In Crete many took to the mountains and their descendants stayed there; on the mainland, where the Minoan culture had never struck deep outside the palaces, they took to the hills or carried on as in pre-Mycenaean times. But the precarious and unusual sophistication emanating from Crete naturally survived best and revived earliest in the exceptionally favourable and relatively secure environment of the islands and settlements off the Anatolian coast; in Rhodes and Kos, at Halicarnassus—a pre-Greek name—and at Mitylene: so "Whatever was left of Cretan love for nature, passion for movement and colour, fondness for realism and truth to life, gave its heritage to the Greek world on Ionian shores."[1]

In Ionia at least Minoan/Mycenaean personal names survived the dark centuries; many are in Homer, some borne by Trojans; as e-ko-to–Hector; ta-ta-ro–Tantalos; pa-do-ro–Pandarus; o-re-tu–Orestes; a-ki-re-u–Accilleus; de-u-ka-ri-go–Deukalion;[2] indeed, in view of the cumulative evidence that the Mycenaeans spoke Archaic Greek, the first prehistoric civilization in Europe is now seen, as might be expected, never to have been sundered from the brilliant historical civilization of the Greeks that succeeded it.

Europe thus owes the origin of its most creative culture, to which modern civilization is still in debt, to a Mediterranean people of archaic stock in the exceptionally favourable maritime environment of Crete and the Peloponnese, whose sea-borne culture was assimilated and militarized by Greek-speaking Achaian Indo-Europeans who, in the climax of the Bronze Age, established a more far-flung hegemony. Eclipsed for three or four centuries by the Dorian and subsequent incursions and warfare, but never losing its basic Mediterranean economy and way of life, this civilization revived first on the coasts and islands of Asia Minor, then spread in its full creative brilliance to the city states of Greece itself, to become the main inspiration of the Graeco-Roman Antiquity and so of Europe.

[1]Swindler. *op. cit.* p. 108.
[2]Ventris and Chadwick. *op. cit.* pp. 104–5.

IV

The Early Greeks

When by the late second millennium the Mycenaean citadels and palaces were overrun by other Hellenic tribesmen infiltrating into Greece, emigrants from the mainland and Crete rapidly enlarged the colonies already established along the coast of Anatolia and on the adjacent islands or founded new ones. Here gradually, in another favourable setting, a new version of the archaic Mediterranean civilization revived; and although the Ionian Greeks became subjected to Asian landpower, it was from Ionia, as from archaic colonies long developed in Sicily and southern Italy, that early Greek civilization mainly derived, to reach its climax on the mainland in fifth-century Athens. This revival and transformation, in which the hard vigour of an originally steppe people was crossed with the subtlety and skills of the Levant, was decisive for Europe. For Graeco-Roman civilization was bi-lingual, owing its principal inspiration to Hellas. As Maurice Bowra put it: "Behind the power and pomp of Rome, men felt, not indeed very clearly or consciously at first but still with awe and questioning wonder, a driving daemonic force, a sunlit ideal, a perfection of achievement, which was somehow not Roman, even if it accounted for everything that mattered most in Rome."[1] And this brilliantly creative and foreign people—Homer is now sundered from us by two and a half millennia— now seem to us to have even more to say: modern archaeology has taught us much more about their background, the waning of transcendental mythologies has made their realism about the human condition seem better to fit the facts and support their belief that even if "death annihilates all that matters, life is all the more valuable and must be turned to the utmost account".[1] Moreover, the principles of scientific enquiry—of measurement, order, proportion and precision, and all the thrusting uninhibited curiosity now armed with modern technology that dominates our time—are in origin mainly Hellenic.

By about 500 BC many principal Greek cities were well established. Besides the predominant Athens and Sparta, Thebes in Boeotia, on an originally Mycenaean site, commanded a relatively rich agriculture. It would fight the

[1]C. M. Bowra. The Greek Experience. London, 1957. p. 1.
[2]Bowra. op. cit.

Athenians over Plataea which threatened its communications with Corinth, side with the invading Persians and would be the birthplace of the poet Pindar. Corinth, commanding the isthmus joining central Greece to the Peloponnese and dividing the Saronic Sea from the Corinthian Gulf, had been a centre of commerce since Mycenaean times: by the seventh century its rulers had constructed a stone causeway across the isthmus and planted colonies on Corfu and at Syracuse. The city became famous for cosmopolitan luxury, but not for military prowess. On the north-eastern Peloponnese Argos, founded by Dorian Greeks, had become, next to Sparta, the predominant power.

The largest city of eastern or Ionian Greece had long been Miletus. On the coast of Asia Minor near the mouth of the Meander, it conducted a far-flung trade with Egypt, where the Greeks had founded Maucratis, and with the Greek towns of the Black Sea. In the east the fertile island of Rhodes was also already flourishing along with neighbouring Kos, while Sardis in Lydia and Cyrene were already prosperous. To the north Lesbos was well placed for trade through the Dardanelles, and Samos for the trade with Athens.

Such are only the outstanding cities: well before the most brilliant age of Hellas, the political and economic pattern was set, and the creative Greek genius already apparent in the cities of the Ionian coast and islands.

II

The Minoan-Mycenaean world still lived on in Greek religion. Zeus, Father of Gods and Men, is a projection of a Bronze Age *Wanax*, a High King who does justice and preserves the cosmic order. The names of the three principal Greek deities derive from those mentioned as recipients of Cretan and Mycenaean votive offerings: "*di-we*" or *Diwei* is plainly the equivalent of Zeus, *po-se-da-o* of Poseidon, attested both from Knossos and Mycenae, and "Athena is clearly named once *a-ta-na po-ti-ni-ja Athenai Potniai, the Lady of Athens*."[1]

Homer, whose influence was all pervasive in antiquity, derives the character of Zeus "from the attributes of Kings ... in early times",[2]; like a Mycenaean king to his subjects, he is aloof from mankind. The *Iliad* depicts an "heroic", competitive and fierce society in which, save for capricious favours, the Gods are pitiless, and in which every man has his assigned fate according to his nature, sometimes determined by the temporary insanity of passion which may be a God working through him or—in modern terms—by subconscious impulse. Men are wary and pay the various gods their due if they respect the forces of the unconscious, adapt themselves to a plurality of impulses and celebrate the pleasures and variety of life—a wiser course than attempting to repress them in carrying out the impossible commands of the kind of Autocrat that Judaeo-Christian monotheists would project. Translated into the idiom of modern psychology, there is much to be said for the Homeric Gods.

[1]Ventris & Chadwick. *op. cit.* p. 125.
[2]Hugh Lloyd-Jones. *The Justice of Zeus*. University of California Press, 1971.

Apart from theology, the Homeric cult of honour, the mainspring of the narrative of the *Iliad*, still contributes to the Aristotlean idea of the temperate and disciplined "good life"—something very different from modern travesties of the phrase—and the cult of *arete*—all-round efficiency, endurance and cunning depicted in the Odyssey—made for the vigour as well as the often lethal turbulence of Greek politics and for the range of their colonization. Like the Homeric heroes, the Greeks were individualists, and "it is almost enough to point out that it is impossible to translate the word freedom, *eleutheria* in Greek, *libertas* in Latin, or 'freeman' into any ancient Near Eastern language, including Hebrew, or into any Far Eastern language either for that matter."[1] The centuries of chequered and war-ridden freedom, coming between the heavily organized archaic Mycenaean Age and the bureaucratic burdens of the later Roman Empire, saw the climax of Hellenic and Hellenistic culture.

The warrior cult of honour and enterprise had come down into a world very different from that of Homer's memory of Mycenae. For in historic times Hellenic civilization was organized in terms of the city state or *polis*, and this was not a citadel or a palace bureaucratically administered, but something more popular, durable and self-governing; a walled city with a much larger population, controlling a compact territory and commanding intense loyalty from its citizens, who felt themselves to be separate and superior to aliens, and in varying degrees of oligarchy or democracy took part in its politics and administration. The tribal and clan origins of the *polis* persisted among the citizens—always a minority seldom of more than ten per cent—and the ownership of land, not of money, conferred status. When, according to tradition, in 594 BC Solon, the poet and law-giver of Athens, "divided the citizen body into four categories each [was] defined by a minimum property holding. But for the study of the Greek economy, the distinction of the most far-reaching significance, one that continued right through the classical period in both democratic and oligarchic states, was between the citizen and the non-citizen, because it was a universal rule . . . that the ownership of land was the exclusive prerogative of citizens."[2]

The rudiments of such government, common in various forms to the Indo–Europeans who had long been settling on the continent of Europe, included a king, a council of elders and an assembly. The Greeks developed and defined them, and first formulated political theories concerned with the aims of government rather than with maxims of conduct or codes of case law. Already by the time that Homer's poetry was written down, the rule of hereditary kings was giving way to deliberate constitutions whereby either an oligarchy of landowners ruled the state, or, later on, democracies in which the entire body of citizens had a voice. Thus, already, forms of self-government were asserted against arbitrary personal power, and decisions taken by formal voting within small cities in which men knew one another and in which policy was decided by discussion as well as intrigue, bribery and varying amounts of violence. In this kind of polity, created by laws, the rule of law was

[1]M. I. Finley. *The Ancient Economy*. London, 1975. p. 28.
[2]Finley. *op. cit.* p. 48.

fundamental. Whatever the virulence of oligarchic or democratic politicians, they fought out their differences within an agreed political framework and were often united in their detestation of tyrants who disregarded it. While Greek political in-fighting was savage, vituperative and even murderous, the Greeks created original and elaborate forms of self-government, and "no city concealed divine monarchs in mysterious isolation or maintained privileged priesthoods as a separate caste."[1]

Constitutionalism, the least bad form of government, had been invented. It was variously institutionalized. Originally a centre for country people with a temple and agora, the *polis* was a tribal foundation, with archaic divisions into *phylae* (tribes), clans, and *phratries*—literally brotherhoods, deriving from times before the Greeks entered the country and overlapping with localized organizations later introduced. Acclimatized at Athens in the sixth century, and still called *phylae*, the tribal structure was based on villages and civic areas called *demes*—hence "democracy", though in Greece it only included the citizens, always an exclusive body wary of aliens and anxious for "autarchy"— a self-sufficiency generally impracticable.

The legislature also reflected tribal origins. The aristocratic Athenian *Areopagus* was originally composed of ten representatives of the four tribes, elected for life, and from them the Archons or chief magistrates were selected by lot; the council or *Boulé* of four hundred, later expanded to five hundred and chosen by lot from candidates put forward by the *demes*, initiated business, and the Assembly or *Ecclesia* was composed of all the citizens, who could all vote on it. Generally only a small proportion regularly attended; but the right was theirs. The Athenians thus early devised a form of self-government whereby public power could significantly be made responsible to the governed within a structure of checks and balances. And although the landowners and wealthier citizens retained predominant influence until the mid-fifth century, first the power of the heavy-armed hoplites diminished that of the original aristocracy, then that of the rowers in the fleet made for democracy. So a form of citizen-government including free discussion, voting, election by lot and by the fifth century ostracism (exile) of intolerable politicians for ten years without loss of civic rights was elaborated, though assassination was often preferred. In spite of bribery, corruption and political murder, government remained institutionalized.

In Sparta at least after the mid-sixth century, following the Messenian and Helot revolts, the regime was less adaptable. Following archaic customs, the Spartans retained two kings, one of whom had to command the army on campaign: the council of Thirty Elders were all over sixty, and elected for life (which, considering Spartan toughness, might be a long time), by the Assembly of all the Spartiate citizens over thirty, who also elected the Ephors. The Council, as at Athens, initiated business, but the decisions were taken by the Assembly. Other patterns of government appear in the Greek cities, but in principle they are similar in that government proceeded by discussion and vote. Its weakness was in administration; for the essential records were kept

[1]Bowra. *op. cit.* p. 18.

only by clever slaves. Its other and fatal weaknesses were parochial suspicion of aliens, even if Greek, and its exclusiveness. The proportion of citizens in Athens at the height of its democratic expansion was only about 40,000 to 300,000 in the whole of Attica. Usually it was far less.

The city states early spread far beyond the Aegean: they swarmed into Magna Graecia—the America of the Hellenes—into Sicily and Italy and on to Monaco, Nice, Antibes and Marseilles—all Greek names, along the coast of Spain; east up the Marmara to Byzantium and beyond through the Bosphorus to the Black Sea, as well as over to Cyrene in North Africa. And this new Greek world was united, like Old Greece, by common religious festivals and ways of life; all the Hellenes spoke variants of the same language, regarding those who did not as barbaroi from the alleged sound of their speech.

Yet, in spite of this common heritage, the Greeks never got beyond the city state, which even Plato and Aristotle regarded as the height of human political and social achievement. They remained incurably factious, and though they just managed to collaborate enough to defeat the two Persian invasions of 490 and 480-79 BC, they tore themselves to pieces in internecine wars, of which the greatest and most tragic was the long Peloponnesian war between Athens and Sparta, in 431-21 and 411-05 BC. Old Greece never recovered, so that by 338 BC at Chaeronea in Thessaly, the cities were swamped by the more massive but relatively uncouth power of Macedon from the fringe of Greek civilization. The super-powers first of Alexander and his successors, then of Rome, were to master the future, and the original Greek city states had to content themselves with their unchallenged historic and cultural prestige.

III

The economic basis of the mainland city states was very limited: according to Plutarch (c.45-122 AD), who, though he wrote so long after, is here probably reliable, Solon's classification of landowners now made, significantly not by descent, but according to property, put the highest class at those whose estate produced 500 metretae of wine or oil (4500 gallons), or 500 medimni of grain (750 bushels), an amount implying an estate not more than about seventy-five acres; the next class with 300 medimni were rich enough to afford a horse, the third, with over 200, to be heavy armed infantry and the rest too poor to have to do more than attend the ecclesia. The number of Athenian citizens in the early fifth century in a total population of about 40,000 was as yet only about 12,000 of whom less than half were comfortably off, and the rest small farmers or artisans, sailors and fishermen.

The setting was comparatively primitive: in Solon's days the wolves were still a menace and rewards high for taking them, and water so scarce that farmers were urged to share wells. Poultry had arrived in Greece only in the sixth century from the east. Hesiod, or whoever wrote Works and Days, the earliest calendar of the agricultural year, in Boeotia around 720 BC, grumbles as farmers will, about the weather.

When Boreas blows on the Earth
He blows through Thrace, where horses graze; he blows
On the broad sea and whips it up: the earth
And forest mutter;

So

Bind on your feet the fitted ox-hide boots
Lined with thick felt.

And he thoroughly dislikes the sea. People have no need of it if they farm properly, and "*it is terrible to meet catastrophe among the waves.*"

Indeed, the dawn of Hellenic civilization seemed to these mainland contemporaries of Homer an age of Iron, and Greece, even if then better wooded, must have been a hard country; brilliant in light and colour, but austere, for most of the small farmers the scene of a primitive struggle for livelihood.

A certain callousness, as throughout Antiquity, always pervaded a slave-owning society. Much has been made of the contrast between the mass slavery of the great Roman estates, and the domestic and small scale factory slavery of the Greeks; but we do not know the numbers of the slave population, and while it has been claimed on flimsy evidence that there were twice as many citizens as slaves, a modern authority declares roundly, "In short Greece and Italy were slave societies in the same broad sense as was the American South."[1] Even quite poor citizens had slaves, and though slaves could become freed men, and their sons born afterwards free men, a society in which one can buy and sell other people and which takes the situation for granted differs from any in which the "peculiar institution" does not exist. Add to this that the Spartans, like other Greeks in some overseas city states, were a minority holding down an indigenous helot population and deliberately in Sparta itself keeping them poor and oppressed, and the callous side of classical civilization becomes apparent. Given hard-driving overseers, slave labour is not necessarily inefficient, but the immense preponderance of the land in the economy and the abundance of cheap manpower—for in the Roman Empire the free citizen peasants became increasingly degraded—must have discouraged the exploitation of labour-saving inventions when made, and form the background to the indifference or contempt which the ruling minorities felt towards "banausic" pursuits or technological gadgetry—an attitude rooted in the literary and oratorical bias of their education.

On the other hand, both the Ionian and mainland Greeks were brilliantly original in theoretical enquiry about the world. In scientific speculation they were extremely courageous, uninhibited by technological limitations or religious dogma, though conscious of the precariousness of human effort before the fate that their aloof Gods symbolized. Hence an objectivity about both experience and nature. No enquiry was forbidden. For the first time the very basis of the physical world was examined. Thales of Miletus, for example, an enthusiast who is said to have fallen into a well when arguing about the stars

[1]Finley. *op. cit.* p. 79.

and who probably flourished about 590 BC, was the first known geometrician. He declared that water was the basis of physical life and held the pantheistical belief that "all things are full of Gods". Pythagoras—none of whose writings survive, though several works, including the Pythagoras theorem of Euclid, proving that the square on the hypotenuse of a right angled triangle is equal to the sum of the squares on the other two sides—came from Samos, though he migrated to Crotona in southern Italy. Fascinated with musical notes and the intervals between them on a scale, he became obsessed with numbers. He also founded a kind of sect infected by the Eastern belief that the body was a prison to the "soul"—something made of "fire and air". Indeed, he believed in the transmigration of "souls" and supposedly remarked of a puppy "Do not hit him: it is the soul of one of my friends". More sensibly, he instructed his disciples to ask themselves every evening "what good have I done today, and what harm?"—a salutary exercise.

Democritus of Miletus, the pioneer physicist and "laughing philosopher" (c.470 BC), scorned such flights of fancy. He thought that the world was made up of indivisible atoms—they were too small, he considered, hopefully, to be split—that mankind originally was made out of "water and mud", and that the "soul" perished with the body. He was a pioneer of optical theory, believing that objects threw off impressions that stamped themselves on the eye, and he did not in the least believe in the Gods. They were simply, he considered, fantasies due to impressions made by thunder and lightning. It was, therefore, he argued, best not to expect too much of life or get wrought up; rather to live in tranquil moderation as cheerfully as one could, a view later propagated by the English Robert Burton (floruit 1621) as *Dimocritus Junior* in the *Anatomy of Melancholy*.

Hippocrates, born on the beautiful island of Kos about 479 BC, is reputed to be the founder of medical science. Asclepius, a son of Apollo by one of his nymphs, had indeed long before learnt medicine from Chiron the centaur, but he had done so well that Zeus had killed him with a thunderbolt for fear he might make men immortal. He was symbolized by a snake twisted round a staff; two of his sons had supposedly been doctors to the Greeks at Troy; and his shrine at Epidaurus, one of the great health resorts in Antiquity, was already long established. Hippocrates studied first at another temple, still extant, on Kos, then during a long lifetime practised on the Greek mainland, where he died at Larissa in Thessaly. His enduring fame is due to the *Corpus Hippocraticum*, treatises following his methods collected at the medical school at Alexandria in about 300 BC and including the famous Hippocratic code of honour and secrecy, still accepted by physicians.

The contrast between the incantations of witch doctors in prehistoric times (they particularly liked to "trepan" people with headaches to let the evil spirit out), and the long current and accepted beliefs of astrologers, with the methods of the Greek doctors is extraordinary. Here, already, is caution in diagnosis, stress on diet, occupation and surroundings; and they would examine all available evidence rather than attribute illness to the enmity of god or man. Baths, exercise, soothing music, were employed to help the patient right himself. Others, like Pythagoras, let theory run wild: as Empedocles, who is said to have jumped into the crater of Etna in order to disappear and be thought immortal—a gesture that failed since the volcano ejected a sandal—believed that man was composed of the four "humours", fire, air, earth and water, and that the art of medicine was to keep them in balance; a theory that would do much harm over many centuries. Hippocrates and his followers, on the other hand, followed the evidence as they knew it. This initiative, in its context the greatest practical achievement of the early Greeks, owed much to Egyptian and probably Indian medicine, but the Greeks were the first to give it full theoretical definition.

But if, in science, their achievement was brilliant, it was not experimental. They posed the essential questions on the origin of matter and on the causes of natural phenomena, which ultimately formed the agenda, mainly through Muslim sources in the Middle Ages, of the European scientific revolution of the sixteenth to the nineteenth centuries. But there was a characteristic limitation: in spite of all their vigorous and original intelligence, the Greeks quite failed to formulate a method of systematic enquiry based on careful and controlled observation which could have given the lie to the many absurd theories and superstitions readily accepted among intelligent people in Antiquity. The Greeks were ever ready to theorize, but not to test their theories in rigorous experiment. They were deductive, not inductive in their reasoning, and this flaw was inherited by the Romans; hence the dominance of a vast system of myth and divination and astrological theories even during the height of Graeco–Roman civilization.

Such, from the early sixth century, are representative aspects of Hellenic genius in the sciences. Common to them all is the rigour of logic, afterwards turned to speculation about ethics. The early philosophers created a discipline of mind that cut down to essentials with fine self-confidence; a sense of order and proportion which would come to distinguish a powerful and original side of a European civilization, distinctive from most others.

IV

Archaic Greek architecture derived from the wooden and thatched structures of barbarian central Europe; from the posts and lintels of the Chieftain's hall, translated, as already at Mycenae, into the stone megaron. From these beginnings the Greeks created the main forms of European classical architecture. The simplicity and logic of their designs are functional, and the original oblong hut facing east to west became the well proportioned temple, with its pillars, originally timber supports for a low pitched roof, placed outside as well as in. The mathematically correct design and proportion of a Greek temple was combined with cunning devices to create an illusion of lightness, and a strict convention made a temple everywhere recognizable. The Doric style, prevalent on mainland Greece and to the west including southern Italy, where the temples at Paestum are particularly well preserved, and in which the Parthenon at Athens is designed, displayed strong fluted columns with plain circular capitals; the Ionic, dominant in Anatolia and the islands, and apparent in the Erechtheum and parts of the Propylaea on the Acropolis, was more graceful, with unfluted pillars and curved or garlanded capitals; the later, Corinthian, style was far more elaborate, with acanthus leaves and palmetts, popular in the exuberance of Hellenistic architecture. Like that of the sculptures, the gaunt appearance of the temples today is misleading: if marble, they were gilded and touched up with colour; if limestone, they were covered in stucco and painted. But the essential and superb quality of design survives; at the dawn of civilization Greek architects set standards of sanity, proportion and functional elegance. The Athenians, particularly fortunate in possessing good marble quarries, created their masterpieces in the second half of the fifth century, well after the repulse of the Persian attack and the destruction of the original Acropolis; but already by the late sixth century the elegant treasury at Delphi, now restored, was in being.

Greek sculpture, also decisive for European art, had more exotic beginnings, there being little scope for it in the barbarian way of life. Like architecture, it was strictly conventional, and at first, in the seventh century, heavily influenced by the Egyptians. The early youths (*Kouroi*) depicted have a formal Egyptian stance, and stare ahead with an African impassivity; the maidens (*Kore*) have a hieratic fixed smile. All Greek sculpture was originally painted; that of Parian or Pentelic marble discreetly, so that the texture of the marble could show. It was also set off by ivory and gold, so that the austerity it presents, like that of the temples, is artificial. By the early sixth century, the originally Egyptian-style conventions had become more human, as in the satisfied look of the big Moscophoros (calf-bearer, c.575 BC) with the live animal on his shoulders, or the ripple of drapery on the amiable *Kore* of Antenor half a century later, while even the potentially sinister Tricorpor, the three-bodied God of the early Acropolis, has a grin and twists his tail as if he found himself a joke. By the end of the sixth century Greek sculpture is poised for its exploits in the fifth, as the statue of Zeus found near Cape Artemesium, judging his distance when about to hurl a thunderbolt (c.450 BC), or that of the pensive youth of the school of Praxiteles from Marathon, both of which would have had the whites of the eyes conspicuously lifelike.

More intimately revealing, the vase painting develops from the austere abstractions of the geometric style into the full range of naturalistic designs, becoming at their best comparable to the masterpieces of Iran or China. The geometric style signalizes something alien to the Minoan world; it expresses not how things look but the abstract idea of them; not the vivid impressions of life but an order imposed on them—a rationalized order comparable to that of the pioneer mathematicians. The accuracy of these patterns is extraordinary, and when this non-representational art has to include humans and horses, it cuts them down into symbolic forms, as in eighth-century Attic funerary amphorae, or the contemporary lying in state processions with figures, horses and chariots,[1] black on a terra cotta ground.

The life depicted is "heroic", hard and military; with the "development of

[1]See Pierre Devambez. *Greek Painting*. plates 32–4. trans. Jean Stewart. London, 1962.

foreign contacts" through trade and colonization, Egyptian and oriental influences made for a more human style. The Melian and Rhodian vases of the seventh century depict mythological scenes and animals; the Corinthian amphora of Hercules and Cerberus between bands of stylized ivy leaves, or of Europa riding a complacent bull between dolphins, fishes and a heron, are already masterpieces, the bull's silhouette rounded out by lines incised on the buff coloured background.[1]

In Sparta by the mid-sixth century, a fascinating and sophisticated design depicts a King of Cyrene in a wide hat on a ship's deck, supervising the weighing of merchandise, and a Corinthian mixing bowl a boar hunt, the figures and the animal now in red as well as black against a pale ground. By now there was a big export trade in amphorae from Corinth, and Athens was producing a great variety of designs for the home market, many, as the landing of Theseus on Delos, revealing of sixth-century life, particularly for the ships.[2] In contrast, with exquisite economy, an Attic cup depicts a single deer, and the cup by Exekias, Dionysus in his boat, vine clusters drooping from the mast as he sails happily, steering oars neglected, through a dolphin-haunted sea.

The climax of Greek vase painting thus came early, roughly from 530–480 BC with an astonishing variety of mythological, social, hunting and funerary subjects, in which overall design and balance is combined with telling detail and psychological insight. Magnificent as the ceramic skill of the great classical fifth century would be, it never surpassed the power and freshness of this most revealing art, which brings the early Greeks as near to us as does their poetry.

V

The grand epics of Homer, written down by the end of the eighth century, had a "long tradition of poetry which derived its stories and its characters, no less than much of its technique and its language, from Mycenaean times, and was passed on from generation to generation by an oral tradition".[3] Similarly the terrific Greek drama, which set the pattern for Europe, had archaic beginnings. The ritual of Dionysus, god of nature, of animals and the vine, was more homely than the cult of remote Olympian Immortals, and out of its primitive ecstatic and priapic ritual Greek drama developed in all its variety. Tragedy came first: in 534 BC Peisistratus, the successful tyrant of Athens, inaugurated the official Spring Festival of the Dionysia to popularize his regime. After the *dithyramb* of praise to the genial God, three chosen poets would compete to produce a "tragedy", literally "goat song" from *tragos* and *oidas*, "goat singer"—(probably a goat was a prize or sacrifice)—followed by a burlesque parody or "satyr play": comedy, from *komos*, revel-singer, was not evolved until half a century later.

The original tragedy thus emerged from a choral cult hymn, when a single

[1]Devambez. *op. cit.* 50–2.
[2]Devambez. *op. cit.* 75.
[3]Bowra. *op. cit.* p. 20.

actor elaborated points in a dialogue with the chorus; with two actors, a straight narrative of events came to be acted out, with comment from the chorus; with three actors, the dramatic range increased.

During the sixth century rudimentary drama was performed at Corinth and at Athens, but Aeschylus (525–456), who was born at Eleusis in Attica and fought at Marathon and probably at Salamis, is the greatest master "who first built high with massive eloquence the diction of tragedy". He wrote about eighty plays of which seven survive entire, and all but the *Persae*, celebrating the defeat of the Persians at Salamis, "stabbed . . . as fishermen kill tunnies in some netted haul" following Xerxes' insolence towards the Gods, work out the Justice of Zeus in the lives of famous characters in myth and epic. These grim and austere themes range from *Prometheus Bound* for stealing fire from heaven for the benefit of mankind, until he blackmailed Zeus into conniving at Hercules shooting the eagle that nightly devoured his liver—a denouement unfortunately not covered by the play—to the great Oresteian trilogy (c.458) on the God-determined fate of the House of Atreus, which included involuntary cannibalism, human sacrifice and matricide, interspersed by disillusioned comments by the chorus on the human plight. The drama is driven home by an awesome power of language and lit up by flashes of description, as of the beacon signals of the fall of Troy that crossed the Aegean.

> "like the whip lash of lightning . . . the resinous
> dazzle, molten gold, till the fish danced".

Such poetry implies a highly intelligent audience; that the great audience was then there at all seems extraordinary. European drama emerges in these profound and exciting masterpieces, rooted in the epic tradition of Homer and the primeval mythology of Hesiod.

The Greek theatre did not come to its full power until after the Persian wars; lyric poetry, like some of the best art, flourished before them. Theognis in the mid-sixth century BC is an early exponent of lyric verse, sung to a flute for solo performance: Pindar (520–440 BC) is far the greatest master of choral odes, celebrating with trained choirs and more elaborate music the aristocratic victors at Hellenic games. Theognis, probably of Megara, was a disillusioned oligarch who combined rather tedious worldly moralizing with ultimate pessimism—

> When things go well I have a lot of friends.
> But few stay loyal when my luck is bad;
> or Be young my soul! New souls will soon abound
> And soon I'll be inanimate black ground.

In more lively mood, like Anacreon who flourished at Samos in the mid-sixth century and died aged eighty-five from a grape pip that went down the wrong way, Theognis celebrated the love of boys. For in sexual tastes the Greeks were uninhibited; indeed, as Professor Andrewes writes, "to pass over the question of male homosexuality would distort the picture of Greek society." And "it ought to be stated at the start that there are, and have been many civilizations which openly tolerate homosexuality without feeling that they are doing anything remarkable, and that such civilizations are not automatically involved in immediate disaster."[1] This fact of Hellenic life, embarrassing to generations of Christian clergymen and schoolmasters interpreting it to their charges, can now be admitted; not least thanks to a pioneer work written "to fill a no longer endurable gap in our knowledge of the Hellenic people".[2]

An anonymous poet is representative of the ambivalence,

> Zeus came like an eagle to God-like Ganymede;
> As a swan he came to the fair haired mother of Helen (Leda).
> So there is no comparison between the two things.
> One person likes one; another likes the other.
> I like both.[3]

Indeed, at least the upper-class Greeks often thought the love of boys or youths was more elevated and romantic—a cult taken for granted throughout Graeco-Roman Antiquity until the Judaeo-Christian ethic proclaimed it criminal. It was primeval and aristocratic; bound up with war, heroism and political liberty: in the *Iliad* itself the passion of Achilles and Patroclus was more violent than any friendship, and Athenaeus of Naucratis echoed an ancient political tradition when he wrote "Hieronymus the Peripatetic believes that love affairs with boys remained widespread because it often happened that the vigour of young men, joined to their mutual sympathy and companionship, brought many tyrannical governments to an end."[4]

So Theognis already writes:

> You're like a colt, boy, who has had his fill
> Of barley elsewhere, then comes back to me,
> Wanting a gentle rider, a cool spring,
> Soft meadows to run in and some shady woods;

then, less happily,

> If you lead a boy to love, you will be burned
> As if you put your hand in a fire of twigs;

but, comprehensively,

> The man is never happy who does not
> Love horses, and hunting dogs and young men.

Sappho, the most famous and passionate love poet of Antiquity whom even Plato called a "Tenth Muse", was born on Lesbos about 620 B.C. Like Socrates, she loved the young, but preferred girls and places "by cool waters where the breeze rustles through apple trees".[5]

She compared love to a storm that shakes the oaks, and Ovid, no mean

[1]Antony Andrewes. *The Greeks*. London, 1967. p. 215.
[2]Hans Licht. *Sexual Life in Ancient Greece*. trans. J. H. Freese. London, 1932. p. 524.
[3]*Greek Anthology*, I.
[4]*Deipnosophistae*, XIV, (Loeb), p. 606.
[5]*Lyra Graeca*, I. ed. J. M. Edmunds (Loeb). p. 187.

judge and who could read all her works now lost, pays tribute to her passion. We have only a few poignant lyrics, of which the most famous is

> The moon has set and the Pleiades;
> It is midnight and time passes, time passes, and I lie alone.

And there was naturally ample celebration of heterosexual love: of girls with "clear blue eyes like summer seas", of "the soft clasp of snowy limbs", and of the relative quality of their kisses; "no-one", writes Andrewes, "familiar with Greek art or poetry, will be disposed to underrate the strength of marital and parental affection that the ordinary Greek felt":[1] and it would be hard to beat the record of this splendid matron;

> I, Callicratia, bore nine and twenty children and did not witness the death of one, boy or girl.
> I lived to be a hundred and five without ever resting my trembling hand on a staff.[2]

Choral odes did not reach their perfection until the fifth century with Pindar, but they are also very ancient. As early as 776 BC the first Pan-Hellenic festival is said to have been held at Olympia in Etolia in the western Peloponnese. These festivals were the diversion of the aristocrats, and the competitors were well born; the Pan-Hellenic Olympic festivals, part of a cult of Zeus, were celebrated every fifth year in the blazing climax of summer under the July full moon. The victors of these athletic contests were crowned with an olive wreath cut from a sacred tree, placed on a fillet of white wool, and as they and their supporters offered sacrifice, choral songs of victory were sung, followed by a banquet. The prestige of the victors was enormous: they were feted on return to their native cities; statues were put up to them; time reckoned in terms of the five year Olympiads. Representatives of most of the cities attended the games, which combined the advantages of a pilgrimage, a social gathering, a festival of poetry and drama, and a fair: the gatherings at Olympia were paralleled by many others—as from 586 BC the Festival of Pythian Apollo at Delphi in the third year of each Olympiad, and the Isthmian games at Corinth in honour of Poseidon. Originating in pre-Hellenic times, during the autumn there were the women's festivals of Demeter, the goddess of fertility and the land, observed all over the Greek world. The Eleusinian mysteries and the Adonia commemorating the yearly return of Adonis, slain by a boar, to Aphrodite, were famous throughout Antiquity, and also related to the primeval cult of fertility and renewal.

At Athens on a more popular level the vintage was celebrated at a Feast of the Wine Presses, in which the gathering, harvesting and treading of the grapes were mimed. As in medieval Christendom with its Saints' days and religious anniversaries, so this Mediterranean civilization had its pre-Christian equivalents; the Spartans celebrating the memory of Hyacynthus, beloved of Apollo, killed by a discus diverted by a jealous Zephyr; the Athenians the Oschophoria festival commemorating Theseus, and the great *Panathenaia*.

[1]op. cit. p. 215.
[2]Greek Anthology. op. cit. II. 224.

The major festivals, as at Olympia or of Apollo at Delphi, continued to unite the Hellenes, persisting through endemic political conflicts, which often made the relations of the city states a chain of alternate animosities, and which gave rise to rival Leagues of Cities, as well as to opportunities for Persian intrigue, setting the Greeks against one another; indeed, such was the bitterness of inter-Hellenic strife that it was commonplace for exiled faction leaders to seek refuge and aid at the Persian court. Yet in spite of these murderous factions, culminating in the long disastrous war between Athens and Sparta, the Greeks always felt part of a common civilization, rooted in the same religion and literature and expressed in similar architecture and art. For the environment and social pattern were broadly the same: city states of manageable size, based upon a conservative agriculture, with the ownership of land giving social status, and enriched, if they were enriched, by sea-borne commerce extending over most of the Mediterranean and up to the Black Sea. Though the cities were not large, Greek civilization was extensive; and in all the cities life centred on the *Agora* or *piazza*, in a loquacious gregarious existence, lived mainly out of doors in brilliant sunshine, with the women minding the households and slaves doing the more menial tasks and working the mines and quarries. So in contrast to orientals, the Greeks made a cult of athletic sports, not merely of hunting; in the Levantine climate young men competed in the palaestra without the religious inhibitions that made naked-ness seem shameful, and delighted in the competitive display of excellence in any field, physical or mental. Apart from fear at having lost face or guilt at having incurred the wrath of a god which, if not incurred by some hereditary curse, could be propitiated by the right ritual and purifications, this naturally quick-witted and subtle people had already transformed the recitative of primitive cult hymns into tremendous tragedy, against an archaic and pervasive background of Epic poetry vastly superior to anything in contemporary Europe, for it could create characters and move to pity. They had also early devised lyric verse which is still poignant. And along with all this enterprise and zest for *Arete*, went a basic realism about life.

V

The Hellenic Climax

The early Hellenes, who had emerged into history by the eighth century, had established a vigorous far-flung and enterprising culture of city states. They were now confronted with a formidable menace, as the great Asian landpower of Persia under the *Shahanshahs* Darius I and Xerxes moved heavily against them, intent on including them in a vast tributary empire. The Greeks might call them *barbaroi*—aliens in language and way of life—but the Persians were much richer and often more civilized, as in gardening and cuisine, than the mainland Hellenes, whom they regarded as uncouth. For the empire established by Cyrus the Great (559–530 BC) extended over the most ancient and wealthiest civilizations in the world; a relatively recent conquest by an Indo-European people who, entering Iran in the early Iron Age, had settled in the valleys of the Zagros mountains in the south-west, had extended their power at the expense of the Assyrians, and created Ecbatana (Hamadan), originally the Medish capital, the first centre of a united Iran. Cyrus, whose plain tomb at Pasagadae attests his Indo-European origin, had coveted the maritime coast of Anatolia, and having taken Babylon and allowed the captive Jews to return to Jerusalem, had moved west, where by an ingenious stratagem he had defeated Croesus of Lydia near Sardis on the river Hermus, for he had collected all his baggage camels, unloaded them, and sent them with armed riders into battle in the front line; whereat "the Lydian war horses, seeing and smelling the camels, turned round and galloped off ... because a horse has a natural dread of the camel and cannot abide the sight or the smell of the animal."[1] So the Persians had come to dominate the Anatolian coasts and islands and the Ionian Greeks: the perennial tension between Asians and Europeans built up on a frontier that became fluctuating and uncertain, and with the Persian invasion of continental Greece, erupted between two civilizations into the first great set pieces of European history, described by Herodotus, at Marathon in 490, and at Salamis and Plataea in 480 and 479 BC.

After the death of Cyrus in battle on the far central Asian frontiers, and in

[1] *The History of Herodotus* (Rawlinson's translation). Everyman ed. London, 1910. p. 41 (Chs. 78–81).

the brief reign of Cambyses, the young Darius I in 514-13 BC had again moved against the West, as part of a major campaign beyond the Danube against the Scythians, had occupied Thrace and established suzerainty over Macedonia. He would rule, in modern terms, over most of Turkey, Lebanon, Syria, Palestine, Iraq and Egypt, from the Caucasus and the Caspian to the Persian Gulf, from the Araxes in central Asia to the Indus. This gigantic area contains vast expanses of desert and mountain, but Ecbatana and Persepolis, Susa and Babylon, Tyre and Sidon—the Phoenician sea-ports—Memphis in Lower Egypt and Thebes in Upper, were all centres of high civilization.

Nor was Darius I (522-486 BC) an oriental despot crazed with power: he was an able ruler, his personality reflected in his palace at Persepolis, with its fluted columns sixty-five feet high, the tallest columns in ancient architecture. "The style of the decoration achieved under Darius is marked by its clarity, balance, power and firmness, a translation into stone of the very character of his career."[1] He thought it his duty to extend the *Pax Iranica*—for he worshipped Ahuramazdāh, the Great God of Order and Light, whose conflict with Ahriman, the Spirit of Chaos and Darkness, had been reinterpreted by Zarathustra in the early sixth century as the struggle between the Good Mind and the Lie. The monotheist Persians despised the polytheistic anthropo-morphic Greek mythology and the Greek practice of animal sacrifice in which the Gods were conveniently assigned the bones and fat, and the smell was hideous to contemplate. Many Ionian Greeks were content to be part of the Persian empire, which, divided into Satrapies and united by a gold and silver coinage, common weights and measures, and by relatively good roads, had a "volume of trade in the sixth and fifth centuries BC (which) surpassed anything previously known in the ancient East,"[2] and it was, moreover, trade in ordinary produce, not merely in luxury goods. The Jews, in intervals of lamentation, had turned their exile in Babylon to advantage, and established banks, and Darius had commanded that in Iran itself subterranean canals should provide irrigation. The empire too was rich in metals, and there was ample timber in Lebanon and parts of Anatolia. As the shrewd Phoenicians had found, there was much to be said for being subjects of the Great King, whose taxation, while regularly collected and settled, was not excessive, for the sheer size and diversity of the Persian empire prevented systematic oppression and, indeed, its weakness was too great a devolution of power.

In spite of these advantages, in 499-94 BC the Ionian Greeks, resenting the civic domination of Persian-appointed rulers, broke into revolt, while many mainland Greeks, aware of the threat to their timber and corn supplies from the Persian advance into Thrace and domination of the Black Sea, were now alert to the danger. An Ionian League, reinforced by the Athenians, was crushed, and though they held out for two years, the people of Miletus, one of the principal centres of Ionian civilization, were deported in the Asian manner to Susa, and finally to insalubrious exile near the mouth of the Tigris. But the Athenians had committed themselves: Darius now proceeded to mobilize an

[1] R. Ghirshman. *Iran*. Penguin, Harmondsworth, 1954. p. 168.
[2] *op. cit*. p. 186.

immense expedition against them, confident in superior resources and in the political disunity of the continental Greeks.

He had reason to believe in it. But although antagonism between Athens and Sparta and the feuds between lesser cities were endemic, and the internal strife within most of them hardly less acute, the Athenians and the Spartans had both shown extraordinary, if contrasting, vitality. Solon in Athens had defined a constitution which had survived the brief phase, common to most of the cities, when a *Tyrannos*—the word had then no pejorative meaning—had asserted a more broad-based public power against a faction-ridden aristocracy. The regime of the Athenian *Tyrannos,* Peisistratus (c.550-27 BC), had been relatively mild; but his son Hippias had been ousted, and in 507 Cleisthenes, still within the old constitutional framework, had further undermined the influence of the aristocracy by altering the structure of the franchise from the four tribes based on kinship to ten based on area, and by creating demes for local government, not only in the villages but in the cities. He thus, in contrast to the practice of many Greek cities, considerably "democratized" the government, and launched an early version of the democratic experiment (since known as the "open society") which would disgust Plato. It is unlikely that a large proportion of the citizens exercised their rights, but this widening of the franchise promoted a vigour and patriotism which reached its climax in the victory over the Persians and in the climactic bright interval of stability (446-432 BC) which saw the building of the Parthenon and other splendours before the tragic sequel of the Peloponnesian war.

Sparta, on the other hand, which never had a *Tyrannos*, developed a closed society, but one equally forceful; and while the Athenians developed sea power, became the greatest power on land. The difference went back to early times when the Dorians or West Greeks had settled on Sparta, Boeotia, and Thessaly, while the Ionian or East Greek influence, with its Mycenaean provenance, persisted in Attica and most of the islands, a contrast already observed in architecture. Then, when the Spartans of Laconia had conquered Messenia and in the seventh century put down a major revolt there, they had organized themselves, traditionally under Lycurgus, into a very peculiar political and social system indeed. They retained a dual kingship—an institution unique among the classical Greeks—a Council, and Ephors, while according decisive powers to the Assembly of equal citizens, with the whole social order based upon helots and slaves. The full Spartiates—in theory aristocratically equal—were trained to war from childhood. Removed from their families at seven, the boys and adolescents were herded into age groups and subjected to extreme physical hardship, sometimes living off the country, if necessary by theft, and undergoing ordeals; at twenty they were drafted into the army, where they ate in "messes" and slept in dormitories; they remained still under the authority of the Council and the Ephors. Sparta was thus deliberately made a garrison state, geared to war, and the army became professionals with better organization, discipline and supply than any other. The proposals of Plato's *Republic* and *Laws* appear less extraordinary considering that the Spartan state was in being. By the early fifth century, when first Darius, then Xerxes, decided to settle accounts with the continental Hellenes, the two leading cities, open and closed societies, were both well able to defy them.

II

"The mountains", wrote Byron, "look on Marathon and Marathon looks on the sea": and here, in July 490 BC, the Athenian and Plataean hoplites drove the first Persian invaders to their ships. It was their own achievement, for the conservative Spartans, warned by Pheidippides, a professional runner who arrived over 140 miles of hard going the day after he had been dispatched from Athens, had delayed until after the festival of the full moon. But the Athenians had ample warning; they knew that Hippias, the surviving Peisistratid, had "medized", and that, relying on many collaborators, the Persians had already launched one attack, foiled by a storm off Mount Athos: and now, striking direct across the Aegean, they had attacked Eretria on the west coast of mountainous Euboea. Betrayed by collaborators, the city had been destroyed, its people deported. So already when the Persians landed at Marathon, the Athenians had established themselves in the foothills behind the beachhead two miles wide by five long, and now ingeniously got round the extraordinary arrangement whereby the generals representing Cleisthenes' ten tribal areas each took a day's turn at command. For when five voted to attack and five to await the Spartans, Miltiades persuaded them to assign overall command to the *polemarch* or civilian war-archon, who opted for battle.

Miltiades waited for his turn of tactical command, while edging the hoplites nearer the enemy, by ostensibly making timber obstacles to their cavalry, until the Persians, like the Anglo-Saxons at Hastings, were within striking distance of the more efficient force. Then in the small hours after Ionian deserters had reported the Persian cavalry away from camp—presumably pasturing and watering their mounts or with their horses hobbled—as the dawn came up behind the serrated peaks of Euboea the Athenian heavy infantry went in at the run, their main weight against the enemy flanks. Though the Persian centre made headway, their flanks crumbled. They depended on cavalry and archers and wore on their heads the soft hat or turban called the *tiara*, and "about their bodies tunics with sleeves, having iron scales upon them like the scales of a fish and their legs were protected by trousers; and they bore wicker shields for bucklers; their quivers hanging at their backs, their arms being a short spear, a bow of uncommon size, and arrows of reed, while they had likewise daggers suspended from their girdles along their right thighs."[1] Clothed and armed thus, they were crushed at close quarters by the great hoplite swords, shields and six-foot spears, rounded up and slaughtered. For what the figures are worth, Herodotus records that 6,400 Persians were killed for the 192 Greeks buried for special honour under a mound that is there still.

Moreover, as the enemy ships sheered off with the survivors, and a

[1] Herodotus. op. cit. book vii. ch. 61. p. 145.

collaborator's shield flashed its signal from the hills, the Athenians guessed correctly that following their original strategy for which the Marathon landing had been a diversion, the Persians would make for Phaleron, then the port of Athens. So by a forced march of about thirty miles they got there first and the fleet sheered off again. The Spartans, arriving late for the battle, could only proceed to Marathon to inspect the enemy dead; as technicians of war, they were eager to examine the Persian equipment. Though a frustration rather than disaster for Darius, for the Hellenes Marathon was a resounding victory.

Ten years later, again in September, the Persians tried again with a much larger expedition. Xerxes, Darius's son and successor, was in command, an unstable character fated to end by asassination, with a touch of megalomania expressed, as often by such rulers, in grandiose building. As Viceroy of Babylon and then of Egypt he had already savagely put down rebellion, and he intended this time to crush the Hellenes for all time. But in Themistocles the Greek democracy had produced a brilliant leader, and been briefly scared enough to accord him the money from the silver mines at Laureion to build a large fleet. So this time the Athenians were able to strike first at sea: moreover, in 481 BC, the Spartans had formed an alliance based on the Peloponnesian League, and were ready to bring their full land power to bear.

In describing the heterogeneous and picturesque army that the Great King mobilized, Herodotus lets himself go: besides the Persians already described, "the Assyrians went to war with helmets made of brass" . . ., the Scyths wore trousers, outlandish garments to the Greeks, had "tall stiff pointed caps" and carried battle axes: the Indians wore cotton and carried cane bows, the Caspians had scimitars, the Arabians wore flowing robes, the Ethiopians "the skins of leopards and lions and had long bows made of the stem of the palm leaf", with spears tipped with sharpened antelope horns, "and when they went into battle they painted their bodies, half with chalk, and half with vermilion". As for the Libyans, they wore leather and carried javelins hardened by fire, and "the Thracians went to war wearing the skins of foxes upon their heads", with their legs and feet in buckskin made from the skins of fauns; and they had for arms "javelins, with light targets and short dirks".[1] The crack troops were the 10,000 Persian Immortals, so called because vacancies through battle or sickness were at once replaced: and besides their arms, "they glittered all over with gold, vast quantities of which they wore . . . [and] They were followed by litters, wherein rode their concubines, and a numerous train of attendants handsomely dressed." But these impressive and picturesque contingents were organized according to their satrapies, instead of according to their specialized armaments and such huge forces were difficult to handle, less formidable against more professional armies than they looked. Their transport was inadequate, they lived mainly off the country, and they were too dependent on their ships.

They now advanced inexorably. Crossing the Hellespont under their master's eye—he had it symbolically flogged for disrupting his bridge of boats, a gesture more intelligible in view of the Persian's veneration for clear streams

[1]Herodotus. op. cit. ch. 64-75. pp. 146-8.

and corresponding detestation of apparently hostile salt and turbid water—and, cutting a canal behind Mount Athos, the enormous army advanced down the Thessalian coast, accompanied by the fleet.

The Greeks decided to hold them; 6000–7000 hoplites led by King Leonidas of Sparta held Thermopylae, a strategically placed pass then very close to the sea, south of modern Lamia and the Sperkios river, where the gulf of Euboea cuts deep into a mountainous terrain, while the combined fleet was stationed at Artimesion in north Euboea, commanding the Trikeri strait. The Greeks thus forced the invaders to battle on ground of their own choosing. If the pass at Thermopylae had held, the fleet based on Euboea might have crippled the invasion, for the coincident naval battle went well for the Greeks; but although, taking it in rotation to hold the narrow pass, the Greeks beat off the Persian attacks for three days, their assailants found a track over the mountain to outflank the defenders and sent the Immortals up through the oak forest to envelop them. The troops guarding the track retreated to the heights and the Greeks learnt that they were doomed. So Leonidas agreed, as he had to, that the main force should disperse, but scorned to retreat, and with his own force of 300 Spartiates fought to the death.

Xerxes, by Greek standards no gentleman, had his body decapitated and crucified. The occasion is commemorated by the famous lapidary epitaph of Simonides—

"Tell them in Sparta you that pass us by,
That here obedient to her laws we lie."

With Thermopylae overrun, the Hellenic fleet drew back down to Salamis opposite Piraeus, and the Persians devastated Attica and burnt Athens. But the turning point came at sea. The Greek ships were based on modern Kamatero; the Persians lay off Phaleron and occupied the small island of Psyttadea at the eastern end of the straits. Many of the Greeks wanted to retreat on the Peloponnese and defend the isthmus of Corinth: but, according to Herodotus, Themistocles by a brilliant improvisation made up their minds for them and lured the enemy to destruction. For he sent a spy to persuade Xerxes that the Greeks were trapped and all set to escape, so that he ordered a squadron to row round Salamis and block the western channel, while commanding the rest of the fleet to attack. But the Greeks, who had kept at sea all night, by feigned flight led them on; then, with a swift turn—"At once their frothy oars moved with a single pulse"—they charged and rammed the enemy or, smashing their oars, immobilized the relatively light Ionian and Phoenician ships. Hence a horrible confusion: "ship into ship battered its brazen beak"; the Persians were surrounded:—

The sea was hidden, carpeted with wrecks
And dead men; all the shores and reefs were full of dead.[1]

Even the skilled and wary Phoenician admiral was killed; the Egyptians fled; Xerxes, rightly fearing that the victorious Greeks would make for the

[1]"On the side of the barbarians more perished by drowning than by any other way, since they did not know how to swim." Herodotus. op. cit., bk. vii. ch. 50.

Hellespont and cut him off, decided to pull out back to Asia, leaving a large force under the satrap Mardonius to winter in Thessaly, where there was pasture for the horses, and then renew the campaign in spring.

But before leaving, Xerxes received a herald who thus addressed him: "King of the Medes, the Lacedaemonians and the Heracleids of Sparta require of you the satisfaction due for bloodshed, because you slew their king, fighting for Greece": at which, enigmatically, the Great King laughed and answered, pointing to Mardonius, "Mardonius here shall give them the satisfaction they deserve to get."

Mardonius offered favourable terms, which at first the infuriated Athenians rejected: so he re-occupied a deserted Athens, then, warned of a Spartan advance, fell back north-west on Thebes in country better suited for cavalry. But in the following year, at Plataea, south of it, in the biggest land battle of the war, the Persian army was destroyed and Mardonius himself perished under the hoplite spears. The Spartans had obtained their satisfaction; and this decisive victory was clinched when a Greek expedition sought out and destroyed the remaining Persian fleet at Mycale near Samos. Moreover the Carthaginian attack on Sicily, coordinated with Xerxes's expedition, had been defeated by the Sicilian Greeks at Himera.

So the long planned strategy of the Great King, his subject people and his allies, went down before the Hellenes. Though Persian domination would not, as often assumed, have blotted out Greek culture—half the Greek world in Ionia had survived it and the *Pax Iranica* was only occasionally oppressive—the character of Hellenic civilization demanded liberty. Not that politically they made good use of it. Great as were its cultural achievements, the Greek *polis* was a political failure, and even the victory over the Persians had been a near thing. In close up, even that exploit is riddled with treason, bribery and espionage; so intense was the competitive Greek drive for success by any means that the politics of the cities are a kaleidoscope of betrayal, tergiversation and murder, later writ large in the conflict of the Hellenistic kingdoms after Alexander. Anyone still bemused enough to think the high-minded idealism of Plato representative might remember his own account of the rottenness of political action, particularly in a democracy, and that even under the Persian attacks, collaboration with the enemy was constant. As already recorded Hippias, former ruler of Athens, fought for the Persians at Marathon—and even Themistocles, the main Athenian architect of victory, was reinsuring himself; eventually, driven by political factions, he went over to the Persians and was refused burial in Athens; while Pausanias, the Spartan Regent and Commander at Plataea, established himself at Byzantium and attempted, in alliance with Persia, to dominate all Greece, and the career of Alcibiades, notorious for treachery, ended in worse infamy. Neither in their sexual nor their political morals were the Hellenes the honorary public school prefects of Victorian and Edwardian imagination; by such Anglican-Liberal standards, they were "rank outsiders"; and the sequel to their brilliant victory was not a magnanimous peace but a horrible and drawn out war between Athens and Sparta for the hegemony of Greece.

III

The defeat of the Persians was a European event; but the Peloponnesian War, an internecine struggle of classic interest and famous incident, was not of such decisive consequence. The drama is, indeed, tremendous: the dour military professionals of oligarchic Sparta set against the volatile, ingenious, democratic leadership of Athens; the conflict of land against sea power, of vivid and contrasting personalities and ideas. But the unnecessary conflict, like the "democratic experiment" in Athens, is a case history in that abuse of public power which Thucydides at the time, and Plato and Aristotle in the long rueful aftermath, defined as the central evil of politics and which both philosophers attempted in theory to counteract.

The Athenians were forced into expansion: in spite of founding many colonies, Athens and Attica were overpopulated and depended on grain imports, mainly from the Black Sea and Magna Graecia. At first the Athenian empire, with a standardized coinage, long remained loyal, if, even for Athens, trade never outweighed agriculture. The Spartans, on the other hand, were a landpower, their territory much larger than Attica, and though long superior in battle, too stupid to know what to do with their conquests, imposing an archaic and fossilized economy; and since the brunt of the fighting in the long war fell on the Spartiate elite, their number diminished. But Persian subsidies as much as Spartan valour won the war.

The mounting tension began two years after Salamis, when under the leadership of Pericles in 478 BC the Athenians formed the maritime Delian League, originally against Persia and so-called from the tiny and sacred island of Delos, birthplace of Apollo; then, in 454, they removed its treasury to Athens, where some of it was well spent on the splendour of the Acropolis. Pericles (495–429 BC) came of aristocratic family and, in 461, on the assassination of its leader, had become head of the democratic faction. Far from being a "Liberal" forerunner of Mr Gladstone, as Victorian admirers believed, he was a party boss in Athenian politics, who limited citizenship to those who could prove citizen descent on both sides. He increased the power of the Council of Five Hundred against the conservative Council and introduced payment for civic office, converted the Delian League into an Athenian empire, and greatly expanded the Athenian fleet so that it controlled the Black Sea. In 445 he made a "Thirty Years Peace" with Sparta. This peace lasted until 431, and covers the so-called "Periclean Age", which broke down with the Peloponnesian War. His speech celebrating the Athenian dead was made in 430, the year before his death.

The immediate cause of the outbreak of war in 431 BC was a conflict between the pro-Spartan Corinth and Corcyra, the modern Corfu, the greatest naval power after Athens. The Megarans backed the Corinthians, the Athenians Corcyra, so the two major powers were drawn in. In 431, the whole of the Peloponnese, except Achaia and the Argolid, sided with Sparta, as did Corinth, Megara, and Boeotia: but Corcyra, Acharnania and Locris to the West, Thessaly, Euboea, Chalcidice and the whole of Ionian Greece and all the islands save Melos, supported Athens. In 430–29 two plagues of smallpox struck Athens,[1] and killed Pericles. But the Spartans could not break the long walls that joined Athens to the port of Piraeus; the Athenians had not the land power to invade Sparta; by 421 a peace was patched up, and the Athenians started to build the Erechtheum on the Acropolis. But in 416 BC the Athenians, having vainly attempted to coerce the pro-Spartan Melos in the Cyclades between Thera and Sparta into the Delian League, besieged and captured it, massacred all the surviving men on the island, and sold all the women and children into slavery, an atrocity underlined by Thucydides in the famous Melian dialogue in which the Athenians are made to point out "You know as well as we do that right, as the world goes, is only a question between equals in power, while the strong do what they can and the weak suffer what they must."[2]

The Athenians, no longer led by Pericles, but by demagogues of coarser fibre, and seduced by the unstable brilliance of Alcibiades, a young aristocratic careerist, then took a strategic gamble. They launched an enormous expedition against Syracuse, a Spartan ally, hoping to bring the wealth of Magna Graecia to bear on the war. It sailed in mid-summer 415, lavishly equipped and well paid. "The ships being now manned ... the trumpet commanded silence and the prayers customary before putting to sea were offered ... all together by the voice of a herald; and bowls of wine were mixed through all the armament, and libations made by the soldiers and their officers in gold and silver goblets. The hymns sung and the libations finished, they put out to sea, and, first sailing out in column, then raced each other as far as Aegina."[3]

By 413, though heavily reinforced, the expedition had come to utter disaster. The fleet was destroyed, the land army capitulated; Nicias, the commander, was butchered by some Syracusans who had been in correspondence with him and wanted him out of the way. The prisoners were crowded into quarries beyond Syracuse, tormented by heat, cold and stench—not even the bodies of the dead removed—on half a pint of water and a pint of corn a day, in "the worst calamity for the conquered in Hellenic history".

Now, with the waning of Athenian sea-power, the Delian League gradually collapsed; the war spread to Ionia and the islands, as the Spartans, who had ravaged Attica, when the expedition had sailed, with forces too strong for the Athenians who were pent up behind their long walls, again attacked. By 404 BC the war was over.

Anxious to control their restive allies, the Spartans spared Athens itself; but the maritime empire had vanished and a Spartan-sponsored oligarchy of "thirty tyrants" was imposed. Some Athenian power gradually revived, but over the

[1]"A pestilence", writes Thucydides, "of such extent and mortality was nowhere remembered. Neither were the physicians at first of any service, ignorant as they were of the proper way to treat it, for they died themselves the most thickly as they visited the sick the most often; nor did any human art succeed any better." The Complete Writings of Thucydides. The Peloponnesian War. Trans. Crawley. with introduction by J. H. Finlay Jnr. New York, 1951. p. 110.
[2]Thucydides. op. cit. p. 331.
[3]Thucydides. op. cit. p. 356.

first half of the fourth century the city states, including those in Sicily, fought themselves into exhaustion, the only gainers being the Persians and Carthaginians. Then, at the battle of Chaeronea in 338 BC, Philip of Macedon, with more massive resources and a better version of the phalanx of heavy infantry, established an hegemony which, exploited by Alexander and his successors on a scale that dwarfed Hellas, ended the political independence of Old Greece.

This record of intrigue and war demonstrated the political bankruptcy of the city states, made more poignant because many Hellenes were clever enough to know what was going on. The "democratic experiment" in Athens, in particular, had proved on its miniature scale an example of the evils of ideological warfare, political faction, demagogic ambition and popular ignorance; evils analysed by Thucydides with unsurpassed and still highly relevant penetration. For example, of a notorious massacre at Corcyra of one faction by another, he wrote that "the whole Hellenic world was convulsed", struggles being made by the popular chiefs to bring in the Athenians, and by the oligarchs to bring in the Lacedaemonians. . . . "The sufferings which revolution brought upon the cities were many and terrible, such as have occurred and always will occur so long as the nature of mankind remains the same. . . . words had to change their ordinary meaning and take that which was now given them." "The rage of party," he continues, "drove men to extremes," since "such association had not in view the blessing derivable from established institutions, but were forced by ambition for their overthrow". "The cause of these evils", he writes, was "the lust for power arising from greed and ambition". The leaders speciously advocating "political equality of the people" or "moderate aristocracy", in fact "sought prizes for themselves"; and "the use of fair phrases to arrive at guilty ends was in high reputation". Meanwhile, "the moderate part of the citizens perished between the two. Thus every form of iniquity took root in the Hellenic countries"; moreover, "in this contest the blunter wits were most successful for, fearing to be worsted in debate, they boldly had recourse to action . . . Corcyra gave the first examples of the crimes alluded to".[1] This cold and terrible analysis, made in the fifth century BC, deserves to be pondered by anyone tempted to think that violent party "ideological" conflict is a road to Utopia.

Having lived through these hard times, the Greek masters of political thought reiterated that the only remedy was the rule of law, which, controlling the abuse of public power, could make the city state a basis for the "good life" for the minority of its inhabitants who were its citizens.

IV

In this war-ridden and factious society profound and original philosophical speculation was going on. In analysing the scope and limitation of mind, in

[1]Thucydides. *op. cit.* p. 189–191.

ethics and political theory, Plato and after him Aristotle created the vocabulary
of European political thought. The logic early applied by the Ionians to cosmic
and physical speculation was now applied to man and his societies. Plato was
inspired by Socrates, the greatest of "Sophists". He despised the other Sophists,
in part because they taught "wisdom for money"; but Socrates (470–399 BC),
who never took fees, was an hypnotic personality "who", writes Diogenes
Laertius, "was the first who discoursed on the conduct of life",[1] and whose
fascination still lives in Plato's dialogues, in particular in the Phaedo, with its
account of his death, in the Symposium, the Phaedrus, and the Apology.
Socrates was physically hardy and remarkably ugly; over forty years older than
Plato, he had been a hoplite in several campaigns and saved the lives of
Alcibiades and Xenophon; he had been a member of the Council of Five
Hundred and was a well known character in Athens, caricatured by Aristophanes in the Clouds. He lived hard, but loved good talk and good looks, and
argued a great deal, with an assumed humility and ironic humour, deflating
pretentiousness in the pursuit of truth. In this quick-witted and leisured
society, he got a following, particularly among the sons of the oligarchs with
whom he had always been friends, and when, "owing to the vehemence in
argument he was set up on and even kicked, remarked 'Should I have taken a
donkey to law supposing that he had kicked me'?".[2] He was judicially murdered
not because the Athenians objected to his alleged impiety or corrupting
influence—both common charges, but for political reasons by the democrats,
who in 403 had supplanted the oligarchic regimes of the so-called "Thirty
Tyrants" imposed by Sparta. He is not, therefore, as widely believed, a martyr
for freedom of thought, but was put down as an intimate of the oligarchy and
a teacher of the notorious Alcibiades. He was thus the victim of a political
crime; a fate also provoked by his ironical defiance when he said that he
deserved free quarters at the Prytanaeum or Civic Hall, the reward of an
Olympic victor, instead of suggesting exile, and when, in the way of politicians,
the oligarchs, then anxious for reconciliation with the democrats, thought the
philosopher expendable. Ironic to the end, Socrates, handed the cup of
hemlock, asked his executioner "What do you say about making a libation out
of this cup to any God? May I or not?". But when the man answered, "We
only prepare, Socrates, just so much as we deem enough," Socrates drained the
poison with complete calm—of "all the men of our time", wrote Plato, "the
wisest, the most just and the best whom I have known."

    What was it, apart from force of character, and iron will, that so hypnotized

[1]The Lives of Eminent Philosophers, with English translation by R. D. Hicks. Loeb,
Harvard. Revised ed. 1950. 2 vols. Vol.I p.151. Diogenes Laertius wrote the only general
survey of the lives and opinions of the philosophers of Antiquity which has survived.
Little is known of him, save that he wrote about 210–220 AD, and, with insatiable
curiosity and industry, gives very interesting and thorough accounts based on a wide
range of books now lost. Some of his short biographies are rather in the manner of John
Aubrey, and his account of Stoic and Epicurean doctrines are very full. Montaigne
found him very good reading.
[2]The widely accepted story that his father was a stonemason or sculptor and that he was
trained as one rests only on a statement by Douris of Samos (d.280 BC), a sensational
and unscrupulous historian, making at best a crude embellishment of a real tradition.

Plato[1] that he became convinced of a transcendent reality of *"ideas"* or *"forms"* which the *phenomena* accessible to the human mind only partially reflect? Along with this belief went the distinction between the *psyche* and the body, probably derived from Iranian and perhaps Indian thought and which implies the "immortality" of the *psyche*. A familiar example of the first belief is the simile of the cave in Plato's *Republic*. Picture men in an underground cave dwelling, with a long entrance reaching up towards the light along the whole width of the cave; "in this they lie from childhood, their legs and necks in chains, so that they stay where they are and look only in front of them, as the chains prevent their turning their heads round." They would then mistake for reality the shadows thrown by a fire outside of those passing along a wall between it and the prisoners, and projected on the wall of the cave. Such is the human condition, imprisoned by the senses; even when released, men would take long to understand what they saw and few could "face the brightest blaze of being". Only by reason can the permanent "form" or "idea" which is "reality" be apprehended which "once seen, must be the cause of all that is right and beautiful in all things".[2]

Supremely confident in the existence of permanent "forms" and in the power of reason, Plato in the *Republic* declares that "unless philosophers bear kingly rule in cities or those who are now called Kings and princes became genuine and adequate philosophers, and political power and philosophy are brought together ... there will be no respite from evil, my dear Glaucon, for cities, nor I fancy, for humanity".[3] Failing this unlikely event, the rule of impersonal law must be enforced, for thus alone can the competition of ravenous apetites be controlled under the various forms of government which Plato analyses with so much penetration.

Plato had been called the father of lies for propagating a false duality between body and mind and fantasies of abstract "ideas"; a doctrine known paradoxically as "realism", since they alone are "real,", as opposed to the Nominalist belief, later summed up by William of Ockham in the fourteenth century, that "entities"—including such *"ideas"* or *"forms"*—"ought not be unnecessarily multiplied". Plato has also been represented as an enemy of the "open society", since he believes that experts ought to run the state, a claim since made by the exponents of quasi-scientific determinist doctrines. On the other hand, Socrates and Plato insist that the aim of the state should be to promote the "good life" of its citizens, not, of course, of aliens or slaves, the majority of the population; that public power should have a moral purpose and be theoretically justified, not simply exist in its own right. Within the context

[1]Born of aristocratic family in 428 BC, in 387 he founded the Academy at Athens, mainly for the study of mathematics and law; in 367 and 361–0 he visited Syracuse, in the vain hope of establishing the regime of a just and philosophical ruler. He died in 348, and his voluminous works, unlike those of most classical writers, have come down largely intact. Descended from Solon through his mother, he was nicknamed "Plato" either by Ariston the Argive wrestler because of his broad physique, or because of his wide forehead. He was a pupil of Socrates when he was 20, and he lived to 81.
[2]*The Republic of Plato*. Translated with an introduction by A. D. Lindsay. Dutton. New York, 1957. pp. 256–60.
[3]Plato. *op. cit.* p. 206.

of the *polis*, Plato, coming well after the great days of Pericles, and in a memorably imaginative way, thus explored profound problems of philosophy, ethics and political theory in an analysis of perennial interest.

V

During the greatest days of Athens the dramatic tradition created by Aeschylus was further developed by Sophocles and Euripides, while comedy found riotous expression in Aristophanes, who parodied and pilloried the public figures and crimes of his day with urban wit and insight. Sophocles, born in 496, lived to be ninety, and his *Philoctetes*, written when he was eighty-seven, is one of the best of his seven surviving plays. Using two actors, he invented the basic dramatic techniques of the European tragic theatre, creating characters in the round, where Aeschylus had kept them in profile. His characters are caught in macabre situations drawn from Greek mythology and tradition, as in the *Electra* on the fate of Clytemnestra; but they have a new initiative, though the chorus sometimes remains maddeningly detached, remarking, as in *Ajax* when the hero is going mad,

> *"The best advice I can offer is*
> *That you should become more reasonable."*[1]

The tone is impartially fatalistic, with a background of unforgiving Gods,

> *"Who look down unmoved upon our tragedies,"*

tragedies made the more poignant by the beauty of the world.

Whereas Sophocles was a handsome, conservative aristocrat who held public office and command as a general, Euripides, born in 484 BC, was a civilian individualist. He was critical of society as well as of the Gods, with a subtle psychological insight, and a pervading sense of natural beauty going beyond conventional expression; more interested in human situations than in divine justice. Nineteen of his plays have survived, most of them dealing with the tragic conflict between human love and beauty and the atavistic forces of envy and hate, often personified by the capricious Gods. Unlike Aeschylus and Sophocles, he avoided public office, and in old age had become so much disliked that he went into voluntary exile at the Court of the King of Macedon, where he wrote the *Bacchae*, his greatest play, and where in 407 he died. In the *Bacchae*, Pentheus of Thebes represents all prosaic pompous killjoys, and he is torn to pieces by the devotees of Dionysus, the God of wine and revelry, coming from "the Asian seaboard where Greeks and Orientals live side by side in magnificent cities", and whose power the wise Tiresias admits—"We entertain theories and speculations in divine matters. The beliefs we have received from our ancestors—beliefs old as time—cannot be destroyed by any

[1]See A. E. Housman's famous parody. *A Cambridge Scrapbook*. Collected by Jean Lindsay. Cambridge, 1955.

argument nor by any ingenuity the mind can invent."[1] The power and joy of the irrational is accepted.

Aristophanes (c.450–388 BC), of whose life little is directly known, is the first master of fantastic comedy, full of parody, satire, buffoonery and invective touched with occasional poetry. His characters and choruses were sometimes dressed as animals or birds, making highly topical allusions and obscure jokes, all put over with a tremendous gusto and sense of theatre, and not sparing the heroes and the Gods—as Hercules or Dionysus. He particularly detested Socrates, whose "Thinking Shop" he guyed, and, unfashionably in Athens, vindicated the good sense of women against the political and bellicose follies of men.

The range of the eleven plays which survive out of about forty-four is apparent from a few titles—*Frogs, Women in the Assembly, Birds* and *Clouds,* in which Socrates is hung up in a basket.

VI

Meanwhile architecture and sculpture flourished; particularly in Athens, when the temples on the Acropolis were rebuilt after the devastation of the Persian wars. They must have been splendid but cluttered up, without the stark dramatic quality shown today; a blaze of colour and gold and ivory, attesting the wealth of the Athenian empire. Following the thirty-year truce with Persia in 449, the wealth spent on war was briefly diverted under the direction of Pericles to architecture. The great Temple—or *Naos*—of Athene Polias, later known as the Parthenon, was built of Pentelic marble in Doric style. Begun by the architects Ictinus and Callicrites in 447, it was swiftly completed by 438, and only six years later the superb frieze above its thirty-four foot columns, depicting not the traditional mythology, but the Panathenaeic festival to the life. Already in 454 BC Phidias had created the bronze statue of Athene in full armour, the flash of whose crest and gold tipped spear could be glimpsed from the sea off Phaleron; now, in the numinous depth of the temple at the back between the aisles, appeared an even more splendid thirty-nine-foot-tall statue on a pedestal of twelve feet, covered, except for the face, neck and arms and the tips of the feet which were all of ivory, entirely in gold. On the helmet of the great glittering image were a sphinx and two winged horses; in her right hand was a statue of victory, and she rested her left hand on her shield, on which, among other things, Phidias had included portraits of Pericles and himself, so that according to Plutarch the sculptor ended up in prison for getting above himself and in 432 died there.

The *Propylaea* or entrance to the Acropolis was also Doric and splendid. Begun in 437 BC it was completed in five years, and at the western corner was built the small and elegant temple of *Athene Nika*, the Victorious, with

[1]Euripides. *The Bacchae and Other Plays.* Trans. Philip Vellacot. Penguin, Harmond-sworth, 1954. p. 187.

another statue of her holding a helmet for war and a pomegranate for plenty; unlike other Victories, she was wingless, perhaps, it was suggested, so that she should not fly away. But the Ionic Erechtheum housed the most ancient shrine, where stood the archaic wooden image of Athene near her sacred olive tree, and where the salt spring struck by the trident of Poseidon bubbled from the rock. Begun in 421 BC during the interval in the Peloponnesian war, the building was completed in 415, and included the elegant porch of Caryatids, still extant.

Such were the most famous monuments of Athens: there were many more; in Attica, for example, the temple of Poseidon (c.430 BC) at Cape Sunion; at Olympia, in Corinth, at Argos. The great temples at Paestum and Agrigentum in Sicily were built about this time, a relatively coarse but impressive and lasting version of those in Old Greece.

The age of Pericles also saw superb Greek sculpture. The rhythm and proportion already apparent in the earlier ephebe of Kritios, termed by Kenneth Clark "the first beautiful nude in Art", had been inspired by "two powerful emotions that dominated the Greek games and are largely absent from our own: religious dedication and love. These gave to a cult of physical perfection a solemnity and a rapture which have not been experienced since."[1]

Sculpture now aimed at mathematically correct proportions with a hint of movement in repose, and the votive statues of Phidias celebrated not the victors of the games but the powerful image of a God. The marble Apollo (c.460 BC), larger than life from the temple of Zeus at Olympia, who quells the bestial centaurs with a gesture of calm and entire authority, is awesome and severe, the bronze charioteer at Delphi has a powerful symplicity, while the poise and grace of the youths managing their horses on the frieze of the Parthenon are unsurpassed. For all its virtuosity, the skill even of Praxiteles in the following century never achieved such impact; the effect is achieved with the economy of line and apparently effortless mastery of the greatest art, coincident with the climax of Greek tragic drama.

In vase painting, though by the mid-fifth century technique in detail improved, in attempts at perspective the finest work was over: perhaps with the waning of aristocratic patronage, vases tended to become fussy and anecdotal, though very revealing of intimate aspects of Hellenic life. By the end of the Peloponnesian War the home market had collapsed, and by the mid-fourth century even an Attic *Krater* representing a Dionysian scene is ill-executed, and the elaborate virtuosity of another from Magna Graecia, on the admittedly difficult subject of Bellerophon and the Chimaera, seems wasted for lack of design. But if vase painting was past its best, the decoration of new temples and public buildings after the Persian war gave new scope to painters on wet plaster and in tempera on marble and wood. The great murals of Polygnotus at Athens under Cimon and later at Delphi were famous into Roman Antiquity, when the traveller Pausanias described them in detail in the mid-second century AD. They depicted mythological subjects, Odysseus' visit to the underworld or the traditional aftermath of the Fall of Troy, or celebrated

[1]Kenneth Clark. The Nude. Penguin, Harmondsworth, 1970. p. 29.

recent victories, as the battle of Marathon, executed for the Painted Colonnade on the Agora at Athens. Polygnotus had a limited palette of red, black, white and yellow and blended them, and was admired in Antiquity for the sobriety of his colouring compared with more garish Hellenistic compositions; but we have no direct appreciation of his work. Pausanias was not a discerning art critic, and we are reduced to inference from vase paintings of subjects which we know he attempted. What we do know is that he and his school were thought very important, and that painting in the mid-fifth century was evidently striking within its conventions and techniques.

One aspect of Greek life almost eludes us. It was very important and very old. One of the earliest statuettes from the Cyclades of 2200 BC—contemporary with the completed Stonehenge in Britain—is a seated man of alabaster playing a *cithera*, a large lyre; so, when Homer smote his, he had already an ancient tradition behind him. And the great tragedies were performed as music drama. The instruments were never elaborate; the cithera for formal epic, the small lyre for personal or "lyric" poetry, the harp (usually played by women) for "background music". For wind instruments they had the reed pipe or flute, generally depicted double, the syrinx or clustered pan-pipe, and the bronze military trumpet. For percussion they had drums, hand clappers and cymbals. But we have little idea of what they played on them, save that it set off the recitative and dialogue which alternated with elaborate solo singing and choral chants and dances. Only a few fragments of composition have survived, and though Plato wrote on musical theory and was much concerned with harmony and correct intervals, we can only infer the sound. Significantly, Dionysus, in the *Bacchae*, brought exotic music from the East, when

> The triple crested Corybantes drew
> Tight the round drum skin, till its wild beat made
> Rapturous rhythm to the breathing sweetness of
> Phrygian flutes'.

It would seem that Greek music, like modern *bouzouki* rhythms, may well have had more affinity with Asia than with the later "classical" composers of the West.

VI

Alexander and the Hellenistic World

In 404 BC, by unconditional surrender, the Athenian democracy proved that it could not sustain a maritime empire against Spartan landpower and Persian gold; but Lysander of Sparta soon also demonstrated that the Lacedaemonian oligarchy was too oppressive to hold one either. Athens revived, coalitions were formed; but again, backed by Persia, the Spartans broke them up, and in 387 BC, helped by Syracusan ships, they gained control of the strategic grain route through the Hellespont and forced the Athenians and their allies to terms formulated by the *Shahanshah*. Known as the "King's Peace", it brought a brief respite to Greece at the price of abandoning the Ionian cities to Persia, but the mainland Hellenes all still strove for autarchy and the changing leagues concluded were all competitive.

The Spartans now again provoked such resistance that in 371 BC they were catastrophically outmanouvred by the Thebans under Epaminondas at Leuctra, but the Thebans never won lasting hegemony. Finally in 338 Philip of Macedon, using new battle tactics, routed a Theban-Athenian army at Chaeronea, where the Theban Sacred Band perished, and imposed peace on the cities by the League of Corinth. A power on the fringe of Hellenic civilization, but broader based on a country which could better support cavalry and which commanded the timber and mineral wealth of Thrace, now outclassed and dominated the old centres of this brilliant culture, and then came to realize a long cherished pan-Hellenic war of revenge by the invasion of the rich and vulnerable Persian empire. Though murdered in 336 BC only two years after Chaeronea, Philip had already planned the great expedition, and his death gave scope for the genius of Alexander the Great.

The meteoric career of this world historic figure changed the face of western Asia and of Egypt, and brought a Greek army to the Indus; it also acclimatized the idea of world empire to Europe. The original Hellenic civilization was deliberately extended over the Near East and as far as Central Asia; the city of Alexandria planned in Egypt on a scale unknown in the Mediterranean; and in spite of their frequent wars, the successor states of Alexander's empire remained wealthy and well administered, so that when the Romans came to take over, the richest and most durable area of their Empire was always in the East.

II

In 401 BC ten thousand Greek mercenaries, mainly from the Peloponnese, had hired themselves out to the Persian Prince Cyrus, who was attempting to oust his brother, the *Shahanshah* Artaxerxes. One of their leaders, Xenophon, had been a born war-correspondent, who about 370 BC wrote the *Anabasis* or *March up Country*—literally "Journey Up"—and the earliest and attractive self-justifying memoirs by a retired general. Xenophon, c.430–355 BC, came of a wealthy Athenian family and grew up under the shadow of defeat in the Peloponnesian War, in the closing years of which he probably fought. An admirer of Socrates and supporter of the oligarchs, he detested the democrats and left Athens in 399 to serve under the Spartan king Agisilaus, who befriended him and presented him with an estate near Olympia in the Peloponnese. But after the Spartan defeat at Leuctra, he retired to Corinth, where he may have written the *Anabasis*. Written with a sharp eye for detail in a readable and colloquial style, the *Anabasis* contrasts the intelligent if mercurial and argumentative solidarity of the Greeks with the treachery of the Persians and the savagery of the barbarians through whose country the ten thousand, following the defeat and execution of Cyrus, made their way. They marched from the Euphrates through Kurdistan, Armenia and Anatolia to Trapezus, the modern Trebizond on the Black Sea, where famously, they shouted *Thalassa!* (The Sea! The Sea!) at sight of it.

The march, albeit a retreat, had shown, under terrible conditions, what could be done by a relatively disciplined force, and the vulnerability of the Persian Empire: "Indeed", as Xenophon writes, "an intelligent observer of the (Persian) King's Empire would form the following estimate: 'it is strong in respect of extent of territory and number of inhabitants, but it is weak in respect of weakened communications and dispersal of its forces, that is if one can attack with speed".[1] And this was exactly what Alexander did.

He was well equipped to do so. His father had attracted some of the best talent in Hellas to the Macedonian court; Alexander's brilliant intelligence was bent on conquest and the Macedonians had devised a new method of war. The old rectangular hoplite phalanx, eight deep, had generally relied on sheer weight; so once both sides were locked in combat, as Greek met Greek, the shock power that had defeated the Persians at Marathon subsided into a "confused shoving—this is literally what it is called in Greek ... until something gave", and the side which kept its formation usually routed the

[1]*The Persian Expedition.* Trans. Rex Warner, Penguin, Harmondsworth, 1972. p. 77. The book is one of the greatest adventure stories, full of character and detail, and shows the author as an attractive personality, if without the detachment and grim analytic power of Thucydides.

other.[1] The phalanx, though more flexible than often imagined, was also too slow and clumsy to follow up a break through, and although this indecisiveness meant relatively few casualties, wars could drag on. Moreover the Greeks were inept at siegecraft, and even the Spartans were baffled by the Long Walls of Athens.

Philip of Macedon, like many innovators, had restored mobility to battle and created a far ranging professional army. He lightened the hoplite armour—the Spartans had carried seventy-two pounds of it—and armed the Phalanx with the sarissa—a pike thirteen feet long for the front ranks to twenty feet long for those at the back. While this redoubtable formation held the attack or crashed into the enemy, heavy cavalry in numbers unprecedented in Hellenic warfare would charge the enemy in the flank, as at Chaeronea, and generally with a right hook, with as much impact as they could without stirrups, and envelop him as he broke, or strike at his centre if exposed. He also used mounted light infantry, the peltastoi, javelin-men and Cretan bowmen, and developed siege engines and catapults, following Sicilian techniques, originally Carthaginian but elaborated by Greeks.

Alexander gave this mobile force a clear-cut chain of command—regiment, brigade, battalion, company—down to the section of eight men, and the phalanx would swing its serried sarissas first left, then right, like an animated hedgehog, before pointing them at the enemies' faces, clanging their shields and yelling, alalalal-ái. Alexander would lead the cavalry charge himself, at the head of the Companions—Macedonian aristocrats and Greeks of outstanding skills—and supported by his squires, the paides Basilikoi—the "King's boys".

When in 334 BC, still only twenty-four, he launched this army into Asia, he changed the course of world history, bringing an Hellenic way of life into vast territories and creating a great Hellenistic civilization. Alexander is thus a figure of the utmost importance in European history, as well as a subject for medieval Christian and Islamic fantasy and romance.[2]

III

The course of Alexander's conquests belongs more to Asian than European history, but their consequences were momentous for Europe. The idea of Empire was acclimatized to the West when the Kingdoms of Alexander's successors were annexed by Rome, and great territorial monarchies dwarfing the city states were included in a wealthy Near-Eastern-Mediterranean "Cosmopolis".

Alexander's motives were both practical and visionary. Philip had died heavily in debt, and the Macedonians coveted the wealth of the Persian empire, while Alexander needed to win support in Greece by a Pan-Hellenic war against the "barbarians" and a quasi-Homeric glory. One of his first acts in

[1]Andrewes. op. cit. p. 149.
[2]For a vivid account of him, with an excellent sense of place, see R. Lane Fox. Alexander the Great. London, 1973.

Asia was to sacrifice to Athene at Ilium (Troy) where he "dedicated his full armour ... and took down in its place some of the dedicated arms yet remaining from the Trojan War", which he took with him to India and back. "Then Hephaestion, to whom he was devoted, they say, placed a wreath on Patroclus' tomb; and Alexander likewise on Achilles' tomb; Alexander—as is related—accounting Achilles happy that he had a Homer to be the herald of his after fame."[1]

He had to wait long, until the climax of the Roman empire for his exploits to be adequately recorded, and then in prose in Arrian's *Anabasis*. Arrian (c.96–180 AD) was Governor of Cappadocia under Hadrian in 131–7, and became Archon of Athens. He thus wrote at the height of Graeco–Roman civilization and, as a soldier and official, he writes official history. But it is based on the *Memoirs* of Ptolemy Sotor, the *Saviour*, one of Alexander's generals, the first Macedonian ruler of Egypt, and also on Aristobulus, one of Alexander's attendants, a less reliable source. He is particularly good on the details of campaigns and far the best authority on Alexander, whom he presents realistically, though his digressions on omens and sacrifices can be tedious, if revealing.

Although his fantastic exploits, in Iran, central Asia and northern India, ended in 323 BC, when he died of fever in Babylon, aged thirty-two, Alexander was the first European to master great tracts of Asia, and to leave behind a new conception of empire. Though his own empire proved ephemeral, the large kingdoms carved out by his generals became the richest provinces of the Roman Empire. Seleucus seized Antioch, a large coastal city near modern Aleppo, founded Seleucia near modern Baghdad, and dominated much of Anatolia and Persia. But the richest prize was Egypt, which fell to Ptolemy I, who enshrined Alexander's body in a Mausoleum at Alexandria, the city he had founded. Ptolemy II, known as *Philadelphus* (brother loving) because he had killed two of his own, consolidated his father's position, and his descendants would hold Egypt until 30 AD, when Octavian annexed the rich country to Rome.

In Europe by 306 Antigonus *Monopthalmus* (the One-Eyed) had become King of Macedon; his descendants long maintained a Macedonian power against Pyrrhus of Illyria and the Ptolemies, and prevented Celtic and other barbarians from overrunning Greece.

IV

The rise of the Hellenistic kingdoms and the political swamping of the old city states did not alter the overwhelmingly agricultural basis of the economy or diminish the gap between the intellectual and social life of the cities and that of the peasants in the countryside, even more marked in the Greek colonies in

[1]Arrian. *Anabasis of Alexander*, with an English translation by E. Iliff Robson, 2 vols. Loeb. Harvard, 1929. Vol.I. Bks.I–IV. p. 53.

Asia. The intellectual brilliance and sheer power of mind of Plato, whose writings still command a huge readership in translation and massive scholarly investigation, was of course urban and unrepresentative of the vast majority even of Athenians. The leisured introspection, the long and elaborate education—Paidaea—in which youths were trained, which alone in Plato's opinion, could, if properly designed, make them instinctively choose sophrosyne (best translated "harmonious self-control"), assumed that the base need to earn a living could be disregarded and that the pursuit of wealth was "joyless drudgery", best left to the "metics" or resident outsiders. As a more far-flung economy developed, the free peasantry of the original city states, who as citizens had been part of the polis, began to lose ground; some enlisted as mercenaries in the Hellenistic wars, while the foreign slave population probably increased.

As a wider trade now developed, the Persian treasure, hoarded to enhance the splendour of the great King as a store for spectacular gifts and luxuries, was put into circulation and increased the money supply, while the Attic currency adopted since Alexander became a standard medium of exchange, like the elegant Phoenician coinage, with its designs of palm trees and horses, used in Egypt. But the Hellenistic and, indeed, the Graeco-Roman economy, for all the affluence of its upper classes on their estates and in the cities, remained limited; indeed "we must remind ourselves time and again that the European experience since the late middle ages in technology, in the economy, and in the value systems that accompanied them, was unique until the recent export trend commenced. Technical progress, economic growth, productivity, even efficiency have not been significant goals since the beginning of time. So long as an acceptable life style could be maintained, however that was defined, other values held the stage."[1] There was no "fiduciary money in any form", no way of creating credit, and "the strong drive to acquire wealth was not translated into a drive to create capital ... the prevailing mentality was acquisitive but not productive."[2]

In a slave-owning civilization with ample labour, skilled as well as unskilled, it is misleading to apply a Marxist model of "middle-class" capitalists thrusting against "feudal" landowners, and in turn provoking "class war" from a proletariat, since there was no massive capitalist industry in the modern sense, manufacturing was generally limited, and no cities grew up, as in early modern times, around factories; cities were centres of marketing and consumption, not, for all their prosperity, of productivity on a large scale, though craftsmen and all sorts of specialists flourished. Technology was still very limited; no one in Antiquity invented a windmill or even a wheel barrow, and water mills only came in under Augustus: magnificent as would be the aqueducts and far flung the Roman roads, the actual transport, apart from post and army horses, remained by modern standards paralytic, and navigation was still relatively primitive since there were no compasses, and ships even in summer generally coasted rather than strike out across the open sea.

[1]Finley. op. cit. p. 147.
[2]Finley. op. cit. pp. 141 and 144.

Only in the art of war were there changes, for after Alexander's campaigns, his successors used war elephants, the Asian monarchs using the originally Indian variety; the Ptolemies African elephants from the Sudan; and the Carthaginians the smaller variety of the African species, then wild in Libya, modern Algeria and the foothills of Atlas. The Ptolemies also made the camel a universal beast of burden in their development of the archaic Egyptian economy, which they made far the richest of all the Hellenistic kingdoms, without, of course, much benefit to the *fellahin*.

For all its financial and technical limitations, however, within its enormous common market, Hellenistic civilization, like the early Graeco-Roman after it, was wealthy and splendid; a *cosmopolis* in which travel and opportunity beckoned, and where, in a conservative and hierarchical society, there was ample freedom for rhetoricians, philosophers, dramatists and poets to find patrons and even fame.

The *Koiné*, a simplified form of Attic Greek, was universal among educated people of whatever origin, and the boundaries between citizens, freedmen and slaves became blurred in a world that, to use a modern term, was "international". It was typical of the Spartans that they had held aloof from the Pan-Hellenic expedition of Alexander and forbade their citizens travel, and that their archaic social order should provoke internal and civil wars. In this cosmopolitan civilization, which extended from Alexander's foundations in the Punjab to Mauritania and the Iberian Peninsula, exile from one's native *polis* was no longer so terrible, and the social and psychological satisfactions of the *polis* declined. Hence, along with Eastern influences which had long affected the Hellenes, as the universal cult of Dionysus, the spread of philosophies that tried to sustain individuals and make them self-sufficient anywhere and under any circumstances in an "oecumenical" society.

V

The greatest genius of the mid-fourth century had been Aristotle, but he had not been a Hellenistic philosopher. Like Plato, his master, under whom he had long studied and whom he criticized, he was a man of the city state who founded the Lyceum research institute at Athens. Born in 384 BC at Stagira near modern Salonika on the borders of Macedonia, of parents of Ionian stock, his father a physician at the Macedonian Court, he was the first great scientific humanist, a collector and classifier of vast erudition, who also laid down principles of poetry, drama, ethics and politics. Since he was without microscopes or exact timing, his observations are uneven; but his empirical method determines his ethical and political thought, which combines strict observation of what we would term political science with trenchant political theory. In the *Politics*, a tremendous book, though, being based on lecture notes and not in circulation till long after Aristotle's death, it is ill arranged, Aristotle firmly asserts that man is "an animal that lives in a polis", and since all nature has an aim, the object of public power is to promote the "good life" of the citizens.

He thus, in theory, subordinates politics to ethics, and denies, by implication, that might makes right; while, like a doctor, he examines societies to see which are healthy and which are not. This dispassionate analysis, together with his assertion of the need for rule of law, since no one can be trusted with unbridled power, has been of the first importance in political thought.[1]

Yet that is only one facet of his titanic range of mind, so that his influence, first through the Byzantines on Muslim thought, then through the Muslims on Medieval Europe, would prove immense and, when wrong or misinterpreted, paralysing. In spite of, or because of, the challenging difficulties of his exposition—for he had none of Plato's literary genius—this encyclopaedic philosopher of worldly but magnanimous mind "whose busts," wrote Barker, "which seem to be authentic, show firm lips and intent eyes,"[2] proved immensely important and remains of perennial interest.

Though he tutored Alexander and outlived him, to die at Eretria on Euboea in 322 BC, Aristotle belongs to the Classic age of the city state: the Hellenistic philosophers were very different, and attempted to provide a code of conduct which would be universal.

Diogenes, who came from Sinope on the Black Sea, a cultural backwater, and who flourished, if that is the word, in Alexander's time, was known as the "Dog" (Kunis), for his biting remarks;[3] hence the name Cynic. He dressed like an Eastern beggar, carried a wallet and stick, dossed down when he could, unless snug in his tub or derelict cistern, where he claimed to be self-sufficient for all purposes. He thus secured much publicity; save in quotations his writings, one of them an immoralist Utopia, have not survived, but the sect he founded became widespread among those who found the social order of Antiquity hard to endure, as well as among the temperamentally anti-social.

The Stoics were the most important of those influenced by Cynic ideas and their doctrines inspired some of the ablest rulers of the Roman Empire. Their founder was Zeno, a Phoenician from Cyprus, born in 334 BC, who settled in Athens till his death in 262. He taught in the painted Stoa or colonnade—hence "Stoic", and though only fragments of his works survive, Diogenes Laertius, in the second century AD, describes him and them. He was the son of a wealthy merchant who bought him books about philosophy, and when Zeno was shipwrecked at Piraeus with a cargo of purple, he took to doing philosophy in Athens after reading Xenophon's Memorabilia about Socrates. An oracle had told him that to obtain wisdom he should take on the complexion of the dead, "whereupon he studied ancient authors". "He had a wry neck says Timotheus of Athens ... moreover Apollonius of Tyre says he was lean, fairly tall and swarthy, hence some called him 'the Egyptian vine branch' ... Persaeus in his Convivial Reminiscences relates that he declined most invitations to dinner. They say he was fond of green figs and of basking

[1]Ernest Barker. The Politics of Aristotle, translated with an introduction and appendixes. Oxford, 1961, for the best edition.
[2]Barker. op. cit. p. xxvii.
[3]A pillar commemorating him at Corinth was topped by one.

in the sun.""[1] His doctrines were elaborated by Chrysippus and by Panaetius, who influenced Cicero.

Stoic doctrines, even when disentangled from their peculiar and complicated physical explanations of the universe, are exacting and austere; as was Zeno, who reproved the young with brief cutting remarks, and "patient and unwearied night and day, clung to the studies of philosophers". The universal *Logos* or Creative Intelligence, realized in the best men, demanded will power strong enough to attain resignation, self-sufficiency and the proper fulfilment of the duties of one's station within a common brotherhood of mankind. The individual life thus gained significance, merged in the cosmic order and the Justice of Zeus, who controls the world by his laws in whose service alone is freedom; "God is one and the same with Reason, Fate and Zeus." So long as the Stoic acts only according to these principles, he is invulnerable, for he can be harmed only by his own decisions. This "self-imposed imperative" as Kant later termed it, in a different context, makes a man proud and detached, for he acts justly out of duty to himself; he will not overvalue the world, and he will conduct and express himself with dignity.

This austere philosophy proved particularly congenial to ruling Romans, who took themselves very seriously; but the doctrines of Epicurus (341–270 BC), a much more amiable philosopher, also won a wide following. He was born in Samos and in about 306 settled permanently in Athens, where "friends came to him from all parts and lived with him in his garden." Epicurus was no "Epicurean": far from advocating exquisite self-indulgence, he counselled moderation and calm. Diogenes Laertius lists the allegations against him from which his ill reputation may have derived—that he counselled a youth "Hoist all sail, my dear, and steer clear of all culture"—in some contexts salutary advice; that he spent a whole mina a day on his food, and vomited twice a day from self-indulgence, besides calling one of his critics a "jellyfish and illiterate". But such critics "are stark mad".[2] On the contrary, he continues, he was so benevolent that he was honoured in statues of bronze and had disciples in many cities, "such was the siren charm of his doctrines". Tormented by "strangury and stone in the kidney" (he wrote "*Against the Physicians*" in three books), "he entered a bronze bath of lukewarm water and asked for unmixed wine, which he swallowed, then having bidden his friends remember his doctrines, breathed his last."[3] His writings were voluminous, three hundred rolls of them, all lost: "*Against the Sophists*", for example, in nine books; *Of Wealth; Of Magnanimity; Of Fate*, etc.

Epicurus, often wisely at the time, taught his followers to withdraw from public life out of "deference", and to "avoid hatred, envy and contempt". No atheist—"verily there are Gods, but not such as the multitude believes"—he merely accepted that the Gods were entirely aloof from human affairs, and he tried to assuage the fear of death. Since, he said, the universe was composed of

[1] Diogenes Laertius, *Lives of Eminent Philosophers*. Zeno's works, all lost to us save in quotation, were many and comprehensive: on Education and Law, on Poetry, Rhetoric, Homeric problems and a treatise *On the whole World*.
[2] Diogenes Laertius. *op. cit.* p. 537.
[3] Diogenes Laertius. *op.cit.* pp. 545-6.

particularly diaphanous atoms which evaporated at death, one ceased to exist, and lost consciousness. Since the dead knew nothing, there was nothing to fear. "A right understanding that death is nothing", he argued, ... "makes the mortality of life enjoyable, not by adding to life illimitable time, but by taking away the yearning for immortality. Death therefore the most awful of evils, is nothing to us, seeing that when we are alive death is not come and when death is come we are not."[1]

As for human conduct, it should be determined by pleasure and pain; and the best pleasures were "static"; rational benevolence, self-control, keeping out of harm's way, helping one's friends. He gained many disciples.

These Hellenistic philosophers, and there were many others, were not, like Plato and Socrates, questing for truth; they were trying to make men live by reason and so find deliverance, offering the severe Stoic self-discipline or the quietest withdrawal of the Epicureans. Those totally disgusted could drop out, in the Eastern fashion, with Diogenes. Most free citizens went on with their routine pieties, consulted oracles, and offered sacrifices; they enjoyed themselves in spite of wars and political crimes, at the theatres, the baths, the palaestras, and at the many festivals with which the Hellenistic cosmopolis was amply provided. Until the Romans really set their minds to it, direct taxation was light; the rich were expected to take civic and religious offices, which entailed lavish expenditure on public amenities, ritual entertainments and charities, so that, unlike modern super-tax payers, they boasted of their generosity. In a landowning hierarchical society, with no idea of progress, in which the social order was taken for granted save when extreme poverty and oppression sparked off slave revolts, the system worked. The Hellenistic monarchs called themselves "Saviours" and "Benefactors", and part of their public relations was lavish grandeur and display: their largesse and that of wealthy citizens made the Hellenistic world in its sunny climate the scene of a splendid civilization for those at or near the top of it, while the increasing populations of central and northern Europe were still barbarous.

VI

The prosperity of this confident civilization was most apparent in architecture. The original Greek designs of temple shrine and colonnade, the expression of reason and order, Doric, Ionian, or Corinthian, were now spread over vast areas, as Greek cities were founded in western and central Asia and even northern India, while the original colonies developed in Magna Graecia and in Spain. Everywhere save in Egypt where, outside Alexandria and Naupactis, the native tradition carried on, the formula was basically similar—acropolis, temple, agora, gymnasium, civic buildings, theatre and the rest, as it would be in Graeco-Roman times. The Hellenistic civilization must have been as uniform as that of Middle Western United States, but more elegant.

[1] Diogenes Laertius. op. cit. II p. 651.

The Greek cult of competitive and naked athletes, which so shocked the more conservative Jews, now spread over the Near East, and where Greeks had "Medized", now orientals followed Greek fashions. After Alexander Hellenistic buildings could be enormous, florid and baroque; but they were not formless, and still astound us by the scale and apparent permanence of the civilization they represent. For the Hellenistic achievement was massive; and if it simply developed the original classic models and wrought large and exuberant variations on them, it was original in the scale of town planning, and in the engineering behind water supply and drainage; techniques all imitated and surpassed by the Romans.

The many statues which adorned the cities and temples were elaborate and finely wrought—if more naturalistic and anecdotal than their classic prototypes. Praxiteles (floruit c.370–330 BC), whose statue of Hermes carrying the infant Dionysus, found at Olympia, is the only major surviving original, but of whose work many later copies are extant, was a master of sculpture in marble, whose sensuous curves and subtle harmonies combine with the old classic sense of balance, particularly apparent in the Apollo *Sauroctonos* (with the lizard), and in the poise and distinction of the Bronze Boy from Marathon. Lysyppus of Argos, famous for his heads of Alexander, was an early sculptor of portrait busts, a style which proliferated throughout Antiquity, in which the ruler's likeness was sometimes attached, on occasion incongruously, to the perfect body of a God. His work, like that of his followers, was anecdotal, depicting an athlete scraping off the oily dust of the *palaestra*, and fauns and satyrs often up to no good. As Hellenistic civilization prospered, sculpture became more luscious and less taut, as in the Venus of Milos or the all too celebrated romantic Apollo Belvedere, while great virtuosity was shown in mythological or realistic scenes, as in the frenzied coils of the Laocoon or the tediously dying Gaul, once the cynosure of connoisseurs. Increasingly trivial and sentimentalized, much late Hellenistic and Graeco-Roman work is such that Kenneth Clark can write, "No civilization has been so artistically bankrupt as that which, for four hundred years, on the shores of the Mediterranean, enjoyed a fabulous material prosperity. During those centuries of blood-stained energy, the figure arts were torpid, a kind of token currency, still accepted because based on those treasures of the spirit accumulated in the fifth and fourth centuries before Christ."[1]

The drama, like sculpture, became more personal, sometimes trivial. Menander, a well-to-do Athenian, born in 342 BC and, according to tradition, drowned swimming off Piraeus in 291, wrote social comedy, ancestral through Plautus and Terence to Molière. He discarded the classic chorus, though the actors still wore masks, and devised the stock characters who have sustained and sometimes plagued comedy and opera ever since: the ardent lover, the hesitant girl, the heavy father, the fortune hunter, the artful slave who devises the happy ending, as well as minor characters; doctors, confidantes, brash soldiers, stupid farmers, all deployed in complex plots neatly resolved. Only

[1]Kenneth Clark. *The Nude. op. cit.* p. 43.

the *Epitropontes* (*The Arbitrators*) survives nearly entire,[1] and turns on the not very exciting theme of the paternity of an exposed but rescued baby: other fragmentary pieces are *The Girl from Samos, The Girl who gets her Hair cut Short, The Hero*; there are sixty others, unidentified, of which sparse fragments have been collected. He "mirrored human life", and, as W. W. Tarn points out, "he is tremendously quotable—*Whom the Gods love die young. Evil communications corrupt good manners. Conscience makes cowards of the bravest*". And it was not his fault that what he drew with such sharp observation from life became a stereotyped convention.

Menander catered for a wide public, and so now did other writers, both for the learned minority and a big new literate public. Though mechanical printing had not yet been invented, it was an age of cultural systematizing and diffusion; there were plenty of educated slave copyists and writing surfaces made from papyrus reeds and parchment from sheep, goat or donkey skin, so that the libraries of Ptolemaic Alexandria and the other Hellenistic capitals were stocked with rolls by munificent rulers, glad to attract scholars and writers to their Courts. Hence the vast library at Alexandria, said to have contained 700,000 rolls, and the rise of textual critics and grammarians who edited the Greek classics, invented Greek accents, and created systematic philology. Although most of Ancient Greek literature has in fact been lost, we would have even less of it, and not know how much has disappeared, but for the libraries and research institutes of the Hellenistic Age; nor could the Graeco-Roman world have been so permeated with a common civilization had not the educated classes had books available over the whole Empire in unprecedented quantities.

The poets therefore had a wide public. Callimachus of Cyrene, in the mid-third century BC, a librarian and courtier at Alexandria, perfected the epigram—an elaboration of such traditional epitaphs as that on the Spartans fallen at Thermopylae, and now worldly or sentimental. Callimachus also composed an anthology of short stories, some imitated by Ovid, and wrote a catalogue of the library at Alexandria and other encyclopaedic works. Meleager (c.140–85 BC) compiled elaborate anthologies of erotic poetry and of epigrams.

But it was Theocritus who was the most original of the Hellenistic poets. He was probably born in Syracuse about 314 BC but lived in Cos and in Egypt, where he frequented the Court of Ptolemy Philadelphus. He created the pastoral *Idyll*; indeed he so perfected it that he "left nothing for others; his successors are far below him, and Virgil's *Eclogues* seem artificial copies." Alone of the Alexandrians he became a classic ". . . and for the sweetness and mere beauty of natural things Theocritus had a feeling such as no other Greek possessed";[2] for the murmur of "blunt nosed" bees, the stridulation of the cicadas, for the mountain owls that cry to the nightingales. And he made vignettes of rural scenes, as the old fisherman on the rugged rock who "eagerly

[1]W. W. Tarn. *Hellenistic Civilization*. Third edition revised by the author and G. T. Griffith, London, 1952. p. 273.
[2]Tarn. *op. cit.* p. 277.

gathers up a great net for a cast", or the small boy intent on plaiting a cicada cage while a fox robs the grapes he is guarding.[1]

Theocritus mentions more plants and trees in his short *Idylls* than are found in all Homer, and records the ups and downs of love. "Half my life is mine by reason of thy beauty, the rest is lost"; and "when thou wilt, the day I pass is that of the Blessed, but when thou wilt not, it is dark indeed."[2] The beloved is fickle and treats a new flatterer like a friend of three years standing and a tried friend like one of three days.[3] Indeed, the Theocritan shepherds and goatherds were hard hit: "yesterday as he passed he gave me a quick glance from between his eyelids, too shy to look me in the face, and blushed. And love laid a tighter grip upon my heart."[4]

The loves of Daphnis and his girl run more smoothly;

> "Come with me under the wild olives that I may tell thee a tale."
> "Nay, but I fear to bear children, lest I lose my fair looks."
> "But if thou bear children, thou wilt see thy youth dawn again."

The affair proceeds apace.

> "What are you doing, Satyr boy, why do you touch my breasts within my
>   gown?" ... "Stop, someone is coming. I hear a sound.
> It is the cypresses that whisper together of your wedding."

"So", concludes the poet, "in the delight of their young bodies they whispered to one another and their stolen bridal was accomplished. And she rose up and went back to tend her sheep, with downcast eyes though her heart was glad within her. And he, happy in his wedlock, went to his herds of cattle".[5]

---

[1]*Theocritus*, edited with a translation by A. S. F. Gow. Cambridge, 1950. 2. vols I. *Idyll* i.
[2]Theocritus. *Idyll* xxix.
[3]Theocritus. *Idyll* xxix.
[4]Theocritus. *Idyll* xxx.
[5]Theocritus. *Idyll* xxvii.

VII

The Roman Republic

When, after his return from the expedition through Central Asia and Northern India, Alexander received envoys at the Court of Susa from most of the civilized world, one of the delegations had been Etruscan; but there had not apparently been one from Rome. The beginnings of that mighty Republic were prosaic and humble but it gradually achieved the domination of Italy; then, transformed into an empire, came to rule and exploit territories from the Euphrates to Scotland, from the Black Sea to the Atlantic, from North Africa to the lower Rhine. These uncouth peasant farmers overcame their own neighbours in the Sabine and Samnite hills, the Etruscans of Central Italy and the Greek cities of Calabria, Apulia and Sicily; then, after a life or death struggle with the great sea power of Carthage, and still a republic, they mastered most of Spain, Macedonia and Greece and much of Asia Minor. This expansion was originally in part improvised and defensive; like that of the British Empire, unplanned; then, gathering its own momentum, a vast exploitation.

By the early first century BC the original farming stock in Italy was being swamped, the archaic institutions of a city state breaking down before vast responsibilities: a Principate was devised, in effect at first a Monarchy in the Hellenistic fashion, then an Empire, far-flung, military, ruthless and, until the mid-third century, successful. It created the Roman Peace and the framework of European civilization.

It was from the Etruscans, the *Tursenoi* as the Greeks called them, a mysterious people from Southern Anatolia as they themselves believed, that the Romans took most of the trappings for which they are best remembered; Herodotus declares that the Etruscans were driven from Lydia by famine, so that after "sailing past many countries they came to Umbria, where they built cities for themselves."[1] Although they are best known for their elaborate but rustic tomb paintings, the Etruscans appear anything but a funereal people, but full of relish for life; for feasting and music, for horses and showy armaments with double crested helmets; rather vulgar and oriental by classic

[1]*History. op. cit.* I. pp. 50–51.

Hellenic standards—Berenson said of them, with all the acerbity of a famous art historian, that "only through the originality of their incompetence" could their art be distinguished from that of the Greeks. But they were oligarchic and urban; well able to exploit the mineral resources of Central Italy, already prosperous by the sixth century BC, and still flourishing when fifth-century Athens was at its climax.

Their language contributed some important words to Latin. Though its alphabet, akin to Greek, can be read, with its plethora of 'th' and 'ch' sounds it remains unintelligible, save for names and patronymics, and a few words, as *Usil* (sun) and *Tir* (moon). It was certainly not Indo-European, and an inscription found on Lemnos in a language akin to it confirms an Eastern origin, as do early art forms of gryphons and lions and a Babylonish cult of divination by inspection of the victim's liver, inherited by the Romans. Their influence is attested by representative key words in Latin, as *templum*; *fasces*, the bundle of rods round the double axe borne by the lictors; *histrio*, from *ister* an actor; *persona*, mask; even *toga*, from *tebennos*.

Etruscan influence was widespread, over Tuscany and Umbria; north over the Apennines to Felsina (Bologna), up to modern Modena and Piacenza and to Mantua; south to Rome and Capua. It was not until 509 BC, only nineteen years before Marathon, that the Romans are said to have driven out the Etruscan ruler Tarquinius Superbus, and in 480 BC, the year of Salamis, the Etruscans were certainly defeated at Himera along with the Sicilian Greeks, an event that marked the crumbling of their political hegemony, though not of their prosperity. For they long traded armaments, elaborate cauldrons, bronze mirrors, drinking cups, ornaments in ivory, gold and amber, and imitation Corinthian pottery, with barbarian Gaul and with the Celts of Central Europe. A famous example of their wares is the bronze cauldron of Vix in Provence. There was thus, long before the Romans came to power, a centuries-old tradition of craftsmanship in Central and Northern Italy: and, pace Berenson, the archaic and enigmatic late-sixth-century Apollo of Veii and the particularly wolfish Capitoline wolf with her massive jaws, still the emblem of Rome to whom the chubby twins Romulus and Remus were added only during the Renaissance, recall talents destined centuries afterwards to revive in Tuscany. The Etruscans, unlike the Greeks, also knew how to build vaults and arches, and devised the *atrium* round which the larger Roman houses were designed. The massive Etruscan vaulted gates at Perugia still attest their skill. It was under Etruscan domination that some of the most characteristic Roman institutions grew up: less fortunately, it was from the Etruscans that the Romans took the customs of bloody gladiatorial contests, originally part of funeral obsequies, which became their characteristic and repellent contribution to mass entertainment, as the Greeks had contributed the theatre.

II

Rome, according to a tradition supported by the late Republican antiquary, Varro, was "founded" by Romulus, a descendant of the Trojan Aeneas, in 753

BC, in the time of Homer, and modern excavation has discovered an eighth-century huddle of timbered wattle and daub huts on the Capitoline hill, commanding the *Forum Boarium* or cattle market by the Tiber, where today the so-called temple of Vesta, built in about 20 AD, still stands. Here an island in the river made the crossing easy, and the tracks from Etruria, the Campagna and Latium converged. Moreover, although there was no marble nearer than Carrara, the volcanic tufa could supplement the timber and mud brick of which the city was still mainly constructed up to the time of Augustus.

The strategically well placed settlement prospered; by 616 BC it was worth Etruscan overlords taking it over. The *Forum Romanum* was laid out north of the Palatine and east of the Capitol, with the *Via Sacra* running east, and a century later there was a state temple on the Capitol, built about the time of the eviction of Tarquinius Superbus. In contrast to the Greeks, the early Romans had no literature—even for the legend of Romulus, we rely on Dionysus of Helicarnassus; but inscriptions show that by the sixth century primitive Latin was current, originally an obscure pre-Etruscan dialect, spoken by the Romans and their neighbours in Latium, and indebted to the Sabines even for such everyday words as those for wolf, ox and sow; akin to Sicel, Oscan and other Italic Indo-European tongues, but destined to become one of the great historic languages, sonorous, lapidary, compact, directly ancestral to the Romance languages in Europe and overseas. This lucid and compendious speech was particularly well adapted to defining law, as its weight and cadence was for oratory, and it proved a fit medium for administration as well as for majestic poetry and fierce satire.

All the Indo-Europeans who came west had representative institutions, more elaborate in Hellas; but the Romans realized and adapted them in the most practical far flung and influential way. As in the Greek city states, power had originally been vested in a landowning oligarchy; the early Roman and Etruscan "kings" were mainly figureheads and, with the expulsion of the Etruscans, Rome became formally a republic. Its early institutions were already elaborate. The "kings" had always been advised by the Senators or *patres*— "the Fathers", originally heads of ramified families or *gentes*; a hundred at first, then three hundred, and afterwards many more, they represented the *patrician* interest, and they largely monopolized the sacred functions of augers, flamens and the like; the vestal virgins were drawn from their families. In contrast to oriental and later, Christian custom, there was no separate priestly class. The Romans also had an ancient *Comitia Curiata*, or meeting of ten *Curia* from their original three tribes, from whom in theory the *imperium* (supreme authority) was derived, early superseded by a *Comitia Centuriata* or meeting of "centuries" (their smallest military units), its representatives weighted according to ability to afford arms and so tending to oligarchy. Significantly engineers and artificers were in the top class, musicians in the lowest with landless men. This popular assembly, though its powers swiftly diminished, elected the chief magistrates. The system was elaborate: the most stately were the two *consuls* (partners) who wore togas with a purple stripe and were companied by lictors: they wielded the *imperium*, but such was the Roman fear of tyrannical kings that they were elected only for a year and could veto each other's decisions.

They presided over the Senate, which they joined automatically on laying down office, when they also became eligible to be pro-consuls of provinces; and they commanded the armies, if necessary on alternate days, or by dividing the forces: so it is not surprising that the office of dictator, elected for six months, was devised for emergencies.

The Senate retained essential powers of taxation and of making peace or war, but the consuls had great prestige; they represented the state, and their office, though with greatly diminishing power, continued far into imperial times, even into the early Byzantine Empire, and had its echoes in the Western Middle Ages. Other important magistrates were the quaestors (investigators), assistant to the consuls, concerned with financial administration and coinage, with aspects of the law and, under the Empire, with gladiatorial games. The praetors—the title means "leader"—were in charge of various aspects of the law at home and increasingly took charge abroad where they might act as pro-praetors or even pro-consuls. The tribunes, effective by 471 BC, were elected by the plebeians in another assembly, the comitia plebis, by plebiscites, and could veto even the decisions of consuls and paralyse senatorial business. They had no official insignia, but right of access to the Senate, and of having anyone who assaulted them thrown, by an old Roman custom, from the Tarpeian rock on the Capitol. This powerful office, if often controlled by the patricians, often caused political upheavals and was abolished in all but form under the Empire. Military tribunes, on the other hand, were high staff officers in the army.

Such, in simplified essentials, were the important, complex, balanced and sometimes frustrating institutions of the Roman Republic, which set precedents to subsequent history, not least in the United States: they worked well until they broke down before the immense responsibilities of expanding foreign conquests and the flooding in of new wealth, for the Romans, unlike the Greeks, knew how to compromise, maintain archaic fictions, and smother antagonism in a network of procedure and law in which the preponderant power remained oligarchical, resolute and responsible, united by a common interest first in survival, then in victory and plunder.

Within this framework developed the complex ramification of Roman Law. Rooted in custom, "the way of our ancestors" (mos maiorum) and originally unwritten, jus—literally "command"—developed into written law, jus civile first codified in 450 BC in the Twelve Tables of which only fragments survive. This definition marked a compromise whereby the Roman plebs, without bloodshed, wrested the law from being a sacred mystery exploited by the patricians, and made it generally accessible. It developed as mainly personal law, much concerned with property and wills. And here the senior male of a family exercised a heavy handed patria potestas for life, including the right to disinherit, even to put to death, his middle-aged sons. Terror added to family pride. The jus civile also dealt with contract and regulated actions over assault or property. All these complex and sensible procedures were built up gradually as the Praetores urbani (for the City) used their imperium to decide particular cases and the lay judges and juries created adaptations and precedents. In the event, "a flexible and sophisticated law was conjured by interpretation out of primitive origins."[1] People now knew where they were: the weight of institutions and precedent made for rational order, while beyond the Alps Europe was still barbarous.

And since the *jus civile* was confined to citizens, the Romans devised a procedure for outsiders who became increasingly part of their lives. In 241 BC a *praetor peregrinus* (for foreigners) was appointed, as this new branch of law, less bound by ancient formalities, was pragmatically evolved. From rules which appeared applicable to everyone, whatever their personal standing, came the *jus gentium*, or Law of the Peoples, which came to blend with the wider Greek concepts of Natural Law, common to all mankind—the *jus naturale*.

The Roman constitution and Roman law were thus the steady support of the state: the Romans, unlike the Greeks, were capable of consensus; too practical to wreck their city by violent conflict between *patricians* and *plebs*. The dominant patrician interest—they supplied most of the consuls—pragmatically conceded what they must. Not that Roman justice was easy to come by for the poor: the social order depended on status and the ownership of land, so then the round of high civic offices were largely monopolized by the great families of the Republic and, as in Greece, slavery was taken for granted. But in contrast to the originally self-made feudatories of medieval Europe, the Roman patrician families owed their position and prestige to public service.

We owe much to the account of a Greek historian, of the rise of Rome. Polybius (c.200–118 BC), son of a wealthy Arcadian landowner and politician, had been brought as a hostage to Rome, where he became a close friend of Scipio Aemilianus, whom he accompanied to Spain: he was present at the siege and destruction of Carthage. He was an experienced statesman, soldier and traveller—he ventured out into the Atlantic—and he chose a fine theme— how the Roman Republic conquered the Mediterranean world. He is an admirable pioneer of the theory of writing history, well worth perusal on that score, apart from his main history; a realist determined to find out what happened. His purpose was austere: not to excite or entertain, but to fortify the reader against a catastrophe by "recalling the disasters of others". His Hellenistic Greek is cliché ridden and diffuse, but the judgment sound. "The quality in which the Roman Commonwealth", he wrote, comparing it with the Greek politics, "is most distinctly superior in my opinion is the nature of their religious convictions ... I mean superstitions which maintain the cohesion of the Roman State. These matters are clothed with such pomp and introduced to such an extent into their public and private life".[2] They thus maintained an oligarchical power by appealing to deep-rooted conservative instincts by ancient ritual. "Since", he believed, "every multitude is fickle, full of lawless desires, unreasoned passions and violent anger, the multitude must be held by invisible terrors and suchlike pageantry." The "moderns", he considers, "are most rash and foolish in banishing such beliefs".

The Romans thus maintained an oligarchical leadership with popular

[1]L. P. Wilkinson. *The Roman Experience.* London, 1975. p. 40.
[2]Polybius. *The Histories.* trans. W. R. Paton. Loeb. London, New York, 1923 Vol. III p. 395 (VI. 56) only eight of his forty books have survived, the rest are later excerpts and citations.

support, and avoided the dangers of the populace breaking out and, as Polybius puts it, not content even with being "the equals of the ruling caste ... demanding the lion's share for themselves"; for "when this happens the state will change its name to the finest sounding of all, freedom and democracy, but will change its nature to the worst of all, mob rule."[1] The Romans, unlike the Athenians, he considered, had avoided such delusions.

So, pragmatic and compact, the Roman Republic from humble beginnings in its strategically well-placed site, survived internal conflict and external attack, and came united, under the sign on its standards S.P.Q.R., *Senatus Populusque Romanus*, to the mastery of the Ancient world.

III

About 390 BC, nine years after the death of Socrates, the Gallic tribesmen of northern Italy, their main concentration near Milan, descended over the Apennines and nearly extinguished Rome. But the Capitol, saved, it was believed, by the sacred geese, remained impregnable and, with Celtic inconsequence, the invaders were more interested in plunder than permanent exploitation. They were bought off. But not before they had burnt most of the City, though, contrary to widespread belief, the archives of the nascent Republic, such as they were, survived. Alarmed, the Etruscan and Roman cities made brief alliances, and the Romans kept in with the Carthaginians and the Greek colony at Massilia. Gradually they extended their power over Latium; subsequent Etruscan attacks were also defeated, and by the accession of Alexander the Great, the Romans had already mastered the Campagna to the south and were granting citizenship without voting power—a sensible device—to many cities as far down as Capua. By 326 they had captured *Neapolis* (Naples). But as they pushed south to control Sicily, the Romans were to encounter their first Eastern adversary, an adventurer from the backwash of the break up of Alexander's empire.

Pyrrhus of Epirus, born in 319, four years after Alexander's death, and at twelve king of that country, was related to Olympias, Alexander's mother, and shared her murderous ambitions. Ousted from his kingdom, he had fought in Asia Minor and been a hostage at the court of Ptolemy I. Restored by him to Epirus, he had then briefly overrun Macedonia and Thessaly. An expert in Hellenistic warfare against the Antigonids of Macedonia, on which he wrote a treatise now lost, by 281 BC he had allied himself with Tarentum in the heel of Italy; a year later, at Heraclea, he heavily defeated the Romans in their first battle with an army skilled in Hellenistic tactics with cavalry and Indian elephants, the most dangerous kind. This formidable enemy then advanced upon Rome; but the Roman policy of settling military colonies and conciliating defeated rivals paid off; Pyrrhus had to withdraw from Sicily, when the Carthaginians, then in alliance with Rome, undermined his brief mastery of

[1]Polybius. *op. cit.,* p. 399 (VI.57.33).

the island. Finally the Romans just managed to defeat him at Beneventum, east of Naples, and in spite of his victories, he took himself off with a greatly diminished army to Epirus, to perish after further ephemeral conquests in Antigonid Macedonia in an obscure battle near Argos. The Roman citizen army had vanquished their first professional challenge from outside Italy: they had also made contact with rich and elegant Magna Graecia.

The war with Pyrrhus was the prelude to a much more gruelling ordeal. Now involved in Sicily, the granary of the central Mediterranean, the Romans had challenged a power older established and more far-flung than their own, and masters of the sea. Carthage, on a strategically well-placed peninsula which juts out from modern Tunis, attached only tenuously to the mainland and protected by a lake, was an enormous and flourishing city, founded about 720 BC from Tyre, and now with a sphere of influence that included Palermo, Marsala and Messina as well as Sardinia, the Balearic Isles (where Port Mahon derives its name from the Carthaginian Mago Barca), the North African littoral, and round to Oran and Mogador. In 460 BC their admiral Hanno had explored the West African coast and probably much further south. This Semitic state lived by trade; its supreme magistrates, the *Suffetim*, ruled in conjunction with a wealthy oligarchic council and an assembly of merchants who exported olives, dates and salt fish, besides elaborate cedar wood furniture, luxurious beds, cushions and ivory. The Carthaginians also exploited the silver mines of Spain, the lead mines of Sardinia, timber from the Atlas, wheat from Sicily: their only artistic achievement was their coinage, for their ornaments were vulgar, their architecture derivative from Greece, and their religion evidently all that the Greeks and Romans said of it, for archaeologists have found the cremated remains of the children sacrificed to Tanit, their supreme Goddess, whose temple was also the scene of ritual prostitution.

These Eastern cults went along with intrepid warlike and commercial enterprise at sea. They were the greatest explorers of Antiquity, they sank any strangers trespassing on their preserves at sight, and, when they decided to fight Rome over Sicily, they commanded formidable and long-established power. Polybius well sums up the contrast: "The Carthaginians naturally are superior at sea both in efficiency and equipment, because seamanship has long been their national craft, and they busy themselves with the sea more than any other people; but as regards military service on land the Romans are much more efficient. They indeed devote their whole energies to that matter, whereas the Carthaginians entirely neglect their infantry, though they do pay some slight attention to the cavalry. The reason for this is that the troops they employ are foreign and mercenaries, while the Romans are natives of the soil and citizens."[1]

The long Punic Wars—from *Poeni*, Latin for Carthaginians—were in three bouts: in the first, 264–41 BC, the Romans broke the Carthaginian command of the sea, mastered Sicily, save that Greek Syracuse retained independence, exacted enormous reparations, and transferred the huge tribute of wheat hitherto exacted by the Carthaginians to themselves: in the second, 218–201

[1]Polybius. *op. cit.* p. 387.

BC, the Carthaginians, having recouped themselves by extending their power in Spain and in part financed by the Ptolemies of Egypt, invaded Italy over the Alps. Hannibal inflicted crushing defeats on the Romans at Lake Trasimene and at Cannae (216 BC), ravaged Italy, and in 211 threatened Rome itself. But the Romans under P. Cornelius Scipio, appointed Dictator at twenty-six, struck back against the Carthaginian base in Spain and, when another Carthaginian army crossed the Alps, defeated them on the Metaurus. Hannibal, with a dwindling army, held out in Southern Italy; but in 204 BC, Scipio invaded Africa where, two years later, he earned his title *Africanus* by totally defeating Hannibal at Zama in Tunisia. Hannibal fled to Syria where he committed suicide.

The Roman victory had been due to winning command of the sea from Carthage. They had fought sea battles like battles on land. Instead of competing in the old tactics of ramming the enemy in galleys built entirely for speed, with about as much room for anyone else on board besides rowers as a large scale racing eight, the Romans hired Greek crews, learnt to row better themselves, built ships stable enough to carry soldiers and used grappling irons on their flimsy opponents. Once secured, the enemy could be boarded and crushed.

In the second Punic War, Hannibal's spectacular crossing of the Alps gave him the advantage of surprise, but his famous elephants were little good to him. He had twenty-seven, all but one of them the small North African variety between seven and eight feet high, not capable of carrying large howdahs, and most of them died before they got into Italy. The only one that survived to go south was an Indian elephant on which Hannibal rode through parts of Etruria. It was called *Surus*, the Syrian.[1] The Italians had been already conciliated by Roman policy, so that Hannibal's army, which had to live off the country, got little support from the Italian cities: nor could it be supplied by sea. With characteristic realism and obstinacy, the Senate then wore him down by the celebrated Fabian tactics of "delay", invented by Quintus Fabius Maximus *Cunctator*. But the second Punic War could have gone the other way, had the Romans not defeated and killed Hasdrubal, Hannibal's brother, at the Metaurus.

The third Punic War was occasioned by the resilience of Carthage, with its economic skills and advantages, and by the well-known and reiterated advice of Cato, in season and out, that it ought to be destroyed: *Delenda est Carthago*. The war was brief, 149–6 BC: Massinissa of Numidia, an ally of Rome, became embroiled with Carthage; the Romans seized the excuse to intervene, and, after a horrible siege, Carthage was extirpated, the very site ploughed up. Such, however, were the advantages of its position that well before the end of the century a Roman *colonia* had been founded, and by 29 BC Colonia Julia Carthago was a flourishing city; it was enlarged by Hadrian, who embellished it with an enormous amphitheatre and supplied it with an aqueduct. It became the scene of Christian martyrdoms and intense religious controversy, and then

[1]Zeuner. *op. cit.* p. 299.

in the mid-fifth century AD a stronghold of the Vandals. It took the fanaticism of the Muslim Arabs to wipe it out at the end of the seventh century AD.

While this life or death struggle was going on and after it, the Romans became involved in Spain and in Greece, and developed their provincial, or we should say, colonial empire, later further enlarged. Sicily had first been made a province—or colony: by the end of the second Punic War, most of Spain had been brought under Roman control and divided into two provinces; soon, as might be expected, the scene of ferocious resistance which lasted on and off through the mid-second century, until crushed by Scipio Aemilianus, the adopted son of Africanus. In Greece, an Antigonid Philip of Macedon, in alliance with Hannibal and with Antiochus, the Seleucid king of Syria, had attempted to destroy the power of the Ptolemies over Greece and even Egypt itself: so, once free of the second Punic War, the Romans, not liking the look of so great a power in the East, destroyed Philip's army at Cynocephalae (197 BC) proclaiming themselves liberators of Greece. Antiochus, once advised by Hannibal, still had to be reckoned with: he invaded Greece and in 189 BC the Romans defeated him at Magnesia. In 168 BC a final rebellion led to the break up of the Macedonian kingdom: in 146 BC it became another province, an occasion signalized by the Roman sack of Corinth.

Such by the mid-second century BC had been the foundation of the provincial empire. A century later it encompassed the whole of Spain save Portugal and the North-West; south-western France from Narbonne roughly to Toulouse; Provence and large areas of the Alps; Corsica, Sardinia as well as Sicily and Tunisia; the Dalmatian coast, Macedonia, all Greece and the islands, Western Anatolia and the Black Sea coast up to Trebizond; Antioch, too, and a slice of Syria; the Lebanon and northern Palestine. This fantastic expansion, which already made the Roman Republic masters of the entire Mediterranean world, had been achieved in a century: its motive had been originally defensive, then a land hunger and desire for loot writ large. The Roman peace was first imposed because exploitation was hindered without it.

This spectacular success had been due to an imperturbable tenacity and method, baffling to the relatively mercurial Greeks; to shrewd diplomacy, sound military organization and iron discipline, all in the service first of survival then of extending the Roman control of Italy; finally of plunder abroad.

IV

The original Republican citizen army, like the archaically complex Roman institutions, had been on a small scale, very different from the huge volunteer professional armies developed by Marius after 106 BC and elaborated under Julius Caesar and the Principate and Empire, which came to dominate the state so that the Empire itself became a military institution. But the methodical organization was already there; the ferocious discipline, the carefully planned march, the routine of making camp to a fixed uniform plan, unique at the time.

It originally consisted of four legions of 4200–5000 men. In Greek parlance, they were "hoplites conscripted by lot" from the original three tribes, substantial peasant farmers who could afford their equipment, serving for sixteen or, in emergency, twenty years. Three hundred cavalry, selected from those who could provide horses and who were much better paid, were attached to each legion, a number that reflects Roman opinion of their value in battle. Having early had to fight hill tribes and Gauls, the Romans had adapted the Greek phalanx chequer-board to a more flexible formation, each block in three lines. The young *hastati* formed the first, screened by *velites*, light armed youths who wore wolf skins or other distinguishing marks over their helmets and, like the Zulu "Haze", competed for the notice of their elders.

The second line of *principes*, men in the prime of life, were the core of the formation: the *triarii* were the middle-aged reserve. All save the *velites* wore the well known Roman panoply, set off, according to Polybius who gives the fullest contemporary account, by three upright purple or black feathers, which, "surmounting their other arms", made every man "look twice his height".[1] Their weapons were two heavy *pila*, barbed throwing spears nine feet long, haft and head the same length, and two smaller ones, "like hunting spears", with heads that twisted on impact so that if they stuck in a shield it became unmanageable. For close work they had the short double-edged *gladius*, more for thrust than cut: the *triarii* had long defensive spears. The shields (*scutum*) were large; two and a half feet broad by four feet long, of wood and hide, iron bossed and edged.

The Republican legion was extremely well organized. Under the military tribunes and their staff, each class was divided into ten *maniples*—thirty in all—of 100 to 120 men, themselves divided into two *centuries* of 50 to 60 men, under two centurions (*principales*) with non-commissioned officers under them. The centurions, the equivalent of commissioned officers, but not then eligible for high command, were selected for reliability more than dash; the standard bearers for exceptional bravery and physique.

This methodical yet simple organization, intelligible to the illiterate, was reinforced by the most original Roman device, which set them apart from any other contemporary army. Irrespective of terrain, they always pitched camp to the same plan. Leather tents, systematically aligned, were set up in a big rectangle, with a two-hundred-foot space between them and the defences. The headquarter tent was always in the same position: there was regular inspection of pickets and guards. Camp was struck systematically to bugle calls. Watchwords were given and discipline was severe: anyone sleeping on watch was court martialled, stoned or cudgelled, generally to death. The *fustuarium* or cudgel was also inflicted on anyone deserting his post in battle or losing his sword or shield. For collective cowardice decimation was practised, every tenth man killed. Citations and awards, on the other hand, were regularly given for valour.

[1] *op. cit.* p. 321. For the whole account see pp. 311–371.

Such systematic proceedings may well have struck the barbarians as uncanny, the whole carefully guarded marching formation winding along like a sinister snake. It moved slowly but relentlessly, for the weight of equipment was exhausting, including entrenching tools, stakes, cooking pots, rations. Most commanders were careful to rest their men before battle.

Later on, the big professional armies drawn from the plebeians were more elaborately organized and equipped, but the earlier conscript Republican legions of peasant farmers and their allies, in spite of appalling disasters against a genius of Hannibal's flair, conquered Sicily, subdued Spain, destroyed Carthage and riveted the Roman hold on Greece.

V

The economic basis of the early Republic had been the strategic position of Rome, set in the low lying areas of Latium and the Campagna; with political expansion and particularly with the conquest of Sicily, wider opportunities opened up. The land hunger of an originally peasant society, most ravenous among the patrician landowners for whom trade was officially unthinkable, and indeed by 2 BC formally forbidden, had been stimulated by the decline of the fertility of overfarmed land, and the consequences of systematic deforestation. The Agger *publicus*, acquired by conquest, was mainly taken over in holdings of over six hundred acres at a time by the senatorial class, and distributions made to smallholders were tiny—less than five acres; yet the peasant farmers had won the terrible second Punic War and suffered the heaviest casualties; their lives had been the price of the conquests in Sicily, Spain and Macedonia. A depopulated countryside, ruined farms, uprooted vines, devastated olive groves and wasted crops, had marked the tracks of Hannibal's army, and the losses in livestock, farm implements and gear were hard to replace. The manpower of the citizen armies was thus eroded, and the smallholding agriculture that had made the early Republic relatively self-sufficient was breaking down. Add to this the enormous influx of slaves, not merely, as in earlier times, from Italy, but from Spain, Macedonia, Africa, Sicily and Greece, not to speak of captured Gauls, set to work in gangs on big estates or doing work hitherto contributed by small free craftsmen, and social dislocation became severe. The small senatorial plutocracy with enormous estates and the rising *equites* and landed businessmen who farmed the tax-collecting in the conquered provinces—for the Romans as yet had no adequate civil service to deal with their growing and immense commitments—bought themselves more estates and luxurious town houses, and the contrast between rich and poor became more agonizing. The ruined smallholders often moved into Rome, where, still citizens, they sank to the level of a proletariat. Meanwhile, the slaves, encouraged to breed, also mixed with the native stock when given their freedom, so that the Roman population was gradually changed. The swarming metropolis, like modern London or New York, became racially more cosmopolitan.

Ancient society was overwhelmingly agricultural and static; but if large-scale factories were unknown, native craftsmen and skilled slaves from Greece and Asia wrought elaborate bronze vessels, lamps, ornaments and pottery, as early Roman austerity gave place to more luxurious display. But clothing remained strictly conventional; civilians went about bundled up in carefully folded togas, only those of the grandest officials relieved by a purple stripe. Since the women were expected to spend most of their time spinning wool and there were no big textile factories, the rich tried to live off their estates and households for clothes as well as food rather than buy in the markets. Even armaments, in constant demand, could not be mass produced, as there was no coal; all had to be done by wood fires, so that to produce steel took a long time: bronze for armour was more manageable.

The Romans early showed their efficiency in constructing aqueducts. Well before the first Punic War, under the censorship of Appius Claudius Caecus, big aqueducts and reservoirs had been constructed to supply Rome, for under Etruscan influence the Roman architects could already construct arches and themselves had invented a kind of concrete: the Appian Way, south-east over the Apennines, had been constructed by 220 BC, the Via Aemilia, north-west from Rimini to modern Piacenza, by the early second century. Nothing comparable to these feats of engineering, later vastly extended over the empire at its climax, was created by any other western peoples until the Industrial Revolution of modern times. While transport remained extremely slow and it was quicker, though more risky, to go by sea, time, save for politicians and generals intent on critical enterprises, was not yet precious, and, save for the threat from pirates and brigands, one could expect to arrive.

VI

The early Romans were as obtuse in the arts as in literature. Hardly anything survives before the first century BC, though the loot of Sicily and Greece had been pouring into Italy, and the sight of Hellenistic statues had encouraged the Romans to develop the funerary masks copied from the Etruscans into ancestral busts of depressing realism. They wanted likeness, and their Hellenistic sculptors gave it them, wrinkled battered endurance, low cunning and all. The faces show what the *patria potestes* could imply, what the slave households had to fear, and what even the Carthaginians could not overcome.

It was not until well into the first century BC that the Roman elite became more self-conscious and had their appearance idealized. As for painting, battle pictures were apparently commissioned for triumphs, but none have survived, and it was not until about 50 BC that the wealthy Romans commissioned their remarkable landscape wall paintings, designed to give a sense of space to their domestic interiors. It was not in the arts but in utilitarian architecture that the Republican Romans already excelled. The great arched aqueducts and the straight Roman roads showed the force and confidence of Republican Rome, the foundation of the vast expansion under the empire, when civilization was carried north to the Rhine and into Britain, although, as Kenneth Clark puts it, "by the time it got to Carlisle it had become a bit rough." As he writes of a later creation, "the way in which the stones of the Pont du Gard are laid is not only a triumph of technical skill, but shows a vigorous belief in law and discipline. Vigour, energy, vitality: all the great civilisations—or civilising epochs—have had a weight of energy behind them."[1] The Romans of the Republic already had this energy: if their motives were mainly the lust for plunder and power, they had the force to create a framework which held together, pacified, and long sustained the splendid Hellenistic civilization to which they brought their own formidably efficient contribution.

Meanwhile, Roman literature remained archaic until early in the first century BC. In verse and drama it is derivative, but the first surviving and connected Latin prose, Cato's treatise on agriculture, De Agri Cultura, is characteristically Roman.

Marcus Porcius Cato (234-149 BC) came of old plebeian stock from the attractive town of Tusculum near modern Frascati. He grew up to farm in Sabine country, and in the course of a long and varied life had a versatile career, military and political. As Censor in 184 BC his severity became proverbial. His writings were encyclopaedic, including a relentlessly impersonal account of the Punic Wars, in which one of the few heroes was Surus, Hannibal's Indian elephant. There is an excellent vignette of him, contrasted with that of Scipio Africanus, in Wilkinson's The Roman Experience . Though he wrote and orated a great deal, his greatest love was for farming; his treatise on agriculture being his only work substantially extant.[2]

It is a notebook or manual of husbandry, jotted down as the thoughts took him; its charm, as its editor remarks, its "severe simplicity" and its accurate revelation of the old Roman way of life. In its compact prose it is succinct, terse, appropriately "shrewd".

"It is true", he begins, "that to obtain money by trade is sometimes more profitable, were it not so hazardous; and likewise by money lending, if it were as honourable." But the Roman ancients had thought a usurer worse than a thief, and when they would praise a worthy man their praise took this form, "good husbandman", "good farmer"

> "et virum bonum quum laudabant, ita
> laudabant, bonum agricolum, bonumque colonum."

In fact Cato himself did some money lending, and large scale farming with slave gangs, but he is obviously sincere when he declares that "it is from the farming class that the bravest men and the sturdiest soldiers come (et ex agricultura et viri fortissimi et milites strenuissimi gignanter)"; farmers have the best reputations, and the greatest security, and they are least subject to people with subversive ideas (male cogitantes).

These sentiments are the prelude to a fascinating account of the right kind of land to buy, the correct size of the farm and of the best variety of products

[1]Civilisation. London, 1969. pp. 3 and 4.
[2]Marcus Porcius Cato On Agriculture and Marcus Terentius Varro On Agriculture trans. W. D. Hooper, revised H. Boyd, 1934. Loeb.

in their order of importance; a good vineyard, an irrigated garden, an osier bed (for making baskets and the like), a big olive grove, a meadow, and an area for cereal crops—not very important owing to the massive intake of grain from Sicily—a wood, an orchard and a mastgrove for the pigs. Nothing Theocritan and idyllic about Cato. He was a hard driving, cruel master, who classes an older sickly slave with blemished animals or an old wagon, to be sold off—"for the Master should habitually sell, not buy." Cato's directions for supervising his steward and getting the last ounce of work out of his slaves show the grim side of the old Roman virtues. A formidable, not a nice man, his personality and what he stood for is well expressed in his prose, though the text that has survived is less archaic than the original. Characteristically, he had a passion for cabbage. "It is the cabbage which surpasses all other vegetables. It may be eaten either cooked or raw: if you eat it raw, dip it in vinegar. If you wish to drink deep at a banquet and to enjoy your dinner, eat as much raw cabbage as you wish, seasoned with vinegar before dinner, and likewise after dinner eat some half a dozen leaves; it will make you feel as if you had not dined, and you can drink as much as you please."[1]

The first writer of Latin verse seems comically clumsy. Livius Andronicus (284-204 BC) was a Greek slave born at Tarentum (modern Taranto). Brought to Rome, he taught Roman boys Greek, composed the first comedies and tragedies for the official games celebrating the end of the first Punic war, and won fame and freedom as an actor. His translation of the Odyssey into Latin verse became a classroom book. The fragments that survive, in halting Saturnian metre, are wonderfully inept; as the opening line,

   Virum mihi, Camena, insece versutum,

"Tell me, Goddess of Song, of the ingenious man"; or when Athena asks what is going on in Ulysses' hall,

   Quae haec daps est—?

"What means this banquet ... ?"; or when Telemachus puts to sea and orders his men to tie their oars with strips,

   Tumque remos iussit religare strappis.[2]

Naerius (c.270-201 BC) wrote the Carmen Belli Poeni—the Song of the Punic War, the first national Roman Epic. Little of it has survived, and we only have fragments of his numerous plays, some of which were historical. His most memorable surviving verse is a proverb, quoted by Varro,

   Prius pariet lucusta lucam bovem
   Sooner will a lobster spawn a Lucanian cow—

the nearest the Romans could then get to describe an elephant, for the animals had first been seen by them when Pyrrhus invaded Lucania.

But Quintus Ennius (239-169 BC), born in Calabria not far from Brundisium and half Greek, who fought as a centurion in Sardinia against the Carthaginians

[1]op. cit. p. 141. (Ch. CLVI). Readers may like to try this recipe.
[2]See Remains of Old Latin. ed. E. H. Warmington. Harvard (Loeb), 1936. Vol. II.

and settled in Rome, is a major figure. He introduced the hexameter, and already shows the force of the language. Horace said that he was a convivial character, and he is said to have died of gout. He wrote many plays and is a precursor of Virgil, for he tackled the same theme, starting his *Annals* from the sack of Troy and continuing through the tales of the she-wolf and Romulus and the early legends of Rome.[1] He was admired in Hadrian's time, when there was a cult of archaic verse.

His opening line is not exactly elegant, in thought or expression:

> *Musae quae pedibus magnum pulsatis Olympum*
> *Muses who shake great Olympus with your feet;*

but he gets into the swing of the hexameters with his line on Father Tiber

> *Teque pater Tiberine tuo cum flumine sancto*
> *And you father of Tiber with your hallowed stream.*

He vividly depicts the she-wolf slinking into a wood, nodding pine trees and straight cypresses, and evokes the scenes of battle, where the ranks of both sides "bristle" with javelins. A good deal of his verse survives, as he meant it to, for he claimed that he painted the greatest deeds of the ancestors—*pinxit maxima facta patrum.*

---

[1] See *Remains of Old Latin*. ed. E. H. Warmington. Harvard (Loeb), 1935. Vol. I.

VIII

The Augustan Principate

As the rulers of the Roman state, a few thousands among millions whose lives remain almost unknown, emerged from provincial origins, assimilated Hellenistic culture and created a literature which, like the Roman legal and administrative tradition, would set standards into modern times, their archaic political institutions collapsed. The Senate and People of Rome could not control their own armies, by the end of the second century recruited not from the citizen small farmers, decimated and ruined by the Punic, Spanish and Macedonian wars and swamped by foreign slave labour, but from landless long-term volunteers whose professional careers depended upon their commanders. Nor could they administer the provinces that, one thing leading to another, were overrun as the originally cautious policy of the Senate was superseded by a greater lust for plunder and tribute among all classes, not least the People, who by a curious freak of the constitution, in their *Concilium Plebis* could directly appoint a general. For war paid off; and the Roman populace were early assigned the corn tribute from Sicily and citizens in Italy relieved from taxation, apart from the opportunities for enrichment for those able to speculate in the slave trade and in land. Here was the chance for military adventurers to build up a power stronger than the state, and from Marius and Sulla in the first quarter of the first century to Pompeius Magnus and Julius Caesar, assassinated in 44 B.C. at the height of a quasi-regal power, military magnates bribed the populace and fought out their rivalries. Finally, in 31 B.C. the victory of Octavianus, Caesar's heir and great-nephew, over Antony and Cleopatra at Actium gave him supreme and permanent authority.

II

The Roman authorities ruled an area vast even by modern standards in territory, if not in population, reckoned at about 60,000,000. But the responsibilities of conquest were early too much for the Republic. In north Africa, following the extirpation of Carthage, the Numidian King Jugurtha raised war, until Gaius Marius, a tough soldier risen from the ranks, ousted his own commander and cleaned things up. Consul in 107 BC, he dealt with a bigger crisis when, in 105 BC, hordes of Germans spilling over from the forests of Central Europe overwhelmed a Roman army at Arausia (Orange) in Provence, and when Cimbri from the Baltic managed to get over the Alps almost to Turin. Marius radically reorganized the armies, in which recruits without property had in fact long been included. The old *hastati*, *principes* and *triarii* were merged and uniformly armed; the maniples and centuries, using new gladiatorial skills, were rearranged in cohorts, ten to a legion; pay, arms and equipment were provided by the state. These legions soon utterly defeated the Teutones near Aix-en-Provence, then the Cimbri at Vercelli; but they had now become a permanent separate interest, no longer a militia of citizens in arms. The armies were again decisive when, in 90–89 BC, most of the allied Italian cities demanded Roman citizenship and, when refused, attacked Rome itself. A "Social" war devasted the country, and the Romans had to grant citizenship to half a million other Italians, but Roman supremacy survived. The price, however, had been heavy. A whole new interest had arisen which was no longer under the civilian Republic's control; rival generals formed factions in the Senate, and when Marius quarrelled with his subordinate Sulla, Sulla turned his army against Rome, interfered with the constitution and indirectly appointed one of the Consuls.

In 82 BC, Sulla returned victorious over Mithridates, King of Pontus, who had tried to drive the Romans from the Levant. He defeated Marius' soldiers at the Colline gate of Rome itself, murdered five thousand of his supporters, and confiscated their property. As Imperator he reinforced the depleted Senate in a conservative restoration; but the civilian Republic no longer controlled the armies and sovereign power had passed from the Senate and People of Rome to an army commander.

Then, in 73 BC there was a massive slave revolt. Spartacus, a Thracian former legionary and gladiator (the Thracians were the star performers), broke out of barracks at Capua and established a camp on Vesuvius. This slave army defeated two Roman armies and cut its way north to escape over the Alps. But the slaves stupidly refused to leave Italy; their forces broke up and Spartacus returned to the South, hoping to establish himself in Sicily or escape to Greece. Crassus, a subordinate of Sulla, defeated and killed him, and six thousand slaves, their owners unknown, were crucified along the Appian Way.[1]

Such was the background to the most spectacular contest of all between the most famous military magnates of the late Republic, Pompeius Magnus and Julius Caesar, the swirl of whose manoeuvres and conflicts engulfed not merely Italy but the entire Roman world and territories hitherto outside it; and out of these wars, fought with huge armies, emerged the *de facto* monarchy of Julius Caesar, consolidated, after further conflict, by Octavian into the Principate.

[1]Spartacus won undeserved credit with modern revolutionaries; he wanted not to improve society, merely to plunder it.

III

The fame of Julius Caesar (100–44 BC) still echoes down the years. His name, garbled to Tsar or Kaiser, passed to the rulers of the Russian, German and Austro-Hungarian empires; he is commemorated in the Julian calendar and the month of July and, like Alexander's, his fame spread through the East. In India the British monarchs were *Kaisers-i-Hind*. By adding what are now France, Belgium, part of Holland, and the Rhineland to the Roman empire, he altered the civilization of Europe, and his spectacular murder at the height of his power clinched his celebrity. Moreover, though most of his writings have been lost, his apparently impersonal but carefully slanted narrative of the campaigns still speaks directly, and whichever of his various busts is the best likeness, in all of them he looks the part.[1]

In his early career he was overshadowed by Pompeius Magnus who had come to power over the slave revolt. The Senate, afraid of Crassus, had summoned this able young soldier from Spain, and though he had only to round off Crassus's victory, he brought a powerful army. But so far from cancelling one another out, as the Senate had intended, the two generals had combined: Crassus was the more monstrously rich, Pompeius had more legions. Caesar, far the most able of the three and from the beginning set on supreme power, had first to make his way by the usual civilian offices. He came of one of the few surviving old patrician families, entitled to wear the red boots with crescent shaped ivory buckles of his order, but the emphatically plebeian Marius had been his uncle by marriage, and he was connected with that faction, though Sulla, thinking him a lightweight, had not included him in the proscriptions. Brilliantly talented and versatile, Caesar had early shown his flair for apt violence. When, dissipated and debt ridden, *en route* for Rhodes to study oratory he was captured by pirates, he raised his ransom, then with a private gang took and crucified his captors. Financed by Crassus, he obtained the traditional offices; first *quaestor* in Spain then, at thirty-seven and incongruously, *Pontifex Maximus*. By 59 BC he was Consul, already powerful through his lavish handling of a parasitic and

> Bribed electorate, changing sides for silver
> On Sale: One People and One Senate.[2]

In 62 BC Pompeius, laden with wealth, had returned from the East, having annexed Bithynia, Cilicia, Syria and Palestine, and put down the pirates in the Aegean; then, inexplicably, after a triumph, he had resigned his command. Whereat, since the Senate had refused land grants for his soldiers, Pompeius, Crassus and Caesar then formed a triumvirate, the alliance strengthened by Pompeius' happy marriage to Caesar's attractive daughter and only child.

Before the combined power of the triumvirate the Senate and People were overawed, and in 58 BC Caesar became pro-consul, first in North Italy (Cis-

[1] His full name was Gaius (*praenomen*) Julius (*gens* or clan *nomen*) Caesar (*cognomen*). This was the normal order of Roman names, but just as we refer to Shakespeare or Milton, Disraeli or Gladstone, famous Roman historical figures will not here be given their full nomenclature.
[2] Petronius. *op. cit.* p. 131.

Alpine Gaul), then in Trans-Alpine Gaul as well. He soon set about the terrible campaigns in which his raids on Britain in 55–54 BC were only incidents, and subdued all Gaul north of the Alps, while, in the following year, Crassus perished after defeat at Carrhae by the Parthians. In 54 BC the death of Julia had weakened the bond between Pompeius and Caesar, and although in 52 Pompeius was made sole Consul to put down gang warfare between political factions in Rome, Caesar, backed by victorious armies and the loot of Gaul, was now predominant. Ordered by the Senate to resign his command, he defied them; Pompeius prepared for war and Caesar now had to kill or be killed. So in January 49 BC at night, with only one legion, he left his province, Cis-Alpine Gaul, and crossed the Rubicon.

By mid-March he had pursued his rival down to Brundisium (Brindisi) and, by April master of Italy, he was soon mastering Spain. Then, next year appointed Dictator for a decade, with seven legions he followed Pompeius to Greece, where, that August, he defeated him at Pharsalus in Thessaly. Pompeius fled to Egypt, where he was promptly killed. After a risky start, Caesar then ousted Ptolemy XII, formerly a Roman protégé, but retained Cleopatra his sister, the joint Pharaoh, as ruler of Egypt, having apparently fathered her son Caesarion. Then after collecting the arrears due from Ptolemy, he brought back the Egyptian queen on a state visit to Rome, where her exotic ways and wealth scandalized conservative citizens, but not before he had defeated Pharnaces, son of Mithridates in Asia Minor, an occasion when he exclaimed *veni, vidi, vici*; and crushed opposition in North Africa led by Cato of Utica, grandson of Cato Major who, defeated, remarked

Victrix causa deiis placuit sed victa Catoni
The victorious cause pleased the Gods, the defeated Cato.

In 46 BC, when he brought Cleopatra to Rome, Caesar with forty legions, whose pay he doubled, was now master of the Roman world. A combination of military genius and showmanship, akin to that of Alexander and Napoleon, with political gangsterism tempered by an aristocratic clemency and charm, had brought him to the summit of power after campaigns which had extended from Britain to Egypt. The ground covered by these monstrous conflicts, when *"all that Discordia commanded came to pass on earth"*, is astonishing. Nor were they yet over, though in fact a new sovereign power had been wrested from the failing hands of Senate and People and would be used to impose peace.

Caesar had not much time left. An impatient opportunist, who had always improvised, he now lavished vast gratuities on his legionaries, men and officers; he cleared up the absurd calendar whereby festivals no longer coincided with the seasons and lengthened the year to its present 365 days: he ordered the reconstruction of Corinth and Carthage; rationalized many archaic provincial municipal constitutions, and extended citizenship in Cis-Alpine Gaul. He was also magnanimous in victory, with a patrician and risky disdain for implacable opponents; he conciliated Cicero, who had supported Pompeius; but in the eyes of the solid republican senators his entourage remained raffish and his largesse corrupt, and he flaunted his power. He was still avid for fresh conquests, planning a great expedition against Parthia in revenge for Crassus' defeat. Nor had he quite the gangster's instinct for "security". He attended the

Senate without his guards. When on the Ides of March (March 15th) 44 BC he was knifed there by Marcus Brutus and his conspirators, he died with an exclamation of astonishment at Brutus' ingratitude—"*Kai su, teknon* (not '*et tu, Brute*')—you, too, my boy."[1]

The Republican *Optimates* made little use of their *coup*. Caesar's death did not change the fact that the Republic could not control the armies; and the Consul Marcus Antonius, grandson of a famous orator put to death by Sulla, and a former pro-praetor of Italy, one of Caesar's commanders at Pharsalus, had not been struck down. As Consul he could impound Caesar's papers and treasure, and though he amnestied the murderers, he confirmed Caesar's official Acts and conciliated the populace by his oration at Caesar's obsequies. He thus obtained Caesar's old proconsular appointments over Cis-Alpine and Trans-Alpine Gaul, with four legions.

But Caesar's heir was his obscure great-nephew Octavianus, whose father, an *Eques* and son of a banker, had married Caesar's niece, been governor of Macedonia, and been adopted into the *gens Iulia*. In June Octavianus arrived in Rome, at nineteen already knowing how to play his cards. He acquiesced when the Republicans, incited by Cicero's oratory, evicted Marcus Antonius from Cis-Alpine Gaul; but in 43 BC at modern Bologna, he joined forces with his great uncle's lieutenant against their Republican enemies. He even countenanced his atrocities; that December Cicero was murdered, his head and hands dispatched to Marcus Antonius: three hundred senators and two thousand *equites* were butchered. Then, with Italy cowed, they sought out Brutus and Cassius in Greece: by 42 BC at Philippi, between modern Kavalla and Salonika, the Republican army had been destroyed and Brutus and Cassius had committed suicide.

The victors divided the Roman world. Octavianus took Italy and the West, and in 33 BC exacted an oath of loyalty from the Italians, afterwards extended; Marcus Antonius took the East, where the Parthians were a menace, and which included the client state of Egypt, whose Pharaoh, still Cleopatra, whom he met and loved at Tarsus and whom he married, put immense wealth at his disposal, in addition to his riches from the Eastern provinces.

Gradually the partition lapsed into war, a conflict in conservative Roman eyes between the virtue and simplicity of western ways and the corruption symbolized by the East. It culminated in 31 BC when Octavianus' army cut their enemies' supply line to Egypt at Corinth and his fleet blockaded them from the entrance to the Gulf of Patras. Off the promontory of Actium, crowned with a temple to Apollo, and where the Gulf opens on to the Ionian sea, a naval battle took place, 400 war galleys against 500 from the east. But Octavianus had the initiative and had tampered with the eastern commanders; they sheered off out of the fight, and, at a prearranged signal, Cleopatra with the treasure chest fled with her galleys for Egypt. Marcus Antonius followed. In Egypt, on a false report of her death, he killed himself, and the now middle-aged Cleopatra, having failed to attract the young Octavianus and knowing

[1] Suetonius. *History of the Twelve Caesars.* I.32. Trans. P. Holland. Ed. J. H. Freeze. London, 1930.

the Roman populace, applied the famous asp rather than make a show in his triumph. He annexed Egypt and kept it firmly under his direct control; he was now, even more than Caesar, the master of the Graeco-Roman world; unlike Caesar, he remained so for forty-four years and he founded and greatly extended the Principate and Empire.

IV

While Caesar had been the impresario of his own genius, Octavianus was careful to mask his power; while in fact appropriating the authority of the Senate and People he appeared a steady and conservative Saviour of Society. His level eyes, "clear and shining", writes Suetonius,[1] broad forehead and tight mouth, still attest his calculating mind, and the Roman Revolution was made to last. The incompetence of Senate and People to administer an empire or control the armies necessary to defend it had left no alternative but a disguised monarchy. Octavianus might call himself *Princeps*—but his essential title was *Imperator*, the commander of the armies. So long as the *Imperator* was capable, the central problem had been solved. In 29 BC, after a resounding "triumph", Octavianus formally resigned his emergency powers; but he still controlled most of Gaul and Spain, Syria and Egypt, the main sources of corn supply for Italy, which no senator was allowed to visit without permission. He also permanently retained the tribunician power, held supposedly from the People, thus blocking demagogic attacks; he called himself *Princeps* and accepted the honorific title, *Augustus*. As he puts it in his own *Acts* (*Res gestae Divi Augusti*). "In my sixth and seventh consulships, when I had extinguished the flames of civil war, after receiving ... the absolute control of affairs, I transferred the republic from my own control to the will of the Senate and the Roman People. For this service I was given the title of Augustus by decree of the Senate and the doorposts of my house were covered with laurels by public act and a civic crown was placed above my door. (*xxxiv*)."

He now set about creating the first far-flung Imperial administration in Europe, and save for one disastrous failure in Germany, extending and stabilizing the bounds of Roman control: "the foreign nations which could with safety be pardoned I prepared to save rather than destroy." (*Acts iii*). There had been nothing similar in the west before; it adapted a Hellenistic administration and Egyptian financial method to a civilization based on the cities on which it depended, for its roots were never deep in the countryside.

But after three generations of civil war, the first objective of the *Imperator* was to control the legions. He reduced them drastically to twenty-eight, mainly Italian; but then under stricter discipline and stationed most of them in the border provinces remote from the intrigues of the capital and under his own *de facto* control. After the campaigns of Caesar, the Romans confidently reduced the armies—feeling as Vegetius would put it, "what couldn't a few

[1] *op. cit.* II, 79.

Romans do against a multitude of the Gauls, or dare against the might of the Germans—or against the Spaniards, though they had better physique, or the Greeks who had more technical skill?" He also created a combined Roman police force and fire brigade seven thousand strong, to put down political riot and crime, and a network of demoralizing espionage and delation, the curse of all authoritarian regimes. He then gradually built up a professional salaried administration; the governorships, including that of Egypt, assigned not to senators or pro-consuls but to *equites*, the prestige of whose already affluent order he systematically enhanced, while he manned the main bureaucracy from his own freed men. The Senate, with diminished powers, was formally exalted, and a committee of senators supposedly advised the *Princeps*, who in fact took his own decisions. It was a conservative settlement, emphasizing the old distinctions of status and protecting property, though shifting the actual sources of power—a mixture of social and economic restoration and administrative innovation.

As a saviour of society, Augustus restored the old religious cults and austere morality; undermined, it was widely thought, by cosmopolitan Greek fashions. The *Ara Pacis* or Temple of Peace, (13 BC), created by Greek sculptors, which, restored, in part survives, is of studied simplicity; its reliefs depicting a procession of what was, in effect, an Imperial family—domestic, not pompous or even warlike. The figures even converse; the children look up. In contrast to the monuments of Susa and Persepolis or the bas reliefs depicting Assyrian violence, here is serenity and an Italian peace. This cult of the family and of the ancient rites of harvest and the agricultural year, of springs and gardens, fertility, and sacrifice, was still widespread, in spite of the scepticism expressed by Polybius, while the minority touched by Stoic philosophy had a wider view, from which, whatever its brutal beginnings and current cruelties, the empire at its climax drew strength. The idea of a *ius naturale* common to all men, and the expression of a cosmic order, had been developed by Cicero in his *de Republica* (54–52 BC). It was now, ironically, canvassed by the regime that had killed him, which claimed that its laws reflected a cosmic order and aimed at the *beata civium*—the "well being of the citizens"—that Cicero had defined. It was typically Roman; "stable with wealth, rich with resources, specious with glory, honourable with virtue". Such is the high but practical purpose glorified by Virgil; if often mocked by exploitation in an acquisitive but economically static and slave-owning society, it would not be without influence during the climax of the Roman Empire, nor was it entirely forgotten. A colossal task was undertaken, and in part fulfilled; the order on which all civilization depends, imposed. It was based on massive slavery; out of a Roman population of at most a million and a quarter, four hundred thousand were probably slaves. Though manumissions were constant and freed men became important in administration and business, the gap between the plutocratic rulers and the masses widened, as the free born citizens were pauperized and levelled down by taxation and obligations of service. In the Augustan age the elaborate Latin of the bilingual upper class which continues through the great days of the empire was already different from the popular speech and writing, as witness the contrast between the elaborate cadences of Cicero, the compact and intense style of Tacitus, and the lucid narration of Julius Caesar with the diffuse, roundabout but effective idiom of the early Augustan Vitruvius whose practical and comprehensive *De Architectura* is ancestral to medieval Latin.

Within this limited upper class, we know the Romans better than we do the Greeks. While, following Julius Caesar, the "second Alexander", emperors larger than life extended or defended the boundaries of the civilized world or fought across it, we can glimpse more intimate life: the Romans are the first Europeans whose letters have extensively survived. Among the wealthy with their vast estates, their villas among the hills or by the sea, an easy way of life sometimes encouraged a kindly *humanitas*, promoted by Epicureanism and by the milder forms of Stoic philosophy. Reading the stern ironic moralizing of Tacitus, or the scandalous and probably exaggerated disclosures of Suetonius, one is apt to think Roman life all political murder, intrigue and debauchery; but save at the hectic summit, and sometimes even at that summit, there must have been affection, enjoyment, content, and *otium—otium* does not mean idleness, but the enjoyment of private as opposed to public life. In a huge and unhurried civilization there was leisure in a good climate, and the teeming life of the cities and the routine of the countryside must have given some satisfaction to millions in the long periods of peace. Although the centre of political gravity shifted as the emperors became more itinerant and dependent on their armies, and finally settled in the relatively austere climate of the Bosphorus, the way of life of Antiquity remained Mediterranean, radiating out from the Central Sea, though it was the achievement of the Principate and Empire to extend it beyond the Alps and to Britain, if never far beyond the Rhine or Danube. And the vital sense of order, method and discipline, came from the south.

As the Imperator (27 BC–14 AD), Octavianus established a form of Hellenistic monarchy, characteristically disguised as *respublica restituta*. *Princeps* or First Citizen, a multi-millionaire, and worshipped in the provinces as Saviour and Benefactor, he was the permanent *Imperator* of twenty-eight legions and their equivalent auxiliaries. This *Principate*, based in Italy, saved the Roman world; brought the armies under conrol and devised a relatively light yet efficient bureaucracy. In spite of the shortcomings of the Julio-Claudians, under Tiberius, and in a more cosmopolitan way under the Flavian dynasty founded by Vespasian (69–79 AD) and continued by adoption, this authority imposed the classic *Pax Romana* and developed into the vast empire of Trajan and Hadrian—both Spaniards—and of Marcus Aurelius. The peace lasted from Augustus to its collapse under Commodus, Marcus Aurelius' son, who, succeeding in 180 aged eighteen, suddenly went out of his mind, spent his time with gladiators, and in 193 had to be strangled.

It was a predatory but internally long a peaceful Empire; at its climax from Augustus to the Antonines, it included Gaul, Roman Britain, the Rhineland, and the line of the Danube; under Trajan, Dacia (part of Romania); beyond it. To the East it included all Asia Minor and Armenia, Syria and Palestine, and to the south Egypt and all north Africa. It was a tremendous cosmopolitan civilization, comparable in scale and influence to Han China for the Far East, and to Iran for the Near East and Northern India, and it determined the religion and culture of western and eastern Christendom. It is the most important institutional and cultural fact of European history and its extensions overseas.

But in one vital aspect the Gods did not send luck. Augustus married twice; by his first marriage he had one beautiful but temperamental daughter, Julia: by his second, to Livia, wife of Tiberius Claudius Nero, whom he compelled to acquiesce in divorce, the marriage was happy but childless. He therefore, in 23 BC, married Julia to his nephew Marcellus, and on Marcellus' death the following year, to his able general and right hand man, Agrippa, by whom Julia had two sons, Gaius and Lucius Caesar. On Agrippa's death in 13 BC, Julia, to her disgust, was assigned to another formidable soldier, Tiberius, Augustus's stepson by Livia's first marriage, who had reluctantly divorced his wife. The marriage, a personal disaster, proved a necessary reinsurance: Gaius and Lucius both died young, and Augustus had to adopt Tiberius as his heir, though Julia's escapades had become so notorious that Augustus had her banished to an island, where Tiberius, on accession, had her starved to death. Thus the succession, of necessity kept within Augustus's family for fear of new civil wars, was only arranged by tortuous manoeuvres and adoption, and the architect of the Principate had no heir of his own line. So the high mortality and small surviving families even among leading Romans haunted the Empire; Trajan, Hadrian and Marcus Aurelius would all succeed by adoption and the chances of personality would saddle the Empire with a Nero, a Domitian, a Caligula and a Caracalla.

The other, but in the long run the greater danger to the Principate and Empire was external, and even Augustus failed to deal with it. The incursion of the Teutons and the Cimbri had been a terrible warning, and the Romans were strategists enough to know the answer. The extended their hold on the Eastern Alps over Rhaetia (Austria and Bavaria), Noricum, Pannonia and Moesia following the line of the Danube. They also tried to extend Caesar's conquests east from the Rhineland to the Elbe, and planned the conquest of the Marcomanni in Bohemia which would have given them a relatively short and defensible frontier from Bohemia to the mouth of the Elbe on the North Sea on the western side of Denmark. In 9 BC Drusus, Tiberius' brother and stepson to Augustus, reached the Elbe. Most of what is now Lower Saxony was annexed, garrisoned and secured with blockhouses. But not strongly enough; so long as Bohemia was unsubdued, the colony was open to attack, and the semi-nomadic pastoral proto-Saxons fiercely resented the Roman policy of settlement and exploitation. A major strategic campaign was therefore planned to be directed by Tiberius to master Bohemia and consolidate a frontier from there to the Elbe estuary; but there were dangerous revolts in Moesia (northern Jugo-Slavia) and Pannonia (modern Hungary), and the campaign had to be postponed. When in 6 AD Varus, an intimate of Augustus and experienced in Africa, took up the governorship of the Rhine and Saxony, the German tribes, too, were planning revenge.

They found a leader in Hermann, chief of the Cherusci, who, as Arminius, had served in the auxiliary Roman army and been admitted to equestrian rank. Since acclaimed a German national hero, he proceeded with exemplary cunning. Varus, a man of taste and a friend of Virgil, lulled into a sense of false security, divided his forces; two legions were on the Rhine, the other three among the Cherusci near the Elbe; and when he returned to winter quarters on the Rhine, on Arminius' suggestion through the Teutoburger Wald, he was surrounded in a downpour and attacked with the full *furor teutonicus* in the forest. His legions and their camp followers were almost wiped out. The Germans failed to exploit their success to the Rhine, and Marbodus of Bohemia contented himself with forwarding Varus' head to Augustus, who for once lost his *sang froid*; but the Romans, already over-strained on the Danube, had had enough; they abandoned Lower Saxony and the strategic campaign to secure Bohemia and a frontier up to Hamburg and the sea, and so changed the prospects of Germany and Europe. The imperial frontier always remained vulnerable on the Rhine and the Danube, and immense areas of German manpower remained untamed. Varus' failure had proved a catastrophe.

Far from these scenes of barbarity and carnage among the bearded, trousered[1] barbarians, afterwards idealized by Tacitus, Mediterranean civiliza-tion came to its classic Graeco-Roman expression. Augustus and his advisers deliberately encouraged an ordered splendour in architecture, art and literature to show that, in Virgil's famous lines,

'*Magnus ab integro saeclorum nascitur ordo*
—*the world's great age begins anew.*'[2]

This policy, in accord with Hellenistic "public relations", does not imply sentimental ideals alien to the realistic *Princeps* and the hard bitten operators who had backed him; it advertised and glorified a strictly practical purpose.

Beside the *Ara Pacis*, and the original Pantheon, the temple of all the Gods transformed and greatly enlarged into the present domed structure by Hadrian, Agrippa and his engineers and architects had spacious squares and colonnades laid out on the newly cleared *Campus Martius* between the embanked Tiber and the old City; Carrara marble povided the statues of Roman worthies and faced the new public buildings, while the main architecture was now in the more durable burnt, rather than sun-dried, brick. Although the most famous monuments and arches had not yet been erected, Vitruvius, Augustus' principal architect, had already written his masterpiece, decisive for all Europe, the classic statement of the architecture of humanism as he meant it to be. "In the following books", he writes, "I have expounded a complete system of architecture,"[3] which indeed he had, "so that the majesty of the Empire should

[1]Garments for which, writes Wilkinson, the Romans had an "irrational contempt". *op. cit.* p. 142.
[2]*Eclogue.* IV 5.
[3]Vitruvius. *On Architecture,* ed and trans. F. Granger. 2 vols. London and Harvard. (Loeb), 1955. Little is known of him save that he was old by 27 BC, when the book appeared, that he had been surveyor of artillery ("Scorpions" and *ballistae*) to the army, and been well endowed by Augustus so that he could write, in his demotic Latin "*et ad exitum vitae non haberem inopiae timorem*—even at the end of my life I should not be afraid of poverty." The manuscript only survived through a copy made at Jarrow in Northumbria, and so later reached Charlemagne's Court.

be expressed through the eminent dignity of its public buildings." In this admirable work, often cited but too little read, he thought of everything; the environment, the prevailing winds, the acoustics, the radiating plan, the proportions and, not least, the architect, who must be familiar with philosophy, music, history, drawing, mathematics—"by arithmetic the cost of building is summed up",—and who must not be arrogant, but urbane, fair-minded and loyal, "*non sit adrogus sed facilis, aequus, et fidelis*". He must also, of course, have talent. His designs should be commodious and salubrious, away from marshes and "the poisoned breath of marsh animals", and, when planning a town, he should be careful to put the shrine of Venus outside the walls to diminish adolescent lust inside, and Mars's shrine outside too, to diminish armed riot.

Such, apart from his famous doctrine of the four architectural orders, are some representative precepts of Vitruvius; an admirable theorist and crafts-man, whom more modern architects might well heed. Nor were the buildings that he and his school designed mere imitations of Hellenistic models. Roman architecture had already become "forceful and independent" through its Etruscan heritage, through its concrete vaulting, paved streets, huge aqueducts and vaulted sewers, as well as through the *nova magnificentia* encouraged by Augustus.[1]

Most of Roman painting has perished, though a great deal of mosaic has survived; what painting there is comes mainly from Pompeii—a second rate city and resort—and from Herculaneum, both preserved through the eruption of Vesuvius. On the Palatine, Livia, Augustus' consort, had her walls decorated with pleasant representations of fruit trees against a blue background, but the interiors of rich Roman houses owed more to the variety of smooth marble, porphyry and malachite lavished on cool interiors for summer heat—which sometimes framed the landscapes of Augustan fashion which later developed into architectural fantasies comparable to those of early modern European court masques. Some illustrations of a ceremony could be good paintings, as a few of those depicting Dionysian rites from the House of the Mysteries, in a well designed harmony of dull reds, purples and yellows, and there are some fine romantic landscapes illustrating the Odyssey, now in the Vatican galleries. The Romans' love of gardens, particularly of lilies and roses, cypresses and myrtle, obviously extended to such landscapes, but most scenes of Greek mythology are from Hellenistic copy books, and many are as smoothly vulgar as most of the surviving portraits. There are a few tolerable paintings of fruit and glass. But the best creative work came much later, when various techniques in mosaic created fine colours in depth under a sheen of green, blue and gold.

In literature late Republican and Augustan times excelled. Cicero's complex, elaborate and sometimes cloudy eloquence are unsurpassed of their kind in Latin; Caesar's *Commentaries* are models of lucid arrangement, still rewarding if related to the places and people with whom they so faithfully deal; and if

[1]See J. B. Ward Perkins. *Etruscan and Roman Architecture*. Penguin, Harmondsworth, 1970. p. 81.

some of those set to translate them may be glad that only 35 of Livy's 142 books glorifying Roman history have survived, and he was notoriously careless about his sources, they are interesting on Roman prodigies and myths and on the details of the second Punic War. Though he cannot compare with Herodotus, Thucydides or Tacitus, his well-paced narrative, which avoided the constrictions of Annals, suited his propagandist theme.

As Hellenistic culture was assimilated, Latin poetry became suddenly very good. Many of the *neoteroi*—the "new poets", came, like Livy, from nothern Italy; Catullus from Verona, Virgil from Mantua. Catullus, a genius who died at thirty in 54 BC, ten years before Caesar was assassinated, had already transmuted the technique of the Alexandrian Callimachus and the early Hellenic lyric poets into poignant and still familiar Latin love poetry and was skilfully evocative of place. Lucretius, who probably died in 51 BC, in his tremendous *De Rerum Natura* elaborates the doctrines of Epicurus with the unepicurean and puritanical zeal of a convert, constructing a philosophical discourse of lasting range and power.

Where Catullus had been a rebel, Horace was a conformist, whose technical brilliance in adapting Latin to Greek iambic metres combined with worldly insight. He was the son of a freedman, a collector of market dues, who had him educated at Rome and Athens, where he briefly served in Brutus's army and fought at Philippi. Amnestied, he obtained a minor administrative post in Rome, and became a professional writer, to such effect that he was accepted into the circle of the rich patron Maecenas, friend and backer to Augustus, who during the campaign of Actium left him in charge of Rome. Maecenas presented Horace with his Sabine farm. Horace now won much celebrity and made many friends, and his poetry is shrewd as well as moving. He chose great public themes and treated them in memorable miniatures, as the self-inflicted fate of Regulus, as well as reflecting on the vicissitudes of love. His work, too familiar for much quotation, combines a didactic strain with playfulness. He enjoyed, indeed, a mellow form of moralizing Stoicism, as in his portrait of the just man who, if the world crashes about him, remains impervious amid the ruins.

By contrast, Ovid (43 BC–18 AD) was a lightweight immoralist, concerned in his *Ars Amatoria* with erotic themes, who showed a slick technical skill exploited in the fantastic *Metamorphoses*. His dexterity made him popular in the raffish cicles frequented by Julia, and in AD 8 he found himself relegated to Tomi (Costanza) on the Black Sea, where he spent the rest of his life lamenting his exile. His erotic poetry and smooth versification made his work much admired, particularly in the Middle Ages.

Virgil is the greatest and most representative Latin poet. Born in 70 BC of farming stock near Mantua, he studied at Cremona and Milan, and then in Rome. He was befriended by Mycaenas and Octavianus himself, and groomed to be the Laureate of the Augustan Restoration. He later lived mainly in or near Naples, and in 19 AD set out for Greece. Arrived in Megara, he went down with fever and returned to Brundisium where, that September, he died. His *Eclogues* (*Selections*, 37 BC) are modelled on Theocritus and, though lacking his lively insight into character, Virgil most melodiously evokes the countryside, and in *Eclogue IV* sweeps into the famous prophecy of the return of the Golden Age. The *Georgics*, ostensibly a treatise on farming in the tradition of Hesiod, though not in his manner but smooth and amiable, superbly depict the landscape of Italy. The *AEneid*, a great epic, was written not, as Homer wrote, to celebrate the exploits of embattled heroes, but the foundation of the Roman state by the Trojan AEneas. Under the command of fate and often against his own feelings, he laboriously fulfils his public destiny: *Tantum molis erat Romanam condere gentem.* (So heavy was the task of founding the Roman nation.)

Yet there is nothing vulgar or boastful in Virgil's epic; rather a celebration of the Stoic virtues combined with public duty, yet haunted by the poignancy of beauty and by a melancholy feeling for human fate:

Sunt lacrimae rerum et mentem mortalia tangunt.

(There are tears in everything and death haunts the mind.)

Virgil was a perfectionist, who in his will left instructions that the *AEneid* should be destroyed. They were countermanded by Augustus.

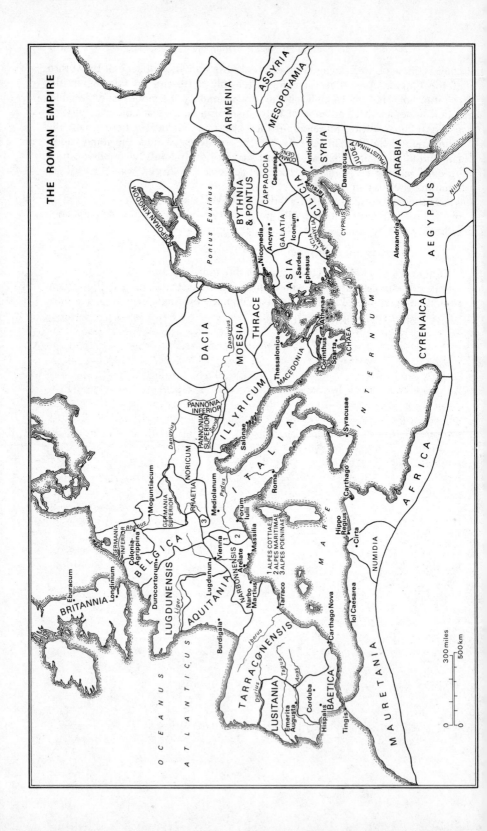

THE ROMAN EMPIRE

IX

Imperium Romanum

While the often lurid politics of Imperial Rome have since loomed large, the personalities of the Caesars, if occasionally decisive, probably affected their subjects less than Roman historians near the centre of power have led posterity to believe. Once the *Pax Romana* had been imposed under Augustus, the provinces in all their variety developed in their own way; in a cosmopolitan world civic patriotism was strong yet compatible with the official cult of empire, and Augustus himself had ordered the foundation of Saragossa, Avignon and Trier. In the east the great Hellenistic cities, Alexandria, Antioch, Pergamum, continued to flourish; Carthage revived and the Carthaginian cities in Spain, like the Greek ones in South Italy and Sicily, still prospered; Trajan and Hadrian both came from southern Spain. Egypt continued to produce the wealth increased under the Ptolemies; Old Greece remained poor, but retained its cultural prestige and the schools of rhetoric at Athens and on Rhodes their following. Moreover, under Claudius the Empire was extended over Mauretania and much of Britain, and under Trajan over Dacia—the modern Transylvania: the area of civilization broadened out. Although the Jewish religion was tolerated and Jews everywhere exempted from military service, only the Zealots of Jerusalem rose in revolt against Hellenization and were crushed, first by Vespasian and Titus, then by Hadrian, but the northern barbarians who had broken into Provence and northern Italy and been defeated by Marius were long kept out, and the Parthians, the most formidable enemy, contained within their own borders. The cosmopolitan empire was long at peace.

The occasional brief convulsions and reigns of terror in Rome can be set against decades of steady administration, and in a civilization so much decentralized they were not dangerous, so long as the armies were kept under control and did not revert to the days of Marius and Sulla, Pompeius and Caesar, and fight one another across Italy and the Provinces, and so long as the population of the capital were amused and fed, and client rulers kept in line. An economically and socially conservative society could proceed at its own slow momentum, without the prospect of any take off into higher productivity or of revolutionary oceanic exploration, but without being dragged by its own

accelerating technology into unknown dimensions of change. During the first
and second centuries AD, Graeco-Roman civilization reached a broad plateau
of stability and achievement; not so creative as in late republican and Augustan
times, but mature and confident under Hadrian; architecturaly baroque under
the Antonines, and, like eighteenth-century England, able to define and
elaborate its own law and appreciate its own past. Arcane and powerful forces,
within and without, were at work to undermine it, and have fascinated
historians from Gibbon until today, but his opinion that the period from the
death of Domitian in 96 AD to the accession of Commodus in 180, was that
"in the history of the world during which the condition of the human race was
most happy and prosperous", may well, in European terms, be true for those
privileged to enjoy the advantages of this magnificent, overwhelmingly agricultural, slave-owing civilization; particularly if they could retire at will from
the hectic life of the City itself, with its vast population living off subsidized
or free "bread" and entertained by "circuses"—not just the extremely risky
chariot races in which Nero excelled, but bloody mass gladiatorial combats,
fights with and between exotic and incongruously matched animals, and the
spectacle of criminals being "thrown to the lions"; so that sometimes every
lion had its Christian, while thumbs up, not as generally supposed thumbs
down, signalled death.[1]

II

Of the "successors of Augustus", Rostovtzeff rightly remarks, "it cannot be
said that the conditions under which they lived were wholesome."[2] They were
on wary terms with a plutocratic but politically frustrating Senate, and, if they
wanted to last, on good terms with the legions—particularly the Praetorian
Guards, and lavish with their entertainment bribes to the Roman populace.
Tiberius (14-37 AD), a veteran of severe campaigns in Germany and the East,
was an able soldier and administrator who consolidated the Principate, but
without political finesse or mercy. Ruling mainly through Sejanus, the Prefect
of the Praetorians, who plotted to succeed him and whom he executed, he
spent his declining years a recluse on Capri. "Corpulent he was," writes
Suetonius for what he is worth, "big-set and strong, of stature above the
ordinary, broad between the shoulders and large breasted, in all other parts of
the body in congruent proportion ... He had an ingenious and well-favoured
face ... and a pair of great goggle eyes in his head such as (whereat a man
would marvel) could see even at night in the dark. His gait was with his neck
stiff and shooting forward with a countenance bent and composed lightly to
severity."[3] Caligula, the son of Tiberius' nephew, Germanicus, was also

[1]Wilkinson. op. cit. p. 206. note 23.
[2]M. Rostovtzeff. Rome. Trans. J. D. Duff. Ed. E. J. Bickerman. Galaxy Books. O.U.P.
New York, 1960. p. 194.
[3]Suetonius. op. cit. III, p. 68. According to Suetonius he had condemned persons hurled
from cliffs on Capri and beaten to death by boatmen if they survived the fall, and he
indulged in what used to be called "nameless orgies". (op. cit. III, pp. 43-4)

paranoiac, became crazed with power, and by 41 AD was assassinated, the murderers crying out *"Hoc Age!"* (Take this!) and *"Accipe ratum!"* (Here, take it sure!), though his German guards, late but loyal, killed some of the assailants and for good measure a few Senators, not in fact implicated.

Claudius, his uncle (41–54 AD), who in 43 AD clinched the conquest of Britain, was originally elevated *faute de mieux* by the Praetorian guards, whom he lavishly rewarded. Though cleverer than generally depicted, and intermittently autocratic, he was an eccentric dominated by freedmen and women, and, having executed his third and dissolute wife, Messalina, he was probably poisoned by his fourth one, Agrippina, with a mushroom. Nero, his stepson by Agrippina, succeeded him. He appeared an adolescent of promise, but proved a stage-struck megalomaniac and matricide, whose vast "Golden House" overlooked a lake on the site of the present Colosseum. He was an expert charioteer in the races of the Blues and Greens, which already enthralled the capital and would enthrall the Byzantines, flaunted his apparently omnivorous lusts, though Tacitus says that they were "subordinate to his cruelty" drove Seneca and Petronius to suicide, and governed mainly through two freedmen; Narcissus, the richest man in his empire, and Tigellinus, "by birth obscure", writes Tacitus, "a beastly boy and a vicious man". He debased though beautified the coinage, lost control of the legions and provoked such hatred that in 68 AD he was forced to cut his own throat, exclaiming *"qualis artifex pereo!"* (What a musician perishes in me!) Such people, personally, were the Julio-Claudians.

The initiative then passed to the legions in the provinces, and the year 69 became the "year of the four emperors". The elderly Galba was proclaimed in Spain, but, arrived in Rome, was cut down by the Praetorians (again only his German guard remained loyal), and his head was sent to Otho, who had accompanied him from Spain. The legions in Germany proclaimed Vitellius, and defeated Otho's troops in Cis-Alpine Gaul, so Otho committed suicide in his tent. Nor did Vitellius last; notorious as a glutton, he was ousted by Flavius Vespasianus, backed by the legions in the East and on the Danube. After street fighting in Rome, Vespasian became *Imperator*.

Vespasian (69–79 AD) had no hereditary claim whatever. He was a veteran of Sabine farming stock with a wry, salty wit who had fought in Britain and in the East. He restored the central authority, ostensibly reverting to Augustan practice: in fact, as *Imperator*, he depended on the armies. Caring nothing for the luxuries and trappings of supreme power, he restored order, accumulated revenue, depleted by the fantastic expenditure of Nero and by the cost of the internecine war, tightened up the discipline of the Praetorians and the legions. He also quelled a fierce Jewish revolt, and his eldest son, Titus (79–81 AD), delighted the legionaries by bagging a dozen Zealots with as many arrows during the final siege of Jerusalem. He, too, proved a formidable ruler, commemorated by the arch still standing between the Forum and the Colosseum, opened in 80, the second year of his reign. But he died of fever in 81, whereat his brother, Domitian—a puritanical and murderous character, who called himself "Master and God" and had the chief vestal virgin buried alive, apparently without just cause[1]—proved both tyrannical and incapable. He was stabbed to death in a palace revolution. So ended the Flavians.

This catalogue of intermittent crime, vouched for not merely by Suetonius but by the great historian Tacitus, was now suspended. Nerva (96-98), an aged and respected aristocrat "with the manners of a cheerful Cato", adopted another able soldier. Trajan (98-117) was an outstanding commander and statesman. Born of originally Italian stock near Seville, at his accession Governor of Upper Germany, he proved a shrewd and methodical administrator—as witness his correspondence with the younger Pliny; he is best remembered by the detail of his famous column (113 AD) depicting his campaigns against the Dacians. But his risky invasion of Mesopotamia was defeated by the "turbanned Parthians" with their "bedizened Kings",[2] and he died in Cilicia on his way back to Rome.

Hadrian, his adopted successor and collateral relation, proved a talented and versatile ruler, the greatest traveller of all the emperors, who spent twelve years of his reign (117-138) away from Rome. This cosmopolitan statesman settled the Eastern frontier by agreement: like his friend Arrian, he had been Archon of Athens where he had built the great temple of Olympian Zeus: he quelled another Jewish revolt under their Messiah, Bar Cochba—"Son of the Star", and built an enormous retreat still partly extant at Tivoli.[3] Long passionately in love with the Bithynian boy Antinous who died in 130, mysteriously, in Egypt, he founded Antinoopolis in Egypt, and put up hundreds of statues to his cult. Hadrian also built the present vast dome of the Pantheon and his own huge mausoleum became the Castel Sant' Angelo.[4] But he remained a capable soldier: never lost grip on the legions: at his accession had at once put down several of Trajan's disaffected generals and, a veteran of many campaigns, he built Hadrian's wall in Britain. Feared and distrusted by the Senate, and disliked by conservative Romans for his love of Greek civilization, he wielded a more autocratic power than Augustus. Under Trajan and Hadrian the empire appeared at its most prosperous and invincible.

Hadrian adopted a reliable stay-at-home official, Aurelius Antoninus, named Pius because he insisted on deifying the unpopular Hadrian—(his own last word is said to have been "aequanimitas"-"calm"). He proved a stop-gap for the young Annius Verus, who, adopted by Antoninus, reigned as Marcus Aurelius (161-180). He had to deal with the first major barbarian incursion since Marius had defeated the Teutons and the Cimbri: in 167 Ballomer, king of the Bohemian Marcomanni, broke through the passes of the Julian Alps and besieged Aquileia on the Adriatic, but by 173 Marcus Aurelius had driven the invaders beyond the Danube. The Meditations of this introspective Stoic

[1]The Letters of the Younger Pliny. Trans. & Ed. B. Radice. Penguin, Harmondsworth, 1969. p. 118.
[2]Martial. Epigrams, Bk. X. LXXII, ed. W. C. A. Ker, Loeb: Vol. II. 1922.
[3]More a palace than a "villa", on a scale surpassing Versailles.
[4]See Marguerite Yourcenar's Memoirs of Hadrian. London, 1955, for an impressive attempt to re-create his personality, perhaps most tellingly evoked by the bust, with its alertness and sense of strain, in the Uffizi Gallery in Florence. Here also is a convincing bust of Vespasian, apparently scanning far horizons on campaign.

emperor have won him an awesome and rather depressing reputation. He was a fine ruler and a considerable warrior. As already recorded, with the accession of his son, Commodus, who reacted against his high-minded father, the beginning of the decline of the empire set in.

III

Though in social and economic terms there were no great changes, the difference in outlook in literature between late Republican and Augustan times and the age between the Principate and the accession of Commodus is striking. Compared with Livy, Tacitus (56–120 AD), the Roman equivalent of Thucydides, who, after going in fear for his life under Domitian, wrote freely under Trajan, is far more profound, with his compact, ironic and memorable power of phrase. He was probably born in Gallia Narbonensis, and he married the daughter of Agricola, governor of Britain (78–84 AD), whose biography he wrote. He held high office as *quaestor*, *praetor*, and under Nerva, as *consul*, and served as *pro-consul* of the province of Asia. He writes as an administrator with full access to official documents, though his history is dramatic and personal.[1]

Seneca is a moralist in the tradition of Cato, but sententious and diffuse. Petronius' fragmentary *Satyricon* (c. 64 AD) is a unique confection of realism and fantasy, probably "written for a circle of Nero's intimates and for a *jeunesse dorée* of low habits and refined tastes; qualities that militated against its survival intact through periods when growing Christianity went hand in hand with increasing intellectual barbarism."[2] It is extremely original, at once satirical, as in the notorious portrait of Trimalchio; indignant about politics, as in the verse; and funny, as in the tale of Eumolpus at Pergamum.[3]

Martial, "born", as he writes, "of the Iberians and Celts" and a citizen of Tagus "with stiff Spanish hair", frequented Rome under Nero, though his earliest epigrams, broadening and sharpening a Greek tradition, appeared in 80 AD, the year of the opening of the Colosseum. Titus gave him a small pension and honorary equestrian rank; but he was always poor, and in 100 under Domitian returned to Spain, where he died. He is notorious for an obscenity acceptable in his own time, and for his concentrated hatred, but more memorable for his feeling for nature and youth—the perfume of apples ripening in their winter chest—and for his delicate sentiment. (XI. XXVI)[4]

[1] He wrote the *Annales ab excessu Divi Augusti* 14–68; the *De Origine et Situ Germanorum*, and the *Histories* of which only books I–IV and part of V survive. See R. Syme. *Tacitus*. 2 vols. Oxford, 1958.

[2] J.P. Sullivan. *The Satyricon of Petronius*. London, 1968. p. 254. q.v. for an excellent study. There seems little doubt that the author is the *Petronius "Arbiter"*, one of Nero's courtiers, who had been pro-consul of Bithynia, and who is portrayed by Tacitus as one whose way of life was "unconventional with a certain air of nonchalance" that "charmed people all the more by seeming so unstudied", (*Annales* XVI, 17–20) and who was driven to take his own life by Tigellinus.

[3] Petronius. *The Satyricon and Fragments*. Trans. J. P. Sullivan. Penguin, Harmondsworth, 1965. pp. 94–6.

[4] Martial. *Epigrams*. Trans. W. C. A. Ker. *op. cit.* Vol.II.

Of Juvenal little is known: he was born at Aquinum in central Italy in 60 AD and lived on well into the reign of Hadrian, when he died, probably in 129. Like Tacitus, he was wise enough to lie low under Domitian, and wrote his first satires, "because he could not help it", under Trajan. His formidable hatred was comprehensive and he set a tone long afterwards imitated, attacking the follies and corruption of Rome, going for women with particular ferocity, but also sending up homosexuals in a dialogue in which a catamite complains of the difficulties of his life. In his last book he attacks almost everything; ambition, life itself. And he does so with compelling power, Latin being well suited for such forays. Lucian on the other hand, though also a satirist, is light hearted and writes prose. He was born about 117 AD at Samosata in Anatolia, and became a barrister in the great city of Antioch, then took to lecturing about literature in Greece, Italy and Gaul. In the reign of Antoninus Pius he settled in Athens, and died about 185 as a high official in Egypt. His chosen targets are bogus philosophers as in *Philosophies going Cheap*. The scene is a large auction room, the proprietors Zeus and Hermes, who remark "We've got a wide selection of philosophic systems for sale" ... "Hey you Pythagoras, come down and let the gentleman look at you." Lucian also attacked bogus oracles, and the not so private lives of the Olympian Gods as in *Conversation in High Society, The new Sleeping Partner, The Beauty Competition*, etc. This lively satirist is still highly topical.[1]

Another entertaining writer, Apuleius, born in Numidia, educated at Carthage and Athens, and widely travelled in the East, flourished as a neo-Platonic philosopher under the Antonines and wrote the only complete short novel that has survived, known as *The Golden Ass*. It recounts the picaresque adventures of a young man who is changed into the animal, though ultimately restored, with the help of a priest of Isis, by eating roses; a release with the symbolic overtones of an Eastern religion, a mixture of fantasy and mysticism and satire. The book includes the charming story of Cupid and Psyche. These two representative writers show that this, increasingly baroque, time was both sophisticated and original, and has been too much played down. And since the civilization was bilingual and preoccupied with the past, many important writers used Greek; as the Plutarch, Arrian, and the Lydian Pausanias, who wrote a detailed description of Greece (175) for knowledgeable tourists. They still give a whiff of pungent and pagan Mediterranean life, having survived, incongruously, at the heart of centuries of Christian classical education.

The standard of education was very high, and literacy probably more widespread than it would be again until the eighteenth century. Galen, born at Pergamum in 130, was considered the greatest physician since Hippocrates. He studied in the East and at the medical school at Alexandria, and by 164, in Marcus Aurelius' time, he was famous in Rome. Like Aristotle, he was a physiologist—he dissected apes—and managed to dispel the current illusion that the arteries were filled with air. He wrote voluminously and ninety-eight of his treatises have survived. Given the limitations of its surgery and its lack

[1]See Lucian. *Satirical Sketches*. Trans. with introduction Paul Turner. Penguin, Harmondsworth, 1962.

of anaesthetics, Antonine medicine, though helpless before the great plague of 166, was better than anything until recent times, with its cult of spas, fresh air, baths, massage, relatively efficient sanitation and belief in the *vis medicatrix naturae*—the healing power of nature given a chance.

Architecture was now both colossal and elegant. The interior of Nero's reprobated Golden House was decorated in excellent taste, its characteristically Italian "grotesques" long afterwards much imitated. "Peculiar to Rome", writes Rostovtzeff, "were the vast and luxurious *thermae*—public baths with athletic grounds which served also as clubs and restaurants; and also the noble halls, called basilicas, which were used for Law Courts. No Hellenistic capital could rival the public parks, hygienic markets, and splendid shops of Rome. Apart from all this, the palace of the Emperors rose on the Palatine, and their magnificent tombs on the banks of the Tiber"; moreover "the towns in the provinces, in proportion to their means kept pace with Rome."[1] The Circus Maximus for chariot racing was gigantic—the equivalent in Constantinople being one of the finest sites in the city—and even the horrible Colosseum is monstrously impressive.

But transport was still very slow, the main and most reliable beast of burden was still the ass, long ago first domesticated from Nubia in Egypt. For obvious reasons it was seldom eaten, though its skin provided parchment: unjustly despised and a by-word for stupidity, it was admired for its sexual prowess; for, writes Zeuner, 'the sex life of the ass is spectacular and full of temperament ... and the beds of married couples were adorned with Ass's heads.'[2] Mules, bred from jackasses and mares, were also popular mounts, as surefooted and smoother paced than horses; preferred by Nero, a preference he shared with later princes of the Church. The Romans, as one would expect, admired the peacock, which came from India, though "needless to say, they ate it",[3] and by the mid first century AD they had imported the pheasant from the Caucasus; they also, characteristically, invented *foie gras* at the expense of geese.

The pig, native to Europe, continued to be held in "universal esteem"; it was omnivorous and hardy, and its by-products often delicious. Only the Jews refused to eat it; perhaps in part because of their nomad origins, for "it is difficult to imagine how nomads could have coped with the art of pig driving, since the animal is notoriously unaccommodating in this respect."[4] Rabbits, native to the Iberian Peninsula to which they were long fortunately confined, were imported by the Romans to eat: they escaped, with predictable consequences, though they only reached England in the late twelfth century, and in the nineteenth century on Portland, in Dorset, the people still called them "they furry things". Though sugar cane was already raised in India, honey was the only source of sweetness in Antiquity; bee-keeping was essential and universal, among the barbarians, who liked mead, as well in the civilized lands. Wax was also essential for writing tablets, an improvement on clay. Since the

[1]Rostovtzeff. *op. cit.*, p. 251.
[2]Zeuner. *op. cit.*, p. 28.
[3]Zeuner. *op. cit.*, p. 456.
[4]Zeuner. *op. cit.*, p. 260.

only form of soap was a repellent decoction of goat fat and wood ash, olive oil was used, though it must have created problems in the public baths.

Roman cuisine was elaborate. Apicius wrote the *De Arte Coquinaria*[1] in the days of Trajan and Augustus. All these amenities implied security and leisure, and for centuries, at the heart of this slave-owning civilization, these were generally achieved.

The *Pax Romana* had succeeded. Yet at the heart of the great but derivative civilization we detect pessimism; where Julius Caesar and Augustus were proud and confident, Hadrian is introspective and Marcus Aurelius lacks zest. Cicero believed in the republic, Virgil in the civilizing mission of Rome; but Tacitus holds up German barbarians as a moral example to Rome, Juvenal scarifies society and Lucian laughs at it. Even Hadrian, the most talented Emperor, was addicted to astrology, long a widespread obsession. If men no longer peered with much conviction at the steaming entrails of sacrifice, they cast immensely elaborate horoscopes by the planets and the stars. Technology, as already emphasized, remained generally static, and the idea of using capital for sustained investment to supply expanding markets unfamiliar; beneath a minority urban culture the vast majority of the population continued their routine of conservative agriculture in their own way. Trade was, indeed, far flung: the Chinese had long exploited silkworms, but only on Cos had Europeans used a different species to produce a fragile gauze-like silk, mainly for women; it was thought rather indecent for men. So the Romans had to import their silk at vast expense through Central Asia by Indian intermediaries, and though in 166 Marcus Aurelius' envoy observed silkworms at the Court of Han China, it was not until 536 that Syrian monks smuggled them to the west in a hollow cane, the resulting industry being at once monopolized by Justinian. Jewellery and spices were obtained from India; incense, much in demand to assuage the reek of sacrifice—"burnt offerings"— from Southern Arabia; the amber trade, interrupted by the Celts and the Suebi, was reopened under Nero, to whom diamonds were never available: he had to content himself with emeralds and rubies. Apart from the slave trade, external commerce was mainly in luxuries, and it drained the empire of much of its gold.

Imperial government was mainly concerned to collect land taxes, harbour dues and municipal tolls from the provinces, not with "developing" them. "What is missing ... is commercial or capitalist exploitation. The Ancient economy had its own form of cheap labour and therefore did not exploit provinces in that way. Nor did it have excess capital seeking the more profitable investment, associated with colonialism." There was no constructive economic policy: "the whole tax structure was regressive and became increasingly so as the years went on."[2] Magnificent as the superstructure appears, in fact, while its intellectual creative drive was on the wane, its foundations were also slowly beginning to subside.

[1]Martial says of him, *Ipse quoque ad cenam gaudebat Apicius ire, Cum cenebat, erat tristior ille, domi.* Apicius himself liked to go out to dine, he got more depressed dining at home.
[2]Finley. *op. cit.* pp. 158 and 165.

IV

Since they were illiterate, the barbarians outside the imperial frontiers in northern and central Europe cannot speak for themselves. Tacitus, unconvincingly, depicts some Germans as "Noble Savages", but even to him, as to other writers, the barbarians appear "shaggy"—as the Gauls in *Gallia Comata*—and enormous, as they would have seemed to shorter Mediterranean people, and the German speech "like the barking of dogs". They were also murderous and moody; their aristocracy bone idle save when hunting or at war and plunder, and their tribal way of life totally incompatible with ordered civilization; but there were a great many of them, and their arms—if not their artillery—were often technologically as good as the Roman, while their agricultural yields in settled areas were probably as good as anything achieved there until the twelfth century.

Archaeological evidence is the most revealing. As Piggott well writes, it "shows us a rudely barbarous society whether in *Europa Celtica* or *Germanica*. The Celtic feasts described by Posidonius, or the Irish Tales (the Ulster Epic *Tain bo Coulaign* describing events of the first two centuries BC), "show us swaggering, belching, touchy chieftains and their equally impossible warrior crew, hands twitching to the sword hilt at the imagined hint of an insult ... wiping the greasy moustaches that were a mark of nobility, 'moved by chance remarks to wordy disputes ... boasters and threateners and given to bombastic self dramatization', as Posidonius coldly remarks."[1] Celtic sexual habits were promiscuous and omnivorous: Athenaeus of Naucratis (floruit 150 AD) remarks "and among the barbarians the Celts also, though they have very beautiful women, enjoy boys more, so that some often have two loves to sleep with on their beds of animal skins."[2] Even Tacitus, who admired German valour and monogamy—"they go singing to war"—and their fiery grey eyes, yellow hair and large limbs, reckons that they "scorn to obtain by labour what they can get by plunder"; lie about all day in winter by the fire, too lazy even to hunt, and were drunkards, brawlers and gamblers, and, we may add, bores. So long as the empire could keep them out, taking in only as many as could be absorbed, civilization remained secure. It was only with their massive irruption in the mid-third century, which coincided with a major Parthian attack, that it was jeopardized. The Roman peace established by Julius Caesar and Augustus was further secured under Trajan, Hadrian, and Marcus Aurelius.

The price paid by the barbarians had been heavy. Julius Caesar, for example, had massacred whole tribes of Celts and Germans to the extent of well over a million. But his Gallic war, fought outside Provence and Gallia Narbonensis, founded modern France. He subjugated the Sequani in Franche Comté, the Aedui in Burgundy, the Averni in Auvergne: in collaboration with the Aedui he destroyed about a quarter of a million Helvetii, Swiss Celts migrating west to get away from the Germans, after two years preparation and burning "all

[1]Piggott. *op. cit.*, p. 229.
[2]*Description of Germany*. III. On their Domestic Life and Behaviour. *Loeb*, Vol. VI.

their twelve towns and four hundred villages ... and also the whole of their grain except what they intended to carry with them",[1] to avoid any temptation to retreat. He also cut to pieces the formidable German Suebi at the strategic sites of Besançon and Belfort, and massacred the Belgae north of the Marne and the Seine and around the Western Ardennes, the Nervii in Hainault and Flanders at Mauberge, the Atrabates near Arras, and the Atuatuci at Namur. Having subdued modern Normandy and Brittany, Caesar broke the sea power of the Breton Veneti, with their big leather-sailed ocean-going ships: he could then establish garrisons at Angers, Tours and Orléans. Finally, the main resistance under Ambiorix and Vercingetorix, who devastated the countryside to paralyse the Roman armies, was defeated in 53 BC at Gergovia near Clermont Ferrand. But after this record of atrocities, surpassing those of Europeans against Africans in the nineteenth century, Gaul with potentially richer agricultural resources was becoming by the next century more prosperous than Italy.

Once they had become part of the empire, the Western barbarians settled down: outside the *limes* flanked by a broad stripe of deliberate desolation, they often remained semi-nomadic pastoralists, despising agriculture, though there were widespread areas of settlement if not of peace. Since about 600 BC the salt mines at Hallstatt in Austria had been systematically exploited, and since then large dogs had become common north of the Alps: hounds and bulldogs were bred by the Hallstatt Celts. One of the prized exports of Britain and Ireland would be hunting dogs. Warfare, at least in summer, was of course constant, as witness the fine helmets and shields and the big hill forts with elaborate fortifications as at Bibracte with walls three miles round, and Maiden Castle in Dorset, munitioned with sling stones. Chariot warfare had come in from the East, and the Celts were ferocious head hunters, who sacrificed men as well as horses: they had come originally out of the Steppe, and as Grousset remarks 'wherever you go in the nomad world there is the same smell of blood.'[2]

They remained politically incoherent: quite outclassed by the Mongoloid Huns of the fifth century, with their skill in manoeuvre and discipline within the horde. The Germans, more capable of ephemeral alliances, had a cult of destruction for its own sake, deliberately slighting captured weapons and loot, and pitching them into bogs in a frenzy of sacrificial excitement; a custom useful to archaeologists if not to anyone else, and in principle similar to the "potlach" feasts of earlier, Megalithic, times. On the other hand, particularly, as might be expected from its Bronze Age prosperity, in Denmark and the neighbouring Baltic lands between the Oder and the Vistula, the chieftains had acquired enough wealth by the time of Augustus to be buried in state, with drinking cups, ladles and dishes, in the correct Italian style, displaying "the responses of flamboyant barbarians to sudden opportunity for exotic

[1]Caesar. *Conquest of Gaul*. Trans. S. A. Handford. Penguin, Harmondsworth, 1951. p. 41.
[2]Quoted by Piggott. *op. cit.* p. 231.

display and affectation",[6] and an alluring taste for half-understood exotic things.[2]

Roman traders and native intermediaries followed the old trade routes from the Adriatic to the Baltic in search of amber and slaves, and, whether by war—great quantities of gold coins have been found near the scene of Varus's disaster—or by commerce or by diplomatic gifts, Roman artefacts and coinage circulated widely in the barbarian world. The two societies strongly contrasted, the one living under northern skies in thatched crofts of timber and clay or in long houses with the living quarters up wind of the animals and raised on mounds as in Friesland or built from wattle and turf; the other as at Trier, north of the Alps, on the Moselle in planned cities of tiled masonry, with paved streets, piazzas and colonnades.

It was not until 258–260 AD that the barbarians made a permanent break through on the Rhine–Danube frontier and that by 272 the strategically important Dacia was overrun. It was the beginning of the widespread Gothic and Germanic infiltration and attack, which by the late fourth century would be stimulated by the incursions of the Central Asian Huns. But these folk wanderings and settlements, though they changed Western Europe's rulers, were never overwhelmingly massive. The Neolithic Bronze and Iron Age populations were never extirpated, and in the west of Spain, in Portugal, the Basque country, western France and Brittany they remained racially predominant. In the British islands and Ireland the Anglo-Saxons and Danes never overwhelmed the Celts or the Iberians of the West; the majority of northern Europeans continued their routine agriculture and stock farming, established since Neolithic times. On the civilized side of the *limes* in security, but burdened with heavy and regular taxation, direct or indirect; on the barbarian side, life was more precarious, if undisturbed by systematic exactions of the tax gatherer. But politically and socially the new "barbarians" came to dominate most of the northern peoples within the Empire, while their military and rural hierarchy, chieftain or "king", aristocracy, bards and lawmen, freemen and slaves, foreshadowed the social order of early medieval Europe north of the Alps.

[1]Sir Mortimer Wheeler. *Beyond the Imperial Frontiers.* London, 1954. p. 35.
[2]Wheeler. *op. cit.* p. 53.

X

Imperial Decline and Christian Infiltration

Marcus Aurelius had good reason to feel that he was sustaining the burden of a precarious world order: the barbarian break through on the Danube had been held; but it proved the prelude to other barbarian attacks, and the built-in political, social, economic and psychological weaknesses of the empire became more apparent.

There was not even an agreed method of determining the imperial succession, now again increasingly decided by the armies. A false rumour of Marcus Aurelius' death had prompted Avidius Cassius, a general backed by the legions of the East, to abandon the campaign on the Danube and return to Italy to seize young Commodus, the emperor's son. Marcus Aurelius had put down this revolt, and in 176 tried to secure an hereditary succession by proclaiming Commodus joint emperor with himself. It was only by this expedient that Commodus had succeeded to the empire, and his reign saw a return to a political violence unknown since the days of Domitian. The curse of the Roman empire, the unbridled power of the armies which, apparent since Marius and Sulla, had wrecked the Republic, had reappeared.

Apart from their arbitrary power, the armies also presented a social and economic problem for which there was no solution. As the empire had extended its boundaries it had needed more legions to patrol them, and although many of them could be settled as self-supporting garrison troops in the conquered territories and recruited from barbarian mercenaries, the demands made on the manpower of the empire itself reduced its already limited productivity. Hence a vicious circle: the more manpower was diverted to defence, the harder it became to support the legions, and a professional military establishment, increasingly recruited for the frontiers, made the whole sprawling and relatively undeveloped economy more top heavy.

As already apparent, the very concept of investing capital for increased productivity was alien to the Ancient World: yet not only was it now burdened with larger parasitic armies for the inescapable needs of defence, but it had also to support an increasing and equally parasitic bureaucracy developed out of the administrative practice of the Hellenistic kingdoms taken over by Rome. And the Imperial and plutocratic establishment, heavily weighted in favour of wealth based on land, saw to it that the increasing taxation to support the armies and the administration fell on those least able to bear it. The status of the free citizens had long been in decline; now such was the weight of taxation that they were depressed to the level of small tenant farmers or even landless labourers, cheaper to employ than slaves, now more expensive and difficult to obtain as the empire's expansion ceased.

These monstrous difficulties, which the rulers of the empire had to face with utterly inadequate statistical knowledge, were increased by the deplorable character of a series of ephemeral emperors. After the murder of Commodus, Pertinax, a senior general hastily proclaimed by the Senate, was soon butchered by the Praetorian Guards, to be succeeded by Septimius Severus (193–211), an aristocrat of African descent whose native tongue was Punic and who built the splendid city of Leptis Magna. This able man tried to restore the discipline and morale of the army but at the price of raising its pay and militarizing the whole government: his last words to his sons are reported to have been "Agree with each other, enrich the soldiers, and never mind about all the others." But after his death at York in 211, his son Bassianus, nicknamed *Caracalla* after a peculiar kind of German coat he wore, murdered his brother Geta, and to make tax collecting brisker, debased Roman citizenship by extending it to all freeborn men. Best remembered for the gigantic and still majestic baths he built in Rome, he was assassinated in 217 by his officers in Mesopotamia. The misdeeds of his cousin, the adolescent Elagabalus, passed off as his illegitimate son, who, through the machinations of his mother, an hereditary priestess of the local Baal at Homs in Syria, briefly succeeded to the Empire, were too much even for the third century AD; and after trying to impose the worship of Baal and its rites on Rome, in 222 the youth was also cut down by the Praetorian Guards.

So in 222 AD, the year following the abdication of the last Han emperor of China, and following the murder of the deplorable Elagabalus, Alexander Severus, having survived Elagabalus' attempts to kill him, and himself only fourteen, attained the Empire. A remote connection of Septimius Severus, he is depicted in the *Scriptores Historiae Augustae* as a model youth, graceful, "manly", and well educated. In marked contrast to Elagabalus, he took regular outdoor exercise, answered letters and conscientiously dispatched business; he is memorable, too, for presenting oil lamps for the public baths, hitherto closed at sunset, as well as for completing the baths of Caracalla. But he is depicted as dominated by his mother, and his campaigns against the Parthians and the Germans failed; he was butchered by his soldiers in his tent near Mainz.

By now "the soldiers had become accustomed to appointing their own emperors in a disorderly fashion"[1] and political chaos set in. Decius, proclaimed emperor on the Danube, and the first systematic persecutor of the Christians throughout the Empire, was defeated and killed by the Goths in what is now Romania. Then Valerian was taken prisoner, along with 70,000 troops, near Edessa by Shapur I of Iran; an event commemorated by a great rock carving at Bishapur. The Emperor is said to have been flayed alive, and the Persians,

[1]*Scriptores*. II. p. 181.

who had already taken Antioch, employed the prisoners in building bridges, river barrages and roads. Gallienus, Valerian's son, in command on the Danube, then reorganized the legions, created a mobile cavalry reserve to fight the Germans and Goths in North Italy and the Balkans, and transferred all senatorial commands to professional soldiers. But in 268 he, too, was murdered by his own cavalry commander at Milan. Aurelian (270–75) managed to put down Tetricus in the West (who deserted his own army), and also Zenobia, Princess of Palmyra, in the East, both of whom adorned his triumph, the first in gaudy Gallic attire, the second in golden fetters. He cleared more barbarians from Italy and built huge walls, still partly intact, round Rome itself; but he ruled by terror: one of his civil servants, thinking himself marked for execution, circulated a comprehensive list of other victims, and Aurelian was murdered near Byzantium.

The Empire by now seemed heading for economic ruin: contending emperors had debased the currency and an atrocious inflation had set in: taxation and requisitioning doubled and trebled; farmers deserted the land, peasants terrorized the countryside: the Sassanians were threatening another attack.

In these straits Graeco-Roman civilization was restored and reorganized by a Dalmatian soldier. The Emperor Numerian was remarkable only for his oratory, and, returning from a campaign in the East, had taken to his litter because of an affliction of his eyes: on arrival at the Bosphorus, he was found dead. Whereat the army at Nicomedia proclaimed Diocletian, Prefect of the Household Guard, as Emperor (284–305). Diocletian at once cut down Aper, the Praetorian Prefect suspected of Numerian's murder, with his own hand on parade, thus showing that he meant business and winning the support of the troops. The grandson of Dalmatian slaves, this efficient soldier, like Vespasian, proved methodical, hardworking and constructive: he also knew how to delegate responsibility. He appointed a junior Augustus to rule the West, and in 293 a Caesar to work under each of them. He thus managed through his reign to keep the armies under control.

To improve the administration he also grouped the provinces under twelve dioceses, and, in 301, tried to stop the inflation by fixing prices and wages. Only in this enterprise, like other rulers, he failed.

His *reparatio* was directed, not from Rome, but from Nicomedia in the East, and from Milan and Trier in the West, and Diocletian deliberately enhanced the imperial prestige by elaborate Eastern Court ritual and awesome splendour. He also tried to deal with a social problem long spelling up; the spread of Manichean and Christian cults which had come into the Empire from the East. In religion Diocletian was conservative and wished to restore the traditional Roman rites. First, though he favoured the Cult of Mithras, he attacked the Manichees whose alien and dualist cult he rightly considered demoralizing; then in 298 he ordered the few practising Christians in it to be discharged from the army. Finally in 303 he launched an all-out attack on all Christians, ordered that their Scriptures should be burnt, their churches shut up and their meetings forbidden. The Christian clergy were imprisoned, and in 304 all citizens of the empire were ordered to make the traditional sacrifices to the Gods and the Emperor.

Diocletian's Edicts were not unpopular: the originally Jewish Christians had long been disliked as a weird sect who held aloof from normal festivals and sports, and when Christians refused the formal gestures of sacrificing to the Head of State they were thought anti-social. There had long been popular riots against them, and they had been blamed for fires, famines, plagues and other catastrophes. Moreover, conservatives had long been alarmed at the swamping of the old Roman way of life by alien cults, and afraid that, if the Gods were no longer regularly propitiated, misfortunes would increase. A rehabilitation of the traditional cults seemed an essential part of any *Reparatio*.

The cumulative *malaise* of the Graeco-Roman world since the age of the Antonines had softened up a hitherto confident and forceful civilization, rooted in the hard and brilliant culture of Hellas and the sturdy and methodical early Roman stock: with the acquisition of a vast and wealthy Eastern Empire, Italy had been swamped with exotic luxuries and infiltrated by eastern religions: the Egyptian cult of Isis, the Persian cult of Mithras, and the despairing beliefs of the Manichees. The Cult of the Sun, a more hopeful religion, Constantine would manage to blend with Christianity. A welter of astrological superstition and the dread of demons ("*powers*") of evil from which the various cults offered deliverance, obsessed men's and women's minds. Out of all these eastern religions, so repellent to the outlook of fifth-century Hellas or the Stoic philosphers of the second century, Christianity had emerged. It is necessary to examine its origins.

II

Near the eastern periphery of Empire, where the formidable Parthian power, by the early third century Sassanian, could meet and vanquish the Romans, the Jews of Judaea had still remained unassimilated. Those of the *Diaspora* had settled in Mesopotamia, in the Hellenistic cities, and most heavily in Alexandria; they had kept distinct, but adopted much Hellenistic culture; those of Jerusalem had twice flung themselves with suicidal fanaticism against the might of the Roman Empire.

Since their religion was utterly exclusive and monotheistic, it could not be adapted to the Graeco-Roman Pantheon; and of all people the Jews had long appeared the most unlikely to transform the civilization of Europe.

Christianity, an offshoot of Judaism, thrust out of it rather than breaking away, had long been a tiny and negligible sect, seldom mentioned by the non-Christian writers; yet of all the religions seeping into the Empire from the east, it would now predominate; though it was not until the disasters of the mid-third century that its influence became considerable, and it took nearly three centuries to become an official religion.

Though Christians, not Jews, believe that Jesus of Nazareth fulfilled and transcended Judaism, he had been a Jewish prophet, who, like others, had come from the people and denounced the priestly establishment; and Paul, the principal missionary and interpreter of Christianity, had been a converted rabbi, trained in Jewish and Hellenistic learning. The disciples, depicted, like the Founder and Paul, by generations of European artists, had been Jews; the Christ, the Anointed, the Son of God of one Substance with the Father, had been, as the Emperor Julian had stressed, a Galilaean.

So the Jewish background was important. It was Asian: Semitic and Bedouin; Babylonian; Iranian. Brought out of Egypt by Moses about 1400 BC and about 1000 BC by Aaron into Palestine, the Israelites had established a Kingdom under David which had reached its apogee with the building of Solomon's temple at Jerusalem. But all save Judaea had been overrun by the Assyrians, Judaea itself had been taken by Nebuchadnezzar, and Zedekiah, the last king of David's line, and most of his leading subjects deported to Babylon. The exile, bitter and lamented, had been brief. In 559 BC Cyrus had allowed the Jews to return under Persian suzerainty, and during the fifth century, when Athens was coming to full splendour, the ancient temple had been restored. But the Jews had returned from their exile with new ideas; to the original tribal cult of Yahweh they had added Babylonian and Iranian notions of a cosmic conflict between God and the Devil, and the working out of history towards a final judgement. History no longer, as to Graeco-Roman minds, seemed a cyclic recurrence, but linear and dynamic; myth had become theology. Along with the Jewish cult of the Law and the Prophets, these ideas had been elaborated; and during the brilliant age of Hellenic and Hellenistic civilization and the most creative Roman version of it, this alien, concentrated and formidable religion had been elaborated in a minor territory on the periphery of the Empire.

Minor, but always turbulent. In 66 BC the Jews had risen under Judas Maccabaeus and, though the rebellion had been crushed, had manoeuvred the Selucids by 143 BC into establishing an independent though faction-ridden Hasmonaean Kingdom. In 63 BC Pompeius Magnus had annexed it. Herod, a wily and murderous Edomite prince, whose father had been a friend of Julius Caesar, and who had ingratiated himself with Augustus, had ruled as client king from 37–4 BC; but though he had greatly enlarged and embellished the temple, the stricter Jews had detested him as an Arab.[1] His incapable son, Archelaus, was soon deposed by the Romans and most of the country subjected to direct rule by a Procurator at Caesarea, though another of Herod's descendants remained Tetrarch of Galilee. Such, in essentials, is the political background, with the Jews, hankering for their brief Hasmonaean independence, seething with discontent and internal faction, and the Romans attempting, with no more success than the British under the Mandate after 1922, to pacify the country.

The religious aspect is of more lasting interest. Since the Roman Empire was long officially Christian before its final collapse in the West and thereafter continued in the "Orthodox" Christian East, the myths, folk tales, military

[1] Indeed his record is unsavoury; he murdered the second of his ten wives, and disinherited and killed his eldest son: whether or not he ordered the "Massacre of the Innocents", he was the kind of character who might have done so.

history, prophetic and moralizing books of the Jewish Old Testament as well as the scriptures of the New, would swamp and transform the long-accepted Graeco-Roman Pantheon, many of whose Gods would be demoted to be demons, if much of the old ritual would be adapted, and some of the most ancient popular religions died hard, if at all. Articulate Europe would express itself, until recent times, mainly in a Judaeo-Christian idiom.

It was richly varied and dramatic. The archaic *Pentateuch*, the Five Books of the Mosaic law, had been put together before the Exile; and some of the prophets had lived in the eighth to sixth centuries, nearly as far back as Homer and Hesiod. But the most eloquent and searching, Isaiah and Jeremiah, are post-Exilic; indeed, *Proverbs, Ecclesiasticus, Job, Daniel,* many *Psalms* and the second *Isaiah,* were all written in Hellenistic times, when, for the benefit of the many Jews of the Diaspora now prospering in Alexandria, Antioch and other great cities, the scriptures were translated into the *Septuagint* in Greek. Compared with the Graeco-Roman mythology and ethics, the Jewish scriptures depicted a cosmic and intense drama between an exclusive and often vengeful god and his "Chosen people" obsessed with anxiety to win and keep his tremendous favour. The racialism which had inspired the Maccabean wars and would lead to the Zealot revolts against Vespasian and Hadrian also in milder form inspired the priesthood, who were sustained in Jerusalem by the offerings of the wealthy Diaspora. Christianity was conditioned by their inheritance, though it broke out of it.

The immediate origins of Christianity are extremely obscure – even to the date of the Founder's birth. According to Matthew, who describes the "Massacre of the Innocents" and the "flight into Egypt", he was born in the penultimate or final year of Herod's reign—5 or 4 BC; according to Luke, who relates his birth to the census under Augustus, it was in 6 or 7 AD. The chronology of our own epoch was not invented until about 527 AD by Dionysius Exiguus, a monk in Rome, who, expert by the standards of his time, calculated the event as having occured on 25th December 753 *ab urbis condita* and, in his own terms, got it wrong.[1]

The literally epoch-making choice of *Anno Domini 1* was in fact a compromise. The date of the crucifixion is also uncertain, between 29–33 AD, in the declining years of Tiberius. The earliest of the gospels, Matthew, was not written until, at earliest, 65 AD, over thirty years after the Crucifixion, and Luke not until 100. Yet, distorted as it may be, the impact of the original teaching is extraordinary, with its unusual compassion, forgiveness, even humour, in a homely lakeside setting of Galilaean cornfields and vineyards, along with searing flashes of moral indignation. This prophet was no "gentle Jesus"; but fierce and exacting and apparently making tremendous claims in the light of a life beyond the present. Ironically, indeed, the Founder of Christianity was anti-clerical; he drove the money changers from the Temple; and worse, he claimed that the Kingdom of God was not, as most of the Pharisees and even the pro-Roman Sadducees believed, a temporal dominion,

[1]"Little Dennis": Cassiodorus, for what he is worth, alleges that he was "Scythian"—so perhaps a Slav. He was expert in Canon law as well as in sixth century Mathematics.

the reward of a conscientiously kept bargain with an exclusive Deity, but the instant free bounty of a loving God to anyone capable of sharing it and passing it on. The Gospels thus had potentially something for everyone: a dramatic story, miracles (as had other religions), fulfilment of the scriptures for the Jews; above all the escape—even the "redemption"—of gentile mankind.

Naturally the priestly establishment at Jerusalem, able and conventional men, not all of them pompous and rapacious, but Hebraically upright and expert in the Mosaic Law, detested the itinerant prophet from unimportant Nazareth and rustic Galilee, so different from the stony hillsides of the Holy City. He had made them appear irrelevant; in their eyes, moreover, by apparently claiming to be the Messiah, he had blasphemed. They "rent their clothes", and contrived, with the connivance of Pontius Pilate, who had plenty of other problems on hand, to have him crucified—the usual penalty for treason.

They had reckoned without their victim. Such had been his hypnotic power, that his followers, more than ever convinced that he was the Messiah, since they now believed that he had risen from the dead, had created a cult. They had continued briefly as a minor Jewish sect in Jerusalem; then, dispersed by Jewish persecution, some had taken refuge in cosmopolitan Antioch. Here they had first been termed "Christians"—from the Greek for "Messiah", the Anointed, and "Apostles" (envoys) of the Incarnate God. The orthodox Jews hounded them down; the keenest persecutor, Saul, an Anatolian Jew from Tarsus, who had studied in Jerusalem. Saul experienced a sudden conversion. Now Paul, he became convinced that Christianity provided an escape from the demon-haunted Hellenistic world and could apply not only to the Jews but to the rest of mankind. Convinced that Christ, the incarnate God, had "reconciled" God and the human race, he inspired the originally Jewish-Christian network in Anatolia and Greece with his eloquent and organizing zeal. "Jesus," he declared, "(who) was delivered up for our trespasses and raised up that we might be justified . . . through him we have got access to this grace where we have our standing, and triumph in the hope of God's glory . . . we triumph in God through our Lord Jesus Christ, by whom we now enjoy our reconciliation."[1] Here is the ancient Jewish idea of the covenant fulfilled, but in a wider context. Along with this conviction of being redeemed from "original sin", Paul had caught the most unusual aspect of the Gospel—in a famous passage: "If I have no love I count for nothing. I may distribute all I possess in charity, I may give up my body to be burnt, but if I have no love, I make nothing of it . . ." Thus "faith and hope and love last on, these three, but the greatest of all is love. Make love your aim . . .".[2]

Paul, however, who thought himself "appointed to be the herald of revelation", was also fiercely dogmatic, claiming a monopoly of truth and authority and the right to "make over" those who have got their faith wrong to "Satan", in terms of the ancient Iranian conflict between Truth and Lie. Nor did his idea of love include sexual tenderness and romance, for he

[1]The New Testament. Trans. by James Moffatt. New Edition revised London. 1934. Romans 4 and 5.
[2]The New Testament. op. cit. I Corinthians. X. 13 and 14.

considered marriage a third rate expedient for those without the "gift of continence", merely designed "to avoid fornication", it being "better to marry than to burn", and he denounced all deviant love as "unnatural", a mere "flaming out of lust". This hatred of sex in a world in which it had been generally accepted and publicly celebrated on its own various merits brought a new and alien note into European civilization; morbid, vindictive and censorious. Many humanists, among whom Nietzsche has been the most eloquent, have considered it a blasphemy of the roots of life.

As might be expected, the Christians had long remained a tiny minority. They had already been notorious enough in Rome to be made scapegoats for the great fires which devastated the city in 64 AD, when Nero had them burnt as living torches: otherwise they are little mentioned. They had naturally been thought subversive when they had refused the formal routine sacrifices to the Emperor as Head of State. Tacitus, generally caustic, had thought them "enemies of the human race"; and the relatively humane Younger Pliny, who had them executed only if they obstinately avowed their faith, told Trajan that he had found Christianity "a degenerate sort of cult carried to extravagant lengths ... a wretched cult". Trajan had replied, in a statesmanlike way, that "these people must not be hunted out", but that "if they proved obdurate," the law "must take its course".

On the other hand, Paul, like the Jews, had used the Jewish network to spread his faith; the Christians were well organized; they had elders, overseers or "bishops" and subordinate "deacons"; regular meetings, records and scriptures—the *Acts of the Apostles* had been written by 60 AD, before the gospels; and contrary to widespread belief, the sect already had long included people of substance who could afford fairly expensive catacombs and considerable charity to their own poor. They were close-knit by fervent beliefs; the ritual of baptism and Eucharist, the expectation of the second coming of Christ; and some were fanatical, courting martyrdom. Moreover, the widespread Stoic philosophy, with its rather cold humanitarianism, together with the long internal peace of the empire, had made Graeco-Roman civilization slightly more humane, even to slaves, and Christianity was only one of many emotional and mutually benevolent eastern religions which had long been accepted and assimilated. No-one officially objected to the widespread cult of Mithras, popular in the army, or to the cult of Isis, celebrated, for example, by Apuleius. John's Gospel equates the *Logos*—a Stoic term—with the incarnate Revelation of God focused in Christ: the Christians were indeed too well grounded and dogmatic to dissolve into the fashionable Gnosticism, and too dynamic for the negative cult of public duty, personal self-sufficiency or withdrawal which was the best that Stoics or Epicureans had to offer. Where they had advocated endurance or evasion, the Christians had long offered something rare in Antiquity—hope.

With the "reparatio" of the Empire, their well-organized communities would become important enough for government to abandon Diocletian's persecutions and under Constantine to conciliate the alien but now widespread cult.

XI

Eastern *Reparatio:* Western Collapse

The genius of Gibbon, master of memorable phrase, irony and footnote, has given generations of readers a vivid but one-sided impression of the decline and fall of the Roman Empire. In fact, after the first serious crisis in the mid-third century, it was pulled together between 284 and 337 by Diocletian and Constantine as a military and bureaucratic despotism. Under Constantine, with Christianity an established and endowed religion, it carried on, its capital now economically and strategically better-placed at Constantinople, its golden *solidus* the acknowledged standard of value; and the city remained the predominant cultural power-house of Europe for centuries. It was only in the West that the Empire collapsed, and then not until 476.

To Gibbon, with his eighteenth-century rationalist dislike of religion, the Christian theological debates of the restored empire between Arianizers and Catholics, already acute under Constantine and his successors, appeared repellent; and its culture so inferior to that of classical or even Antonine times, that he played down the unbroken continuity between Roman civilization and the great Byzantine empire which long held off Gothic, Persian, Bulgar, Slav and Muslim attacks; briefly in its richest and most powerful phase under Justinian (527–565); reconquered much of the West and Africa and then converted the Balkan and Russian peoples to Christianity, leaving its mark of autocracy and devious diplomacy most strongly on Kievan and Muscovite Russia, and setting cultural, monetary and administrative standards which long influenced the barbarian kingdoms of the West and kept alive the idea of a Western Empire. That Mediterranean civilization now radiated from Constantinople, not Rome, and that after Justinian's time even the Byzantine rulers of a civilian government spoke Greek have obscured the historic fact that it never became, like the West, sub-Roman, but remained another and formidable manifestation of the old undefeated empire.

On the West Gibbon did not exaggerate. The abdication in 476 of Romulus "Augustulus" from a long bankrupt authority was a belated acknowledgement of the facts. Civilization, long infiltrated and overrun by Germanic barbarians, would so far decline that, even among the ruling classes, writing would appear an arcane magic, and among the clergy only a garbled and often parrot learning was preserved, as in the *Etymologiae* of the Visigothic Isidore of Seville, long misleadingly venerated into late medieval times. It was only through official Christianity, backed by the power and prestige of Rome and of the great landowners in North Italy and Gaul, that some of the learning and the memory of civilization survived. For the intellectuals, the Greek and Latin fathers from Origen to Augustine created a wealth of sophisticated ideas: while, in addition to the startling impact of the Gospels with their promise of Heaven and threat of Hell, the worship of Christ, the miracle-working hero, attracted the barbarians. Further, in Egypt and Syria, two of the least Romanized provinces, anchorites and monks in the Eastern manner set examples that swiftly and strangely appealed to the heathen, so that European holy men and monks turned missionaries, spread Christianity and the rudiments of Mediterranean civilization among peoples whom the Romans had considered beyond the pale.

But the old lay culture in the West also long remained tenacious. After the empire had been given a new lease of life by Diocletian, Constantine and their successors, the Western aristocratic culture revived. Ausonius (310–95), for example, who owned estates near Bordeaux and had great political influence, celebrated the beauty of the Moselle in good poetry: Claudian, an Alexandrian Greek settled in Rome, wrote a technically accomplished panegyric on Stilicho, the half-Vandal commander who defended the City before Alaric's Goths sacked it; and Symmachus (330–402), a wealthy Roman Senator, wrote letters that illuminate his time. Later, Boethius, who, at the cost of his life, served the Ostrogoth King Theodoric, wrote his memorable and needed *Consolations of Philosophy*, and some moving neo-Platonic verse. The highly civilized magnates in Gaul, Italy and Spain, who went to ground on their great estates during the troubles, survived inflation and remained very powerful: they turned Christian, largely monopolized the bishoprics and abbacies, and put their authority behind the Church; significantly, it was now that the Latin vernacular spread conclusively among the country people in France and Spain, displacing Celtic and Iberian. Further, the landowners came to terms with and influenced the barbarian leaders and their warrior elites, whom they sometimes preferred to the despotic military and itinerant emperors, with their tax collectors and their now largely barbarian armies.

So in the East there was restoration; in the West only gradual decline into collapse. And the Eastern Empire, in its new and *parvenu* form, became under Justinian at least rich and spectacular, in the superb architecture of Hagia Sophia and the mosaics of Constantinople and Ravenna. "The impeccable Roman toga ... would still appear on statues of officials and great men. But the great men themselves would have worn a dress as flamboyant as any worn in the Arabian nights: a tight tunic reaching down to the knees, heavily embroidered at the hems; bright stockings; a huge cloak pinned above the right shoulder with a clasp of barbarian origin, its billowing silk sewn with gold thread, decorated with panels of colour appropriate to the rank of the wearer, or with figures with flying dragons and, in the case of pious Christians, with scenes from the Bible. Nor would they have lived in the houses of the past, built four-square around a courtyard; but in intricate palaces, bright with inlaid marble and rainbow coloured mosaics, built from the inside out, to convey by their arcades, by halls on different levels, domed ceilings and heavy curtains a new sense of opulent mystery."[1]

II

When Diocletian slowly pulled the empire together, it had emerged as a debased but viable military and bureaucratic despotism with Eastern trappings, mainly under soldiers from the Balkans.

Diocletian's methods were rough and ready: there were two Augusti, himself in the East, Maximian, by origin a Balkan peasant, in the West; in turn they nominated two Caesars, Galerius in the East, Constantius Chlorus (the Pale) in the West. When in 305 Diocletian retired and his colleague Maximian reluctantly did the same, to be succeeded in the East by Galerius, originally a cattle herdsman, Constantius Chlorus assumed the purple in the West; but in 306 he died at York, not before his eldest son, Constantine, held in effect as a hostage at Galerius's Court, had escaped to join his father at Boulogne by hamstringing all the relays of post horses behind him. Galerius came on his father's side from small landowners near the modern Niš in Jugoslavia; his mother Helena (248–328), Constantius Chlorus' first wife, had worked in a tavern at Drepanum in Bithynia, so he was racially Balkan and Anatolian. There is no evidence that Helena, sainted for having, according to late fourth-century accounts written two generations after her death, found the true cross, and celebrated by the Anglo-Saxon Caedmon in the late seventh, was British, a legend first popularized by the Welsh Geoffrey of Monmouth in 1147. Galerius refused to recognize Constantine as Augustus, so in 307, aged about twenty-two, Constantine proclaimed himself. Having secured the Rhine frontier, Gaul and Spain, in 312 he crossed the Alps by the Mt. Cenis, and defeated the armies of Maxentius, Maximian's son, near Turin and Verona. Then, having secured North Italy and with the speed that made him an undefeated commander, he advanced over the Apennines to Tuscany and to Rome, on Maxentius himself. And during this autumn march the young Augustus had a momentous vision:—a cross of light in the heavens, above the sun, with the inscription *En toutō nika*. ("In this [sign] conquer)[2] So inspired, he had a *Chi Rho*—the first two letters of the title "Christ"—painted on the

<hr>

[1]Peter Brown. *Augustine of Hippo*. London, 1967. p. 26.

[2]"What Constantine probably saw was a rare but well attested form of the halo phenomenon ... analogous to the rainbow, and like it, local and transient, caused by the fall not of rain but of ice crystals across the rays of the sun. It usually takes the form of mock suns or rings of light surrounding the sun, but a cross of light with the sun in its centre has been on several occasions scientifically observed." A. H. M. Jones. *Constantine and the Conversion of Europe*. London, 1948. p. 96. Constantine kept the story to himself, and only many years later confided it to Eusebius, the author of the *Life of Constantine*, published after the Emperor's death. "The victorious emperor himself," he writes, "told the story including his dream of Christ, who commanded him to make a standard ... to me, the author of this work ... and confirmed it upon oath." cited, A. H. M. Jones. *op. cit.* p. 95.

shields of his soldiers, and, following a dream, an elaborate standard (*labarum*) constructed.

Maxentius was fool enough to advance over the Milvian bridge—the one to-day leading to the Castel Sant' Angelo—supplemented by a bridge of boats, and to fight with the Tiber behind him. On 28th October, 312, Constantine engaged him and threatened the bridges; whereat Maxentius' men panicked, Maxentius himself was trampled into the Tiber, whence his body was retrieved and beheaded; and Constantine was master of the entire West.

He was not ungrateful to the Christian God. At a meeting with Licinius, now the Eastern Augustus, at Milan, he prudently agreed to grant religious freedom to the Christians and everyone else, "so that whatever heavenly divinity exists may be propitious to us and to all who live under our rule". This decision, confirmed in Nicomedia in the following year, transformed the Christian Church from a persecuted though widespread sect of perhaps at most 200,000 in an empire now probably of nearly 70,000,000 inhabitants, to a powerful and privileged establishment. For Constantine did not merely tolerate the Christians: he favoured and lavishly endowed them. Sunday, originally celebrating the Unconquered Sun, now became a Christian celebration, and Christian bishops could legislate in their own courts: the emperor himself, the autocrat of an increasingly totalitarian state, would try to reconcile the doctrinal disputes that after more than two and a half centuries of increasingly sophisticated and abstract argument, were disrupting the officially recognized religion. His decision was literally epoch-making, and rendered him a world-historic figure. Yet he remains blurred; for, apart from his own enactments, the main sources are so inferior: Eusebius of Caesarea's fulsome panegyric, whose very authenticity has been challenged, is a sad falling off from the standards of the classic Graeco–Roman writers—a Tacitus or a Plutarch—and Lactantius' lurid "*On the Deaths of the Persecutors*", depicting the mêlée out of which Constantine had fought his way, is fanatically prejudiced.

One thing is plain: Constantine was an outstanding commander: also a conscientious ruler, anxious to propitiate whatever gods there were and fulfil his arduous responsibilities; even wading into depths that the theologians considered their own, reckoning himself *Pontifex Maximus* and even "Thirteenth Apostle". But power politics gave little scope for his Christianity: apart from killing off his rivals, he had his eldest son and his second wife executed, and drove his brother-in-law, Licinius, to suicide. After such political and domestic exigencies, he was prudent to postpone baptism until his death bed— a common custom at the time—so that he could have no more occasion for sin and in 337 enter the next world with his passport in order.

This concern with religion, both personally and for the state, led him in 325, as the sole Augustus after he had eliminated Licinius, to convene the Council of Nicaea to settle the most disruptive conflict in the Church. The Arian heresy, pulverized in the elaborate Nicene creed, turned on definitions of doctrine so minute as still to appear baffling. Yet to Christians they are fundamental. Arius, a Libyan, educated and ordained at Alexandria, questioned the untrammeled divinity of Christ. In the current anthropomorphic idiom, he taught that the Father, transcendent, eternal, and so pre-existent, had created the Son, who was finite and subject to change and so not "of one substance (or essence)" with the immutable Father. Christ was a facet of God, not God himself: the way seemed open for him to become a demi-God and the very incarnation and redemption to be called in question.

Constantine intervened heavily; he saw to it that the heresy was condemned and its principal exponents exiled; Arius, a well-meaning intellectual, to Illyria. He then turned to the probably more congenial task of transforming Byzantium into Constantinople. In the end, anxious to unite the Church and to be on the safe side, he recalled the Arians, including, in 336, Arius himself, and banished Athanasius, bishop of Alexandria, their most redoubtable enemy, to Trier.[1]

But the controversy had not been settled. Bishoprics and high political appointments were involved as the parties became more powerful and Constantine's successors had to take account of them. The extremist Arians would insist that Christ was actually "unlike" the Father; moderates would compromise; he was *homoiousios*, of *similar* substance, not *homoousios*, or *one* with Him. By 360 a Council at Constantinople would abandon the *ousia* and proclaim the Saviour merely *homoios*—"like".

Such ideological conflicts, always endemic in their varied idioms, religious or secular, among intellectuals expounding their abstract ideologies—and Christianity had come a long way since the preaching of the original gospel in Galilee over two hundred and fifty years before—then, as now, provide ample opportunities for the aggressive instincts of mankind; and the waning of Arianism at the end of the fourth century did not prevent its infecting the Visigoths, from whom it spread to the Ostrogoths, Vandals and other destructive converts, leaving the even more destructive Franks to embrace Catholicism. For Wulfila (Ulphilas c.311–382) their evangelist, himself born on the wrong side of the Danube, who had devised a Gothic alphabet and translated the bible for them—though he prudently left out both books of *Kings* as inciting to violence—was an Arianizer, and perhaps misplaced commonsense told the benighted barbarians that a Father was apt to be senior to his Son.

III

The political sequel to the *Reparatio* of Diocletian and Constantine and to Constantine's establishment of Christianity, which had made him one of the most decisive rulers in the history of Europe, was disappointing. His sons at once killed their uncle and most of their cousins, then fought one another over the succession. Constantine II, who ruled Britain, Gaul and Spain, invaded

[1]This clever and turbulent prelate (c.295–373) spent much of his career being evicted from and returning to his See, on one occasion taking refuge in Rome, where Pope Julius I vindicated his views, which reflected the decisions of the Council of Nicaea. He wrote voluminously against the Arians, upon the Creed and the Incarnation, and sponsored a Life of St. Anthony. He is famous for the Athanasian Creed, but did not in fact compose it: it was devised in North Italy.

Italy, where in 340 he was killed by the troops of his youngest brother Constans, who was based in their family's ancestral town of Niš. But Constans, who for ten years ruled the West, Illyria, Italy and Africa, was murdered by a usurping German adventurer in Gaul. The survivor, Constantius II, an Arian, then took over from the East, summoned his sole surviving cousin, Julian, to Milan and made him Caesar of the West.

Destructive as their family conflicts had been, the military power and wealth of these emperors was still immense; Constantius II, writes Ammianus Marcellinus (Vol. II, p. 245), was a tremendous figure; he "sat alone upon a golden car in a resplendent blaze of precious stones whose mingled glitter seemed to form a sort of shifting light";[1] he had streaming dragon standards borne beside him and his heavy cavalry, the *clibanarii* were so smoothly armoured that "they seemed like statues by Praxiteles", and impervious to the bolts even of artillery. He still ruled civilized Europe. To this formidable power Julian succeeded, when the troops under his command refused Constantius's order to go East, and when Constantius died in Cilicia on his way back to reassert his authority.

The only one of this murderous Balkan family educated at Athens and eager for culture, the emperor Julian (361–3), determined to restore the old religion; and though he did not persecute the Christians, he considered their beliefs a superstition. Having "withdrawn" from the Christianity in which he had been brought up, he has been termed "the Apostate". Brought up a Christian in Cappadocia, he had been allowed to study in Athens, where he had lost his faith. He had early proved himself an outstanding general against the Franks, and when the "Germans had been raging beyond their customary manner", had relieved Cologne, Mainz and Strasbourg, and made his headquarters at Lutetia (Paris).[2] After his accession he determined to "put the Persians under the yoke", and so "restore the shaken Roman world"—*ita quassatum recrearet orbem Romanum*. Ammianus Marcellinus vividly describes the campaign, with the "gleaming" Persian elephants looming slowly through dust and heat, and the "iron clad" Persian cavalry and archers.[3]

Unlike most Roman emperors, Julian was abstemious and chaste, his main fault a "touch of vanity" and "talking too much". An outstanding general, he also had the wit to write *The Caesars*, or *Saturnalia*, in which, in the manner of Lucian, he makes Romulus give a banquet to the Gods and the Roman Emperors. Julius Caesar, of course, arrives first, ready to take over from Zeus;

[1]Ammianus Marcellinus (c.330–393) is a baroque and discursive historian with a flair for evoking episode and place. The eighteen books of his *Res Gesta* which have survived are a continuation of Tacitus from 96 AD to cover the years 353–391, and he is famous as the panegyrist of Julian. He was a Greek Syrian of Antioch, a city he called *Orientis apex pulcher*—the most beautiful in the East; and, having served in the Imperial Guard and on campaign, he devoted most of his well-to-do life to his history. He travelled widely and has an entertaining digression on Egypt and the habits of the crocodile: "whoever it meets it pertinaciously attacks with destructive bites—*perniciosis morsibus*". See *Ammianus Marcellinus*, ed. and trans. J. C. Rolfe, 3 vols. Harvard, 1956.
[2]*The Works of the Emperor Julian*, ed. and trans. W. C. Wright, 3 vols. Harvard, 1954, Vol. II, p. 429.
[3]Rolfe. *op. cit.* II, p. 491.

Augustus appears as a chameleon, Tiberius so solemn and grim that he is thrown out, Nero with a wreath which Apollo promptly removes; and when Trajan appears, "it is time for Zeus to look out if he wants Ganymede for himself", while Hadrian is told to "stop prying about", as Antinöus is not there.

Julian also wrote *Against the Galilaeans* which, as will be apparent, even in fragmentary form, is a telling attack. He was killed in retreat from Ctesiphon during his abortive Persian campaign, aged, like his hero Alexander, only thirty-two, having rushed into battle without his mail shirt. Transfixed by a spear through the liver, he died in his tent, his last words an intricate discussion on the nobility of the soul, but though the remark "*Galilaie Nenikekas*—Thou has conquered, O Galilaean"—was not attributed to him until the sixth century, it is apposite. It is, however, unlikely, even had Julian lived another forty years, that Christianity could have been dis-established, and his attempts to revive the ancient rites provoked not only educated but popular resistance.

The outer barbarians now closed in. By 367 a *conspiratio barbarica* nearly destroyed the civilization of Roman Britain; and in 379 the emperor Valens himself was killed by Arian Visigoths at Adrianople. Theodosius I, "the Great" (379-95), whose reign coincided with a cultural and artistic revival, and in part with the reign of the great Chandra Gupta II (375-415) in India, discarded the office of *Pontifex Maximus*, proclaimed Catholic Christianity the sole admitted religion, and commanded all his subjects to profess the Catholic creed. He checked the Visigoths more by diplomacy than by arms, and settled them south of the Danube under their own government as an insurance against other barbarians; a risky expedient, now regularly followed in the West as well.

In 389 Theodosius visited Rome, where he met strong opposition from the conservative Senate. According to the non-Christian Zosimus, they declared that, if they changed the religion which had kept Rome safe for 1200 years, "they could not tell what would happen". But the Western Emperor Gratian (367-383) had already disbanded the Vestal Virgins, and Theodosius now replied that the old ceremonies were too expensive when the armies needed more money from the tax payers, and cut the subsidies for the old ritual. "All the ancestral traditions of Rome (thus) fell into disregard. And so the Roman power and empire was gradually mutilated and became the home of barbarians."[1]

Theodosius even did penance at Milan, a gesture unthinkable to Constantine, at the insistence of Ambrose the bishop, accustomed to dominating the Christian Gratian, for a routine atrocity committed at Thessalonika. After campaigning against a Frankish adventurer, Arbogast, who had set up as Western Augustus in 395, Theodosius died at Milan, having consolidated the wealthy Christian priestly establishment and confirmed its monopoly. Theodosius and his family still appear in elegant imperial dignity on a bas relief on a site among the ruins of the hippodrome in Constantinople. His sons, the

[1]*Histories*, IV, 59.

youths Arcadius (383–408) and Honorius (384–423), succeeded him respectively in the East and West. Both proved incapable; the former looked on powerless when Alaric the Visigoth plundered Greece; the latter took refuge in Ravenna, leaving his realm to be defended by Stilicho, his Vandal father-in-law, assassinated in 408, while Alaric plundered Italy. Arcadius' son, Theodosius II, scholar and theologian, then ruled as Eastern Augustus from 408 to 450, during one of the worst phases of barbarian attrition and Western collapse; but his monuments are the Theodosian law code and the massive double walls of Constantinople, still awesome in size and extent, with their contrasting stone and striped brick and machicolation which set new standards of fortification and guarded the city until 1453.

In the West, meanwhile, disaster set in. In 406 the Germans crossed the Rhine and fanned out into Gaul, where the Vandal warbands had already penetrated and whence they were beginning to move into Spain; in 410 Roman Britain was left on its own to resist the Anglo-Saxons, and Alaric, King of the Visigoths, sacked Rome. Strategically the City had long given place to Milan and Trier, but the event sent shivers through the West and North Africa. By 418 Arian Visigoths had been settled around Toulouse as an insurance against worse barbarians, and were prospecting towards Spain; by the 'thirties the Burgundians were settling around the middle Rhone and the Saone. Then, even more dangerously, the Vandals, originating in Northern Jutland and Southern Sweden, whence they had migrated to Silesia, had got into Gaul and thence by 409 into Spain. Invited by factions hostile to Rome, they had crossed into Africa, and in 439 under the able and treacherous Genseric (439–477) they captured Carthage. Recognized as *foederati*, they soon became independent, took over the estates of the Roman landowners and, converted to Arianism in Spain, persecuted the Catholic Church in Africa though retaining the Roman administration. What was worse, true to their Scandinavian origins, they took to the sea, revived Carthaginian sea power, mastered the Western Mediterranean and threatened the corn supply of Rome itself. Then in 455, bringing their ships up the Tiber in Viking fashion, they plundered the City for a delirious fortnight, carrying off not only vast amounts of loot but the Empress Eudoxia and her daughter. As Arians, they may have felt the raid a work of piety, but by evicting the African landowners and persecuting the Church, then sacking Rome much more thoroughly than had Alaric's Goths, they won a lurid and lasting reputation for destructiveness and gave a perennially topical adjective to our language.

Rome thus had to fight, as Genseric intended, on two fronts, for he had acted in concert with the worst enemy of all, whose nomadic incursions out of Central Asia had originally set his own people on the move out of Central Europe. Since the late fourth century the Huns had been a mounting threat, in a Western extension of a movement radiating from Central Asia. They had long threatened the Chinese, who had observed that "these barbarians should be looked upon as animals and therefore one should not appreciate their friendly utterances",[1] and who in 383 had defeated them at Fei Shui. By 450

[1]Piggott. *op. cit.* p. 250.

other tribes, the "White Huns", would wreck the most creative Hindu civilization in India, at its climax under Chandra Gupta II, still famous for the dramatist Khalidaša and the paintings of Ajanta.

In 441 Attila and his hordes were on the Danube. They soon destroyed Singiodunum (Belgrade); by 443, the year Genseric established his independent kingdom at Carthage, they destroyed Niš and Sofia. But the great double Theodosian walls of Constantinople, built just in time, blocked his advance, and he could only massacre all the Roman forces on Gallipoli and exact a colossal tribute in gold. In 447, having disposed of his brother, Bleda, he overran modern Wallachia and Northern Greece, though he was held at the historic pass of Thermopylae. Then he turned West, where he met his match. The Imperial acceptance of the Visigoths paid off, and Aetius, an outstanding commander, in alliance with the Visigoths of Toulouse, defeated the Huns near Troyes. Gaul had been saved.

Indefatigable, in the following year, Attila, still drawing vast tribute from Constantinople, invaded north Italy and destroyed Aquileia, Padua and Verona and drove the first refugees to the Venetian lagoons. But problems of supply and, reputedly, the prayers of the Christians and the diplomacy of Pope Leo I induced him to withdraw to his headquarters in the Hungarian plain; and here in 453 the now elderly "Scourge of God" perished in the arms of an all too attractive new wife. "Their marriage", writes Gibbon, "was celebrated with barbaric pomp and festivity at his wooden palace beyond the Danube; and the monarch, oppressed with wine and sleep retired, at a late hour, from the banquet to the nuptial bed. His attendants continued to respect his pleasures or his repose, the greatest part of the ensuing day, till the unusual silence alarmed their fears and suspicions ... They found the trembling bride sitting by the bedside hiding her face with her veil, and lamenting her own danger, as well as the death of the King who had expired during the night. An artery had suddenly burst, and as Attila lay in a supine posture, he was suffocated by the torrent of blood ... his body was solemnly exposed in the midst of the plain, under a silken pavilion."[1] The incursions of the Huns, added to the growing power of the Germanic rulers, further diminished the authority of the Empire in the West. In 476 the Arian Odoacer, a Saxon adventurer who had helped another adventurer, Orestes, to depose Julius Nepos, the current Western Augustus, but feeling cheated by Orestes of his reward, occupied Pavia and killed his puppet. He then deposed and surprisingly pensioned off Orestes' sixteen-year-old son Romulus, nicknamed "Augustulus" in contempt, who had taken refuge in Ravenna, and became de facto ruler of Italy. His power was recognized when the emperor Zeno, now the senior Augustus in Constantinople, admitted Odoacer to the incongruous rank of "Patrician", and the barbarian rulers and Senatorial landowners settled down to make the best of each other in Italy, as in Gaul, in the first major barbarian kingdom in the peninsula. The Imperium Romanum in the West was at an end.

[1]Gibbon. The Decline and Fall of the Roman Empire. Chapter XXXV.

IV

When, by Imperial command, Constantinople had been rebuilt in six years, it had been laid out in traditional Hellenistic style, and statues, removed from other cities, were set up in and around the great palace and the new hippodrome. Like the arch of Constantine in Rome, the original Haghia Sophia was conventionally classical with a pillared porch, and it was not until the complete establishment of Christianity under Theodosius I the Great that a more creative period of Sassanian-influenced architecture set in, to culminate under Justinian in the gigantic domed Byzantine Haghia Sophia and in the superb mosaics of Byzantium and Ravenna.

In the West, by the mid-fifth century, in spite of political turmoil, the long timber-roofed Christian basilicas were already grand and austere; the interior of Santa Maria Maggiore (432–440), and of San Paolo fuori le Mure in Rome (386–440), the rotundas of San Stephano at Rome, and of St. Angelo at Perugia, originally a mausoleum for a sister of Constantine.[1] If Pagan Antiquity had been symbolized by gigantic public baths, the rise of Christianity is marked by the cool colonnades of austere basilicas leading to the altar and the apse. Not that their outside was yet distinguished: the churches at Ravenna are of plain brick and roofed, if not by timber, by humble red tiles.

But figure sculpture had now deteriorated. As might be expected, save for the dark haloed and awesome bronze statue of St. Peter at Rome, the right foot since worn smooth by the millennial osculations of the faithful, the few remaining portrait statues of fifth-century worthies have a worn and apprehensive look, sometimes interpreted as spiritual. Though the famous bronze figure of Valentinian I at Barletta is still technically accomplished, the glare in the eyes is barbaric; while the four porphyry generals, or perhaps Caesars, somehow stranded in battle dress by St. Mark's at Venice, demonstrating their obviously false pact of mutual amity after the death of Diocletian, show how far standards of sculpture had fallen since the days of Hadrian.

In wall paintings, the Hellenistic tradition merged more naturally into the Christian; indeed, the lyrical quality of the few remaining pastoral scenes, as in the impressionist painting of Paris on Mount Ida, or of the ritual of Isis being celebrated in a garden, have a similar feel to the settings in some of the Christian catacombs. Nor are the themes dissimilar—the frieze-like anecdote of Orpheus and Eurydice now in the Lateran, and of a child being conducted to another world by Hermes, being concerned, like the Christian paintings, with an afterlife. But early Christianity gave artists new ideas—other than the well-worn themes of Theseus and the Minotaur, the Wooden Horse at Troy, Medea's infanticide, and the adventures and exploits of Hercules—for example with the supposed likeness of the Apostles Peter and Paul and the Christ on the Mount from the Roman tomb in the Viale Manzoni, or with the Christians

---

[1]Mausolea were no longer fashionable, even for the very great (though Theodoric at Ravenna, an Arian barbarian, was naturally a law unto himself), and the colossal Mausoleum of Hadrian was considered by the Christians impiously arrogant. Rotundas for Churches or for commemorating Martyrs were now preferred.

in Paradise among fruit trees and peacocks in the catacomb of St. Calixtus, where a new inspiration is apparent.

These new themes, changing from the early lyrical ecstasy to the more majestic and heavily charged symbolism of the official church, inspire the splendid Christian mosaics of the fifth and sixth century; indeed they transformed a hitherto rather banal tradition in a medium impervious to damp and enhanced by water. The conventional Hellenistic work, familiar from many Roman villas, could be pleasing, as in designs of dolphins and fishes or of symbolic figures of the seasons; but the mosaics of bestial gladiators, the nearest thing that could be got to a coloured photograph, are revolting; even the more famous hunting scenes, though again revealing, are no major works of art, though one from Carthage of the late fifth century showing a tame Vandal on horseback rejoicing in his formerly Roman estate, shows this lout cheerfully assimilated.

The Christian mosaics at Ravenna, at their climax under Justinian in the mid sixth century, were already brilliantly effective in the so-called "Mausoleum" of Honorius' sister, Galla Placidia, who died in 450. It is low built in the form of a Latin cross surmounted by a squared dome, and inside the effect is stunning: in a haze of dark blue and gold, set off by luxuriant green garlands, the "whole curved area is comparable to a soft oriental carpet, indigo in colour and spangled all over with white stars, crosses, rosettes with red seeded centres and corollae of white flowers surrounded by blue and gold rings";[1] two stags, "panting for the water brooks", thrust through convoluted green and gold acanthus leaves towards the waters of life, and Christ, beardless, Hellenistic, and seated on a rock, framed in vegetation, fondles a trusting sheep.

The artists were equally skilled in abstract composition, and purely decorative mosaics with geometric designs to give an illusion of slanting sunlight.[2] Such, in the second half of the fifth century, was the superb prelude to the Byzantine mosaic compositions of the sixth which coincided with, and were designed to promote, Justinian's reconquest of Italy through Belisarius.

V

While Byzantine civilization continued unimpaired, the Catholic Church, with the authority of Graeco–Roman civilization behind it, now came to dominate Western Europe for centuries and remain the most far flung Christian church in the world. It also derives directly from the late Roman empire. In the three and a half centuries that elapsed between the death of the Founder and the full establishment under Theodosius, a powerful and disciplined organization had grown up, and complex and sophisticated theological positions had been defined. The gospel preached in Galilee had inspired a

[1]Guiseppe Bovini. The Ancient Monuments of Ravenna. Milano, 1955. p. 6.
[2]For the best colour reproductions I know, see André Grabar. Byzantium; from the Death of Theodosius to the Rise of Islam. Trans. S. Gilbert and J. Emmons. London, 1966. pp. 117–127.

novel kindliness and hope; it had now been interpreted in terms of an authoritarian priesthood and the terror of a Last Judgement. The alternating hopes of Immortality and threat of Judgement had a powerful impact—about the only thing that could have galvanized so debased a civilization. It was intelligible and clear cut, and it struck home to the people in their most intimate aspirations and fears. Moreover, the sheer grandeur of the Church, as endowed and established, had made it the heir of the secular empire, now in the West tottering to its fall.

The sharp distinction between sacred and secular authority was new, and had been most clearly defined by the genius of Augustine of Hippo in the early fifth century. But long before that, Tertullian, the first of the great Latin Fathers (155–220), who had grown up under Marcus Aurelius and Origen (Origenes Adamantius) (185–254), the most influential of the Greeks, who wrote under the influence of the neo-Platonist Plotinus (206–270), had defined and elaborated their faith.

Tertullian, like Augustine a North African, had been born in Carthage: trained as a lawyer, and converted in 193, he coined the famous phrase "*credo quia impossibile*—I believe because belief appears impossible"—and insisted on the literal truth of the Incarnation (de *Carne Christi*—of Christ's flesh), of the Resurrection and of the Corporeality of the Soul. He made the first detailed exposition of the Lord's Prayer, and insisted on the importance of chastity (de *exhortatione Castitatis*) and of penance. He also violently attacked what he termed idolatry, and eloquently denounced the horrors of the arena (de *spectaculis*). After the thunderous if unclassical Latin of Tertullian, there was little doubt where the Church militant stood.

Origen, an Egyptian Greek, probably born in Alexandria, had been the first great scholar who made an ordered exposition of Christian doctrine based on the Biblical texts. He is much more Hellenistic and philosophical than Tertullian, holding that Cosmic Reason (*Logos*), the principle of the universe, is manifest through Christ, as the Creation expresses the bounty of God.[1] Plotinus, intellectually the most subtle and formidable of these theologians, had propagated the Platonic idea that the world is a pale and distorted reflection of a permanent harmony that transcends it beyond space and time, and Origen argued that Christ, as the expression of the Logos, focused this reality on the world, so that mankind, through Him, could participate in it.

The tide of recorded history has given the impression that these Fathers of the Church, so influential for many centuries, had it all their own way. But they lived under such notorious emperors as Elagabalus and Caracalla, in the political, social and economic decline of the third century, and they had many opponents to contend with as well as the Gnostics and their own heretics, not least the "paganism" of the great Roman families, who looked down on the Christians.

But the most direct attack came from the Emperor Julian; and Julian's representative if fragmentary tract, written at Antioch in 363, was scornful: he

---

[1]The allegation by Eusebius of Caesarea that he castrated himself, so as not to rape the female Christians he instructed, was a malicious gloss on the chastity of his life.

called the Christians "Galilaeans" and Christ "The Nazarene"; "Would not any man", he wrote, "be justified in detesting the more intelligent of you, or pitying the more foolish, who following you, now sink to such a depth of ruin that they have abandoned the everlasting Gods, and gone over to the corpse of a Jew, and slaughter heretics because they do not wail over it in the same way as yourselves."[1]

"Why are you so ungrateful to your Gods", he demanded, "as to desert them for the Jews?" "It is, I think," he wrote, "expedient to set forth to all mankind the reason for which I am convinced that the fabrication of the Galilaeans is a fiction." Julian also rejected the tale of Adam and Eve; God must have known what Eve would get up to, and, anyway, what language did the serpent speak?. And "what could have been more imbecile than a being unable to distinguish between good and evil?"

The Emperor preferred a pluralistic Pantheon of Gods to the exclusive and sole Judaeo-Christian Deity. "Why were the peoples so different—the Celts and Germans so fierce, the Hellenes and Romans inclined to political life, the Egyptians such intelligent craftsmen?" Morality and customs were notoriously relative. It took all sorts to make a world, and all sorts to make a Heaven: what was wrong with Apollo, Dionysus and Heracles, representing the various facets of Godhead? The death of Julian certainly removed a formidable opponent of Christianity.

The most influential and profound of the Latin Christian Fathers was Augustine of Hippo (354-430), whose De Civitate Dei (413-25) is supplemented by his Confessions (401), the first surviving introspective autobiography.

Born of Berber stock to a pagan father and an ardently Christian mother, Augustine came of minor provincial gentry of Thagaste in Algeria, and made his career by his own brilliant talent as a rhetorician; but he never resolved the tensions he inherited.[2] This conflict was underlined when he early became a Manichee, a sect which derived from Mani, a Mesopotamian prophet, whose execution in 276 had not prevented the spread of his religion as far as Europe and Central Asia, whence it would penetrate to China. These unhappy mystics believed that the world itself was misbegotten, a botched-together "smudge" in which Darkness had got mixed up with Light; a conflict also fought out within man himself, in which the "Good mind", derived from the Light, was tormented by the body which derived from Darkness and the Lie.

This typically Eastern conviction of the radical evil of the creation suited Augustine's psychological needs and the political conditions of his day, so he projected it into his vision of the world, conceived of as a dynamic process of conflict between the City of God, composed of the predestinate elect, and the City of the World, whose authority was not intrinsic but could only be "justified" as a "secular" arm of the Church, itself a kind of "colony" planted out on "Earth" from "Heaven". This outlook he expressed in the De Civitate Dei, a work of immense influence for Christian Europe. It expresses a dualism

---

[1]The Works of the Emperor Julian. trans. W. C. Wright. Loeb Harvard. 3 vols. 1954. Against the Christians. Vol. III. p. 373.
[2]See E. R. Dodds. Augustine's Confessions: A Study of Spiritual Maladjustment. Hibbert Journal 26. 1927-28. pp. 459-473.

that struck at the heart of the Graeco-Roman idea of government whereby the "good life" as defined by Plato, Aristotle or Cicero, was its own justification, and not made impossible by the innate wickedness of men or dwarfed into insignificance by the prospect of some "other" world and a judgement. Augustine, living amid the threat to civilization when the Goths had sacked Rome and the Vandals-Arians—liable to torture Catholic bishops to death—were padding towards his own see of Hippo, thought that humanity was so steeped in original sin that it could not rescue itself; the only hope was in God's inscrutable Grace, whereby at least an Elect were saved. Predestination, apparently so grim a doctrine, was thus, in the fifth century, "a doctrine of survival";[1] something to cling to as a last hope, even if it "drew a line across the human race as immovable as the divisional good and evil natures proposed by Mani".[2] Hence the controversy with the Irish Pelagius and his supporters, who optimistically held that man was not predestinate, but capable of salvation by his own efforts. To this day the controversy continues.

It was thus out of political and social disaster that the doctrine emerged, predominant in medieval times and revived today, that man cannot "make himself"; that secular government is intrinsically incapable of creating order and harmony, and can at best be but a "remedy for sin"; indeed, that the human condition is such that only by the inscrutable grace of God can an elect minority be "saved".[3] St. Augustine's reading of the fifth-century facts proved immensely influential. And St. Augustine, his biographer concludes, in his *Retractationes*—or revision of his works—"provided the Catholic Church with what, in future centuries, it would need so much: an oasis of absolute certainty in a troubled world."[4]

VI

While, in a civilization threatened in the East and collapsing in the West, the Fathers of the Church were defining ideas which would condition the mentality of Europeans for centuries, Graeco-Roman literature retained a surprising, if derivative vitality. In spite of barbarian incursions and infiltration, civilized life continued, and perennial interests in agriculture, hunting, dogs and horses, celebrated since Hesiod and Xenophon, carried on. The Romans had always been sensitive to the beauty of gardens, and Ausonius,[5] a nominal

[1] Peter Brown. *op. cit.* p. 407. This subtle and deeply learned work best relates Augustine's own experience to the needs of his time.
[2] Brown. *op. cit.* p. 401.
[3] In modern terms that talent and good will, being due to the chance of heredity, are so rare and "predestinate", that no amount of political change or social engineering can improve the human condition.
[4] Brown. *op. cit.* p. 430. See also his *The Making of Late Antiquity*, Harvard, 1978.
[5] When Gratian was murdered by Maximus in 388, Ausonius retired to his estate, and even after Theodosius the Great had destroyed Maximus, he remained there. He won exaggerated reputation in his day, being compared even to Virgil. There is an excellent chapter on him and what he stood for in Samuel Dill, *Roman Society in the Last Century of the Western Empire*. London, 1898.

Christian, with a pagan education who, from teaching rhetoric at Bordeaux became tutor to the Christian Gratian, afterwards Western Emperor, and so won very high political rank as Consul, shows romantic feeling to the still peaceful landscape of the Moselle, which "brings the honour of Empire to Trier" and which he contrasts with the " . . . tired fields allotted to barbarians, whose luck deserted them in frontier skirmishes".[1] With refreshing felicity, he describes

> "this land of well-tended fields and
> estates set on hills, and cliffs green with vines
> and hedges running along the slopes like
> schoolboys at play, and murmuring below
> in the valley, the Moselle, my new found river,
> hurries along. The pleasant scene
> Recalled to me my home, Bordeaux.
> Its pools, bright as water in crystal goblets
> Mimic the mountain lakes I've seen at dawn".

He observes how

> "Here the scales of chub gleam among the weeds
> Trout and grayling dart out of sight,"

and

> "the casual beat of the salmon's tail
> splashes in the deepest pool."

Here is a painter's eye and sensibility as acute as anything in modern nature poetry; with a touch of humour as well for Lucius the pike, who is "Never invited to dinner".

An artist's vision makes Ausonius describe how "the blue river reflects the shadowed hill", as the Garonne "reflects the rows of his own vines," and create an exquisite miniature of the "makeshift pageants of the painted barges" on the water, while the bargemen run from bow to stern "like boys

> Playing their summer games, and the farmer
> Rests his back and gaily watches their feats
> of skill played on the river's flat surface
> forgetful of the setting sun"

and of

> "the cares of his land."

The rivers of Gaul—Loire, Aisne, Marne, Charente—he concludes, will never be finer than the Moselle, and the cold Alpine streams and even the Rhone

[1]The Last Poets of Imperial Rome. ed. and trans. H. Isbell. Penguin, Harmondsworth, 1971. p. 52. For Latin text see Ausonius. trans. H. G. E. White. 2 vols. Loeb, New York, 1919.

> *"Will admit your glory higher than this*
> *And I will sing your praises to the Garonne."*

That a poem of such accomplished charm could be written during the mid-fourth century shows how tenacious a hold civilization still had on men's minds during that Indian summer of Gallo-Roman decline.

In a harsher setting in North Africa, a Carthaginian poet had earlier written sound advice about hunting and the breeding of dogs. The *Cynegetica* of Nemesianus (c.283-4) is not all romantic; tired of the old fables, the author wants to breed good hounds and to "get out into the fields and find game". He advocates severe culling of each litter; and the surviving puppies must not be confined; they will chew at their posts and gnaw the doors and ruin their teeth. They should be early trained at hares and to "know the urgency of a familiar voice".[1] Rabies was evidently a plague, and its cause unknown—perhaps the sun in the sign of Leo, "contagion" from the earth, or stagnant water—whatever it is,

> *a burning fire grows in the veins and excites*
> *the tissues near the ear and with venomous foam*
> *escapes in snarls that compel the poor beast to bite.*

The best dogs are Greek; Spartan or Molossian hounds; but the British breed are very fast: good ones also came from Hungary and Spain, Libya and Tuscany. The best horses, too, came from Greece and Cappadocia—"their eyes sparkle with energy and restlessness"—but fine ones also came from Calpe in Southern Spain, and their eyes, too, show their spirit: while Numidian horses are bred for hard work and are very enduring:

> *If you race this horse on an open plain you will*
> *Discover that he becomes stronger as he runs*
> *So that towards the end he seems refreshed and leaves*
> *The other horses behind, choking in his dust.*

When feeding a horse it is good to pat him, so that he will relax. Winter should be spent preparing for the hunt;

> *When Spring is about to begin, send*
> *Your hounds into the meadows and urge your horses*
> *to run faster and faster through the drying fields,*
> *We will go hunting before the heat of the day, while*
> *the soft earth still preserves the tracks made in the night.*

In the world of late Antiquity, there were still men who could enjoy an evening on the Moselle or a hunt in Algeria in the dawn; not everyone was preoccupied by political and social conflict or like the baleful St. Augustine with unanswerable questions of theology. Indeed, the accomplished courtier Claudian, who frequented the Court of Theodosius the Great and of Honorius at Milan, and brings the full weight of classical mythology to bear on celebrating the nuptials of Stilicho with Honorius's daughter Maria (an alliance

[1] *Last Poets of Imperial Rome. op. cit.* p. 32.

which would lead to Honorius executing his father-in-law), wrote verse that is relatively competent and boring, ladling abject and insincere flattery on the half-barbarian warlord, pretending that the political match was spontaneous and mobilizing Cupid to persuade his mother Venus to forward the wedding, when "the Imperial Majesty" (in fact reduced to giving his daughter to a barbarian) may "put away its mighty pride" and join the guests.

Rutilius Namatianus, a high official of Honorius' court, seems more human: when he writes of his return (de reditu suo) in the autumn of 416 to his native Toulouse along the coast of Italy, which he is leaving with regret:

> In the half light of dawn the anchor was lifted
> As we left the shoreline the colours were
> Returning and we could see the fields on the hills.[1]

He is very conscious of his Italian past;

> We too, like the Greeks, have a land of great legends.[2]

He still venerates Rome:

"—there is the government of the world", and regards "Minerva who gave us the olive tree and Bacchus who gave us wine" with particular devotion. Rutilius despises both the Jews and the Christians. Overcharged by a Jew ashore, his party pay up with contempt; as to 'Humanis animal dissociale cibis',[3] (literally to 'an animal anti-social towards human food'), representative of a people that 'spend the seventh day as if their God were tired'.[4]

Passing Caprera, he remarks that it is a "dreary place full of men who shun the light" (squallet lucifugis insula plena vivis) who call themselves "monks"—a word from the Greek for "alone"—because they wish to live with no one and "fear fortune, whether good or ill". "Such reasoning", is "the raving of a madman".

The ship proceeds past Pisa, and coasts along by Massa Carrara, where, then as now, "white and shining cliffs of marble" seem to rise from behind the coast—in "a polished brilliance ... bright enough to challenge the white snows".

Here, in the early fifth century, is a calm romantic sense of landscape and a regret for familiar scenes, as there is great feeling for nature in Ausonius' poem on Opening Roses, still famous in English because it stated a theme immortalized by Herrick:

---

[1]Last Poets of Imperial Rome. op. cit. p. 227.
[2]Last Poets of Imperial Rome. op. cit. p. 228.
[3]For a sub-Ovidian Latin of Rutilius see Poetae Latini Minores. Recensuit et emendavit Aemilius Baehrens, Lipsiae Teubingen. 1883, Vol. V. (Bibliotheca Scriptorum Graecorum et Romanorum Teuberiana.)
[4]Last Poets of Imperial Rome. op. cit. p. 231.

It was the Spring of the Year and the
daylight returned on the break of golden dawn.
The biting cold of winter was ended, but a
fair breeze blowing just upon dawn,
gave me a clear warning of the day's coming heat":[1]

It concludes, with surer sentiment than style, after depicting the glistening dewdrops of that fifth-century morning, and the incipient wilting of the flowers,

Collige, virgo, rosas dum flos novus et nova pubes,
et memor esto aevum sic properare tuum;[2]

which can be literally rendered;
  "Gather, girl, roses while they are fresh and you are young; and remember that your years, like theirs, haste away."

[1] *Last Poets of Imperial Rome. op. cit.* p. 70.
[2] Wright. *op. cit.* Loeb. Vol. II. p. 280.

BOOK III

THE MAKING OF CHRISTIAN EUROPE

XII

Merovingian Gaul

When the poet Rutilius made his way back from Italy to his estates in Gaul, he was returning to the most prosperous area of the Western Empire: it would be from sub-Roman Gaul that the main force of a French-speaking Catholic civilization would derive and France would eventually replace Italy as the cultural centre of Western Europe. For when the Byzantine Empire, still flourishing and intact, tried to reassert its authority over Italy, the peninsula was politically wrecked in the conflict, and the Ostrogothic realm founded by Theodoric (493–526) replaced by new Lombard barbarians, who, in contrast to the Ostrogoths, "looked on most things Roman with a surly brutal incomprehension".[1] Rome itself was ruined, its aqueducts cut in the conflict; and the Papacy long became in truth the "ghost of the Roman Empire, sitting crowned upon the grave thereof".

When Odoacer had deposed the last Roman Emperor of the West he had not set up another, reckoning to obtain a freer hand. But it was decided in Constantinople that another barbarian and potential menace should replace him. The emperor Zeno, in the vicissitudes of his career, had owed much to the support of Theodoric, King of the Ostrogoths. Originally based on Pannonia, the modern Hungary, Theodoric had lived as a young hostage in Constantinople, and, though he never learnt to write, he had absorbed the standards of the Eastern empire in one of its richest and most creative times. With his subjects *foederati* in Dacia and Moesia, Theodoric was appointed *Magister militum* and Consul, and in 489 he was launched against Odoacer in Italy. He had defeated him on the Isonzo, and by 495 had taken Ravenna and dispatched Odoacer with his own hand. Two years later he became the officially recognized ruler of Italy under Constantinople.

Theodoric was an Arian Christian, following Ulfilas; but his reign is commemorated by the splendid Byzantine-style churches and mosaics of St. Apollinare Nuovo in Ravenna, and by his own massive and unique mausoleum. He became the most powerful and civilized of the barbarian rulers, and

[1] L. H. Butler. *The Western Middle Ages.* in *The Concise Encyclopaedia of World History.* Ed. John Bowle. London, 1971. p. 188.

extended his influence by political marriages with the barbarian royal houses of the West. Based on strategically placed Verona and on Ravenna, then a focus of sea-power and easily defensible, he could even reach out over the Maritime Alps and annex Provence. Under his rule, although Goths and Romans had their own separate laws and intermarriage was forbidden, barbarians and sub-Romans might have settled down together and a single government still have controlled the peninsula. But, as an Arian, Theodoric had incurred the implacable hostility of the Catholic Church; moreover, as often in barbarian realms, his dynasty collapsed. In 526, on Theodoric's death, his daughter Amalasuentha, wife of the short-lived Eutharic, became regent for her son Athalaric; but in 534 the boy died, and Amalasuentha, relegated to an island on lake Bolsena by the hostile faction of her cousin Theodahad, was murdered there in her bath. So ended the house of Theodoric the Ostrogoth. Then Justinian, now became Eastern Emperor, decided to re-impose Byzantine authority by arms.

While the most promising of the barbarian kingdoms had risen and collapsed in Italy, a new and formidable power had appeared in Gaul. The Franks had for centuries been settled as barbarian *foederati* on the Rhine; long notorious for treacherous ferocity, the Salian Franks had settled around the Yssel in Brabant and between the Scheldt and the lower Rhine; the "Riparian" Franks on the middle Rhine. Hereabouts the emperor Julian had defeated them, though by 415 they had recovered enough to burn Trier, the northern capital of the West. The origin of their royal house is mysterious: of the romantically named Pharamond there is no proven trace;[1] Merovech—the supposed founder—hence "Merovingian"—was, allegedly, the son of a Sea God—*"bistea Neptuni Quinotauri similis*—a beast of Neptune like the Minotaur", who had raped his mother while she was bathing in the North Sea. The effective founder was Childerich of Tournai, east of modern Lille, in Flanders: exiled to Thuringia, he had so much attracted the local queen Basina that she had pursued him to Flanders, and there given birth to Chlodovech[2], (Clovis): the first Merovingian of European fame.

Chlodovech (481–511) succeeded at fifteen to no great inheritance, though his father had campaigned down to the Loire: he had a small personal war band of "antrustians", backed by perhaps six thousand warriors in an unattractive part of Belgium, if he could satisfy their ambition for land and loot; and his first campaign was against the redoubtable Alammani, who, blocked by Theodoric from invading Italy, had moved north from around the great stronghold of Meersburg on Lake Konstanz up to the Rhine: Chlodovech, who is said to have appealed to Christ during the hard fought battle, routed them near Köln. Then, turning south-west, he attacked the sub-Roman principality of Syagrius at Soissons, mastered some of the best land in France and secured Paris, already important under Julian the Apostate.

The Catholic bishops of sub-Roman Gaul reported to Rome the rise of this new barbarian power; Chlodovech was not yet Christian, but, at least, he was

---

[1]See Samuel Dill. *Roman Society in Gaul in the Merovingian Age*. London, 1926. p. 9ff.
[2]The spelling probably reflects the sound of primitive Flemish speech.

not an Arian convert: moreover, he had married Chlothilde, daughter of Gundobad, King of the Burgundians and, though her father was an Arian, she was a Catholic. By 496 Chlodovech, having taken his time and considered the feelings of his tribesmen, had been baptized a Catholic Christian at Rheims by St. Remigius (St. Remi). The bishop had laid on an already impressive ritual—streets overshadowed with coloured hangings, churches adorned with white ones, and in the baptistry perfumed tapers gleaming through clouds of incense, and he had remarked, being "skilled in the art of rhetoric, 'Meekly bow thy proud head Sicamber' (a patronizing name for a Frank, derived from a lesser tribe); 'adore that which thou hast burned, burn that which thou hast adored'." The historic alliance between the Papacy and the French monarchs had been secured.[1]

To the Catholic convert Chlodovech the heretic Arian Visigoths of Aquitaine now seemed legitimate prey. "It irketh me somewhat", he said, 'That these Arians hold a part of Gaul. Let us go forth and with God's aid bring the land under our own sway'; and this speech finding favour with all, he assembled his army, and marched on Poitiers. . .".[2] Chlodovech, like Constantine, was both a cunning and a militant convert, remarking of the Passion of Christ, "If I had been there with my Franks I would have avenged His wrong." So to secure his left flank, he attacked the Burgundians around Dijon and drove Gundobad south to Visigothic protection at Avignon, protesting that he could never become a Catholic and "worship three Gods"; then in 507, Chlodovech marched west against the Visigoths in Aquitaine and himself killed their king, Alaric, at the battle of Vouillé, south of Poitiers. He captured the rich Arian cities of Toulouse and Bordeaux, and his son, Theuderic, would have taken Arles, had Theodoric's army from Italy not blocked him. It was the first incursion of the Catholic north against an heretical south, repeated, centuries later, in the Albigensian crusade.

Chlodovech was now the greatest power in all Gaul; he returned to Tours, where envoys from Byzantium presented him with a purple tunic and a cloak, and accorded him the title of Patrician and Consul, "*Summum bonum primum in mundo*, the greatest prize and highest honour in the world". He was hailed, at a safe distance, as *Novus Constantinus*—the new Constantine of the West. He established himself at Paris in the Ile de la Cité and in due course in 511, fifteen years before the death of Theodoric, he was buried in the church of St. Geneviève on the south bank. "Here was a warrior of Beowulf-like stature who yet forewent the barrow and the windy headland and was content with a Christian grave in a Parisian church. All the same, finds in later Merovingian graves would warrant the guess that the *novus Constantinus* would have been laid to rest with at least a selection of the pagan symbols dear to his race.'[3]

[1]Gregory of Tours. *History of the Franks*. Trans. by O. M. Dalton. Oxford, 1927. Vol. II. p. 69.
[2]Gregory of Tours. *op. cit.* II. p. 75.
[3]J. M. Wallace-Hadrill, *The Long-Haired Kings*. London, 1962, p. 183. The Merovingian royalties were early distinguished by their long hair: they were *reges criniti*. When Chlodemer, son of Chlodovech, had mistakenly left his two sons in the care of their grandmother Chlothilde, their wicked uncles, Childebert and Chlothair, got hold of them and sent their grandmother scissors and a naked sword, signifying that she should

But, whatever his motives, Chlodovech, unlike the Arian Theodoric, was *rex Catholicus*: with the Latin Church behind him, "ruling a Christian *regnum* that was Roman in expression".

A sub-Roman way of life had proved sufficiently entrenched in Gaul to assimilate the most vigorous of the barbarian peoples who, under the Carolingian Franks, would create the revival of learning and form the political structure of Medieval Western Christendom. When the attempt of the Byzantine Emperor Justinian to reconquer Italy and North Africa had failed after its first success, the initiative in reviving and extending Christian civilization in face of the terrible Scandinavian and Muslim attacks of the seventh and eighth centuries had to come from the north-west.

II

Since Constantine had established his capital on the Bosphorus, the eastern empire had maintained the habit of Christian administration. The eastern areas had always been the richest and best organized part of Graeco-Roman civilization, and Constantinople the natural centre for the trade of the Black Sea and the Levant. The "Byzantines", as we term them, more colloquially *Visantíni,* continued to call themselves *Rhomaioi,* and, until the seventh century, to use Latin as their official tongue; while their fleets and armies, like their bureaucracy and their system of taxation, entirely outclassed anything in the now barbarized West. With the introduction of the gold *solidus*,[1] a stable coinage had been achieved after the raging inflation of the third century, and although the gulf between the plutocrats and the poor had widened, the social revolution under Diocletian and Constantine had brought many able men from the lower ranks of society into the governing class. Moreover while in the East respect towards the distant Senate in Rome had been vague, the adoration of the Christian *Autokrator* in person had now produced a more active loyalty.

Theodosius the Great in the late fourth century had reigned with the full backing of the Church in Italy as well as in the East, and "a sense of otherworldly mission affected the Roman State. The Christian emperor, too, would have to answer to Christ for the souls of his subjects. In the West this

choose between their having their hair or their throats cut. Chlotilde replied at once that she would rather have them dead than shorn; whereat the wickeder uncle (Chlothair) knifed the eldest boy and when Childebert tried to save the other, knifed the younger one as well. Such was the Merovingian obsession about hair, and such Merovingian family life. During the decadence of the dynasty their long hair was about the only asset that the *rois fainéants* possessed, as they were trundled round on ceremonial occasions in ox-waggons. It was worn, on the evidence of the coinage, parted in the middle and shoulder-length.

[1]As Peter Brown points out in his brilliant description of *The World of Late Antiquity*, (London, 1971) "the Latin slang of the provinces was [now] immovably lodged in their official vocabulary: a classical Roman should have called the new gold piece an *aureus*; nobody called it anything but a *solidus*—a 'solid bit' ".

idea made weaker rulers even more susceptible to the demands of the Catholic clergy; while in the more firmly based eastern empire, it added yet another deep note to the swelling register of the imperial autocracy."[1] So when Justinian (527-565) succeeded his illiterate uncle Justin (like so many rulers of the eastern empire, originally a Balkan peasant), he became a ruler of colossal political and religious prestige, on a level completely beyond the most powerful barbarian rulers of the West, and the inheritor of an immensely rich and powerful realm. Convinced of his mission as Augustus and representative of God on Earth, he believed it his duty to improve the organization of his empire and to extend its bounds. Before his accession he had married Theodora, a Cypriot beauty of shady origins and high intelligence, whose realism and courage sustained him in his onerous task. They appointed Belisarius, a cavalry commander of genius, as Magister Militum, who at twenty-five, with massive wealth and seapower behind him, defeated the perennial enemy, the Persians, and the encroaching barbarians from Europe as well. In 532 Belisarius and Narses, an elderly Armenian eunuch and *praepositus cubiculi*—Grand Chamberlain—helped Justinian and his consort put down the dangerous Nika revolt in Constantinople, when Constantine's cathedral was burnt down, so that Haghia Sophia had to be built instead; and in the following years Belisarius was despatched against the wealthy Vandals of North Africa, who had long threatened the corn supply of the capital and Byzantium sea power on the Levant.

   Once a by-word for ferocity, the Vandals had succumbed to the seductions of civilization:

> "In Africa", writes Procopius, "the Vandals had taken to luxurious habits, and used to indulge in baths, all of them, every day, and enjoyed a table abounding in all things, the sweetest and best that the earth and sea produce. And they wore gold very generally, and clothed themselves in the Medic garments, which now they call Seric (silk) and passed their time, thus dressed, in theatres and hippodromes and in other pleasurable pursuits, and above all else in hunting [they hunted with cheetahs]. They had dancers and mimes and all other things to hear and see which are of a musical nature ... and most of them dwelt in parks which were well supplied with water and trees, and they had a great number of banquets, and all kinds of sexual pleasures were in great vogue amongst them."[2]

So these formerly destructive barbarians were now soft; incapable of sustaining the hardships which the native Berbers could face, and the Byzantines could disrupt the resistance of such discrepant allies.

   So successful was Belisarius that by 535 he had invaded Sicily and captured Naples, and in the next year Rome itself. By 540 Ravenna had been taken from the Ostrogoths, weakened by dynastic strife after the death of Theodoric. Justinian, however, now recalled Belisarius, in fear that he might set himself

[1]Brown. *The World of Late Antiquity*. *op. cit.* p. 108.
[2]Procopius. *History of the Wars*, with an English translation by H. B. Dewing. Loeb. New York, 1914. Vol. II. p. 257.

up as an independent ruler in Italy,[1] and in 551 appointed Narses, his subordinate, to the Italian Command. But although he defeated the Goths, again secured Rome, and in the nature of things could be no dynastic rival to Justinian, after Justinian's death in 565, Narses, too, was recalled, leaving, in contrast to Belisarius, bitter memories of cruelty and rapine. The attempts to restore direct imperial rule in Italy thus partially failed, though the Byzantines long ruled Sicily and part of the Italian South, and by crippling the relatively civilized Ostrogoths, let in the Lombards, far more savage overlords.

These Germans had arrived belatedly in the South from an unpromising area around the Lower Elbe and the Lüneburg Heath, whence they had understandably migrated to Pannonia; here their chieftain Waccho (510-546), who had displaced his uncle Tato, had managed to rule them in territories along the Danube and around Lake Balaton. His descendant, Alboin, now led them over the Alps; and by 572 he had captured Pavia, along with the famous "iron crown"—so-called because it was believed to include a nail from the True Cross, not because it was wholly of that metal. But after the exploit Alboin, all too representative of his people, went too far: detesting his father-in-law, he forced his wife to drink from her father's skull, a gesture thought extreme by her kinsmen and even by many of his own followers, who murdered him. But the Lombards, or Langobardi, remained in control of North Italy, which still bears their name; and it was only by calling in the Franks that the Papacy could counteract their originally baneful influence. For further reinsurance as well as in Christian duty, the Popes also secured other faithful Western allies, the hitherto heathen Anglo-Saxons, to whom in 596 Pope Gregory the Great sent Augustine of Canterbury to convert Aethelbert of Kent, who had married Bertha, a niece of the Merovingian Chilperic.

III

Contrary to much popular opinion, the barbarians were few compared with the indigenous populations of the Western Empire: only in Roman Britain were the traces of civilization blotted out, and then only in the south and east. The campaigns of Chlodovech against the Burgundians and Visigoths devastated only relatively small areas, and at all levels the Gallo-Roman way of life carried on; the more so because the illiterate barbarian overlords depended on literate churchmen trained in Roman law and administration. When towards the end of his reign, Chlodovech directed that the famous Salic laws be drawn up, they remained basically Germanic, but they were arranged by a sub-Roman hand. Estates were not simply occupied by the barbarians without compensation; tenure had to be secured, agreements drawn up: sometimes, since the new owners were more interested in hunting than in agriculture, the old owners managed to keep the better land.

The subsistence economy that had supported the great sub-Roman estates

[1]The legend that Belisarius ended his career as a blind beggar is quite untrue: he was merely retired, after a phase of imprisonment.

through all the troubles did not break down, nor did luxury trade and the valuable tolls and customs dues that went with it. There were still plenty of Jews in Merovingian Gaul—they tended to support Arian rather than Catholic rulers—and they flourished on the slave trade as well as on lending money to tax collectors who had farmed out their functions and, bilked by subordinates, needed to meet their own obligations; they also subsidized the clergy, who, anxious for promotion, had to give substantial presents to royal and noble patrons. Chilperic, in a moment of exasperation, ordered the Jews to be rounded up and given the choice of being blinded or baptized; but they remained ineradicable—a living testimonial to the prosperity of a land in which they chose to remain.

For communications had never broken down. The great Roman roads were still usable, transport by water slow but relatively sure. Anyone important or on important business could afford sufficient escort against brigands, and count on hospitality in some monastic house. There was no breakdown in the way of life of the upper class and their dependents, who could command plenty of slave labour: no 'revolt of the masses' from the routine of an hierarchical society, even if the hierarchies had changed. The advent of the barbarians brought no freedom for the serfs: only new masters. Indeed, after Chlodovech's campaigns in Aquitaine, the slave markets were glutted. And a pre-industrial society could not be paralysed or bankrupted by "strikes".

The breakdown of the old Imperial authority with its crushing exactions had sometimes even given new life to old cities, where the *curiales*, who had been driven to evade municipal office, took it on again, glad of the pompous titles of the old order. Sub-Roman Gaul, now becoming France, was a naturally rich country, though since transport in bulk was slow, local famines could develop, and if a murrain struck the cattle or sheep, little could be done for them. Nor could anything be done about bubonic plague, which struck down rich and poor alike, or about the other epidemics before which the physicians were helpless. The occasional splendours of royalty and magnates, of which the chronicles make much, were accompanied by hordes of beggars and cripples who flocked to solicit charity.

Such charity was often forthcoming. The Church taught that by giving alms Christians acquired merit; and the most famous saint in sub-Roman Gaul was St. Martin of Tours, who as a young officer had given half of his fine great military cloak to a beggar. Hence the many foundations, often by pious women, for the cure of lepers, the sick and the poor, and the gift of immense estates to the Church by magnates anxious to escape God's judgement on their sins. The inhuman apathy towards suffering encouraged by anonymous modern urban life does not seem to have been usual in the "Dark" Ages.

When not at war, the aristocracy, barbarian and sub-Roman, who regularly intermarried, enjoyed hunting; wild boar and stag were their main quarry, passionately pursued. Vast tracts of woodland were assigned to the chase; red deer were hunted with staghounds, buck hounds pursued fallow deer. Venison, doubly prized when cattle were small and scraggy, and delicious when properly hung, became a mainstay of itinerant royal and princely households, where already, by the time of Ausonius, the limited Mediterranean cuisine had become enriched with northern plenty.

But the decline of civilization brought centuries of inferior wine. The great Falernian wines of Antiquity had been vintage wines, matured for years in amphorae containing about 6½ gallons stoppered with wax. Though less effective than the bottles stoppered with corks which came in during the seventeenth century, this method had allowed classification by vintage years and high standards of quality. But when the Romans acclimatized Italian vines in France, wine began to be kept in wooden casks in which full maturing is impossible, and "until the nineteenth century AD there came out of France no great wine which could challenge the fine old vintage wines of the ancient Greeks and Italians."[1] As the import of good wine in amphorae fell away, and the vineyards on the Garonne and Moselle became established, the native growths, stored in casks, superseded the Italian wine, and barbarian overlords, who wanted quantity more than quality, were content with what was to hand. Doubtless many of them, and most of their followers, swilled ale and mead, native drinks of the north. The clergy, who needed wine for ritual as well as refection, cultivated the vine where they could, thus helping to maintain a Mediterranean way of life.

IV

While the sub-Roman Western Empire had been in part rehabilitated by the Merovingian kings, the Eastern Empire had been flourishing. In 532-7 in Constantinople Justinian's architects had created the superb and enormous structure of Haghia Sophia, one of the finest buildings in Europe. Its sheer size, like that of St. Peter's in Rome, still dwarfs those who enter it through the huge doorway above which Constantine and its founder are still commemorated in black and gold, while pastel greys and golds enhance the diffused effect of light beneath the enormous dome. "In Haghia Sophia everything conspires to produce the impression of an immense space ideally organized. From the main door of the nave, looking along the axis of the church towards the apse, the beholder can appreciate the noble sweep and majestic proportions of the vast interior, with its supporting columns and walls covered with polychrome marbles. His gaze is drawn towards the mighty vaults overhead which—apparently so cumbrous when seen from the outside—seem to float in air, released from the pull of gravity, the moment one has entered the church. No praise is too high for the skill with which the architects ... exploited all the possibilities of sunlight."[2]

This Byzantine metropolitan architecture, though in direct descent from the Roman empire, was extremely original; a contrast to the long wooden-roofed

[1] H. Warner Allen. *A History of Wine*. London, 1961.
[2] Grabar. *op. cit.* pp. 93-4 q.v. for the impressive engineering skill behind the central dome.

basilicas of Italy, and different even from the churches of Byzantine-dominated Ravenna.

Here, already, the so-called mausoleum of Galla Placidia had shown how splendid mosaic could be: now the mosaics of St. Apollinare in Classe, commissioned by Theodoric c.520, and those of Catholic San Vitale, as altered by the Byzantines, show sumptuous colour and stately design. In the former the saint himself stands arms extended in the old posture of prayer, in a setting of stylized flowers, landscape, and sheep symbolizing his congregation. The walls are decorated with a processional frieze of martyrs—a form of decoration that has come a long way from its origins in Sumeria, Babylon and Iran, while, probably at Theodoric's direction, a picture of his palace is included between whose columns stood portraits of the Arian dignatories of his Court, on whom Justinian's officials had white fringed curtains superimposed.

For his own mausoleum Theodoric had commanded a massive structure in his own lifetime; in imitation perhaps of Hadrian's mausoleum in Rome, it is circular and set off by cypresses. Covered with a monolith of Istrian limestone, it was designed to contain the porphyry sarcophagus of the Ostrogothic monarch himself. It is a monument less to piety than to a megalithic force then quite beyond the resources of any barbarian ruler in the Trans-Alpine west.

San Vitale also has more of a political than a religious message. Begun in 521, it was consecrated under Justinian in 547, ten years after *Haghia Sophia*. It is not a basilica but a domed octagon divided by eight pillars and a surrounding ambulatory. The most striking mosaics are purely Byzantine. In the lower panel of the apse is the Basileus Justinian himself, the deliverer of the Catholics from the Arians, crowned, haloed and bejewelled in full imperial regalia and bearing a great golden paten for the Eucharist. On his right, his corvine and ascetic countenance contrasting with Justinian's soldierly and weather-beaten look, paces the archbishop of Ravenna; on his left, with the wary, guarded and preoccupied expression of their kind, walk his civilian officials, while beyond them and setting them off by their own red, green and gold colours stand the young barbarian palace guards. And opposite moves the cortege of the crowned Basilissa, Theodora; her high-strung clever face with its great eyes under a canopy of green and gold, dominating her chamberlains and court ladies.

Against their plain gold background all these figures are curiously abstract and timeless; their impact, unlike that of Rembrandt's advancing "Night Watch", depending more on colour form and design than on any sense of depth. Originally propaganda reinforcing the campaigns of Belisarius, the mosaics in their own right still exist as great works of art.

If we consider the discrepancy between the two civilizations, the Merovingian West naturally produced nothing to compare with these splendours, save some derivative ornaments enlivened with originally Scythian animal motifs. The transfigured Christ from Niederdollendorf is barbarically inept; a Christian version of the Giant of Cerne Abbas, without the virility, and surmounted by a radiating halo like that of a pagan sun God. But the Merovingian jewellers, imitating Byzantine designs, were skilful in cloisonné work, setting garnets in silver gilt filigree; the brooches, found as grave goods long into Christian times and used to fasten cloaks on the left shoulder, have a barbaric size and richness. The only original inventions are reliquaries, then in such demand, in which the priceless and coveted remains of local saints could be kept, and, if necessary, transported out of harm's way. These objects, wrought with elaborate gold filigree patterns and encrusted with garnets and pearls, are in a tradition long afterwards elaborated by Fabergé for almost equally Philistine royal patrons. Naturally the early Merovingians, like the late Romanovs, loved expensive ornaments; as witness the gaudy attire of Queen Arnegunde (c.560), a contemporary of Justinian, lately discovered beneath St. Denis near Paris, her violet tunic covering white-stockinged cross-gartered legs, and overlaid with a red mantle fastened by great brooches of hammered gold. The widespread Merovingian custom of burying their most prized possessions with the dead continued.

V

The literature that has come down from these barbaric times in the West is sub-Roman. In the Eastern Empire, at a time of great wealth and vigour, Procopius of Caesarea wrote a first-hand account of Justinian and Belisarius's campaigns against the Persians, the Vandals and the Goths, as well as of the *Nika* riots of 532, and a full account of the principal buildings put up in Constantinople in the reign of Justinian and Theodora. He also wrote a *Secret History* in which he bitterly denounced them both, and Belisarius as well, thus setting a tempting precedent for later historians, in most of their lifetimes subservient to the current establishment. As already apparent, he is a sound military historian and a sharp political observer.

In the West standards were different. Cassiodorus (480–575), the principal sub-Roman administrator under Theodoric, who survived to end his life in a monastery which he founded on his own estates near Squillace, Calabria, was an able statesman and diplomat, contending with immense difficulties and well aware of them. Yet he will overload his state papers with curiously childish digressions and platitudinous reflections. His letters are particularly illuminating on how Theodoric's government, itself half barbarian, dealt with the Trans-Alpine barbarian powers—as when he sends Gundobad of Burgundy a waterclock, a present which will increase his respect for Romano-Ostrogothic technology. Clovis, too, had asked for a harper, and Cassiodorus, on behalf of Theodoric, after much pedantry about the theory of music (a *"chord"* is so called because it moves the heart, *"cordem"*), urges his colleague Boethius to find one: "be sure to give us this Citharoedus, who will go forth, like another Orpheus, to charm the bestial hearts of the barbarians."[1] In his *Institutions of Divine and Human Study*, Cassiodorus attempted an outline of all knowledge, and, legislating for generations unborn, defined the discipline of the "Humanities" in the *Trivium* and the *Quadrivium*.

[1] T. Hodgkin. *The Epistles of Cassiodorus*. London, 1888. Bk. II. letter 40.

Boethius (480–524) is less representative of his time: he was a neo-Platonist with a passion for order and lucidity. His *Consolations of Philosophy*, written in prison when he was awaiting execution, attained a wide and lasting influence—on Dante's Italian poetry and on Chaucer, for example, who wrote neatly, following him, *"For the nature of thinges ne took not hir beginninge of thinges amenused and inparfit, but it procedeth of thinges that ben al hool and absolut."*[1] For the "happy fortune of Boethius was that his teaching was taken up by the poets. There can be little question that Boethius, more than any other philosophic author, helped the great schoolmen to retain a general comprehensive view of the world as a whole, in spite of the distractions of their minute enquiries."[2] Boethius, concludes Ker, "somehow or other felt what was most wanted in the intellectual confusion in which he lived." Undaunted, at a time of chaotic decadence, he crystallized the compensating idea of harmony, a fusion of Platonic and Christian ideals:

> *O felix hominum genus*
> *si vestros animos amor,*
> *quo caelum regitur, regat.*

freely rendered by Dante, as translated

> *"Fortunate human race, if your minds*
> *are ruled by the love that moves the*
> *sun and the other stars".*

The letters of Sidonius Apollinaris,[3] a Gallo-Roman landowner and aristocrat, born at Lyons in 432, who owned estates near Clermont Ferrand, of which town he later became bishop and where in 485 he died, are illuminating through a fog of pretentious language. "His life was passed in times too stirring for him to be able to escape completely from them; and of these times and their manners he was a careful observer. His power of observation is indeed his only literary quality which posterity can still recognize as a merit. As an observer he was singularly detailed and precise: in another age such a man might have made a first rate naturalist or field archaeologist. In his description of the Frankish prince Sigismer, every detail of dress and armour is precisely described; and his portrait of Theodoric II, the Visigothic king, makes him live as does no other historical figure of the century."

The Visigoth Theodoric II of Toulouse (not to be confused with Theodoric the Ostrogoth of Ravenna) was a well conducted barbarian, with a most "gracefully curved nose", and his lips were "delicately moulded", "not enlarged by any extension of the corners of his mouth". He was so carefully shaved that he seemed younger than he was, and he had a "milk white" neck above well-shaped shoulders. Beneath a prominent chest his waist elegantly "receded", while his thighs were "hard as horn" and his knees "free of wrinkles". Moreover he had small feet. He got up early, and, after exercise, he worked

[1] Cited by W.P. Ker. *The Dark Ages.* London, 1904, reissue 1955, p. 109.
[2] Ker. *op. cit.* p. 110.
[3] *The Letters of Sidonius.* Trans. O.M. Dalton, Oxford, 1915. They are also translated, alongside the Latin in the Loeb edition by W.B. Anderson. Harvard, 1965, 2 vols.

quite hard giving audiences and doing business; he then took his main meal at about eleven, served with fine linen and scarlet cloth to guests on couches, combining, says Sidonius, "Greek elegance, Gallic plenty and Italian briskness". After that, he would inspect his stables; then, after a siesta, perhaps go hunting wild boar or stag. He could also spin dice "with finesse" and when playing never lost his temper. Indeed, he liked to "throw off the stern mood of royalty", and, Sidonius confides, "my own opinion is that he dreads being feared." After supper he would sometimes "admit the banter of low comedians"; but he drew the line at hydraulic organs or tambourine girls, since "he only liked string music that comforts the soul." Here in Aquitaine was no mead-swilling ruffian, his hair plastered with rancid butter, like the savages of the north, but a Romanized Visigothic monarch; an évolué, considerate and confident enough to command his guards, who wore skins, to stand well back in the room when he was giving audience.[1]

Sidonius is not always so explicit: like Cassiodorus, he can be overwhelmed with pedantic detail, "saying in ten words what he could say in one", and "unable to say a straightforward thing in a straightforward way". He can be "typical of that failure of nerve, that spectre of intellectual cowardice, which is characteristic of the last productions of this pagan culture".[2]

Gregory of Tours (Georgius Florentius), who lived much later, was also a Gallo-Roman aristocrat. In 573 he became Bishop of Tours, and retrospectively composed a sensational catalogue of Merovingian crime. He wrote, as he admits himself, elementary Latin—"Non tibi latet quod sim inops litteris." "It cannot be concealed from you that I am inept at letters." But he is a born raconteur and gossip, and the crudity of style well suits his subject. He is also, unlike Cassiodorus or Sidonius, childishly superstitious, recounting in contrast to the dynastic murders of his day the ascetic practices of the more saintly clergy. As for example, of Pope Gregory the Great, "such was his abstinence in eating, such his wakefulness in prayer, such his zeal in fasting that his weakened stomach seemed hardly to support his frame."[3] Standards had changed in Gaul since Ausonius had celebrated the oysters of Bordeaux.

The lurid cruelties of the Merovingian women that Gregory records were committed in a society at once wealthy yet stricken with famine and plague— "Behold how all the people are smitten by the sword of Divine Wrath." Processions singing psalms and hymns wind through plague-stricken streets to the shrines of martyrs in the hope of intercession, and the clergy exhort the wretched people to repent. Indeed, their own main weapon war fear of the lord—as witness the rueful saying reported by the dying and wicked King Chlothaire, "surprised at the ways of heaven in dealing with great persons". "Wa! quid putatis qualis est ille rex caelestis qui sic tam magnos reges interficit!"[4] By refusing communion or to celebrate mass the clergy could exert some sanctions, and Gregory constantly interlards his chronicle of assassinations and

[1]See Anderson. op. cit. Vol. II, pp. 378 ff.
[2]C.E. Stevens. Sidonius Apollinaris and his Age. Oxford, 1933. p. 176. q.v. for an excellent account with full bibliography.
[3]History of the Franks. op. cit. Vol. II. p. 425.
[4]"Wa! What sort of a God is this King of heaven, who thus kills such mighty kings."

blood feuds with tales of how a holy Abbot healed acute toothache by a touch; how a dove descended upon a particularly promising handsome and aristocratic youth (who grew up to be Abbot Aredius) and which refused, in spite of all the boy's efforts, to go away; how the Blessed Abbot Salvius apparently died, but, reviving at his own funeral, gave a detailed account of heaven and how sorry he was to come back from it. Meanwhile, Queen Fredegund had solved a problem of blood feud at Tournai by inviting its three leading exponents to a banquet, seating them at the same bench, and after the table had been removed, according to Frankish custom, and they were drunk, having them all beheaded at once by three men with axes; whereupon, not unnaturally, "the banquet broke up".

By the end of the sixth century, in spite of the conversion of the barbarians in the west, the deceptive stability of the sub-Roman world of Ausonius, and even of Sidonius, had collapsed into violence, hysteria and superstition, while Byzantium in its own way carried on unbroken the civilization of the Roman empire.

XIII

Europe at Bay

While Gaul was sinking into sub-Roman Merovingian barbarism and Italy being pillaged by Lombards from the Baltic, a new threat to Christian Europe was building up. In September 622—a date from which the Muslim era begins—Muhammad made his *Hijra* (emigration) from Mecca to Medina and, before his death ten years later, had united most of the tribes of Arabia in a militant religion. His *Caliphs* or Deputies used Arab manpower and camelry to attack both the Byzantine and Persian empires, which had recently, and conveniently for the Arabs, exhausted themselves in mutual conflict; and by 636, only four years after the Prophet's death, had defeated the Byzantines on the river Yarmuk and overrun Syria. Enfeebled by religious conflicts between the Monophysite and Orthodox factions, and by the internal strife that had followed the end of Justinian's dynasty, when the Emperor Maurice had been murdered by his soldiers in 602, the Byzantine provinces put up little resistance; in 642 the Caliph Umar-ibn-al Khattāb took the great city of Alexandria, nor did Antioch long resist. Established at Damascus in Syria, the Ummayad Caliphs of this rich oasis launched a full scale attack on Constantinople itself. In 673 and again in 717 the Arabs were beaten off, mainly through the Byzantine secret weapon of "Greek fire", thought to have been a mixture of petrol, sulphur, naphtha and quicklime, which, discharged through hoses, ignited on contact with water, while the great Theodosian walls withstood the assaults of the Bulgars and Avars, tribes out of Asia now infiltrating the eastern Balkans.

In 711, at the other extremity of Europe, the Arabs, having overrun North Africa, crossed the Straits of Gibraltar into Spain, where they swiftly conquered most of that difficult country from the Visigoths and even raided deep into Gaul, until caught in 732 by the Frankish Charles Martel near Poitiers. Gaul was cleared, but the major part of the Iberian peninsula, the greatest western stronghold of Roman civilization, and, since the conversion of the Visigoths to Catholicism in the late sixth century, of militant Catholic Christianity, was lost. Further, the Arab conquest of North Africa, hitherto, save for the brief phase of Vandal domination, an integral part of the Roman and sub-Roman empire, meant that Europeans lost command of the western

Mediterranean and the trade routes across it. The Arabs, on the other hand, now commanded the resources of the two oldest and richest civilizations of the Near East, Egypt and Mesopotamia, and swiftly assimilated the adminis-trative skills and cultural riches of Iran. Under the 'Ummayads of Damascus, and after 750, under the 'Abbāsids of Baghdad and the 'Ummayads of Cordova, Muslim civilization was far richer and more elaborate than anything in Europe outside Byzantium, and in these early and creative stages eagerly exploited the learning of Graeco-Roman Antiquity. Compared with the elites of great cities of Islam, most semi-barbarous western Europeans were simply rustics.

But in addition to erosion of civilization from within, and dilution by barbarians who at least respected the Antique culture, Europe now had to face fanatical Semites and Berbers, inspired by religious hatred against the Infidel.

In these circumstances the papal alliance with the Franks again proved its worth and the basis of further strength. Gregory I the Great, Pope from 590 to 604, was a wealthy Roman landowner who had been Prefect of the City before becoming a monk and a diplomat at the court of Constantinople. He reorganized the basis of the Papal temporal power in Italy and beyond, wrote a subtle treatise on *Pastoral Care*, and extended the Papal control over most of the monasteries and missions that had grown up spontaneously beyond the Alps. He sent St. Augustine to Canterbury, not, as the Venerable Bede charmingly narrates, on impulse,[1] but as part of a deliberate policy to extend the Papal-Frankish collaboration by winning over Aethelbert of Kent, and also by asserting Roman authority over the far-flung Celtic Church, long flourishing on its own.

Untiring though he was, the great Pope was a physical wreck. "The austerities of his monastic days had shattered his constitution, and during the last fourteen years of his life he was never free from illness. He suffered frightfully from indigestion."[2] And this condition may have been aggravated by a liking for *retzina*[3] (*vinum resinatum*), presumably acquired among the Byzantines at Constantinople.

Otherwise vehemently austere, he removed from his entourage all but "grave clerics and ascetic monks". He was also extremely superstitious: witness

[1]Bede writes, "We are told that one day some merchants who had recently arrived in Rome displayed their many wares in the crowded market-place. Among other merchan-dise, Gregory saw some boys exposed for sale. These had fair complexions, fine cut features, and fair hair. Looking at them with interest, he enquired what country and race they came from. 'They come from Britain,' he was told, 'where all the people have this appearance.' He then asked whether the people were Christian or whether they were still ignorant heathens. 'They are pagans,' he was informed, 'Alas!', said Gregory with a heartfelt sigh, 'how sad that faces of such beauty conceal minds ignorant of God's Grace. What is the name of this race?' 'They are called Angles,' he was told. 'That is appropriate,' he said, 'for they have angelic faces, and it is right that they should become fellow heirs with the angels in heaven.' " . . . Bede. *A History of the English Church and People.* Trans. L. Sherley-Price. Penguin, Harmondsworth, 1955. p. 98.
Gregory long remembered the boys, for he later instructed a Papal official in Gaul to buy some English slaves of seventeen or eighteen to be brought to Rome and trained as interpreters.
[2]F. Homes Dudden. *Gregory the Great.* London, 1905. Vol I, p. 243.
[3]Dudden. *op. cit.* p. 245. 'cognidium' = *Konias Oinos* = *vinum resinatum*.

the compilation of legends known as his *Dialogues*, translated into Anglo-Saxon by Bishop Waerforth of Worcester, in which he narrates visions of angels and demons, anecdotes of temptations of the devil overcome and homely tales of minor miracles; of talking animals and of rivers that overflow, but when rebuked return to their normal courses. A Goth, who had kidnapped two children, refused all Bishop Fortunatus of Todi's persuasions to give them up; so the bishop cursed him. Next day the barbarian was thrown from his horse and broke his hip; whereat he hastily had the captives returned, and begged the holy man to intercede for him. The good bishop then cured him at once by a sprinkling of holy water.

This kind of thing induces even the great Pope's admiring biographer to write, "My conclusion is that Gregory had no capacity either for weighing and testing evidence brought forward by others, or for drawing correct inferences from what fell within his personal observation"; one can, however, accept a certain credulity in anyone with the imagination to transmit the famous tale of the devil on the lettuce. A nun plucked and ate a lettuce without first making the sign of the cross, and became "possessed". At the exorcism which followed, the devil cried out "What have *I* done? What have *I* done? I was sitting on a lettuce and *she came and ate me.*" (Dialogue I. 4.).[1]

II

In spite of the Arab conquests, the Papacy retained an ardent following in the Iberian Peninsula. By 589, at the Council of Toledo the hitherto Arian Visigothic King Reccared had declared for Catholicism, impelled in part by the need for Papal support against the Byzantine reconquests under Justinian. Even Catholic and Arian bishops had been reconciled in imposing a powerful Church, backing capable rulers and giving them a sacrosanct authority. Under Recceswinth (649–672) the Visigothic laws were codified and their relation to the other peoples in the peninsula defined. When the Arab invaders arrived, they found the Spaniards—both Visigoths and Iberians—far too set in their ways and united by a powerful religion to be culturally overwhelmed by Islam; and a distinctive Mozarabic or "mixed-arabized" civilization grew up, blending Byzantine, Italian, Iberian, Visigothic and Arab influences. Moreover, Asturias in the far north-west, facing the Bay of Biscay, remained Christian and undefeated, and would include the renowned shrine of St. Iago de Compostela, with its relics of the Apostle James, who, it was believed, had himself evangelized parts of Spain. And out of this difficult country in the north-west and the Carolingian Spanish March, afterwards Catalonia, in the north-east, a centuries-long *reconquista* would be launched, backed by a Visigothic civilization which had survived enriched among Latin-speaking peoples during the seventh and eighth centuries. The long-haired Visigothic aristocracy, originally nomadic herdsmen, who had been relatively few, would now become the most

[1]cited Dudden. *op. cit.* p. 353.

zealous crusaders for the Roman Church. The Spanish crusades are much more important than the ephemeral and more celebrated ones in the East, and this crusading zeal, also expressed in fine architecture and religious art, persisted in the Spanish conquests in Central and South America as well as in Spanish support of the sixteenth-century Counter-Reformation in Europe.

When in the mid-fifth century in Gaul the Huns had been beaten off and Anglo-Saxon *foederati* were getting their hold on Eastern England, out in the far north-west St. Patrick (c. 389–461), a Romanized Briton, had arrived in Ireland. He had been kidnapped by Irish pirates at fifteen, had escaped from what is now county Wicklow as an attendant to a leash of wolfhounds bound for the mouth of the Loire, and become a monk on the Isle of Lerins, off Cannes. He had then studied at Auxerre and returned to Ireland under orders to look after Christians already there, and established himself at Armagh.

Never subdued by the Romans, the Irish were still a tribal society; even their monasteries were tribal. Their bards and lawmen had always had much prestige, and once the tribal chieftains had been converted, Christianity had spread with the prestige of the aristocracy behind it; like the Druids, Christian bishops and abbots could safely cross tribal boundaries, while the rulers could assign tribal property to monasteries. Celtic Christianity thus became part of a prehistoric society; Mediterranean Christianity had originally been urban, but here bishops were not tied down to dioceses or local clergy to a parish. And these mobile Celtic clergy proved extremely enterprising: St. Columba, who was both an abbot and a clan chieftain, founded a monastery in the remote and beautiful island of Iona, from which he evangelized the Picts of Dalraida and even those of north-eastern Scotland who lived round the Moray Firth. The Irish now no longer raided Cornwall; they established religious communities there. Further, in due course, they made dangerous voyages, as had their ancestors in Megalithic ages, as far as the Orkneys and Shetlands. Though the Welsh clergy, surviving directly from sub-Roman times, remained irreconcilable to the heathen Anglo-Saxons, whom they hated too much even to try to convert, the Irish Celtic Church created a remarkable Christian culture in a relatively secure area of Europe, out of which missionaries journeyed direct to the continent. In the early seventh century, when the Arabs were overrunning Spain, St. Columbanus founded a monastery at Reichenau, west of Lake Konstanz, and died in North Italy at Bobbio near Genoa, having established good relations with the Ostrogoths. When control of the Mediterranean and Spain was being lost, the Irish were studying at Clonmacnoise, and creating masterpieces of book illumination and metal work.

But their most lasting external influence was through Scotland and Northern England, where Celtic Christianity from Iona infiltrated to the East with the conversion of the Picts, and was brought to bear on Anglian Northumbria. King Oswald, nephew of King Edwin and, like him, slain by the heathen, founded Lindisfarne, off the Northumbrian coast, the eastern equivalent of Iona, and accepted Aidan, a monk of Iona, as its head.

Meanwhile in southern England, where Christian communities had been established for over a century before the Anglo-Saxon invasions, the Roman clergy had extended their influence. Following St. Augustine's mission (596), the conversion of Kent and the foundation of the sees of Canterbury, London and Rochester, Bishop Birinius, an Italian consecrated at Genoa, had become Bishop of Dorchester-on-Thames in 635, and after conversion of Cynegils, king of the West Saxons, his son, Cenwalh, appointed Agilbert from Merovingian Gaul Bishop of Wintoncaester (Winchester) in the heart of Wessex. Bored with him because he could not speak Saxon, the King soon appointed a Saxon bishop, whereat Agilbert retired to Gaul and died Bishop of Paris, where his sub-Roman sarcophagus, badly mutilated, survives. By the 'sixties of the seventh century, Mercia had been converted, and Bishop Chad, who preferred to undertake his preaching missions on foot rather than on horseback, became the first Bishop of Lichfield.

The West Saxons and even the Mercians now had their bishops, and in 664 the Roman delegates at the Synod of Whitby managed to persuade the Celtic clergy to accept the authority of Rome, even in the crucial matter of the correct date of Easter, always a problem of great importance to the Christian churches. When in 669 the Byzantine Greek Theodore of Tarsus became Archbishop of Canterbury, he was able to consolidate the English Church in parishes, while the Celtic clergy, if still footloose, had been brought at least to acknowledge him. So while the Arabs were threatening Byzantium, overrunning North Africa, the Balearic Islands and Spain and dominating most of the Mediterranean itself, the Papacy extended its alliance with the Franks to include both the Anglo-Saxons, the Iberians and the Celts of an Atlantic world. And from this new base the Church would evangelize the Germans and the Scandinavians, hitherto outside the sphere of Roman control even at its greatest extent.

III

"The identification of the Church with the whole of organized society is the fundamental feature which distinguishes the Middle Ages from earlier and later periods of history."[1] Although the outlook of Christendom was profoundly alien to that of Graeco-Roman civilization at its climax, it still had the august and lasting prestige of the Roman empire behind it even in the West, and in the East by direct descent the Church now represented civilization itself, its ideas being worked out to the minutest detail. The monastic movement, as disciplined by the rule of St. Benedict, was already as strictly based on theory as would be the more elaborate twelfth-century edifice of scholastic thought built up by St. Thomas Aquinas. The earlier rule of St. Basil, on which it was in part based, makes plain by question and answer the "mandate" handed down by Christ: *Diliges dominum Deum tuum ex toto corde tuo et ex toto animo tuo ... diliges proximum velut teipsum.* "Love the Lord thy God with all thy heart and all thy being ... and love thy neighbour as thyself."[2] Benedict

[1] R. W. Southern, *Western Society and the Church in the Middle Ages*. Penguin, Harmondsworth, 1970. pp. 15–16.
[2] Migne. *Patrologie Latine*. Vol. 103. *Codex Regularum* 487 ff.

of Nursia (480–547), born near Spoleto in Umbria, had founded no order; but the *regula* or rules he had laid down for the conduct of the monastery he founded on Monte Cassino were so practical and relatively humane that they were widely adopted by the communities which had long spontaneously grown up over western Europe to maintain worship, and preserve continuity and ordered peace in the increasingly hideous world of sub-Roman collapse and barbarian brutality.

Protected by the aura of sanctity and well enough endowed to be self-sufficient, these disciplined communities, like those in the Buddhist East, were venerated as part of an accepted religion and of the social order, alike by the rulers who endowed them and by the populace. The *Opus Dei*, the *Work of God*, was thought as essential as government or agriculture; for the monks were *at work*, praying away against the devil and all the maleficent demons that infested the land; moreover, the monasteries could provide for their founders' younger sons and daughters.

The price paid for calm and security was severe; and Benedict wisely decreed a year's trial while the novice tested his "vocation": after that, residence was for life. The abbot had supreme power; property was held in common, and routine exactly regulated; six hours a day for prayer, five for manual work, four for reading. Life was a vigil "because we do not know when the Lord may come."

The Benedictine rule stressed self-control: "continence" not only in sex, but in "anger and grumbling", "scandal and backbiting". Diet was austere, for the demons who assailed solitary monks at night "derived from a full belly"; dress was plain, but suited to the climate.

All the Benedictine monasteries followed the same plan: a basilican church and cloister, a dormitory, a refectory, supplemented by novice quarters and an infirmary, a bakery and brewhouse and farm buildings. The calm monotonous routine sustained on principle a good will which included the unattractive, the ill and the old.

The Rule spread gradually to older foundations—Monte Cassino itself was soon sacked by the Lombards—but it was not until the Carolingian revival of the ninth century that it became predominant. By then the Benedictine monasteries were producing most of the great ecclesiastics of the day and had trained many of the missionaries—Irish and Anglo-Saxon—who had carried Christianity to the Germans and Scandinavians. Not least of the Benedictine contribution was in music and liturgy, which gave some dignity and beauty to cloistered lives and impressed Christian laymen with the religious awe which was their main and often only protection.

IV

While the Byzantine Empire had been fighting off the Arab attack, the Bulgars had settled along the southern plain of the Danube and in the Maritza valley, an immediate menace to Byzantiun; while western Slav peoples, probably originating around the Pripet marshes north-west of Kiev, had spread into Poland, Bohemia and Moravia, and the southern Slavs had early penetrated deep into the Balkans and even into southern Greece. The Byzantines still held their own, as they had against the Goths, by war and by superior civilization, and by converting these barbarians to Christianity. Long under Scythian domination, the Slavs were a mainly peasant people, who had not devised the violent mythology of warlike and treacherous Gods created by the Germans, but who propitiated spirits of the waters and the woods. Some of them had already suffered the depredations of the Bulgars, a Turkic people who had originated from Central Asia and settled first on the Volga, and whose relatives, the "Black" or Volga Bulgars, had remained there. Incited or conscripted by the Bulgars, the Slavs in the Balkans had supported the Bulgar attacks against Justinian's Constantinople, and by 681, coincident with the mounting Arab threat, the Bulgars were exacting tribute from Byzantium. Their leader, Krum Khan (802–814), justly described by Professor Trevor-Roper as "dreadful", defeated the Byzantine emperor Nicephorus I and used his silver-mounted skull as "a drinking cup for use in merry barbarian potations".[1] He was the first of the Bulgars to establish his rule from Sofia. But it would not be until 865 that the Bulgars would be converted to Christianity, an event recorded by a revealing picture of the baptism of their Khan Boris by the Orthodox rite of total immersion.

The Eastern Slavs, ancestors of the Russians, spreading out along the great rivers between the Baltic and the Black Sea, clearing the forest and practising their peasant agriculture, had by now accomplished colonization on which the exploitation of the Goths, the Avars, the Khazars and the early Kiev-Russians was based, and their trade in furs, wax and particularly slaves was already worth development by the Swedes or Varyagy, who were mastering the rivers and developing cities out of tribal trading posts by the ninth century. Here in conditions akin more to those of untamed North America than to western Europe a great potential power began to grow up in huge areas unknown to the Romans save as a source of slaves, while the East Slavs looked to Byzantium for civilization and religion.

Thus, in spite of the new threat of Muslim attack in eastern Europe, as well as in the West, the Christian Church, Orthodox or Catholic, survived and even extended its influence. But the contrast in standards of civilization was still so great that the Byzantines often preferred their Muslim enemies to the semi-barbarian West, even considering Islam as a recognizable if extreme heresy of Christianity. Nor did Arab fanaticism prevent their assimilating much originally Hellenistic culture which might not otherwise have survived; Justinian had closed the university at Athens, but the great centres of Muslim learning welcomed humanist scholars from Constantinople, and the refugee

[1] H. R. Trevor-Roper. *The Rise of Christian Europe*. London (revised edition), 1966. pp. 54–5.

'Ummayad rulers of Cordova accumulated a library that included much translated Greek learning.

The rift in Europe in wealth and civilization was becoming deeper and would be widened when the Papacy tried to revive the western empire. More to the point, both the eastern and western areas of Christendom had survived the Muslim attack, and shown the vitality to bring in new peoples with massive manpower and potential wealth into the orbit of Mediterranean civilization.

V

When he describes how Theodoric's daughter, the Ostrogothic Queen Ama-lasuentha, was deprived of control of the education of Athalaric, her son, Procopius writes that the magnates declared that even Theodoric would never allow any of the Goths to send their children to school; for he used to say to them all that, if the fear of the strap once came over them, they would never have the resolution to despise sword or spear. They asked her to reflect how her father had "invested himself with a Kingdom which was his by no sort of right, although he had not so much as heard of letters." *"Therefore, O Queen,"* they said, *"have done with these Tutors now."*[1]

Such was a representative barbarian attitude; and it persisted for centuries in the West, leaving learning entirely in the hands of the clergy. While the Byzantine gentleman remained steeped, like Procopius himself, in his version of classical humanism, and a civilian bureaucracy continued in control, in the West the exclusive powers of the literate Churchmen were confirmed. And during these crucial centuries, when through the bottleneck of the new barbarism only about ten per cent of the literature of Graeco-Roman civilization was preserved and transmitted, it was through an exclusively clerical medium that it survived. Not that even the ablest churchmen valued it for its own sake: Gregory the Great, whose influence was enormous, was wary of the influence of "pagan" literature. Living among the ruins of a once splendid and prosperous city, where the palaces of the great Roman families were closed and in decay, their shrines shut up and haunted, said the Christians, by evil spirits, their libraries dispersed; where vegetation that, as Cassiodorus had observed, was "the peaceful overturner of buildings" had made another century's headway, and where the breakdown of the aqueducts had led to desiccation on high ground and to stagnant marshes on low, the Pontiff alone represented a new and incongruous incarnation of the empire. For Rome, four times sacked by the Lombards during the sixth century, its splendid classical buildings plundered, its once prosperous countryside pillaged, and its population diminished from over a million to perhaps 40,000, was already becoming a centre of Christian pilgrimage. As in Moscow, once the seat of autocratic Tsars, the workers and tourists of the world now shuffle past

[1]Procopius. *History of the Wars*, with an English translation by H. B. Dewing. New York (Loeb), 1914. Vol. III. p. 19.

the embalmed body of Lenin in his Kremlin shrine, so, even more incongruously, in the city of Augustus, Trajan and Hadrian, the faithful from all over western Christendom flocked to the great church of Constantine, since beneath lay the body of the Apostle Peter. After all, at the Resurrection, he would have the keys.

So far had come the despised Christian religion, an offshoot of Jewry, itself long ago apparently extirpated by the might of Rome. The most prized trophies of Gregory's residence as envoy of the Pope in Constantinople, where he did not even bother to learn any Greek, were an arm of St. Andrew and the head of St. Luke.

Under such conditions, if Papal strategy remained astute, Christian learning was hard put to it to survive, as will be apparent from the *Etymologies* of Isidore of Seville and the importance of the work of the Venerable Bede in Northumbria.

The *Liber Pastoralis* of Gregory the Great, laboriously translated by Alfred of Wessex and his collaborators into Anglo-Saxon, opens with advice of perennial value for those entrusted with the selection of bishops about the best sort of candidates. They should be skilled in leadership and administration, but not arrogant or ambitious, and of course lead respectable lives; and selectors should beware of too much loquacity, preferring those who "take care not to talk inordinately, even of that which is right".

The ideal bishop, according to Gregory, must be capable of meditation, with the resources in himself on which to draw for his essential task, which was not administration, but to attract his flock by example, by teaching and sympathetic understanding. He must have psychological insight, adapting his admonitions to his audience. "Different admonitions are to be addressed to the wise in the world and to the dull." He should elicit the good in some of his flock, without by the same words encouraging the failings of others—"preach humility to the proud without increasing the terror of the timid." And he must also observe individuals closely, like a "physician of the soul". Nor should he "draw the mind of his hearer beyond his strength, lest ... the string of the soul being stretched beyond that it can endure, be broken."[1]

He should be humble and companionable; and even when imposing discipline, considerate. Yet his love must not be "enervating"; nor should he be so unworldly as to neglect secular business, or as not to be able to distinguish between virtues and "virtuous-seeming vices" or not to know how to deal with them when detected. "Sometimes the faults of subjects are discreetly to be winked at; but to be shown that they are winked at." Gregory gives examples of the kind of preaching suitable to various types of people.

Such in the late sixth century, amid the times of the utmost peril and degradation of the West, was the subtlety of mind of Gregory the Great.

This psychological insight, even cunning, was precisely the best means of dealing with the barbarian converts which the spontaneous activities of the monks and local clergy were already bringing into Christendom. It has never been lost by the Catholic Church.

[1]Dudden. *op. cit.* I. pp. 230 ff.

To modern minds the elementary learning the Church had to offer seems less attractive, though it was well suited to the age. Isidore of Seville's *Etymologiae*, the most important encyclopaedia of its time, is the *fons et origo* of much medieval learning, and contributed to many of the *Vulgar Errors* still being confuted by Sir Thomas Browne in the seventeenth century.[1] Since Isidore Hispalensis based his work in part on Cassiodorus, it is often misleading, but it is extremely comprehensive and it was widely copied and read. It is, indeed, the early seventh-century equivalent of the latest *Encyclopaedia Britannica*, and embodies immense effort and ingenuity. Setting the tone of much medieval learning, it is particularly imaginative on animals, transmitting legends long extant. Elephants, for example, have particularly good memories (i.e. never forget), the Romans, he narrates, at first called them Lucanian cows. The unicorn, which often fights with the elephant, stabs him in the belly with his impenetrably hard horn, but ("so they assert", writes Isidore, with unwonted caution, "who have written of the nature of animals") "a virgin can subdue him simply by opening her bosom to him, whereat, putting aside all ferocity, he places his head there, goes to sleep and gets captured."

Beavers are called *castores* from *castrando*. Knowing that their testicles are useful as medicine, the moment they see the hunters, they castrate themselves and "amputate their virility with bites". The bear, *ursus,* is so called because it licks its young into shape with its mouth—*ore suo formet*. The wolf, *lupus,* derives from the Greek *Lukous,* so called because "in the rage of its rapacity it kills everything that it meets." For it is *rapax enim bestia*, a rapacious beast, *et cruoris appetans*: it "seeks blood". The fox is little better, *vulpes* from *volus pes*, swift of foot. It never runs straight, but twists about through difficult places: it is indeed *fraudulentum animal*, very deceitful, and it eats carrion.

Dogs, on the other hand, (*Canis* from the Greek *Kuōn*) are so called from the sound (*canore*) of their barking: they are the most sagacious of animals, answer to their names, love their masters and guard their homes. Tigers are named after the *Tigris*, fastest of rivers, because they are so swift. The lamb (*agnum*) is so called because it knows its mother—"*statim balatu recognoscat vocem parentis*" "it at once recognises the voice of its parent by the bleat." The camel is so called because it kneels down when being loaded and curves its back, and the Greek for curve is *Kamone*. It bites its enemies in battle, will allow only its own master on its back, and cries a great deal when its owner

[1]St. Isidore of Seville (560-636) probably came from Cartagena, which had been recently brought under Byzantine rule. In 600 he became archbishop of Seville, and in 633 took part in the important synod of Toledo which decided that a native Spanish liturgy should be adopted. With immense industry he also wrote biographies of leading characters in the Bible (*De ortu et obitu patruum*), treatises against the Jews and against heretics, and undertook the daunting task of narrating the history of the Goths, the Vandals and the Suebi. There is an edition of the *Etymologiae* edited by W. M. Lindsay: *Isidori Hispalensis Episcopi Etymologiarum Sive Originum*. Oxford, 1911. It would almost defy translation, since most of the derivations come from misleading Latin analogies and puns, but anyone who edited and translated Isidore would make a much needed contribution to learning.

dies. The *panther* is so called because it is so friendly to all other animals (*quod omnium animalibus sit amicus*, and the Greek for *omne* (all) is *pan*. The billy goat is a lascivious animal and apt to butt; *lascivius animal* and *furens semper ad coitum*, its eyes are, therefore, always looking sideways out of lust, and it has got its name from "*hirci oculorum anguli*".

Isidore ranges over many even wider fields of information and definition; he has a whole chapter on the World and its geography; one on rustic economy, another on buildings and fields, another on ships and clothes. Why is the sea called *mare*? Because, of course, its waters are bitter (*amarati!*). Fights are called *pugna* because originally they were fought with fists. A tumult is the result of *Timor multus*, "much fear". Arrows, *sagittae*, are so called from *sagaci ictu*, a keen blow, that is *veloci ictu*, a swift blow. The sword (*gladius*) is so called because *gulam dividit*, it cuts the throat, *id est cervicem secat*, "that is to say, cuts off the head". *Vomer*, a plough, is so called because it heaves or vomits up the earth. More importantly, Isidore managed to transmit the idea that kings, who derive their title (*rex*) from *regendo* (ruling), only legitimize it by just rule ... and cites the terse proverb "*Rex eris si recte facias; si non facias, Rex non eris*" "You will be king if you do right; if you do not do right you will not be king." This simple sentence, intelligible even in the seventh century, sums up an essential maxim of civilized government. Further, he defines law as "something drawn up not for private advantage to anyone, but for the common good of the citizens"—a particularly valuable point when barbarian conquerors lived under their own law, distinct from that of the sub-Roman peoples. Along with his wild inaccuracies and sheer genius for false analogies, Isidore's massive work of defining the meaning and origins of words brought a much needed coherence into a chaotic world.

Two generations after this Visigothic archbishop in Seville had completed his immense task, the Venerable Bede (Baeda 673–735) out in the Far North-West in recently converted Anglian Northumbria was then writing much the best history in western Europe. Born at Wearmouth, near Durham, he was orphaned at seven and placed in St. Peter's, the Benedictine monastery there, under its founder and abbot, Benedict Biscop, who travelled widely on the continent and collected a good library. In 682 the boy was transferred to another Benedictine monastery, St. Paul's, at Jarrow; when Ceolfryth succeeded Benedict Biscop as abbot. There were six hundred monks in the two monasteries, and in these very large communities Bede spent his entire life of study and teaching. Here Roman and Celtic influences blended, and Northumbrian scholarship became famous on the continent.[1] In contrast to Isidore, Baeda was careful to test his authorities and weigh evidence, and he has an eye for vivid circumstantial detail; as when King Aethelbert of Kent takes care to receive Augustine at Canterbury out of doors, in case the Christian priest should use magic, or when King Edwin of Northumbria "sat alone in silence for long periods, turning over in his mind what he should do, and which

[1] King Alfred translated, or caused to be translated, the Latin *History of the English Church and People* into Anglo-Saxon. A good modern translation is by Leo Sherley-Price, *Bede. A History of the English Church and People*. Penguin, Harmondsworth, 1955.

religion he should follow." Hagiography, which in Gregory of Tours seems tedious and superstitious, comes alive through Baeda's homely and telling detail, and his narrative is well planned, his judgements magnanimous and fair. This quality makes him the first major English historian, and at a time when hysterical panegyrics or denunciation—as in the rhetoric of Gildas—had long been predominant. The "Venerable Bede", coming from a country recently renowned for its savagery, is an early exponent of a vigorous Christian civilization—not, like Gregory of Tours or Gildas, sub-Roman. He combines Benedictine discipline, method and order, with the freshness and poetry of the new Anglian feeling for Christianity, which was to inspire the Anglo-Saxons on their dangerous missions to their kinsfolk in Germany and Friesland and contribute to the vigour of the Carolingian revival.

VII

The overall decline of Western European power and civilization during the seventh and eighth centuries is reflected in architecture and art. The Byzantine achievements of the age of Justinian were not prolonged into the time of the iconoclastic movement; hostile, like the Muslim religion, to representational sculpture and painting. Only from Visigothic Spain has some fine architecture survived, and the feel of the early Lombard Court has been all too well caught by the comic, lively, and particularly Germanic vulgarity of the sub-Roman gilded copper helmet depicting King Agilulf, second husband of Queen Theudelinda, trying hard to look dignified in his chair of state, supported by ridiculously fierce guards, by common looking winged victories and by trousered and hairy figures prancing forward with his regalia. Under Byzantine influences, however, the Lombards afterwards patronized some good sculptors, who at the church of St. Maria in Valle at Cividale in Friuli wrought figures of dignity, simplicity and grace.

The Visigoths were more original and excelled in creating illuminated manuscripts, in which the Spanish love for yellows and reds predominates, setting off swarthy and formalized faces under black hair. Contrary to popular opinion, "the Visigoths contributed more than the Arabs to the characteristically southern Spanish horseshoe arch, which was already known to the Spanish Romans and belonged in Spain to an older tradition than that of the Muslims."[1] In Galicia and Asturias, which remained unconquerable, the Spaniards built their own elaborate version of Romanesque which survives at Oviedo.

Most ancient and most original of all, the Celtic Church in Ireland and western Scotland adapted the megalithic tradition of standing stones and menhirs to Christian symbolism: elaborate crosses date from the sixth and seventh centuries, and intricate Celtic patterns, gold, red and green, frame the manuscripts of the Gospels produced by the blend of Celtic and Anglian

[1]See R. Altarmira. *A History of Spanish Civilization*. Trans. P. Volker and J. B. Trend. London, 1930. pp. 414 ff.

Christian culture in Northumbria, as in the Lindisfarne gospels of the late seventh century, completed when Bede was still young.

These things were new; more original than the splendid but old fashioned loot in the ship burial at Sutton Hoo in Suffolk, where the craftsmanship is exquisite, but closely akin to Merovingian ornament, and the most prized treasures are derivative from Byzantine work. For the Northumbrian illuminations are harbingers of the Carolingian revival, and draw on Celtic and Anglian inspiration; evoked, indeed, in part by Catholic Christianity, but something out of the north, independent of the Mediterranean world.

XIV

Charlemagne and the Carolingian Revival

In 754 the last and hopelessly incompetent Merovingian Childeric III was deposed, shaved, given a hair cut (*depositus et detonsus*), and relegated to a monastery by his own *Praefectus Aulae*.[1] This Prefect of the Palace was Pepin, son of Charles Martel, the Hammer (so-called because he had hammered recalcitrant clergy, not because he had defeated the Saracens "*apud Pictavium civitatem*", near Poitiers). The Merovingians had long been decadent; their only assets their empty royal titles, their long hair and untrimmed beards. They had only one small manor of their own; and when they had to go to the annual tribal Mayfield or anywhere else, they went in a ceremonially archaic ox-wagon (*carpento*) driven *rustico more*—in rustic fashion—by an oxherd or ploughman (*bubulco*).

Pepin's *coup* had been approved by Pope Zacharias and confirmed by his successor, Pope Stephen II, as expressing the facts of power; and a new and formidable dynasty now prevented the Franks from going the way of the Ostrogoths and the Lombards. Three dynamic personalities, Charles Martel, Pepin and Charlemagne, took charge and, building on one another's work, created the political framework of Western Europe. Charlemagne's empire was over-ambitious, without the economic and administrative foundation for such a vast hegemony, and it collapsed through the perennial weakness of all the barbarian dynasties, the partition of the inheritance among younger sons— a partition they would have carried out for themselves had it not been formalized to avoid bloodshed. Charlemagne's own achievement (768–814) owed much to the death of his younger brother Carloman, after a joint reign of only three years.

Charlemagne was thus able to assert his powerful personality unhampered, and become the most important ruler in European history since Constantine. This large, vigorous and many-sided man, probably best portrayed by his moustached profile on his silver *denarius* (*denier* or penny), and certainly not by the aged and white-bearded patriarch of medieval legend, was the first

---

[1] The French translation "*Maire du Palais*" gives a wrong impression translated literally into English, since an English "Mayor" is generally a harmless civic worthy, with a faintly comic touch. "Prefect of the Palace" gives a better sense of power.

German permanently to change the political face of Western and Central Europe. Already by descent *Rex Francorum et Langobardorum ac Patricius Romanus*, he inherited the alliance of the Franks with the Papacy; reaffirmed when, in 753–4, Pope Stephen II had wintered in Gaul and obtained Pepin's guarantee of the Papal patrimony in Italy against the Lombards, implemented the following year when Pepin had invaded Italy, been crowned King of Lombardy at Pavia and proclaimed *Patricius Romanus*.

Offsetting the Muslim conquests, Charlemagne shifted the main political weight of Central Europe to the Germans, already in the Rhineland, Franconia and Hesse converted, mainly by Anglo-Saxon missionaries, to Catholic Christianity. He now forcibly included the Saxons, hitherto part of a prehistoric Danish-Baltic world, and made the Bavarians, who had tended to look to Italy, politically part of Central Europe. He thus increased Western influence in Bohemia and Poland, and strengthened the European defences against raids from Central Asia, and against the Magyars in the following century. He confirmed Pepin's Italian policy by annexing the Kingdom of Lombardy and with it most of Italy, as well as pushing east into Croatia where the Croats managed to resist him. His gruelling and mighty wars wore down the heathen Saxons, drove back the Moors to the Ebro, and expelled the Asian Avars from Pannonia;[1] only the Bretons, their native intransigence reinforced in the fifth century by immigrants from Cornwall, managed to defy him. It was as a Frankish warlord, not through the title of Western Emperor, suddenly and without his authority, conferred on him on Christmas Day, 800, by Pope Leo III, that Charlemagne won his immense prestige.

The event was crucial in European history, for the revived Western Empire would continue, in medieval times "Holy" as well as Roman, and in theory dominate European politics until the days of Charles V in the sixteenth century; then, as an hereditary attribute to the Habsburgs, continue until in 1806, when Napoleon abolished it. But its existence soon set off a conflict between empire and Papacy that long rent Christendom, for Leo III had "created not a deputy but a rival, even a master ... that action was the greatest mistake the medieval popes ever made in their efforts to translate theory into practice."[2] Charlemagne himself, alleges Einhard, so resented the Pope's sudden "crowning of him" that he declared "he would not on that Christmas morning have entered St. Peter's had he known what was a-foot ..."

Though the revival of the Western Empire, in abeyance since 476, reaffirmed the common civilizations of Latin Christendom, and would in time revive the Caesaro-papism of Constantine at the expense of the Papacy, it had little immediate effect. The now Greek-speaking Byzantines, themselves under the Empress Irene (officially "acting Emperor"), regarded Charlemagne as an

---

[1]The Avars were particularly fierce; when they had audience with the emperor Justin II, a Byzantine poet described how they "walked like Hyrcanian tigers when they are let out of their cages in the circus", and how, when they prostrated themselves, "their long hair fell forward over the carpets."

[2]R. W. Southern. *Western Society and the Church in the Middle Ages*. Penguin, Harmondsworth, 1970. p. 99.

uncouth upstart and the bishop of Rome as just another Patriarch; so they refused to recognize the title until 806.

Charlemagne remained a tremendous personality in his own right. The following description, paraphrased by many historians, comes directly from Einhard's *Gloriossimi Imperatoris Karoli Regis Magni, Vita et Conversatio*. The author, a well-born German monk of Fulda, had escaped the self-conscious alembicated Latin of the sub-Roman elites in Italy and Gaul, or the contamination of popular sub-Roman jargon; he therefore writes in a clear and readable style, based probably on Suetonius' *Lives of the Caesars*, but without Suetonius's appetite for scandal. Written about 814–821, his biography is realistic and convincing, without excessive glorification of his hero. Together with the many surviving *Capitularies* or Orders issued by the Emperor, it gives a credible picture of the King. He was a vigorous extrovert, with a fine gusto for life—"*corpore amplo et robusto, statura eminenti*"[1]—stout and outstandingly tall—with white hair, large lively blue eyes and a merry and genial countenance—*facie laeti et hilari*, though his "clear" voice was "not consistent with his size". He had ample sexual appetites ("of Charles's virtues", wrote Gibbon, "chastity was not the most conspicuous"), and he raised a large family by four successive wives and several concubines. He was an affectionate parent, and, probably out of political caution, prevented his fine daughters from marrying, saying tactfully that he needed their company. He was also a great athlete, hunting the bison and boar in the Ardennes when not on campaign, and an expert swimmer—"unsurpassed by anyone". He loved steam baths in the Roman fashion—hence his palace at Aachen,—"by the warm springs"—, and he liked to have his courtiers share these amenities. As one would expect, he liked his food, particularly roast game, and would complain of "the inconvenience of fast days"; but he was temperate in eating as in drink, and, unlike most of the Merovingians, he detested drunkenness. He was very talkative, *eloquentia copiosus et exuberans*, and learnt enough Latin to speak it fluently, though he "understood Greek better than he pronounced it." He even tried to learn to write: *temptavit et scribere*, but failed, having started to learn too late in life.

Charlemagne deliberately encouraged learning, not only for his clergy but for his magnates. He had their sons taught at the Palace School, and, like King Alfred, insisted on translations being made into the native language. But though he submitted, and caused others to submit, to the arid grammatical discipline imposed by the Englishman Alcuin (Ealhwine) of York, whom he had met and recruited with handsome offers at Parma in 781, he never aped cosmopolitan Italianate culture. He made a point of dressing in the Frankish style, with linen undergarments, a tunic, cross-gartered stockings and a cloak

[1]*Oeuvres complètes D'Eginhard. Réunis et traduits par A. Teulet.* (Paris, 1840), p. 8. (Latin with French translation.) Notker Balbulus, "the Stammerer" (840–912), a monk of St. Gall in Switzerland, though not, like Einhard, a contemporary, adds some anecdotes to Einhard's picture; but he is credulous and silly in the monkish manner, and anxious to distort Charlemagne's personality for the benefit of the Church. A translation of his *De Carolo Magno* is included in Lewis Thorne's *Einhard and Notker the Stammerer, two Lives of Charlemagne*. (Penguin, Harmondsworth, 1969), which also gives an excellent translation of Einhard, with notes, but without the Latin.

or furs, and refused to wear "foreign clothes" except on one occasion in Rome "at the Pope's request". He also set store by old Frankish heroic poetry, which he commanded to be written down. Unhappily, his successor, Louis the Pious, with excessive religious zeal, had the manuscripts destroyed.

At once rooted in his tribal past and customs, yet a European figure, and the first Western Emperor since 476, Charlemagne's prestige was enormous. Haroun-al-Raschid, the Abbasid Caliph in Baghdad, thought him worth conciliating; and when Charlemagne asked him for an elephant, sent him "the only one he had". It was named Father of Destruction, so presumably it was a war elephant, and it survived the northern climate for eight years. Charlemagne sent in return fine Friesian cloths, "white, grey, crimson and sapphire blue", and Frankish and German hunting dogs.[1]

Like most able monarchs, Charlemagne was a great builder, his principal Cathedral at Aachen being closely modelled on San Vitale at Ravenna; he also built palaces at Mainz and Ingelheim, restored many old palaces and forts, and gave vast endowments to the Church, particularly in the Rhineland.

In theory Charlemagne was as absolute as any Byzantine Autocrat, ruling both church and state. "The will of the Emperor", runs one of his Capitularies of 802, recorded at Aachen, "is absolute; his ban cannot be questioned, and let no one in any respect act contrary to his will or precepts." Yet the Capitula give the impression of intense but uncoordinated activity, from major decisions of policy to general moral supervision of clergy as well as laymen. Thus, after issuing his reformed denarius, Charlemagne declares, "understand quite clearly our edict that in every place, every town and every market this new denarius is to be accepted by all at the same worth." And again, trying to fix prices, he declares it worth "twelve loaves". There follows a general admonition that if an "altercation" arises between a cleric and a layman, the local bishop and count shall meet to decide unanimously who is in the right.[2] Charlemagne then turns to forbid people to destroy trees and ponds and to forbid laymen to enter monasteries and make a noise, thereby disturbing the brethren. If, however, they are local magnates (who perhaps as founders or benefactors had property rights in the foundation), the noise must be put up with.[3] By the Salzburg Statute of 799 those concerned are commanded "to sing better in church", and "not in such a rustic way as hitherto." The behaviour of monks and nuns constantly concerned Charlemagne and his Counsellors. Nuns should never be allowed to wander about ("vagare") or monks to enter taverns; and in 802 the Emperor is particularly "shocked and grieved and disturbed" to hear of sodomy among them. He insists that this sin be stopped. "Let this be notified to all ... nowhere else in our whole realm is this evil so prevalent as among those whom we wish to be the most chaste and holy." He threatened "to take such a vengeance that no-one would dare to perpetrate this sin again."[4]

The officials of Charlemagne's Curia administered an empire of daunting

[1]Notker. op. cit. pp. 147–8.
[2]Migne. Pat: Lat: vol. 97, p. 198.
[3]op. cit., p. 206.
[4]Capitula Aquisgranense. p. 17.

size. It extended from the North Sea to the Mediterranean and Adriatic; over the Alps far down into Italy, into Croatia, and over much of northern Spain. Yet the organization of the Court was domestic and rudimentary: a Count of the Palace, a Chamberlain, a Chancellor, a Seneschal and a Butler.

Charlemagne's power was indeed more effective in war than in peace. The large armies that intermittently fought and deported the Saxons for thirty-three years must have been fairly well organized; but the provincial adminis-tration under Prefects and Counts was inadequate, and the rudiments of a decentralized feudal society of largely self-supporting sub-Roman *beneficia* accorded to the magnates, with sub-Roman titles of Duke (*Dux*) and Count (*Comes*), in return for military service, who themselves gave land to their own *vassals*, can now be discerned. The Frankish magnates, Addvadus, Serimfrid, Eriwardus, filius Herigildi, Wondulf and Sigugath, to whom the *capitularies* were dispatched, do not sound promising material for an imperial bureaucracy needed to rule half Europe. Even the itinerant royal envoys (*missi dominici*), the two counts and one bishop, sent out to investigate the condition of the counties and royal estates, would vanish on their long, slow and well-paid peregrinations in early summer and not return until the fall, when it would be hard for government to act on any recommendation they might make. So when the great Emperor died of pleurisy in his seventy-first year, it is not surprising that the Carolingian empire began to break up.

It did so less rapidly than it might have, since two of his sons had predeceased him, leaving Louis the Pious, the third of them and ruler of Aquitaine, to succeed to an undivided realm; but on Louis' death in 840, the vast inheritance was fought over by Lothar, the eldest of Louis' sons by Ermingarde, who inherited the title of Emperor and most of Italy; Ludwig, King of Bavaria; Charles the Bald (son of Louis' second wife, Judith Welf), now based on Gaul; and Pepin, Louis' grandson, based on Aquitaine. At the hard-fought battle of Fontenoy, near Auxerre-sur-Yonne, Ludwig and Charles heavily defeated Lothar and Pepin II in a victory for the Germans and Northern French over the southern armies from Italy and Aquitaine; and in 843, by the momentous treaty of Verdun, the Carolingian empire was divided.

Lothar was still accorded the title of Emperor, but his territories, extending from Friesland through the Rhineland and Lorraine and over the Alps to Southern Italy, were strategically hard to defend and impossible to administer. Ludwig "the German" took over the German-speaking East, while Charles the Bald settled for the West; his boundaries the Meuse, the Saône and the Rhone. Pepin, the nephew, was left out. The partition was similar in principle to many arranged among ephemeral western emperors and Caesars during the late Roman Empire; but since it now corresponded to the nascent and lasting linguistic, economic and racial divisions of the continent, it took root. The German and French civilizations went their own ways, and the Western Empire, always an over-ambitious project, lost whatever viability it had. Neither Germany nor France was yet in being; the dynastic strife of the Carolingians had made it necessary to invent them.

Even these arrangements were challenged. Until 877, Charles the Bald ruled the western kingdom; but the western succession soon lapsed into a contest

between various *epigoni*, now mainly distinguished by their physical peculi-
arities. Charles the Bald's son, Louis "the Stammerer", having sub-divided his
realm between three short-lived sons, Ludwig "the German's" successor,
Charles the Fat, ignoring the claims of his youngest cousin, Charles the
Simple, tried to reunite the whole empire. In vain; the task proved too much
for him, and he was deposed; whereat Charles the Simple (898-922)—not
perhaps all that simple—managed to secure the Western inheritance. Bald,
Fat or Simple, none of the lesser Charleses had the force and genius of Charles
the Great. The Carolingian Empire retained its fateful divisions.

II

It had always been shadowy, based upon a primitive economy and rudimentary
feudalism. The Belgian economic historian Pirenne believed that after the
Muslims had overrun Sicily, Sardinia, Corsica and the Balearic Islands,
Christian commerce in the Western Mediterranean had been paralysed: it is
now know that, apart from the flourishing trade between Venice and
Byzantium, Pisa, Genoa, Marseilles and Barcelona were still in business with
Africa and the Levant. Notker asserts that "the King of the Africans" sent
Charlemagne a "*Marmerican*" lion and *murex* dyes; Charlemagne's elephant
was consigned to Pisa; and if these transactions are hardly representative, they
show that the harbours could take substantial cargoes. None the less, by the
time of Charles Martel, the West had become a predominantly rustic economy,
in which economic, social and military power was based on the ownership of
land. Only the slave trade still flourished, as in the times of Gregory the Great,
now supplied with fresh drafts of heathen by enterprising Vikings and Jews.
Nor were even the Christian Anglo-Saxons above disposing of their superfluous
relations in this way, or any Welsh that they could lay hands on, though the
main catchment areas remained in Eastern Europe.

In this rustic and predominantly stagnant economy the golden *Bezants* of the
Eastern Empire became rare and unpractical: Charlemagne had therefore
abandoned the gold standard and minted his silver *denarii*: gold did not return
to the West for centuries.

If in relatively good times this rural society could be self-sufficient, it was
liable in bad ones to local famine, made the more serious since the old Roman
roads had further deteriorated. And here the Church, with its vast estates,
hoarded treasure and systematic accounting, came through better than the
secular lords; it could even, without exacting interest, alleviate local distress;
for the clergy, in the tradition of Antiquity, took the conservative landed
subsistence economy for granted, and were hostile and contemptuous towards
trade, as well as condemning interest as the sin of "usury".

But the most important social and political consequence of the decline into
a rustic economy derived from the urgent needs of defence. It had been proved
in the East and in Byzantium that the best—though not the infallible—answer
to the incursions of the steppe nomads on their swift ponies, trained to rapid

manoeuvres in battle, was the heavily armed horseman on a large trained war horse. His elaborate equipment, though not such a complicated panoply as that of the Byzantine cataphracts, was extremely expensive, and the only way to endow him became by landed *"benefices"* or *"fiefs"*, held in return for military service and worked mainly by serfs of varying status. Since the adoption of stirrups, probably in the time of Charles Martel, cavalry had become even more invincible, so that a small number of these armoured professionals, trained up from boyhood to hunting and war, dominated the battlefields. Hence, quite naturally, this commonsense answer to the needs of defence, following the breakdown of the large well-organized Roman armies, complete with supply train, camping equipment and siege engines, was the rise of the heavy-armoured "knights"—the "paladins" of the *Song of Roland,* among whom fighting bishops are included. This "feudal" and essentially personal improvisation was not a "system": it was an answer to the collapse of one.

Under Charles Martel and Charlemagne it was already proving effective; but it also proved a long-term challenge to any central authority, particularly in the context of the dynastic partitions and rivalries of later Carolingian times. Even the power of the kings came to derive not so much from their title or sacred prestige, but from their domains and status as the greatest of all feudatories, increased by conquests. Thus though the nucleus of the French monarchy came to be Paris and Orleans, the royal household, like that of the Angevins in England, long moved about over scattered estates, consuming the produce. In this context even the word "feudalism" is too abstract. As has been wisely observed, "As a general rule medieval historians do well to avoid words which end in *ism* . . . words which belong to a recent period of history and their use injects into the past the ideas of a later age."[1] Since the whole feudal relationship was intensely personal, much depended upon the personality of the King and whether he was a great enough warrior and negotiator to control his magnates, to whom at least in theory he was "overlord".

Meanwhile, the knights already set the tone. Along with the all-pervasive churchmen, they dominated Christian Europe for centuries. "So", as Lot puts it with some acerbity, "the French aristocracy elaborates itself: turbulent, martial, ignorant, scornful of things of the mind, incapable of serious political concepts, basically selfish and anarchical,"[2] but an essential improvisation for European defence.

It was badly needed, for the reigns of Charlemagne's descendants in the ninth century saw the worst of all the barbarian attacks—the Viking assault out of prehistoric Scandinavia, coincident in the next generation with the Magyar raids out of the Eurasian steppe.

If war was thus institutionalized, so was its peacetime equivalent to which all the Frankish upper class were devoted—hunting. Enormous areas had been set aside in Merovingian times for the chase, in which all the nobles were trained from childhood and in which the higher clergy also took part. They

[1]R. W. Southern, *Medieval Humanism and other Studies.* Oxford, 1970. p. 29.
[2]Ferdinand Lot, *La Fin du Monde Antique et le Début du Moyen Age.* Paris, 1954. p. 456.

hunted bison and boar as well as deer, wolves and elk, with hounds bred for the purpose. Huge tracts of territory were also set apart for the Carolingian hunts, where so much was "waste" that they served as good a purpose for harbouring game as for cultivation; and in "undeveloped" northern Europe the cry of hounds and the sound of hunting horns would have brought a wilderness to life. Hawking, too, was a sport shared by Christian and Muslim royalties and aristocracies, and immense sums would be given for falcons, fascinating in the air and elegant on the wrist. Primitive and wretched as the lives of most of the peasants who formed the bulk of the population must have been, the rulers, from Charlemagne, his Dukes and Paladins downwards, had their luxuries and excitements in peace as in war.

III

Charlemagne had been able to extend his mastery of the Germans in part because much of Central Germany had already been converted to Catholic Christianity. It was thus only in the north-east that he met a stubborn pagan resistance, for the Saxons were still fiercely devoted to their ancient Gods. As is apparent from the works of Bede, the Gospel as interpreted by the Celtic and Anglo-Saxon converts had an energy, freshness and charm lacking in the theologically more complex religion of Italy and Byzantium; moreover, the Anglo-Saxons genuinely felt it their duty to bring their kinsfolk in Germania into the light.

It was in England too that the earliest and best surviving Germanic poetry and prose had been written down. The oldest and mainly heathen poem, written down in the late eighth century, commemorating events coincident with the main Anglo-Saxon settlement in Britain, but which had taken place in southern Scandinavia and Central Europe in about 520, is the epic of *Beowulf*. It depicts an intensely martial and Germanic world, in which rulers are judged entirely by their prestige as warriors and by their generosity in bestowing gifts, and where, next to the excitement of battle, the best thing in life is feasting in the mead hall, merry and warm, shutting out grim memories of winter frost and icy seas. The outlook is military and materialistic; concerned with treasure and loot and personal honour. The Christian God appears mainly as a supreme war lord. It is a horrible world, which nineteenth-century academics have romanticized.

It is all the more peculiar that a Germanic people with such traditions, long notorious for their atrocities and feared and detested by the Welsh, should have produced Christian poetry of such moving charm. Caedmon, the earliest Anglo-Saxon Christian poet (c. 657), was an illiterate cowherd, who, ruminating on the scriptures as read aloud to him, turned them into Anglo-Saxon verse.

The Jehovah of the Old Testament now appeared as a mighty war lord, who had put down Satan and disloyalty and transformed the rebel angels into devils: "Because they would not honour him in deed and word, therefore Almighty God set them, vanquished in a darker pit down under the earth in swart hell."[1] *Elene* describes the adventures of Constantine the Great's mother, Helena, in seeking and finding the True Cross. She appears as "stately and warlike", escorted by "blithe warriors", and standing no nonsense from the Jews who tried to conceal the precious object. With their delight in battle and destruction, the Anglo-Saxon poets paraphrased a Latin poem on Doomsday, an event accompanied by bitter cold and ice as well as fire: with their instinct to moralize, they muse upon the varied fates of men, whose gifts and miseries are so different. "To one the joy in youth; in one success in war, mighty warplay; to one, a blow or stroke, radiant glory; to one cunning at chess"; while "some scribes become wise." Another "shall gladden men gathered together, delight those sitting on the benches at the beer when the joy of the drinkers is great."[2] The first of the Teutonic peoples to become literate reveal a broad picture of Anglo-Saxon life and the unusual combination of imaginative sympathy with fairness and common sense.

Winfrith, known in religion as St. Boniface (675–755), and martyred thirteen years before Charlemagne's succession by the heathen Frieslanders, had been the principal Anglo-Saxon missionary to the Germans. Born near Exeter in Devon, he had penetrated to Thuringia, Franconia and Hesse, east of the Middle Rhine; and after working in Bavaria, had become Archbishop of Mainz. In this capacity, sanctioned by the Pope, he had anointed Pepin after he had superseded the Merovingians. He had also founded the abbey of Fulda, where Einhard, Charlemagne's biographer, had begun his career. His colleague, St. Willibrord, also an Anglo-Saxon, became the first bishop of Utrecht. The Irish missionary St. Columbanus had much earlier arrived in Burgundy, where he had founded the monastery of Luxeuil; but in 611 he had transferred his mission to Metz, the northern shores of Lake Konstanz and Bregenz. Though he had died at Bobbio in Italy, among the Lombards, he had evangelized part of south-eastern Germany.

Through these missions Charlemagne found vital areas of central Germany under a Church which he himself controlled, and here he lavishly endowed cathedrals and monasteries, as also in the lands that he conquered further East. Carolingian clergy spread to Bohemia; and the politically momentous sequel was the spread of Catholic Christianity in central and eastern Germany. For by 966 the Poles and Western Slavs had established rudimentary principalities there, looking to the Catholic, not the Eastern Orthodox creed and civilization, while Bohemia, if later a scene of heresy, would also become culturally part of the West.

In originating this missionary enterprise the Frankish Church had played little part; the conversion had been mainly the work of Celts and Anglo-Saxons. Lot considers that the wealthy Gallo-Roman Church had been so corrupted with the superstitious cult of relics that its "propaganda was incapable of converting the Friesians, Saxons and South Germans."[3] In any

---

[1] *Genesis B.* (probably ninth century) is in effect on the subject of Paradise Lost. *Anglo-Saxon Poetry*; translated by R. K. Gordon, p. 112. Everyman, 1949. This selection gives the best general impression of the literature.
[2] *Anglo-Saxon Poetry. op. cit.* p. 351.
[3] Ferdinand Lot. *op. cit.* p. 453.

event the new north-western converts, along with the Papacy and the rudimentary defensive feudality of the Carolingian empire, combined to counteract the Muslim and Avar attacks, to found the resistance to the Viking incursions of the tenth century, and even to absorb the Norsemen and turn their energies to account.

IV

Probably the most important contribution of Charlemagne and his advisers to European civilization was not political: it was the introduction of a legible script in which most of the sparse surviving literature of Graeco-Roman Antiquity has been preserved. Without the Carolingian revival there could have been no Renaissance either in the twelfth century or in early modern times. As Kenneth Clark has put it, "what with prejudice and destruction, it's surprising that the literature of pre-Christian antiquity was preserved at all. And in fact it only just squeaked through. In so far as we are the heirs of Greece and Rome, we got through by the skin of our teeth."[1] By the late eighth century two kinds of script were current: the uncial or capital, and the cursive. The former, in which the scriptures were copied, was formal and sacred; the second was used in the sub-Roman Lombardic, Visigothic and Merovingian realms mainly for secular business. When the Germans were converted, the Carolingian script was devised to elucidate the cursive and provide a hand-writing for the German monasteries; the Irish and Anglo-Saxon missionaries to the Germans also clarified the Latin cursive script, and they were backed by the Papacy, anxious not so much to preserve "pagan" literature, to which Gregory the Great had been intensely hostile, but to train and equip a better-educated clergy. The Germans, already by nature laborious, were persevering copyists, and, supplemented by the copyists in the Duchy of Benevento in southern Italy, they preserved most of the Classical Latin poetry which has survived, and nearly all the prose.

The copyists were encouraged by the patronage of Charlemagne's own court at Aachen, where he had collected scholars from England, Italy, Gaul and Spain, with whom he mixed on familiar terms, the circle inventing Classical nicknames for one another, in conscious imitation of their misunderstood version of Antique civilization. And this Carolingian fashion affected the Court of Alfred the Great of England (871–899), who saved Christian southern England from the heathen Danes and by 886 occupied London, and who was determined that the secular rulers of England as well as the clergy should be literate. For Alfred had the books then considered important—as Boethius' *Consolations of Philosophy*, Gregory the Great's *Rules of Pastoral Care* (*Liber Regulae Pastoralis*), and Orosius' *World History against the Pagans*, translated into Anglo-Saxon. The Carolingian minuscule script, which spread widely and rapidly, was equally useful for the recording of law and secular business, and,

[1]*Civilisation. op. cit.* p. 17.

revived by the Humanists of the fifteenth century, it remains to this day the basis of our own print.

In architecture and wall painting the Carolingian age was still sub-Roman or derivative from Byzantium, including even the splendid domed octagon of the Royal Chapel at Aachen built by Odo of Metz, and the kind of learning propagated by Alcuin at the palace school was grammatical and rudimentary. But it was widespread, since the sub-Roman episcopal and monastic schools had survived in Gaul, and in old-established centres as those at Tours and Corbie near Amiens, as well as in the newly founded German monasteries, diligent copyists were at work in their scriptoria.

The Scriptures were so rare and precious that they were given heavily jewelled or ivory bindings and exchanged as presents by royalty; nor was the art of writing entirely despised. When recording or copying the Word of God the writers are depicted as inspired, as in the ivory of St. Gregory taking a rapid dictation from the Holy Ghost in the form of a Dove, or in the illustration of St. Matthew swept by a rushing wind of inspiration in the Gospel Book of Archbishop Ebbo of Rheims.

In contrast to the dull sub-Roman figures on the Grandval Bible of Moses bringing the Ten Commandments to some apprehensive Jews, the engravings on rock crystal of Susanna and the Elders made for Lothar II in the mid-ninth century show lively narrative skill as the figures gesticulate in their quasi-Roman dress. But with the Utrecht Psalter, completed about 820, only six years after Charlemagne's death, we are in a new world, as with flowing and economical line an artist of genius depicts so much going on at once, in a flutter of draperies and a brisk movement of coracle-like boats.[1]

[1] See *The Dark Ages*. ed. D. Talbot Rice. London, 1961. p. 283. q.v. for admirable illustrations of Carolingian architecture and art.

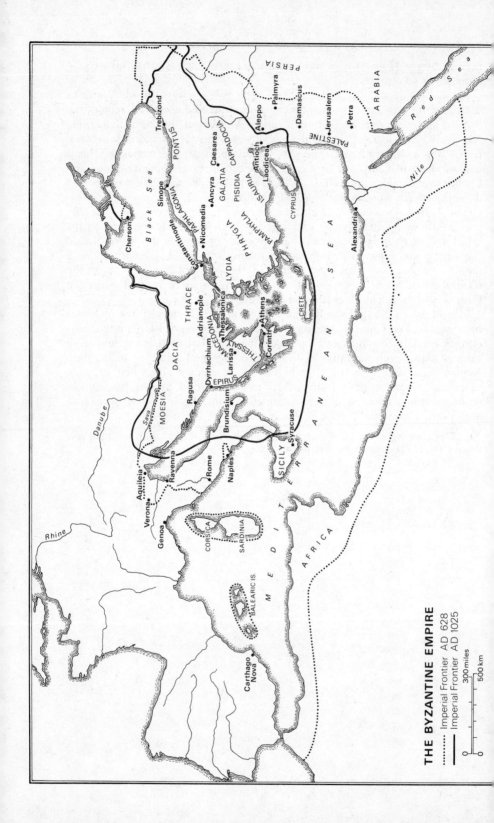

THE BYZANTINE EMPIRE

.... Imperial Frontier AD 628
——— Imperial Frontier AD 1025

0 300 miles
0 500 km

XV

First German Reich: Byzantium: The Norsemen

In the tenth century, after the break up of the Carolingian Empire, the main centre of Western power settled in the Germanies. German military might in Christian guise stopped the Magyars, now the scourge of Central and even Western Europe, thrust out eastwards along the plains of Brandenburg and Pomerania and the Baltic coast, and determined that the Bohemians, the Magyars and the Poles would adopt Catholic, not Eastern Orthodox, Christianity. But by reviving Charlemagne's empire, albeit in truncated form, and by relying so heavily upon the Church in Germany to administer the unmanageable first German *Reich*, the western emperors became involved in Italy and with the Popes, so that the Empire never became really viable, either north or south of the Alps. The western heirs of the Carolingian empire, on the other hand, after a period of eclipse, began to build up a French monarchy over a smaller but ultimately more manageable area. Meanwhile, coincident with the Magyar incursions from the steppe, the most destructive, mobile and wideranging of all the barbarian invaders created devastation around the coasts from Friesland to the Mediterranean, as the Scandinavian Vikings, with command of the sea, harried the unwieldy dominions of the later Carolingians, occupied half of England and the better ports of Ireland, and finally settled, first in Normandy, then in England, southern Italy and Sicily, creating the most efficient realms of the eleventh century. These Scandinavians, traders as much as pirates, also occupied a great swathe of eastern Russia, and developed the political and economic framework of the first Russian state.

Such were the fortunes of what the Byzantines still regarded as the undeveloped western hinterland of their own visibly superior civilization; the only one which was still metropolitan and well organized; rich and powerful enough not only to fend off the attacks of Bulgars, Slavs and Muslims, but to radiate its civilization outwards over the Balkans and Kievan Russia during one of the most creative periods of its existence.

II

Professor Arnold Toynbee considered it provincial or "bizarre" of western

European and American historians to disregard so much of Byzantine history, when Byzantium was still a going concern in direct descent from Antiquity, and "ignoring the history of the rest of the civilized world from Greece to China and from China to Meso-America and Peru," to "concentrate attention from 476 onwards on the barbarian successor-states of the Roman Empire in the empire's derelict western provinces."[1] Yet barbarous as these people must have appeared to the Byzantines, they were destined to affect the rest of mankind so profoundly in modern times that their origins remain retrospectively of great importance.

With the break up of the Carolingian Empire, the Germans briefly shoulder their way to the centre of Medieval European history and determine as much as do the Byzantines the cultural and religious frontiers of Middle Europe. For the claims of the Carolingians to the Empire having lapsed, the Germans revived them: on the death of Ludwig the Child, the last of the legitimate descendants of Ludwig the German, the German magnates elected one of themselves, styled, for want of a better title, Dominus rerum—"Lord of Everything". He was Konrad, Duke of Franconia, and failed; so in 1916 Heinrich, Duke of Saxony, nicknamed the "Fowler" because hawking when the news of his election arrived, was chosen to succeed him and founded the Imperial "Saxon" dynasty. He proved the military leader that the Germans wanted and admired. In 933 he defeated the Magyars at the battle of the Unstrutt, and in the following year defeated the Danes near their own border: when he died in 936, his prestige was almost comparable to Charlemagne's. His son Otto (Otto the Great 936-73) was therefore formally elected to succeed him and crowned at Rome with neo-Carolingian ceremonial. Thus in 962 was inaugurated the first German empire or Reich.

It was not easy to govern. It lacked the anarchic feudal magnates who were defying the later Carolingians in France, but the great tribal duchies presented an almost equally difficult problem, though it was from the Dukedom of Saxony, long the most resistant to Christian civilization until forcibly converted by Charlemagne, that the emperor's own main power derived. Extending from the mouth of the Elbe and the sandy coast of the North Sea down to the woods and hills of Thuringia and Franconia, Saxony was a major source of fighting manpower from tribes notoriously fierce since their ancestors had massacred Varus's legions. With Saxony behind him, the Lord Heinrich began to re-assert the old Carolingian claims over the Dukes of Lotharingia, Franconia, Bohemia, Swabia and Bavaria, re-create the Carolingian alliance between the counts and the great bishops and secure the revenues of his own large but scattered royal domaines. The dukes at least could not claim their rights by tribal descent; they had been military leaders appointed by the Carolingian emperors: so Otto later handed over Bavaria to his brother Heinrich, rightly surnamed "the Quarrelsome", and the whole vast and vulnerable territory of Lotharingia to another brother, Bruno, archbishop of Cologne. He also created new bishoprics under his own control as he resumed

---

[1]Arnold Toynbee. Mankind and Mother Earth, a narrative history of the World. Oxford. 1976. Preface p x.

the Carolingian drive to the east, pulverising the heathen Wends and Slavs into Christianity, and even endeavoured to create an archbishopric at Magdeburg which would have been a kind of northern Rome.

Heavily dependent on the German clergy, Otto also became dependent on the Pope. In 950 the inheritance of the Lombard Kingdom of Italy fell to a woman, the Princess Adelaide. There was a rush to take over the heiress and her lands, in which Otto himself determined to be the victor; and in 951 he made his first expedition over the Alps, a move which at once provoked rebellion in Germany from his disappointed rivals, including Heinrich the Quarrelsome and Liudulf of Swabia, Otto's own son.

These struggles were now eclipsed by a major Magyar attack. These originally Finno-Ugrian and Turkic people had originated between the Volga and the Urals; driven west over the steppe by the Turco-Ugrian Petchenegs, they had formed a tribal grouping known as the Ten Arrows, or in their own tongue *on-ugur*—whence the name *Hungaria*. By 889, by English reckoning in the reign of Alfred, they had reached the estuary of the Danube; then, led by their paramount chief Arpád, had occupied most of Moravia and crossed the Carpathians into the congenial plains of the Middle Danube. Based on what is now Western Hungary, they had raided far into Germany, Northern Italy and France for loot and slaves, though after their defeat on the Unstrutt, some of their leaders had come to terms with the Byzantines and Orthodox Christianity. They were nomadic horsemen and skilled archers, difficult to catch.

In 955, at Lechfeld near Augsburg, Otto the Great caught and utterly defeated them, winning a European prestige and much adulation from his chroniclers, though his victory was widely attributed to the magical properties of the Holy or Winged Lance, still in the Hofburg at Vienna, which contained a Holy Nail from the True Holy Cross. In due course, the defeated Magyars reluctantly decided that German Catholicism was better worth adopting than Byzantine Orthodoxy.

Otto, again like Charlemagne, now became deeply involved in Italy. In 961, anxious for a freer hand over the Church in Germany, he gladly answered the appeal of John XII, a particularly disreputable Pope,[1] for help against the factions in and around Rome. His reward was to be crowned in February 962 by the Pope in St. Peter's. He soon found himself in a hornet's nest. Having rescued the patrimony of St. Peter, the Emperor expected the Pope to hold it in subordination to himself; but John XII was spirited and all too worldly: he decamped to the pleasant resort of Tivoli and, allied to his former Roman enemies, raised a fierce Italian opposition to the detested Germans in Rome. And so when Otto, backed by his lusty army of occupation, convened a Synod which deposed John XII, the Romans refused to elect the imperial nominee. Otto managed to impose him, and having to reckon with the Byzantines in southern Italy, in 972, following the embassy of Luidprand of Cremona to Constantinople, he obtained the reluctant recognition of his title as Western

[1] It is alleged by the Chronicler Benedict of Soracte that the young Pontiff was mad on hunting and on women. He was, indeed, according to Gregorovius, the 19th century German historian, the runner-up to Benedict IX for Papal depravity.

Emperor from the *Autokrator* and the hand of Princess Theophana for his son, afterwards Otto II.

Otto I also had an octagonal imperial crown made at Reichenau, near Konstanz, for his coronation—erroneously known as the "Crown of Charlemagne" and still among the crown jewels in the Kunsthistorisches Museum in Vienna. It has eight hinged plaques of gold, so that, as was often necessary, it could be folded up and transported for ceremonial purposes or for safety. Magnificently ornamented with precious stones and pearls or with enamelled representations of Christ, King Solomon and the prophet Isaiah, it originally had had pendilia, like the Visigothic and Lombard crowns, and the arch was added only in c. 1024. The colour harmony of pale stones in a setting of gold filigree is particularly attractive. Charlemagne is often represented wearing it, though it was not made until a century and a half after his death.

When he died in 973, Otto the Great had gone a long way to creating a sound regime in the Germanies, and had re-created the prestige of a diminished empire, but he had been forced to overreach himself in Italy. Otto II even became involved in Sicily when he was defeated by the Muslims, and in 983, the year of his death, he suffered a much more damaging defeat by the heathen Slavs in the Nord Mark between the Oder and the Elbe. Already the over-extended *Reich* was attempting far too much.

Otto III (996-1002), who came to the empire at sixteen and died at twenty-two, was half Greek and highly intelligent. He was also, on his Saxon side, one of the first German romantics, who saw himself as a second Constantine. The youth appointed his tutor, Gerbert of Aurillac, one of the outstanding scholars of his day, as Pope Silvester II. Born 950, he was a redeeming intellect of the last part of the tenth century, which needed one. Born in Aquitaine, he studied in the monastery at Aurillac in Auvergne, and visited Catalonia and Rome, where he taught the young Otto II, who afterwards made him abbot of Bobbio. Otto III made him archbishop of Ravenna and fixed his election as Pope. The "Young Augustus" even presided over the theological discussions he arranged, opening the proceedings with impeccable and diffident royal sentiments: "Meditation and discussion, as I think, make for the betterment of human knowledge, and questions from the wise rouse our thoughtfulness." Gerbert collected all the rare manuscripts he could get and had them copied: such was his reputation for omniscience that he acquired a posthumous reputation as a magician.[1]

Otto wore Byzantine clothes and cultivated Byzantine manners, very conscious of being the heir of Augustus, Constantine and Justinian, as well as of Charlemagne. He opened the tomb of Charlemagne at Aachen, who was found upright in a chair, and himself pared the nails which had grown through the Imperial gloves. The short-lived Otto III is the first royal aesthete and amateur archaeologist of European medieval history, romanticizing a policy which had originally depended on the German clergy and so on the Pope, but which was now unrealistic. It was to bring much evil both to the Germans and

[1]See Osborn Taylor. *The Medieval Mind*. Vol. I, pp. 282-294.

the Italians and leave the main initiative in Catholic Europe not, as seemed likely in the tenth century, to the Germans, but to the Normans and French.

The Saxon emperors, more successfully, had continued Charlemagne's drive to the East on a broad front, bringing Catholic Christianity with it. Forced back into Hungary after their defeat at Lechfeld, the Magyars turned to the victorious faith: their prince Vajk married a Catholic Bavarian princess, took the name Istvan (Stephen) (997-1038), and, with German help, soon imposed Christianity by the sword and became a saint. The Czechs, too, had been brought into the German Catholic fold, and their "Good" Duke Vaclav or Wenceslas, murdered at twenty-two and never in fact the venerable monarch of the carol, had already been an exemplary Catholic in the early tenth century by the time of Athelstan. The Poles also became officially Catholic, and the pro-Catholic, pro-German policy of Miecsko I was continued by Boleslaus the Brave (992-1025), maternal grandfather of Knud of Denmark and England.

Right across eastern Central Europe the Catholic tide had spread, and Otto the Great planned to extend German-Catholic influence east of the Elbe where technologically superior Germans and converted Poles were united in exterminating pagan Old Prussians, Wends and Balts, whom they already considered sub-human.

This north-eastern enterprise was not much approved of by the Papacy: anxious for German support against the Byzantines and the factions in Rome itself, the Popes, after a taste of German occupation in their own city, were wary of an extension of German power through a projected archbishopric of Magdeburg on the Elbe.

Further, they could now count on new and faithful supporters in the north-west. The Anglo-Saxons had long been ardent Catholics, and had established a rich and civilized realm. Alfred the Great (871–99) had beaten off the first Viking invasions, and his descendants, Athelstan and Edgar, had been powerful monarchs, dominating the island and respected throughout the north. And although under Ethelred the Redeless (*No Council*) (978-1016), the "golden age" of the West Saxon kingship had collapsed before another Danish attack, Knud the Mighty (1017-1035) had not destroyed but taken over a wealthy and relatively well organized realm, which he had made part of a maritime Scandinavian empire. And Knud, in spite of ferocious Viking origins, had proved an ardently Christian monarch, anxious for recognition at Rome, whither he had made pilgrimage in state. Moreover, having helped to convert the Germans, Anglo-Saxon missionaries had been helping to bring the Scandinavians into Catholic Christendom.[1]

In the looming conflict between Empire and Papacy, the Popes could now count not only on their traditional understanding with the French kings which went back to their alliance with Clovis, but now also on Anglo-Saxon and Anglo-Danish support; when William of Normandy, that Latinized Viking, invaded England, he would do so with the blessing of the Pope, who would also find well placed allies in the Normans of southern Italy and Sicily.

[1]It needs to be said yet again that if he defied the sea, it was not out of stupid arrogance but to show his courtiers the limits even of royal power.

III

In spite of the German Catholic drive into Eastern Europe which had encompassed the Poles, the West Slavs of Bohemia, the Magyars of the Hungarian plains, and the Croats in the north-western Balkans, Orthodox Byzantium remained far the most powerful influence in Eastern Europe; among the Southern Slavs, the Bulgars and, in Kievan Russia, radiating its civilization over all the south-east and far into the north.

The legacy of Justinian and his dynasty had enabled the Byzantines to defeat the Muslim Arab attack, if not on Egypt and Palestine, on the City itself. In 717–18, Leo the Isaurian had beaten off the most serious assault, and his descendants had continued to rule until the deposition of the Empress Irene in 803. Basil I (867–86), a contemporary of Alfred the Great, had then inaugurated the Macedonian dynasty whose belligerent policy east and west had produced a great period of Byzantine wealth and power, coinciding with the reigns of the later Carolingians in the West. The usurpers Nicephorus Phocas and John Tzimisces had been equally formidable, and the restored Macedonian dynasty came to its climax under Basil II *Bulgaroctonos* (Bulgar slayer) (986–1025), a contemporary of Knud.

With the Bulgars subdued, the empire was at a peak of power and influence, with far the best organized army in Europe. Its nucleus, the four mounted regiments of Imperial Guards, were supported by elite Varangian axemen— the *Hetaeria* or Imperial Guard proper, mainly recruited from the North. These expensive troops, not lightly risked, were supplemented by espionage and diplomacy: indeed "the real strength of the Byzantines lay in the intelligence with which they faced their various enemies ... The Franks, they observed, were victims of their own rashness; they could be led into ambushes. Their commissariat was bad and hunger tempted them to desert. They were insurbordinate to their commanders and they were corrupt."[1] The Turkish light horsemen, the Byzantines observed, could not break disciplined infantry, and, once caught, could be ridden down by heavy armed cavalry; while the Slavs were dangerous only in hill country. As for the Arabs, though they had huge armies and could move fast, they were often laden with plunder and easily demoralized by cold weather and rain.

The Byzantine government was itself still strictly centralized under the *Basileus-Autokrator*, and mainly administered by eunuchs; having no descendants and being barred from the throne, they were not considered dangerous. They dominated the civil service and "for a boy to be really successful, it might be wise to castrate him. Even the noblest parents were not above mutilating their sons to help their advancement, nor was there any disgrace in it."[2] Decisive power was thus civilian and often emasculated, to the disgust of the virile feudatories from the West.

To this central administration the twenty-five provinces, Eastern, Western

[1]Steven Runciman. *Byzantine Civilization*. University Paperbacks, London, 1975. pp. 142 ff.
[2]Runciman. *op. cit.* p. 144.

and Maritime, the last including Crimea, Dalmatia and Sicily, were subordinate; the pattern was extended when the expansion of the empire threatened to give the border barons a dangerous independence, and so continued until the loss of vital and extensive territories in Anatolia after the Byzantine defeat at Manzikert in 1071 by the Seljuk Turks; and even then, on a reduced scale, until the occupation of Constantinople by the Franks and Venetians of the Fourth Crusade in 1204.

In comparison with the West, the Byzantine government was immensely rich with colossal gold reserves. Taxation was systematic, through "head taxes", "hearth taxes", and land taxes on rural and urban property. Nicephorus I, himself a professional financier with the ingenuity of his kind, taxed unearned income as "treasure trove". The Byzantine tax collectors knew all about death duties, customs dues (at 12½%), and levies on imports. With a freer hand than modern governments, they even managed to control inflation by limiting the money supply. The smuggling in of slaves duty-free was prevented, and the state itself went into business in the silk factories and in the lucrative corn trade. "The whole system of taxation, by giving the emperor a constant supply of cash and thus enabling him to maintain his huge bureaucracy and his standing army, put him in a far stronger position than any western ruler or calif."[1] During its most prosperous time in the ninth and tenth centuries, the Byzantines dealt in slaves, furs, honey and wax from Kievan Russia, in wheat from Dacia (now Romania), and in wine and oil from Italy, Crete and the coast of Asia Minor, while they largely monopolized the valuable spice trade from Africa and Asia. They imported raw materials, wool and hides and wheat from the undeveloped north, and themselves exported such prized luxury goods as brocades and silk robes of state. Their *bezant* was the only gold coinage in Europe.

Such were the rewards of Constantine's foresight when he chose so well placed a site for the new capital of the late Roman empire; and with so much wealth the Byzantine emperors managed to overcome the fierce religio-political disputes which became the curse of the City, while diverting the populace, in Roman fashion, by subsidizing the chariot races between the Blues and the Greens which kept them in a fever of relatively harmless if often politically tinged excitement. The arts flourished: the splendid mosaics of Justinian's time were supplemented by carved ivories of subtle texture and workmanship while, after the suppression of the Iconoclastic movement which tried to delete the human figure from all sacred art, Byzantine artists developed *Ikon* painting of often baleful grandeur, which would influence Italian and, more lastingly, Russian art.

All this grandeur had its politico-religious purpose; and the Byzantines had long been converting the Balkan peoples to Orthodox Christianity. St. Cyril and St. Methodius, their two most famous missionaries, had been invited into Central Europe by King Rostislav of Moravia in 863, and only later, when driven from Moravia by Catholic Germans, had their Orthodox followers brought the Glagolitic Script, originally designed for the Moravians, to the

[1]Runciman. *op. cit.* p. 100.

Bulgars and southern Slavs, and so launched the writing which would be adopted in Kievan Russia and then in Muscovy.

The Bulgars had permanently adopted Christianity in 865, when Boris I (852–889) (a descendant of Krum Khan who had killed the Emperor Nicephorus and used his skull as a drinking cup) had accepted Orthodox Christianity, in fear, according to tradition, at a picture of Hell painted by a missionary monk, but probably also for political advantage. His *Khans* and *Bagaturs* had been converted wholesale, and under Simeon the Great (893–927), who styled himself Tsar, the first phase of Bulgarian Christian civilization had flourished, leaving remarkable Armenian-influenced churches and monasteries as its memorials. This over-extended realm had in due course collapsed before internal rivalries and Byzantine attacks, which had culminated when, in 1014, Basil II *Bulgaroctonos* had defeated and captured a Bulgar army at Cleidion, and blinded fifteen thousand captives, leaving one in a hundred with one eye to guide the others, thus causing the Tsar Samuel to die of rage. So had ended the first Bulgarian hegemony.

By the late twelfth century the already waning Byzantine power had been less able to control the difficult area against new enemies. The Serbs, unlike the Bulgars, had not been nomads, but peasants long mainly settled in the valley of the Drina and its vicinity in the north-west. They were tribesmen and clansmen led by *Zupans*. In 879 *Zupan* Mutimir had been converted to Orthodox Christianity. Though Simeon the Great's Bulgar empire had threatened the Serbs, they had refused to accept Byzantine aid at the price of subordination; and by the mid-eleventh century they had established their own main bastion of resistance to all comers in Montenegro and around Kotor. By the twelfth century the Venetians were strong enough on the Dalmatian coast for the Serbs to play them off against the Byzantines, and under the mid-twelfth-century Stepan Nemanja they would become a power for Byzantium to reckon with.

But it was not among the southern Slavs of the Balkans that Byzantine influence was most important. It was in Kievan Russia, and later in Muscovy, that the Byzantine empire would find its most powerful successors. Here the eastern Slavs had been organized by Scandinavian enterprise, as in the West the latinized Scandinavians of Normandy had organized the most efficient realms; and it was this cross between Scandinavian rule and Byzantine religion and cultural influence which determined the future of Kievan Russia, so called from *Ruotsi*, the Finnish name for the Swedes.

IV

Of all the outer barbarians who attacked the remnants of the Roman Empire, the Scandinavians had been the most ferocious. They were also among the ablest, the most enterprising and the most adaptable. The Northmen in the West and the Swedish Vikings in Russia had an eye for trade—not least in slaves—as well as for piracy; and, when assimilated, they showed a great flair for administration and legal procedure. To some wretched monk, hitherto immune in the Far West, who saw these savages sending up his monastery in flames and smoke, looting its reliquaries, not for the contents but for their gems, and making off down an estuary in their war boats before the local defenders could get at them, the Vikings must have appeared as much a scourge of God as the Huns or the Magyars; and all the worse, since, commanding the sea, they could strike without warning when and where they would. Yet the descendants of these pirates created a far-flung network of maritime trade lacking since Carolingian times and, once settled and partially tamed, built up the two most efficient realms in Europe in England and Sicily and the political and economic framework of Kievan Russia.

Nineteenth-century historians, who thought war romantic, glorified these originally horrible people, who had raised heroic valour to a murderous cult and whose religion was a weird blend of fatalism and anthropomorphic fantasy, akin to, but without the grace or humour of, Greek mythology. They shared with the Homeric Greeks a cult of proud self-reliance and personal honour; quick to sense an insult, tenacious in avenging it; stern in their judgment of men and, ideally, unmoved by the changes of fortune in a world where even the Gods are doomed. Like the Germans, they held nothing so disgraceful as treachery towards a friend; it made a man a *nithingr*. They combined boasting in their cups with a passion for litigation and must have been tremendous bores. The jolly idea of them as gallant and colourful masters of the waves would have been unintelligible to their victims, who could only pray to God to deliver them "from the fury of the Northmen". And fury it was: the *Berserkirs* ("bearshirts" or "bear-pelted") literally "howled" as they went into battle. Here, in fact, was prehistory undiluted, and prehistory out of the cold and darkness of the far north, territories almost unknown even to the best geographers of Antiquity.

Seasoned in a grim environment, the Vikings were realists with an ironical grasp of essentials laconically expressed; like some modern Scandinavians, introspective and apt to exceed in drink. In campaigns they relied on speed and discipline: since Neolithic times the Scandinavians had used skis of animal bone, and their "snake" ships or *snekkjas,* the foundation of their success, were so light and flexible that they could ride over rather than crash through the waves carrying a crew of forty men rowing twenty oars a side. But these ships were not, as commonly believed, those used for exploration in Atlantic voyages as far as Greenland and North America, which were made by "round" *kaufskips* (merchant ships) which relied more than the *snekkskips* on sail. Only the biggest warships, the *drekurs,* had the famous *dragon* prows, and might be 69 feet long by sixteen broad. Skilled navigators as the Scandinavians were, their sea battles were tactically rudimentary; they would tie their ships together in line abreast, so leaving no room for manoeuvre, and, like the Greeks and Romans, convert a sea fight into the nearest they could to a land battle. In these encounters bows were important, and on occasion three dozen arrows were allotted to each rowing bench.

Their tactics on land were more advanced. Unlike anyone else since the Romans, they made huge permanent base camps with deep ditches and palisaded barricades.They were good enough horsemen to round up and ride the horses of the neighbourhood under attack, which may not be saying much; but they fought on foot in the *skaldborg* (shield fortress) round a battle-standard, with long axes and two-edged slashing swords to which they gave loving nicknames, as *Byrnie bitr* (mailshirt biter), *Fotbitr, Leg bitr*. Only the leaders had helmets and mailshirts, until great kings like Knud in the early eleventh century could afford crack household troops or *huskarls*, whose panache rivalled that of the Scandinavian and Anglo-Saxon Varangians of the Byzantine emperor's guard. Like the other Germanic peoples, the Vikings loved a feast and enriched English and American English with the word *steak* (from *Steikja*, something *stuck* on a spit); they also, as is well known, "seem to have been men of some thirst; their potations—though probably rare save in the most prosperous circles—were alcoholic in the extreme and because of the impurities contained in the drink, they must have had the most frightful hangovers."[1]

Nor can the hangovers have been improved by their burial customs. On the Volga in the early tenth century, slave girls would voluntarily die with their masters, along with horses and cattle. To the thumping of staves on shields the girls, bemused with drink, would be ritually violated by successive warriors, muttering thickly if unconvincingly, "tell your master I have done this out of love for him." The unfortunate girl would then be strangled, and finished off by an old woman known as the "angel of Death" who knifed her between the ribs. More simply, they would bury a dead man's favourite wife alive and unprotesting beside him.

In contrast to these hideous rituals, the elaborate expression of prehistoric custom, the heathen religious festivals in autumn, mid-winter and spring after the isolation of winter, were more genial. They took place in the "crowded warmth of the Hall" with "Big Fire" in the centre, where "gorging beef, horse meat and pork, rich with blood and fat, rank with garlic, the draining of horn upon horn of thick ale must have led to a rapid breakdown of reserve."[2] The heathen cult gatherings, fairs, public assemblies, horse racing and horse fights, were never put down by the Christians. Conversions to Christianity were often tentative and political. Some professed "conversions" had their rewards, as for the wily old pirate described by Notker, furious when fobbed off with inferior garments. "Since there were as many as fifty heathen clamouring for baptism and the fine set of Frankish garments, adornments and arms that had to go with it at the Court of Louis the Pious, the King had ordered some old shirts to be cut up and be tacked together to make tunics or to be run up as overalls. 'Look here,' roared the old Viking, 'I've been through this ablutions business about twenty times already, and I've always been rigged out before with a splendid white suit, but this old sack makes be feel more like a pig farmer than a soldier. If it weren't for the fact that you've pinched my own clothes and not given me any new ones, so that I should feel a right fool if I

[1]Peter Foote and David Wilson. *The Viking Achievement*. London, 1970. p. 166. a detailed and comprehensive survey on which much of this account is based.
[2]Foote & Wilson. *op. cit.* p. 402.

walked out of here naked, you could keep your Christ and your suit of reach-me-downs too.' "[1]

More constructively, heathen methods of rudimentary self-government, backed by elaborate customary laws, had a great future. The *Thing* or public assembly of free men, with its *Law Speaker* and clearly defined procedures, contributed to the development of law courts and eventually of parliamentary government, and the method of nominating a neutral group to find a verdict which was "declared", instead of relying on the archaic "compurgation" by kinsfolk and friends who swore to the accused's innocence, would in due course contribute to the evolution of trial by jury.

The innate commonsense of these people made them accept strict discipline in their war boats. Men could join at eighteen and still be fighting at sixty; all ties of kinship were superseded, all swore not to flinch before an enemy of equal strength and equipment and to avenge each other. No word of fear must be uttered, however grave the crisis, and, significantly, all loot had to be brought to the *stang* (pole); grumbling, complaints and argument (they were a litigious people) were forbidden, and all information was to be brought to the captain alone. No wonder that experienced raiders under such a code generally outclassed the local levies and undisciplined feudatories who opposed them.

Accustomed to disciplined piracy, the Vikings were as much traders as raiders; indeed, they were the greatest traders of their time. Their horizon was vast: not even the Friesians, the destruction of whose fleet by Charlemagne and his successors had probably opened the way for the Vikings, had been such efficient exploiters of the cold northern seas. And their range was oceanic; round the Low Countries down to Normandy and so up the Seine to Paris and on to Burgundy, or straight across the North Sea to England and on to Ireland, or round Brittany to the mouths of the Loire and Garonne, then out across the Bay of Biscay to Spain and Portugal and so through the Straits of Gibraltar into the Mediterranean to southern Italy, Sicily and the Levant. They even colonized parts of Iceland, briefly southern Greenland, and reached the fringe of North America.

Eastward, the Swedish Vikings were just as enterprising, penetrating from Novgorod down the great rivers to Kievan Russia, linking the produce of northern forests with the markets of Byzantium and even penetrating beyond into Central Asia. They traded with Central Europe through Regensburg in Bavaria into Hungary, and the northern route from Lübeck on the Baltic through the Gulf of Finland to Novgorod above Lake Ilmen gave access due south to Smolensk and east to Yaroslav and even Kazan on the Volga.

So the eastern Swedish Vikings, named by the Russians *Varyagy*, established a far-flung exploitation and widening political control over vast areas of forest and swamp, and over the fertile agricultural land around Kiev, united by slow navigable rivers and by stockaded forts and trading posts, which in winter over the ice and in summer through the swamps and rivers kept communications open and trade on the move. Like all Scandinavians, the *Varyagy* knew a good thing when they saw one, and by 988 Vladimir I, Grand Prince of Kiev, on

[1] In *Two Lives of Charlemagne. op. cit.* p. 169.

condition of obtaining a Byzantine princess in marriage, abandoned his pagan gods, his five wives and eight hundred concubines,—"an extravagant number even for a Viking—a figure probably improved upon by the chronicler to demonstrate his baptismal transformation",[1] became an Orthodox Christian and saw to it that his subjects, in droves, did the same. It was then that the Cyrillic Script was adopted for secular as well as religious writing.

A succession of formidable Scandinavian Princes now ruled Kievan Russia. Vladimir's grandson, Yaroslav the Wise (1034-54), a more successful contemporary of Edward the Confessor of England, made far-flung dynastic marriages with the royal families of Norway, France and Hungary. His son Izyaslav confirmed his racial affinities by marrying a Pole, while Yaroslav's grandson improvidently married Gytha, one of Harold Godwinsson's daughters.

The first Russian state was thus closely connected both with Byzantium and with Middle and Western Europe; and it was not until the catastrophe of the Mongol invasions in the thirteenth century that cut it off from Catholic Christendom that Kievan Russia collapsed, and Muscovy, not Kievan Russia, gradually emerged as the centre of Russian government and civilization.

V

By the eleventh century the most dynamic peoples in Europe were the Normans of the West and southern Italy and the Varyagy of Kievan Russia: the German rulers, for all their military might and technology, their manpower and the prestige of the revived Western Empire, termed "Roman" by Otto II but not "Holy" until the reign of Friedrich Barbarossa (1150-90), were wasting their energies in the impracticable task of managing the Germanies and Italy at once, while the French monarchy, founded by Hugh Capet (987-96)and destined for greater success, as yet controlled only a small area around Paris and Orléans. It did not then even control Chartres or Blois, and the territory north of Amiens was ruled by the Count of Flanders.

In 878 the main army of the Northmen, defeated by Alfred the Great in Wiltshire, had retreated to the Low Countries, where, three years later, they had sacked Charlemagne's palace at Aachen, and in 885-6 they besieged Paris, where they were bought off by a more than usually incompetent Carolingian, Charles the Fat, with a Danegeld far surpassing that raised a century later by Ethelred the Redeless in England. Defeated in the Netherlands by the East Franks at the battle of the Dyle near Maastricht, they had then settled under their leader, Rollo, in the rich territory of the Lower Seine, ceded to them in 911 as the Duchy of Normandy.

Here in a manageable and fertile area, a breeding ground for fine horses, they had prospered. In spite of their internal feuds, they had also multiplied, and their predatory younger sons were not content to settle for exploiting the

[1] F. Drovnik. *The Kiev State and Western Europe.* in *Essays in Medieval History.* ed. R. W. Southern. London, 1968. p. 10.

lush farms of Normandy, but cast covetous eyes on the island kingdom of England, already part of a Scandinavian empire, and on southern Italy and even Sicily, a more exotic prize, long fought over by Arabs, southern Italians and Byzantine Greeks. Duke William the Bastard, son of Robert I the Devil, Duke of Normandy, had harboured the royal Cerdinga refugee Edward Athling, afterwards Edward the Confessor of England, and now claimed to have obtained from him the reversion of the English throne, while in draughty strongholds and timbered manor houses in Norman winters the barons and their sons mulled over the exploits of their countrymen in the south.

Though far richer and more civilized and with a more deep-rooted system of government, the insular and conservative Anglo-Saxons and their Anglo-Danish masters had not adapted to the new cavalry warfare of the continental feudatories. Moreover, in the fall of 1066, they had to fight on two fronts. Having defeated and killed the formidable Viking Harald Hardrada at Stamford Bridge in the north, King Harold of England marched south with his *huscarls* and encamped, without the Roman routine of digging in, within striking distance of a superior force. For William of Normandy, whose army of professionals had been allowed by the incompetence of the Anglo-Saxons in disbanding their fleet to land near Hastings, defeated Harold's expert axemen in hard fought battle by a combination of archers and heavy cavalry who by a "feigned flight" disrupted an ill-disciplined but gallant and obstinate defence.

The crucial battle imposed the Norman yoke on England and decided that a strong, relatively centralized government would control the country, hitherto, like the Germanies, divided into tribal areas, here called earldoms. Tragic at the time for the English, the brutal Norman Conquest, with its French-speaking aristocracy, was the foundation of English power.

Away in the south the administrative genius of the Normans found even greater scope. By 1016 Norman adventurers had been reconnoitring southern Italy, and in 1071, only five years after Hastings, Robert Guiscard, already Duke of Apulia and acknowledged by the Pope, had seized Bari, commanding the exit from the Adriatic and the Byzantine supply route from Constantinople. As determined and able as William the Conqueror, this fierce and cunning son of a minor Norman baron, Tancred de Hauteville, had begun his career as a mercenary captain in Calabria; by 1076 he had captured Salerno and by 1082 Durazzo and Corfu. He thus made the Normans masters of southern Italy and the Strait of Otranto, and the principal allies of the Papacy against the Germans. In due course they became masters of Sicily. They thus established a formidable Mediterranean power, extremely well governed; the scene of a brilliant civilization blending Arab, Latin and Byzantine culture.

As R. W. Southern writes of the Normans: "From their bastion in Normandy they went out to conquer England and southern Italy and take a leading part in the Crusades. They seemed to have a knack of being in a vital spot at the right time. They came to England at a time when the country was wavering between a closer approach to or a wider alienation from the culture and organization of Latin Europe, and they settled the question in favour of the first alternative for the rest of the Middle Ages. They went to southern Italy in a dark and troubled time when Latin, Greek and Moslem influences jostled uneasily side by side, and they settled the question in favour of the first of these influences once and for all."[1]

In eastern Europe also the Varyagy were just as decisive: and modern research has emphasized the predominantly Scandinavian origins and affiliations of the Chief Russian princes up to the close of the eleventh century. Indeed West or East, the Vikings adapted themselves brilliantly to civilization and the influence of their immediate descendants was out of all proportion to their numbers. More than any other barbarians, they had initiative, administrative and legal ability and luck.

[1]The Making of the Middle Ages. op. cit. pp. 28-9.

XVI

Resurgence of the West

The resurgence of the West in the eleventh century, based on the increase in population and wealth which led to the cultural efflorescence of the twelfth, was handicapped in the Germanies and in Italy by the conflict of Papacy and Empire which long rent Catholic Christendom. It was in Norman England and Sicily, then gradually in France, that more efficient realms developed, while on their western frontiers the Germans lost ground and in south-east-central Europe in the Ostmark never fully consolidated their power. Only along the Baltic, where resistance was relatively weak, were they able to confirm their hold.

Perhaps fortunately for the West, the tedious and apparently futile conflict between the Popes and the emperors set back the political development of central Europe by disrupting the union of Church and State which continued in Byzantium; in time it also enhanced the prospect of a more diverse and dynamic civilization, if the vision of a cosmopolitan Christendom controlled by the Catholic Church faded before the consequences of the struggle, and the Church lost in authority what it had briefly gained in temporal power.

Historically considered, the conflict grew out of the very success of the Church and the responsibilities it entailed, along with the failure of the Carolingian empire. As the successors of Charlemagne grew weaker, more itinerant, less wealthy, they could no longer endow or even protect; indeed, for the primary needs of defence and revenue they might even plunder Church property and, to the detriment of the clergy, appoint archbishops whose loyalty was more to themselves than to Rome. For the clergy the only alternative protector to the monarch was the Pope, and it is significant that most of the *False Decretals*, attributed to Isidore of Seville—who better?—and to a *"Pseudo Isidore"*, were probably produced to enhance papal authority not in Rome but by the clergy at Rheims or Tours about the year 853.[1] The success of the

[1] The *False Decretals* of *Pseudo-Isidore* were supposedly papal decretals fomulated before the Council of Nicaea; others were genuine decrees by Councils of the Church; others were mainly forged letters supposedly written by Popes from Silvester I in the time of Constantine to Gregory II in the early eighth century. They also included the *Donatio Constantini,* fabricated a hundred years earlier by a papal notary in the service of Pope

Church had also increased the volume and complexity of appeals to Rome as the sole fount of Canon Law—far more lucid and comprehensive than anything else then available. Add to this the rise of "reformed" or novel monastic orders under direct papal jurisdiction, along with the increased dependence of the lay rulers on the higher clergy, and the friction between Papal and Imperial authority and over papal or lay investiture of bishops becomes more intelligible.

Albeit, the conflict was basically ideological and so irrational. Muslim fanaticism and the onslaught of the Viking heathen had created a corresponding fanaticism among the Christians, naively expressed in the contemporary accounts of the first Crusade and in the immensely popular *Chanson de Roland*. The Pope became the equivalent of a Caliph—a *"Deputy"* or Vicar of St. Peter. Moreover, under Leo IX (1049–54), doctrinal disputes with the Byzantines had come to a head. The eastern emperors resented the papal alliance with the hostile Normans of southern Italy, and the Popes wished to assert their independence. Connoisseurs of Arian heresies will appreciate why the Byzantines objected when the Catholics added *Filioque* (*and* from the Son) to the Creed, and implied that the Holy Spirit proceeded also from Christ as distinct from God, thus undermining the doctrine of the Indivisible Trinity— Three in One. Nor, after their experience with the Bulgars, could the Byzantines be blamed for insisting that only total immersion was adequate for baptism. Further, they argued, the Catholics fasted on the wrong day and, at considerable moral risks, allowed priests to shave. These grave differences— and the first is not, as often represented, a quibble but profound—were now magnified by political conflict.

So Leo IX had recourse to his archives which contained the forged *Donatio Constantini*. Though included among the *False Decretals*, it was older: it had been fabricated in 753 when Pope Stephen II was about to venture into Gaul to win the support of Charlemagne's father, Pepin, against the Lombards, who had wrested the originally Byzantine Exarchate of Ravenna from the Papacy. Pepin, who needed Papal recognition after usurping the Merovingian throne, had duly expelled the Lombards and then, although the Byzantines demanded the territory, handed it over to the Pope. Apart from a mutual interest which is the secret of successful political accord, Pepin had doubtless been impressed when his experts informed him of the *Donatio* whereby Constantine was alleged to have handed over Rome and the entire West to the Papacy and migrated to Constantinople in part to leave the Pope a clear field. The essential passage ran, "Behold, we give over and relinquish to our most blessed Pontiff Sylvester, our palace, our city of Rome and all the provinces, palaces and cities of Italy and the western regions, and decree that they are to be controlled by him and his successors." Even Constantine and the Byzantine emperors were represented as the mere holders of a "benefice" from God and

Stephen II, and based in part on the even earlier *Legenda Sancti Silvestri* (c. 480) which alleged that Constantine, having been cured of leprosy by Silvester I, had made his lavish Donation in gratitude.

subordinate to the Pope, who was God's representative, not His vassal. Pepin, like Clovis, had found a powerful, perhaps a dangerously powerful ally, and Leo IX and his successors, in good faith, exploited this document, which was widely accepted until shown up by Laurentius Valla, a Renaissance Humanist in the fifteenth century.

Gregory VII (1073-85), a Tuscan-born Cluniac monk, formerly Cardinal Hildebrand, now carried these claims further. He was as much inspired by the vision of a united Christendom under the Catholic Church as Lenin by dialectical materialism and World Revolution, and determined that a celibate church, in the world but not of it, should become the supreme spiritual authority of Christendom and of the whole earth. Even the Byzantines would be subordinated. And in such an "ideological" conflict, the Popes held strong cards—"the unparalleled advantage which the papacy had over other institution was its own storehouse of ideological memory, the papal archives."[1]

Medieval society reflected in theory the hierarchy of Heaven in which Christ was the Supreme Judge. As the "soul" was thought pre-eminent over the body, so the Church, responsible through the Pope to St. Peter and so the Christ, was in theory superior to any lay power. According to Gregory VII, both eastern and western emperors were the "secular arms" of the Papacy—no new doctrine promulgated by Cluniac reformers, but one as old as St. Augustine's view of government. So, as "deputy of St. Peter", Gregory VII claimed Divine Sanction for his commands, since "the whole universe must obey and revere the Roman Church." It was the claim of a Priest-King—Rex-Sacerdos.

With the logic of the ideologically obsessed, Gregory categorically stated his position. That no Pope could be judged by anyone: that the Roman Church had never erred and could never err: that the Pope alone could depose emperors: that the Pope can absolve subjects from their allegiance. And he alone can depose, restore or translate bishops: he alone can call general councils of the Church and authorize that an appeal to the papal court inhibits canon law judgments in inferior courts, and, for good measure, that "all princes should kiss the Pope's feet", while a duly ordained Pope was "undoubtedly made a saint by the merits of St. Peter".[2]

Such claims, even in the eleventh century, must have seemed staggering. And to the young emperor Heinrich IV, who had just emerged from a struggle for the succession, they appeared to make the management of the Germanies impossible. He decided to strike first. In 1076, ten years after Hastings, he therefore convened a Diet of German magnates at Worms at which he declared this impossible Pope deposed. So Gregory excommunicated him, many German magnates broke into rebellion and Italian cities into revolt, while the Pope prepared to come to Germany himself and "mediate" at Augsburg. To forestall this obviously weighted "mediation", Heinrich at once himself crossed the Alps in a particularly bitter winter by the Mt. Cenis, and, dressed as a penitent, intercepted the Pope at Canossa—a shrewd move.

[1]Walter Ullmann. The Growth of Papal Government in the Middle Ages. A Study in the ideological relations of Clerical and Lay Power. London, 1955. p. 262.
[2]Dictatus Papae. cited R. W. Southern. Western Society and the Church. op. cit. p. 102.

Gregory could hardly refuse him as a "penitent", though he kept the emperor waiting for three days in the cold, and then absolved him only on the condition that he would hold the projected arbitration. But Heinrich, contrary to popular belief, had scored a diplomatic victory: what with one thing and another the arbitration was never made. He had also taken an ambiguous oath, promising to make an agreement according to the Pope's advice, "unless some positive hindrance should prevent him or myself".

Thanks to the papal excommunication, the rebellious princes now elected another emperor—Duke Rudolf of Swabia. The war dragged on, and in 1080 Gregory excommunicated Heinrich again. But the second excommunication fell flat: a Diet at Brixen again declared the Pope deposed and set up the archbishop of Ravenna as an anti-Pope, Clement III.[1] Then Rudolf of Swabia was killed in battle, and Heinrich IV mustered an army big enough to cross the Alps, overcome the Italians, and lay siege to Rome, which he captured in 1084. But while Heinrich IV was crowned by his own Pope, Gregory defied him from the Castle of St. Angelo, originally Hadrian's tomb.

The alliance concluded in 1058 between the Normans of South Italy and the Pope then bore fruit. Gregory was rescued by Robert Guiscard, Duke of Apulia, whose expert Normans and Saracens drove off the Germans, but subjected Rome to a sack which apparently surpassed even that inflicted by the Vandals. The cause of these catastrophes then died at Salerno, convinced, as such fanatics are, that he had always been right, and reputedly declaring with self-regarding bitterness, "I have loved justice and hated iniquity, therefore I die in exile."

Yet the defeat of Gregory VII was only apparent. By stating his claims with such clear and uncompromising authority with its appeal to the medieval passion for ordered hierarchy in a confused world, he had enhanced the prestige of the Papacy; and when another Cluniac, Odo of Chatillon-sur-Marne, became Pope as Urban II (1088–99) and revived Gregory's project for a crusade to rescue the Holy Places from the Muslims, it was the Pope not the Emperor who launched the first Christian *Jihad*. By the exorbitant extremity of his claims Gregory VII had shown himself expert in spiritual and political warfare: he had created a tremendous and compelling Myth.

II

The forces in Europe behind the Gregorian claims to supreme authority had long been building up. During Merovingian, Carolingian and Ottonian times rulers and clergy had been united in the effort to keep society going at all and preserve it from heathen and Muslim attacks, and in the process of defence the idea of Western Christendom had been defined and taken root. It is

[1]But without the agreement of powerful German bishops. One of them, Benno of Osnabrück, prudently hid in a cavity behind the altar at Brixen while the election was going on, then stole out again back to his place, explaining that he had never left the church.

apparent not simply in the writings of the Cluniac churchmen but in the *Chansons de Geste* popular among the most enterprising secular class—the knights: the idea was the equally militant equivalent of the idea of Islam.

Monasticism, too, a negative ideal of withdrawal and self-sufficiency in a disintegrating civilization realized by the Benedictine monks, had now become more various and dynamic. The inspiration of the change had originated at Cluny, a Benedictine foundation in Burgundy founded in 910, by English reckoning not long after the death of Alfred. Owing to the piety of its lay founder, William Count of Macon, it was entirely autonomous, and under the protection of the Pope. Among monasteries, as among English public schools, it seems that there is always need for the reformer, and St. Berno, the first abbot, having won wide repute by his austerities, was soon being called in to advise and "reform", as was his successor, St. Odo, a contemporary of Athelstan. At Sarlat, at Limoges, at Sens, at Fleury, the seductions of an already French way of life had led to certain indulgences: they were now stopped. And naturally in Rome itself, more ancient and prestigious foundations were all too obviously in need of "reform".

Abbot Odo was a busy and famous man: and an astute one. He would first approach the lay patrons, pointing out that if the lives of the monks on their foundations were unedifying, their prayers would no longer work even for founders and founders' kin. With the patron's backing, he would then descend upon the monastery and after a brisk campaign of enquiry and exhortation, form a "cell" of committed monks with whom, until his return, he could keep in touch. This since familiar technique developed closer and more lasting ties, and by the late eleventh century a network of "reformed" Cluniac abbeys and priories had spread over the West, centred on Cluny itself. Moreover, the power of, as it were, the Central Committee at Cluny was confirmed when in 1075 the abbot was exempted from the authority of the local bishop and made responsible only to the Pope. The relatively easy Benedictine rule was tightened up and the essential *opus Dei* made more elaborate, while architecture and sculpture became more colourful and splendid, and a stricter uniformity of discipline was imposed. Gone were the days when unpredictable Irish missionaries wandered over the continent and set up communities where and how they would: the Burgundian abbots now aimed to know who was doing what everywhere and when they were doing it.

In due course the zeal of the Cluniac Benedictines was eclipsed by the Cistercian or "White Monks", founded in 1098 at Solesmes, also in Burgundy, where perhaps the local traditions of good living already made temptation unusually severe. Three years after Urban II had launched the First Crusade, they were established at Cîteaux on the Côte d'Or, south-east of Dijon, repudiating the comforts of their original monastery.[1] They sought not to change the Benedictine rule, but to make it stricter, more "unworldly". Having renounced the normal means of support from tithes and rents and services, the Cistercians had to work: *"laborare"*, they said, *"est orare"*—"to work is to

[1] The Abbey, almost destroyed during the French Revolution, was restored in the late 19th century.

HOLSTEIN

Danzig

Hamburg *Elbe*

Bremen

ALTMARK

S A X O N Y

Utrecht

Münster

LOWER
LORRAINE

Bruges

Ghent

BRABANT

Cologne

Liege

HAINAULT

K I N G D O M

Verdun

Metz

FRANCONIA

Nuremberg

Main

O F

THURINGIA

LUSATIA

MEISSEN

Oder

Vistula

P O L A N D

S I L E S I A

Breslau

Poznan

KINGDOM OF
BOHEMIA

MORAVIA

K I N G D O M

O F

F R A N C E

UPPER
LORRAINE

ALSACE

SWABIA

BURGUNDY

Regensberg

Danube

Augsburg

Munich

AUSTRIA

Salzburg

Vienna

STYRIA

KINGDOM OF

HUNGARY

G E R M A N Y

BAVARIA

TYROL

CARINTHIA

Danube

FRIULI

Aquileia

CARNIOLA

Lyons

K I N G D O M

Rhône

O F

A R L E S

VERONA

Padua

Veroná

Venice

Po

Milan

Brescia

Pavia

Cremona

K I N G D O M

LOMBARDY

O F

Genoa

Bologna

Ravenna

Pistoia

Florence

Pisa

I T A L Y

TUSCANY

Siena

Arles

PROVENCE

Marseilles

PAPAL
PATRIMONY

Rome

Barletta

Naples

K I N G D O M

O F

Palermo

Messina

S I C I L Y

Syracuse

THE MEDIAEVAL GERMAN EMPIRE

—— Boundary of The Empire

0   200 miles

0   300 km

pray". The crowded ritual of the *opus Dei* was diminished as the brothers went to work in the fields. They made a cult of hardship and they admired hermits: in an almost Manichaean austerity they renounced not only the pleasures of bed and board, but the pleasures of learning, art and music.

Ironically, in the event, their resolve to go out into the wilds led them to riches. The virgin soils they tilled proved fertile; the empty moors and downs proved excellent sheep runs, and they became the pioneer ranchers and sheep masters of the Middle Ages. Their communities were freer than those of the Cluniacs, being deliberately de-centralized and linked only with the mother house; moreover, they admitted lay brothers, even if illiterate, to help with the farming and with minding the sheep.

Though each house had internal autonomy, all the abbots met annually at Citeaux and discipline was everywhere the same. Much of the original inspiration came from an Englishman, Stephen Harding of Sherborne in Dorset, but the main expansion of the Order occurred under the leadership of St. Bernard, terrifyingly austere and eloquent, appointed abbot of Clairvaux in 1115; the most spectacular expansion thus belongs to the twelfth century when the Cistercian spirit caught the imagination of a vigorous age.

III

If the visions of ascetic monks and the policies of fanatical Popes were one source of a new European energy, the mounted knight with his Christianized cult of prowess was another.

Heavy armed cavalry, originally employed in Iran against the raiders from the steppe, had come by late Roman times to dominate the battlefield, and the use of stirrups, which had probably come in from the East, had greatly increased their impact, already dominant in battle in Carolingian times. Even the Byzantine cataphract, hung about with a whole panoply of various weapons, was now outclassed by the West European knight, who, clad in ring mail over leather, protected on his left side by a long triangular shield, and seated well back in his great war saddle, could now charge home with the lance and swing down with a heavy sword, or, if he were a fighting bishop, strike with his mace, without toppling from his mount if he missed. Such armour, like the trained war-horses, was extremely expensive, and the knight could not struggle into or out of it without help; the war horse or *destrier* had to be fresh for battle, and the knight required a second mount to ride on the march, so that the whole unit comprised at least three horses, including a baggage animal, and men to look after them, as well as a squire or serjeant to arm and disarm him. Indeed it has been estimated that one "lance" implied a unit of six men, "like the crew of a battle tank".[1]

No one could survive, still less master, such specialized warfare unless trained to it from boyhood, and these elite fighting men had long been a

[1]Michael Howard. *War in European History*. London, 1975. p. 3.

professional class, their station determined by the quality of their arms and horses. At a time when coinage was scarce, they needed land and peasants for their upkeep, hence the "feudal" improvisation already described, whereby a man held land in return for the military service that went with it.

And with the land went the strongholds to protect it. Over most of western Europe, in one form or another and mainly in open country, this "feudatory" class had grown up. But they were not yet *noblesse*. The collapse of the social order of Antiquity, with its Senators and great landowners, had been paralleled by the break-down of the archaic barbarian social distinctions, reflected in contrasting *wergilds* or blood prices between the Woden-born and the rest; and in a fluid society men of peasant and even of servile descent had carved out their own fortunes. Late Carolingian times had also provided careers for talent, particularly for military talent, and it was an "age of short pedigrees".[1] The crucial test was the possession of armour, weapons and a good warhorse: that, not as in the later Middle Ages heraldic quarterings and descent, determined status; only military efficiency secured the all important fief and the castle, seigneurial rights and way of life, that went with it.

By the eleventh century, when the *Chanson de Roland* was popular, an aura of heroic romance began to transform the crude reality of feudatories and feudal warfare, and a common *esprit de corps* to develop among the knights. They looked down on paid soldiers hired by the monarchs, as already William Rufus was hiring them, while a new cult of elegance and even foppery came in among the younger knights at Court, which shocked the Churchmen, who sensed what they called the " Norman vice". The late Carolingian feudatories had been much more barbarous and illiterate, and had spent their time hunting when not at war, which of course included *guerre couverte* or private war, and *diffidation* or formal defiance of an overlord—a correct and admitted procedure. Nor had there yet grown up the elaborate law of arms that formalized late medieval conflict: let loose against the heathen, the Carolingian feudatories had enjoyed uninhibited rapine and slaughter, as would the Crusaders who took Jerusalem.

Once in possession of a fief, the feudal seigneur had to find openings for his younger sons; there were often many of them, and from such a background some of the greatest Noman families emerged. In southern Italy Tancred d'Hauteville sired a large family of successful predators, and many of the minor adventurers and younger sons who "came over with the Conqueror" to England obtained large Anglo-Saxon estates and founded famous families.

IV

The religious fervour of the clergy and the faith, adventurousness and lust for plunder of the knights combined when in 1095 Urban II at the Council of

---

[1]See M. Bloch. *La Société Féodale, les classes et le gouvernement des hommes*. Paris. p. 12.

Clermont launched the First Crusade. He already wanted to assuage the in-
fighting of the feudatories by extending the "Truce of God", to divert their
energies against the Infidel, and also perhaps to heal the schism of 1054 by
according the Byzantines the help they had asked for, after the invasions of
Anatolia by the Seljuk Turks, rather than to promote the more hazardous and
dangerous enterprise of recapturing Jerusalem. In the event, he loosed upon
the eastern empire a horde of barbarous Franks who horrified the astute and
sophisticated Alexius Comnenus, and whose bad manners his daughter Anna
Comnena vividly described, and who, save for the governor and his guards
who bought themselves off, massacred all the Muslims in Jerusalem.

The Pope had followed up his address at Clermont by travelling extensively
through France, preaching the Crusade, commissioned his bishops to do
likewise and sent out special preachers as well. If his object was to divert the
more ferocious knights from their internal feuds and depredation, he succeeded, for the response was well nigh hysterical. *"Facta est igitur motio valida
per universos Galliarum regiones*—there was a great stirring of hearts throughout the Frankish lands."[1] The Pope had promised that the Crusaders would
save their souls and that "if any of them lacked anything, God would give
them enough", so they "began to sew the cross on the right shoulders of their
garments", eager for an adventure that promised fortune in this world and
salvation in the next. Ascension Day 1096 was fixed for the start of the crusade
and contingents were raised from northern and southern France, from Flanders
and Lorraine and from the Normans of southern Italy led by Bohemund of
Otranto, the disinherited son of Robert Guiscard himself. No monarchs took
part: William Rufus preferred to consolidate his own realm and get his hands
on Normandy, the inheritance of his feckless elder brother Duke Robert
"Curthose", one of the leaders of the crusade.

Meanwhile enthusiasm had spread to the populace in the Rhineland,
Flanders and northern France, already disturbed by plague and famine and
incited by one Peter "the Hermit", who lived near Amiens. In the spring of
1096 hordes of them with their women and children, dazzled by escapist
fantasies, set out for Jerusalem; making a good start, they thought, by
massacring the Jews of Köln, Worms, Mainz, Trier and Metz. After all, the
Jews, they had been taught, had been the greatest enemies of Christ.

Their piety brought them no reward. In Hungary the Magyars, in reaction
to the policy of St. Stephen, who had imposed Christianity by the sword, were
in revolt against German-Catholic domination, and although Lazlo I, when he
died in 1095, had restored Christianity and the authority of the crown, his
nephew and successor Kalman, one of the more sinister figures in Hungarian
annals, was embroiled in family strife. So the country was in more than its

---

[1]*Gesta Francorum et Aliorum Hierosolamitanorum.* Trans. and ed. R. Hill. London, 1962.
This anonymous eyewitness account was probably written by a minor southern Italian
knight in the following of Bohemund of Otranto, the ablest leader of the First Crusade.
This edition contains a first rate introduction explaining the political situation among
the Turks and Arabs in Palestine and the racy and simple Latin is briskly translated.
The narrative concludes with a guide to the Holy Places, so one is glad to know that the
narrator survived.

customary disorder, and the Magyar nobles, finding the bedraggled pilgrims an irresistible target, reverted to the pagan habits of the steppe and wiped most of them out. Those that survived from these and other peasant hordes attacked and robbed Byzantine cities, and were shipped hastily across the Bosphorus by the emperor, where they subsequently hung about the main body of the knights in rags, took to cannibalism, and inspired the Turks with revulsion and even fear. Their leader, Peter "the Hermit", survived to get in at the kill when Jerusalem was taken.

This sinister anticipation of popular anti-Semitism and folly is the obverse to the more effective enthusiasm of the main First Crusade. For the Crusade of the Knights was a success. After severe hardships as they crossed the arid interior of Anatolia in summer—it had not occurred to them to take water skins till the local people suggested them—they beat off Turkish attacks, and by 1098 captured the strategic city of Antioch. When, in the following year, after the Fatimid Arab rulers of Egypt had managed to recapture Jerusalem from the Turks, the Crusaders had the sense to advance down the coast as if to threaten Egypt; the Arabs withdrew their main force down to Ascalon, whereat it was relatively easy, even in the heat of July, to turn up into the hills and capture Jerusalem, while keeping communications open with the shipping at Jaffa.

Division among the Muslims had played into their hands. The Shi'ite Arabs of Egypt, like the Persians, despised the crude and recently converted Sunnite Turks, and had snatched Jerusalem from them while they were preoccupied with the siege of Antioch. But the Crusaders thought the Turks better fighters, while the Turks had a saying that "only Turks and Franks were true knights" and looked down on the Arabs. Though the Turks used prisoners as targets for archery, the idea that the "Turk is a gentleman" goes back a long way.

The worst hardship of the siege of Jerusalem was thirst; but the Crusaders managed to construct a great tower from which they jumped onto the walls and penetrated the city as far as Solomon's Temple, where they "made such a slaughter that they waded ankle deep in the enemies' blood—*Talis occisio ut nostri in sanguine illorumpedes usque ad cauillas mitterent.*"

The Arab Emir then surrendered, and, looting and weeping, the Crusaders cut down the inhabitants till they reached the Holy Sepulchre and burnt the Jews, given quarter by Tancred, Bohemund's nephew, on the roof of the Temple. Not since Hadrian had razed it to the ground had the Holy City seen such a massacre.

Having ordered that the Saracen corpses be piled up outside the walls and burnt, "because of the stench", the Crusaders descended to the plain at Ascalon by the sea, where they routed the Arab army, which retreated at speed to Egypt.

In spite of their victory, the Franks who now occupied part of Palestine remained a garrison, not a settlement. They were generally too stupid and fanatical to create the blend of civilizations achieved in Sicily or Spain, and remained a tiny "colonialist" minority ruling a "native" population. They were reinforced by celibate military orders, as the Templars, so called since their original headquarters was near the site of the Jewish Temple in Jerusalem, and the Hospitallers, or Knights of St. John, whose original duty was to take care of the sick: these Orders, founded respectively in 1119 and 1115, were expected to protect the swarming pilgrims who now flocked to the city.

Since the Crusaders were dangerously few and commanded unlimited labour, they built enormous strongholds at strategic places, such as the enormous Krak des Chevaliers. But the occupation survived mainly because the Turkish Sultans of Baghdad had other concerns in mind and thought it not worth mopping up. These European feudal outposts of *Outremer* were never more than a fringe, and depended mainly upon the sea power of the Venetians, the Pisans and the Genoese, who were the main beneficiaries of the Crusades, and had been accorded depots for trade at Acre, Tyre, Sidon and Tripoli.

Indeed, the Crusaders in occupation depended on the west as does modern Israel, though the fringe was much longer, extending from Antioch down to Gaza. Apart from its stimulus to trade and perhaps ideas, the success of the First Crusade was deceptive and led to the waste and disasters of the Second and Third. Far more important and more constructively expressive of European resurgence were the Crusades in Spain, with the *Reconquista* beginning with Alfonso I of Castile's capture of Toledo in 1085 and followed up in 1099, the year when the eastern Crusaders took Jerusalem, by *el Cid's* capture of Valencia. Though they would have their setbacks, the Spanish Crusaders were to achieve permanent results, since the Muslim civilization was so widespread and deeply rooted and its architecture and way of life so well adapted to the Iberian Peninsula, that the Spanish Christians, though boasting of their northern Visigothic descent and at first utterly destructive, would adapt themselves to the civilization and economy they had conquered and become part of it.

Even the crusades along the Baltic coast, not undertaken until the thirteenth century, would have more direct consequences for Europe than *Outremer*. The Teutonic Knights, founded in 1191 at Acre during the Third Crusade, would be diverted by their Grand Master, Hermann von Salza (1210), a follower of the emperor Frederick II from Palestine, to exploiting the long-standing German drive against the Lithuanians, Wends, Balts and old Prussians of the north-east. For he could grasp that it would be strategically far more promising to crusade with superior armaments and with the weight of an expanding German populations behind him than to waste resources on an inadequately based campaign in Palestine. So, after a crusade against the Kumans in Hungary, the Teutonic Knights would launch themselves against the heathen Prussians on the Vistula, starting campaigns which extended into Livonia and won great estates for the Order and its successors, creating the hard core of the Prussian military tradition; something again of more significance in European history than the states of *Outremer*.

V

The Cistercians and the Crusaders had a massive increase of population behind them and a much more vigorous economy than the static, conservative

and agrarian social order of Carolingian times. Since Antiquity the predominant social order had always been based on land, and even at the height of
Graeco-Roman civilization there had been little idea of capitalist investment
and enterprise. The Church, with its dislike of "usury" and its contempt for
"trade", had inherited this outlook, and the barbarian warrior aristocracies had
shared it. Now, in conditions in principle similar to those of colonial North
America, if in a better climate, there were more mouths to be fed, and during
the eleventh and twelfth centuries great tracts of country hitherto waste were
colonized. Forests were cleared, marshes drained, meadows irrigated, polders
reclaimed from the sea. All this could best be done by free peasants,
emancipated from the serfdom of the manor with its *corvées* and obligations;
landlords who wanted their vast areas of waste developed had to offer
favourable terms.

And already there existed models of relative freedom. The towns had always
been anomalous in an agrarian feudal society, but the better placed ones had
survived. Venice had always flourished on the trade with the Levant, under
the nominal suzerainty of Constantinople; the ports of southern Italy, under
Norman protection, had outlasted the Muslim attacks and traded with the
enemy; London and Rouen, Bruges and Ghent, had increased their trade in
corn, wine and wool, fish, hides and timber, ranging round Brittany to Spain
and Portugal and along the Friesian coast to Denmark and the Baltic. Now
that the Vikings had been tamed, a whole new sphere of Baltic enterprise had
opened up, while the ancient trade routes across the continent to the south,
never entirely disrupted, were now reviving.

All over the Continent new towns, *villeneuves, neustadten, novgorods* were
being founded—one manifestation of the great work of reclamation which
from the end of the eleventh century transformed the soil of Europe ...
"Throughout the area occupied by the old Carolingian empire, the growing
density of population brought about a great increase in the number of
inhabited centres, from which labour pushed its way energetically across the
waste lands to conquer fresh fields."[1]

With the revival of European trade and the expansion of the economy,
money became more important, and landlords tended to commute labour
services and tribute in kind for cash. Society also became more mobile. The
cult of pilgrimages increased; that to St. Iago de Compostela was already as
well established by the eleventh century as that to Rome in the ninth.
Merchants banded together for safety on the long and perilous journeys they
had personally to undertake, and great cosmopolitan fairs grew up, protected
by a special "peace" and encouraged by special privileges. They flourished
most thickly on the trade routes from Italy through the south of France up to
Flanders, in Champagne and Brie; already by 1115 there was one well
established at Troyes; and the fairs culminated in the Flemish hucksterings
and jollities of Ypres, Lille and Bruges. Here the raw materials and textiles of
the north were exchanged for the silks, spices and luxuries of the south, as the

[1]H. Pirenne. *Economic and Social History of Medieval Europe.* Trans. I. E. Clegg.
London, 1936. pp. 74-5.

two most advanced urban industrial areas—the Low Countries and Northern Italy—linked up. Merchants also came from the Germanies, Scandinavia and the British Isles, as well as from Spain and Portugal. It was in the twelfth and thirteenth centuries when, in default of better organization, the principal merchants themselves had to come, that the fairs reached their climax, but by the eleventh they were already established.

Sustaining this activity and the colonization in north-eastern and central Europe that went with it, the technological improvements, which had come in by Merovingian times, had long made for greater productivity. The ox-drawn heavy plough, with a coulter to start a furrow, was presumably familiar to Isidore of Seville in the early seventh century, when he defined the plough as "vomiting up" the earth; the horse collar, which, incredible though it may seem, Graeco-Roman civilization had never invented, so that the horses even of Hadrian's time had to work half-throttled by their harness, had been adopted during the most dismal period of cultural decline, and by the twelfth century the windmill had often supplemented the long-established water mill.

The most tangible memorials to this resurgence are the huge Romanesque cathedrals, monasteries and churches which have survived, intact, restored, or in ruins. The Normans, in particular, were tremendous builders and as ruthless as the Victorians in scrapping what they thought old fashioned. From the original timber strongpoint on a strategically placed mound encompassed by a ditch, grim and colossal donjons were constructed, as at Loches where the size of the stone blocks even today seems staggering, and the great Hall of William Rufus at Westminster, though restored and elaborated under Richard II, is so massive that, like the central keep of the Tower of London, it is still little changed.

Considering that, according to the sagas, the Scandinavians habitually burnt each other's homes with the owner inside, it is peculiar that stone strongholds were not more widely built before the tenth century. Doubtless the experiences of the First Crusade, when the knights saw the elaborate Byzantine castles and were forced to become more professional in the art of sieges and defence, contributed to the new standards apparent around 1100, while the Normans in Sicily had artificers trained in Byzantine and Saracen techniques, and those in England unlimited, if sulky and unwilling, Anglo-Saxon labour. Apart from the timber stockade, vulnerable to fire, even if wet hides were hung over it, the most primitive and obvious refuge was the stone tower, already evolved in prehistoric times in Ireland and Sardinia, but most efficiently developed in the cities of Italy, where the perennial feuds of the townspeople were fought out in a confined space. If hardly the best defence for a long siege, the tower could be a refuge until help arrived.

The need for permanent strategically placed strongholds to contain the Viking attacks has already been observed: and such places on a ford or river bend, as on the Rhine, could as easily become a base for fleecing the local populace and traffic as for protecting it. Further, since the whole status of a great feudatory with holdings scattered over wide areas depended on the strength of his principal castle, and siege-craft remained relatively primitive, a habit of more massive building set in. In England during the reign of Stephen, when endemic civil wars centred on the reduction of such strongholds, it was generally achieved only by starving them out.

Though many of the crusader castles were enormous masterpieces of design, it was not until the late twelfth and the thirteenth century that really elaborate castles, such as those built by Edward I to hold down the Welsh, were built in Europe; the eleventh-century strongholds were still comparatively primitive and were used normally only in a crisis and as depots, for they must have been very uncomfortable.

But the really massive Romanesque architecture was sponsored by the Church. It was originally an enlargement of Roman building, a vista of round arches supported by massive piers and heavily cemented walls, supplemented by groin vaulting when two barrel vaults, joined at right angles, were combined. This innovation produced the rib-vaulting of Durham Cathedral (1104) which is far higher than the roof of any Christian Roman basilica, and more impressive. The porches, as those in the Byzantine style at St. Mark's at Venice, were used to instruct the illiterate in the main lessons of the Bible; but instead of mosaic there was now sculpture, with a background of decoration. The sculptors were thus given new scope, as in Ancient Hellas, and by the 13th century at Chartres they would take full advantage of it. The great cathedral of Santiago de Compostela, in the north-west corner of Spain, is designed with wide ambulatories to accommodate the swarms of pilgrims who already frequented the long route down through France, itself punctuated by shrines and churches in elaborate Romanesque style. As at the Cluniac abbey of St. Pierre at Moissac, with its swirl of tense human figures and fabulous beasts round a majestic bearded Creator over the west door, where, Kenneth Clark writes, "the chief sculptor ... seems to have been an eccentric of the first order, a sort of Romanesque El Greco," and where since "Cluniac ornament seems to have been painted, as manuscripts show us, in bright primary colours ... [the beasts] must have looked even more fiercely Tibetan than they do today."[1]

This kind of sculpture reaches a macabre culmination at Autun and at Vézelay in Burgundy, where weird motifs are elaborated with a primitive but skilled exuberance, though at Vézelay the quasi-Hindu efflorescence erupts around one of the calmest, lightest and loftiest of Romanesque naves under arches contrived in alternate light and dark stone.

In more outlandish parts, as in English villages, the porch decoration was extremely crude, often mere beak heads and zig-zags, and sometimes a rudimentary carving of a crusader finishing off a Muslim by a spear thrust, as at Fordington, Dorset.

Impressive and magnificent as the interiors of Romanesque cathedrals still appear, as do the great striped patterns of Durham or Norwich, or the intricate designs of Ely, they were designed for colour, and today give but a faint impression of their originally stunning effect.

[1]Kenneth Clark. Civilisation. op. cit. p. 38.

VI

At the beginning of the twelfth century, in spite of the conflict of Empire and Papacy at the summit, and vestiges of paganism at the bottom, society was still united by common beliefs, and the fighting men could be depicted, humbly as at Fordington and more grandly at Compostela, in battle against the heathen. And as well as the Romanesque building and its decoration, that witness the resurgence of the time, we now have a new epic poetry. The outlook of the knightly class is now summed up and sublimated in the first famous epic in old French. In the original, *La Chanson de Roland*, composed about 1110, is a splendid poem, swinging along in brisk stanzas to be sung to primitive lute or guitar in a stately rhyming metre.[1] This "*style noble*" introduces us at once to Charlemagne—

> *Carles li reis, nostre emperere magnes,*
> *Set ans tuz plein ad estet en Espaigne,*

"now full seven years in Spain." He is no longer the German-Frankish ruler of history, but

> *L'emperer Carles de France dulce*—"of sweet France."

The plot is simple and memorable—how the villain Ganelon, by his bribed connivance with the Muslims, betrays Charles's nephew Roland, Count of Brittany and his friend Oliver to their deaths at Roncesvalles—a fate sealed by Roland's arrogant pride which deserves punishment.

> *Li soens orgoitz le devreit ben cunfundre.*

Apart from its high poetic merit, the poem creates character and is full of revealing detail. The *destriers* (war horses), like the swords, have names, *Tachebrun, Veillantif*; a Muslim has "nothing white about him but his teeth"; Ganelon at a crisis "draws his sword *two inches* from its scabbard"; Turpin, the fighting archbishop of Rheims, cries "*Fel seit ki ben n'ferret*"—"Shame on him who doesn't strike hard"—and the Norman French idea of a tribute suitable for the Arab ruler to send Charlemagne includes bears (*urs*), lions and harriers, seven hundred camels and four mules laden with "Arab gold".

Charlemagne, "two hundred years old", is much given to enigmatic silences and slow of speech:

> *Sa costume est peroler a lieser.*

He tugs his beard and swears by it, and twists his moustache:

> *Si duist sa barbe a faitad sun Gernun,*

and in general seems sadly preoccupied.

This picture of him, with its stress on his beard and immense age, doubtless

---

[1] See *La Chanson de Roland* ed. with a French translation and notes by J. Bédier. 2 vols. Paris n.d. (c.1930), from the Digby MSS in Norman French written down, c. 1170, in the Bodleian Library at Oxford.

contributed to later legend. The barons, from Roland and Oliver downward, have a touchy sense of honour, which dominated their lives and deaths, and God appears as the supreme feudal overlord, to whom Roland in death "offers his glove for the redemption of his sins" and in final quittance for duty done. And always in the background

> Halt sun li pui et li val tenebrue
>   High are the mountains and deep the valleys of the Pyrenees.

It is a clear cut, luminous, coherent and simplified French world, very different from the murky Teutonic setting of *Beowulf*, with its mists, meres and monsters, and in which Beowulf's shaggy companions ride round his smoking pyre on the headland over which the mysterious "dragon" has been "pitched".

XVII

Twelfth-Century Renaissance

The surge of crude vitality which developed in western Europe during the eleventh and early twelfth centuries created in its own idiom an intellectual vigour without parallel since the most creative days of Antiquity, and as important as the better known Italian Renaissance of humanism and classical scholarship. Like Gothic architecture, it was new; and its most lasting and original legacies were the European universities and those affiliated to them beyond Europe, the spontaneous development of banking and merchant guilds in the increasingly independent towns, a new and "romantic" courtesy to women of which vestiges still remain, and the beginnings of vernacular European literature.

As might be expected when, perhaps fortunately, central government—unlike that of Byzantium—was weak, the earliest universities grew up spontaneously, as scholars congregated around an outstanding master, and developed first for practical studies in law and medicine. People, not buildings, first made a *universitas*, a word then applicable to any corporation; and the mainspring, though not the origin of the movement, as of the Crusades, was in France, where the Italian initiative, begun at Bologna for law and Salerno for medicine, was paralleled by the study of theology and the "arts". The logic and vigour of medieval theology and metaphysics was first fully expounded by Abelard, an intransigent Breton; its full rather desiccated scholastic elaboration was expounded by the German Albertus Magnus and the Italian St. Thomas Aquinas in an attempt to prove religious faith by logical argument.

The earliest university at Bologna was strategically set at the foot of the Apennines, where the road ascended the mountains on its way to Florence and Rome. Here the full text of Justinian's *Digest* was rediscovered; and by 1100, only a year after the first crusaders had captured Jerusalem, Civil Law was being elaborately studied. Such expertise made careers, and sharp-witted young men flocked to make them; while the study of Church or "Canon" law, stimulated by the controversy between ecclesiastical and secular powers, offered "glittering prizes" for those skilled in nice argument, already in English reckoning in full swing by the early twelfth century, during the reign of Henry I, the first really industrious administrator among the Norman kings. These eager young lawyers on the make, secular and clerical, soon got themselves organized, particularly if they were foreigners who had to cope with Italian life. Independently of their teachers, they formed "corporations" and elected "Rectors".

This beginning is paralleled in the rise of a more useful science. At the medical schools at Salerno Muslim standards had long been set, superior to those of western Christendom. Hippocrates and Galen were translated, but by the time of the First Crusade, students were practising a more empirical medicine. And neither the law schools nor those of medicine were entirely dominated by the Church.

Beyond the Alps, on the other hand, in the Gothic north, the universities emerged from the cathedral schools which derived from Merovingian times and were always concerned with religious studies and the arts. The most flourishing were in and around Paris. Bilingual in Latin and their native tongues, young scholars flocked there from all over the West; the most talented to become cosmopolitan humanists and theologians, more deeply read in classical learning than the Carolingian grammarians; as the Englishman, John of Salisbury, who became Bishop of Chartres, and Walter Map, the courtier and wit, or the Welsh Giraldus Cambrensis who wrote an autobiography and described the Papal Court.

Moreover, the ablest men were original. St. Anselm of Aosta (1033–1109), Abbot of Bec in Normandy and Archbishop of Canterbury, had already in his *Monologion* (1077) and *Alloquium de Dei Existentia* (1078) claimed that reason could prove the existence of God, as a being nothing greater than which exists, thus already investigating a topic which would concern generations of philosophers including Descartes, Hegel and Kant. Nor did he shrink from investigating why God had become Man, *Cur Deus Homo?*, formulating a doctrine of Redemption important to theologians. Such was the vaulting intellectual ambition and scope of a contemporary of William Rufus. But it was Peter Abelard (1079–1142), a wayward and irrepressible genius, who launched the attempt to prove theological beliefs by elaborate logic which was to culminate a century later in the all-embracing *Summa Theologica* of St. Thomas Aquinas.

Abelard came of minor nobility of Le Pallet in Southern Brittany, and his redoubtable intransigence seems Breton—perhaps he may also have had Cornish descent. As a student at Paris he early quarrelled with his instructor, then as a teacher himself at Notre Dame de Paris he started an affair with his pupil Héloise, niece of one of the Canons. Héloise bore him a son, Astrolabius, and under pressure from the Canon and against the wishes of Héloise, concerned for Abelard's career, in 1118 he secretly married her. This, however, was not enough for the infuriated Canon Fulbert, who set on ruffians to castrate him; a vengeance, as a French biographer writes, "as cruel as it was irremediable". Abelard, lucky in medieval conditions to survive, wisely became a monk at St. Denis, where with singular tactlessness he asserted that the cherished relics of Dionysius the Areopagite were bogus. After a short spell as a reforming abbot at St. Gildas de Ruys in his native Brittany, where the provincial monks tried to kill him, Abelard resumed his brilliant lectures in

Paris. But in 1121 his *Treatise on the Trinity*, always a difficult subject, had been denounced and burned by the authorities, and now, as his following increased, he was denounced by St. Bernard and condemned by the Pope. After that he died at Chalons-sur-Seine. Héloise, relegated to a convent, lived down her past, became its abbess and long outlived him. Since Abelard's *History of Calamity* has survived and many letters, much sentimentality has been lavished on the affair of Abelard and Héloise, from which Héloise emerges with more credit than her instructor, caught as they both were in the conventions of the time. Abelard wrote a poem for their son, the unwitting cause of the *Historia Calamitatum*: Héloise, with maternal good sense, solicited the Bishop of Paris to give him a prebend.

Abelard's impact was astonishing, and in reinforcing good resolute dogma by dialectic and mobilizing what he knew of "pagan" writers, he set a new fashion. His most famous work, the *Sic et Non, Yes and No*, presents the pros and cons of such fundamental problems as "whether or not one can believe in one God" (*Quod sit credendum in Deum Solum, et contra*), and if the sacrament is *essentialiter* the flesh and blood of Christ; "the first key to wisdom is interrogation," he insisted, and "from enquiry we perceive Truth", while such reasoning "sharpens the wits of the young". Naturally the conservatives thought Abelard a menace—"too clever by half"; better, they thought, to stick to simple faith.

Be that as it may, Abelard deployed his unbridled rationalism untrammelled by empirical research, free as air, and, with all the charm of novelty, overreached the limits of mind, attempting to explain the universe and prove faith by logic, and syllogistically dividing unanswerable problems into "definitions" (*distinctio*), followed by arguments, pro and con, then stating the final solution. A brilliant orator, he had genius and magnetism, along with the vanity and exhibitionism of his kind.

As he was born in the reigns of Philip I of France and of William Rufus, it is remarkable that any one took notice of him. Thanks to the power of the Church and its monopoly of learning, such theologians, born before the invention of print, surprisingly proved influential in a society otherwise dominated by illiterate barons and sustained by an illiterate peasantry.

Abelard was a pioneer: the University of Paris was not formally founded until about 1150, eight years after his death; Oxford not until about 1170; Cambridge was not incorporated until 1209, and most of the Spanish universities—Salamanca, Valladolid, Seville—until well into the thirteenth century. Many celebrated French ones, as Poitiers, Avignon, Bourges, date from the fourteenth century and none of the German universities was founded until the later Middle Ages—as Basel, Tübingen, Freiburg, while the old Scots universities date from the fifteenth century. It took generations for the scholastic impulse to work itself out and extend to Catholic Central and Eastern Europe, as in the Universities of Prague (1347) and Cracow (1397).

But their Latin-speaking learning was entirely cosmopolitan, and since most people were illiterate, this learning created an elite drawn from all sections of society, save the serfs. Some of the greatest princes of the Church, as Pope Adrian IV, or Suger, Abbot of St. Denis and Regent of France in the mid twelfth century, were of humble origin, rising as high civil servants in royal governments; others made considerable careers in the service of magnates whose huge scattered properties needed supervision; later on, other scholars were friars, more independent of patronage and so perhaps better able to concentrate on learning. As the numbers of students increased with the great expansion of population in the thirteenth century, "colleges" were founded for their protection and discipline, for the rough and tumble penury of student life—familiar from their racy Latin songs—must have made it hard for students to work, "town and gown" riots could be lethal, and graduates needed peace and security to follow the long courses prescribed for "advanced" degrees. Spontaneously, and without the endowments and bureaucracy now thought essential, these brisk urban communities built up a tradition; accumulated books, devised oral examinations, created a world of entirely unpractical intellectual stimulus and excitement, all under the shelter of the Church, transcending nationality and the lust of military conquest. *Hospita in Gallia nunc me vocant studia* sings a German student going into France in his jaunty Latin,

> *Vale dulcis patria, suavis suevorum Suevia*
> *Salve dilecta Francia, philosophorum Curia!*[1]

The basic curriculum was extremely limited; but it was rigorous, deriving from Carolingian times. The *Trivium* inculcated Latin grammar and rhetoric, logic and eloquent argument: then the scholar struck out in the more ambitious *quadrivium*, which included mathematics, geometry, primitive astronomy, and music. The study of the Bible was supplemented by commentaries and books of collected opinions—*Sententia*—(hence "sententious"), or based on lecture notes. Abelard maintained that pagan authors could illuminate scripture since "God had revealed himself outside the Church", and the extraordinary feat of the thirteenth century school men was to assimilate Aristotle into the framework of dogma in *"disputations"* in which tabulated adverse arguments are stated first, then systematically refuted. These metaphysical constructions, totally devoid of experimental foundations, sharpened the argumentative wits of twelfth century schoolmen, and perverted their minds from more useful activities, though providing much satisfaction to those concerned.

Thus in mind, as in politics, medieval civilization sought to explain unfathomable mysteries; but at least it dispelled much of the fear which for barbarous generations had pressed down on generations of Europeans, and it has been claimed that "the greatest triumph of medieval humanism was to make God seem human."[2] This dubiously hopeful belief probably encouraged people to face the world with greater confidence, thus restoring *La dignité humaine*. Certainly this aspect of the twelfth-century renaissance shows a new confidence in life and in the capacity of mind: as when Anselm, an archbishop who was the contemporary of the barbarous barons of the First Crusade, had the sheer confidence to "prove" by argument the existence of God, and to

[1] My studies now summon me a visitor to Gaul. Farewell dear native land, sweet Swabia of the Swabians: Greetings! beloved France, home of philosophers!
[2] R. W. Southern. *Medieval Humanism and Other Studies. op. cit.* p. 37.

raise questions which have kept philosophers arguing for centuries. There had been nothing comparable since the most creative days of Antiquity and such élan marks the emergence of a vigorous society more at home in the world, if not yet attempting to exploit it by scientific method.

II

The other original and spontaneous medieval invention was urban. With the revival of trade and of Roman Law with its rational and written procedure, the towns and the transactions of merchants became better organized. They varied according to origin and locality, from Byzantine Constantinople and Arab Córdoba, which entirely outclassed any others, through the surviving towns of the Roman empire, generally seats of bishoprics, to the big cosmopolitan ports of Italy, Venice, Pisa, Genoa, Amalfi, down to local strongholds under the protection of a great lord or bishop, which served both as market centres, as refuges, and perhaps, with special licence, as the site of a mint.

Within these various settings, alien in a rustic feudal society, there grew up the *bourgeoisie*. Some cities, as Venice or Genoa, were rich enough to become republics, acknowledging no superior and negotiating as equals with kings. Most remained under at least the nominal authority of their local lords, to whom they owed feudal obligations, but from whom they often bought rights of internal self-government or *franchises*. If they could raise their own taxes and militia, they had more regular resources available than most of the great feudatories or even kings. And their liberties, written and exact like their own systematic accounting, were better defined than the personal and customary obligations of feudal order—or disorder. Custom was being superseded by written rights, recorded as in business.

The mentality of the townsmen naturally became different from that of the rural feudatories and peasantry in the north, if in Italy the nobles, too, became urban. It was cash and business sense that counted, not descent, and the towns were governed by a council of the wealthier families who elected a "Mayor" or "Provost" from themselves for a limited term of office, an oligarchic election in which the occasional popular assemblies had little influence. This sponta-neous development had been paralleled by spontaneously formed guilds of craftsmen and tradesmen of the same calling, which originally protected both producer and consumer, preventing competition and maintaining quality of goods. No one could practise a craft save by a long apprenticeship and by customary methods. But as the merchant guilds developed, with capital behind them, composed not of local craftsmen but of merchants who bought and sold in bigger markets and so accumulated more wealth, the town oligarchies developed, along with their "bankers" (originally money changers so called from the benches they sat on), lawyers and accountants, to form an *haute bourgeoisie*, in their way as proud and exclusive as the nobility who despised them, and who, unlike the merchants of Antiquity, thought not so much of buying land as of putting capital to productive investment. Here is a development as original and socially even more decisive than the rise of universities.

Huddled in their cramped and plague ridden walled towns, disinfected by periodical fires, they were apprehensive of attack, and soon, with competitive merchant capitalists dominating the old craft guilds, the townspeople observed each other with sharp and often malicious eyes. They became quicker in the uptake than the proud feckless barons, rustic knights or peasantry; more witty and sceptical; while the magnates of Rome had their roots in great slave-run estates, these people were out for profit. A new outlook is discernible, more methodical, more specialized, and, outside the *haute bourgeoisie*, a new radical discontent, critical of any "establishment", even of the Church, and "anti-clerical", as in the north Italian republics.

III

The most showy manifestation of the new twelfth-century vitality remained the nobles and their dependants, now becoming more stratified within their own class. The Eastern Crusades had taught some of them new fashions, and more sophisticated notions of heraldry (most of the technical terms are originally Persian) had come in, along with new luxuries; eastern carpets instead of rushes on the floor, portable hangings for draughty rooms; dress, following Byzantine and Sicilian fashions, now included "damascene" silks and coats of soft camel hair for the rich. Cooking became more elaborate and complicated, enlivened by spices from the East. Far from devouring roasted hunks of beef, as had Charlemagne, some of the richer and more courtly thirteenth-century barons would have scooped up brightly coloured *mousses* with spoons, and the Crusaders had first met and enjoyed cane sugar in Egypt. The elaborate cuisine of the Levant was applied to the more plentiful materials of the north-west.

The barbaric decoration of helmets goes back to the Bronze Age and to Celtic times, and the Vikings had made themselves more fearsome by horns projecting from their helmets, as the Franks and Anglo-Saxons had applied the serried tusks of wild boars: most barbarians in all continents have invented a more or less terrifying get-up for battle. But the medieval knights had another reason for vivid and conspicuous badges: William the Conqueror at Hastings is shown in the Bayeux tapestry tilting his helmet back off his face to disprove the rumour that he was dead; by the time that the conical helmet had been superseded by the circular helmet which could not be tilted back, the wearer had to identify himself by heraldic devices on shield and surcoat, the latter having come into fashion to protect the knight from the heat of the sun on chain mail which, worn over leather, had driven the early crusaders desperate with discomfort and thirst. The knights had also adopted the Muslim custom, probably derived through Persia from Central Asia, of putting pennons on lances, and the originally Asian custom of pounding drums, brought to reverberating climax by Timur Lenk as described by Ibn Khaldoun in 1401, who sat his horse to the thunder of drums "till the air shook".

With greater wealth and longer lineage the knight became self-consciously knightly in a way that the rough and ready self-made predators of Carolingian times had never been, and in feudal custom, as in the hunting field, a ritual grew up. The original granting of a fief had been simple: the vassal had put his hands between those of his lord and knighthood had been conferred by a clout on the back of the neck. Now, with more leisure, wealth and pride of descent, the ceremonial became elaborate, and a mystique of knightly honour grew up. Now the young candidate had to confess his sins, take a bath, and keep a vigil before an altar; then in the morning to be girt with belt, sword and spurs. Thus fully accoutred, he knelt before his lord who tapped him thrice with the flat of his sword and once, perhaps playfully, with his gauntlet on the cheek.

By the late twelfth century a new cult of *courtoisie* towards women had grown up, directed by convention by young bachelors towards supposedly inaccessible married ladies, who swooned over the romances of Geoffrey of Monmouth, whose writings were fashionable. It seems incongruous in a society still so tough, where the main concern of illiterate and knightly youth when not at war was with dangerous tournaments and stag, boar and wolf hunting. But it proved historically important; as Court circles were imitated, it enhanced the social standing of women. Instead of shutting them up, as did the Muslims in harems, the Christian aristocracy, following southern French fashion, invited them to go through doorways first, helped them to do many things they could quite well do for themselves, and enthroned them as arbiters in "*Courts of Love*". This did not prevent them having it both ways, and there are many records of invincible women defending castles and administering fiefs, nor is the convention as incongruous as it looks. Feudal institutions provided mainly for eldest sons, and the Courts of kings and great lords attracted the younger sons who hung about until they got their chance of making their fortune through war or by marriage to an heiress. Some, brought up to the life of the camp and the comradeship of arms, as at the fashionable and flashy court of William Rufus, became casually homosexual—to the disgust of St. Anselm, who denounced the fashion to the King himself. "If it is not speedily met with sentence of stern judgment coming from you and by vigorous discipline coming from the Church, the whole land," he warned, "will I declare become little better than Sodom itself." Strong words, but Rufus brushed them aside. "Enough," he said, brusquely, "say no more about it."[1]

By the later twelfth century others, unsatisfied by the local wenches available, started pining in the fashionable convention for "mistresses", a word which lacked its present connotation. Hence much showing off.

Tournaments, starting as mock battles staged to take prisoners and still very dangerous (*conflictus gallicus*—a *melée*), became formalized in the thirteenth century into "jousting". By defeating a series of wealthy opponents in single combat and obtaining their ransoms, a young knight of no fortune could make

[1]Eadmer. *History of Recent Events in England.* Trans. G. Bosanquet, with foreword by R. W. Southern. London, 1964. p. 50.

one: the career of William the Marshal, Earl of Pembroke, was based on a round of successful tournaments on both sides of the Channel, followed by fame equivalent, on its much grander level, to that of a modern cricket or football star, and by marriage to an heiress.

Under the veneer of good manners within their own class, the knights must have been arrogant and exclusive, an attribute accepted in an hierarchical society. They certainly looked down on clerks who could write as low-born technicians; even King John of England did not "sign" Magna Carta, but only had it sealed; not because, like the Conqueror (who could just make a cross), he could not write, but because it would have seemed below his dignity to do so on so formal an occasion. Chivalrous *courtoisie* did not extend to tradesmen, still less to peasants; though knights, if not then their ladies, would have been on easy terms with game-keepers and the like. But peasant *"villeins"* (from *villani*, men of the *villa*, an old Roman word) were regarded as brutish and uncouth, which by courtly standards they were. The word "villainous", after all, derives from them.

IV

Yet these *villeins*, from whom most modern Europeans and their descendants overseas derive, sustained the exotic civilization of Church, towns and aristocracy. As Piggott writes, "The essential rural economy which was to become historical Europe has roots which strike very far back into prehistoric antiquity."[1] The origins of the peasantry were at least Neolithic, for changes of rulers had been demographically superficial, and even the migrations of the *Völkerwanderung* had seldom been massive. Some of the peasants were descended from *coloni* in the late Roman Empire who had kept some hereditary tenure, if subject to forced labour on the demesne, and to payment in kind and later in money to their lords. Others, *borderii*, were in effect serfs; descendants perhaps of slaves on the big Roman estates still existing under the Merovingians. Degraded as the peasants were, and *adscripti glebae*, tied to the soil, they were not feckless migratory barbarians, idle when not at war, like the primitive Germans; and if they got little out of the small surplus they created, their energy was harnessed to relatively civilized ends. At the price of constant toil in a technologically primitive society they raised their own families, and were not, in the West, like the slaves on the Roman *latifundia* or in the slave states in North America, herded like animals and sometimes sold separately from their wives and children.

Moreover, in the north the primitive open field system with its strip cultivation, derived from barbarian times, made at least for equality in hardship and, save for famine years, subsistence. On a diet mainly of coarse bread, porridge, onions, garlic and cheese, supplemented by occasional pig meat and poultry, washed down for the more prosperous by great quantities of ale at all

[1]*Ancient Europe. op. cit.* p. 258.

hours (the English despised the French for drinking water and eating "bread right brown made of rye"), the peasants' hard lives were at least adapted to the seasons in a natural rhythm, quieter and more human than that of a modern megalopolitan slum.

With the greater prosperity of the thirteenth century, the peasants in Western Christendom were able collectively to buy themselves charters which limited the powers of their lords, and individually to secure tenure of their holdings; in Eastern Europe, on the other hand, where lands had been won by conquest and the peasantry were of Slav, Lithuanian, Lettish, Balt, and Wendish origin, they were levelled down into a common servility by landowners of alien descent, a contrast fateful to the future of Europe into modern times.

Though separated by so deep a social gulf from their superiors, the peasants had long assimilated the Christian religion in a form they could understand; though the Christian veneer was sometimes thin over pagan practices, local saints equated with older gods, strange ceremonies of the old religion still performed and the usual sexual jollities continued thinly disguised, medieval society was generally pervaded from top to bottom by common beliefs. The Church had cleverly taken over the main pagan feasts of the agricultural year, and the cult of the relics of local saints was widely followed. When famine and pestilence struck, the people were united in begging their saints to intervene and protesting their penitence before God.

The little colour in their lives came from the ceremonies of the Church; as in megalithic times when the stones of Carnac, Avebury and Stonehenge were dragged into place by a work force that believed in the cult, so now the people, including the peasantry, dragged great loads of stone to build the cathedral at Chartres. Societies which, like fifth-century Athens and twelfth- and thirteenth-century France, believe in themselves and are united by a common creed and purpose, erect the most lasting monuments and devise the most influential ideas. Universities, princely courts, bustling towns, and a peasantry that believed in their religion combined to make the high Middle Ages one of the most creative epochs in European history.

V

The most impressive manifestations of this cosmopolitan Christian civilization which symbolize and sum it up are the splendid Gothic cathedrals of the twelfth and thirteenth centuries; and the superb sculpture and stained glass, a new invention designed both to enhance the splendour of the buildings and to familiarize the illiterate majority with the essentials of the Christian faith. Where the Romanesque cathedrals were sustained by the sheer mass of their walls, and got their effect by breadth as much as height, the new Gothic[1]

[1] It was retrospectively and contemptuously so called in the fifteenth century by neo-classical architects who disliked it as northern and Germanic, and who regarded the Goths as particularly barbarous owing to their sack of Rome under Alaric.

soared upwards on interlaced arched ribs above slender columns, and held
lateral thrust by flying buttresses. A natural architecture for the north, where
rain and snow demanded high-pitched roofs and great windows for light, and
where the forest pervaded men's imagination, it was also typically medieval in
following an overall design, like an ordered scholastic argument, and just as
fantastically ambitious as the theology of St. Thomas who sought to explain
the universe. And the size of these enormous buildings with their pointed
arches, derived perhaps from the East, was out of all proportion to the
resources of the still mainly rustic society which financed and built them.

Gothic developed gradually out of the ambitious Romanesque of Autun and
of Durham, which contains the finest high rib vaulting in Europe, and its first
great patron was Suger, Abbot of St. Denis in France (fl. 1136), where it first
came into fashion; Laon, Noyon, Soissons and Sens were all built in the twelfth
century, and the greatest masterpiece of all was begun at Chartres in 1194
after the earlier Romanesque cathedral had been burnt down. Amiens, with its
staggering elaborate west front, was begun in 1220, the same year as Salisbury,
the most perfect thirteenth-century Gothic English cathedral; and by the end
of the century the style had spread over most of Europe, to northern Italy at
Siena (1227), the Rhineland, and into Hungary and Bohemia, though not to
southern Italy where classical and Byzantium influence was too strong.

The architects were not, as often supposed, clergy, but respected and well
organized lay professionals. Some of them won personal fame; as in the
thirteenth century that widely travelled Picard, Villard de Honnecourt, whose
sketchbook shows the grasp of geometrical and engineering principles that the
creators of these soaring and complicated edifices must have possessed.[1] As
John Betjeman puts it, they were "engineers in stone".[2] Since their designs
were functional and the cathedrals were designed to drive home the teachings
of Christianity, sculptured figures were grouped about the main portals
depicting the Passion of Christ, the Resurrection and, particularly, the Last
Judgement, which most of the congregations doubtless had good cause to fear.
Hence opportunities for sculptors, opportunities which they took, as over the
centre doorway in the west front at Chartres, with Christ enthroned, or the
elongated figures which flank the great west door. As Kenneth Clark writes,
they are carved "in a style as still and restrained and classical as [that of] the
Greek sculptors of the sixth century". He goes on to speculate "that whereas
the chief master's style is absolutely Greek in the simplicity and precision of
every fold. Was it really Greek .. in derivation? Were these reed-like
draperies, the thin straight lines of the fluted folds, the zigzag hems, and the
whole play of texture which so obviously recall a Greek archaic figure, arrived
at independently? Or had the Chartres master seen some fragments of early
Greek sculpture in the South of France . . . ?"[3] He concludes that he had.

Indeed, some of the statues at Chartres in poise, economy of design and
serenity of aspect can compare with the best Greek and Chinese sculpture;

[1] And also that he had studied statues from Antiquity. See P. Frankl. The Gothic:
Literary Sources and Interpretations. Princeton University Press, 1960.
[2] Ghastly Good Taste. New Edition. London, 1970. p. 26.
[3] Kenneth Clark. Civilisation. op cit. p. 55.

but the stained glass, an original twelfth-century invention, is unique—the finest in the world, surpassing anything made since. It was devised partly through the inspiration of the paintings which, themselves imitating mosaics, decorated the broad wall spaces of Romanesque cathedrals and churches, and in part through following the illumination of manuscripts then coming into fashion. For its object was to illustrate; as Suger declared, "to show the people what to believe". The oldest glass is the best, as exemplified in the west window at Chartres (c. 1150) which was part of the original Romanesque building and survived the fire. For a relatively primitive technique got the finest effects, and it was simple: the glass was made of one part river sand to two parts beechwood ash, with some charred bracken added and a little salt. This was "kept red hot for several hours, and it is no accident that Chartres became a centre for glass making, for in the surrounding districts a particularly fine river sand is found."[1]

Glass made of sand and wood ash is light green; but under intense heat the Chartres glass could turn pink, red or purple from the manganese in the bracken; yellow can be obtained by adding iron, red from copper, and blue from cobalt. "With these somewhat primitive means the glaziers obtained a range of colours of unsurpassed splendour," and "between these rich primary colours fine gradations of tone were effected, perhaps more by accident than design—olive green . . . a neutral brown and a soft purple merging into brown or pink." The glass, being coloured throughout, had to be made very thin to let through the light, and the "tonal beauty of the older windows is in part due to the very imperfection of this technique. The unequal thickness of the panes, the inclusion of little air bubbles and grains of sand create sparkling refractions of light."[2] But the artists were responsible for the faultless juxtaposition of colours. Later methods of painting enamel on to plain glass and firing it in could not get such brilliant effects.

Once made, the glass had to be fitted into the intricate framework which held it in great panels against the light. The result, still of staggering richness, must have been enhanced when most of the interior of the building had been covered in a dull red wash, with scroll work perhaps in black, so that the pilgrim "walked into an unimaginable painted wonder . . . an attempt . . . to create a semblance of Heaven on earth, with their stone, colour, music and ritual."[3]

The only things comparable to the medieval stained glass are the best mosaics of late Antiquity, and, splendid as they are, they do not have the full translucency of the finest windows. As old Persian rugs, made with vegetable dyes, far surpass modern imitations, so stained glass made by the old methods outclasses anything made in modern times. The variety of effects is vast, ranging from large figures of kings and patriarchs, sometimes realistically portrayed with dark eastern faces, and broadly outlined in bold designs, to the extremely complicated "storied" windows giving the human descent of Christ

[1] Alfons Dierick. The Stained Glass at Chartres. Hallweg. Berne. p. 4, on which this account is mainly based.
[2] Dierick. op. cit.
[3] John Betjeman. A Pictorial History of English Architecture. London, 1972. p. 31.

or narrating a series of biblical stories. The most decorative French invention
was the "rose" window, which achieves a complicated distribution of coloured
light through small jewel-like apertures. And these windows were not presented only by royalties, ecclesiastics and magnates, but often by merchant or
craft guilds.

The military architecture of the twelfth century remained fairly simple,
though extremely massive and formidable; as at Chateau Gaillard, Richard I of
England's great stronghold on the Lower Seine, or at the castle of the counts
of Anjou at Angers. Both in town and country the nucleus of defence was the
keep; in the latter, surrounded by earthworks with a bank and a ditch. But the
keep alone was inadequate to house a garrison and its horses, so that walls
were extended around it. The knights still did not regularly inhabit these
strongholds; they preferred to live in hunting lodges and manor houses and
retreat to the castles in emergency. Moreover, the really massive and elaborate
castles such as Chateau Gaillard or Chinon were built by kings or very great
noblemen who alone could afford them, and are not representative of anything
but the exotic life of courts. But it is not until the late thirteenth century that
castle building comes to its expansive climax, as in Edward I's immense castles
in Wales, and the most spectacular relics are those which have been enlarged
and lived in during the later middle ages.

The typical life of the twelfth-century nobility was not, unless a major war
was going on, one of mail-clad clanking garrison duty, through echoing
staircases as the guards were changed, but rather one of leisured idleness
during which the nobles moved about from one manor house to another on
their scattered estates, and in which the main excitement was hunting and
hawking or organized jousting with entrance fees graded according to rank.

VI

There was thus time enough for elaborate sentiments of love to become the
fashion, particularly when the climate was genial, and the vernacular poetry of
the *Langue d'Oc* or *Midi* was gay, sensual and short-lived. Its exponents were
the *troubadours*, of whom William Count of Poitiers (1071–1126) is the best
known. They were mainly rather precious courtiers, either magnates themselves or impoverished gentry who gravitated to the courts. But they were
original in creating the classic forms of French poetry—the *aubade*, the
pastourelle, the *ballade*, the *virelai*. They imitated the Arabs and celebrated the
dancing girls captured during the Reconquista in Spain, making a cult of girls
and women which the Merovingians of either sex would have thought soft.
This sort of thing was snuffed out in the thirteenth century by the northern
barons let loose by Innocent III against the *Midi* in the Albigensian "crusade".

In the north, in the *Langue d'Oil*, the vernacular poets emerged later; but
they had a more popular audience, as did the *trouvères* at the early twelfth-
century court of Thibaut, Count of Champagne, and the *jongleurs* among the
bourgeoisie of the thriving cloth towns, as at Arras. Later on, as one would

expect, an urban public relished the satires of the Parisian Rutebeuf (1256–85), already in the sharp and knowing Gallic tradition. Rutebeuf is the first knock-about French poet and satirist who attacked the Church, the university establishment and the Friars, castigated his public for not supporting Louis IX's crusade against Tunis and complained of his own poverty in racy colloquial terms. He is a world away from the *Chanson de Roland*.

The *jongleurs* also recited stories of *Renard the Fox* and *Tibert the Cat*, probably of Flemish origin, for the characters have German-sounding names, though they may have come originally from the East. From c. 1250 we have the romance of *Aucassin et Nicolette*, written to be sung in prose and verse, which has more human interest than the long rather maundering allegories of the slightly earlier *Roman de la Rose*, both of which were immensely popular and widely imitated.

Out in the West in the mid-twelfth century, Geoffrey of Monmouth on the south Welsh border, with Celtic romantic imagination, had launched the popular legend of "King Arthur" who ruled all *Ynys Bridan*, the *British Isle*, in the *Historia Regum Britanniae*, dedicated to Mathilda's half-brother, William of Gloucester, thus bringing Welsh folk tales, though not the Welsh vernacular, into fashionable European court literature.

By the late twelfth century, the Germans devised the *Nibelungenlied* (c. 1190), the weird and tragic epic resuscitated by Wagner, with its surly giants, capricious water sprites and valkyries who pounce on those fated to die in battle, all pervaded by the anger of murky, passionate, incalculable and envious gods. It is in the same descent as *Beowulf*, with a similar obsession with violence and gloom and fate, and culminates in cosmic Teutonic disaster. The German court poets, on the other hand, would use French forms, as in the poems of the *Minnesinger* Walter von der Vogelweide (d. c.1228), who achieves a singularly natural freshness; as in the well-known *Unter der Linde an der Heide* "under the lime tree on the heath", and who in his political verse would take the side of the German emperors against the foreign Pope, concluding, as the conflict between them mounted, that "honour was dead". But the *Minnesinger* would remain court poets, and would never, like the French *jongleurs*, have a wide popular audience. In the development of German literature their influence was limited and evanescent.

XVIII

Imperium or *Ecclesia?*

While these creative and original cultural and social movements were setting in, European power politics at the summit and their military and political consequences rumbled like an intermittent thunderstorm around Western Christendom. A cosmopolitan civilization, officially united by Catholic Christian beliefs, was afflicted by a contest between Empire and Papacy for an impracticable power, each side claiming divine sanction for supreme authority.

The other disaster for Christendom was that in 1204 Byzantium, the centre of Orthodox Christian civilization in Eastern Europe, but since 1054 officially schismatic in Rome, was crippled by the Fourth Crusade, when the Venetians diverted the Western Crusaders to wreck their trade rival and plunder its sphere of influence. So, while in Catholic Christendom "secular" and "spiritual" powers fought each other and left the way open for the rulers of dynastic realms to assert a secular and absolute sovereignty, and even decide their subjects' religion, in Orthodox Christendom the defences of the East were weakened against a new enemy, the Ottoman Turks, while political and doctrinal conflict rent the Balkans, and after the destruction of Kievan Russia by the Mongols, Muscovy became the "Third Rome"—the Orthodox heir of Byzantium.

Both Emperors and Popes operated on a European scale, and it is astonishing, given the communications at the time, how much territory the Emperors traversed and what immense projects they attempted during a struggle which lasted from the accession of Friedrich I (Barbarossa, Red Beard as the Italians called him) in 1152 to the death of his grandson Frederick II (*il re Federigo*, to his Sicilian subjects, and to himself Fridericus)[1] in 1250.

Friedrich Barbarossa (1152–90, emperor, 1155) seemed the ideal feudal king. He was extremely handsome, a soldier and ruler of untiring energy and panache, with the knightly virtures of charm, good manners and lavish generosity. He had vast and romantic ambitions, and he was also a formidable legislator and diplomat. He could read Latin, though apparently he could not

[1]He is said to have had the thumb of a secretary cut off for spelling it Fredericus.

speak it fluently, and he was steeped in the history of the Roman Empire as it was then understood, as well as in the newly revived Roman Law, so that he believed himself the heir not merely of Charlemagne (whose canonization he arranged) but of Constantine and Justinian. He claimed nothing less than *Weltmacht* as leader of all Christendom; but for the Italians he was always merely *Imperator Theutonicus*.

In Germany he at once had to face constant disorder and private war, and the already ancient feud between Welf and Waiblingen, which, as a descendant of both families, he attempted to assuage. This feud went back to the death, without descendants, of the emperor Heinrich V (of Hohenstaufen and Waiblingen), who had married Mathilda of England, when, passing over his nephew, Friedrich the One-Eyed of Swabia, the electors had chosen Lothar of Supplinberg, Duke of Saxony. Lothar had married his daughter and heiress to Heinrich Welf, Duke of Bavaria, and their son, having inherited both Duchies, had been known as Heinrich the Proud. His son, Heinrich the Lion, had inherited vast territories and become the head of the Welf interest, as Barbarossa was head of the Waiblingen or Hohenstaufen factions. When the conflict spread south of the Alps, the Italians, unable to pronounce the German names, termed Welfs and Waiblingens, Guelphs and Ghibellines. The former generally fought for the Pope, the latter for the Emperor.

After being chosen King of Germany by the Electors at Frankfurt, Friedrich proceeded by boat down the Main and Rhine in slow medieval state to Trifels, then by land for his coronation at Aachen. He proclaimed a general "land peace" to stop private war, hanged persistent and eminent offenders and destroyed their castles. In 1155 he made an example of the Count Palatine of the Rhine and ten of his followers by reviving an old Frankish custom whereby knightly offenders had to carry dogs for a mile—a shocking disgrace.[1]

The problem of the great tribal Duchies was even more urgent, and Friedrich, who in 1153 had come to a friendly understanding by correspondence with Pope Eugenius III, tried to divert the energies of the turbulent *Reichsfürsten* to the East. Heinrich the Lion, for example, son-in-law of Henry II of England and Aquitaine, was given a free hand against the Balts, Wends and Slavs. By 1160 he had founded Lübeck and, in rivalry with Albrecht the Bear of Brandenburg, extended German power and colonization far to the north-east. Friedrich himself supported the pro-German faction in Poland, and in 1158 created Wenzel of Bohemia a puppet king. Most importantly, he solved the dispute over Bavaria between Heinrich the Lion, who founded Munich in 1158, and Heinrich Jasomirgott (so called for his favourite expletive) by creating a separate Duchy of Austria for the latter. He also attempted, without much success, to enforce his own rule over Burgundy. Like the Saxon emperors, Friedrich depended heavily on the great churchmen, whom he

[1] It is not known what sort of dogs. Boxers or hunting dogs would have been unwieldy; Dachshunds, though all too articulate, would have been more portable. There could have been danger as well as disgrace: medieval dogs were often savage, and one method of execution was to hang a criminal up with a dog, then beat the animal, which, in rage, savaged the bound victim's face. This was done at the execution of a Brugeois assassin of one of the Counts of Flanders in the twelfth century.

appointed himself and whose property he took over if opportunity served. He thus revived the old investiture controversy and provoked the wrath of Adrian IV, the only English Pope.

So his settlement of Germany was precarious, for he had won the support of the *Reichsfürsten* only by giving them too free a hand, and weakened the imperial power just when in France, England and Sicily the kings were creating centralized realms. From being a relatively simple pattern of tribal duchies, Germany became divided into a much greater number of feudal principalities, even more impossible to govern. Such improvisation had been inevitable, for the country had to be settled somehow before Friedrich could assert his imperial power over Italy; and then the constant expeditions he made over the Alps jeopardized his work in Germany.

In 1154 he first set out for Rome where, in difficult circumstances that winter, Adrian IV was elected Pope (1154-59).[1] For the Romans, led by the revolutionary Arnold of Brescia, had set up a shortlived republic, and the Normans of the south refused to recognize Adrian's election. Friedrich could only be crowned in the early morning, and the Romans attacked the Lateran, to be dispersed by the German troops. Pope and Emperor then prudently left for Tivoli; but after Friedrich had returned to Germany, Adrian IV concluded an alliance with the Normans, a policy considered hostile by the Emperor. Relations, always uneasy, were not improved when the Pope wrote to Friedrich in language which implied he had conferred the empire upon him as a "*benefice*" or fief.

By the second Italian expedition of 1158, Adrian was inciting the citizens of Lombardy to revolt, and was only prevented by his death in 1159 from excommunicating the Emperor. This Englishman had time, however, to grant Ireland to the Angevin Henry II, since all islands converted to Christianity belonged to the Papacy, and since the King, it was hoped, would be able to civilize the Irish.

Early in his reign, Barbarossa thus came in conflict with the Pope and was distracted from the government of Germany by his Italian ambitions. And well he might be. In 1158 he had crossed the Alps with 6000 knights and their attendants, a host so big that they crossed by four different passes; he then captured the great city of Milan, and at the Diet of Roncaglia forced the Lombard cities—republics anomalous in a feudal world and despised by Barbarossa and his Knights—to restore the imperial *regalia* of rights of taxation, customs dues and river and canal tolls. The infuriated Italians rose in revolt. Whereat Barbarossa razed most of Milan to the ground. This atrocity, like others by armies of occupation, proved counter-productive; and by 1167 the

---

[1]Nicholas Breakspear, a native of Langley, came of obscure origin, and began his career as a monk in the neighbouring abbey of St. Albans. He became a servitor in the abbey of St. Rufus, Valence, of which he became prior. In 1146 he was made Cardinal of Albano and sent on a mission to Norway, where he founded the see of Drontheim. As Pope, as a follower of the policy of Gregory VII, he was uncompromising; and although he depended on the Germans to establish his authority in Rome, he refused Friedrich the kiss of peace until he had led his palfrey by the bridle in view of the army. Thus the poor boy from St. Albans disputed the primacy of Christendom with an emperor.

wealthy cities had sunk their mutual animosities in a *Societas Lombardiae*—a Lombard League. Lying across the imperial communications with Germany, it proved extremely dangerous.

Still determined to clamp his power on all Italy, even on the Normans, in 1167 Barbarossa occupied Rome, where Alexander III (1159–81) took refuge near the Colosseum, then fled to Gaeta and on to Benevento. By now it was August, and the German camp was stricken with epidemic fever: in his forced retreat over the Apennines, Friedrich's best officers and most of his army perished. With only a few followers he managed to reach Susa, whence he returned to quell disturbances in Germany. He had united the Pope, the Lombard cities and the Normans against him.

Undeterred, in 1174 Barbarossa again crossed the Alps, but without the support of Heinrich the Lion, his most powerful subject. Two years later he was utterly defeated at Legnano, north-west of Milan, where the Milanese defended their standard on its *carroccio* or wagon so well and counterattacked so fiercely that Friedrich himself had to fly the field.

Forced to accept reality at last, he prostrated himself in the porch of St. Mark's at Venice before Alexander III. Then, having made peace with the Lombard League, he returned to Germany to take his revenge on Heinrich. Based on the Swabian domain, on Franconia and the Palatinates, Friedrich, with the help of the imperial cities—of which Regensburg and Nürnberg were the most wealthy—managed to drive his most dangerous enemy from Germany and secure his own position in the short, if not the long, term by assigning Heinrich's lands to the major princes. In 1184, at the Diet of Mainz, with his Italian defeats behind him, Friedrich appeared supreme in Germany, though he had succeeded only by putting too much weight on tenuous feudal ties and diminishing the power of the crown. It was impossible to rule Germany and be *Imperator Theutonicus* of Italy as well.

But Friedrich was still determined to master the Italians; and in 1186 he negotiated a marriage of the first dynastic consequence between his son Heinrich and Constance, heiress of Norman Sicily, the richest realm in Europe. He thus caught the Papacy between two fires, made it possible for Heinrich to occupy Italy and Sicily as the Emperor Heinrich VI, and also the extraordinary sequel—the fantastic career of his own grandson, Frederick II.

But Barbarossa was finally distracted by yet another obligation. Grave news had arrived from Outremer: the Kurdish prince Salah-al-din had united the hitherto rival powers of Baghdad and Cairo, defeated the Christian occupying army at Hattin west of Lake Tiberias, and threatened Jerusalem. In 1198, the now ageing Emperor set out on his last impracticable quest—the Third Crusade. Two years later he was drowned in the river Saleph—the modern Gocksu in southern Asia Minor, "a fatal and odious river", writes a contemporary, "in which—what grief!—this entirely shining example was extinguished!" "For the emperor, though dissuaded by his companions, (*dissuadentibus his qui secum erant*) insisted in entering the river to refresh and wash himself (*ad refrigerendum se et lavandum*)"; but he got tired and began to sink and, though they tried to reach him by swimming and on horseback, he was carried away.[1] "Having dined after intolerable labours," says another account, "since he wished to bathe in the said water and so refresh himself by swimming" he was unexpectedly submerged.[2]

II

Eight years after Friedrich Barbarossa had perished, and with him his attempts as the "secular arm" of a cosmopolitan Christendom to dominate most of Europe, Lothar of Segni, Innocent III (1198–1216), endeavoured to become its spiritual overlord with more success. Lothar of Segni came on his father's side father's side from nobility in the Campagna, on his mother's from the aristocracy of Rome. He studied Canon law at Paris and Bologna, and was only thirty-seven when elected Pope. He had an untiring grasp of detail and administrative flair, and his private life was austere. He saw himself as the moral arbiter of Christendom; comparing his own power to that of the sun and the Imperial power to that of the moon—"the lesser light". He was only fifty-five when he died of malaria at Perugia. He was a statesman and administrator rather than a theologian, though he laid down the dogma of Transubstantiation which later caused so much conflict.

His objectives, like those of Adrian IV, were those of Gregory VII; but given a new precision by a great lawyer and administrator, the head of a vast organization centring on the Roman *curia*, a bureaucracy which far surpassed anything else in the West at the time. If anyone could have imposed a spiritual leadership by authority rather than persuasion or example, Innocent III might have done it; but his authoritarian claims, pushed further by Gregory IX, Innocent IV and Boniface VIII, led to schism and conflict with the laity. Certainly, however, he raised the temporal power of the Papacy to new heights and canalized the enthusiasm of the Dominican and Franciscan friars in a counter-reformation against heresies that then, as much as in Luther's time, challenged central doctrines of the Church, so that the Papal Inquisition was now first devised, though it was not fully launched until the pontificate of Innocent IV.

Gregory VII had considered himself the "Vicar" of St. Peter: Innocent III claimed to be the "Vicar" of Christ. As such he claimed "plenitude of power" over all Christians, clerical and lay. At the great Lateran Council of 1215 he and his advisers tried to make the Church separate and superior to the rest of society; celibate, authoritarian, disciplined, and efficient; ruled by a priest king or "*Gubernator Mundi; minor Deo, sed ultra hominem*, the Ruler of the World, less than God but more than Man", who could judge princes and be judged by none. Innocent also insisted on auricular confession, thus enhancing the hold of the priests over their flocks, the *oves Christi*—the sheep of Christ; and he

[1]*Historia Peregrinorum. Monumenta Germanica Historica, Tomus* V. Berlin, 1928. p. 172.
[2]*Cum vellet balneare in eadem aqua, et ita se refrigerare vellet natando. Epistola de Morte Friderici Imperatoris. Monumenta Germanae Historica.* V. p. 177.

ordered the clergy to cultivate learning and eloquence, and denounce sexual sin, while he himself freely excommunicated even princes for it. Convinced of his rectitude and authority, he plunged into power politics with a clear conscience as part of his duty to secure order, justice and peace. Once committed to assert Papal authority by force, Innocent III became enmeshed in the tortuous and violent expedients which increased under Gregory IX and Innocent IV.

The two major commitments were over the succession to the empire and over the Papal States. Barbarossa's son, Heinrich VI, had managed to occupy most of Italy and Sicily. Apparently set to realize Barbarossa's design, he had died in 1197, the year before Lothar of Segni became Pope. He had left two potential Hohenstaufen heirs; his brother Philip of Swabia, and his son "Federigo", aged three. Anxious to break the German hold on the Papal States, and claiming the right to arbitrate, Innocent III now deliberately pushed Germany and Italy into a new bout of Guelph/Ghibelline warfare by backing Otto of Brunswick, son of Heinrich the Lion and grandson of Henry II of England, as Guelph candidate for the Empire. But, passing over the prior claim of Federigo, as he was a child, the Germans in 1198 defied the Pope and elected Philip of Swabia; ten years later he was assassinated by Otto of Wittelsbach, to whom he had refused the hand of his daughter. Being in the habit of fencing with the emperor, Otto arrived at court with a drawn (and sharpened) sword, and on Philip's declaring that he had no mind to fence that day, remarked that he had no mind to fence that day either, and ran the emperor through.

The Ghibellines then turned to the other Hohenstaufen heir, Federigo, King of Sicily. Whereat Innocent III switched his support to young Federigo, already his ward, as the lesser evil than Otto IV, who had failed to vacate the Papal States, in the hope that he would be more amenable, *sperans quod melior patre foret; sed qualis pater, talis filius, et etiam longe deterior fuit inventus*.[1] For when in 1211 the Ghibelline faction in Germany elected the boy to the empire as Frederick II (1211–1250), he was to prove the most dangerous and brilliant enemy of the Papacy.

III

The long term strategy of Friedrich Barbarossa when he had married his son Heinrich to Constance heiress of Norman Sicily in 1186 had now paid off. Young Frederick was now both King of the cosmopolitan Mediterranean *Regno* of Sicily and emperor-elect of the huge Hohenstaufen realm in Germany.

The *Regno* was always his most valuable possession. Long so well organized and wealthy that it surpassed any other kingdom, Norman Sicily had been

---

[1]"Hoping that he would be better than his father. But like father, like son, and he was found to be far worse." *Chronica Fratris Salimbene de Adam, Ordinis Minorum.* ed. O. Holder-Egger in *Monumenta Germaniae Historica*. Vol. VI. Hannover, 1905–13. p. 359.

better administered even than England, the other insular Norman conquest, where successive and ferocious Norman kings had consolidated a base for the more centralized government of the Angevin Henry II. In Sicily the descendants of the original adventurer, Tancred de Hauteville, had reigned over a polyglot court in which Byzantine, Muslim and Catholic Christian influences were blended into a brilliant civilization, still commemorated by the superb and spirited decorations of the Capella Palatina at Palermo and in the elegant cloisters at Monreale, where a Mediterranean sun glitters on the spiralling mosaics of column and capital.

The *Regno*, a kingdom since 1130, when Roger II had obtained the recognition of the Pope, had long been solvent and tolerant. Here pagan Antiquity had never quite given place to medieval Christendom, and the same riches in corn, wine, flocks and fish that had long made the island a prize fought for by Greeks, Romans, Carthaginians and Vandals, and the setting for some of the best Greek and Latin pastoral poetry, were now protected by a Norman fleet financed by the best organized exchequer in Europe outside Constantinople. By the Assize of Artano Roger II (1127–54) had imposed laws after Justinian's Code, and a financial system based on the Arab *diwan*, using Arabic numerals instead of the clumsy Roman reckoning.

Another event had then intervened. Roger II's attacks on the Byzantine empire in Greece had failed, and William II, known as "The Good", presumably in contrast to his father, Roger II's successor, William "The Bad" and most of his other relations, had lost Salonika; the Normans had thus been compelled to concentrate on the compact Sicilian kingdom itself and on Southern Italy, where in 1138 Roger II had conquered Naples. Such was the kingdom that Barbarossa's grandson, young Frederick, had inherited.

In 1212 Frederick's fortunes had further changed, when a German delegation had arrived in Palermo to offer him the German crown. He had accepted it, and, proceeding to Genoa by sea and crossing the Alps to Coire, he had descended on Konstanz, which he had occupied a few hours before Otto IV. He had then established himself at the great castle of Hagenau in Alsace, where the hunting was excellent.

Then, two years later, in 1214 Frederick had another stroke of luck. Philippe Auguste of France totally defeated Otto IV and his English-backed coalition at Bouvines and ruined him: symbolically the French King sent young Frederick Otto's Imperial banner. So, in July 1215, Frederick was crowned at Aachen and his title soon confirmed by the Fourth Lateran Council in Rome; that December he presented his son young Heinrich to the Princes of the empire at Nürnberg. By 1219 the child was elected King of the Romans.

IV

When in 1216 Innocent III died, still comparatively young, he had thus sustained a major political defeat in the thunderous conflict at the summit of Christendom between Empire and Papacy. But he had proved a great administrator of a better-organized and more comprehensive European Church, and if his ventures into power politics at the summit had proved disastrous, he had been more successful in harnessing the enthusiasm of the new Dominican and Franciscan friars to combat heresy and invigorate Western Christendom.

When in 1198 Innocent III had become Pope the *Cathari* heretics of Languedoc, who had found patrons in the ill-organized dominions of Raymond VI, Count of Toulouse, were already becoming a menace. Following the Manichees of Persia, who had influenced St. Augustine, they believed that the Creation itself was evil; a casualty in the eternal struggle between the Good Mind and the Spirit that Denies, between Light and Darkness. These deleterious, if plausible, doctrines had first taken root among the Bulgar Orthodox Christians, and by the mid-tenth century among the Bulgars in Constantinople itself, where in 1100 the emperor Alexius Comnenos, after shipping off the First Crusade to Asia Minor and Palestine, had one of the Bulgar leaders burnt. But in Bulgaria they had not been extirpated: their influence and organization had spread to Bosnia and thence into the Catholic West, into northern Italy and southern France, where the weaker brethren among the heretics got a bad name. Indeed the term "Bulgar"—in French "*bougre*"—became, and has remained, pejorative.

These *Bogomils*, as they called themselves after their founder Bogomil (Old Slavonic for "God-loving"), spread their conviction that God could not have been responsible for anything so appalling as the Creation, so that the world was the domain of Satan. The Creation, they declared, had been a botched mistake: the only way to salvation was a complete renunciation of the world. This view of life, perhaps propagated by heretical Armenians, had won many adherents. They had created a vast organization extending from Central Asia to the West, and their ascetic elite of *Cathari* or "Purified Ones" claimed to have escaped the bondage of the Creation and become part of the World of Light and Good Mind. The great majority of the heretics, called *Believers*, made no pretence at attaining such virtues, but denied all morality in a world hopelessly corrupt. The supreme crime, they believed, was to get children, thus mixing up more Light and Darkness. So long as this consequence was avoided, they advocated, and may well have practised, an unbridled and omnivorous sexuality.

From the centre of this religion among the Bogomils in Bulgaria, "bishops" and missionaries had been sent out to the West, and even quasi-bishops established in Toulouse, Carcassonne and Albi, as also in Milan, Florence and Bergamo. They ministered to congregations drawn mainly from artisans, though a few disillusioned aristocrats also became *Believers*, if not *Cathari*, whose austerities were very exacting. Soon this underground movement had its influence in politics, business and village life, and when, in 1208, a papal legate arrived to deal with this parody of the Church, he was assassinated.

The challenge to the Church was total. The heretics denied that the Incarnate Christ had redeemed the Creation, and so undermined the concept of a coherent and basically benevolent cosmic order which the Church had built up. God had failed, and so had Christ: the Church was a fraud, and, if anyone was in charge, it was the Devil. Some heretics believed that he was a fallen Angel; others that he was a God in his own right, a belief which linked up with primeval cults of the old pagan gods, still widespread in superficially Christianized areas. The doctrine took on better in the realistic south than in the relatively sentimental north, and encouraged the revival of a paganism that was never far below the surface. Moreover, it attracted many intelligent people, all too experienced in the facts of medieval life.

The proliferation of heresies was in part a symptom of the twelfth-century intellectual resurgence; for a thousand years in the West few people had been in a condition to invent abstractions, and the intellectuals at Charlemagne's court had been preoccupied with grammar and rhetoric. A popular common ground was dislike of the wealth and pride of the Church and of priestly pretensions, so that even those who rejoiced in the Creation and accepted the Gospel thought the Church irrelevant. Of these other and potential heretics St. Francis of Assisi (1182–1226) is the most famous. The son of a well-to-do cloth merchant, he enjoyed wealth; then he suddenly became converted to extreme asceticism. But, unlike the Cathari, he had an unmedieval love of nature and animals; he renounced his inheritance, disowned his family and preached with missionary zeal what must have appeared to most people an hysterical cult of universal love. If the Cathari dropped out of organized society and relied on the charity of the Believers for sustenance out of loathing for the Creation, St. Francis became a homeless beggar for love of it. He is said to have had particular powers over animals. He converted a wolf at Gubbio from its predatory ways in return for regular rations, and was on excellent terms with various birds. As a Holy Man he carried conviction among the Muslims when in 1219 he visited Egypt, and even entered the Muslim camp where he was well received.

Innocent III, with a shrewd eye for the needs of the Church, canalized both the enthusiasm of St. Francis and his followers, and also that of a more intellectual band of brothers founded by a Spaniard. Indeed Domingo de Guzman—St. Dominic—set out specifically to combat subversion by the Cathari. St. Dominic (c. 1170–1221), unlike St. Francis a masterful organizer, came of minor Castilian nobility. In 1203 he accompanied the Bishop of Osma to Provence, where he encountered Cathari. He was authorized to preach against them at Toulouse by Innocent III, after its capture by the North French crusaders from Raymond VI, its Count, brother-in-law to the excommunicated John of England, who had married Isabelle of Angoulême. In 1215 Dominic went to Rome, and may have encountered St. Francis on the journey; in the following year his Order of "Black Friars" was sanctioned by Honorius III. It was developed with great strategic insight and by 1220 its method of government was devised at Bologna, where, after extensive travels in France and Italy, the founder died in the following year. Both these originally mendicant orders were distinct from the monks: they lived and preached among the laity, and called themselves fratres—friars or "brothers". Their influence proved pervasive, not least at the courts of kings, in the towns, and in the universities, where many of the most famous scholars were friars. The tolerance and insight of Innocent III had mobilized their zeal for the Church.

In case persuasion did not work, by the 1230s the Papacy would also organize its own *Inquisition* against the heretics, fully professional and independent of any amateur lynching by the populace or of the efforts of local bishops and princes. So the counter-attack on heresy, signalized by the Albigensian crusade, at its height from 1208 to 1218,[1] in which the barons of northern France had destroyed most of the culture of the Midi, now went on apace. By the end of the thirteenth century the heresy had been stamped out; its hierarchy had disintegrated, and the Church Triumphant and its Inquisition controlled north Italy and southern France and became established in Spain. The Inquisition was, however, rejected by the Teutonic peoples, including the Scandinavians and the English. Konrad of Marburg, its main protagonist in Germany, was assassinated in 1233; and later in northern France the converted heretic Robert le Bougre, so called since he never lived down his *Cathar* origins, was deposed for excessive rigour. Though the Papacy issued the Bull *Ad Exterpanda* of 1252—that heretics could be tortured, flogged and starved, condemned to life imprisonment and confiscation of property and handed over to the "Secular Arm" to be roasted alive in an *auto-da-fé*, or "act of faith"—the Inquisition thoroughly took root only in north Italy, southern France, and, of course, in Spain, where it would long remain popular.

V

While Innocent III had been contending with heretics in Provence and northern Italy, Frederick had been securing his realm in the Germanies. With the death of the great Pope, his prospects looked deceptively good. He was no longer the "Boy from Apulia"—a term originally not of romantic admiration but of scorn—but the King of Germany and prospective *Imperator semper Augustus* of the secular *Imperium* of Christendom; an empire part of the Divine order of the world, as the Pope was head of its spiritual order. But in pursuit of this vision, and to gain the support of the Church and the great German princes, Frederick, like Barbarossa, had paid a heavy price. By 1220 he had granted immense privileges to the German Church, making it a realm within the realm, and further encouraged the fragmentation of lay principalities initiated by Barbarossa.

Frederick, though crowned at Aachen, was still technically only Emperor elect: he therefore in the autumn of 1220 descended on Italy through the Brenner to be crowned by the new Pope, Honorius III, at Rome. Having lent himself to spectacular festivities in the City, he was soon crowned with the Crown of Charlemagne. Then he returned to Sicily, the realm he cared most about, to set that, too, in order.

Now at the height of his power, "radiant", as he wrote, "with the glory of the title of the Caesars" and *semper Augustus*, Frederick II, *Immutator* (Transformer) rather than *Stupor, Mundi,* was a handsome man; well built, of

[1]See Jonathan Sumption. *The Albigensian Crusade.* London, 1978, for a good account.

medium stature, with auburn hair and blue eyes. The Franciscan Minorite friar Salimbene, though bitterly hostile, accorded the emperor a reluctant admiration. "Callidus homo fuit, versutus, avarus, luxuriosus, malitiosus, iracundus. Et valens homo fuit interdum, ... iocundus, delitiosus, industrius, legere, scribere et cantare sciebat et cantilena et cantiones invenire; pulcher homo et bene formatus, sed medie statura fuit. ... vidi enim eum et aliquando dilixi." "He was an adroit man, cunning, avaricious, lustful, malicious and hot tempered. Yet he was a proper man all the same; witty, charming, hard working. He knew how to read and write and sing and how to compose tunes and songs ... He was a handsome man and well made, though of middle height. For I have seen him, and at one time admired him."[1] He had spoken Arabic from childhood and could speak several other languages. Elaborately educated (he had never, as alleged, been a "waif" in Palermo), with a sceptical and practical turn of mind, he lived like an oriental despot, with a harem, eunuchs and a travelling menagerie, and he wrote a standard treatise on hawking, De Arte Venandi cum Avibus, Of the Art of Hunting with Birds; a most unmedieval fruit of exact observation and experience,[2] in which, he wrote, "our true intent in the book is to describe things as they are—'ea, quae sunt, sicut sunt'." He also inspired the Liber Augustalis, an extremely able treatise on legislation, in which he assumes the Emperor to be a "living law".

During his long absence in Germany, the Regno had fallen into disorder. Some of the Muslims had taken to brigandage in the mountainous western part of the island; while the Sicilian barons, the Pisans and Genoese had to be brought to heel and the central administration tightened up.

But Frederick was haunted by a promise he had made at his coronation at Aachen: anxious to retain the support of the Church, he had sworn to go on crusade. And these obligations both Honorius III and the new pope, Gregory IX, now held over him. Inevitably, since the Church clung to its temporal power, Empire and Papacy were still at odds. The papal states in Tuscany and Umbria and the cities of the Lombard plain lay athwart the communications between the Sicilian realm and Germany, upon which the Popes, intent on the territories in Tuscany and the Mathildine lands as the basis of their wealth and European influence, dreaded the Emperor's incursion. Gregory, therefore, sought to weaken the Emperor by insisting on an irrelevant and deleterious campaign to Outremer,[3] its manpower coming from Germany and its transport

[1]Salimbene. Chronica. op. cit. p. 349.
[2]Far the best biography is T. C. van Cleeve. The Emperor Frederick II of Hohenstaufen. Oxford, 1972, a massive and definitive piece of American research with an ample bibliography.
[3]A Children's Crusade of 1217 had been led by a twelve-year-old boy called Stephen from the Orléannais. Though discouraged by Philippe Auguste himself, he had collected a huge following of children and adolescents at Vendôme, and conducted them to Marseille, confident that the sea would open before them and that they could march to Palestine. Some were shipwrecked off Sardinia; others captured off Algeria and sold as slaves, some last heard of in Baghdad. In Germany another boy called Nicholas collected a similar following and, crossing the Alps, some by the Gotthard, others by the Mt. Cenis, they trudged to Genoa, Pisa and Ancona. Few of them even put to sea, but fewer returned to their homes.

and finance from the *Regno*. So in 1227 Frederick renewed his ten-year-old crusading vow, and, following the death of his first wife, Constance of Aragon, he prepared the way to fulfilling it by a marriage to Yolande, the fifteen-year-old queen of Jerusalem, daughter of Jean de Brienne.

The failure of Louis IX's expedition to Egypt in 1221, in which Damietta had been surrendered, owing, it was said, to the misguided tactical interference of the clergy who had tried to "lead knights", had made Frederick's procrastinations the more exasperating at Rome; and in the following year he had taken his vow again, promising to set out not later than 1227. But, before that, he needed to cow the Lombard cities, a task which during 1226 he unsuccessfully undertook, and when the relatively mild Honorius III was succeeded by Ugolino of Ostia, a nephew of Innocent III, as Gregory IX, it was clear that the prime object of the Papacy was to get the emperor to the East and in his absence to undermine his power in Italy.

By the spring of 1227, tempted by free transport and German pay, crusaders from over most of Europe had flocked to Brindisi. Naturally plague broke out, and though he had started, Frederick II himself fell ill; Gregory IX promptly excommunicated him, and although in 1228 the emperor sailed for Cyprus and Outremer, he sailed excommunicate. Obviously Frederick had to succeed: thanks to divisions among the Muslims and his own diplomacy he did so, and by February 1229 he had secured a settlement whereby the Christians obtained an enclave including Jerusalem, Nazareth, and Bethlehem, while retaining the coast with its ports and strongholds from above Beirut to south of Jaffa. It was a civilized settlement, based on mutual interest, negotiated between two highly intelligent men of the world—the excommunicate Emperor and the Sultan Al Kāmil.

But it had been obtained not through killing Saracens but by diplomacy; though highly favourable to the Christians, it lacked the general sanction of the peoples involved. "It was not a general treaty between states, but between two men both of whom were capable of a tolerance and friendliness towards the opposing side which their followers did not share."[1]

Palestine, then as now, was no place for rational compromise. Though Frederick had brought off a brilliant diplomatic success, the more fanatical and representative Churchmen thought of a crusade as a chance for killing infidels even more than of rescuing the Holy Places; they also resented that the Muslims should have access to their own Holy Place, the Dome of the Rock. When the excommunicate emperor crowned himself King of Jerusalem in the Church of the Holy Sepulchre, the Christian patriarch of the city became his bitter enemy. Nor did the settlement last. In 1244, ten thousand Khwarasmian Turks, in league with Ayub, the Arab ruler of Egypt, took and sacked Jerusalem and massacred most of the Christian inhabitants—men, women and children. It was the end of the Christian hold on the city.

Early in June 1229, long before this sequel, Frederick II had landed back at Brindisi: temporarily reconciled with the Pope, and no longer excommunicate, he could turn to exploit the *Regno* in the most creative and culturally brilliant

[1] van Cleeve. *op. cit.* p. 220.

period of his rule, commemorated by the neo-classical bridge tower of Capua and the luxuriously appointed Castel del Monte in Apulia: "Like Frederick's De Arte Venandi cum Avibus, these splendid structures are the affirmation of Frederick's yearning for the majesty of ancient Rome and the expression of his insatiable urge to artistic creativeness."[1]

He had already in 1224 founded the first state-sponsored university in Catholic Christendom at Naples to train administrators and diplomats in his service and forbidden his subjects to study anywhere else. But he was not now content just to develop his power as a neo-classical tyrant of Sicily and southern Italy; affairs in Germany demanded his attention, for his eldest son, Heinrich, King of the Romans, now rose in rebellion, convened a meeting of his supporters at Boppard-am-Rhein, and even approached the King of France and the Lombard cities for an alliance. In May 1235 the Emperor, with his favourite son, Conrad, the child of Yolande of Brienne, crossed the Alps, accompanied by an exotic entourage of Saracen mercenaries, Ethiopian slaves, camels, leopards and apes and a vast store of money raised in Sicily. Deeply impressed, the Germans deserted young Heinrich who, at an assembly at Worms, prostrated himself in penitence before his infuriated father. Frederick was inexorable and consigned the youth to prison at Heidelberg, then at Melfi, in southern Italy. Six years later, summoned to his father's court, Heinrich, rather than face Frederick, evaded his guards, rode his horse over a bridge spanning an abyss near Mortorano and perished.

The reconciliation with Gregory IX had always been hollow; Gregory continued to incite the Lombard cities against the emperor, and in 1239, after Frederick had defeated the Milanese at Cortenuova, excommunicated him again; then in the following year summoned a General Council of the Church to Rome to depose him. Whereat the Emperor's Sicilian and Pisan ships intercepted a Genoese convoy of prelates en route for Rome, and they were imprisoned in chains—a "sacrilegious act" not forgotten or forgiven.

After the virulent and presumably senile Pope died aged over a hundred, the Holy See had to be kept vacant for two years. Then Sinnibaldo Fieschi, supposedly a Ghibelline, had been elected as Innocent IV (1243-54); but he proved just as intransigent. In 1245, having fled to Lyons, he summoned another General Council of the Church, attended mostly from the West, and again declared the Emperor deposed. There seemed nothing for it but to extirpate the Pope, then within the territory, not of France, but of the empire. But Frederick had first to secure his communications in Italy, and turned aside to reduce Parma. And here in 1248 he suffered total defeat, abandoned his expedition over the Alps, and retired to southern Italy. There his prospects improved, for the Pope, still demanding unconditional surrender, was widely blamed for the vendetta and the troubles it caused. But now, with the tide turning in his favour as seldom before, in December 1250 Frederick II died of an "excruciating" dysentery at Castel Fiorentino, not far from Lucera near Foggia, and so, said the Churchmen, "mala morte obiit"—"he came to a bad end."

[1]van Cleeve. op. cit. p. 246.

With him the Hohenstaufen empire collapsed. His eldest son Heinrich had been driven to suicide; his favourite son, Conrad, King of the Romans, was never crowned and died four years after his father; Manfred, who was illegitimate, briefly ruled Sicily, but was ousted and killed at the instigation of the Pope by Charles of Anjou, son of Louis IX; Frederick's son Henry by his third wife, Isabella of England, sister of Henry III (to whom to mark this final reconciliation with the Welf interest the emperor had sent three cheetahs), was left a fortune, but never secured the Kingdom of Jerusalem bequeathed to him. To complete the tragedy, Conradin, Frederick's grandson, aged fifteen, attempting to secure his inheritance in Italy, was defeated at Tagliacozzo and beheaded on the main piazza at Naples.

Frederick was regarded by many contemporaries, including Salimbene, as the Anti-Christ; and historians have since presented him as an agnostic or radical sceptic. He was in fact both a Mediterranean and a Medieval man, who made a cult of Antiquity as the scholars of the fourteenth-century Renaissance would do, and considered himself *Caesar semper Augustus* in direct succession; but he never questioned the concept of Christendom and of the Emperor as the universal ruler, God-appointed to control the *Imperium* as the Pope controlled the *Ecclesia*. He merely wanted to keep the *Ecclesia* in its place. As an intelligent cosmopolitan he was tolerant of other faiths, but the charge that he preferred the Muslim faith to Christianity "has no foundation in fact": he merely respected Muslim science, medicine and astrology. He was a cruel and capricious tyrant; his ablest and most faithful minister, Pietro della Vigna, driven apparently to try to poison him, was blinded, and killed himself by dashing his head against a wall. And Frederick was merciless in imprisoning and tormenting his enemies; but the tales of his pioneer experiments in vivisection are based only on the assertions of Salimbene, and even he dismisses other and similar rumours as not worth recording.[1] He evidently had a mordant and unbridled wit, as when he remarked that when God chose Palestine as the Promised Land He cannot have seen his own Sicily, and it was a stock charge that any apparent freethinker was an "Epicurean", who disbelieved in a future life, *quod non esset alia vita post mortem*. But if he once said that there had been "three great imposters—Moses, Christ, and Muhammad", he generally took the Christian outlook for granted. The unrestrained hostility of Frederick towards the Popes ... "originated solely in his belief that

[1]As that he took two men and after they had dined sent one of them for a siesta and the other out hunting, and "that evening had them both cut open in his presence, wanting to see which one had digested his food better." (The doctors concluded that the one who had slept had assimilated it best, a commonsense conclusion which could have been arrived at, in the way of many such experiments, with much less pain.) He also, it was alleged, shut a man up in an air-tight wine cask to die to demonstrate that there was no "soul" to escape (*ut de homine quem vivum includeret in vegete, donec ibi moretur, volens per hoc demonstrare quod anima totalitur deperit*) (Salimbene. *op. cit.* p. 351). The story that he shut up new-born children to find out what language they would speak if they had no one to talk to carries more conviction: "for he wanted to know whether they would speak Hebrew, Greek, Latin or Arabic or the language of their parents." So he instructed the nurses to suckle and bathe them but in no way to speak to them or pet them. But "he laboured in vain—*laboravit in cassum, quia pueri sive infantes moriebantur omnes*—for the boys or infants all went and died." (*op. cit.* p. 352).

the Pope, in the guise of God's vicar on earth and oblivious of his spiritual obligations to mankind, was determined to appropriate to himself the God ordained function of the emperor".[1] He also publicly burnt heretics to uphold the Divine Order. For all his Mediterranean realism and his "wanting to see things as they are", Frederick II was a man of his time; a fact borne out—and he was not a German for nothing—by the impracticable and typically medieval ambitions of universal empire which clouded his Norman Sicilian realism and curiosity, and to which, like his grandfather Barbarossa, he devoted his formidable abilities and ambitions in vain.

VI

The high and farflung conflict of Papacy and Empire had overshadowed the flourishing European civilization which reached its intellectual climax in the scholastic philosophy of St. Thomas Aquinas. In 1263, long after the death of Fredrick II, the Dominican St Thomas (1225-1274), was directed by Urban IV to assimilate the recovered writings of Aristotle to Christian philosophy. His *Summa Theologica*, in over a million words and 769 *quaestiones*, explains the entire Cosmos; from *De Deo, an sit* (of God, whether He exists,) down to the degrees of Sin. Politics are an aspect of the Divine purpose for 'communities', in which alone men can fully live. This vast metaphysical construction, created with sublime disregard for the disorders of the time, is one of the most extraordinary feats of the thirteenth century. But it was even longer after the collapse of the empire that its ideal was enshrined by a great Italian poet.

Dante Alighieri (1265-1321) was born in the year of the death of Manfred and the break up of the Court of Palermo, from which the main inspiration of vernacular Italian poetry had derived. The son of a minor Florentine banker, he became deeply involved as a Ghibelline in the city's politics, and in 1301 was driven out by the Guelf faction, who supported Boniface VIII. He wrote his treatise, the *Monarchia*, to support the emperor Henry of Luxembourg, and dedicated parts of the *Commedia* to the Ghibelline Can Grande della Scala of Verona. Dante had early fallen in love with Beatrice Portinari; a passion intensified when he met her again at eighteen; but she married another, and in 1290, she died. The romance was sublimated in the *Commedia* in which an idealized Beatrice admitted the poet to heaven. In 1318 Dante left Verona for Ravenna, where in 1321 he died, like Innocent III, of malaria.

Dante perfected a "*new style*": it was based on a medieval Florentine tradition combining Troubadour romantic love with a neo-Platonic, mathematically precise and symbolic medieval cosmology, expressed in a simple, concentrated and poignant vernacular. The *Vita Nuova* (c. 1293), and *Divina Commedia* (1310-21) are written in the originally Provençal twelfth century *terzia rima* or triple rhyme, and so called because written as a sequel to Virgil's *Aeneid*, technically to Dante a *Tragedy*. Written in colloquial Italian, the

[1]van Cleeve, *op. cit.* pp. 537-8.

Commedia begins grimly in Hell and ends happily in Heaven: it is the first vernacular poem to attempt a grand cosmic theme in the Virgilian way. Steeped in the best classical literature then available, in Aristotle's *Ethics*, and in the *Summa Theologica* of St. Thomas Aquinas, Dante designed the *Commedia* as a tour of Hell, Purgatory and Heaven. The enemies of the Divine cosmic order are assigned their punishments and rewards, according to their legends or to their hostility or loyalty to the Ghibelline ideal of universal empire descending from Rome.

This ideal is also depicted with immense ability in the *Monarchia* (1309), Dante's masterpiece of political theory, which supplements the *Commedia*. The greatest villain of Dante's cosmos is Lucifer, who first disrupted the cosmic order, and to whom is assigned the deepest pit in Hell, where, triple-mouthed, he eternally devours Judas, Brutus and Cassius, the next greatest sinners, who betrayed Christ and murdered Caesar, the founder of Empire; others, not least Dante's political emenies, are suitably punished, along with other famous and flagrant sinners of deeper or lesser dye, those in purgatory sustained by hope. Finally, with the inspiration of Beatrice, the poet glimpses Heaven.

This extraordinary and wonderfully organized fantasy is essentially medieval, with its vision of cosmic order worked out in living detail; and the *Imperium* for which Frederick II had fought is depicted as reflecting the Divine purpose, since it alone can impose universal peace on the temporal world, and only in peace can human faculties be fully realized in that "beatitude of life which consists in fulfilling its own being" thus "keeping potential intellect constantly actualized in speculation and action since God and Nature make nothing in vain."[1] A supreme authority Dante insists—not without relevance today—is essential to peace and so to civilization, and "the office of monarch is necessary for the well-being of the world."

So, in ironic contrast to the facts which had decided that the *Imperium* and the ordered Christendom for which it stood had long ago been broken by the claims of the *Ecclesia* for temporal domination, Dante defined, with a magic power of phrase which launched vernacular Italian poetry, the idea which the conflict between Frederick II and the Papacy had shattered, a conflict which was still continuing between Boniface VIII and the King of France, now the beneficiary of the collapse of the Empire and the most powerful monarch in Europe.

[1]See the *Monarchia* in a translation of *The Latin Works of Dante Alighieri*. ed. P. H. Wicksteed. Temple Classics, London (reprint), 1934.

XIX

The Atlantic Realms

In contrast to the far-flung ambitions of the Hohenstaufen and the Papacy which had brought both *Imperium* and *Ecclesia* near collapse, the feudal monarchs in the West were consolidating their relatively manageable realms. The most successful were the French Capetians and, after they had abandoned their ambition of continental empire, the Angevin Plantagenets of England. The former, with originally very small domains, but with the consistent backing of the Church—an alliance which went back to Clovis—very gradually imposed their overlordship on the great natural regions of France in all their rich variety: over Normandy and Flanders, Champagne and Blois; eastward over Burgundy; south-west over Poitou, Aquitaine and Toulouse; south over Provence; eventually in the far west over Brittany; regions which formed the richest and most populous area in Western Europe. When the German kings had been distracted by the ambitions and obligations of empire on both sides of the Alps, the Capetian monarchs were enforcing their feudal rights over their own original territory and then beyond.

Philippe I (1060–1108), son of Henri I and Anna of Kiev, managed to link up the county of Sens with Paris and Orléans, fought the Duke of Anjou and William the Conqueror and supported Robert Curthose against his brother, William Rufus—*fortissimum Regem Anglium*. Philippe's son Louis VI le Gros (1108–37), *juvenis jocundus, gratus et benevolens*, says Suger, the Abbot of St. Denis, who became his principal minister and who wrote his life with a sense of drama and place rare among medieval chroniclers, was fortunate in the death of William Rufus—(*subito inopinata sagitto percussus*—[1]suddenly struck

[1]Suger. *Vita Ludovici Grossi Regis*—*Vie de Louis VI le Gros*, ed. et trad. H. Waquet. Paris, 1929. Suger writes that he himself heard Sir Walter Tyrel ("this Tyrel") deny that he had shot the king and swear that "he had never come into that part of the forest that day where the King was." (p. 13).
Suger (1081–1151) came of humble birth on the estate of the abbey of St. Denis, to the service of which he was early vowed by his father. At the school of the Priory d'Estrée he made friends with the young Prince Louis, and, after studying near Fontevrault and Marmoutier, made his name defending the rights of St. Denis against the bishop of Paris. He became provost of Berneval in Normandy, and on Louis' accession entered his service as an administrator and diplomat. He attended a Lateran

by an unexpected arrow). Exploiting his own feudal overlordships and interior lines of communication, Louis systematically put down rebellious local feudatories, though, forced in 1119 to attack Chartres, he refrained from burning town and cathedral when clergy and townspeople appeared bearing the Holy Chemise (*camisiam*) of the Blessed Mother of God. In 1113 he made a tentative peace with Henry I of England over Normandy, but Henry in the following year married his daughter Mathilda to the German emperor Heinrich V and instigated him to attack Rheims. This invasion set off one of the earliest manifestations of French patriotism, generally considered not discernible until the battle of Bouvines fought by Philippe Auguste in 1214. "Having long conceived a hatred against the Lord King Louis," writes Suger, "the Emperor Henricus assembled as big a host as he could of Lotharingians, Germans, Bavarians, Suebi and Saxons, . . . and plotted to attack Rheims by stealth." But Louis VI rallied his magnates because it was his feudal "prerogative" to summon them to defend his realm, if the subjects of any other king dared to attack his own. Then, advancing on the enemy with what men he could, he "invited all France to follow him in force" (*tota Francia sequatur potenter invitavit*).[1]

He got a vigorous response. The "unwonted audacity" of the Germans had already infuriated the French, and "the Knights came in from all sides, remembering their ancient valour and former victories." An enormous host now awaited the German invasion (*Theutonicorum incursum*), while the magnates of the realm took council, saying "Let us boldly advance over towards them (*transeamus audacter ad eos*) lest it be said that the proud presumption with which they have invaded France, mistress of these lands, remained unpunished." Others advised the army to wait until the invaders had advanced enough to be cut off, so that they could be massacred without pity "as if they were Saracens", and the bodies of "these barbarians" exposed to the wolves and ravens. Redoubtable French women brought up wine for their men, and bandages and water for the wounded.

In the event, Heinrich V decided to call his invasion off, "preferring ignominy to defeat", and the French won a famous and bloodless victory, "the same as or better than if they had triumphed in battle."

Having thus asserted at once a feudal and even national leadership, Louis VI continued to concentrate on the possible and put down rebellions in his own domain; even when over sixty and grossly overweight, lamenting to his intimates that "one could hardly ever combine experience with full strength"[2] and "hardly transportable", he harried the rebels to the end and died of the flux with edifying piety at Paris.

His son Louis VII did not live up to his inheritance, and allowed his important dynastic marriage to Eleanor of Aquitaine to end in divorce. As has

Council, and Imperial Diets in Germany, and in 1122 he was elected Abbot of St. Denis, which he reformed and embellished, for he was a great patron of the arts. Closely involved in the government of the realm, in 1147 he was appointed Regent during Louis' absence on the Second Crusade. He wrote his *Vita Ludovici* during the years 1138–44, immediately after the death of Louis VI.

[1]Suger *op. cit.* p. 220.
[2]*op. cit.* p. 271.

been rightly observed, "Eleanor of Aquitaine was probably not a suitable wife for a sensitive man,"[1] nor had she behaved well on the Second Crusade, but "for personal considerations Louis sacrificed France." For Eleanor was promptly married to Henry Plantagenet of Anjou who in 1154 succeeded to England, and who came, mainly through her inheritance, to rule more of France than the French King. Louis VII consoled himself with the characteristically French remark that while Henry II "lacked for nothing valuable; horses, gold and silver, silks and jewels", at the court of France, they had "only bread and wine and gaiety".

The next Capetian, Philippe Auguste (1180–1223), proved the ablest medieval architect of the French monarchy. He consolidated the strongest realm in western Europe, including Normandy, Anjou and Touraine, and mastered Flanders and Toulouse. In 1214 he utterly defeated the Emperor Otto IV at Bouvines in Flanders in a battle of European significance, and foiled the concerted invasion of John of England from La Rochelle, thus opening the way for Frederick II in Germany and putting John at the mercy of his barons in England so that he had to concede *Magna Carta*. Philippe then centralized his government through royal non-feudal *baillies*, while exploiting his feudal rights to the full. While Barbarossa had despised and fought the Italian Communes, Philippe extended his support and authority by making the French ones his vassals. He also turned the Albigensian Crusade to account; after Simon de Montfort's death at the siege of Toulouse, his son, unable to resist the revived power of the Count, made the French King, as his feudal overlord, his heir. Philippe Auguste thus got a hold on the Midi, as well as on the whole of the Channel coast. So strong were the French kings that they, and not the Papacy, became the predominant partners in that ancient alliance, and the French realm, like French civilization, became the strongest power in western Europe.

After Louis VIII (1223–6) had carried on his father's consolidation, the sainted Louis IX, (reigned 1226–70) became the moral arbiter of Western Christendom; a position conclusively abdicated by Frederick II, Gregory IX and Innocent IV. He was at once the supreme feudal overlord and the saintly "father" of his people, as described by his contemporary Joinville: "Maintes fois avint que en estel il se alloit seoir au bois de Vincennes apres sa messe, et se acostoioit à un chesne, et nous fesoit seoir entour li. Et tuit cil qui avoieut a faire venoient parler a li sanz destourbier de huissier ne d'autre."[2] He would then take the petitions in order. He even made the monarchy popular by intervening to settle the grievances that followed the exertions of the royal *baillies*, and conciliated the magnates by a fair interpretation of feudal rights. Nor was he naive in his dynastic policy, for he consolidated the French hold on the Midi by marrying his son Alphonse to the heiress of the Count of Toulouse, and his son Charles of Anjou to the daughter of the Count of

---

[1] K. N. Bell. *Mediaeval Europe 1095–1254.* Oxford, 1911. p. 85.
[2] "Often it happened that in summer he would go and sit in the Forest of Vincennes after Mass, and settle himself under an oak tree and make us sit round him. And any one who had business with him came to speak with him without hindrance from an usher or anyone else."

Provence. The threat posed by Henry II, when in control of Aquitaine, of cutting off the French monarchy from the Mediterranean was thus finally scotched, and in 1266 Charles could go on to evict Manfred of Hohenstaufen from Naples and Sicily and kill him, and order the execution of young Conradin, last of the Hohenstaufen.

II

Across the Channel another realm was also being consolidated, at first as a means to continental empire. Henry Plantagenet (reigned 1154-89) was a Frenchman from Anjou brought up on the Loire, where the sun is powerful enough for vines to flourish and the light sufficiently brilliant to make the colours of the English landscape seem tame. Bilingual in French and Latin, Norman through his mother Mathilda, Henry II regarded England mainly as a source of revenue for his war against the French Kings and his own sons, incurred in France as Angevin emperor of territories that extended, in right of his own inheritance and of his wife, from the Channel to the Pyrenees, and from Gascony and the Bordelais eastward through Sarlat across to Le Puy de Dôme and the headwaters of the Loire. Now overlord of some of the most fertile areas of France, he could threaten Toulouse and even Provence.

The position of the English monarchs was exceptionally strong: since William the Conqueror had won the island by the sword, in feudal law all the land was technically his own; moreover William Rufus had been able and ferocious, and Henry I (1100-37) highly intelligent and methodical as well as ruthless. Exploiting both the existing Anglo-Saxon chancery, with its charters, records and writs, and the ancient English shire courts, Henry I had centralized the administration on his own *curia* or household, thus linking it with indigenous local government, and had established a new Court of Exchequer to collect taxation and keep accounts, as well as sending out itinerant justices to the shire courts. In spite of the setback to royal authority during the disputed succession between Mathilda and Stephen of Blois, Henry II inherited an exceptionally well established form of government to restore, develop and exploit.

A restless and dynamic character, mainly pursuing his own profit, he and his administrators created the most efficient government in the West next to that of Sicily, and made himself overlord of Wales and Scotland, and even of Ireland. Though, in the medieval way, he was himself constantly on the move, he established the Exchequer and the law courts permanently in London, far the largest and richest city in the realm; and he asserted the royal authority throughout the land by regular assizes held by royal judges. He also strengthened the growing landed establishment and kept its support of the crown by protecting the rights of property and inheritance, providing writs which could be applied for to bring disputes into the King's courts. In contrast to contemporary practice in Barbarossa's Germany, litigation superseded violence. The King's power became something more positive than being merely the guardian of custom or even that of the supreme feudal overlord, while the decisions made and recorded in the royal courts built up into a formidable body of "Common" law—so called because common to the whole realm. This achievement was rooted in Anglo-Saxon, Norman and Scandinavian procedures, and, along with the use of juries to find out the facts, it made for a more centralized, business-like routine within a manageable area. Even the spectacular dispute over the rights of Church and State—the English aspect of the conflict between Papacy and Empire, which in 1170 culminated in the murder of St. Thomas Becket and the temporary humiliation of the King, ended in compromise; for Henry II in fact continued to appoint bishops, and if a few criminal clergy escaped the royal justice, the rule of the King's law was not seriously impeded.

Henry's sons, incited by Eleanor of Aquitaine, regularly rebelled against their father, but their attacks affected his continental empire far more than his English realm. Although his vast continental ambitions failed and he died in rage and frustration at Chinon and he is buried at Fortevrault, where his thick-set effigy remains, Henry II and his administrators created a strong realm, a *communitas regni*; though still feudal in expression, it included the whole land, and proved strong enough to survive the expensive, glamorous adventurer, Richard I (1189–99), *Coeur de Lion*, who swore "Ho! Ho! By God's throat!" and spent less than a year in England during his entire reign, though he won European knightly fame.

Moreover the Angevin failure on the continent, which culminated in the loss of Normandy and Anjou themselves, made the English barons more insular and increased their solidarity. Already by 1215, by imposing *Magna Carta* to stop John's overdriving of his feudal and Household powers, they created a precedent of bringing the *communitas regni* to resist further encroachments by the Crown which led to the assertion of greater liberties in other contexts at home and overseas.

For *Magna Carta* is a feudal document, concerned with feudal grievances paralleled in contemporary documents in France and Spain; but it could and would be re-interpreted, as when a clause promising that "no (feudal) scutage or aid shall be imposed save by common consent of our realm" would be broadly and inaccurately interpreted as meaning "no taxation without representation" in seventeenth-century England and in America in 1776.

Henry II had exploited an increasingly prosperous realm. Population was rising, waste being colonized, and the great sheep pastures being developed which were giving England its immense medieval wealth in wool. Gone were the days of Viking pillage and baronial depredation; London could now hold its own with the great continental cities, its exports extending to the Low Countries and the Baltic—mainly in raw materials, wool, hides, fish and cheese—and its imports derived mainly from Gascony, Rouen and Bordeaux; timber and cordage from the Baltic, luxury goods and armaments from the Rhineland and Italy. Other ports also flourished; Bristol, Southampton and King's Lynn. Coal was already exported from Newcastle to Flanders. After two generations of relative security, the level-headed and businesslike qualities of the English are already apparent.

This prosperity made the thirteenth century in England, as on the Continent, a time of growing civilization; but the still cosmopolitan monarchy did not share this wealth. Henry III (1216–72), son of John and Isabelle of Angoulême (between Poitou and Périgord), was a Frenchman, determined to keep up with the Capetian and Hohenstaufen; a great patron of architects and artists, with a Poitivin, and, after his marriage to Eleanor of Provence, a Provençal entourage. His household government, dominated by the court and by the great bishops, provoked the resistance of an increasingly insular baronage determined not now to destroy, but to control the royal establishment, and now claiming themselves to represent *le commun de Engleterre*. In the ensuing conflict, which culminated in civil war, Simon de Montfort the younger, the King's brother-in-law, attempted to put the crown in commission to a council of magnates, but in 1265 he was killed at Evesham; after that the government of the realm was virtually taken over by the King's able son, the Lord Edward, afterwards Edward I.

In the conflict, both sides had needed all the help they could get, and summoned representatives of the gentry of the shires and of burgesses to attend *parlements* of the Royal Council and magnates, a decisive innovation which involved newly important elements of the realm in government. Here, quite unintended, was an important departure; as the gentry and burgesses grew more powerful, it would make for the transformation of a feudal into a parliamentary monarchy.

While the rise of the French kingship was immediately more decisive for continental Europe, the consolidation of the central government and early parliamentary institutions of the compact and insular English realm would have an even more important future, not least beyond the Oceans.

III

In the tenth century the Arabs or "Moors" dominated most of the Iberian peninsula; by the end of the twelfth the *Reconquista* by the Christians of the north had left the Moors with only the small mountainous and tributary state of Granada and a strip of territory along the south coast from Almería past Málaga to Gibraltar. The Christian states claimed descent from the Visigoths and their original nucleus had been around Oviedo in the north-west, then, by the early tenth century, around León, from which Castile broke away. Then Sancho III Garcia of Navarre (1005–35) had mastered Castile and most of León; his second son, Fernando I (1035–65), inherited Castile, while his fourth son, Ramiro I, obtained Aragon, founded in 1035. The Christian states with their fluctuating boundaries and confused successions—doubly confounded by the prevalence of the name Alfonso among the rulers of them all—found it hard to collaborate. Fernando I of Castile by 1064 had captured Coimbra and reached the Mondego. With neo-Visigothic implications, he had become *Yspanus Rex*. By 1085 Alfonso VI of León and Castile (1065–1109), a contemporary of William the Conqueror, had captured the prosperous Moorish city of Toledo in 1185, a turning point of the Reconquista. The crusade was now stepped up by the influence of the Cluniac "reformers"; the Spanish Church, which had gone its own Visigothic way for centuries, was subordinated to the authority of Rome. Spain became more part of Western Christendom, more influenced by French civilization. But though, in the words of el Cantar de mio Cid (c.1140), Les Moros llaman Mahómet et los Cristianos santi Yague,[1] there was still enough tolerance between the predominantly rural Christians and the urban Muslims for Alfonso VI to try to be "Emperor of the two religions"—over a "third Spain", Muslim but not African.

After the fall of Toledo, however, the Spanish Moors invited the help of the Berber Almoravids (al-murabitin—the "fortress dwellers" of the Holy War), a fanatical sect who had conquered Morocco, founded Marrakesh and even mastered Northern Nigeria. Complete with camels, negroes with hippopotamus-hide shields and thunderous drums, they totally defeated Alfonso VI near Badajoz in 1086, in the year after he had taken Toledo, and brought new bitterness into the war. Meanwhile, in 1094 the Castilian Rodrigo de Bivar, el Cid (from the Arabic Sidi, lord), had taken the rich south-eastern city of Valencia and held it till his death; while Alfonso VI had greatly advanced the Reconquista. Indeed, he had proved "an extraordinary monarch" who had displaced two brothers and outlived his five wives, had won half Spain and lost it again and brought the Roman Church into Castile and León and had filled them with Muslim gold.[2]

The assault on the Andaluz continued on various fronts, with a new intolerance. The short-lived Alfonso "the Battler", King of Galicia, got as far as Córdoba and Granada, though, battling once too often (against his own side), he was slain by Alfonso VII of León in 1134.

The Almoravid power was now in decline; but a new army of fanatical Berbers from the Atlas mountains now entered Spain: the Almohads (al-muwahhidun, the united) had captured Marrakesh, by 1162 carried the Jihad to Granada and by 1195 defeated the Christians of Alarcos. But in 1212 the great Christian victory at Las Navas de Tolosa, where they cut through the bodyguard of chain-linked negroes guarding the Caliph's tent, gave them command of the upper Guadalquivir, and under Fernando III of Castile (1217–52) and León (1230–52) the Christians won Córdoba (1235) and Seville (1248).

So, while Empire and Papacy were locked in conflict, the Spanish crusade had almost entirely succeeded. Compared to the Moorish "opening up" of Spain, as they had called it, in the eighth century, it had taken a long time, but the Spanish realms had been disunited. The main conquests had been made by the hard-bitten fighters of Castile and León who took over at Andaluz in the South: and the Aragonese, and Catalans of the Spanish March, originally cleared of the Moors by Charlemagne's armies. They now followed the logic of geography on the eastern side of the Spanish watershed and concentrated

[1]"The Moors called on Mahomet and the Christians on St. James."
[2]Harold Livermore. A History of Spain. London, 1958. p. 109. q.v. for a fine general survey on which this account is in part based. For a further treatment see D.J.F. O'Callaghan. A History of Medieval Spain. Cornell, 1975, to which I am also indebted.

on the east coast—on Valencia; they also took to the sea, captured the Balearic Islands, went on to Naples to become a great Mediterranean sea power and penetrated to Greece.

The Moors had proved no match for the northern knights; and their Caliphate based on Córdoba had lapsed into *Taifas*, disunited city states with their surrounding dependencies, often long tributary and relatively easy to reduce. Following the pattern later discerned by their great historian Ibn Khaldoun, many Muslims had lost their original élan and settled into an easy luxurious urban way of life, so that they were often more alarmed by their fanatical Berber allies than by the Christians. Indeed, the line between two civilizations had long been blurred; but not the predatory purpose of the Crusaders. The famous poem of the *Cid*, in contrast to the archaizing and romantic *Song of Roland*, is a tale of practical success, told in plain Castilian. The *Cid* invades *al Andaluz ganer su pan*, to "win his bread". His exploits are not fantastic and those concerned are historical persons: he is happily married, not yearning for a "mistress", and he marries his daughters to royalty. He ends, not as Roland and Oliver in tragedy, but in worldly triumph. He is a lucky *campeador*—a warrior, a chivalrous but predatory and realistic hidalgo.

IV

The Kingdom of Portugal hived off early from the rest of the Iberian Peninsula, but there was no racial cause for the division. The original *Portucale* was very small, extending from the Minho behind Valencia down to the Douro inland from Oporto, and after the final Spanish conquest of Coimbra on the Mondego, the area was assigned to Count Henry, brother of the Duke of Burgundy, and to Teresa, the bastard daughter of Alfonso VI, who had married Constance of Burgundy. After Henry's death, Teresa offended the Portuguese magnates by her amorous intrigues, and in 1128 was driven from the country; but their son, Afonso Henriques (1128–85), became the principal founder of Portugal, extending the *Reconquista* to the south, and in 1147, with the eager collaboration of English, Flemish and French Crusaders, massacred the harmless Mozarabic (Arabized) Christians, like the Jews living long in safety under the Moors, and captured Moorish Lisbon, already a centre of oceanic commerce and of the study of geography and navigation. In 1179, after becoming a vassal of Pope Alexander III and in the year before the accession of Philippe-Auguste, Afonso Henriques was formally recognized as King of Portugal.

"Liberation" by the *Reconquista* was often disastrous to the Mozarabic Christians and Jews who had been allowed to profess their religion under Moorish rule; but the most fanatical crusaders could not permanently destroy the skills in the agriculture, horticulture and irrigation which were at first the basis of the economy, and though the *Reconquista* proved a set-back to civilization, the vineyards and orchards were still cultivated, the irrigation tended, while the tough Portuguese fishermen still brought in their catch: the Sephardic Jews, originally from Salonika, naturally survived. But the ferocity of the conquest led to much deliberate resettlement and to collaboration between the royal government, the Cortes and the municipal and local councils, along with grants of forcis (charters) to the towns. Strong by right of conquest, as in England, the monarchs were able, in collaboration with the Cistercian monasteries, to develop a country which had originally owed its civilization to the Romans, the Moors and the monks.[1]

The first Portuguese king of popular fame is, significantly, Dom Denis (1279–1325), o Rei Lavrador, the royal "farmer" or "labourer", who was mainly concerned with irrigation and forestry (Portugal was particularly rich in timber for ships), as well as with founding the university of Coimbra (1290), with creating a fleet of war galleys propelled by free rowers, not by slaves, and with encouraging marine insurance. In contrast to the habitually insolvent monarchs of most medieval realms—as most of the English Plantagenets—this provident king, also a poet sensitive to graceful girls and landscape, was careful always dinheiro tiver—"to have money in hand".

Thus the Kingdom of Portugal with its long coastline, combining Atlantic rain with Southern sunshine, developed differently from Castile, based on the high, often barren plateau of the interior, with its extremes of climate, or from Catalonia, with its French and Italian connections; for in spite of its apparent geographial unity the Iberian Peninsula has always been the scene of intense regional and so of political divisions. Yet both the Spaniards and the Portuguese inherited the centuries-old civilization and economy created by the Moors, and symbolized by the tinkle of fountains in the enclosed gardens of Seville, and the green and white Moorish tiles in the Old Palace at Sintra.

V

So by the late thirteenth century the peoples of the Atlantic coast of Europe, in Graeco-Roman times on the periphery of a Mediterranean civilization, but destined to become the four great European oceanic colonizing powers, had been organized into relatively coherent and prosperous realms by secular monarchies, often in collaboration with representative parliamenz or cortes and municipalities, which had been fitted into a now obsolescent feudal social order. Frederick II had been the great exemplar of a lay power, and if he had been a spectacular failure, his struggle with the Papacy had made it more dependent on the French kings, its traditional allies, and cleared the way for French cultural and political supremacy based on vast revenues accumulating from the richest and most populous country in Europe. In England, the very failure of the Plantagenets to maintain their continental empire had in fact strengthened the realm by making the magnates more insular and more at odds with the cosmopolitan and insolvent court, so that in the conflict with the monarchy a new solidarity came about between the magnates, the gentry and the burgesses, both now represented in a central parliamenz. Pulled

---

[1]See J.B. Trend. Portugal. London, 1957, for an illuminating and highly readable account, with emphasis on the civilization and economy.

together by the able Edward I (1272–1307), *Scotorum Malleus*—the Hammer of the Scots—the English asserted their power over the Scots and the Welsh, the former provoked to lively and successful patriotic resistance, the latter, vehemently protesting, held down by garrison castles.

In Spain the long eviction of the Moors had left a lasting crusading and predatory tradition, symbolized by the Cross and the Sword, and carried on by Spanish military Orders; the Knights of Calatrava, for example, spontaneously organized in the mid-twelfth century after the Templars had failed to hold the city against the Almohads; the Knights of Alcántara, originally from Salamanca, and the Order of Santiago of Compostela. Proud and intensely individualistic, their religion a fighting creed, the Spaniards had conducted by far the most successful of the Crusades, and overrun a civilization so well established that they had to adapt to it. The Aragonese and Catalans were set on Mediterranean objectives, and Pedro III of Aragon, having married Constance, daughter of Frederick II's bastard Manfred, determined to evict Charles of Anjou from Naples and Sicily. The Portuguese had now achieved a close solidarity, blending Moorish and Christian civilization with a complex mixture of race; they were becoming united in a more businesslike exploitation of the singular economic advantages of their country, and then more aware than the Castilian Spaniards of the prospect of oceanic enterprise of which they would become the European pioneers.

XX

Central Europe and the Balkans: The Waning of Byzantium

The defeat of the Hohenstaufen had led to competition for the empire. The Electoral Princes of Germany were agreed only on two things: that the new emperor must be harmless and that he must be rich; so they had favoured candidates on the fringes of the empire or even outside it. William, Count of Holland, elected with the support of the Rhineland cities King of the Romans and crowned at Aachen in 1248, never extricated himself from the feuds of the Low Countries, and perished in battle with the Friesians on the icy polders near Alkmaar early in 1256. A Spanish candidate, Alphonso X, *el sabio*, was wise enough to withdraw his candidature; and Richard of Cornwall, the reputedly wealthy brother of Henry III of England, after much reciprocal entertainment in the Rhineland cities, was elected, crowned in 1257, and, mainly an absentee, filled the vacancy until his death in 1271.

Then in 1273 the Electors thought they had found their man: Rudolf of Habsburg or Aarsburg on the Aar east of Neuchâtel, a wealthy yet peripheral magnate in what is now Switzerland. They had in fact found the ancestor of the most cunning and tenacious dynasty in European history, who in due course succeeded, where the Hohenstaufen had failed, in making the empire hereditary in their House.

Rudolf (1273–91) at last abandoned the Imperial claims on Italy, and concentrated on the possible. Having come to terms with the Hungarians in common hostility to the Czechs, who claimed overlordship over Austria, Styria and even Carinthia, he cleared Premysl Ottokar II out of Austria and set about founding a reliable power base in the Danube valley.

But whatever the pretensions of the emperors, the most powerful monarchy in Europe was now French; and when Boniface VIII in the Bull *Unam Sanctam* asserted claims to Papal supremacy in France as extreme as those formulated by Gregory IX, the realistic Philippe IV the Fair (1285–1314), grandson of Louis IX, felt strong enough, with his subjects' support, to incite an emissary to lay violent hands on the Pope at Anagni, an outrage from which the Pontiff succumbed within a month. For good measure, the King confiscated and plundered the wealth of the Templars on trumped up charges of heresy and moral turpitude; an example followed by Edward II of England, of all people. The sequel led to further degradation of the Papacy, known as the "Avignon Captivity", when from 1309–78 the Popes, dependants of the French kings, resided there in the elegant palace still extant.

So while the long *Reconquista* drove the Moors but not their civilization from all but the extreme south of Spain, and French, English and Portuguese realms were consolidated, the former into the greatest power in Christendom, the empire lost most of what authority it had in the Germanies and became based for the first time on the Habsburg power on the Danube.

II

The strategic bastion of Bohemia, from which the Marcomanni had defied the Romans and made their incursion to the Adriatic at Aquileia, had long been infiltrated from the east by Slav tribes who had swamped the Marcomanni and beaten off the Avars. The leading tribe, the Czechs, had emerged in the tenth century from the collapse of the formidable kingdom of Moravia to which in 863 the missionaries Cyril and Methodius had originally been assigned; and their first ruler, and founder of the Premyslid dynasty, had been Premysl, by repute originally a ploughhand.

Under German influence Catholicism had spread, and in 929, in the time of Athelstan, the young prince and afterwards patron saint Vaclav—"Good King Wenceslas"—had been murdered by his pagan brother Boleslav, rightly termed "the Cruel". His cruelty had paid off, for he reigned from 929 to 967, and his long rule and that of his son, Boleslav II (967–999), consolidated a realm that included the Slovaks to the East, originally part of Great Moravia. A Catholic bishopric of Prague had been established, and in spite of a continuing habit of fratricide, the Premyslids survived. Vladislav II (1140–73) had been made King of Bohemia by Barbarossa and the rich silver mines developed, much forest had been cleared for agriculture, and the ancient trans-European trade between the Baltic and the Adriatic gradually revived. With this wealth behind him, Premysl Ottokar II (1253–78) had extended his overlordship to Austria and Styria, even to Carinthia and down to the Adriatic, thus providing Bohemia with a sea coast.

This extension did not last: Rudolf of Habsburg combined with the Hungarians to drive the Czechs back to their original boundaries, and in 1278 the Hungarians defeated and killed Premysl Ottokar II at Dürnkrut.

His successor, Vaclav or Wenceslas II, who had encouraged German settlers to develop the country, now turned his ambitions north-east, and in 1300 got himself elected King of Poland after the breakdown of the indigenous Piast dynasty, an honour that brought the Premyslids no good; for in 1305 his successor Wenceslas III, the last of his House, was assassinated by the infuriated Poles. Though the Premyslid monarchs, fluctuating authority proved ephemeral, it had contributed to a strong Czech sense of solidarity.

III

The other western Slavs, the *Polanie*, or "people of the fields", had emerged under the rule of the Piast princes by the mid tenth century in an area which included the headwaters of the Oder and the Vistula, but which was also the main geographical corridor between Europe and western Asia, on the northern part of the broad isthmus between the Baltic and the Black Sea. The Poles were at once culturally and in religion an outpost of Western Christendom, yet racially different; part of the Slav world. Their earliest centres had been Krakow in the south near the junction of the Bohemian mountains and the Carpathians, and Gniezno in the central corridor near modern Poznan, directly halfway between modern Warsaw and Krakow, the original stronghold of the *Polanie*. By 966, under Prince Mieszko I, who, as already remarked, had married one of the daughters of Sweyn of Denmark and so become the grandfather of Knud, they had been converted to Catholic Christianity and accepted the overlordship of Otto the Great, for Mieszko was an ardent westernizer. His son Boleslaw I, the *Brave* (992–1025), became the first King of Poland and, turning east, briefly occupied Kiev. Kazimierz the *Restorer* (1039–58) had put down the fissiparous nobility, and Boleslaw the *Bold* (overbold, for he was driven into exile) and Boleslaw *Wry-mouth* (1102–38), a contemporary of Henry I of England and Louis VI of France, beat off an attack by the ubiquitous Emperor Heinrich V, and conquered and converted the Pomeranians around modern Szczecin (formerly Stettin) and near Rügen on the Baltic.

The Piast monarchy thus had wide horizons, extending from Kievan Russia to Denmark, and wider ambitions; moreover they were staunch allies of the Hildebrandine Papacy. But Boleslaw *Wry-mouth* divided his dominion among his sons; the senior line became based on Krakow, the burial place of the Polish kings, and the others on Gniezno, Poznan and Masovia in the north. The Piasts thus became unable to defend or to control a naturally incoherent country, and in 1173 Mieszko the *Old* was driven even from Krakow, while in 1226 the Polish Konrad of Masovia was reduced to calling in the Teutonic Knights to subdue the heathen old Prussians and Lithuanians to the north, so admitting even more dangerous neighbours. Hence, too, the invitation to Wenceslas III of Bohemia to the throne, and its murderous sequel.

This political confusion, and the independence of the Church and nobility that went with it, had not prevented the economic development of the country; vigorous here as in most of Europe during the twelfth and thirteenth centuries, and in Poland much due to German settlers and Flemish colonists settled along the Baltic. Moreover the Jews, expelled from many western areas by misdirected crusading zeal, were welcomed in Poland, where they settled as *Ashkenazim* distinct from the *Sephardim* of Spain and Portugal, and multiplied in special quarters in the towns.

The original Polish peasantry had little share in this prosperity, often due to foreign initiative, and under military masters they were being depressed into serfdom. None the less, the Catholic religion had taken deep popular roots, and the wealthy Churchmen had built and embellished distinguished Roman-esque architecture. There was a particular cult of St. Adalbert who had resigned the bishopric of Prague to convert the Old Prussian Balts, and had been beheaded by that recalcitrant people,

IV

On the broad plain of the Alföld beyond the Danube which forms the western extremity of the vast Eurasian steppe, and in the undulating Dunántál, the Roman Pannonia on the more European side of the river, the Magyars, now officially Christian under German Catholic influence, formed a wedge of Finno-Ugrian and Turkic stock between the Western Slavs and Southern Slavs of the Balkans. An originally tribal and nomadic society, they were now settled on the land, and Geza I, the first of the Arpáds, who had attempted to combine Christianity and paganism, saying that he was "rich enough to afford two gods",[1] had established his capital with Bavarian support at Esztergom in the Dunántál. His son István (St. Stephen, 1000–1038) had married a sister of the Emperor Heinrich III, and having been sent a crown and a cross by Pope Sylvester II, the mentor of Otto III, he had been crowned King on Christmas Day 1000.[2] St. Stephen, like Knud of England, thus became one of the major princes of Catholic Christendom, proved a munificent patron of the Church, and managed to control the restless and belligerent Magyar nobility. But his successor and nephew, Peter, had been killed by his brother Andrew; himself evicted in 1060 by Béla I (1060–63). László I (1077–95)—later canonized— restored the authority of the crown and the church; but his nephew Kalman (1095–1116) called the *Bookman*, since he had been intended for the Church, blinded his brother Almos and his infant nephew Béla. The child survived, however, to rule as Béla II (1131–41), and by the mid twelfth century the Magyars, in spite of Byzantine resistance, had dominated Croatia and much of Dalmatia. Béla III (1173–96), though brought up in Constantinople, opted for the Catholic West, married a French princess and made himself king of Croatia, which he ruled through a Viceroy or *Ban*, as well as becoming overlord of part of Galicia east of the Carpathians. His reign was prosperous; but after a disputed succession, the Magyar nobles forced Andrew II (1205–35) to accept the Golden Bull of 1222, a *Magna Carta* that went wrong, whereby they all obtained a formal right of resistance to the kings and their officials.

The Mongol invasion of 1241–2 now utterly devastated the country, and in the aftermath Béla IV (1235–70) had to rely on the nobility to build and garrison the chain of forts which were the best answer to further Mongol incursions and to form the heavy cavalry for counter-attack. The crown was further weakened by Lázló IV "the Cuman" (1274–90). His mother had been

[1]C. A. Macartney. *Hungary*, a short history. Edinburgh, 1962. p. 17.
[2]The circlet of the crown still preserved is Byzantine, probably presented in 1075, but the closed top portion may be contemporary with St. Stephen. See Macartney. *op. cit.* p. 13 note.

of that fierce tribe, he took after his pagan maternal forebears, and he had to be killed. Andrew III, a collateral Arpád, whose mother was Venetian, proved intelligent and well intentioned, but he died young and childless in 1301, with no direct heir.

The Arpád dynasty, now at an end, had managed to bring the Magyars within Catholic Christendom, lavishly endowed the Church, and encouraged the immigration of German settlers, particularly into the towns, as well as establishing a Francophil court and extending their own authority over Croatia, Southern Galicia and a fringe of other *Banats*. They had survived the transition from a nomadic to an agricultural economy and kept the Magyar nobles within bounds; but they had not, as had the Monarchs of France or England, established a centralized authority. Hungary was dominated by restive and martial magnates who had risen above the free gentry, who themselves still maintained their full liberties. Like the Polish aristocracy, they all lived off a subject peasantry and were susceptible to the lure of impracticable conquest beyond ill-defined borders, while the authority of their kings was precarious and intermittent.

V

The centre from which civilization had radiated into Eastern Europe and the Balkans since Antiquity had always been Byzantium, which, in spite of the doctrinal schism of 1054 with the Catholic West, had here still retained its preponderance. Now the eastern empire, as already related, received a mortal blow; not from Asian enemies it had long defied, but from the Christian West. The Venetians, in rivalry with the Genoese, had long conducted a lucrative trade with Byzantium and its dependencies along the Adriatic coast, in Greece and in the islands; they now diverted the Fourth Crusade from fighting the Infidel in *Outremer* to clinching their own commercial domination of Constantinople and the Levant and plundering the schismatic Byzantines.

Innocent III's project of another crusade had excited the barons of north-western France. Now in 1201, realizing that it would be prudent to travel by sea, in collaboration with barons from northern Italy, they had begun to negotiate with the Venetians. The Doge was the aged but astute Enrico Dandolo, of whom Villehardouin writes that "this distinguished man had good reason to stay at home, for though he had fine eyes, he could hardly see, because he had lost his sight from an injury to his head. But he was stout hearted" (*"que perdue avoit la veue par une plaie qu'il ot el chief. Mais parere de grant cuer"*).[1] He had promised to build transports for 4500 horses and 9000

[1]Geoffroi de Villehardouin, *Conquête de Constantinople,* ed. M. M. de Woilly, Paris, 1882, p. 38. There is an English translation by M. R. B. Shaw, *Joinville and Villehardouin: Chronicles of the Crusades*, Penguin, Harmondsworth, 1963. Villehardouin never doubts that God was entirely on the side of the "pilgrims". He was himself one of the leaders of the Crusade, and he is the first considerable vernacular historian of France. Villehardouin himself secured a fief in Messenia in the Peloponnese.

squires, and other ships for 4500 knights and 20,000 foot sergeants, along with nine months rations for the men and fodder for the horses, and all for 5 marks per horse and two marks per man—the horses presumably taking up more room and consuming a greater bulk of fodder. It was estimated that 85,000 silver marks would meet the bill. Amid scenes of wild enthusiasm the Venetian populace had ratified the bargain made by the Doge. But when, in June 1202, the crusaders converged on Venice and took up their quarters on the island of San Nicolo di Lido prudently provided by the Venetians, it was found that far too few had arrived to raise the required sum. The Doge then suggested payment for the transport in kind; the King of Hungary, he said, had taken Zara, the main Venetian port of the Adriatic coast; perhaps the Crusaders could recover it for them? The 34,000 silver marks outstanding could then conveniently be won by the conquest.

With little choice, for they had run up some heavy bills in Venice while on the island of the Lido, the crusaders complied. By November the harbour of Zara was taken by spectacular assault, and despite the protests of the Cistercian abbot of Vaux that Christians ought not to attack Christians, the city was besieged, heavily attacked and forced to surrender.

Events in Constantinople now played into Venetian hands. The emperor Isaac II Angelus had been deposed and blinded, and in 1203 his son, who had taken refuge with his father-in-law, Philip of Swabia in Germany, arrived in Zara begging for help against their supplanter, Alexius III. Venetians and Crusaders took up his cause; the fleet was diverted to Constantinople.

After stiff resistance, the defenders using a fire ship—a *mult grant enging,* sent down wind—the hitherto impregnable city was occupied by the Byzantine claimant who was restored as Alexius IV. He had been lavish with impracticable promises, including bringing the entire Byzantine empire under the Roman Church, and providing 200,000 marks for the "pilgrims".

By the spring of 1204 he had been strangled by the Byzantines; led by a usurper, they rose against the heretic barbarians from the west and their detested Venetian allies. So in April the Crusaders sacked the august city of Constantine, the focus and protector of Christian civilization in Eastern Europe. The plunder was fantastic: gold, silver and jewels; silks and furs—"*Si granz li gaaienz faiz que nus ne vos en sauroit dire le fin ... Toz les cheirs avoirs que oncques trové en terre*"—"The booty so great that we do not know how to tell you the end of it ... all the treasures that have ever been found in the world." And all this taken by twenty thousand men against over four hundred thousand in the strongest town in the whole world and the best fortified—*en la plus fort vile qui fust en tot le munde et lo mielz fermée.*[1]

A Flemish adventurer, Baudouin de Flandres et Hainault, became emperor, and the Byzantine empire in Greece was carved up into feudal fiefs: the Italian Boniface of Montferrat became "King" of Salonika, there was a "Frankish" Duke of Athens and a Catholic Prince of Achaia; but the Despotate of Mistra in Sparta reverted to the Byzantines and became a memorable centre of Byzantine culture, still alive in the frescoes of the Pantanassa. The Venetians

[1]Villehardouin. *op. cit.* pp. 146–8.

occupied the best commercial sites of wharfs in the city and took over Euboea and Crete, which they briskly developed, as well as many of the lesser Greek islands. But a singularly incongruous and inefficient feudal disorder settled on Old Greece, and restive western barons defied the sketchy authority of the usurpers in Constantinople, doubly unpopular since the Venetians had ousted the Orthodox Patriarch.

Baudouin de Flandres did not last long: he was killed in 1205 in battle with the Bulgars, and although his brother and successor, the able Henri de Flandres, tried with some success to hold the impossible inheritance, after his death in 1216 the incongruous feudal regime began to break down. When in 1261 Michael VIII Palaeologos of Nicaea returned, the original Byzantine empire was past repair; though by diplomacy, including even a formal submission to the Pope, which infuriated most of his subjects, he thwarted the designs of Charles of Anjou of Naples and Sicily, and in 1282, incited the Sicilians to the notorious massacre of the French known as the "Sicilian Vespers".

The Turks, meanwhile, were closing in from the east; it was impossible for the Byzantines to fight both the Catholic Christians and the Muslims at the same time. The Fourth Crusade had done its work, and only the shrewd Venetians had reaped their harvest, still apparent in the architecture of their depots along the Dalmatian coast, and memorable for their vineyards in Crete from which the Portuguese would plant the vines of Madeira.

The crusade of 1204 was a catastrophe for Eastern Europe. Byzantium survived only "as one state amongst other states as strong or stronger" and the crippling of its power was disastrous for the southern Slavs. "Hitherto, vassal or free, they had regarded Constantinople as the centre of their universe, the source of their culture and religion. Now suddenly and unexpectedly they were orphaned."[1] In contrast to the consolidation of the Atlantic realms, the Balkan peoples were never stabilized.

VI

Three major Byzantine states survived; the most powerful at Nicaea in Anatolia, whence in 1261 a legitimate Greek emperor had regained Constantinople; the others were at Trebizond on the Black Sea towards the eastern boundary of the empire, the other in Epirus in the west. In the Balkans, over difficult country, broad but superficial Bulgarian and Serb dominations now succeeded each other, while in Greece French, Italian and even Catalan feudatories fought over Attica, Corinth and the Peloponnese, as western adventurers now diverted their energies from unrewarding Outremer to what had once been Hellas.

The attack of the Fourth Crusade on Constantinople had been the Bulgars' opportunity, and in 1205 their pent up hatred for the Greeks had erupted

[1] N. H. Baynes & H. St. L. B. Moss. Byzantium. Oxford, 1949. p. 359.

against the now Latin empire. Baudouin I, less than a year after his coronation, had been outmanoeuvred, captured and murdered by Tsar Kaloyan Āsen of Trnovo, who had already conquered Niš and Belgrade and, making the best of both worlds, obtained a royal crown from Innocent III. Under Ivan Āsen II (1218-41) this second Bulgarian realm now extended from the Adriatic to the Black Sea, for he had subdued even the redoubtable Albanians, and Trnovo became the centre of the second creative phase of Bulgarian medieval culture, with its Church under an Orthodox Patriarch and still memorable for fine architecture and frescoes.

As for the Serbs, in 1167, their Chieftain Stefan Nemanja, with Venetian aid, had more than held his own against the Byzantines, and having built the foundation of a Serbian realm, abdicated to become a monk on Athos. His son and successor, Stefan II (1196-1228), became King of the Serbs, known as "Stefan the First Crowned" after his coronation by his uncle St. Sava, who had returned to the "world" from Athos, and in effect founded a national church independent of Constantinople.

Stefan Uros I (1243-76), in a relatively peaceful and prosperous reign, relied heavily on the support of the Venetians; Stefan Uros II (1281-1321) subdued Bosnia and most of Macedonia; but he had to blind his rebellious son. But the blind Stefan Dekenski Uros III, restored in 1322, led the Serbs in 1330 to victory over the Bulgars at Velbuzd.

His illegitimate son, Stefan Dushan (1331-55), strangled his father; he then became the first Serbian Tsar, the ruler of a far-flung but ephemeral hegemony. He was the one Balkan ruler who realized the importance of uniting all Christians against the Turks; and by 1345 he had conquered all Macedonia and western Thrace and mastered Epirus and Thessaly. He established his capital at Skoplie and drew up and tried to enforce the *Zakonnik* Law Code and to administer his realm on the Byzantine model. He also worked with a Council of his magnates and on occasion summoned the lesser nobility to a *sobor* (parliament), so he won unusual support and prestige. Yet Serbia remained predominantly agricultural and feudal, with an Italianate merchant class confined mainly to the Dalmatian coast, and even the Serbs failed to assimilate the martial Bosnians, Dalmatians, Albanians, Macedonians and Bulgars whom they had conquered. When in 1255 Stefan Dushan died on the way to attack Constantinople, his realm disintegrated.

Like the Bulgars, the Serbians were soon overwhelmed by the Ottoman Turks, who first in 1371 at the battle of the Maritza crushed the Bulgars; and then at the fatal field of Kossovo in 1389 inflicted final disaster to the Serbs. Both the Bulgar and Serb empires had failed in the impossible task of pacifying the Balkans, after the Byzantine empire had virtually collapsed. But both left traditions of martial and autonomous orthodox Christian civilization which lived on in folk memory until the nationalist movements of the nineteenth century. Once the Byzantine power to protect them from Asian invaders had gone, Greeks, Bulgars and Serbs, divided by mutual animosities, were helpless before the Ottoman armies which increasingly outclassed anything in Europe. While in the West medieval national realms were consolidated, in the Balkans, as in Poland and Hungary, the effort failed.

XXI

The Mongols and Kievan Russia

The other major set-back to Central and Eastern Europe and the Levant was the swift and devastating Mongol incursion of the mid-thirteenth century. It was a new version of an ancient theme, the onslaughts of the predatory nomads of Central Asia on the surrounding settled lands. Attila in the fifth century had penetrated deep into France and northern Italy; but now the Mongols proved even more destructive than the Huns. They originated, not from Central Asia, but from the Far East in the area which now includes the Buryatskya republic of the U.S.S.R. east of Lake Baikal and north of modern Mongolia: the so-called Tatars came from even further east around the upper Amur which enters the sea opposite Sakhalin, itself on the Sea of Okhotsk. Tatar was the West's generic name for all the Mongols.

They had been organized by a leader of genius. Temudjin was the son of a minor Mongol chief; after a childhood of atrocious dangers, he had made himself supreme over all the Mongol clans as Genghis—the Inflexible—Khan. His objective, within the range of his knowledge, was quite simple: the conquest of the world. Though widely believed to have been the greatest architect of ruin in world history, he was in fact, in his utterly ruthless way, a methodical and far ranging organizer. All centred on the Mongol royal family and the Mongol ruling tribe, whose laws were promulgated through the great *Yasa* or Imperial Decrees.

The Mongols, save for the immediate royal family, were all equal before the supreme Khan, who took no other title, and though they elected him in their assemblies or *Kumiltays*, they were all bound on pain of death to his service.[1] Their armies were simply and logically organized, in units of ten, a hundred, a thousand and ten thousand, all under iron discipline, and, again on pain of death, no man could move from his assigned unit into another. Their small sturdy horses could cover vast distances, and each Mongol had from one to four remounts on campaign; they were essentially archers, but well equipped for close combat with sabres, axes, lassoes and nets, and they practically lived

[1]For the best account in English see G. Vernadsky and M. Karpovich. *A History of Russia*, Vol. III. *The Mongols and Russia*. New Haven, 1953.

in the saddle. In battle they would manoeuvre to signals from black and white pennants and from lanterns at night, and they charged home only when their arrows, lethal up to three hundred yards, had crippled or demoralized the enemy. They could exist for weeks on fermented *koumis* (mare's milk) and raw meat—"accursed raw-eating Tatars" as the Russians called them.[1]

The Great Khan himself organized an elite imperial guard, and further decreed that, "if there be found in the horde moonlike girls", they were to be collected for the Khan and his family to make their choice, keeping the most moonlike ones, and "kindly" dismissing those rejected, to serve the Royal Dames. As the conquests increased, Genghis Khan would present his immediate family with literally thousands of slaves and colossal plunder.

The first Mongol objective had naturally been China; but after their main force had sacked Peking, devastated the great centres of the old Han and T'ang civilizations and begun to take over the entire Ch'in empire of northern China, Genghis Khan had commanded an invasion of Central Asia. The literate Uigurs of the Tarim basin south of the Altai had been cowed and assimilated, as had been the Turkic tribes of the Khara-Khitai. The combined hordes had then swept into Afghanistan where they destroyed Herat and most of its inhabitants, and on into Persia where they took Hamadan. Other hordes had moved directly west and, having defeated the Georgians of the northern Caucasus, utterly routed their first Europeans when in 1222 they out-manoeuvred and destroyed a big Russian army led by the Grand Princes of Kiev and Smolensk on the banks of the Kalkha near the Sea of Azov. Not even the Polovtsi, driven into alliance with the Russians, could stand up to them; and Mongol atrocities were calculated as well as instinctive—the penalty, to serve as a warning, if a city refused the first demand for surrender.

But it was superior Mongol discipline, mobility and planning that made them invincible. The Mongols proper had been kept alert during the bitter far eastern winters by vast organized hunts, which served as practice for manoeuvres, and, when on campaign in Russia, they would fight in winter. It was this mobility and hardihood, not their numbers—since grossly exaggerated— that outclassed the relatively slow-moving Russians or ill-disciplined feudal armies, Hungarian or German. Since they objected to agriculture as such (it wasted good pasture), they despised and hunted the peasants of Eastern Europe, and are thought to have halved the population of Hungary. Moreover, after they had captured Chinese experts in siege warfare, even fortified towns did not stop them; and when they massacred the inhabitants, they decapitated everyone, to make sure that no one escaped by shamming dead: hence their penchant for making pyramids of skulls.

These brilliantly organized barbarians, under commanders from east of

[1]This appetite for raw flesh particularly horrified Europeans. Joinville recorded that they put "uncooked meat between their saddles and the tails of their coats, and when the blood is well pressed out they eat it quite raw." *Chronicles of the Crusades. op. cit.* p. 287.

In fact they invented what is still called the "Tartar beefsteak". (The correct spelling is Tatar. Tartar derived from a medieval pun, which equated Tatars with the inhabitants of Tartarus, that is, of Hell.)

Outer Mongolia, now fell on Europe. The attack on south Russia had been merely a reconnaissance; and when in 1227 Genghis Khan died and was succeeded as Supreme Khan by his son Ogodai, there was a pause. Then in 1231 the Mongols overran northern Persia and Azerbaijan; in 1236 eastern Georgia; then under Batu Khan, grandson of Genghis, they again invaded Russia. They took and sacked Riazan and, in 1238, Vladimir, Suzdal and Moscow. They even got as far north as Novgorod, though they failed to take it. In 1239 came the greatest disaster: Batu Khan's own horde utterly destroyed Kiev, the main centre of Russian civilization, and another horde destroyed Krakow, the main Polish capital. In 1241 even the Teutonic Knights of Prussia were routed at Liegnitz. Batu, meanwhile, had swept into Hungary and routed the Hungarians at Mohi.

But central and part of Western Europe were now spared further devasta-tion. Not through their own efforts—Frederick II and Gregory IX were more concerned with their own quarrel:[1] but because, by the end of 1242 Ogodai Khan, who was subject to a common Mongol weakness in prosperity, had drunk himself to death in Karakorum and Batu raced back across Asia to secure his dynastic position. Central Europe was abandoned, but the Mongols maintained their grip on Russia, with lasting and fateful effect.

II

The Eastern Slavs, who under Scandinavian impulsion since the days of Ryurik who had founded Novgorod in 862, had built up a civilization of trading cities along the rivers of Western Russia and assimilated Orthodox Christianity and Byzantine culture, had long created a flourishing area of Christendom in touch with the Baltic, Scandinavia and the West, but based on the original Slav settlements. Yaroslav the Wise in the mid-eleventh century, and Vladimir Monomakh, who was half Greek, had married into the royal families of the Catholic West, and architects and artists trained in Byzantium had been invited to their courts. And, following Byzantine example, the Russians had written revealing Chronicles, still full of interest. As for example the account in the *Laurentian Chronicle of Vladimir* (980–88) of the original conversion to Christianity. "When the Prince (Vladimir) arrived at his capital, he directed

[1]The Catholic Christians long maintained a silly fantasy that Wang-Khan of the Kereit was really *Johannes* and so the Christian "Prester John", and that the Mongols, despite cogent evidence to the contrary, could be converted to Christianity and become allies against the Muslims. Hence the mission in 1245 of Friar John Pian del Carpino, sent to Mongolia by Innocent IV, and the mission of Friar William de Rubriquis, sent in 1253 to Karakorum to the Court of Mangu Khan by Louis IX. Both wrote vivid accounts of their travels; but neither Pope nor King gained much from their missions. Mangu Khan replied with the utmost arrogance giving a list of Central Asian potentates that he had crushed, demanding a yearly tribute from the French, and concluding "If you refuse to do this we will destroy you as we have destroyed the kings already named." Joinville. *op. cit.* p. 288. For a good introductory account of these missions and of the Mongol way of life, see John Bradford. *Nomad Empires of Asia* in *The Concise Encyclopaedia of World History*, ed. John Bowle. Second Edition. London, 1971. pp. 168–186.

that the idols should be overturned and that some should be cut to pieces and others burned up:[1] [and he] sent heralds throughout the whole city proclaiming 'If anyone, whether rich or poor, beggar or slave, does not come tomorrow to the river he will be an enemy of mine.' When the people heard that they went gladly, saying "If this were not good, the Prince and his boyars would not have accepted it."

Outside the cities, the converted people were not settled in manors as in the West but in village communities or *mirs*, but the tariffs for homicide according to status of the victim are similar to the Anglo-Saxon codes: offenders are fined for "cutting down a landmark oak", and the Princes attempted, as in England, to pin down responsibility for punishing crime on local "guilds"; ordeal by hot iron was prescribed for major thefts, by water for lesser ones. There are glimpses of Russian family life, already temperamental; as when a girl refuses to marry the man chosen by her parents, and, compelled by force, tries to make away with herself, the parents shall be at fault before the bishop.[2] The famous *Testament* of the most successful ruler of Kievan Russia, the great Vladimir Monomahk, so called after his grandfather, the emperor Constantine Monomakos, exhorted his sons "without fear of death or war or wild beasts (he had himself survived beng 'stamped on' by an elk) [to] do a man's work." One is reminded of the benevolence of King Alfred the Great when the Russian Prince advises, "Pass no man without a greeting: give him a kindly word." And he warns his heirs not to depend on their *druzhina* (retinue) or *voivody* (officials), but always on themselves: to get up early, refrain from too much strong drink, and "never to put down their weapons without a quick glance round."

The relationship of princes with subjects was complicated by the extraordinary rules of family succession, so that when a senior prince died, the next brother might succeed him from a junior principality and all, as it were, might move up or across a step. Hence the *Suzdal Chronicle* (1175–76) records how the people of Vladimir, involved in a consequent dynastic war, said to their Prince Mikhalko, "Either make peace, Prince, or else look after yourself." To which, with what appears a curious open-mindedness, the Prince, ready in the Russian way for discussion, replied "You are right. Why should you perish because of me?" He then left them, and the people of Vladimir "saw him off with tears."[3] One city got rid of a prince who had married a priest's wife, declaring that they would keep him but "would not bow down to her." So he chose to go.

The Church obtained vast endowments and comprehensive liberties: its courts were early independent, and, in contrast to western practice, the lay power accepted that the wives and children of married clergy, as well as monks and nuns, and the physicians, bakers, brewers, free men and slaves who looked

---

[1]They deserved it. Standing on a hill outside Kiev, Perun, with a silver head and gold moustache, Dazh'bog, Stribog, Simar'gi and Mokosh had been accorded human sacrifice. See *A Source Book of Russian History from early times to 1917*. ed. G. Vernadsky *et al*. New Haven, 1972. p. 26.
[2]Vernadsky *op. cit*. p. 40.
[3]Vernadsky *op. cit*. p. 43.

after them, were all outside its jurisdiction. As might be expected in trading cities, there are laws about the affairs of merchants; if, for example, a trader with money on board belonging to another suffers shipwreck, he need only pay back the money by instalments, since "his ruin was from God."

Upon this long established and civilized society and its eastern outposts, vulnerable because more dependent on trade than on broad-based agriculture, descended the Mongol hordes, when "in the winter of 1238 the godless Tatars, with their Tsar Baku came from the east to the land of Riazan" demanding a tenth of everything—including horses. "They surrounded the city with a palisade, took and burnt the town, sworded some, shot some down with arrows and flung them into the flames." Then "these accursed godless ones" pushed on westward. Years after, when Carpini passed it the site of Kiev was still reduced almost to nothing, and the place and countryside littered with skulls and bones. Only Novgorod in the north near Lake Ilmen survived, protected by its flooded marshes, and in 1240, fighting a war on two fronts, proved strong enough, under Alexander Nevsky, grand Prince of Vladimir, to defeat both the Swedes on the Neva, and in 1242 the Teutonic Knights on the ice of Lake Peipus though they had conquered East Prussia, Livonia and Esthonia. These victories stopped further invasions from the west; but the Russians remained almost cut off from the Baltic just when they were being cut off by the Mongols from the Black Sea. And the Mongols, with their Turkic subordinates, were there to stay.

Much has been made of the *Pax Mongolica* since the Mongol rulers were animists with a respect for their own *Shamans* and tolerant of other religions; because they organized an official post service with relays of horses to keep themselves informed about their colossal empire,[1] and because they fostered commerce from which tribute could be raised. It was in fact a peace of death and demoralization. Summoned to the Golden Horde at Batu Serai on the Volga on the northern shore of the Caspian, or sometimes even to the Great Khan's court at Karakorum in Mongolia, the Russian Princes did not know whether to expect promotion or death. Many, including Alexander Nevsky himself, and later the grand Princes of Moscow, came to terms with the enemy; some Russians even took service with the Great Khan in the Far East. Most Russians became inured to a regime of arbitrary and tyrannic power, remote, inexorable and feared: servility and deviousness best made for survival.

But Orthodox Christianity and much of the civilization of Russia carried on; the cathedral of Sancta Sophia at Kiev, built about 1036–46, long before the Mongol attack, somehow survived and can compare with Haghia Sophia at Constantinople or with Ravenna. At Novgorod the early twelfth-century church of St. George had first displayed the characteristic Russian "onion" dome, better adapted to the northern climate than the rounded Byzantine kind. St. Dmitri's at Vladimir (1193–97) has austere elegance, adapting the Western Romanesque style of decoration to Russian traditions. Ikon painting, acclimatized by the twelfth century, developed on its own lines in the

[1] The Khans gave strict orders to those concerned to spare their mounts.

monasteries when Russia was cut off from Constantinople and the West. The main preserver of the Russian culture was the Orthodox Church.

But the Mongol conquest was a brutalizing disaster. Most of the original Mongols having returned to their homelands and to China, Turkic *vashkaki* tax collectors were ubiquitous, exacting tribute at first in furs and silver, based on a census which also served for regional military conscription of fixed numbers of men and horses, worse than any tax. Nor was there any way for Princes to escape the summons to the Golden Horde or to Karakorum, or of ensuring safety when they arrived. Mikhailo of Chenizov, ordered to bow to the Mongol sacred fire, refused, and was at once executed with knives. Sometimes the Mongol "Peace" prevented the old feuds between cities over the succession, and Mongol-Turkic administration set more efficient standards; but it would not be until September 1380 that Dmitri Ivanovitch Donskoi would rally the Russians to combine in a great counter-attack. "Let us go against the accursed Godless, impious and dastardly eaters of uncooked meat and [the Khan] Mamai for the Orthodox Christian Faith and all Christians." St. Boris and St. Gleb would appear in the sky along with the *Archistrategos* Mikhailo, and the Tatars would be routed at the battle of Kulikovo Pole—the snipe meadow.

Two years later, the Tatars, to be sure, would sack and burn Moscow, but the catastrophe would not eradicate the nascent Muscovite power. Originally a stockaded settlement, enlarged by Daniel Alexandrovitch Nevsky and by his son Yuryi (1303–25), Moscow proved well enough rooted in the forested area to survive Mongol-Turkic attack, and then even the attack of Timur Lenk. If the Muscovite princes would perforce collaborate with the Golden Horde, their heirs would create an hegemony more Eurasian, formidable and massive than that ever achieved by Kievan Russia.

XXII

The Northern Periphery

On the periphery of north-western and northern Europe, in lands which the Romans had never occupied and hardly explored, prehistoric peoples had long been emerging into civilization. Their world was pervaded by the sea; the north Atlantic with its rain-drenched cloudscapes and enormous rollers pounding in from Dursey Head and Valencia in Cork and Kerry, up to Iona and Ardnamurchan, and Dunvegan on Skye, and away past Cape Wrath and the Orkneys to Norway. It produced brave, hard and practical people, and an impressive literature from Iceland in sagas written down in the mid thirteenth century in which the dour and prosaic characters, unlike those of medieval romances, knew exactly what they were about. Denmark, the most culturally sophisticated and strategically well placed of the Scandinavian countries, was also pervaded by the sea, its peninsula and islands set in the North Sea and the shallow but icy Baltic, giving access to Poland, Finland, Esthonia and Russia. The contrast between this maritime environment, particularly in its Atlantic aspect, with the land-bound countries of central and eastern Europe was entire.

II

One realm early consolidated was Scotland, and it proved strong enough to establish and retain its identity against the predominant English for many centuries, and even after the Anglo-Scottish union of 1707. It also developed in the course of time tenacious links with France, Scandinavia and the Low Countries.

The Kings of Scotland had originated in the West, in Dalraida, and Christianity mainly in Iona. The MacAlpin dynasty had been Celtic; but by the early ninth century Kenneth MacAlpin had extended his overlordship to the east coast. When the usurper Macbeth of Moray had supplanted Duncan MacAlpin I, his reign had proved successful but ephemeral; defeated at Dunsinane and killed at Lumphanan, he had been ousted by Malcolm MacAlpin Canmore (1057–93), whose marriage to Margaret, brought up in

Hungary and sister of the Anglo-Saxon Edgar Atheling, had brought continental influences to Scots civilization.

After the Norman Conquest of England, Normans had penetrated to the lowlands, and a Norman feudal aristocracy and gentry settled in, bearing famous names of Scots history—as de Valeys (Wallace), de Brus (from Brix in the Cotentin), Balliol (from de Bailleul). Although the basic contrast between the Celtic, Gaelic-speaking, tribal Highlands and the settled Normanized lowlands with their predominantly Scandinavian and northern English population continued, the originally Norman landholders became long enough established to combine with the MacAlpin kings to resist English encroachment: William Garbel or "the Lion" was of sufficient consequence to begin the "auld alliance" with the French; and by the time that Edward I, Scotorum Malleus, moved against Scotland, a national resistance led by William Wallace (captured and executed in 1305) proved too strong even for him. Still more for his incompetent successor, Edward II, whose elaborate and decorative army was utterly defeated in 1314 by the Scots led by Robert de Bruce, Earl of Carrick and King of Scotland (1306–29), at Bannockburn; a victory of pikemen and disciplined cavalry over ill-deployed archers and undisciplined mounted knights. By 1328, the year before Bruce's death of leprosy,[1] Scotland had been recognized as independent by the Treaty of Northampton.

The Scots monarchs had been only intermittently first among equals in a feudal society riven by vendettas. The Bruce himself had stabbed the Red Comyn in church, so that his own grandson, the child David II, incurred a feud from the Comyn's kin, and the English took advantage of a disputed succession to put forward their own candidate. In 1333 the young Edward III routed the Scots at Halidon Hill, though they had been prudent enough to refuse his challenge to come down from an unchivalrously strong position to fight on more level terms. Moreover, the Stuart dynasty, descended from Robert the Bruce's daughter Marjory and Walter, hereditary Steward (Stuart) of Scotland, seldom had luck: the heirs were often children, and when adult, singularly apt to get captured, so that the Scots had to ransom them at frightful cost. James I was captured at sea in 1406 and, understandably, not ransomed for eighteen years; when redeemed,.he proved himself formidable, but was murdered in 1437. James II personally stabbed a Black Douglas, and in 1460 got blown up by a cannon, too eagerly supervised. The main achievement of James III, who succeeded to the throne aged nine, was to obtain Orkney and Shetland by marrying a Danish princess.

The Scots Crown, though strong enough to lead a popular resistance to the English, was never a Parliamentary one, grounded in the alliance of a strong centralized Conciliar royal government with the gentry and the middle classes, but remained, even up to the time of James VI of Scotland and I of England,

[1]The Black Douglas of the day took the Bruce's heart in a silver casket to be buried in the Holy Land, but on the way could not resist fighting the Moors on a Crusade in Spain. Flinging the casket into the midst of the enemy, he charged after it, saying that he would follow the Bruce as he always had, only to be cut down by Moorish scimitars. Fortunately the casket was retrieved and brought back, to be interred, after its adventures, in Scotland.

when in 1603 the Stuarts inherited England, at the mercy of feuding magnates, churchmen, and recalcitrant clansmen, worsened in the sixteenth century by the clash of virulent sectarian dogmatists.

The situation of the Welsh had been unfavourable since the Roman occupation of Britain, when their Druids, in spite of vigorous imprecations and contorted magic, had been cornered and massacred by the legionaries on Anglesey. The very word "Welsh" signifies "foreigner" in Anglo-Saxon, and was applied to the original inhabitants of Britain driven into the mountains. Although far more of them survived in the West Midlands and the West Country than was once assumed and intermarried with German-Danish invaders, by language and temperament they were far more incompatible with the Anglo-Saxons than were the Lowland Scots; they even detested their supplanters so much that they had no interest in converting them to Welsh Christianity, and long refused to collaborate with the missionaries from Rome and Frankish Gaul. Loquacious, excitable, quick to take a point or a sheep, they maintained their own language and their own fine habit of song—part of a prehistoric Celtic society, mainly pastoral. Driven into relatively poor country, they were apt to live by raiding one another and their neighbours along the Welsh border, and they were recruited as mercenaries from the days of William Rufus to those of Charles I, giving an undeserved bonus to their English enemies by introducing them to the Welsh long bow.

Their main and inexpugnable stronghold was in the mountains of Snowdonia. Here Gruffydd Prince of Gwynedd had held a sketchy sway in the days of the Norman Henry I, and his son, Owain, had successfully resisted the campaigns of Henry II. The Lord Rhys of Cardigan had been a glamorous leader of revolt, and his grandson, Llywelyn the Great, had taken advantage of John's conflict with his barons to regain much territory overrun by the English.

But the Welsh achievement was negative; they had not the resources to strike at all far into England, though they preserved their language, literature and way of life, well described by the Norman-Welsh Giraldus Cambrensis in his *Descriptio Cambriae—Description of Wales* (1194). The Welsh occasioned much concern and expense to Edward I, who named his highly unsatisfactory heir, Edward II, as the first English Prince of Wales.

If the relationship of the English with the Scots had been stark and with the Welsh lively, their relationship with the Irish early proved tragic. Here at the north-west extremity of Europe was an island strategically placed at a singular disadvantage to itself and to its neighbours. Never occupied by the Romans, it had remained the setting of a prehistoric tribal society, belligerent, incoherent, and technologically primitive. Here the last of the Celtic Iron Age aristocracies, once the overlords of half Europe, had been washed up. Calling themselves Gaels and the country Erin, they had preserved the "heroic" way of life and literature of their continental forebears, while exploiting the native *Firbolg*, perhaps of Iberian origin. Like the Gauls in Caesar's time, they had tribal strongholds, but not their own ports and towns: these had been founded by the Vikings—the Norse *Finngall*, the "fair-haired foreigners", and the Danish *Dubhgall*, the "dark-haired foreigners"—mainly as ports—Dublin, Cork, Waterford and Limerick.

In spite of the high culture and missionary exploits of the age of Colum-banus, the "high kings" or Ard Rí originally established at Tara in Meath by Niall in the late fourth century, had but a shadowy authority, and their descendants, the Ui Neill, were hard put to maintain even that.

Thus disunited and at odds among themselves, the Irish fell a relatively easy prey to Norse invaders; and even when, as near Clontarf in 1014, they won a battle, they typically forgot to guard the most famous of their High Kings, the aged Brian Boru, who, too old for battle, was slain in his tent by a stray Viking making off to his ship. The death of Brian Boru, who had come nearest of the Ard Rí to bringing political coherence and cultural revival to the island, marked at least the end of the worst Viking attacks, and the Norsemen of the ports, traders as well as pirates, became assimilated with the rest of the population. But the endless rivalries of the petty "Kings" of Munster and Leinster, of Meath and Connaught and of their followings, prevented the rise of any central authority; while the Normans who had mastered South Wales were now awaiting their chance.

In 1138 King Stephen created Gilbert de Clare Earl of Pembroke, and his able son Richard—known as "Strongbow"—soon observed the opportunities for conquest across the Irish Sea. The more so since Henry II, not a man to forgo an advantage, had obtained a Bull from Adrian IV. The English Pope, who claimed that under the Donation of Constantine all islands belonged to the papacy, had authorized him to conquer Ireland, a permission he now passed on to "Strongbow" as the man best placed for the enterprise. In 1170 "Strongbow" therefore landed at Waterford, with 1200 to 1500 men, nominally to support the MacMurrough of Leinster,[1] against Rory O'Connor of Dublin, King of Connaught. He promptly defeated O'Connor and occupied the city, and when Henry II, wishing to assert his authority and to evade the aftermath of Becket's murder, arrived in Dublin in the following year, he was the first ruler of England to set foot in Ireland, and now officially, with Papal sanction, Dominus Hiberniae, Lord of Ireland.

He was followed in 1185 by Prince John, with an entourage of Anglo-Norman courtiers; and when King in 1210, he proved far more successful in Ireland than anywhere else, imposing the essentials of Anglo-Norman admin-istration in the area under his control, introducing a sound coinage and appointing the most famous tournament-champion in Western Europe, Wil-liam the Marshal, to govern the part of the country where the King's authority could be enforced. William married "Strongbow's" heiress and an Anglo-Norman-Irish regime was clamped on eastern and part of central Ireland, now divided into the counties of Dublin, "Strongbow's" territory of Leinster, and the de Lacy Earldom of Meath. In the kingdom of Cork or in Desmond, in Connacht and in Tir Connail and Fermanagh in the north-west, the indigenous Irish, barefoot, in saffron kilts and black cloaks, consoled and stimulated by

[1]Who had offered him his daughter Eva in marriage, and reproached him for not coming sooner with a touch of poetical diction, "The swallows have come and gone yet you are tarrying still." "Strongbow" married the girl, thus setting a significant precedent, for the Anglo-Normans became closely related to the Irish tribal aristocracy.

usquibaugh and by itinerant bards and harpers, continued their traditional way of life until Tudor times.

III

While the Western European monarchs were becoming stronger within compacter realms, the rulers of Scandinavia became less able to control their nobles, and all the monarchies except Denmark remained elective. The independent small farmers—the Vikings who stayed at home—also lost ground before the major land-owners, before the Germanized middle class in the relatively sparse towns, and before the wealthy Hansa merchants who had their own quarters and privileges.

Norway, with its vast expanse of forest, fjord and mountains, with communications mainly by sea, could support only a small population for its size, and its people had been in the forefront of Viking raids and colonization, not least in Iceland, colonized by about 850. The originally Swedish Ynglinga dynasty, so called because, like the Merovingians, it was thought to be descended from a God—the God Yngve, better known as Fray,—had emerged from pagan prehistory with Harald *Fairhair* (872–930), a younger contemporary of King Alfred, whose son, Erik *Bloodaxe*, briefly King of York, was ousted by his younger brother Haakon (934–61) who had been brought up at Athelstan's court at Winchester, already a place of piety and learning. Retaining this imprint, he became known as Haakon the *Good*, for he attempted to acclimatize Christianity; but he was killed by the heathen Danes. By contrast, another Ynglinga, Olaf Trygvesson, a great-grandson of Harald *Fairhair*, was brought up at Kiev, began a Viking career at twelve, and took part in the second wave of Viking attacks on the England of Aethelred the Redeless. From England he tried to master and Christianize Norway, landing at Trondheim, but perished in 1000 AD fighting the Danes at the battle of Svold, leaping into the sea and sinking beneath his shield rather than surrender. He was celebrated as the "ideal" Viking, all the more poignantly since he died young. But Olaf *Digre*—the *Stout*—made the best of both worlds: after raiding in the Baltic and in Friesland, he was converted to Christianity in England, then, taking advantage of Sveyn of Denmark's preoccupations there, he crossed to Norway and so far Christianized the people that he established bishoprics before he was driven out in 1028 by the Dane, Knud the *Mighty*. After taking refuge in Kiev, he attempted to regain power, but perished in battle against the Danes at Sticklestad, where an eleventh-century church marks the place, for he was afterwards made a saint.

These struggles for power, which could be held only by the axe and which were hard to enforce in depth, were superficial, save that during them Sweden became part of Christendom; the temporary union of Norway and Sweden by Magnus IV Eriksson (1319–74) did not last, unlike that of Norway and

Denmark under his son Haakon VI, who in 1369 married Margarethe, daughter of Valdemar Atterdag, King of Denmark.

The permanent realities of Scandinavian history were social and economic: reflecting the contrast between the large areas of forest and fjord in Norway and of forest and lakes in Sweden with the sea-girt lowlands of Denmark, always much more susceptible to continental and urban influences and, after the collapse of Knud's Anglo-Danish empire, concerned with continental ambitions, where Norwegian ambitions were oceanic.

About 874 Ingolfur Arnarson, finding the rule of Harald *Fairhair* of Norway oppressive, had migrated with his household to Iceland, and settled at Reykjavík on the ice-free south-western coast. He was followed by other men and women of substance from western Norway, Orkney and Shetland, also threatened by Harald's power. They found a grim country, mainly plateau at over 1600 feet with glaciers and mountains, including Hekla, an active volcano, rising to five thousand feet. At best, only a quarter of it was fit for cultivation and pasture. But there were then beech forests, as in Denmark; the grass was good for sheep, and the sea and rivers teemed with fish; nor was the climate so appalling as might have been expected from the latitude, since the Gulf Stream brought relatively mild air and rain to the west and south-west coasts.

Arnarson had found the large island deserted, save for a few Irish hermits who wisely made off, no one knows whither. Contrary to popular belief, the Norwegians were not particularly "democratic"; their local *Tings* or assemblies were dominated by the *Godhi* or chief landowners; and when in 930 they set up the *Allting* for the whole island, the oldest Parliament in western Europe, the *Godhi* in fact made the laws and dispensed justice. But they were all intensely litigious, and men were esteemed almost as much for their knowledge of the law as for physical prowess. Nor was there much social distinction between the landholders and lesser men; all were farmers and fishermen and esteemed for their skills and cunning—including being able to "swim like a seal". By about 1000 AD, mainly for political reasons, the leaders accepted Christianity, but the so called "Icelandic Commonwealth" remained so ridden with family feuds that in 1262–4 the islanders voluntarily submitted to Haakon IV the Old of Norway, who took over the country as a personal fief.

In the thirteenth century Icelandic poetry and prose sagas were written down: bored presumably in the dark bitter winters, they had always listened to *Skalds*, as Braji the Old who, at a safe distance, had sung the praises of Harald *Fairhair* in a dialogue between a Valkyrie and a raven, as they followed him in pursuit of the corpses in his wake. Egil Skalagrimsson, one of the most celebrated of these *Skalds*, captured by Erik *Bloodaxe*, composed in a night a song glorifying his captor and so escaped execution: it was called the *Head Ransom*.

The Icelanders preserved much archaic German mythology collected in the poetic Edda in the late thirteenth century, of which the most powerful is the *Voluspá* or Prophecy, (c. 990), foretelling the *Doom* or *Twilight of the Gods*; also the *Havarmal* or (rather platitudinous) *Sayings of the High One*, and the *Flyting of Loki*, who mocks the gods. The prose Edda, composed by Snorri

Sturleson (1170-1241)[1] a landowner who lived near Reykjavík, to illustrate old poetic forms and metaphors, preserved other bloody-minded Teutonic legends, as well as some more recent Scaldic verse. The medieval Icelanders however have been best remembered rather for their own prose sagas of homespun, litigious, ordinary life, written about their own forebears in the tenth and eleventh centuries and their protracted law suits and feuds. The most famous, the *Njal Saga*,[2] delineates character with moving skill, and the *Laxdaela Saga* describes a family over five generations. The fierce and practical women often determine the outcome, sometimes settled by "giving careful notice in the hearing of all men at the Hill of the Laws", with witnesses called and arbitration accepted; more often, by wholesale murder and the burning of massive but wooden homesteads with their owners as well—the fate of Njal, that just and enduring man. The qualities admired are steadfastness, common-sense, cunning, grasp of the law, laconic self-control, a biting tongue and a biting battle axe. Victorian romantics, as William Morris, who admired muscular heroes even when not Christian, may have over-praised these dour tales, but they depict Icelandic life in homely and convincing detail and often with a novelist's insight. This grim northern literature contrasts with the contemporary romantic and precious cults of Chivalry and Courtly Love at the luxurious and sophisticated courts of southern France and Italy.

IV

Of all the Scandinavians the Swedes were the last to emerge out of a grim but fascinating prehistory, and while the Norwegians had looked to the North Sea and the Atlantic, they had looked to the Baltic and the east. In 829 in the days of the Carolingian Louis the Pious, a redoubtable Frankish monk named Ansgar had the strategically correct inspiration to mitigate Viking violence by converting the Scandinavians at home, and he had set out to Birka in Sweden near Lake Mäleran, west of modern Stockholm. Intercepted by Vikings, he had lost all his gifts and gear, but he was well received at the Court of Bjorn, King of the Svear, and allowed to build a church. Long after, as Bishop of Hamburg, though evicted from his city by Vikings, who burnt it and forced him to retreat to Bremen, he set out again to convert the Svear, but they were now so preoccupied by their successful enterprises in Russia that they were less interested in Western Christendom.

Prehistoric heathendom was strongly rooted among the people, whose main common ties derived from the network of cults centred on Uppsala, north of

---

[1] He was an Icelander born of distinguished ancestry, ingenious enough to turn the hot springs or Gesyrs of the island to good for heating a hot tiled bath, and Law Speaker for the Icelandic High Court. Unhappily this scholar and antiquary got mixed up in politics in Norway and fell out with Haakon the Old, who forced him to return to Iceland and, when he did so, had him killed.

[2] Trans. as *The Story of Burnt Njal* by G. W. Dasent, Edinburgh, 1861. See W. P. Ker. *Epic and Romance*, London 1897, 2nd Ed. 1908, for much illuminating criticism of the sagas.

modern Stockholm, where every nine years macabre ceremonies were carried out. Nine men, one for each year ahead, were hanged in the sacred grove and left to rot, and with them were hanged dogs and even horses—a feat that must have taxed the priests' sacrificial skills. This stinking charnel house, designed to propitiate the gods, was the most sacred shrine of the old religion, whose principal deities were Thor the Thunderer, who looked after the weather and the harvest, Odin the god of war, and Freya or Frigg, the god of sex. This cult was still going strong among the peasants well into the eleventh century, after the country had become officially Christian; as witness "the Norse court poet and diplomat Sigvat, who ... tells how one evening he came to a homestead; the door was closed; and in answer to his questions the people within roughly bade him begone, for they were busy with holy things, a sacrifice to their household gods. 'I fear the wrath of Odin' said the wicked woman. 'We worship the old gods.' "[1]

In spite of the tenacious resistance, the growing power and prestige of the Ottonian empire and church in Germany, followed by the conquests of Knud the Great, who claimed the overlordship of all Scandinavia as well as of England, brought increasing pressure to bear on the Swedes. Olof Scötkonung (c. 995–1025), and his descendants St. Erik and Knud, who founded Stockholm, gradually imposed Christianity as the official cult; by about 1070 the groves and temples at Uppsala were destroyed.

Swedish trade and colonization in Russia were now in the hands of well-established immigrants, and the native Swedes became more concerned with Germany—or rather the German traders with them as a "backward area". But the Finns—a Finno-Ugrian people—more "undeveloped" than the Swedes seemed the easiest target, and became the objective of a "crusade" by way of the Åland islands which led to the establishment of a Swedish aristocracy and Swedish type of culture in Finland. And in the early thirteenth century the Swedes unsuccessfully attacked the heathen Esthonians, already victims of the Danes.

With the death of Erik Eriksson (1226–50) there came a change of dynasty. Since the King was childless and the monarchy elective, the choice fell on Valdemar Folkung, Erik's nephew by marriage, soon deposed by his younger brother Magnus Ladulås (d. 1290). The new dynasty, though working in collaboration with the Church, whose ties with Rome were now better acknowledged, found it hard to hold their own against the magnates, and came to rely upon Germans who were developing the mineral resources of the country and the fur and timber trade.

This dependence provoked the Swedish magnates in 1318 to drive King Birgir Magnusson from the country, and in 1319 to elect the boy Magnus VI Eriksson, already King of Norway, to a strictly limited power; an arrangement formally defined in 1350. But by 1363 the nobles, with German help, had expelled Magnus; not, however, before he had betrothed his son Haakon (VI) of Norway to Margarethe, daughter of Valdemar IV Atterdag of Denmark in

---

[1]Ingvar Andersson. A History of Sweden. Trans. C. Hannay. Stockholm/London, 1955. p. 34. This is the best short general history of Sweden.

the hope of strengthening his position against the Swedish magnates by creating a Danish Norwegian union which might include Sweden—a policy which Margarethe would follow up by the Union of Kalmar.

V

Danish enterprise during the Viking age had been mainly directed against England, Ireland, Friesland, the Low Countries and France, and on into the Atlantic and the Mediterranean. They had obtained their richest continental prize in Normandy, the springboard for the conquest of England, already Anglo-Danish since the reign of Knud the Mighty. The Danish peninsula and islands were on a much more manageable scale than the untamed areas of forest and mountain that formed a back of beyond to the Norwegian and Swedish realms, and though the Danes lacked the iron and copper mines of Sweden or the Swedish wealth of fur and timber, their undulating but low lying lands in Jutland, Fyn and Zeeland were strategically well situated, commanding the exits from the Baltic, and well suited for agriculture and pasture.

The richest of all the Scandinavian countries in prehistoric times, Denmark was now the principal base of the western Viking campaigns, and contains the great Viking royal barrows and rune stones of Jelling, the ship grave of Ladby near Kerteminde, where a heathen magnate was buried with his horses and dogs, as well as the great fortress settlement of Trellenborg, laid out with a mathematical precision unknown since Roman times, and the great *Dannevirke* defence against the Germans. In the early ninth century Gudrun and Hemming, heathen Jelling kings, had mastered most of the country, but it had not been until 960 that Harald Blaatand (*Blue Tooth*), son of Gorm the Old, had been converted to Christianity. Sweyn I (*Forkbeard*) was still heathen when he conquered much of England, and died near Gainsborough falling from his horse when threatening to destroy the shrine at Bury St. Edmunds, after seeing a vision, it was said, of the saint himself in armour advancing to the attack.

Knud the Mighty, his son by Swietoslava, daughter of Mieszko I of Poland, the first Viking prince to become a major Western European power, became a full convert to Catholic Christianity, and brought Denmark into the tide of eleventh-century civilization, now culturally dominated by the French and the Roman Church. This French influence always continued in Denmark, all the more valued since German influences were inevitably so powerful. Under Knud's successor, Sweyn II, the Church was well established, as witness the Romanesque churches that survive, and under his descendant Valdemar I (1157–82) the Great and under Absalon, Bishop of Roskilde, the Danes reached out across the Baltic to conquer the island of Rügen and forcibly Christianize the pagan Wends. Wisely, while strengthening the *Dannevirke* against Henry the Lion, Valdemar I did homage to Friedrich Barbarossa. His son Valdemar II, *Sejr* (the *Victorious*) (1170–1241), took advantage of the conflicts in Germany caused by Frederick II to obtain an even freer hand in the East. In collaboration with Albrecht, Bishop of Livonia and founder of Riga, head of the German Knights of the Sword, and with the converted Wends, he attacked, subdued and converted the Finno-Ugrian Esthonians, whom he heavily defeated in 1219 at the battle of Tallinn on the northern coast, when the *Dannenbrog* standard fluttered down from heaven, expressing the approval of the Almighty for this feat of arms. The Esthonians long put up a gallant resistance; but the Danes temporarily managed to secure Tallinn and most of northern Esthonia from their allies the Knights.

Valdemar *Sejr* had won European prestige, and was able to marry first a Czech then a Portuguese princess. But these adventures over the Baltic and new cosmopolitan horizons had not done the Danish monarchs much good at home and Valdemar IV *Atterdag* (1321–75), father of the princess Margarethe who married Haakon VI of Norway, had to consolidate his position in Denmark, while intriguing in north Germany to enhance his power along the Baltic coast. By 1350 his efforts to strengthen the monarchy provoked rebellion, and the so-called "Land Peace" of Kalundborg, defining the rights of king, magnates and people. Moreover, the recovery of Skåne, and the capture of the important Hansa town of Visby on Götland, provoked a major attack by the Hansa cities in collaboration with the discontented nobles of Jutland, so that Valdemar was compelled to acquiesce in the Treaty of Stralsund which enhanced the privileges of the Hansa, themselves now in decline. Such were the events which led up to his daughter Margarethe's ambitious policy of uniting the three crowns, mainly against the Germans, by the Union of Kalmar.

In spite of having the best maritime strategic position of all the Scandinavian realms and having a more westernized civilization looking to France, the Danes were always, as in prehistoric times, vulnerable to German attack; nor had they a sufficient base to dominate any substantial continental sphere of influence in north Germany or even Poland. Hence the policy adumbrated at Kalmar, which they failed to persuade the Swedes permanently to accept.

The purpose of the Union of Kalmar was to strengthen the three crowns of Scandinavia against their own magnates and against the spread of German domination. Though Haakon VI of Norway had died young, his widow Margarethe of Denmark secured the succession of their son, Olaf of Norway, to the throne of Denmark, and when in 1387 the boy died, she herself took over as "Sovereign Lady" of Norway and Denmark, and had managed to become "Sovereign Lady" of Sweden as well.

In 1397 she selected her great-nephew, Erik of Pomerania, her male next of kin, to rule jointly with her, and after the magnates of all three states had been convened at Kalmar, the child was crowned King of Denmark, Norway and Sweden in June of that year, a coronation reinforced by a plan drafted for the Union of Kalmar.

In 1412 Erik succeeded Margarethe and married a sister of Henry V of England, but he failed to carry the Swedes into the Union. The Union of Denmark and Norway (including Iceland) lasted until 1814, but in 1439 Erik was deposed from Sweden, by 1448 the Swedes had in effect left the Union and though, following the Halmstad Constitution of 1483, the Union was revived, the disruption took until 1523 to be formally recognized, and the redoubtable Margarethe's dynastic project had failed.

VI

So round the north-western and northern peripheries of Europe from Ireland and western Scotland to Norway, Denmark and Sweden, to Esthonia in the eastern Baltic and to Finland, peoples hitherto on the fringe of a civilization still culturally based on the Mediterranean, if now also deep rooted in France, were brought into the orbit of Christianity and of medieval kingship. Their racial origins and environment were entirely un-Mediterranean and un-Roman; and they brought new and often contrasting qualities to European civilization, as, for example, the native Irish contrasted with the Scandinavians in physique and temperament.

The main impact of the Scandinavians on Europe had hitherto been made by Norsemen who had left their lands; now the Scandinavians who had stayed at home created their own realms; not so politically efficient as those created by Norman conquerors overseas, since the native Scandinavians grudged power to their kings, but destined, when the economic centre of gravity for Europe shifted to the Atlantic oceanic states, to a major future overseas, not least in North America.

IV

The Rise of Dynastic States

XXIII

Signoria and Humanism in Italy

Though the dilapidated Empire, still Holy and Roman, remained in theory the summit of Christendom, and by the fifteenth century decisive influence north of the Alps passed to the French Kings, the brilliant city states of Italy now asserted a workable secular power, afterwards justified according to Machiavelli by itself. The original civilization of northern Europe had come from the Mediterranean; now a civic and courtly Humanism with a better understanding of the culture of Antiquity, itself derivative from city states, gradually transformed the outlook of educated Western and Central Europe through successive phases of what came to be termed the Renaissance.

The Italians of the *Trecento* had launched a new appreciation of the writers of Antiquity. Petrarch (1304-74) had sought out manuscripts and made a rather pedantic cult of Cicero's elaborate Latin; Giovanni Boccaccio (1313-75), son of a French mother by a Florentine father, had been a banker in Naples before he settled in Florence, where he composed his *Decameron* (1349-51) during the years of the Plague, and survived to turn to ill-rewarded classical scholarship. The great architect Brunelleschi (1377-1446) began his superb Duomo at Florence in 1420, by English reckoning five years after Agincourt, and the brilliantly versatile Alberti (1404-72) became the first architect whose treatise on his subject (1452) can compare with that of Vitruvius; while Donatello (1386-1466) in his St. George and his equestrian Gattamelata made splendid new departures in European sculpture. Coluccio Salutati (1375-1466) was the first celebrated Humanist to be head of the Florentine Chancellery.

Spreading out from originally republican Florence, this new Humanism extended first over the other Italian cities and states, then, in the sixteenth-century High Renaissance, over northern Europe and into Spain and Portugal, making the Italians again culturally the most important people in Europe, while in the Netherlands wealthy and thriving cities became the cultural beacons of the north.

These city states, Italian and Flemish, had their roots in the Middle Ages; but they had risen by commerce and banking, they were incongruous in the feudal world and their outlook was business-like and methodical. Italian political theorists now began to derive the state's authority not, as had Dante, from a Divine Cosmic order, but from a secular commonwealth of the citizens, as did Marsilio of Padua, or simply as workable power justified by itself, as would Machiavelli. The Italians in practice and theory were making the cosmopolitan pageant of universal Empire and ecumenical Papacy insubstantial.

II

North of the Alps, only those emperors based on relatively compact territories had been successful. Two dynasties emerged and one lasted into modern times: the Luxembourg kings of Bohemia whose power had culminated in the fifteenth century under the Emperor Charles IV; and the Habsburgs, one of whom married the heiress of the Luxembourg line.

The first Luxembourg King of Bohemia to attain the Empire was Henry VII (1308-13), the emperor admired by Dante. Then a Wittelsbach Duke of Bavaria, the emperor Ludwig IV (1327-45), employed the English philosopher William of Ockham and Marsilio of Padua in political warfare against the Papacy, now, after Philippe le Bel of France had deposed Boniface VIII, "captive" in Avignon.

But the Luxembourgers soon regained the Empire. Henry VII's son John had married the Premyslid heiress of Bohemia; he proved a royal knight errant, that "Blind King of Bohemia", who finding the din of battle irresistible and determined to "strike just one stroke" with his sword, had been guided by his pages to his death in the melée at Crécy, probably knifed by Welsh auxiliaries. But his son and heir, Charles, escaped from the battle and made Bohemia the leading power in Central Europe.[1]

Elected King of the Romans in 1334 and Emperor (1346-78) as Charles IV, this able King of Bohemia in 1348 founded the University of Prague and transformed the city. He rebuilt the Karlstein Castle in the fashionable French style and commissioned the Charles IV bridge, as well as fostering mining, glass making and the brewing of good Czech beer. Then, as Emperor, he promulgated the Golden Bull of 1356 designed to make elections to the Empire more coherent by limiting the Grand Electors to the Kings of Bohemia, the Dukes of Saxony and Bavaria, the Markgrafs of Brandenburg and the archbishops of Köln, Mainz and Trier. Charles IV brought French and early Renaissance culture to Central Europe, and even persuaded his French queen to learn Czech. Since his authority was based on a prosperous and relatively well organized kingdom, he also brought new life to the Holy Roman Empire.

His elder son, the Emperor Wenzel (1378-1400), lacked his father's flair for government: he preferred hunting and the pleasures of the bottle, and sold

[1]Brought up at the Court of Charles IV of France, he had been given a new start by having his original name, Wenzel, changed to Charles on being married to the sister of Philip VI. His daughter, Anne of Bohemia, married Richard II of England. He was a versatile linguist, a cosmopolitan humanist who invited Petrarch to Prague and wrote an autobiography, *Vita Caroli IV* (Trans. Bede Jarrett. *The Emperor Charles IV*. London, 1935)—still worth reading.

Imperial honours to the highest bidder, including the Dukedom bought by
Gian Galleazzo Visconti, tyrant of Milan. His brother Sigismund, King of
Hungary, in effect had to take over the Empire, as King of the Romans
(1411–33), though he arranged for Wenzel's titular rehabilitation from 1411
until his death in 1419, and himself became Holy Roman Emperor only from
1433 to 1437.

But Sigismund, after a life of overwhelming responsibilities in Bohemia,
Hungary and Germany, later to be described, died without a male heir, and
the Empire passed to an even more successful dynasty. Albrecht V of
Habsburg, King of the Romans (1438–40), had married Sigismund's heiress,
the last of the Luxembourgs. Then on Albrecht's premature death, his cousin,
Friedrich of Habsburg, became the emperor Friedrich III (1440–93), and the
Habsburg policy of prudent marriage would be confirmed when Maximilian I
(1493–1519), Friedrich III's son, married the immensely wealthy Mary of
Burgundy and the Netherlands, heiress of Charles the Bold.

So the Holy Roman Empire survived. But mainly as an instrument of
dynastic aggrandizement; first based on a Central European Czech realm and
then as what became an inherited title added to the accumulating realms of
the Habsburgs, who had themselves originated in northern Switzerland and
had become based on Vienna. In a more realistic world, the once great
visionary and cosmopolitan European institution of the Empire had thus
become an instrument of Central European dynastic politics.

The Papacy also had survived successive attempts at control by Councils of
the Church by transforming itself into a vigorous Italian Renaissance principality with more limited aims, at the long term price of losing much of its hold
on the northern peoples, hitherto, in their comparative naivety and simple
faith, among its most loyal supporters. Both Empire and Papacy had thus been
adapted to the more businesslike temper of the age in which the pace was
being set by the Italian city states, whether commercial republics like Florence
and Venice, or the civic *Signoria* exploited by adventurers whom their
contemporary Chaucer called "tyrants in Lombardy".

III

These tyrants who exploited the *Signoria* of city states—the word means
originally the "estate" or "entourage" of a Prince—were reviving a very
ancient tradition in a society where an urban way of life had never been
entirely disrupted since Antiquity, and of which Frederick II's secular *regno* in
Sicily had been an expression.

These city states were at once military and commercial, and their humanist
ambience was reflected in the new artistic style of Giotto. Born in 1265, in
1304 he had decorated the Arena Chapel at Padua with rounded figures
dramatically grouped in space in a way afterwards developed by the great
classic painters Raphael and Poussin. Though ardently Christian, he gave an
unmedieval and anthropocentric dimension to painting, so that he "belonged

to the world of solid realities, the world created by the bankers and wool merchants for whom he worked", while "Dante belonged to the earlier Gothic world of St. Thomas Aquinas and the great cathedrals."[1]

This more realistic outlook, originally the result of thirteenth-century economic expansion, was now enhanced as an economic recession, coincident with plague, struck fourteenth-century Europe. During the high middle ages of the twelfth and thirteenth centuries population and colonization had greatly increased; but although more land had come under cultivation, the techniques of agriculture had not improved enough to keep pace with demand. Hence inflation and sometimes famine, a fall in population and the abandonment of marginal land. What, within its limited technology, had been a prosperous economy had begun by the early fourteenth century to decline; in the west the manor, the basic social and economic foundation of feudal society, had begun to change as peasants bought themselves out of servile obligations, hired labour became more mobile, and production began, not merely for subsistence, but for a market. The feudal host, too, had been for long superseded by mercenaries and "indentured" professional soldiers.

On the surface the great feudal kings and magnates continued their flamboyant and insolvent adventures and way of life, but they were becoming more dependent on money. Edward III of England, for example, defaulted on enormous debts to Florentine bankers, and the Peruzzi, the Bardi and the Acciaioli all went bankrupt between 1343 and 1346. So sometimes, as with the French fiefs in Greece, the bankers took over their clients' titles and estates. In Italy the evil legacy of the conflict of Papacy and Empire continued in the feuds of Guelphs and Ghibellines and in rivalries of various tyrants who employed foreign mercenary *condottieri,* while Philippe VI, the first Valois King of France, and Edward III managed to launch the Hundred Years War which intermittently devastated France for generations. And while the two most powerful Atlantic realms were thus embroiled, the Tatars continued to oppress and brutalize the Russians, also overrun by Poles and Lithuanians in the aftermath of the Mongol attacks, and although the Croats and Hungarians fiercely revived, the Turks were now extending their hold on south-eastern Europe.

In this fourteenth-century anti-climax to the creative twelfth and thirteenth, the worst recorded plague in European history now killed at least a third, and in the cities probably more, of the population of the continent. There had been such epidemics before, as under Marcus Aurelius and under Justinian; but not on such a scale. Three kinds of plague now became epidemic: one the bubonic plague, thought to have originated around the Gobi desert from fleas on the Manchurian marmot, otherwise "a beguiling squirrel-like creature."[2] But for reasons unknown, it was above all *Rattus Rattus*, the tough, nimble, by

[1]Kenneth Clark. *Civilisation.* op. cit. p. 85.
[2]Philip Ziegler. *The Black Death.* London, 1969. p. 26. The term Black Death is not contemporary, being first used in Sweden *(Swarta döden)* in 1555, probably a rough translation of "pestis atra", the dreadful plague. The term was used in England after the Great Plague of London in 1665, to distinguish the medieval catastrophe from the current one.

nature vagabond black rat which made the move: they infested Tatar encampments and, according to one contemporary source, the Tatars deliberately passed the plague on. Infected themselves during a siege of the Genoese depot at Cassa in Crimea, they had catapulted plague-stricken corpses among the defenders, who had fled to the west.

The second kind of plague infected the lungs; it was even more infectious, spread by the victim's breath, and where the bubonic variety killed within one week, the pulmonary plague killed within hours. The third, also a septicaemic kind, was utterly fatal and carried by the ordinary fleas *(pulex irritans)*, which swarmed in medieval households.

Black rats had also long infested the grain cargoes from South Russia; and by October 1347, Genoese galleys from Crimea brought the plague to Messina and Catania in Sicily. In the same year it appeared at Marseilles and began to spread up to Bordeaux and Avignon. By January 1348 it was brought to Genoa and Venice and spread to Pisa, Florence and Siena; by that winter it was in Paris, and, probably through the Channel Isles, it appeared at Melcombe, now part of Weymouth, whence it spread to Bristol; while from Southampton it spread to London, East Anglia and the Midlands. By the spring of 1349 it had got into Wales—"we see death coming into our midst like black smoke, a black plague like halfpence. It is a grievous thing that they should be on a fair skin."[1] The Scots, at first delighted that the English were stricken, mounted a major raid from the forest of Selkirk; but they were soon stricken themselves ("God and Seynt Mungo, Seynt Ninian and Seynt Andrew scheld us this day and ilka day for Goddis grace and from the foule deth that Yngleesh men dyene upon").[2]

During 1348-9 the plague was raging in the Rhineland, in Frankfurt-am-Main and Vienna. Medieval housing,[3] malnutrition and stark ignorance combined to render the physicians helpless. The clergy would parade their relics and images, and lead barefoot processions intoning penitential psalms. Their dogmas had long rendered empirical research impossible: in 1300 that proud Pontiff, Boniface VIII, had forbidden dissection of the human anatomy because it was the image of God. Grotesque and eleborate theories, inherited and distorted from Galen, stultified the doctors, themselves with little authority compared with the priests. They advised bleeding, warned against hot baths, which "opened the pores", and recommended the effluvia of latrines as a disinfectant.

The peoples reacted according to their already discernible national temperaments. The better-off Italians wisely fled the cities and amused themselves intelligently in ways described in Boccaccio's *Decameron*: the wealthier French took to hectic gaiety and mordant wit about each other; the Germans to hysteria, self-flagellation, and to massacring the Rhineland Jews, accused of poisoning wells; the English grumbled and endured, but "for one reason or

[1]Ziegler. *op. cit.* p. 190.
[2]Ziegler. *op. cit.* p. 198.
[3]Of London, Ziegler writes, "The medieval house might have been built to specifications approved by a rodent council as eminently suitable for the rats' enjoyment of a healthy, carefree life." *op. cit.* p. 152.

another . . . did not indulge in the massive disorders in which others found an outlet for their emotions."[1] The inspired contribution of the Pope was to proclaim 1350 a Holy Year, which would bring thousands of pilgrims to increase the population of plague-stricken Rome.

Providentially the epidemic had by then abated. There were now not enough peasants to till the soil and tend the cattle. Thousands of Jews in the Rhineland and in Switzerland had been murdered, often burnt alive: only in Poland were the authorities so convinced of their value that they managed to protect them from popular hate. In Spain the disease killed Christians and Arabs impartially, and brigands terrorized parts of the countryside. Mysteriously, some areas suffered less than others; the worst sinks of infection were the ports and the trade routes, but "the inclinations of the rats must have been the most important cause" (in some places the indigenous brown rats fought off the immigrants). But "the smell of death was over the whole of Europe."

This catastrophe did not suddenly wreck medieval civilization: with surprising resilience, its more creative areas revived, though the infection remained and flared up for centuries; but the Black Death hastened a transformation already going on, and tended to make men more sceptical of established institutions; more pessimistic, more tenacious of limited objectives and less naive about visionary ones. Where the vitality of feudal society had been rural, drawn from the mutual obligations of the manor or its equivalent and conditioned by ancient customary law, the vitality of early modern times, regulated by commercial Roman-style law, would emerge more from the cities; in particular from those of central and northern Italy and the Low countries, from the Hansa towns of the Baltic and their hinterland, and from the now oceanic enterprise of the Portuguese.

IV

In the early fourteenth century, the political condition of Italy, described in lurid detail in the spirited pages of Sismondi,[2] had hardly been promising. Petrarch, for example, then the greatest Italian humanist, despaired of his times and regarded political life with disgust. But since the days of Barbarossa, the vitality of the Italian republics had been irrepressible; with no monarch to crush them and sustained by flourishing long distance commerce, by cosmopolitan banking, and by the extension of their territories, republican communes had emerged. Most of them were republics governed by patrician families through *Signorias* or Councils; and in spite of internal strife with the craft

[1]Ziegler. *op. cit.* p. 133.
[2]Jean Charles de Sismondi (1773–1842) is famous as both economist and historian. A Genevan Swiss of Italian descent, in 1789 he took refuge from Genevan politics in England, then in northern France, where he wrote his *History of the Italian Republics* (1809–18). This was a highly tendentious popular work designed to present the Italians as the champions of liberty and enlightenment; a thesis hardly borne out by the facts he presented with such gusto, which have greatly contributed to the popular conception of Renaissance politics.

guilds, they had bought themselves out of their old obligations to the emperors or to their bishops.

But the conflicts between urbanized nobles and bourgeois patricians had been exploited by adventurers: they had monopolized civic offices of the *Signoria* and, held on to them, organized their own gangs and, in the aftermath of the Guelph-Ghibelline conflicts, seized power and kept it by cunning methods, military and civilian.

The principal states were now Venice, Milan, and Florence, and after 1377, when Gregory XI returned from Avignon, to be succeeded by Urban VI (1378–89), Rome with the extensive states of the Church, and also the Kingdom of Naples. Lesser cities, Verona, Bologna, Pisa, Siena, Mantua, manoeuvred to maintain and enhance their threatened independence and became centres of vivid literary and artistic culture. Such was the political setting of the early Renaissance, in which the Italians developed the secular city state, republican or despotic, as a deliberately constructed institution; even, as Jacob Burckhardt put it, as "a work of art".[1] These city states had no moral basis, merely successful power; their practice would be analysed by Machiavelli; justified in terms of national realms simply because they were useful, by Hobbes; writ large in terms of nation states, it would dominate the modern world.

If we disregard its prototype, the Sicilian *Regno* of Frederick II, the first major Italian architect of such a *Signoria* was that genial ruffian, Can Grande della Scala, tyrant of Verona (1312–29),[2] who conquered Padua and Treviso, Feltre and Cividale, and died aged forty-one. Without hereditary or feudal status, such opportunists had to use the utmost intelligence and finesse; hence their patronage of scholars and artists who advertised their upstart and competitive courts: and there followed, "worked out in detail, the purely modern fiction of the omnipotence of the state".[3] Such was the vitality and wealth of the cities that, as in those of ancient Hellas, the sort of political crimes chronicled by Thucydides and Machiavelli failed to wreck a brilliantly creative civilization.

Among the major powers of Italy, Milan had early fallen under the control of a Ghibelline archbishop whose great-nephew, Matteo Visconti, had been made Imperial Vicar General by the emperor Henry VII. His descendant Gian Galeazzo Visconti had greater ambitions. In 1385 he lured his uncle Barnato, the reigning tyrant of Milan, to Varese near Lake Como and poisoned him in prison. Though a paranoiac despot, Gian Galeazzo proved highly successful. He captured Verona and Padua, and threatened Venice; and although the Florentines engaged against him Sir John Hawkwood (*Giovanni Acuto*), fresh from the Hundred Years War, he mastered Parma, Piacenza and Bologna, crossed the Apennines and took over Perugia, Siena and Pisa. He still failed to

[1] See his classic *The Civilization of the Renaissance in Italy*, still, in spite of important criticism that he exaggerates its neo-pagan aspect, an inspiring book.
[2] He sits his horse, to this day, above the restored della Scala tomb in Verona, looking very pleased with himself, as if just returned from successful sack and pillage; his great helmet tilted back, his sword upright.
[3] Burckhardt. *op. cit.* p. 5.

defeat Florence; but he established Milan as a power comparable to Venice, and could well afford the Dukedom he bought from the emperor Wenzel, King of Bohemia.

In Florence the republican tradition was stronger, and almost as predatory; the republic took over Arezzo, and in 1406 conquered Pisa and Livorno. But by the mid-fifteenth century an immensely rich banker, Cosimo de' Medici, won *de facto* control, and at his death in 1464, he had established the predominance of his family. He was only one of many such patricians who had made their fortunes out of banking or cloth making, and rigged the originally democratic civic franchise into an oligarchy by monopolizing the rotating offices of the *Signoria*. With mounting affluence, this early fifteenth-century patriciate had launched Florence into a "golden age" of intelligent patronage of literature and the arts, not unlike that of the Periclean Athens they imitated. Like the Athenians, the Florentines had emerged victorious from dangerous attacks, from the war against the Papacy of 1377-8, and the war against Milan concluded in 1402: they were proud and rich and very intelligent. The wealthy patricians built themselves villas in the surrounding countryside and revived the old Roman cult of gardens; their sons, taught by Humanist scholars, became fascinated, as had been the leisured young Athenians, with the pleasures of discussion and learning, and the Florentine oligarchy came to rely on professional bureaucrats headed by Humanist Chancellors, as Leonardo Bruni (1414–44) who succeeded Salutati and wrote a *History of the Florentines,* and Manetti (d. 1459) who wrote an unmedieval tract *On the Dignity and Excellence of Man.*

These quick-witted, versatile and confident people, far enough south to enjoy Mediterranean sunshine, yet braced by a cold winter climate, had penetrating minds and sure aesthetic taste, and they knew a great artist when they saw one—as Ghiberti, whose Bronze Doors on the Florentine Baptistry (1424–52) won immediate applause, or his pupil, the sculptor Luca della Robbia. Benozzo Gozzoli (1420–98) and Sandro Botticelli (1444–1510) were patronized by the Medici, and the latter influenced by the cult of Platonism that came in with the Byzantine Joannes Argyropoulos, professor of Greek at Florence (1456–71). Cosimo himself, the main founder of the Medici greatness, who expanded his business by developing branches in France, England and the Netherlands, was an enthusiastic book collector as well as a patron of the humanities and the arts. He was also a hard man of business, as apparent from his worn, intelligent and determined profile as he sits with folded hands in a plain red furred gown in his portrait in the Uffizi. His grandson Lorenzo, given the courtesy title *Il Magnifico* since he had none in his own right, proved just as able and alert; as when, in 1478, he escaped assassination (instigated by Pope Sixtus IV) at the moment of the elevation of the Host in the Duomo at Florence.[1] The *Magnifico* survived in wealth and grandeur, though excommun-

---

[1] The would-be assassin foolishly steadied himself for the blow by putting his left hand on the *Magnifico's* shoulder when about to strike home with the right. But Lorenzo reacted to the touch like a Russian cat: leapt up, smothered the blow with his cloak wrapped round his own left arm and whipped out his sword. The foiled assassin (a clergyman) then decamped, but was apprehended and dispatched.

icate, until 1492, the year in which Columbus discovered America. With the French invasion of 1494, the Medici were expelled, but after a republican interval restored by Spanish arms in 1512.

The wealthiest city-state was the Republic of Venice which had defeated Genoa after long naval wars in the Levant, and, having exterminated various Slav pirate nests in the Adriatic, was now immensely rich. With a Doge elected for life, power shared by a Council of Ten and secured by a network of delation and espionage combined with spectaular pageantry for visitors and populace, this Republican oligarchy not only commanded great wealth, but the most sophisticated diplomatic service of its day. In effect, it was the heir of Byzantium, and well deserved the symbolic possession of the bronze horses from the Byzantine hippodrome that still adorn St. Mark's Cathedral, itself redolent of the East.

In spite of their competitive belligerence, the city-states of Milan, Florence and Venice all had a common interest in creating at least a balance of power and keeping out foreigners; by the Peace of Lodi in 1454 they combined to make a defensive alliance for forty years. It did not work so badly as might have been expected.

In Central Italy, however, the return of the Popes from Avignon hardly made for peace: in spite of the Great Schism (1378-1417), and the Conciliar movement which had both threatened their authority, Martin V (1417-31) and a succession of Popes rehabilitated the prestige of the Papacy, as did Nicholas V (1447-1455) when he celebrated the jubilee of 1450. They tried to defend the vulnerable Papal states which extended from Bologna through Imola, Faenza and Forli in the Romagna round to Urbino, and so over the march of Ancona down through most of Central Italy as far as Rome itself. South of Rome, vulnerable to any power that controlled Naples, lay the Campagna and the coast down to Terracina.

When Nicholas V celebrated the jubilee of 1450 he inaugurated the full Renaissance Papacy: it would last until the sack of the city by the army of the Emperor Charles V in 1527. To make the transformation the Popes, most of whom were Italians, had to become Renaissance Princes and *politiques,* intriguing and fighting for survival in fiercely competitive times. Financially they were a medium power, with revenues rather less than half those of Venice, but the discovery and development of the alum mines in the Tolfa mountains in 1462-80 greatly increased revenues, since alum was essential for cleaning wool and leather and there was then no other known source outside Turkey. The Popes had to contend with the over-mighty Roman families in the City and on large estates around it, as well as control the families of the near independent "Vicars" who ruled in the Romagna. While the more forceful Popes wanted to create a Papal monarchy, and the College of Cardinals wished to control it, there was a fever of "nepotism" and family plundering of the revenues, already strained by a proliferating bureaucracy. The Papacy was not hereditary, the tenure generally brief, and each Pope felt it his family duty to make hay while the sun shone. "If the Pope became a Prince the cardinals had little alternative but to become courtiers and succumb

to the attractions of high life, ostentation and political intrigue. This was what
most of them did."[1]

Nicholas V, a lavish if undiscriminating patron of literature and the arts,
had begun to transform late Medieval Rome, the run-down market town and
centre of fluctuating pilgrim traffic that had survived among the gigantic ruins
of Antiquity, into the splendid capital of Catholic Christendom envisaged by
Julius II and realized by Paul III, a change symbolized by the contrast between
the dilapidated and ungainly façade of the old St. Peter's and the classic
grandeur of the new. Under Sixtus IV (della Rovere) (1471–84), Rome became
a real Renaissance capital, and by 1475 the humanist Platina, who wrote on
the Lives of the Popes,[2] had been appointed Prefect of the Vatican Library.
The reign of Alexander VI (Rodrigo Borgia) (1492–1503) had given openings
mainly to astute secretaries and diplomats; the Borgias, by origin provincial
Spaniards from Valencia, were not great art patrons, and Cesare, Rodrigo's
son, celebrated the downfall of Granada by staging a bull fight in Rome.

Nor were they the amateurs in poison they are still widely believed to have
been; there is no evidence, for example, that Alexander VI and Cesare Borgia
poisoned themselves by mistake with a delicacy designed for someone else;
probably the Pope died and Cesare became ill from acute malaria caught
during a Roman August in 1503. The crimes of the Borgias have, indeed, been
grossly exaggerated, since generations of historians have uncritically accepted
the propaganda of their enemies. The Florentine Guicciardini, a partisan of
the Medici, incorporated the most virulent of the legends in his famous Storia
d'Italia written much later in 1536–40. Lucretia is described when she was
Duchess of Ferrara, by the contemporary biographer of the Chevalier Bayard,
as "able to give wonderful festivals and banquets in the Italian fashion"; and,
even after partaking of them, he described her as "gentle and amiable to
everyone"; her son, Ippolito d'Este, became a cardinal, and as governor of
Tivoli created the Villa d'Este (c. 1550), thus surely redeeming any authenticated family crimes.[3]

It was after the Borgia regime, under Julius II (1503–13) and Leo X
(1513–21), that Michelangelo and Raphael were given full scope. With
Michelangelo (1475–1564) a new "heroic" aspiration appears, apparent already
in the David created for the Florentines to symbolize their brief and austere
republicanism under Savonarola, a statue which, as Kenneth Clark has
remarked, compares with Donatello's version as Beethoven does with Mozart.

[1]Denys Hay. Europe in the Fourteenth and Fifteenth Centuries. London, 1966. p. 293.
[2]On Nicholas V he writes, "He was commendable for his liberality towards all,
especially learned men, whom he advanced with money, court preferments and
benefices, whom he would sometimes set upon writing some new thing and sometimes
upon translating Greek authors into Latin, in so much that the Greek and Latin
Tongues, which have lain hid for six hundred years, at last regained their splendour to
some considerable degree." The Lives of the Popes from the Time of our Lord Jesus
Christ to the Reign of Sixtus IV. Translated by Paul Rycaut, and continued by him
after 1471 to the present time. London, 1685. Modern edition ed. W. Benham, B.
Platina, The Lives of the Popes, vols XI-XVI, London, 1888.
[3]See Michael Mallett. The Borgias. the Rise and Fall of a Renaissance Dynasty. London,
1969, pp. 242–243; q.v. for a clear, readable, and impartial account.

This cosmic vision was expressed at the behest of Julius II on the roof of the Sistine Chapel in Rome, most movingly in the vision of God bringing Adam to life.

In the large Kingdom of Naples and Sicily, the long aftermath of the fall of Frederick II and the execution of Conradin had continued. The sequel to the massacre of the Angevin French at the "Sicilian Vespers" had been that the Spanish rulers of Aragon, descended from a daughter of Manfred, had taken over the island: they had a formidable Catalan fleet and had already occupied Sardinia. But the Angevin descendants of Charles of Anjou, who had destroyed Manfred, had kept their hold on Naples, where their family vendettas were played out against a melodramatic setting. The senior branch, in a far-flung medieval way, became highly successful rulers of Hungary; and, wishing to keep their domination of Naples, married Prince Andrew of Hungary to his cousin Queen Joanna I (1326–82). But she found him repellent, so had him assassinated; whereat King Louis of Hungary arrived with an avenging army. The dissolute and murderous Queen, now married to Louis of Taranto, took refuge in Avignon, where, as Countess of Provence, she sold the entire city to the "captive" Pope. Armed with the proceeds, she returned to Naples, and by 1352 she was rehabilitated and re-crowned. She then made a major error: at the opening of the Great Schism, she backed the wrong Pope, and even harboured Clement VII at Naples. Urban VI, himself a Neapolitan, excommunicated her and commissioned her cousin, the Angevin Charles of Durazzo, to deal with her. So he put her in prison, and, appropriately, had her smothered under a large feather bed. Though she had married a third husband, James III of Majorca, and finally a roving German adventurer from Brunswick, as well as conducting many unofficial amorous adventures, she died childless.

She was briefly succeeded by her murderer. But Charles of Durazzo's son Ladislas, after a hectic career, died young, and his sister became queen as Joanna II (1414–35). But Joanna II proved no better than Joanna I. "Distracted by love affairs and at the mercy of favourites," she too died without offspring, and the original Angevin dynasty perished miserably.[1]

Joanna I's caprices had appalling consequences. She had not been able to decide whether to leave her kingdom to Alfonso V of Aragon or to René of Anjou. So Alfonso V, "the Magnanimous", who had ruled Sicily since 1416, gradually took over Naples and became a major power in Italy, determined, in alliance with the Sforzas of Milan, to keep the French out of the Peninsula. But though Ferrente, his bastard, who succeeded him to Naples (but not to Sicily, still less to Aragon), managed to survive internal conspiracy and foreign threats, Charles VIII of France inherited the Angevin claims, and on Ferrente's death in 1494, he invaded Italy. The relative stability achieved by the Peace of Lodi in 1454 was over, and the age of massive foreign intervention had begun, to end in Spanish domination.

Italian political theory reflected the facts of Italian politics. It has already been recorded that in the early *Trecento*, in the days of Can Grande della

[1] See Denys Hay. *op. cit.* pp. 179–180, for much light on these imbroglios and a pedigree. Those seeking a closer look can read E. G. Leonard. *Les Angevins de Naples*. Paris, 1954.

Scala of Verona, Marsilio of Padua had adumbrated a secularized theory of the city state. He had set aside the claims of the Church itself to be ruled by a Council of Christendom, and derived public authority from the will of the civic oligarchy. Now, after much more varied experience of politics and diplomacy of the High Renaissance, a shrewd Florentine civil servant, Niccolo Machiavelli, had assumed that a secularized state power was a law unto itself and justified it simply by success.

Born the son of an unsuccessful lawyer in 1469, at San Cascano near Florence, Machiavelli escaped the elaborate archaizing education of his richer contemporaries, and continued to write hard-hitting prose. In 1498, after the fall of Savonarola, he became head of the Second Chancellery in the Republican Government, and was sent on diplomatic missions to France, to Cesare Borgia in 1502, to Rome in 1503 and to Emperor Maximilian I in 1507 and 1511. He also organized the Florentine militia, which in 1509 captured Pisa. With the return of the Medici in 1512, Machiavelli was dismissed, imprisoned and tortured: he was then rusticated to his small but beautifully situated farm near San Cascano, where he wrote The Prince (1513) and The Discourses (1517) and attempted to regain favour and employment under the Medici. In 1520 Cardinal Giulio de' Medici, afterwards Clement VII, gave him the small appointment of Historiographer to the Florentine state, a favour which alienated the Republican party. In 1527 he died without regaining the power he had lost in 1512. He wrote many dispatches and reports as well as a treatise On the Art of War and a comedy Mandragola, in which he broke away from the stereotypes of the classical Roman theatre and delineated his repellent characters more from life.

In a trenchant and forceful style Machiavelli analysed how in fact power was obtained and why it was lost. He wrote as an early modern Florentine administrator and diplomat, submerged in the practice of his craft,[1] making a coldly objective analysis.

Having risen from humble beginnings to the summit of Florentine affairs and of international diplomacy, but then been dismissed, imprisoned and tortured, Machiavelli was understandably embittered. Arguing that it is "safer" for a ruler to be feared than loved, he writes,"Because it is to be asserted in general of men that they are ungrateful, fickle, false, cowards, covetous and as long as you succeed they are yours entirely; they will offer you their blood, property, life and children, as is said above, when the need is far distant, but when it approaches they turn against you.[2] Since such is human nature and since it does not change, only the most vigilant foresight and ruthless cunning can win and keep public power; the Prince must combine the qualities of the Lion and the Fox, come out boldly on the side of other Princes whom he considers likely to win, and when enemies have to be destroyed, destroy them entirely at one blow, because they can avenge themselves of lighter injuries, but of more serious ones they cannot." And if injuries should be done at one blow, benefits should be spaced out. There is nothing new in these conclusions:

[1]See H. Butterfield. The Statecraft of Machiavelli. London, 1955.
[2]The Prince. Chapter XVII. Everyman edition.

they are implicit in Thucydides, in Aristotle's account of revolutions, and in Polybius: but no one had before set them down as precepts.

Not that Machiavelli is confident that they will work. Chance or "Fortune" rules at least half men's lives: "I hold it to be true," he writes realistically, "that fortune is the arbiter of half our actions, but she still leaves us to direct the other half or perhaps a little less."

A typical High Renaissance Humanist in his intense admiration for the republican Romans, and a patriot in his admiration for the Florentine republic, Machiavelli, unlike most Italians, admired the republican Swiss, and thought the Germans less corrupt than the Latin peoples. But he discarded any hope of the cosmopolitan Christian order envisaged by Dante, and still hankered for by Marsilio, and he defined, without batting an eyelid, the principles on which great dynastic national states and supranational states have ever since conducted foreign policy. "When the entire safety of our country is at stake, no consideration of what is just or unjust, merciful or cruel, praiseworthy or shameful, must intervene. On the contrary, every other consideration being set aside, the course alone must be taken which procures the existence of the country and preserves its liberty."[1] Such was the first modern theory of the State.

V

Just as Venice and Milan were well placed to command the trade from the Levant and Italy over the Alps to Northern Europe, so the cities of the Low Countries could focus the trade of the North Sea and the Baltic, the Rhineland and north-eastern France; and now, with better ships and navigation, the Atlantic trade with the Mediterranean, the Iberian peninsula and south-western France. There had thus arisen prosperous cities and manufacturing centres in an economic and social pattern similar to those of northern Italy though in a very different climate and among very different, Flemish-speaking people, without the Italian versatile intellectual brilliance and distinguished style. At Bruges, Ghent and Antwerp they early developed technically proficient art, the foundation of the painting of the Northern Renaissance, which would culminate in the work of Rubens and Rembrandt. And the Dutch Christian humanist Erasmus soon won European influence.

Like the Italian republics, the Flemish cities were incongruous in a feudal society, but by dynastic chance and policy they were ruled by old style Valois Dukes of Burgundy, whose combined possessions made them immensely rich. There was thus more of a late medieval flavour about the Flemish cities; but they were governed, as were the Italian republics, by Councils made up of the hereditary *haute bourgeoisie,* of the representatives of the major merchant guilds, and even of the lesser craft guilds, for all were united in keeping the unskilled workmen and labourers in their place. The wealth of these oligarchies, only occasionally challenged by popular revolts, soon put down, made them recalcitrant to their feudal overlords, whom they defied or bought off.

[1]*Discourses*. Trans. N. H. Thompson. London, 1883. Bk. III, Chap. XLI.

The heavily fortified castle of the Counts of Flanders at Ghent still underlines the relationship of the Counts with the medieval city.

By the mid-twelfth century, following the German colonization to the East, great trading cities had also arisen along the Baltic. Of these Lübeck, north-east of Hamburg, itself on the Elbe and so facing the North Sea, was by far the most prosperous; strategically well placed for trade with Copenhagen and with Malmö in Sweden. With the economic expansion of the twelfth and thirteenth centuries German cities had spread east along the Baltic coast, as Danzig, Rostock, Stralsund, even Riga. In 1293 Lübeck took over the island of Götland. The raw materials of the "colonial" areas of the East, including Novgorod, were exchanged for the manufactured goods of the West, while Bruges and Ypres imported vast amounts of raw wool from England, another "colonial" area, to which Cologne exported wine and armaments. The Hansa merchants developed Swedish iron and copper mines as well as exploiting the herrings for which there was an insatiable demand.[1] A whole network of commercial interest united the cities of the north, and by the Law of Lübeck in 1263 they had combined, to put down piracy and regulate the life of the sea, even setting up lighthouses and placing buoys. These merchants established Hansas and depots—the equivalent of the "factories" in which European "factors" would live in the Asian East—and, like the Venetians and Genoese in Constantinople, they had their own privileges. So great was the prestige of these wealthy foreigners, known to the English as "Easterlings", that "sterling" long remained the word for a sound currency.

Further south, in Central Europe, many prosperous German towns had also been established, as at Nuremberg, Ulm and Augsburg, and the great Rhineland cities, Köln, Mainz and their dependencies. The weakness of the emperors and the resulting disorders forced these oligarchies into informal defensive groups, never so close as the arrangements of the maritime Hansa cities.

The recession of the early fourteenth century and the Black Death gave a setback to their prosperity, and anyway most of these towns were small, and the Bourgeoisie socially long despised by the fighting aristocracy. But while the population everywhere remained predominantly peasant and rural, a powerful interest had established itself north of the Alps; and where Mediterranean civilization had been urban since its origins, in much of the north the rise of civic republican oligarchies was an innovation, particularly in areas outside what had been the Roman Empire. These communities encouraged a thrusting and businesslike mentality, a method and routine alien to the rural or courtly feudal world, and many erstwhile serfs once bound to the soil found that "town air made them free".

This liberation, even if it meant that the serf merely changed into a member of an urban proletariat, for it was hard even for able men to rise in the close oligarchic civic and guild hierarchies, was limited by a further consequence of

---

[1]The "soused" or Bismarck herring was invented long before Bismarck and exported more easily after proper casks had been devised in the thirteenth century to contain it in quantity.

the social and economic changes of the thirteenth century which now momentously emphasized the contrast between Western and Eastern Europe.

In the West the fall in population had made the surviving peasants better able to bargain with their landlords; once labour dues on the demesne were commuted for cash payments, it was impossible to keep the peasants "bound to the soil". The ancestors of a free "yeomanry" appeared; peasants who had taken over more land and farmed it well for a market. The break up of the ancient manorial system had been their opportunity: some of them even made their fortunes as sheep masters or cattlemen, exploiting urban markets for wool and leather and meat. By contrast, in the "colonial" lands of the East, where on the terms of the original settlement the peasant had been free, the landlords went in for large scale cereal crops cultivated by peasants who had been tied closer to the soil and whose obligations to the lords had been increased. In areas under far-flung but shallow and fluctuating political realms, as in Poland, Lithuania and Hungary or under the iron heel of the Teutonic Knights who had settled in East Prussia, the peasants could not expect protection by the kings, or even by their local lords. Even the minor nobility increased their irresponsible liberties as the kings had to bid for their support. In Poland for example, by the end of the fifteenth century, the peasants were still officially bound to the soil by the authority of the realm. In Prussia vast estates were exploited to grow wheat with peasant labour, and the "Junker" class, totally distinct from the rest of the people, peasant or bourgeois, began its baleful existence.

In Russia, of course, the destruction of the Kievan city-states and the long brutalizing Tatar regime which had followed had further depressed the peasants into servitude. This contrast between Western and Eastern Europe would have profoundly important consequences.

VI

The most emancipated of all peasants were the Swiss. Taking advantage of the unique defensive advantages and strategic situation of their country, they had revolutionized the art of war, as the Welsh with their long bows had in the West. The nucleus of their Confederation—the only permanently successful one in the Middle Ages—were German-speaking peasants of the forest cantons of Uri, Schwyz and Unterwalden around Lake Lucerne. Since they commanded the approach to the important Gotthard pass into Italy, their strategic position was strong, and when in 1218 the Habsburg-Laufenberg counts had added the overlordship of Schwyz to that of Aargau, in 1240 the men of Schwyz had got a charter from the Emperor Frederick II, bringing them directly under his own authority. With the downfall of the Emperor, and the election of Rudolf of Habsburg to the empire, Schwyz was again threatened; and in 1291 the three cantons formed their historic "Everlasting League", consolidated (in German) by the Pact of Brunnen in 1315, after the Swiss had utterly defeated Leopold I of Habsburg at Morgarten in that year.

The nucleus of the Confederation had been peasants, but peasants living on a major trade route, and their interests had coincided with those of Lucerne, Zurich and Berne, all cities that joined the Confederation between 1332 and 1353. The lowland territories of Glarus and Zug were also included. By now the Habsburgs had obtained the Tyrol on the eastern flank of the Swiss and Leopold III attacked Lucerne; but in 1386 the Swiss defeated and killed him at Sempach; and in 1393 the Confederation was further defined in the *Sempacherbrief.*

The Swiss now began to think of expansion on the Italian side of the Alps, and in the north they were joined by the wealthy and old established city of Basel on the Rhine. They then became involved with the attempt of Charles the Bold (*Carolus Audax*, Duke of Burgundy) to extend his power over Alsace and Lorraine, an ambition countered by a League of Cities: Basel, Colmar, Mulhouse and Strasbourg. And when in 1476 the Duke hanged a Bernese garrison at Grandson, the Swiss combined to defeat him there and at Morat, following up the victory by helping to kill him in 1477 at Nancy.

Their military prestige all over Europe was now immense; and the weapons displayed in the Chateau de Chillon show why: the Swiss were particularly apt with the pike and the double handed sword. They became extremely belligerent and commanded high pay as mercenaries, reaching the height of their prestige during the second half of the fifteenth century and providing the Papal Guard, a service still performed in a way more ornamental than belligerent. In spite of these extraneous interests, most of the peasants continued farming and the towns their commerce: the Confederation was maintained. In the heart of a Europe still apparently dominated by monarchies and quasi-feudal aristocracies, these bourgeois-peasant republicans already flourished.

VII

The early fourteenth century was the turning point into late medieval and early modern times, not only because of the collapse or transformation of the high medieval institutions of Christendom, and the emergence of Italian city states, but also because the ideas that had inspired them and reached their climax in the late thirteenth century in the elaborate metaphysical constructions of St. Thomas Aquinas were now undermined. It is therefore necessary further to examine two early philosophers already mentioned.

William of Ockham (1280–1347) had been Franciscan, educated at Oxford, who believed that the "realist" philosophers, following Plato, had over-reached themselves and were talking nonsense. He was born at Ockham, Surrey, and studied and lectured at Oxford until 1322. Accused of heresy by the Chancellor of the University, he was sent for examination to Pope John XXII at Avignon. Here he was incarcerated for four years, but escaped by night, "with one cardinal", says his editor, "in hot pursuit"; he got to Aigues Mortes, whence, with two others accused of heresy he was "swiftly conveyed by dinghy to a warship" sent by the Emperor Ludwig IV from Pisa. Having joined the Imperial Court and army at that city, he returned with the Emperor to Germany, where he "attacked the established system of the time with at least the candour of Tacitus and something more than the courage of Juvenal," pouring out pamphlets in support of the Imperial cause; and, though his work in philosophy proved more important, showing himself a deadly enemy of the Avignon Popes, and indeed of the whole Papal claim to supreme authority. In his *De Imperatorum et Pontificum Potestate* he anticipated the "Protestant" claim (the word only came in after the conclusion of the Council of Trent in 1563) that there is no need for intermediary priests between the laity and God.[1] Ockham asserted the "nominalist" doctrine that only particular objects existed and that the concept of universal abstract ideas alone being real and permanent beyond the flux of time and experience was moonshine. He coined the memorable phrase that "entities ought not to be multiplied unless they have to be," *entia non sunt multiplicanda praeter necessitatem,* which became known as "Ockham's razor". This instrument, applied to the luxuriant metaphysical under- and over-growth long fashionable, produced devastatingly stark results. Ockham had, indeed, anticipated the scepticism of Hume and Kant and accepted the limitations of mind: like Kant, he also asserted that "will", not intellect, was the means of the moral realization of personality. This doctrine, which presents experience and the universe as a mystery unfathomable by mind, could bring the whole Gothic edifice of Thomist abstract logic crashing to the ground and put pause to the attempt to explain the universe elaborated in the *Summa Theologica.*

Gradually the doctrine filtered through; it unsettled Luther's mind, and Thomas Hobbes in the mid seventeenth century, still trained in scholastic method, was in fact a "nominalist". The main stream of philosophy would accept the limitations of mind, until metaphysical ideas came back with the Romantic movement in the early nineteenth century, and Hegel, in convoluted German, claimed to understand "the inner go of things by speculative cognition", thus inaugurating a phase of philosophical debauchery now mercifully again out of fashion.

Ockham's destruction of metaphysical beliefs also proved extremely import-ant for the development of empirical science. For once Descartes (1637) had been reduced to accepting the limitations of consciousness to a mere "*cogito ergo sum*—I think, therefore I am", faith became, as it were, a separate department from reason, and the world could be studied objectively and so understood and exploited without apparent prejudice to religion. The thoughts of this peculiar Franciscan—summoned from Oxford to Avignon, but surpris-ingly never declared heretical—are thus of first rate historical importance, coinciding as they had with the emergence of a more practical outlook, particularly in the Italian and Flemish towns and among the more cunning and systematic rulers both in Italy and in the north.

William of Ockham had also made devastating attacks on the Papal temporal

---

[1]C. K. Bampton's edition of his spirited polemic includes a valuable introduction (Oxford, 1927) from which I quote.

power; but he is mainly important as a philosopher. His contemporary, Marsilio of Padua (1278–1342), is more important for political thought. He was the first practising physician to write political theory, an Italian who thought in terms of the government of cities and elaborated a theory of the secular state. His *Defensor Pacis* (1324) (The Defender of Peace) owes much to Aristotle's *Politics*, a book which, as a member of a city state, he understood better than the scholastic clergy who had tried to interpret it. In the turmoil of late medieval and early modern Italian politics, Marsilio had tried to define the conditions for *Tranquillitas*, and argued that the temporal power of the Church has been the main cause of the political strife in Italy. His objectives are worldly, not transcendental: the state should be a "community" in which "men not only live like animals and slaves, but live well." Marsilio is here directly in the pre-Christian tradition of Aristotle, and anticipates the Humanism of Spinoza.

The law of the state, which is distinct from Divine Law, is of its own making, and it originates from the *"civium universitas"*—the "community of the citizens". This community is naturally not a democracy of all of them, but an oligarchy, such as the *signoria* then prevalent in all the cities, of the *valentiorum*—the more influential and well-to-do elected by or reflecting the will of the "general congregation of the citizens", with the executive power in the hands of a "public force" which can be either one man or several. Having constructed his secular model, quite independent of the Church, Marsilio had proceeded to sweep away the claims of Papacy and Church hierarchy to temporal power. The priests, he claimed, should be advisers, "doctors of souls—*medici animarum*"; not directors and intermediaries with God. The government of the Church—and here his work became politically topical— should be in the hands of a General Council of Christendom, a *legislator humanus* in which laymen as well as clergy should be represented. This project, he believed—and indeed it would be widely supported, if violently opposed by the Popes—could reform and rehabilitate the Papacy and purge the Church of a temporal power and wealth incompatible with the example of the teachings of its Founder. And the lay power, unhampered by clerical interference, and at last self-sufficient, could then organize itself effectively on its own level.

So a philosopher and a political theorist of the early fourteenth century had made radical departures from the Thomist total explanation and from the vision of a United Christendom dominated by the Papacy, and had substituted the idea of a self-sufficient lay state, still Christian and acknowledging a General Council, but based on emergent human will. In their rarified way, these ideas had reflected and in time enhanced the massive social and economic changes which, accelerated by the economic recession and the Black Death, by the subsequent development of cosmopolitan banking and commerce, and by the Humanist liberation of mind, were bringing in a new phase of European civilization of which Machiavelli would analyse the political facts.

XXIV

The Western Realms Consolidated

It was not apparent to most contemporaries that the political and social initiative in western Europe was passing to bankers, merchants and administrators, or that the increasingly powerful monarchs were being forced into more businesslike methods of government; nor did they themselves think in such terms. It has been well observed, "A society in which martial prowess is held in such high esteem, is not likely to remain long at peace. It is wrong ... in the Middle Ages to regard the peaceful condition of things as the natural one: it was not."[1] The old spectacular dynasts and fighting nobility still occupied the foreground: old hierarchies are tenacious and the magnates and lesser knights maintained exclusive and conservative traditions. The monarchs, indeed, were now better established; for, contrary to much received opinion, "any description of the relations between a ruler and his greatest subjects in terms of natural antagonism is misleading. They were his most respected subjects, he had been brought up among them to share their tastes and prejudices, if they absented themselves from the court it could only damage his prestige."[2] Moreover, within their now more settled royal caste, the monarchs could better extend their influence and their possessions by dynastic marriages. Subject always to feuds within the royal families, which the grant of huge appanages and dukedoms to younger sons had fostered, the structure of the western realms was now becoming set: the problem was to make them solvent and to raise taxation for the paid armies and artillery trains which had superseded the feudal host.

The fighting establishment, after the decline of the old feudal society, was thus given a new "bastard" feudal lease of life and it still carried on. It could do nothing else; the cosmopolitan order of warrior kings, magnates and knights, now with longer pride of pedigree bound up with complicated rights of inheritance, had evolved an exclusive code of "chivalry" and defined complicated cosmopolitan "Laws of War" within its own class.[3] The full elaboration

[1]Maurice Keen. A History of Medieval Europe. London, 1967. p. 12.
[2]op. cit. p. 86.
[3]See Maurice Keen. The Laws of War in the Late Middle Ages. London, 1965, for an illuminating study.

of heraldry and of the functions of literate heralds dates from this time, and the famous Orders of Chivalry, as the Garter or the Golden Fleece, would be a flourish of a waning social order, self-conscious renewals of the past.

With this emphasized aloofness came greater class hatred. The peasants who had survived the Black Death were now relatively prosperous, and governments passed laws to keep them in their social place, to fix wages and to tie them to their parishes. The Peasant Revolt of 1381 in England was a protest not against penury and famine, but, as so often where there is social friction, because a more prosperous class was being held to their old social status and heavily taxed—*"Lokke that Hobbe robbour* (the Treasurer) *be well chastysad,"* they said. The *Jacqueries* and *Bauernkriegen* in France and Germany were more a protest against ruling class mismanagement, novel taxation, and wars now conducted as a business or continued informally by mercenaries out of employment in time of peace.

For dynastic conflicts were now exploited for profit, at once romanticized by the exaggerated cult of chivalry[1] and debased as mercenaries lived off the land. Thirteenth century knightly warfare was in fact obsolescent before well armed infantry like the English archers at Agincourt, the Swiss pikemen at Nancy, or the Portuguese and English in 1384 at Aljubarrota. The thoroughly "unsporting" hand gun or arquebus (*Hakenbüchse* or "hooked" gun) and rudimentary cannon were coming in; but war was still the main *raison d'être* of royalty and the natural employment of a large and destructive vested interest established at least since Merovingian times. Naturally no one took much notice of Marsilio of Padua and his *Defensor Pacis*.

In these circumstances we must look below the surface and see how the excesses of the old order, at once romantically flamboyant and intensely predatory, drove the rulers of the Atlantic realms to a more businesslike and centralized form of government, administered by "new men" capable of industrious routine, using the methods originally devised in the Italian cities and the Netherlands, and bringing with it the more realistic political and even economic strategy apparent in early modern times.

II

The most important and striking example of this tendency is the foundation of what became the absolute monarchy in France, which, paradoxically, emerged from the degradation of the French Kingship during the "Hundred Years" War (1337–intermittently–1453).

Originally an old-style ordeal by battle, the conflict was immediately occasioned by the accession of the first Valois king, Philippe VI, which enabled Edward III of England as the grandson, through his mother Isabella, wife of Edward II, of Philippe IV (Capet) le Bel, to claim the French throne by

[1]See J. Huizinga. *The Waning of the Middle Ages.* London, 1924. Chapter VII. *The Political and Military Value of Chivalrous Ideas.*

descent from the senior line.[1] The first part of the war from 1337 to 1360 went very badly for the French, who could not adapt themselves to the English tactical innovations, such as using deadly professional archers and fighting on foot. It was a war for plunder: the English, in alliance with the ever-intransigent Bretons, with recalcitrant Normans of the Cotentin and with the Flemings, with whom they had close economic ties through the wool trade and through common political hostility to the hated French overlords of Flanders, launched a series of successful chauvauchées into the French King's territories. They captured Caen and, though they failed to get to Paris in 1346, won a great victory at Crécy near the estuary of the Somme; then, after a long siege, occupied Calais, which they would retain until 1558. In 1356 another great raid into south-western France in collaboration with Gascon troops led to another stunning victory near Poitiers and to the capture of the French King Jean II, a knightly, chivalrous but unpractical monarch. Indeed, Froissart's account of the King's efforts to surrender is unintentionally comic. In peril during the retreat on Poitiers, King Jean heard a French knight serving with the English say "in good French", "Sire, Sire, surrender yourself." "The King, who found himself very disagreeably situated" (and was evidently fussed), "asked 'To whom shall I surrender myself? Where is my Cousin, the Prince of Wales? If I could see him I would speak to him' ". "Sire", replied Sir Denys, "he is not here; but surrender yourself to me and I will lead you to him". "Who are you?" said the King. "Sire, I am Denys de Morbeque, a Knight from Artois, but I serve the King of England because I cannot belong to France, having forfeited all I possessed there" [for murder]. The King then gave him his right hand glove and said "I surrender myself to you." The Prince, who had feared for the King's life, was delighted to welcome him in his "small pavilion of crimson colour", and ordered wine and spices, which "as a mark of the great affection, he presented to the King himself."[2] Froissart is still indispensable for a vivid and detailed account of these times, and particularly good on Crécy.[3]

By the mid-fourteenth century Edward III had learnt enough to provide better for supply and even recreation. "I must inform you", writes Froissart, "that the King of England and his rich lords were followed by carts laden with tents, pavilions, mills to grind their corn and forges to make shoes for their horses—(good strong horses transported from England)" ... "Upon the carts

[1]Philippe le Bel's three sons, Louis X, Philippe V and Charles IV, had died in rapid succession without heirs between 1316–28, thus opening the way for their first cousin, Philippe VI, son of Charles, Count of Valois.
[2]Froissart. The Chronicles of England, France and Spain. Everyman Edition. London, 1906. pp. 64–7. Froissart (c.1337–1410) was born at Valenciennes, and became secretary of Philippa of Hainault, afterwards the queen of Edward III. He knew Flanders intimately and was a courtier of the Duke of Brabant; he also visited Scotland and was in England during the reign of Richard II. He describes the war as a splendid sport, in which the royalties and knights behave with exquisite consideration to each other, in a setting of glittering pageantry: then, with entire callousness, describes appalling atrocities. As Huizinga writes, this "sober and accurate description of outward circumstances sometimes acquires tragic force just because it leaves out all psychological speculation"; he compares Froissart to a "photographic plate".
[3]Froissart. op. cit. pp. 44 ff.

also were carried several boats, skilfully made of boiled leather, and large enough to contain three men, so as to enable them to fish any pond or lake ... The commonality, however, were compelled to use whatever provisions they could get. The King had, besides, thirty falconers on horseback with their hawks, sixty couple of hounds and as many greyhounds so that everyday he took pleasure in hunting and fishing."[1]

In 1360 a Treaty was arranged at Brétigny, near Chartres, apparently after Edward III, scared by a shattering hailstorm, had vowed to Our Lady of the Cathedral to make peace. It assigned King Jean's colossal ransom and the whole of Aquitaine to the English—with Ponthieu and Calais as well. And although nine years later the war broke out again, and the French under Charles V "the Wise" (1337–80) and Bertrand du Guesclin managed to regain a great part of these territories and devastate most of the rest, the English presence in France and the English dynastic claim continued.

Richard II (1367–1400), unlike Edward III, was not interested in war: he preferred to assert the prerogative of the Crown at home and enjoy the most sumptuous court in Europe (to ratify peace, he even married as his second queen, Isabella, daughter of Charles VI of France); while Henry IV, the usurping head of the junior Lancastrian branch of the Plantagenets, who deposed and killed Richard as a tyrant, was too ill and precariously placed to renew the wars. But his son, Henry V, with his doubtful title, was anxious to assert all his rights, and distract his subjects from private wars and conspiracy at home. Moreover, the essential strategic conditions for a new campaign had now been fulfilled: there was a major power in France, hostile to the French Crown; this time the great Dukedom of Burgundy, which now included Flanders and most of Holland. For in 1363 Jean II, in his open-handed way, had granted away Burgundy as an appanage to his youngest son, Philippe le Hardi,[2] who by his marriage to the heiress of Flanders had soon brought a much wealthier Burgundy into the orbit of England, since the Flemish cloth industries depended on English wool. Then Charles VI (1368–1422), Charles V's son, had gone mad in 1392,[3] and the Valois family had been further disrupted by the quarrel between his uncle, Louis d'Orléans, and his cousin, Jean Sans Peur, Duc de Bourgoyne, over the control of France. The feud had mounted until in 1407 Orléans had been murdered in Paris at the avowed instigation of the Burgundian Duke. France was also further divided between those who, following the Burgundian factions, opposed the Popes at Avignon during the Great Schism, and the Orléanists who backed them.

Here was the English opportunity, and Henry V took it. Hence the extremely risky campaign that, starting with the slow and difficult siege and capture of Harfleur, which had prevented a planned march on Paris and Bordeaux, ended in the spectacular victory of Agincourt, afterwards celebrated by Shakespeare with so much nationalist rhetoric. This victory, tactically comparable to those of the Swiss against the Habsburgs and Burgundians, as

---

[1]Froissart. op. cit. p. 71.
[2]So called from his brave conduct at Poitiers, for which his father wished to reward him.
[3]He became violent and smashed plates and furniture, though under the delusion that he was himself made of glass, and so could not move.

obtained by infantry and archers against knights, brought more than the loot and ransoms of the previous century: it won the Crown of France. But although to reinforce his claim Henry V made a dynastic marriage with the daughter of the insane Charles VI, Henry's premature death in 1422 left the English with more than they could hold, and utterly dependent on their Burgundian allies. Moreover, though the infant Henry VI grew up to found Eton and King's College Cambridge, he proved quite unable to cope with his responsibilities, having presumably inherited a streak of insanity from his Valois grandfather.

The English could still, however, count on the vital Burgundian alliance,[1] since in 1419 Jean Sans Peur of Burgundy had been murdered on the bridge of Montereau by an agent of the Dauphin, heir of Charles VI, in revenge for the assassination of Orléans in 1407. The English still occupied Normandy, Paris, and most of the valley of the Seine, while the crazy Valois King and the understandably shifty and neurotic Dauphin were based on Bourges or Chinon. Under the terms of the Treaty of Troyes (1420), John, Duke of Bedford, brother of Henry V, proved a capable regent for the child Henry VI, officially also King of France.

With the death of Charles VI and the accession of the Dauphin as Charles VII, the French fortunes changed. The superior resources of France were gradually brought to bear, following the imposition of regular taxes through the taille (hearth tax) and the gabelle (salt tax); the provinces occupied and plundered by the English became more restive; and in 1429 an inspired peasant girl of eighteen, Jeanne d'Arc from Lorraine—her fervour and magnetism reminiscent of the leaders of the Children's Crusades but politically directed—induced Charles VII to sanction a successful relief of Orléans, besieged by the English, and to ventuure to Rheims for the coronation without which no French King could command his full thaumaturgic powers. In reaction to the romantic nationalistic halo accorded her in the nineteenth century, Jeanne's influence has been unduly disparaged: such eccentrics—and she was a formidable eccentric of sturdy stock, well able to handle difficult horses and wear heavy armour[2]—could then win widespread if ephemeral followings, and her capable and hardy leadership enhanced French morale, as witness the jubilation among the English and Burgundians when she was taken. Handed over to the English by her Burgundian captors, she was convicted of heresy at a political trial designed to discredit the coronation of Charles VII, and in 1431 burnt in the market place at Rouen. Her conviction for heresy had made Charles VII wary in his own interest of trying to protect her, but in 1456 he went out of his way to have her memory rehabilitated from all taint of it.

Much more serious than the brief influence of an inspired peasant girl, the collapse of the Burgundian alliance destroyed the entire English strategy. In 1435 by the Treaty of Arras, Charles VII bought peace with Philippe le Bon

[1]For the best survey of the whole war see Edouard Perroy. La Guerre de Cent Ans. Paris, 1946.
[2]Her father was a substantial farmer, and her two brothers afterwards made successful military careers as Bailly of Vermandois and Captain of Chartres.

of Burgundy by handing over the attractive territories of Macon and Auxerre; and in the following year the English evacuated Paris.

Gradually their whole position became eroded. By a royal ordonnance of 1439 the French King had created a standing army, the gens d'ordonnance; and by 1445 they amounted to twelve thousand professional soldiers with artillery. With the Burgundians reconciled with the French, the English had to make the best terms they could, and though Henry VI was married to Margaret of Anjou, niece of Charles VII, Normandy and Maine were lost to the English; and in 1453 Gascony as well, when Sir John Talbot, first Earl of Shrewsbury, long seasoned in border wars against the Welsh and Irish, and famous in the campaigns in France—Ducum Angliae omnium strenuissimus et audacissimus— was defeated and killed in the assault on the castle of Castillon on the Dordogne.[1]

The horrors of civil war and foreign occupation had evoked a cynical response in the mordant genius of François Villon, born in the year of the execution of Jeanne d'Arc. He writes in the tradition of Rutebeuf of the precarious and hectic life of the Parisian underworld,[2] which he lights up with flashes of haunting beauty, as in the famous refrain "Mais où sont les neiges d'antan?"[3] During a career in total contrast with Chaucer's English respecta- bility, he cuts through the conventions of allegory and romance to observe life, not from near the top, but from the gutter and even the steps of the gallows. And where the English Langland grumbles and moralizes in a general way, Villon expresses the agonized sensibility of a highly educated and already disorientated French intellectual. The Hundred Years War had left its mark on French civilization by bringing in more realistic literature.

It also proved, on the public and political level, the making of the French monarchy. The crown was forced into organizing a large and permanently recurring revenue from a potentially wealthy realm much larger than England, and to do so on its own authority. The nobles, with typical irresponsibility, had resisted this extension of regal power in a revolt contemptuously termed the Praguerie in reference to current disturbances in Bohemia—but Charles VII proved able to quell it and, under the urgent circumstances, he could also ignore the various regional parliamenz. The Hundred Years War was won by paid professional soldiers and artillery, and the French monarchs emerged with the standing army and the guns which, exploited by the realistic, cunning and

[1]This old warhorse was one of the earliest senior commanders north of the Alps to be shot in battle, being hit in the leg by a bullet from a culverin.
[2]François Villon (1431–63?), born in Paris as François de Montcorbier, took the name of Guillaume de Villon after a canon of the Parisian house of St. Benoit de Betourné, who had been his benefactor. He studied at the Sorbonne, where in 1452 he took his master's degree. Three years later he had the misfortune to kill a priest in the cloisters of St. Benoit, and was banished. Reprieved, he robbed the Collège de Navarre and fled to Angers; an occasion on which he composed his Petit Testament leaving imaginary and appropriate possessions to friends and enemies. By 1461 he was in prison at Meung, where he wrote his Grand Testament. Again arrested for robbery and riot, he was condemned to the gallows, a sentence commuted to banishment in 1463. The time, cause, and place of his end have never been fully substantiated.
[3]"But where are the snows of yesteryear?"

tenacious Louis XI, would in time render them, after many vicissitudes, the absolute masters of the most powerful realm in Western Europe.

III

In England the war had united the aristocracy and their dependants in a new way behind the throne. While in the thirteenth century continental wars had been unpopular, in the fourteenth they had paid off; and while the French regional parliaments had lost what political power they had, in England since the wars of Simon de Montfort against Henry III, the Parliaments had come to include representatives of the gentry and the townspeople. By 1327 it had been taken for granted that the Commons were an integral part of Parliament, and by 1361 the Crown, working through a Conciliar government in London, was collaborating with the Justices of the Peace to keep some order in the counties through regular petty sessions and quarter sessions. This alliance between Crown and gentry was of cardinal importance and survived the disorders of the late fifteenth century occasioned by the chances of dynastic incompetence and strife, but not by the intrinsic structural weakness of the monarchy. Moreover by 1362 the gentry and the burgesses in the Commons had increased their greatest source of strength, their influence over the grant of supply, when Edward III had agreed not to levy the most essential of the taxes—the wool tax—without their consent; and by 1376 the Commons were also electing their own Speaker. It is of course premature and misleading to speak of a "Lancastrian constitutional experiment", but King, Lords and Commons (and their petitions) had become an accepted pattern of government: the Commons, though sometimes terrorized by rival Court factions, had to be taken account of. Policy was naturally still in the hands of the King's Council and justice administered from King's Bench; but an originally feudal monarchy had become parliamentary. Moreover the Crown now had better control over the Church: some of the greatest bishops, as William of Wyckeham, were royal civil servants who collaborated with the lawyers and lay bureaucrats of central government; Henry Beaufort, Bishop of Winchester, made a cardinal in 1426, was the illegitimate son of John of Gaunt, legitimized by Gaunt's nephew, Richard II. He had been one of the Protectors of the Realm during Richard II's minority; he then became Chancellor, and after Henry V's death, he used his immense wealth to help finance the expenses of the Crown and his diplomatic skill to negotiate a peace with the French after the death of Bedford and the collapse of the Burgundian alliance. On his death in 1447 Henry VI characteristically remarked when offered a legacy, "My uncle was very dear to me and did me much kindness when he lived. May the Lord reward him! Do with his goods as ye are bound to do: I will not have them." The days of Anselm and Becket, archbishops of a cosmopolitan Church whose allegiance was to Rome, had long faded into the past, and a worldly royal cardinal had become a needed pillar of an insular state.

The other side of the medal was the growing unpopularity of the clergy all over western and central Europe. Most of the people were still Christian; but they questioned the monopoly of the Church, its wealth and its politics. The Popes at Avignon were in schism, with three Popes at once, while priests neglected their parishes and held several livings (often in consequence of the Black Death), and with the increasing rapacity of churchmen on fixed incomes in a time of inflation, the now increasingly literate laity became critical of clerical pretensions and of the natural failure of the clergy to live up to the high strung celibate ideals once propagated by Innocent III. On the highest European level the Conciliar Movement tried to reform the Papacy by congresses of Christian clergy and laymen, as at Konstanz in 1414-18 and Basel in 1431. But on the provincial level there was a proliferation of heresy, particularly in England, where Wycliffe formulated a devastating attack in the vernacular on the heart of Catholic doctrine, and in Bohemia, where the perennial dislike of the Czechs for the Germans added nationalistic force to the Hussite Revolt. The disorders and savage class conflicts in Flanders and in Germany, and demoralization following the Black Death and the Hundred Years War in the west, encouraged a preoccupation with mortality and with the torments of purgatory and hell, always part of the Christian teaching that pride of life and sexual impulse were wicked and would incur "Judgement". Ancient pagan beliefs in magic and sorcery were not far below the surface and, even among the educated, astrology was considered a science until the days of the emperor Rudolf II (1576-1612) and even of Wallenstein in the seventeenth century.

In England the Lollards or "mumblers", as their enemies called them, already displayed the puritan hatred of life and pleasure which were to become so powerful in the seventeenth century, and attacked the Church hierarchy with prurient zest. For John Wycliffe (1330-84) was the first and all too articulate spokesman of the Non-conformist Conscience. He was no follower of Ockham, but a conservative "realist" who repudiated the official authority of the Church and proclaimed with St. Augustine that salvation depended on predestinate Grace. In feudal terms, he argued that all Christians "held" their life "tenure" and its sequel "direct" from God, whose word had been made manifest in the Bible. He also denied the doctrine of Transubstantiation in the Mass and of the priests' authority to dispense salvation through it. But unlike the Cathari, he did not regard the world as the botched work of the devil; he was a Christian who sought to relate men directly to God through the study of the translated Scriptures—an idea that appalled the scholastic experts, who claimed, not without reason, that the multitude would only profane and misunderstand them. His followers posted on the doors of St. Paul's Cathedral and of Parliament at Westminster, a list of denunciations in English which denied the supposed miracle of the sacrament and attacked the wealth and, of course, the deviant morals of the clergy, as well as denouncing the splendours of late medieval architecture, and the kind of art patronized by the Court, as by implication that minor masterpiece, the Wilton diptych, commissioned for Richard II. It is not surprising that Henry IV, the Lancastrian usurper, afraid of the political and theological implications of Lollardry, should have devised the statute *De Hereticis Comburendis* in 1401, against such radical subversion.

But politically, by the late fourteenth century, the English parliamentary monarchy had become well established, both at the centre and in the counties; strong enough for Richard II to attempt to turn it into a despotism in the style of early Renaissance Italian tyranny and well enough grounded for Conciliar government to survive the Lancastrian *coup d'état*, the disorders following from the incapacity of Henry VI, and the backwash of the Hundred Years War.[1] Contrary to long received opinion, Edward IV and Henry VII did not create a "new Monarchy", but rehabilitated the old one of which the House of Commons was an accepted and regular aspect.

The English language, long superseded by Norman French, had now come back into its own, and Geoffrey Chaucer (1340–1400) had become the first English vernacular writer of outstanding genius; indeed then the greatest vernacular writer in Europe. Chaucer came originally of a Suffolk family, but was born a Londoner, son of a wealthy merchant, with close connections with the Court. He became a page in a noble household and at nineteen fought and was taken prisoner and ransomed in France. In 1366 he married Philippa Roet, sister of John of Gaunt's third wife, the widow of Sir Hugh Swynford, and later became one of the esquires in the household of Edward III. He travelled in Spain on business for John of Gaunt and on diplomatic missions to Genoa and Florence, where he read Dante and Boccaccio. In 1374–86 he was appointed Comptroller of the Customs of Wool, at a substantial salary, and continued to act as a diplomat on behalf of the new king, Richard II. In 1382 he also became Comptroller of the Petty Customs and in 1385 a Knight of the Shire for Kent. In 1389 he held the sinecure office of deputy forester of North Petherton, Somerset. His fortunes, though he complained of them, survived the deposition of Richard II, and Henry IV augmented his pension. He died in London and was buried in Westminster Abbey, the first poet to be accorded that honour. Though an official of a cosmopolitan Court, bilingual in French and English, who had travelled in France and Italy, Chaucer is intensely English in his humorous, ironic and tolerant observation of character, which he can hit off in a phrase. To this day he remains intelligible, a writer to fall back on, still relevant. Langland, too, is early modern, the slow beat of his verse well adapted to the perennial moralizing of English poets, ancestral to Hardy and Auden.

IV

The hitherto prosperous Flemish cities, since 1369 under the Dukes of Burgundy through the marriage of Philippe le Hardi and Margaret, Countess of Flanders, had suffered from the recession of the early fourteenth century, which had also brought to a head the class conflict between the French or Frenchified overlords and the cities, and, within them, between the *haute*

[1] The battles of the so called "Wars" of the "Roses" between 1455 and 1487 occupied only about four months of the thirty-two years, and, like the Thirty Years War in Germany, had far less effect than was once believed.

bourgeoisie and the lesser craftsmen, not of course out for a "democracy", but, like trade unions, to assert their own monopolies. And beneath these struggles, the Flemish peasantry, speaking a patois unintelligible to their "betters", attempted savagely destructive revolts, aimed not merely against the rich but, like the English Peasants' Revolt in East Anglia, against literate minorities as such.

It would be tedious to record the atrocities and counter-atrocities committed by the uncouth citizens of Ghent and Bruges and their rulers, ably assisted by the brutish peasantry during those times. Froissart, who knew the country only too well, had described how the men of Ghent, led by a brewer of metheglin (mead), Jacob van Aarteveldt, rose against the Count of Flanders, and drove the Count into France; an occasion seized upon by Edward III to make his landing in Flanders after his victories at Cadzand and Sluys on the Scheldt at the beginning of the Hundred Years War, and establish himself at Antwerp; but such revolts seldom lasted or stood up against armoured knights.

The decline of the cloth industry on which the prosperity of the Flemish cities was based was more serious. The craft guilds forced up wages and clung to obsolete techniques, so that suicidal protective tariffs crippled trade, and cloth workers migrated to Florence and to England, where they were encouraged to settle.

In overseas trade the English would now slowly draw ahead, following objectives set in the *Libelle of Englysche Polycie* (1436). It advocated the encouragement of international commerce backed by substantial capitalists operating on a continental scale from the Baltic to Spain and from Venice to Southampton. Across the Channel the interests of Jacques Coeur (1395–1456), *argentier du roi* to Charles VII of France, were now cosmopolitan. His vast fortune was based on trade from Narbonne and Montpellier with the Muslims in the Levant, for which he had obtained a dispensation from the Pope; he had then become master of the royal mint in Paris and rich enough to finance the King's campaign to rid Normandy of the English. He had agents at Barcelona, Avignon, Rouen and Bruges, and became, and lived like, a multi-millionaire. But his wealth provoked such envy that, in 1450, the King imprisoned him and confiscated his profits, and he was forced to begin a new career by escaping to Rome, where Pope Calixtus III put him in command of a fleet sent to relieve Rhodes then besieged by the Turks. The enterprise killed him, but this cosmopolitan banker, admitted to the highest social circles,[1] and wielding immense influence, is a portent in early modern history, symbolic of an alliance between kings and monied men, both served by a host of agents and administrators with a new professional expertise.

In due course and by such policies the wealth of the Low Countries was built up again, not by the old and vulnerable cloth manufacturers, ruined largely through protectionist, inflationary and conservative craft guilds, but by a commerce and finance conducted on a European scale with far greater capital behind it. Though not yet surpassing the enterprise of the Italians, who long

[1]A privilege which cut both ways. He was so intimate with royalty that he could be accused of poisoning Charles VII's mistress, the elegant Agnes Sorel.

kept their lead, until the discovery of the route to the East Indies round the Cape and of the wealth of Central and South America shifted the main opportunities of commerce to the Oceans and the Atlantic states, many cities of the Low Countries, France and England, like those of Northern Italy, were becoming more modern in the techniques, the routine and the objectives of business.

The gorgeous and extremely accurate style of painting of Jan and Hubrecht van Eyck (floruit 1422–41) developed under the patronage of Philippe le Bon of Burgundy whose Chancellor, Nicolas Rolin, is included in Jan van Eyck's famous picture of the Madonna and Child against a prospect of a receding river seen through arches. Philippe le Bon also brought Claus Sluter to Dijon, where he created the superb sculpture of the tombs of the Burgundian Dukes. Jan van Eyck was also commissioned to paint the rich cosmopolitan merchants, as in the portrait of the domestic bliss of the Arnolfini of Lucca, an amiably realistic piece of observation, including a faithfully observed mongrel dog. If these masterpieces have all the colouring of medieval book illumination, they are also meticulous in depicting the detail of princely and upper-bourgeois wealth, and the worn and wary faces of those who accumulated it.

V

"A dry, barren, impoverished land, 10 per cent of its soil bare rock; 35 per cent poor and unproductive; 45 per cent moderately fertile; 10 per cent rich. A peninsula separated from the continent of Europe by the mountain barrier of the Pyrenees—isolated and remote. A country divided within itself, broken by a high central table land that stretches from the Pyrenees to the southern coast. No natural centre, no easy routes. Fragmented, disparate, a complex of different races and languages and civilizations—this was—and is, Spain."[1]

In spite of these disadvantages, by the late fifteenth century Spanish monarchs united the country, and soon became the rulers of a vast American empire.

In 1469 the marriage of Ferdinand of Aragon and Isabella the Catholic had led ten years later to a joint monarchy which could draw on the constitutional, administrative, commercial and diplomatic experience of both the Mediterranean power of Aragon and the man-power and crusading military tradition of Castile, at last freed from dynastic civil war.

As already remarked, the natural division of the country between the lands facing the Mediterranean, Aragon, Catalonia and Valencia, and the inward looking central area of Castile and new Castile, with its contacts towards the Atlantic through León to Galicia and Asturias, and towards Portugal through Estremadura, was emphasized by the discrepant weight of population—then far greater in the interior—and by contrasting ways of life. The interests of the Catalonians had long been mercantile and maritime, extending over

[1] J. H. Elliott. *Imperial Spain 1469–1716*. London, 1963. Prologue.

Sardinia, Sicily, Naples and even the Levant, where there had been Catalan Dukes of Athens. They had long fought the Genoese over the trade in corn, spices and cloth; but the economic recession of the fourteenth century and the Black Death had hit them hard, while Alfonso the Magnanimous, by attempting to rule the country from Naples, had lost grip on the Spanish inheritance on which his original power had been based, and broken down the constitutional collaboration between the merchants and the crown that had served the country well. Hence class conflict, and by 1462 revolt and dynastic strife.

Castile had developed differently. The vast flocks of sheep which had multiplied since the introduction of the merino strain around 1300, and which had been organized under the *mesta* which supervised their migration to and from their summer pastures, had led, as in England, to the rise of a rich trade in wool both with Flanders through San Sebastian and Corunna, and often in Genoese ships through Seville with Mediterranean markets. Not much of this wealth had found its way to the Crown, weakened then less by over-expansion abroad than by internal conflict. In 1350 Alfonso XI of Castile had been succeeded by his son Pedro, termed the Cruel (1350–69). But his cruelty had not paid off: his bastard brother, Enrique of Trastámara, had defeated him at Montiel, knifed him after the battle, and won the throne as Enrique II (1369–79): and though John of Gaunt, Duke of Lancaster, whose brother, the Black Prince, had backed Pedro, thereupon married Pedro's daughter, and through her claimed the throne, he claimed in vain.

The Trastámaras survived; but Enrique II's son Juan I (1379–1390) failed to win Portugal, and Juan's grandson, Juan II, married twice: by Maria of Aragon he had a son Enrique IV (1454–74); by Isabella of Portugal, a daughter, Isabella, termed "the Catholic". The Castilians, however, called Enrique IV the "impotent" and refused to recognize his own heiress, and Isabella, his half sister, claimed the throne. Rejecting French or Portuguese suitors, she married Ferdinand of Aragon, a youth of her own generation who could bring immediate and skilled military aid in the struggle for the succession. Hence, after Isabella, the last of the Trastámaras, had secured the throne in 1474 and Ferdinand had succeeded to Aragon in 1479, the powerful and momentous union of the two crowns. Under the leadership of Castile, they mopped up the last Moorish state of Granada, annexed the Canary Islands, in 1492 gave Columbus his chance, and launched the pent-up energies of the Spaniards into Atlantic oceanic empire.

A sardonic Spanish vernacular literature now began to flourish. The dynastic conflicts which had led up to the union are reflected in the plays and poems of Juan de Encina of Salamanca (flor: 1500) who sarcastically depicted St. Antony succumbing to his temptations and used a parody of pastoral subjects to express his disillusionment with life and the clergy in a manner which anticipates the ironic humour of Cervantes. Torres Naharro, his contemporary, also wrote drama which developed the old morality plays to deal with secular subjects in a style which anticipates the techniques of Lope de Vega and Calderón. There is a direct transition in Spain from medieval convention to vernacular realism.

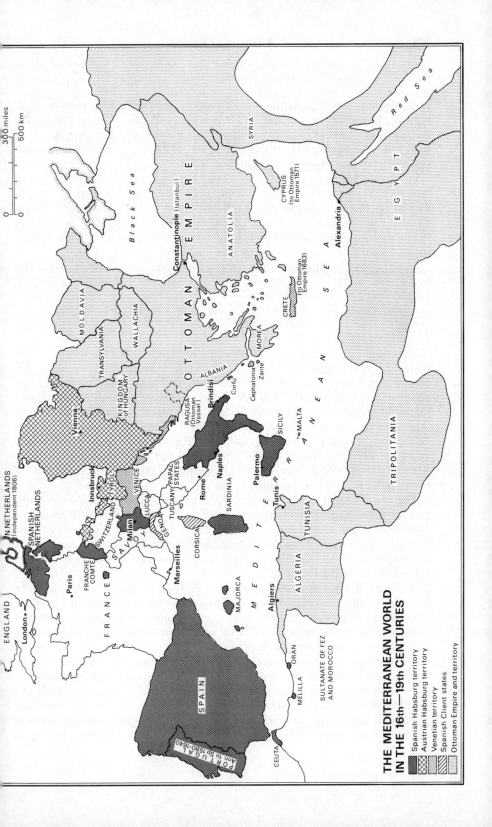

**THE MEDITERRANEAN WORLD
IN THE 16th — 19th CENTURIES**

Spanish Habsburg territory
Austrian Habsburg territory
Venetian territory
Spanish Client states
Ottoman Empire and territory

300 miles
500 km

Red Sea

SYRIA

CYPRUS
(to Ottoman
Empire 1571)

Black Sea

Constantinople (Istanbul)

ANATOLIA

OTTOMAN EMPIRE

MOLDAVIA

TRANSYLVANIA

WALLACHIA

KINGDOM
of HUNGARY

Vienna

ALBANIA

MOREA

Zante

Cephalonia

Corfu

RAGUSA
(Ottoman
Vassal)

Brindisi

CRETE
(to Ottoman
Empire 1669)

Alexandria

E G Y P T

A E G E A N   S E A

SICILY

MALTA

Palermo

Naples

SARDINIA

Rome

PAPAL
STATES

TUSCANY

LUCCA

GENOA

Milan

VENICE

S A V O Y

INNSBRUCK TYROL

SWITZERLAND

FRANCHE
COMTÉ

Paris

FRANCE

Marseilles

CORSICA

MAJORCA

Algiers

ALGERIA

TUNISIA

Tunis

TRIPOLITANIA

M E D I T E R R A N E A N   S E A

Innsbruck

SPANISH
NETHERLANDS

N.NETHERLANDS
(independent 1806)

ENGLAND

London

SPAIN

PORTUGAL
Ann to Sp 1580-1640

CEUTA

MELILLA

ORAN

SULTANATE OF FEZ
AND MOROCCO

VI

In contrast to the Spaniards, the Portuguese monarchs and most of their subjects, following the example of Dom Diniz, had continued to collaborate for practical objectives. Moreover they had defeated the dynastic claims of Juan I of Trastámara, King of Castile, to whom on the death of Ferdinand I the legitimate succession to Portugal had fallen.

His claim had been contested by Ferdinand's widow, but a more effective leader of Portugal had arisen in a young nobleman, the Master of Aviz, who, backed by the anti-Spanish merchants of Lisbon and the Chancellor Avaro Pais, had murdered the widowed queen's Spanish lover and driven her from the city. She had fled to the Castilians, who had taken over her claim, leaving the question to be decided between Juan I and the Master of Aviz.

So in 1384, the Spaniards and French were besieging Lisbon, while the Portuguese, under their constable, Nun' Alvarez, and reinforced by English archers hired by Lisbon merchants at Southampton, faced them in a well-prepared position at Aljubarrota. Portuguese and English maintained an unmedieval discipline until, in the August heat, their opponents had been exasperated into attack.

The resulting Anglo-Portuguese victory was decisive for Portugal and the house of Aviz. The Master of Aviz became João I, and in 1386 consolidated a commercial treaty of Guimarez made with the English in 1372, into the political and commercial Treaty of Windsor, a lasting alliance. João I also married Philippa, a daughter of John of Gaunt, and they established a highly sophisticated court; their third son, the Infante Dom Henriques (Henry the Navigator), proved a consistent promoter of the voyages of exploration which colonized the fertile island of Madeira in 1420 and, coasting down the West African shores, would later bring vast wealth to Portugal by discovering a route to the East Indies round the Cape.

Thus in Portugal, as in the other Atlantic states and in the Netherlands, commercial and practical interests began to emerge through the foreground of conventional late medieval dynastic warfare as described by Froissart, and the Portuguese tradition of monarchy working to develop the country's resources and commerce, established by Dom Diniz, was given a new dimension by João I, the founder of the House of Aviz.

As in Spain, there is a satirical strain in Portuguese vernacular literature, to be most tellingly expressed by Gil Vicente in the early sixteenth century, who, bilingual in Castilian and Portuguese, wrote satirical and anti-clerical comedies which, despite their medieval court conventions, pay an unmedieval attention to realistic undercurrents of village life.

But the most memorable evocation of the Portuguese who laid the foundations of the exploits of Vasco da Gama, remains the magnificent painting by Nuno Gonçalves, appointed in 1450 Court painter to Afonso V (1432–81). The *Polyptych of São Vicente* combines superb composition, detail as lovingly accurate as that of Jan van Eyck, and colouring which is more subtle than even the Flemish painter generally achieved. This genius depicted character with a precision and sympathy which goes deeper than even many of the Italian portraits, whose subjects are so much on parade; and the homely weather-beaten features of Dom Henriques of the House of Aviz and Lancaster contrast with the etiolated refinement of the kneeling figure thought to be Afonso V, while the androgynous saint himself, at once vulnerable and authoritative, diffuses a sense of peace over the supporting groups of hard bitten ecclesiastics, solemn soldiers, fishermen, and men of business, skilfully deployed. "Much of the success achieved was daring novelty in those days ... the monumental composition which relied on triangular schemes: the daring shown in the use of tint, such as the treatment of the white of the monk's robes, the golden hue of the saint's dalmatics ... obtained through the use of gold tints, not through gold leaf ... the gradations in grey; the prodigious advantages taken of the various planes, a fact which is most remarkable in the construction of the features, the sculpture-like modelling of the figures ... the differentiation of the tissues and metals, the innovations in the representations of the shadows and in the use of violet shades."[1] The painting is in an egg tempera, not in oil, with a sober range of colour, without the overemphasis on gold on which the Flemish and Burgundian patrons probably insisted.

[1] João Couto. *Nuno Gonçalves, O Poliptico de S. Vicente*, Estudios Cor. Lisboa, 1954.

XXV

Central European Disintegration: The Turks: Muscovy

The decline of the empire and the waning of Byzantine power had given a freer hand to the rulers of Central Europe: in the wake of the Mongol invasions their realms now had a final military and cultural success, before the steadily encroaching Turks conquered the Balkans and threatened Vienna, and the power of the *Tsars* of Muscovy, who now considered themselves God's appointed heirs of a "third Rome", became more formidable.

The Poles had a common interest with the Danes and Swedes in resisting German domination of the Baltic; but the Poles were more continental-minded than the sea-going Danes, more concerned with Hungary and Bohemia. After the assassination of the Czech monarch of Poland, Wenzel III, Wladyslaw I, termed the Short, who came of the old Piast line, had been crowned king in Krakow in 1320. Threatened by the Teutonic Knights, who had seized Dantzig and tried to cut the Poles off from the Baltic, Wladyslaw married the daughter of Gedimynas, Grand Prince of Lithuania (1315–41), an alliance that would lead to the important union of Poland and Lithuania.

The Lithuanians, already in 1261 briefly converted to Christianity under their king Mindangas, had soon killed him and reverted to paganism. And no wonder: they were related to the eastern Old Balts, and to the irreconcilable .Old Prussians; and time out of mind, they had settled in out of the Eurasian steppes on the flat, sandy and forested country south of Riga; they were now, like the Poles, set to expand south-east in the wake of the Tatar devastation of Kievan Russia. Vilnius in Samogitia, south of Esthonia and Livonia, was their principal base; and, under Grand Prince Gedimynas they had already spread into the area around the Pripet marshes and the upper Dnieper. Kasimir III the Great of Poland (1333–70), who succeeded Wladyslaw the Short, was himself half-Lithuanian, and collaborated in an expansion which included most of Kievan Russia. Abandoning Pomerania to the Teutonic Knights, he turned south-east and occupied eastern Galicia, including Lwów, and from Krakow, where in 1364 he founded a law school, the nucleus of a university, he tried to administer the whole of Poland.

On his death in 1370, Poland passed briefly into the spectacular empire of his nephew, Louis the Great of Hungary, but in 1382 reverted to Kasimir's younger daughter Jadwiga, who in 1386 married her cousin Jagiello, Grand Prince of Lithuania, baptized a Catholic in the previous year. He changed his name to Wladyslaw and was crowned King of Poland as Wladyslaw II, creating under the Jagiello line a dynastic union of Poland and Lithuania confirmed in 1401 at Radom. It led to useful results, when in 1410 a combined Polish-Lithuanian army defeated the Teutonic Knights at Tannenberg, and it was further confirmed in 1413 by the Pact of Hordlo, when Poland-Lithuania became a joint realm of the Jagiellos that would last until nearly the end of the sixteenth century.

Under Kasimir IV Jagiello (1447–92) the Poles and Lithuanians combined to overrun larger areas of White Russia and of the Ukraine, where, with their connivance, Ruthenian *Kazaki* (freebooting *Cossacks*) were occupying some of the most fertile parts of Russia and warring against Tatars and Turks. Poland-Lithuania thus expanded broadly if superficially over large debatable territories; but its rulers, committed to fight both Russians and Tatars and Germans on the Baltic, had to concede too much to their magnates. Moreover, they were Catholics, controlling the whole of the Baltic-Black Sea isthmus, whose subjects were mainly Orthodox Christians; a situation not much assuaged by the foundation of the *Uniate* Church, basically Catholic, with Orthodox ritual.

Both Poles and Lithuanians were dashing horsemen, fighting men aloof from their subjects. The Poles, who set the tone, were divided into *Pani* (magnates), *Szlachta* (gentry) and serfs. *Pani* and *Szlachta* alone had political rights, and their exclusive Diets had no popular roots. The central Diet had a built-in majority of warriors—*woiwodes* (war lords) and *castellani*; and, unlike the contemporary English and Catalan Parliaments, it had no burgesses. By 1652 any member could paralyse decisions simply by saying "I object": a privilege known as the *free veto*, much prized by a temperamentally independent and privileged gentry.

So, in spite of an imposing Catholic façade, far-flung dominions, and wealth enough to sustain a westernized Court and to patronize Italian architects and sculptors who created memorable palaces in Krakow, the Polish-Lithuanian realm of the Jagiello kings was spectacular and glamorous but impossible to govern: just when the western monarchs were creating centralized states with more systematic and competent administration, as that of Louis XI in France and Henry VII in England, the Poles, part of a fluctuating and wildly ambitious military empire, ruling a population who were mainly serfs and a middle class in part of immigrant Germans but mainly of Ashkenazim Jews, failed to create the kind of realm which, even if devoid of natural frontiers, could survive the resurgent pressures of German and Muscovite power.

II

In Hungary, the same pattern of cosmopolitan, far-flung, but precarious authority had emerged. After the death of Andrew III, the last of the Arpáds, the Angevin Charles Robert of Naples, whose mother had been the sister of

Kasimir the Great of Poland, had been crowned in 1310 King of Hungary (1310–42), in the emphatically Hungarian city of Szekesfehérrar, the ancient stronghold of the Arpáds. With the backing of the Church and his own military prowess, "Carobert" had quelled the more obstreperous Magyar lords and occupied Bratislava on the Danube east of Vienna. He had then by French and Italian methods of administration created about the most efficient government in Central Europe.

His son, Louis the Great (1342–82), thus came into a rich inheritance, which he fully exploited. He captured the fine port of Dubrovnik from the Venetians, then, after the death of the Serbian Tsar, Stephan Dushan, in 1355, he dominated Bosnia, northern Serbia and western Bulgaria. When, in 1370, he also succeeded his maternal uncle Kasimir III the Great to the throne of Poland, he presided over the largest, if not the most manageable, realm in Europe. Louis the Great was a Frenchified knight, anxious to win renown; but he was also shrewd enough further to develop the gold mines of Transylvania, whose proceeds he spent on Italian and French architects and artists as well as upon the pursuit of military prestige. The reigns of the Angevin Carobert and Louis the Great, contemporaries with the English Edward II and Edward III, mark the apex of medieval Hungarian civilization, and the tradition of his Francophil Court with its glamour and charm long lingered in the country.

On the death of Louis the Great in 1382, he was succeeded by Sigismund of Luxembourg, who had married his daughter, Maria of Hungary. But as the son of the Czech emperor Charles IV, Sigismund was marked out for even greater responsibilities. Elected King of Hungary in 1385, in 1411 he would become King of the Romans and so of Germany; then in 1419, on the death of his half brother Wenzel IV, he would become King of his own native Bohemia, where he had to contend with the Hussite revolt. Finally he would be elected Holy Roman Emperor (1433–37), and become preoccupied with organizing Councils of the Church to end the Great Schism. Sigismund would thus be increasingly distracted from his original duties as King of Hungary.

But in one important aspect his obligations as Emperor and King of Hungary coincided. He was deeply concerned in both capacities with the mounting menace of the Ottoman Turks in the Balkans and Central Europe.

But as a Czech monarch Sigismund commanded little support in Hungary, and was diverted from the essential task of resisting the Turks by the Hussite movement in Bohemia, his own principal base. He had to buy the loyalty of the Hungarian magnates by concessions injurious to the throne, and by founding the Order of the Dragon, the oldest Hungarian Order of Chivalry; but the Hungarians prided themselves on descent from Attila, and one Magyar noble representatively remarked "By God, I am no servant of thine, thou Czech swine."

Even as defender of Hungary against the Turks as well as a cosmopolitan patron of Rennaissance art and learning, Sigismund incurred further Hungarian resentment by exacting heavier taxes; and his successor and son-in-law, Albrecht of Habsburg, reaped the harvest. A ferocious peasant revolt erupted, disastrous in itself and in its sequel, for Albrecht crushed it with extreme cruelty, taking a leaf out of the Turkish book and impaling the leaders. Already in Poland by Louis the Great's decree of 1374 the serfs had been placed entirely at the mercy of their owners; now, in Hungary as well, the peasants were further degraded. The resulting hatred and demoralization did not make for effective resistance to the Turks. And when in 1396 Sigismund instigated and led a European crusade against them, it came to disaster at Nicopolis on the Danube, when the Sultan Bajazet captured Jean Sans Peur of Burgundy and many other western knights, and so clinched the resounding Turkish victory over the Serbs at Kossovo in 1389. The Ottoman Turks were now masters of the Balkans and threatening Hungary itself.

In Hungary there was a final rally. Following the death of Albrecht's son, Ladislas Postumus of Habsburg (1440-46), a Luxemburger through his mother, John Hunyadi, a Vlach magnate and mercenary captain from Transylvania and Voivode of that area since 1441, became Regent of Hungary. Hunyadi organized a more professional paid army; and in 1456 when, after the fall of Constantinople in 1453, the Turks advanced to besiege Belgrade, he relieved the city. But he died of "camp fever", as had young Ladislas of Habsburg, the last of the Luxemburg line. So in 1458, Hunyadi's kinsman, Mathias Hunyadi, famous as Mathias Corvinus from the raven on his coat of arms, was elected to the Hungarian throne. Hailed, with polite intention, as *Attila Secundus* and married to a daughter of the House of Aragon, he proved an able statesman and warrior. He first raised *Hussars*—Hungarian light cavalry famous for their gallantry and style—as well as being a great patron of Renaissance learning who collected the celebrated Corvina library, fortunately dispersed before the Turks could destroy it *in situ*. He died in 1490 and was the last really able elected king of Hungary with European prestige.

III

There were, as already described, two relatively well placed dynasties in Central Europe; the Luxemburg Kings of Bohemia who, with Charles I and IV, had obtained the Empire, and the Habsburgs, who were pursuing a steady policy of aggrandizement by marriage and by collaboration between all branches of their family. The Luxemburg kings controlled the strategic bastion of Bohemia and commanded its mineral wealth; the Habsburgs had extended their power from their base at Vienna over Styria and Tyrol. Now Bohemia was riven by sectarian strife and the divergent duties of kingship and empire. The Emperor Charles IV, after a highly successful reign over Bohemia, had been succeeded by Wenzel IV, King of the Romans; then by Charles's second son Sigismund, King of Hungary, and by 1433 emperor. But during the Great Schism Sigismund had been confronted by the first heresy in Europe with formidable military backing on a national scale. The Hussite wars were more an expression of Czech national feeling against the cosmopolitan Empire and the German-dominated Catholic Church than of fanatical devotion to religious doctrine, though religious animosities fanned the flames in a prelude to the seventeenth century Thirty Years War, when religion cloaked and enhanced a power struggle between the Catholic Habsburg emperors and the Protestant Princes in the Germanies.

John Huss (1369–1415) had assimilated the essential doctrine of Wycliffe that the final authority for Christian beliefs was not in the Clergy but in the Bible, and, like Wycliffe, he had inveighed against the wealth and pretensions of the established Church. He came of a peasant family in Southern Bohemia, and by 1401 was Dean of the Faculty of Philosophy in the University of Prague. Like Wycliffe, he was a conservative "realist" who defended the Thomist philosophy against "nominalist" innovations, mainly German. But he also took over the "Bethlehem" Chapel at Prague, founded by followers of the mystic puritan, Jan Milic, a bishop who had renounced all worldly position and specialized in redeeming prostitutes. Huss preached and wrote in Czech, though if, as alleged, he simplified the spelling, it is hard to imagine what it must have been like before. Huss believed in predestination of an Elect, and shared the Lollards' puritanical hatred of the originally Mediterranean Catholic cults and of the artistic and architectural grandeur that displayed them. Wenzel IV had shielded this essentially academic figure from the persecution of the authorities, but Sigismund was determined to make an example of him. During the climax of the Great Schism, Huss was excommunicated, and in 1412, after he had denounced the sale of indulgences by the emissaries of the anti-pope, John XXIII (1410-15), he was rusticated from Prague. But he was not left in peace, as Wycliffe had been, in the country. Huss was summoned by Sigismund to the Council of Konstanz under inadequate guarantees of safety, and accused of heresy. He never, as had Wycliffe, denied transubstantiation; rather he had exalted the eucharist, claiming that the laity ought to have wine as well as bread in communion, so that some of his followers were called *Calixtines*, as they demanded the *chalice*, and others *Utraquists*, as claiming communion of *both kinds*. But he was convicted of heresy and burnt, as had been his associate, Jerome of Prague.

This was not the end of Huss. He had become a martyr; and five hundred of the nobility and gentry of Bohemia banded together against the already discredited Pope. They hated the German clergy and they coveted the rich Church lands. Further, the peasants were incited by preachers who promised them a Christian communist millennium. In Prague the Czechs, led by a renegade monk, inaugurated one of their historic customs by throwing German magistrates from a window in the Council House on to the pikes of the mob below. Huss's followers went far beyond their founder in extremist doctrines; and they found an able leader in Jan Žižka, a soldier who came of minor Czech gentry and who had early lost an eye in battle. He had fought at Tannenberg against the Teutonic Knights, and after the death of Wenzel IV, he organized the militant Hussites against Sigismund in a new way. They had assembled in a camp that they called, in the Old Testament way, Mount Tabor, and Žižka invented the new technique of using wagons in *laager* along with pikemen, arquebusiers and rudimentary artillery not only for defence but for attack. In 1420, five years after Agincourt, he routed Sigismund's army at Vitkov and Vyseland. The Czechs then established a government of "estates", but the war went on. In 1422 the redoubtable Žižka, though he lost his remaining eye at the seige of Rabi, again defeated Sigismund at Nemacky Brod, and quelled dissident Adamite Communists among his own following. By 1424 he was dead of the plague.

The Hussite wars, the first major religious wars between Christians in Europe since Arian times in which both sides were evenly matched, have been romanticized by Protestant historians and Czech nationalists: the spectacle of these fanatics roaring their hymns as their wagons creaked and trundled into battle not only in Bohemia but in Germany and Poland, would seem to an impartial eye a prelude to the seventeenth-century Thirty Years War, itself set off by another Czech revolt against the Empire, and, immediately, a distraction from the main task, then urgent for Central Europe, of organizing a spoiling attack on the Turks. The motives too are similar; the nobles' and gentry's desire for the Church lands are a foretaste of the princes' exploitation of Luther, while the millenarian and chiliastic preachers' vision of social revolution anticipate the Anabaptists' regime at Münster.

The Hussite wars ended in compromise. In 1434 the Catholic and "Calixtine" nobles combined to defeat Prokop—the successor of Žižka—and his peasant army at Lipany, and in 1436 Sigismund, now emperor and having previously agreed to the Compact of Prague, was restored to the shaken throne of Bohemia.

IV

The one really solid dynastic achievement in Central Europe, and destined to spread far beyond it, was now the accumulation of Habsburg power, extended in 1477 by the marriage of Maximilian, son of Friedrich III, Holy Roman emperor (1452–93) to Mary, heiress of Charles the Bold of Burgundy, into a pan-European dimension. When most other dynasts, as the Valois and Plantagenets, fell into bitter internecine feuds, the Habsburgs, though they had their differences, concerted their policies by vesting the authority of their House in all the males of the family, of whom the eldest was admitted to be the final authority. Already in 1379 by the Treaty of Neuberg the family possessions had been peacefully divided between Albrecht III, Archduke of Austria and his brother Leopold III of Tyrol, Carinthia and Styria. Finally the entire family possessions were united under Friedrich III, the last emperor to be crowned in Rome by the Pope. Though he failed to assert his authority as emperor or collect the revenues to which he was entitled, Friedrich III was clever and popular; he made a good marriage with Eleanor of Portugal, and launched his family into dynastic greatness by arranging the decisive Burgundian marriage of his son Maximilian. It was in his reign that the famous line was written *Bella gerant alii, tu, felix Austria, nube.*[1]

So, while in Poland and Hungary glamorous and far-flung realms had created memorable court cultures, but failed to develop effective central government

[1]Others may make wars, you, happy Austria, marry.

or to prevent the increasing oppression of the peasantry, and in Bohemia, after the remarkable achievements under Charles IV, Czech dislike of the Germans had led to a national support of an originally academic heresy, and to the first major armed heretical revolt, foreshadowing that of Luther and its seventeenth-century sequel; in Austria, Styria and Carinthia, on the other hand, in south-eastern Central Europe in the lands where the Turkish encroachment would have to be met, the Habsburgs had established an increasingly formidable power, drawing on resources extending far beyond their original territories. It would long dominate Central Europe, belatedly protect the continent from further Turkish attack, and even, under the emperor Charles V attempt to make the Empire again a dominant force, more than it had been even in the twelfth and thirteenth centuries.

V

The tentacles of Turkish conquest had long been extending far into the Balkans; it was now only a matter of time before they would close in on Constantinople itself. The Central Asian conqueror Timur Lenk, after enormous depredations in Transaxiana and South Russia, and after subduing Iran and Afghanistan and sacking Delhi, had taken Baghdad, invaded Egypt and in 1402 was besieging Ankara. Here the Turkish Sultan Bayezet was totally defeated and taken prisoner, and the Turkish attack on Constantinople set back by half a century. But by 1430 the Turks had captured Thessalonika and by 1444 defeated another ill-organized Christian crusade at Varna on the Black Sea, thus confirming their hold on Wallachia and Moldavia as well as on the country south of the Danube. Nor had the west made good use of the breathing space that Timur Lenk had indirectly accorded them. In 1438 the Council of Florence had forced through a union of the Catholic and Orthodox Churches, a measure detested by most of the Greeks, many of whom so hated the Catholic Christians that they felt it "better to suffer the Sultan's turban than the Cardinal's Hat". The Emperor Friedrich III had neither power nor money; the French were paralysed by the aftermath of the Hundred Years War; the potential crusader, Henry V of England, had been succeeded by Henry VI, a half-imbecile *dévot*, and the Spaniards had their own infidels to fight. The Venetians even considered that their trade might benefit if the Turks took over Constantinople and brought political stability to the faction-ridden Byzantine state, and the Genoese, who detested the Venetians too much to co-operate with them, were now hard put to it to defend their own base in Italy from local enemies. When the pacific and elderly Murad II was succeeded by his young son Mehmet II, determined for the glory of Islam to conquer *Qustantiniya*, intelligent, well educated, a good linguist, formidable and cruel, the doom of the city appeared inevitable.

Mehmet II proved an able strategist and tactician. He grasped that the Turks must win command of the sea and he understood that the ancient and enormous land walls could not stand up to the concentrated fire of big guns; in emergencies he was resourceful, and he had absolute and unified command of 80,000 men. The Byzantine emperor Constantine XI Palaeologus was more than twice Mehmet's age; an honourable man, who refused to escape from the doomed city and prepared to die rather than submit;[1] but he had at most only 7000 men to defend the city, an area of fourteen square miles.

By 1452 the Turks were closing in. They built the strategically placed fortress now known as Rumeli Hissar and launched a considerable fleet on the Sea of Marmara. The Christians, in reply, constructed a strong boom across the entrance to the Golden Horn. Meanwhile the largest cannon ever constructed was being brought into action. An Hungarian engineer had offered his services to the Byzantines, but they could not afford his fee: he therefore went over to the Sultan who offered him four times as much, as well as unlimited facilities and labour. He had thus been able to construct a bronze cannon 26 ft. 8 in. long, and proportionately thick, which could fire a stone projectile weighing twelve hundredweight. This monster was now dragged from Adrianople by sixty oxen and, with others of slightly less calibre, placed to bombard the part of the walls considered most vulnerable.

When in 1453 the assault was launched, and the Turks failed to break the boom protecting the Golden Horn, the Sultan commanded that ships be dragged over land by oxen from the Bosphorus behind Pera, the Genoese trading settlement, and launched into the Golden Horn, thus threatening Venetian and Genoese shipping and greatly increasing the area of walls that the sparse defenders had to guard. For six weeks, the unremitting and terrifying bombardment was continued, until the ancient Theodosian walls began to crumble, and at the cost of heavy losses among the auxiliary *Bashi-Bazouks*, a foothold was obtained for the crack Janissary troops to go in. By an appalling oversight, a postern gate in the second and highest line of walls, used for sorties by the defenders, had been left unlocked and unguarded; the Janissaries took it and its tower by assault; the emperor and his principal commanders perished in the battle, and the Turks captured Constantinople.

According to Muslim custom, they were allowed three days to plunder the city; then discipline was restored. Apart from personal cruelties, as the execution of the Megadax Notoras, his son-in-law and his youngest son, since the father preferred to see the boy decapitated rather than yield to the Sultan's lust, then to die himself, Mehmet II made a statesmanlike settlement. Thus Christians were now a *milet*, second class citizens under Turkish rule, but their religion and commerce were tolerated. The Venetians, though they had belatedly sent a fleet to relieve the city, which had turned back when informed of its fall, had not been far wrong: after a few years under the new regime, Constantinople—now Istanbul—began to thrive, and its population to increase under a regime that was at least secure.

In the long term the effects on Christendom were more serious. The Turks now had a permanent imperial capital on European soil with immense strategic

---

[1] The contrast between the Muslim and Christian leaders and the setting, course and consequences of the siege and its outcome are comprehensively described in Sir Steven Runciman's masterly *The Fall of Constantinople 1453*. Cambridge, 1965, which the reader is strongly recommended to consult.

advantages; they could confirm their hold on the Balkans, on Moldavia and Wallachia, on Greece (Athens in 1456) and upon many of the Islands. They could take their time in evicting the Knights of St. John from Rhodes; they could even drive the Venetians from important towns on the Adriatic. "The Grand Turk", with his disciplined and uniformed Janissaries, their thunderous bands and superior firepower, commanded better armies than any European monarch, and the neo-Hellenic cultural and artistic life which had flourished during the last decade of the restored Palaeologoi was submerged. To this day in the Seraglio palace at Istanbul, reminiscent of airy Mughal palaces and far more elegant than the contemporary ostentation in the west, can be observed, in unbroken sequence, the superb state robes of the Sultans of a Turkish empire that extended for centuries from the Tigris and Euphrates to the Danube. Such was the fate of the city of Constantine and Justinian.

VI

The Russians firmly believed that Constantinople had fallen as a punishment for its emperor's apostasy in accepting the Union of Florence of 1438 with the Catholic Church. They remained themselves strictly Orthodox, uncontaminated by compromise with the West. And they were now becoming extremely formidable; their main power base in Muscovy was in the forested zone north of the steppe, with Moscow, a natural centre of river transport, well to the east of Lithuanian attacks. The Tatar menace had now diminished, when in 1445 and 1449, in part through Muscovite diplomacy, the Khanates of Kazan and Crimea had separated from the Golden Horde at Sarai and started to raid each other. The Grand Princes of Moscow, who had collaborated with the Tatars to survive, were now asserting their independence, and in spite of occasional Tatar raids, unobtrusively extending their power. Ivan III, the Great (1462–1505), was the first Grand Prince to assert his independence of the Tatars, refuse tribute (1480) and call himself *Tsar*. He incorporated Riazan and Tver into Muscovy and in 1471 mastered distant Novgorod, carrying off its famous *veche* (town bell) to Moscow, and making peace conditional on Novgorod renouncing its old alliance with Lithuania. The long subjection to the Tatars had increased the Muscovite respect for autocracy, and the Tsar, who recruited Tatar troops, so adding to his massive resources of man-power, discarded the ancient popular assemblies, as at Novgorod, and was better able to control the magnates or *boyars*, who had absolute power over their serfs and who had increased their enormous appanages during the Muscovite expansion in which they had joined. Ivan also developed a nobility of military service in return for grants of state land. The Russian Autocrat, in his fastness deep in Muscovy, thus escaped from the predicament of the Polish, Lithuanian and Hungarian monarchs, whose power was hamstrung by their own nobles and gentry; like the monarchs in the west, he laid the foundations of a centralized and powerful state.

It remained Eurasian: Ivan III imported Italian architects to build the

Kremlin and artillery experts to train his army, and in 1472 he married an Italianate niece of the last Byzantine emperor; but Muscovy was not deliberately thrust forward as the heir of Byzantium; it became so by a turn of fate. There was no other great Orthodox power left, and the Orthodox clergy and their followers accepted the accomplished fact as the work of God.

Hence in 1512, long after the fall of Constantinople, the monk Philotheus could write to the Tsar Vasilyi III, "The Christian empires have fallen, in their stead stands only the empire of our ruler ... Two Romes have fallen, but the third stands and a fourth there will not be."

XXVI

The Iberian Sea-borne Empires: Charles V

"This is the story of heroes", wrote Camoens in the opening canto of *Os Lusiades*, "who leaving their native Portugal behind them, opened a way to Ceylon and further, across seas no man had ever sailed before."[1] Here is "the first epic poem which in its grandeur and its universality, speaks for the modern world",[2] and it celebrates the world-historical shift in the balance of power between Europe and Asia, which makes a contrast between medieval and early modern times. Once the Portuguese had rounded the Cape of Good Hope, come to dominate the Indian Ocean and establish themselves in the Far East, western Europeans had outflanked the hitherto vastly more powerful land empires of Asia, whose civilizations had always been more massive than anything in the West since Graeco-Roman times. Add to this the discovery of America, an even more epoch-making event, and western Europeans, who had hitherto looked to the Mediterranean as the focus of trade and political power, became aware of entirely new oceanic horizons and began to create sea-borne empires of settlement and colonization which would last until the twentieth century and change the face of the world.

The Portuguese had long been feeling their way down the coast of Africa in search of gold and slaves, and incidentally voyaging out into the Atlantic in search of legendary islands. Dom Henriques (Henry the Navigator), the third son of King João I, had backed these ventures with money and influence; and already by 1420, following the chance discovery of Santos, Madeira had been colonized and soon planted with sugar cane from Sicily and vines from Crete. But the main objective was still Africa, where the Portuguese hoped to by-pass the Sahara by sea and make direct contact with the non-Muslim pagan states of Black Africa.

Their objectives were still medieval; to win gold and spread Christianity. Like his cousin, Henry V of England, Dom Henriques was obsessed with the idea of a crusade; and for him, as for the Spaniards, it was a crusade in Africa. He was not much interested in trade and, if occasion served, preferred a direct

[1]Camoens. *The Lusiads*. trans. W. C. Atkinson. Penguin, Harmondsworth, 1973. The "Lusiads" were the sons of Lusus, the mythical founder of Portugal.
[2]C. M. Bowra. *From Virgil to Milton*. London, 1945.

attack on Morocco. "The memorial which he wrote in 1436 urging an attack on Tangier, and his own gallant but inflexible conduct in command of the enterprise, both recall the pages not of Camões but of Froissart. All this is far from the Renaissance with its bright, lively curiosity, its clear hard sense of expediency, its passion for human fame, its love of learning and the arts. ... Though he was a generous patron of sailors and cartographers, the story of a school of astronomy and mathematics at Sagres is pure invention. Certainly this pious and chivalrous ascetic was no Renaissance humanist."[1]

Yet the Portuguese explorations were well planned, with the backing of government and with the advice of the experts and cartographers who had long frequented Lisbon. And in the dynastic war with Spain which extended into one over the trade with West Africa, settled in 1483 by the Treaty of Alcaçovas, the Portuguese obtained the advantage when their monopoly of the Guinea trade was recognized.

But the Spaniards kept the Canary Islands, though in 1420 the Portuguese had got there first. The archipelago had been known to the Romans in the first century BC[2] and to the Arabs since the late tenth century, while the indigenous Guanches, tall people with blue eyes and light hair, perhaps descendants of Palaeolithic stock, who lived in caves and worshipped dogs, long resisted European encroachment. Adventurers from France had early settled Lanzarote, one of the eastern islands, and acknowledged the King of Castile as their feudal overlord: hence the Spanish claim, and although the Portuguese had arrived on Gomera, one of the mountainous western islands, they were unable to maintain a settlement.

Meanwhile, they had pushed on south, and by 1456 discovered the uninhabited Cape Verde Islands, so-called because far out in the Atlantic off Cabo Verde and Dakar in Senegal. They were volcanic islands with a mountain, Pico, over 9000 feet high, and an excellent harbour—Porto Grande—on the island called São Vicente. It proved a convenient depot for the slave trade out of West Africa, and the islands soon supported a mulatto population descended from negroes and Portuguese, who now had the monopoly of the Guinea trade in gold, pepper and slaves, and the duty, imposed by the Pope, of converting the negroes to Christianity.

With the accession of João II, the Portuguese consolidated their hold on the West African coast: they built stout forts, as the fort at El Mina, with stone imported from Portugal; at once strong points and trading posts in the sweltering "Negrolands" where Atlantic rollers swept up to a coast of tropical rain forest.

It now became apparent that the Bight of Benin did not lead to Asia, but that the African coast turned south; so the Portuguese, who took with them stone columns they called padrãos which they set up at key points in sign of possession, followed it further, discovered the mouth of the Congo, and brought back Congolese negroes to Lisbon, where they were warmly received. By 1486 the explorers had reached Walvis Bay, and in 1487 Bartolomeo Diaz,

[1] J. H. Parry. The Age of Reconnaissance. London, 1963. p. 36.
[2] They had called it Canariara since it was infested with large dogs.

fetching a course far to the south, rounded the Cape without knowing it and reached the Great Fish river in South Africa. His crew then refused to proceed east.

So it remained for Vasco da Gama, ten years later in 1497, in the reign of Manoel "the Fortunate", and five years after Columbus' discovery of the West Indies, to set out with a well found expedition for India. He sailed from Lisbon with two three-masted ships of about two hundred tons, a larger store ship and a small caravel, and he commanded 170 men. The expedition, unlike that of Columbus, was the culmination of long and systematic enterprise, with a well-born commander backed by the Court and the merchants of Lisbon, designed to secure direct access to India and the Spice Islands of the Far East, and as a crusade to spread the Catholic religion. Dom Vasco da Gama (1460–1524), Count of Vidiguerira, who came of distinguished family in the Alentejo, proved a fine sea commander, diplomat and ruler. On his second voyage in 1502 he was made Admiral of the Indian Seas, and went out a third time as "Viceroy of India" in 1524. He died in Cochin in modern Kerala in that year, leaving a large fortune in Portugal.[1]

The expedition was well timed. Leaving Lisbon in July, the ships made for the Canaries and then for the Cape Verde Islands; then, fetching a course far out into the Atlantic, reached Natal on Christmas Day, at the height of the southern summer. They proceeded up to Mozambique, Mombasa and Malindi, where they obtained a pilot who knew the Arabian Sea, and who took them in three weeks to Calicut, the main centre of sea-borne trade in Southern India. The return voyage was less successful. With the August monsoon against them, it took nearly three months, during which many of the crew died of scurvy, the curse of all these expeditions. By September 1499 da Gama was back in Lisbon where he was enthusiastically acclaimed.

It was one thing to make this reconnaissance, another to establish a trading empire. The Arab traders, who had long profitably monopolized the Indian Ocean and the spice trade, incited the Indians against the Europeans; so da Gama was sent out again with a considerable fleet which completely out-gunned the flimsy armaments of the Arab dhows and bombarded Calicut itself. Having established supremacy at sea, he obtained a useful trade treaty with the Indians, ratified at Cochin on the Malabar coast. Indeed, the Portuguese developed a profitable local trade exporting Indian textiles for pepper, for cinnamon from Ceylon, and for nutmegs and cloves from the Moluccas; but to undersell the Venetians in Europe they needed to control the Arab trade to the Levant.

Under Afonso Albuquerque, their greatest Viceroy, they therefore acquired a major naval base at Goa, then at Malacca, commanding its Straits, as well as at Ormuz at the entrance to the Persian Gulf, and briefly, on Socotra, at the mouth of the Red Sea. They were now able to disrupt the Arab trade with the Levant, and, keeping their own vital route round Africa open to Lisbon, almost to monopolize the spice trade in Europe. Moreover, once in control of the

[1]See The Three Voyages of Vasco da Gama. Ed. H. E. J. Stanley. Hakluyt Society. 1869.

Malacca Straits, they founded Macao on the China coast and developed trade with Canton, bringing back silks from China and trading with Japan.

Unlike the Spaniards, they never founded a military empire: their ambitions were for trade. They accumulated great wealth and lavished it on their extraordinary Gothic Manueline buildings, in which, as at Belém in Lisbon, late medieval architecture is festooned and embellished with ornament imitating ships' ropes and the creatures and seaweeds of the ocean. By intelligent and tenacious foresight, systematic organization and fine seamanship, the Portuguese had achieved their objective—to exploit directly the spice trade with the Far East. In doing so they had opened up a whole new field of predatory enterprise for Europeans, brought them into contact with the elaborate civilizations of Asia and Indonesia and, less happily, the Asians in touch with their own.

II

When in 1492 Christopher Columbus sailed with three small ships from the harbour of Palos near Cadiz, he had the same objectives. Don Cristóbal Colón (1451–1506) was the son of a weaver, Dominico Colombo, of Genoa and Savona. Since he had reddish hair and a pale complexion, he may have had Lombard descent, and he early went to sea in the western Mediterranean and the Levant. In 1474 he fought for Portugal in a battle against the Genoese off Cape St. Vincent, and was lucky to swim ashore near Sagres clinging to an oar. After settling in Lisbon, then the most active centre of cartography, Colón voyaged to Iceland; then, after his marriage to Filipa Perestrello in 1478, he lived at Porto Santo opposite Madeira, where his brother-in-law was in command. Returning to Lisbon, he elaborated his project before putting it to the King, who was already fully occupied with the other more reputable scheme that resulted in Diaz passing the Cape and the sequel under da Gama. In contrast with da Gama, Colón failed and found something else, setting off a train of events even more extraordinary and bizarre.

Unlike the Portuguese commanders, he was no aristocrat, but an adventurer of genius, obscure origin and obstinate determination, obsessed by an idea. Convinced, like contemporary experts, and unlike the best minds of Antiquity or Medieval Europe, that the earth was round, Columbus grossly miscalculated its size. He thought he could get to Japan by sailing west and struck the New World of the Americas instead. It was only after the Portuguese had rejected him that he sailed in the service of Spain and opened the way for the monarchs of Castile to rule an enormous territorial empire in lands hitherto entirely unknown to Europeans. He had first put his project to the Portuguese in 1484; they were too expert to take it seriously; and so two years later he obtained an interview with Fernando and Isabella in Córdoba. Preoccupied with the attack on Granada, they appointed a commission of experts under the Bishop of Talavera which, with Spanish deliberation, sat for four years and then turned his project down. Columbus, meanwhile, had won the support of Diego de

Deza, a professor at Salamanca, who as tutor to Don Juan, the heir to the throne, had access to the Court. He also convinced two friars, who, in league with one of the Queen's confessors, persuaded the King and Queen to see him again. Columbus, with great audacity, demanded high terms: to be made admiral and Viceroy, with reversion to his descendants, of the lands he would discover, and 10 per cent on all resulting trade. So entire was his confidence that the royalties, with the surrender of Granada in prospect, and perhaps looking out for new projects, were impressed; Isabella had always regarded the enterprise as a crusade. And Columbus had now acquired just the collaborator he needed in Martin Pinzón, a shipowner of Palos near Cadiz.

Early in August 1492, the *Santa Maria*, a medium-sized ship under Columbus' command, and two caravels, the *Pinta* and the *Niña*, commanded by Pinzón and his brother, Vicente, put out from Palos with eighty-eight men and made for the Canary Islands. Here, for nearly a month, they prepared for their audacious voyage. On September 6th they set sail, and with the northeast trade wind behind them, they made good speed; Columbus was an able navigator, and in five weeks, by October 12th, they sighted the coral sands of one of the then well-wooded Bahamas. The indigenous Arawak Amerindians, who, pathetically, welcomed the intruders, called it Guanahani; Columbus at once christened it San Salvador; afterwards the English, prosaically, called it Watling Island. Apart from its sub-tropical climate, there was not much to attract the Spaniards, but they ceremoniously annexed the island for the Catholic Monarchs. Raccoons that scuttled under the cedar trees, and flamingoes that rose from the shore had little appeal, though the sea turtles may have come in handy.

Columbus now proceeded south-west, convinced that he was on the way to Japan. So they missed Florida and the north American continent and arrived off Cuba and the north coast of Haiti, which Columbus promptly christened Hispaniola—"Little Spain": but here the *Santa Maria* was wrecked, and Columbus, leaving a settlement behind him, sailed for Spain. With favouring winds and current, he made north-east to the vicinity of Bermuda, then due east to the Azores, and so, under stress of weather, not to a Spanish port, but to Lisbon, where the *Niña* was not entirely well received.

But Fernando and Isabella were delighted; they at once commanded Columbus to organize a second much larger expedition, and arranged that the Catalan Borgia Pope, Alexander VI, who depended upon the Aragonese of Naples, should issue an important Bull—*Intercaetera* (1493). It created a theoretical boundary from north to south a hundred leagues west of the Azores and the Cape Verde Islands, beyond which all land to the west should be in the Spanish sphere of influence and all to the east in that of Portugal. This ambitious arrangement, modified by shifting the line many leagues further west for the benefit of the Portuguese, was ratified in 1494.

Columbus' second voyage, made with seventeen ships, set out in September 1493 from Cadiz: it was designed for the settlement on Hispaniola, the base for further exploration. But it arrived off Dominica, one of the Lesser Antilles. It then proceeded to Cuba and Jamaica, but found the settlement on Hispaniola destroyed. Leaving his brother, Bartolomeo, to found Santo Domingo, long the administrative capital of the Spanish Indies, Columbus returned to Spain. He had not yet struck the mainland of the Americas.

In 1948, on his third voyage, he came nearer to it, observing the continental fresh water tide of the Orinoco off Venezuela as well as discovering Trinidad; but at Santo Domingo he found the settlers in anarchy. Unable to restore order, in the following year he was superseded and sent back to Spain in disgrace. Whatever his genius, it was impossible for a low-born Genoese foreigner, with a trumped-up title and coat of arms, to dominate the arrogant younger sons- of feudal-minded hidalgos and other military adventurers of Castile. Columbus had wanted to create trading settlements and develop commerce with Asian civilizations which he never reached; the settlers wanted battle, gold, land and slaves.

In 1502, on his fourth voyage, Columbus at last reached the mainland of Central America, but it was only the repellent coast of Honduras; and when he coasted south and discovered Costa Rica, his ships proved unseaworthy. He always maintained and believed that he had found the Far East: but the discoverer of the New World never got beyond the Bahamas, the West Indies, Honduras and Costa Rica.[1]

Columbus rightly won fame for his epoch-making reconnaissance; but it was the second phase of mainland conquest that won Spain a great empire. In 1513 Vasco Nuñez de Balboa, first of the ruthless *Conquistadores*, founded Darien on the Caribbean shore of the southern isthmus of Panama; then, having sighted the Pacific before stout Cortés ever set eyes on it, in 1519 he founded Panama.

There followed the fantastic exploit of Hernán Cortés and his men in taking over the rich and populous Aztec empire of Mexico. He launched it in 1519 from Cuba, landed at Vera Cruz, then marched through forbiddingly difficult country up to the high central plateau of Mexico, where, with six hundred men and some Amerindian allies, he mastered the lake city of Tenochtitlán, the heart of the predatory Aztec empire. The famous campaign is told in detail by Bernal Diaz, who took part in it.[2] By 1521, while in Europe Charles V was contending with Luther's heresies at Worms, the Spaniards, with six hundred men, a few ships' cannon, and sixteen horses, had conquered Montezuma'a entire realm and driven the kidnapped Montezuma himself to death. Execrated and stoned by his own subjects for appeasing the Spaniards, he lost the will to live.

The most elaborate civilization in central America became tributary to Castile. Then, after careful reconnaissance from Panama, in 1531 Francisco

---

[1]After his failure as governor, Columbus, though received by Fernando at Segovia, died in frustration, but by no means in poverty, at Valladolid. His son, Diego, who had been brought up at Court, married into the aristocracy and inherited his father's titles of Admiral of the Indies and Governor of Hispaniola. The best biography is by S. E. Morison, *Admiral of the Ocean Sea: a life of Christopher Columbus* (2 vols, 1942); see also his *Christopher Columbus, Mariner*. 1956. F. Fernandez Armesto has written a good short account: *Columbus*. London, 1970.

[2]Bernal Diaz. *The Conquest of New Spain*. Trans. J. M. Cohen. Penguin, Harmondsworth, 1963.

Pizarro, a "cut-throat of undiscoverable origins",[1] with only one hundred and eighty men and thirty-seven horses, set out from Panama to conquer the Inca empire of Peru.

Traversing jungle and mountain passes of appalling difficulty, within a year they had captured the reigning Inca, Atahuallpa, and garotted and burnt him; they then plundered much gold, and by 1533 mastered an empire that extended from Quito to northern Chile. Vast areas of South America had become subject to Charles V, already since 1517, as Charles I, ruler of Spain and vast territories in Europe, and by 1520 crowned King of the Romans and in effect Holy Roman Emperor.

So the two Iberian powers, both after their kind, expanded into sea-borne empires: the Portuguese, intent on commerce around the coasts of the ancient civilizations of Asia, with their power based on command of the sea and on keeping their trade route open to and from Lisbon round the Cape; the predatory, crusading Spaniards, intent on gold and land, the military and clerical masters of Amerindian cultures hitherto unknown to Europeans or anyone else; themselves the exploiters of civilizations long highly developed socially and artistically, but technologically and militarily quite incompetent before the invading Europeans, and unable also to resist the impact of European disease.

Along with high adventure went tragedy; and although owing to the intervention of the Catholic monarchs and high ecclesiastics, the Spanish official administrators and clergy were more humane than is generally represented, the Amerindian population was hideously diminished. The sequel belongs to world history: but the Iberian sea-borne empires now began to affect Europe.

III

The Catholic monarchs, following their policy in the Iberian Peninsula, had been careful as far as they could not to allow any independent quasi-feudal powers to the conquerors of the Aztec and Inca empires, or to the settlers of Spanish America in the Caribbean. Isabella was particularly concerned that the Amerindians should not be too severely exploited and, following the policies already imposed in the Canary Islands which often formed precedents for Spanish rule in the Americas, the home government sometimes managed to diminish the brutality of the colonists. Resentment by the creoles—the indigenous colonists—against the peninsulares formed a constant theme of Spanish American history until it culminated in the early nineteenth century in the revolts of Bolívar and San Martín; but, during the sixteenth century, the hand of the home government and its bureaucracy was heavy and fairly effective. While the exploitation of the conquests was naturally slow and the influx of gold and silver from Spanish America took longer to cause inflation in

[1] J. H. Parry. op. cit. p. 126.

Europe than was once supposed, the Spanish Crown managed to draw an increasingly massive revenue from the Americas, while, even at the height of the wars with the English and the Dutch, the treasure fleets were only once seriously interrupted. The effect of Columbus' discoveries was gradually to give a much needed increase to the revenue of Castile, under whose jurisdiction they were firmly placed.

The scope of Castile thus became imperial: "the conquest of Granada, the discovery of America, and the triumphant emergence of Spain on to the European political stage lent unparalleled lustre to the new State created by the Union of the Crowns, and set the seal of success on the political, religious and economic reforms of the royal couple ... Castile—its most pressing domestic problems momentarily solved—was ready to throw itself into new experiences, cultural or political, with all the energy of a nation released from long confinement ... Already to the Castilians, Castile was Spain; and already it was being beckoned towards a still greater future, as circumstances both at home and overseas inexorably cast it for an imperial role."[1]

IV

The circumstances at home went far back into European history, resulting in an unforeseen twist in dynastic succession. The Emperor Charles V (de facto 1520-55), a grandson, through his mother Juana, of Fernando and Isabella, now inherited a fantastic accumulation of Spanish, Habsburg and Burgundian territories, and made the last neo-medieval attempt, based on Spain and Spanish-American wealth, to revive the Holy Roman Empire, realize the ideal of Dante's *Monarchia* and unite a divided Christendom against the Turkish menace in Hungary, the Levant and north Africa. This titanic effort of a methodical, conservative and conscientious prince, no great warrior, but a dedicated *politique* and diplomat who held tenaciously to his objectives, became the central theme of European politics. He failed, but he and his son, Philip II, convulsed a continent in strife.

The laborious dynastic policies of Fernando and Isabella had been distorted by the high death rate then usual among royalty. Determined to unite Portugal with the rest of Spain, they had married their eldest daughter Isabella to Prince Afonso of Portugal. On his death, she had been passed on to King Emmanuel of that country, and when she, too, had died, her sister Maria had taken her place.

Even higher politics now intervened. After Charles VIII of France, following up his claim to the Angevin inheritance in Naples, had invaded Italy and threatened the Aragonese in Naples, Sicily and Sardinia, in 1495 Fernando managed to create a "Holy League" of Spain, the Borgia Papacy and the Empire, supported by England, against the French. And here the most crucial dynastic union had taken place: a double marriage between the Infante Juan,

[1] J. H. Elliott. *op. cit.* pp. 115 and 119.

heir to the Catholic monarchs, and the Archduchess Margaret of Habsburg, daughter of the Emperor Maximilian I, which was reinforced by the marriage of the Catholic monarch's daugher, Juana, to the Archduke Philip of Habsburg, Maximilian's handsome son, through his mother, heir of Burgundy and the Low Countries. The pact had been further clinched when the Infanta Catherina of Aragon had been married first to Arthur, Prince of Wales, the heir of England, then to Henry VIII.

All these careful plans had gone wrong. In 1498 Isabella of Portugal died, followed the next year by her infant son Miguel. Most important of all, the young Infante Juan was dead within six months of his marriage, exhausted, it was rumoured, by his efforts to continue his dynasty. So in a manner unforeseen and undesired, the Infanta Juana, who already showed signs of madness, became the heiress of Fernando and Isabella, and in 1504, on her mother's death she inherited Castile. She soon proved incapable of government, and her husband, the Archduke Philip of Habsburg, was an alien in Spain. Moreover, their son, Charles of Ghent, was being brought up in Flanders.

So Spain became saddled with a foreign Habsburg dynasty and part of a European-Imperial inheritance; and when in 1516 Philip the Handsome died prematurely, Charles of Ghent, a gawky Flemish-looking youth with a peculiar lower jaw, came as Charles I into the whole Spanish inheritance, which now itself became inextricably entangled in the affairs of the Low Countries and Central Europe, the springboard of his Herculean attempt as Charles V to revive the Holy Roman Empire.

Charles V's possessions were immense. In 1519, on the death of Maximilian, he inherited not only the Burgundian Netherlands through his grandmother, heiress of Charles the Bold, but all the Habsburg lands in Germany and on the Danube down into Styria and Carinthia and round into Tyrol, as well as, in his own right through his mother, Castile and Spanish America, Aragon and the Aragonese possessions of Naples, Sicily and Sardinia. In the person of this youth of nineteen, soon, after immense bribes to the electors, King of the Romans and Holy Roman Emperor elect, for the first time in centuries the august title was backed by immense potential European power, and for the first time ever by resources that were extra-European.

Now, coincident with the gradual shift of economic enterprise to the Americas and the Far East, the Holy Roman Empire became once more central to European politics.

V

But Charles V would find it as hard as had his predecessors to fulfil its overwhelming responsibilities. Three main problems confronted him. The intransigent ambitions of France, long the most aggressive and formidable power in the west, and not above making alliance with the Grand Turk; the outbreak of militant popular and expanding heresy in the Germanies, exploited, as had been the comparable if milder heresy of Huss, by power- and land-hungry princes and nobles; and the formidable advance of the Turks in Central Europe and the Levant, along with the growing Muslim naval power based on North Africa. To contend with all these difficulties Charles V had to assert his unpopular authority over a potentially divided Spain, secure his possessions in Italy, and keep his communications open between the Low Countries and Franche Comté and between Germany and Spain through Italy.

The French historian Braudel has amply demonstrated the immense difficulties of transport and communications with which all sixteenth-century rulers still had to cope at a time when winter regularly slowed down or even paralysed land transport and shipping, when transport was still archaic, maps unreliable, roads and bridges in disrepair, and news a "luxury".[1] In spite of these obstacles, slow and devastating wars were conducted which disfigured an otherwise brilliantly creative age, when in spite of increasing foreign domination, the Italian and Flemish artists painted superb masterpieces, architects transformed the appearance of Rome, and the Italians culturally inspired the northern peoples who were creating their own "Renaissance" and outclassing them in economic and political power.

The conflict between France and the Empire was mainly fought out in Italy, where it was essential for Charles V to keep control of Milan and Genoa and to keep open his communications with Austria and the Germanies, as well as to maintain his hold on Naples and Sicily. It was, indeed, in the campaigns in southern Italy that the new striking force which briefly made the Spaniards the military masters of Europe was evolved. Gonçalvo de Córdoba, who had won his reputation as the *Great Captain* at the siege of Granada, had organized the Spanish infantry into heavily armed but mobile companies of pikemen and arquebusiers. By 1534 the Spaniards developed the *tercios* which became the terror of Europe. They were large units of up to 3000 men in twelve companies, who combined the Swiss defensive power in a phalanx of long pikes with the offensive power of firearms. These *tercios* could stand up to cavalry, break their attack, and shoot them down. They won for Spain the domination of Italy.

The French invasion under Charles VIII had already ended in fiasco, though in 1495 the king managed to break out of the trap set by the Italian League at Fornovo and escape to France; his successor, Louis XII (1498-1513), after initial success, had been defeated at Novara and also forced out of Italy; but Louis' nephew, Francis I (1515-47), returned to the attack, and in the year of his accession, defeated the Swiss mercenaries at Marignano. But the French occupation provoked a hornets' nest of resistance; and when, in the autumn of 1524, Francis I again crossed the Mt. Cenis and recaptured Milan, in the following February a combined German and Spanish army closed in on the French as they besieged Pavia. The defenders broke out while the Imperial army attacked; the French knights, caught in the meadows round Pavia by the

[1]See Fernand Braudel. *The Mediterranean and the Mediterranean World in the Age of Philip II.* trans. S. Reynolds. Fontana, London, 1972. 2 vols. This book is essential for the understanding of the sixteenth century in Europe, a rare masterpiece of research and exposition.

Spanish pikemen and arquebusiers, were routed, and Francis I himself captured
and deported to Spain. Henry VIII, then in alliance with the Emperor, ordered
bonfires in London; but Charles V in Madrid took the news phlegmatically
and merely returned to his chapel royal to give thanks for it. Now master of
Italy, he intended, he said, to proceed to his main objective, a crusade against
the Turks.

With farsighted statesmanship Charles did not try to ruin Francis I. He
refused Henry VIII's pressure for a joint invasion of France; but in 1526 by the
Treaty of Madrid, he supposedly obtained French consent to his inheritance
of the Duchy of Burgundy and the abandonment of French claims on
Charollais, Artois and Flanders, as well as of their claim on Milan, Naples and
Sicily. But, released, Francis I at once repudiated the treaty as exacted by *force
majeure*, and formed the League of Cognac with the Pope, Venice, Florence,
and Henry VIII. Charles, however, retained his domination of Italy: his troops
occupied Milan and Rome, and in 1527, following ancient barbarian custom,
his unpaid German army sacked it.

Thus medieval history was re-enacted: Charles V's attempt to revive the
Empire fanned the embers of the old Guelf and Ghibelline feud, and the
Popes, Leo X (1513-21) and, more deviously, Clement VII (1523-34) in
traditional manner, tried to thwart the Emperor's effort to organize Christendom. The Spanish grip on Italy remained: in 1529, by the Treaty of Cambrai,
the French accepted the accomplished fact, obtaining in return the recognition
of the French de facto possession of Burgundy. This Spanish domination, long
to continue, would be confirmed in the general European settlement made in
1559, after Charles' abdication, by the Treaty of Cateau-Cambrésis; the French
monarchs, none the worse for abandoning the lure of Italy, could then
consolidate themselves position in France and pursue the less impractical
objectives towards the Rhine opened up by the confusion worse confounded in
the Germanies by the consequences of the Lutheran revolt.

VI

This German problem had haunted Charles V almost since his accession. As
in the conflict between Empire and Papacy in Italy, medieval themes again
emerged, now north of the Alps, but with greater power. Luther, like Huss,
and Huss's followers, detested the Mediterranean cults enshrined in an
Italianate Church, and appealed, like Wycliffe, to the authority of the Bible.
He also, like Huss's disciples, embodied the nascent nationalism of his people;
as they had rallied Czech national feeling behind them and preached and
written in the Czech language, so Luther, a far greater genius than Wycliffe
or Huss, was representative of the Germans. Born in 1483 at Eisleben, the son
of a copper miner and brought up there and at Mansfeld, he entered the
University of Erfurt in 1501. His father, who had done quite well in his
business, wished him to be a lawyer, but in 1506 Luther insisted on becoming
an Augustinian monk. After taking his degree at Wittenberg, he returned to

teach at Erfurt under Johan von Staupitz, Vicar-general of his Order, in whose defence he was sent in 1510 to Rome. Like many northerners, the earnest young provincial was deeply shocked by the Roman way of life, and returned disgusted with the lavish Papal Court of Julius II. By 1512 a Doctor of Divinity, he succeeded von Staupitz as professor, his main task to expound the Bible. In 1515 he was made a prior, and assigned pastoral work as well. His career had thus been outstanding, when in 1517 he became the centre of resounding controversy over the sale of Indulgences in the diocese of Mainz. After the political crisis of 1517–21, and translating the New Testament into German, Luther married Katherine von Bora, a lapsed nun.

To Charles V Martin Luther presented a nagging problem that would not go away. His force and eloquence were combined with a brutal coarseness of language that brought a new vulgarity into theological disputes, and his bull-headed obstinacy made him politically formidable: he thought with the blood. A spreading, raucous and popular controversy was launched over a traditional grievance, the sale of Indulgences; this time for a far better objective than most, the rebuilding of St. Peter's at Rome. It created sufficient stir for the many German princes, their eyes on the Church estates, to fish in the muddy waters in its wake. Here, as in Hussite Bohemia, was a heresy that impinged on politics.

In 1517, Luther nailed no less than ninety-five theses on the door of the *Hofkirche* at Wittenberg. His basic principle, discovered after long-wrestling introspection, was that "the just shall live by faith"; it followed that "works"— that is ritual, relic worship, and the whole accumulated and spectacular structure of the Church which had come down from sub-Roman, Merovingian, Frankish and Ottonian times and been organized by Gregory VII and Innocent III—were superfluous. So Luther appealed to the "Christian nobility of the German nation" to "reform" the Church. The Medici Pope Leo X naturally excommunicated the renegade monk: in the winter of 1520, to the delight of his students, Luther publicly burnt the Bull. No characters could have been more incompatible than Leo X, hedonist and art patron, and Luther, the religious mystic and popular evangelist.

Luther's doctrines were now fashionable and caught on. Brought up in the "nominalist" philosophy of the School of Ockham which accepted the limitations of mind, he wished to clear away what he considered the pretentious scholastic structure of Thomism and get back to the early Fathers and to the Gospels. He thus appealed to many intellectuals attracted by novelty and by the Renaissance cult of getting back to the sources of the Bible and the Classics, while his hearty German eloquence delighted the people, as well as serving the turn of the princes and nobility, determined to diminish the cosmopolitan Catholic emperor's authority and to get their hands on the Church property. Luther also composed tremendous hymns—as the *Ein feste Burg ist unser Gott* written in 1524. By the time of his death at Eisleben in 1546, Luther had attracted a huge following. Moreover he was the first heretic of genius to exploit the new power of print. Moveable type, as opposed to wood blocks, had been invented by John of Gutenberg in 1454, the year after the fall of Constantinople. By 1516 the Dutch humanist Catholic, Erasmus, had won European celebrity by editing the New Testament from the Greek, alongside his own Latin version, thus challenging the authority of the venerable, official and inaccurate Latin Vulgate. His witty and elegant *Colloquia* and *Adages* also brought him wide popularity among the educated. But Erasmus had appealed to an elite: Luther instinctively went for a mass public, and of course the voice of Erasmian Humanism, though it proved pervasive and lasting, was swamped in the popular uproar. And Luther's ideas soon spread far beyond Germany.

The English establishment became uneasy. As Tunstall, Henry VIII's ambassador to Charles V, wrote of the "boke intitylde *De Babylonica Captivitate Ecclesiae*", "They say ther is moch moo strange opinions in hit nere to the opinions of Boheme. I pray God kep this bok out of Englond."[1] Huss's followers had been the first heretics to incite a nation to arms; Luther, a compulsive pamphleteer, set off a far greater national and cosmopolitan combustion. It was impracticable to suppress his works: Archbishop Warham of Canterbury wrote to Wolsey that the University of Oxford was "infectyd with the heresyes of Luther," and that it was "a sorrowful thing to see how gredily inconstant men, and specyally inexpert youth, fallith to new doctrynes, be they never so pestilent, and howe prone they be to attempt that thyng that theyre forbeden by thair superiors."[2] Anxious to obtain the title *Fidei Defensor*, Henry VIII himself denounced Luther, mainly with his own pen, in the *Assertio Septem Sacramentorum* which was presented to Leo X, who admired the binding and, after considering the titles "most Orthodox" and even "Angelic" for the monarch, accorded him his wish.[3]

Luther replied, with a certain coarseness, that the King had demonstrated "how well he could soil a lot of paper", and Henry, not to be outdone, described the reformer in a letter to Charles V as a "dilapidated, sick and evil-minded sheep"—the sixteenth-century equivalent of "deviationist pig". The pamphlets sold briskly and the publishers—though they took risks—enjoyed an early experience of the power of the press in a popular mass market.

In 1521 Charles V, Holy Roman Emperor Elect, but aged only twenty-one, convened the Diet of the Empire at Worms where much other urgent business awaited their attention. Summoned to appear, Luther, under the protection of the Elector of Saxony, ringingly declared his mind. "So long as I cannot be disproved by Holy Writ or clear reason, so long I neither can nor will withdraw anything, for it is not criminal and dangerous to act against conscience. So help me God—Amen."

Naturally Charles V supported the Church. His ancestors, he declared, had all been its faithful sons, and had bequeathed him a heritage: "thus I am

---

[1]Cited in Edwin Doernberg. *Henry VIII and Luther.* London, 1961. A work which admirably catches the spirit and idiom of the times.
[2]Doernberg. *op. cit.* p. 9.
[3]The title was of course revoked from Rome in 1535 and '38; so Henry in 1543 had the Papal title made hereditary by Act of Parliament, with the incongruous addition *et in terris caput supremum et immediatum post Christum Ecclesiae Anglicanae* (and on earth supreme head, immediately after Christ, of the Anglican Church); and the Protestant English monarchs still employ it.

determined to hold fast to all that has happened since the Council of Konstanz, for it is certain that a single monk must err if he stands against the opinion of all Christendom. Otherwise Christendom itself would have erred for more than a thousand years. Therefore I am determined to set my Kingdom and dominions, my friends, my body, my blood, my life, my soul upon it. For it were a great shame to us and to you, members of the north German nation, if, in our time, through our negligence, we were to let even the appearance of heresy and denigration of true religion enter the hearts of men." He now regarded Luther, he concluded, as a notorious heretic and hoped that they all, as good Christians, "would not be wanting in their duty."

Luther was at once hustled away by his supporters to the Wartburg, under the protection of the Elector of Saxony, where he set about translating the New Testament into German (1522), and personally worsted the devil in several encounters. He became a major political figure in Europe, backed by succeeding Electors of Saxony, the Landgraf of Hesse and the Elector of Brandenburg. But he was not interested in organizing an independent Church, or even in formulating a generally acceptable creed among his own followers. He left this to his Augsburg companion, Melancthon. While the "Protestant" princes founded the Schmalkaldic League, which Henry VIII, now at odds with Pope Clement VII, with characteristic and treacherous pragmatism was now anxious to join, Luther was much more concerned with debating the minutiae of the "real presence" in the Sacrament. He was also horrified at the popular radicalism and even peasant revolts which in 1524 had started in the Schwarzwald, and which his challenge to authority had encouraged. So he dashed off a particularly virulent pamphlet *Wider die räuberischen und möderischen Rotten der Bauern*—(Against the thieving and murderous Hordes of the Peasantry).

The affinity of Luther with Huss and the "opinions of Boheme", observed by Tunstall, was thus confirmed: Huss, through his followers, had roused militant Czech nationalism, as Luther on a greater scale roused that of the Germans; and as Žižka had put down the Bohemian radicals, so Luther did his best to destroy the peasants, whose real grievance was, as usual, mainly about the Game Laws.

In spite of the efforts of both Pope and Emperor, Luther set off a lasting conflict in the Germanies deeply disruptive of Church and State; but politically he was no radical, and he came to inspire the mild Protestant Lutheran churches established in Germany, Scandinavia and beyond Europe, in which, under the accepted rule of the lay power, his followers have worked out their aimiable, unpretentious and docile version of Christianity.

VII

Soon after Luther had been condemned as a heretic at Worms, Charles V's third major problem came to a crisis. The Turks under their Sultan Suleimān the Magnificent (1520–66) captured the strategically important island of

Rhodes. Taken over by the Knights of St. John of Jerusalem in 1309, it had long been a base for Christian sea-power in the Levant: behind its massive fortifications, still largely intact, the Knights, whose national *auberges* with their blazons still remain, had put up a skilful and tenacious defence lasting six months and had been allowed an honourable capitulation. But the town and the beautiful island, so celebrated as a centre of rhetoric and study in Antiquity, fell to an alien Muslim people out of the wide spaces of Anatolia which stretch away into Asian lands that dwarf Europe. The Knights, all of aristocratic lineage—the French had to show eight quarterings on their arms, the Germans, even more *hochgeboren*, sixteen—came also from Castile, Aragon, León, Portugal, Italy and England; they wore a white cross on scarlet mantles, and were collectively immensely rich. Under their Grand Master, Villiers de l'Isle Adam, they retired to Viterbo, then to Nice.

Charles now intervened. It was essential, he believed, that their military prowess should be deployed against the infidels, and he chose the strategically placed island of Malta for their new domain. There may well have then been more trees on the barren island than there are now, and it had fine harbours; in 1530, along with the indefensible asset of Tripoli in North Africa, it was assigned to the Knights as a perpetual fief for the token annual rent of a falcon. The strategic insight of Charles V and his advisers would later be fully vindicated: when in 1565 a huge Turkish expedition, reinforced from Algiers, attacked the island, after an epic resistance which aroused passionate interest throughout even a divided Christendom, they would be foiled when a Spanish counter-attack was launched to raise the siege from Sicily.

The victorious Grand Master, Jean de la Valette, would then consolidate their strategic success by building the elaborate and massive fortifications of Valetta, protecting the Grand Harbour; and with Malta secure, in 1571 the Turkish naval power in the Levant would be crippled by the resounding Christian victory at Lepanto.

All this was far in the future. An immediate continental threat of Turkish attack still loomed up over Eastern Europe;[1] and following the death of Mathias Corvinus in 1490, his successor, Ladislas *Dobze*, "all right", so called since he at once agreed to his magnates' demands, had gravely weakened the Hungarian realm. There had been peasants' revolts, hideously suppressed; finally in 1526, under Louis II, who was killed in action, the Hungarians were again crushingly defeated by the Turks at Mohacs.

But Charles V, a true Habsburg, had already settled a family problem and strengthened the defences of Hungary by a dynastic marriage. He had been careful to remove his younger brother Ferdinand from Spain, as a potential rival; what more politic than to settle him with an ample appanage on the Habsburg lands in Eastern Europe, reinforced by the dynastic alliance with

---

[1]Contemptuously addressing Francis I, Suleimān the Magnificent could write: "I who am the Sultan of Sultans, the sovereign of sovereigns, the shadow of God on earth, ... I Sultan Suleimān Khan, son of Sultan Selim Khan, son of Sultan Bāyāzid Khan: to thee, who art Francis, King of the land of the Franks." Cited in P. K. Hitti. *History of the Arabs.* London, 1960. p. 714. This book gives a valuable version of European/Muslim relationships from the eastern point of view.

Hungary and Bohemia which could be brought to him by Anne of Hungary? This momentous decision, taken to solve the problem of Ferdinand's future, extend the already tentacular Habsburg power and strengthen the landward defences against the Turk, had also divided the Habsburg family into two branches; one assimilated the Empire, the other commanded the military might of Spain, much of Italy, and the growing resources of Spanish America.

This fateful move altered the political future of Europe, if its immediate dynastic purpose failed. In May 1521, at Linz on the Danube in Austria, Ferdinand, now Archduke of Upper and Lower Austria, Styria, Carinthia and Carniola, married Anne of Hungary. In return for Ferdinand's renunciation of his claims on heritable lands in Burgundy and Spain, Charles had made over to him the entire Habsburg lands in the Germanies, while it was arranged that once Charles, still Emperor elect, had been crowned Emperor in Italy, Ferdinand should become King of the Romans and have the reversion of the Empire. And in July the new dynastic alliance had been consolidated by the marriage of Charles's and Ferdinand's sister Mary, to King Louis II of Hungary.

The Turks meanwhile were besieging Belgrade, and the news arrived of the fall of Rhodes. Four years later in August 1526 when the Hungarian army came to catastrophe at Mohacs, and King Louis II died without an heir, the remnant of the inheritance passed to Ferdinand's wife, Anne of Hungary and so in due course, after much difficulty, into the Habsburg net.

If the Turks had not been stopped, the dynastic policy of Charles and Ferdinand had won unexpected success. It was followed up when in October 1526 Ferdinand was elected, in part through the hereditary claims of his wife, King of Bohemia, and in the spring of 1527 crowned in Prague. True to Habsburg tradition, Ferdinand continued to collaborate with Charles V, and a front was improvised across Central Europe from Bohemia to the Middle Danube down to the Eastern Alps against the Turkish advance. And that year Charles V himself, reverting to the earliest dynastic objectives of Fernando and Isabella, had married in Seville his cousin, Isabella of Portugal, so spreading the vast Habsburg interest over the Portuguese sea-borne trading empire, now, having "opened the way to Ceylon" and beyond it, well established in India and the Far East.

VIII

When the Portuguese had established themselves at Goa, and Cortés and Pizarro had conquered the Aztec empire in Mexico and the Inca empire in Peru, and so opened a new phase of world history in which Europeans would long predominate over all other civilizations, the Europeans themselves in their own continent were preoccupied with internecine warfare. Charles V and Philip II, the rulers who gained most by the new oceanic discoveries, were concerned more with neo-medieval objectives of restoring the Holy Roman Empire as part of a Counter-Reformation provoked by the most successfully disruptive heresies in the history of the Church.

Preoccupied also with fending off the encroachments of the Turks on land and sea, Charles V had worn himself out in the last effort to unite Western and Central Europe, and his son, Philip II, would bankrupt his governments in a Counter-Reformation crusade. So to contemporaries what now seems the really epoch-making event of the time, the oceanic discoveries and exploitations which made contact with other civilizations hitherto unknown, appeared subsidiary to traditional objectives, and to an old-fashioned attempt to revive a dynastic version of the Holy Roman Empire at a time when the predominant political power of the future was already manifest not in cosmopolitan institutions but in the sovereign great state. Yet the "heroic" quality that Camoens celebrated in his epic of Portuguese discoveries is not entirely absent at least from the titanic effort of Charles V to realize, at last, the ancient concept of a United Christendom.

IX

Despite the efforts of Charles V, the ideological conflict that Luther had set off through Germany had now become fully translated into politics. After, in 1524, the Catholic states had formed the League of Ratisbon, by 1526 the Protestants had formed the League of Torgau, which developed by 1531 into the League of Schmalkalde. The Catholics were stronger in the ancient civilized lands; in Bavaria, Austria and the Rhineland: the Protestants in Saxony and the north, in Hesse and Brandenburg, lands much more recently converted. What had begun as a quarrel among monks was taken up by the Electoral Princes, glad for an occasion to create disorder and perhaps increase their territories. The divisions of the *Reich* had been chronic for centuries; now they would culminate in far flung ideological conflict. The heresies seething in Europe since the time of Innocent III had now riven the fabric of the European Christendom that Charles V was trying to defend.

In the Swiss city of Zurich, meanwhile, another peasant of genius, Ulrich Zwingli, born in 1484, a year after Luther, had absorbed Erasmian ideas of reform and the cult of the Bible. He had studied at the universities of Vienna and Basel, and in 1518, after serving as chaplain to Swiss mercenaries in Italy, became "people's priest" at Zurich Cathedral.[1] Like Luther, he sought salvation through the study of the New Testament as newly edited by Erasmus in Greek, and by faith rather than "works". He soon became an evangelical preacher expounding the scriptures in relation to current events, with a strong feeling for Swiss nationality against the encroaching great powers. So in Zurich, as in Germany and later in England and among the Dutch, Protestant beliefs succeeded in part, and perhaps mainly, as an aspect of nationalist feeling against foreigners. Like Luther, Zwingli reacted against conservative

[1] He had been spirited enough to get rusticated from Vienna University, to win disapproval among the more censorious Swiss as a musician, and in 1516 to have had an affair with a barber's daughter, characterized as "sordid" by the New Cambridge Modern History (Vol. II, pp. 97–8).

Thomist "realism" but found no constructive alternative in the fashionable "nominalism", and, zealous for humanistic reform, he drew up no less than sixty-seven articles against the Pope. He hankered for the rule of "Godly Magistrates", for he was no theocrat, and by 1525 his influence had so pervaded Zurich that the Mass was officially abolished. He also preached that the Swiss should disentangle themselves from service as mercenaries to foreign powers who cared nothing for them, and asked of this occupation—so lucrative to those who provided the cannon or pike fodder—"is that what Christ taught us?" He provided good Swiss wooden vessels instead of plate for a commemorative communion, and encouraged spontaneous "prophesying" during church services; so Zwingli's doctrines, milder than the Lutheran beliefs on the crucial subject of "original sin" which he thought of as a "disease" rather than as implying "guilt", took on widely, not only in Zurich but beyond in Basel, Konstanz and even in Strasbourg, whence they would spread to England, in the reign of Edward VI, at first more effectively than Luther's.

Unfortunately for him, Zwingli had patriotic political ambitions; he managed to create a Christian Civic League of northern Swiss cities, including Berne, ready, if need be, for alliance with the German Protestant League of Torgau, and in 1531 the League attempted economic warfare—a field in which all Swiss were then as now sensitive—against the Austrian-dominated Catholic cantons of the Confederation. The Catholic states, stung to the quick, launched a war, and that year, at the battle of Cappel, Zwingli and his army, in spite of having thirteen preachers to inspire them, were cut to pieces, and the body of the reformer, armed with a huge Swiss sword and a great Swiss axe, was burnt. In the division of Switzerland between Catholic and Protestant cantons, the memory of this confrontation persists.

Zwingli's doctrines were elaborated by the Swabian scholar Johannes Oecolampadius (d. 1531), and by Heinrich Bullinger, who spread Zwinglian doctrines by the printed word and by the ramified and cosmopolitan correspondence so characteristic of the time.

While Luther and Zwingli had preached doctrines that were socially fairly conservative, Luther denouncing the Peasant uprisings in Germany and Zwingli desirous of "godly magistrates", some of their followers and fellow-travellers in the Protestant Schism, like those of Huss, had become more radically subversive in ideas and practice.

Of these the Anabaptists attracted the greatest horror and reprobation of both Catholics and Protestants. In 1523 Zwingli at Zurich had admitted that he thought it doubtful if children, too young for understanding of the mysteries of Christian doctrine, ought to be baptized. The children were thus, of course, put at grave risk. Since, according to the Catholics, unbaptized infants went to Hell, or at best to Purgatory, most parents thought it worth taking the risk that they might not understand what was going on and baptizing them in early infancy. A whole gaggle of Protestant intellectuals and radicals, of whom Thomas Munzer, a leader of the German Peasants' revolt of 1524, became particularly dogmatic, now debated the question, and a splinter group of Zwingli's followers moved out from Zurich to Zollikon on the lake, convenient for baptizing adults by total immersion. The Council at Zurich then declared

that the Anabaptist leaders ought to be drowned by permanent total immersion, and in November 1526 one of them was tied to a hurdle and met a
watery end.

But the surviving Anabaptists provoked greater horror among the *bien
pensants* by preaching pacifism and even an approach to community of goods:
expelled from Zurich, their missionaries penetrated to Tyrol and Moravia,
where they had major success among the descendants of the followers of Huss,
and began, in medieval fashion, to preach of the Millennium and the Second
Coming of Christ. In 1528 Hubmaier, the most successful missionary, was
burnt as a heretic, and his wife, for good measure, was thrown into the
Danube, with a heavy stone tied round her neck.

But in spite of the attentions of the authorities wherever they appeared—as
in Ulm and Strasbourg—the Anabaptists proved hard to eradicate. We hear of
them in the winter of 1535 at Amsterdam, where seven men and five women
of their persuasion cavorted naked through the streets in the cold crying out
"Woe, Woe, Woe! The Wrath of God!" They had done it, they explained,
before they were executed, as a sign that they spoke the *naked* truth.[1] The
only thing to do with them, thought Charles V's government, was to burn the
men and bury the women alive.

X

For Charles V, the commotions set off by Luther, Zwingli, Calvin and the
lunatic fringe of Anabaptists and their political followers and exploiters were
one more obstacle to his overriding purpose, to mobilize Christendom against
the Turks. And the need was becoming more urgent: by 1529 an Albanian-
Greek pirate, a *renegado* called Kizr, nicknamed Barbarossa from his beard,
and officially named Khey-ed-Din Pasha—Protector of the Faith—by the
Sultan, had captured Tunis and Algiers. The Knights of Rhodes, established in
Malta only in the following year, could not yet command the central
Mediterranean, and by 1534 a large Turkish fleet under Khey-ed-Din was
ravaging the Straits of Messina and even the Neapolitan coast. The French,
meanwhile, had long been negotiating with Constantinople and two years later
would make an alliance with the Grand Turk.

It was imperative, whatever the situation in Germany, or the intentions of
Francis I, the behaviour of Henry VIII or the lunacies of the Anabaptists, to
reassert Christian sea power, and by May 1535, the year after Henry VIII had
broken with the Church of Rome, Charles V mobilized a massive expedition.
It had been laboriously prepared against Tunis, ostensibly to restore the
legitimate ruler, Mulay Hassān: caravels from Portugal, war galleys from
Genoa under the famous Andrea Doria, a great fleet of transports to carry
twenty-five thousand Spanish and German pikemen and arquebusiers and six
hundred cavalry assembled off Genoa, to be reviewed by the Emperor himself.

[1] *New Cambridge Modern History.* Vol. II. *op. cit.* p. 127.

By mid-June, in brilliant weather, the expedition arrived off Tunis: they soon captured the outlying fort of La Goletta and by a brisk land attack, pressed home in spite of dust, heat and thirst, captured Tunis and liberated twenty thousand Christian captives. Charles V had fought in the thick of the battle, and acquitted himself as the Christian knight he was determined to be. But although most of the Turkish ships were captured, Khey-ed-Din, now supreme Admiral of the Sultan's fleet, escaped to Bona, whence he fled by sea to Algiers where he had galleys in reserve. The pirates had been defeated but not extirpated.

But the expedition was considered a resounding success;[1] in August Charles returned to Palermo and Monreale, where he was acclaimed by the Sicilians as "Conqueror of Africa". He then crossed to Naples, where he made a triumphant entry and kept Christmas and Carnival in his Aragonese kingdom. In April 1538 he entered Rome.

He had intended to follow up his success by a conclusive attack on Algiers; but found that Francis I, who had married his son Henri II to Catherine de Medici and intent, as usual, on Milan, had invaded Savoy and Piedmont; Charles was therefore forced to divert his armies from the Crusade to attack Provence. The Spaniards now controlled the Western Mediterranean, but the pirate base at Algiers remained intact, and it was beyond the logistic powers of the Christian fleets to launch a successful attack at so great a distance on the main Turkish strategic position in the Levant.

In Rome Charles V had attempted to win the support of Pope Paul III—he even offered in medieval style to fight Francis I in personal combat, the prize being Burgundy for himself if he won, Milan for Francis if Charles lost.[2] All he got was the offer of a Council to be held next year to consider the case. Meanwhile the attack on Provence to be co-ordinated with an invasion of France from the Netherlands, had bogged down, after the French had successfully defended Avignon. So Charles retired to Spain, and an armistice was patched up with the French which led in 1538 to the Truce of Nice. But it was not until another bout of war that by the Treaty of Créspi in 1544, the French abandoned their claim to Milan and Naples and the Spanish domination of Italy was recognized, to last until the early eighteenth century, with profound political and cultural effects. Even the republic of Florence had been extinguished when in 1530 an imperial army had restored the Medici. Most significant of all, the Habsburg-Valois conflict would now be fought out across the Rhine.

Charles was now freer to deal with the heretics in Germany, whose position had been weakened by the defection of one of their principal patrons, Philip, Landgraf of Hesse, who had deserted his wife for another woman whom he had then married, an act which Luther had encouraged but advised him to conceal. The Landgraf, deeply offended, had gone over to the Emperor, deserting the Schmalkaldic League, and his example had soon been followed

---

[1]It is recorded in telling detail in the tapestries designed from sketches made by the Dutch painter Vermeyen on the spot, now in the *Kunsthistorisches* Museum at Vienna.
[2]Karl Brandi. *The Emperor Charles V.* Trans. C. V. Wedgwood. London, 1939. p. 378.

by Prince Maurice of Saxony, to whom Charles had promised the reversion of the electorate now held by John Frederick, his cousin, the son of Luther's original protector. In 1547 the Lutheran army was routed at Mühlberg on the Elbe. But the victory proved politically inconclusive: most of the Catholic German princes remained set on crippling the Emperor's power and the Lutherans remained irreconcilable.

Maurice of Saxony, dissatisfied with his rewards, now deserted Charles V, and in 1552 by the Treaty of Chambord with the new French King, Henri II, arranged that the strategic fortresses of Metz, Tours and Verdun should be ceded to him as Viceroy General of the Empire in return for his support of a Lutheran rebellion. Immediately the French pressed their strategic advantage, occupying the Lorraine bishoprics and severing Charles' connection with the Netherlands. The German Princes then pursued Charles to Innsbruck, where he was forced to flee over the Brenner and up to Villach. Ferdinand of Austria intervened, and in 1554 at Passau the Princes abandoned the French alliance.

But the French had got a fateful foothold in Alsace and Lorraine, and the power to intervene in the politics of the Germanies, clinched by the seizure of Metz in 1552, which Charles V failed to recapture. This menacing fact overshadowed the sensible compromise over religion arranged by Ferdinand of Austria in 1555 by the Peace of Augsburg, and only reluctantly accepted by Charles V. The Princes, not the sword or even the Emperor or the Pope, were now to settle the religions of their own territories—"Cujus regio," it was written, "ejus religio"—"to whom the realm, his the religion."

By 1555, after the humiliating flight from Innsbruck and the fiasco before Metz, it was obvious that Charles V's attempt to revive the Holy Roman Empire as a universal monarchy had failed, and that autumn he decided to abdicate. In a speech to the Knights of the Golden Fleece and the Councillors and ministers of the Netherlands, he recapitulated his long labours: "nine times he had visited Germany, six times Spain, four times France, twice Africa, and twice England. Now he was preparing to make his last journey, to Spain . . . He was at the end of his strength . . . he was tired even to death and desired only to give his own lands to [his son] Philip, the empire to Ferdinand."[1] In January 1556 Charles abdicated from Castile, Aragon, Sicily and the Indies, and in August left the Netherlands by sea for Spain. Landing near Santander, he proceeded to Estremadura, and in the following year took up residence in a luxurious imperial villa in the grounds of the Monastery of San Jeronimo de Yuste, to which he had transported the favourite canvases among the Titians he owned. Prematurely aged and crippled by gout, the former Emperor settled down to make the best of a beautiful prospect and an excellent climate.[2] But not for long: on September 21st, 1558 Charles V died; his grand memorial remains in the Chapel of the Escorial, commissioned by Philip II.

Philip II, his successor, had lost no time in defeating the French. By 1557

[1]Brandi. op. cit. pp. 633-4.
[2]The story that he "rehearsed" his own funeral is false—a distortion of reports of the requiem masses celebrated for his father and grandfather. Nor was he the gourmand he was said to have been by Spaniards unaccustomed to Flemish standards of cuisine.

they had been routed at St. Quentin, and he had clinched the Spanish hold on Flanders; but by then neither the Spanish nor French governments could continue the war, for that year both went bankrupt. So in April 1559 the Peace of Cateau-Cambrésis marked a lasting peace of exhaustion. The French gave up Savoy and Piedmont and their claims on Flanders, along with their claims on Italy, already conceded at Créspi; but they retained Metz, Toul and Verdun. The main significance of the Treaty was to admit the European supremacy of Spain with its control of Italy and its Spanish American empire. As has been well observed, "the centre of gravity of Europe, indeed of the world, broke away from the lands of central Europe", for the abdication of Charles V had settled the matter. Spain now became predominant, the Germanies politically of little account, and France would be torn by internal friction. Yet the Treaty of Cateau-Cambrésis was successful, for it was "the charter of a new Europe, gravitating towards the west, where the Atlantic Ocean would bring oceanic trade and colonization, but while it bought a phase of comparative peace and prosperity in the Germanies, in central Europe it weakened the empire before the Turkish menace, and soon for Italy, the Italy of golden cities, decadence. The path of the future lay, even more than in Spain, across the Atlantic and the seven seas of the world."[1]

IX

This shift of economic enterprise to the Iberian peninsula and the north-west is marked by the rise of Antwerp to the climax of its prosperity. In 1499 the spice staple for the trade with Portugal had been established there at the expense of Bruges, already in decline. Antwerp thus added an immensely lucrative trade with the Iberian peninsula through the Atlantic and Channel to trade with England and the Baltic, and encouraged it by improvements along the banks of the "route of Walcheren" through the Scheldt; the Portuguese and Spaniards needed grain, and if the delays and uncertainty of the great voyages round the Cape made the trade a gamble, the market for relatively cheap spices in northern Europe was insatiable. Antwerp was also the natural focus both for English cloth and for the textiles now being manufactured in southern Germany, as well as for the mineral wealth of the mines of central Europe and Tyrol. With Flemish manufacturing in decline and with the fully justified hostility between Ghent and Bruges and the Emperor Maximilian I, merchants of Antwerp obtained increasing political and economic favours from the Habsburgs, to whom they gave consistent support.

Linked with the rise of Antwerp had been that of the banking house of the Fuggers of Augsburg, international financiers of unprecedented scope, without whom the wars of Charles V and Francis I would have been impossible. The Fuggers had started as Swabian weavers and made their first capital by manufacturing textiles in Augsburg, some of which they exported to the

[1]*New Cambridge Modern History.* Vol. II. p. 358.

Antwerp market; they had then won control of the silver mines of Tyrol, Carinthia and Hungary in return for loans to Maximilian I. By 1508–27 they had obtained a lease on the Papal Mint and were exploiting the Antwerp spice trade with wealth from the silver mines, so that by 1519 they could raise half a million florins to secure the election of Charles V as King of the Romans. Jacob Fugger II "the Rich" had speculated, with lucrative results, in the spice trade not only in Antwerp but also in the more expensive spices still brought in to Venice from the Levant; his cosmopolitan activities extended from Krakow to Antwerp, Lisbon and Seville, and Charles V, deeply dependent on him, made over to him the revenues of old and proud Spanish Orders of knighthood as well as the monopoly of mercury from Spain. Jacob II was a munificent benefactor and built the *Fuggerei* almshouses long extant in Augsburg. His son, Anton (d. 1560), came to the rescue of Charles V with nearly half a million florins when he had fled from Innsbruck in the most humiliating crisis of his reign, and had financed the extremely expensive election of Ferdinand as King of the Romans.[1] Like the Rothschilds, the Fuggers organized a rapid and far-flung intelligence service through the Fugger newsletters, and the scale of their operations eclipsed those of the pioneer fifteenth-century French financier, Jacques Coeur.

As a hub of such activities, Antwerp became the first centre of international finance in the north; as well as handling an immense trade in commodities, as German metals, Portuguese spices, English and German cloth, German and Spanish wines, and grain, timber and cordage from the Baltic. The wars in Germany and Italy created an increasing demand for armaments, and German armour and weapons found eager purchasers among the English and the French, while Flemish and Rhineland cities competed with one another for the splendid bells that, then as now, rang out from their cathedrals. And the humming cosmopolitan commerce of Antwerp was paralleled by the more provincial and Breugelesque fairs of Bergen-op-zoom.

These commercial activities were traditional; the vast financial capital operations that raised money for governments were something new. The final bout of Charles V's war with France demanded huge credits, and Henry VIII, as well as squandering his plunder from the English monasteries on the war, borrowed huge sums in Antwerp. The risks of default were obvious; but interest rates about 12% to 15% were correspondingly high. It was now possible to mobilize wealth in a way impracticable even in the fifteenth century, and the political and ideological strife that rent Christendom may at least have benefited the economy by encouraging the mobilization and circulation of money, in a world increasingly concerned with new oceanic interests opened up by the Portuguese and the adventurers of Spain.

[1]The later Fuggers lost interest in their business and became book and art collectors; one wrote on the breeding of horses; another became Bishop of Regensburg, and one Jacob in the early 17th century became Prince Bishop of Konstanz. The religion which went along with the rise of Fugger capitalism was emphatically Catholic.

XXVII

New Horizons: Old Obsessions

In 1520–1 a Spanish expedition of five ships, commanded by the Portuguese Fernão de Magalhães, better known as Magellan, and completed by his Basque navigator, Sebastian Del Cano, surpassed the explorations of Vasco da Gama and Columbus. Penetrating the desolate and dangerous Straits of Magellan, they crossed the Pacific in ninety-nine days and arrived at the Philippines, where, at Sebu, Magalhães and forty men were killed by the Philippinos, but whence, after loading up with cloves at Tidore in the Moluccas, del Cano brought the surviving ship, and 17 men out of the original 265, back to Lisbon round the Cape; they had circumnavigated the world. Fernão de Magalhães (1480–1521) came of minor Portuguese nobility of Oporto. After being a page at Court, he went east in 1505 and fought in the expeditions to Cochin and Malacca which he helped to capture in 1511. Back in Lisbon in the following year, he fought in North Africa, but in 1514 was refused promotion and dismissed by King Manuel. So in 1517 he offered his services to Charles I of Spain, afterwards the Emperor Charles V, at Seville, informing him that the Moluccas would be found by sailing west to be within the Spanish sphere of influence. Setting out with five ships, he made Tenerife, then crossed to Brazil, whence he coasted down to Rio de Janeiro. At St. Julian he quelled a mutiny; then, proceeding south, found the long-sought south-west passage through the straits that bear his name. Traversing them in a month during the southern summer, he made north-west into the Pacific and with three ships and famine- and scurvy-stricken crews, arrived in the unknown Philippines where he met his death. Del Cano, in the eighty-five-ton *Vittoria*, wisely unwilling to face the Magellan Straits again, returned round Africa.[1]

No one had ever sailed round the world before; the exploit proved the theory that the world was round, but that the Pacific was much vaster than the best of the cartographers had calculated; so enormous that the attempt to get to the Orient by sailing west, though at last achieved, was considered uneconomic, and in 1529 Charles V by the Treaty of Saragossa sold his rights

[1]There is an eye witness account by Pigafetta, trans. and ed. Lord Stanley of Alderley. Hakluyt Society, Vol. 82.

to the Philippines for 350,000 ducats to the Portuguese, already in control of the Moluccas. This mistake would be rectified when in 1564 Miguel de Lagaspi brought over an expedition from Mexico and captured Sebu and Manila. Here, in collaboration with the Portuguese, the Spaniards developed an immensely lucrative trade exchanging cheap and plentiful American silver for Chinese silks. The "Manila" galleon sailed regularly from Acapulco for Manila before the north-easterly trade wind and returned very slowly across the central Pacific; the silks were then transported to Vera Cruz and so to Seville.

Though the Spanish authorities disliked this drain of silver and confined it to Mexican specie, "the Manila galleons nevertheless, continued their hazardous but always profitable sailings till the end of the eighteenth century. Manila remained all this time the meeting ground, half way round the world, of the heirs of Columbus and Vasco da Gama; a triumph of maritime communication in defiance of probability."[1]

Charles V remained entirely preoccupied with Europe and the Turkish menace: but he had wider horizons than Charlemagne or Barbarossa or even Frederick II; and American silver began to finance his laborious, determined and impracticable revival of the Holy Roman Empire, the policy that would merge into a Catholic "Counter-Reformation" backed by his son, the dedicated Philip II, after 1580 with Portuguese as well as Spanish colonial wealth behind him.

II

Charles V, who regarded himself as the "standard bearer of God", was an immensely powerful dynast, but his colossal and incongruously composed inheritance was almost impossible to administer, and under him late medieval Christendom, its cohesion always precarious, was breaking up.

Politically the predominant fact of power had long been the emergence of national realms under sovereign princes served by bureaucracies as good as the Italian and financed by cosmopolitan bankers, of whom Charles V's supporters, the Fuggers of Augsburg, were now the most influential; and although a network of dynastic marriages had been designed to stabilize shifting alliances, they remained unreliable. Charles's most formidable rival had always been Francis I of France, who had inherited a throne so well consolidated by Louis XI that it had remained unimpaired by the failures of Charles VIII and Louis XII in Italy, for France was the most heavily populated and potentially rich country in western Europe.

Charles's own power base was also national—in Spain as united by the Catholic kings, while England, after the eclipse of monarchy under Henry VI, had emerged under Edward IV and Henry VII as a power to be reckoned with, and the Swedes were throwing off the control of Denmark and under the

---

[1] J. H. Parry. *op. cit.* p. 196. The capture of the "Manila" galleon by Commodore Anson during his voyage round the world in 1740–4 was regarded as the highlight of his own circumnavigation.

new Vasa dynasty becoming an independent power. Charles's own inheritance in the Burgundian Low Countries was restive and hard to manage, and the rival states of Italy, of which the Papacy was the most disruptive, invited foreign interference and proved a battle ground for Spain and France; while the perennial disunion of the Germanies provided openings for French diplomacy and military intervention after the Spanish domination of Italy had been secured, so that for centuries the main European conflict between Habsburgs and Valois took place north of the Alps.

As if the political causes for instability and war were not enough, the religious schism launched by Luther, precisely defined by Calvin, and exploited by their patrons in Germany and France, further disrupted Christendom and perverted what might have been a Humanistic reform of the Church into fanatical ideological conflict. It had looked in the early sixteenth century as if the Christian Humanists of the Renaissance, who had set themselves to clarify the original text of the Bible and hoped through the Conciliar movement of clergy and laity to get rid of the obvious abuses of the Church, might attain their purpose. Desiderius Erasmus had brought the light of reason to bear on Biblical scholarship; but the Humanist cult of the Biblical texts in fact challenged the authority of the Church that Erasmus wished to reform, and the Catholic humanist Sir Thomas More thought it best to show up the evils of his time by writing an amiable *Utopia*, a revival of a classical form of satire.

These Christian Humanists had won celebrity through the new medium of movable print. But it was not Humanist reason and compassion that caught the ear of a vast new public: it was caught by the prophets and the ideologists, and the problem that finally defeated Charles V was the breakdown of his authority over the Germans following the politically disruptive influence of the Lutheran and Calvinist Schism.

For the other and even more disruptive ideologist was now Jean Cauvin or Calvin (1504–64). Born at Noyon in Picardy, son of Gerard Cauvin the secretary to the Bishop of Noyon, and of his wife, daughter of an innkeeper of Cambrai, Calvin was brought up and educated in the Bishop's family, the Hangests of Cambrai, and destined for the Church. He studied at Paris under the humanist Cordier, showed brilliant promise, not least in disputations, and became a friend of the Hellenist Budé. By 1528 he was studying law at Orléans and after further study of Greek and Hebrew in Paris, he wrote a commentary on Seneca's *De Clementia*. In 1534 he became converted to Luther's beliefs, and after writing against the Anabaptists, wrote a preface to his own French translation of the Bible and removed to Basel. Two years later he settled in Geneva. Briefly expelled, he lived at Strasbourg, but, recalled to Geneva in 1541, he devised the *Ecclesiastical Ordinances* to regulate the Presbyterian Church. He dominated the city until his death and saw to it that Geneva had a good water supply and sanitation, as well as a Calvinist Academy of which the building survives.

Where Luther had given the Protestant Schism inspiration, Calvin, the founder of the world-wide Presbyterian Church, was an organizer of genius. Both singularly well represent the characteristics of their people—Luther, cloudy, emotional, impulsive, apt to over-do everything, but docile to public authority; Calvin lucid, systematic, logical. Both were incapable of compromise.

Converted to Luther's ideas, Calvin abandoned a congenial and distinguished Christian humanist circle in Paris, and in 1536 at Basel, wrote his famous *Institutes of the Christian Religion* in Latin. They were occasioned because Francis I had accused the Protestants in France of being Anabaptists, a charge that horrified Calvin as much as it would have Luther, and which he was determined to refute by defining Protestant doctrine. By 1539 the *Institutes* had been translated into French and by 1541 they were circulating in a large edition.

Calvin, like Luther, was obsessed with original sin, and deeply influenced by St. Augustine. The only glimmer of hope was the "inscrutable decree" whereby God had predestined a minority of the Elect, irrespective of merit, for salvation. Thus at least some part of the human race would escape Hell, though since the Elect were predestinate—for the human will was not free— there was no hope for most of mankind. Again like Luther, Calvin had been trained in the sceptical Nominalism of the school of Ockham, and lived in a philosophically bleak world, unconsoled by the busy unbridled rationalism of the Thomist schoolmen, who, having plenty to believe in and play with, were less worried about original sin. Moreover, Calvin believed that God, "offended" by Adam's rebellious pride rather than by the concupiscence which had occasioned the Fall, was exacting a terrible vengeance on mankind, so that a strictly imposed discipline was urgent to avoid it. And who better qualified to discipline the flourishing exponents of original sin than the Elect?

So this logical French scholar, trained not only in theology but in the law, returning to Geneva in 1541, worked out and propagated his view that men attained salvation not simply by the Lutheran direct approach of man to God, but were brought to God, who sought them out, by the agency of the Church of the Elect. And whenever the Elect felt the conviction of being "called" and that "Christ was in the midst of them", there was a cell of the True Calvinist Church. Such a Church existed for the service of God and, if elected by the congregation, represented the inspiration of Christ. Hence Calvin believed that a hierarchy was justified; and hence the criticism that "new presbyter [was] but old priest writ large". Hence, too, a build-up of Pastors, or "Ministers" who preached and administered the sacrament, of Elders who supervised the people's morals, and of Teachers who inculcated the correct interpretation of the Scriptures.

Though, in the event, this structure proved extremely authoritarian, in Calvin's view such a hierarchy, based on constant discussion between representatives of the congregation, expressed the Spirit of Christ working through the flock; but the Presbyters on the higher levels of organization had control of appointments and finance; and the General Assembly, elected by the Presbyteries, formed an annual Court of General Supervision.

Far from liberating the common man, Calvin's system, which proved extremely tenacious and gave great scope for men of ability and ambition, saddled his followers with an oligarchy quite as onerous and much less picturesque than that of the Catholic Church. Drawing its strength both from the grass roots and from the concentration of authority, it formed a party organization in the modern sense within the secular state, and it was cosmopolitan. With its stress on preaching, it enabled eloquent and didactic Pastors and Presbyters to arrogate to themselves the authority of God. As Calvin himself wrote: "as if the congregation heard the very words announced by God himself"; "What is the mouth of God", he asked, "it is a declaration ... of his will, when he speaks to us by his Ministers. If (in brief) we desire salvation, we must learn to be humble disciples to receive the doctrine of the Gospel and to hear the Pastors whom he has sent to us, as if Jesus Christ himself spoke to us in person." The preacher was indeed an "envoy" sent by God.[1] Calvin himself loved preaching, and by 1549 preached on every day of alternate weeks as well as twice on Sundays, expounding, exhorting, laying down God's law.

So many people felt sure that they were "called" to be of the Elect that Calvin's version of Christianity took on even more widely than had Luther's; and since Calvinism was extremely well organized and firmly grounded in the study of the Bible, it proved the most widespread and powerful form of Protestant belief. It appealed particularly to the argumentative Lowland Scots, to the prosaic Dutch and English "puritans", and especially to those who tried to found an ideal community, ruled by the Elect, in New England in North America.

Though Calvin did not advocate theocracy, the Calvinists at Geneva established an authoritarian regime as intolerant as that of the Catholic Inquisition; and in 1553 they tried and burnt the Spanish physician Miguelo Serveto (Servetus), a pioneer Unitarian who had questioned the doctrine of the Trinity and so got himself burnt in effigy by the Catholics at Vienne and in the flesh by the Calvinists at Geneva.[2]

The fate of Servetus was symbolic of the wave of ideological persecution which has made the immensely vigorous and creative sixteenth century as notorious as our own for cruelty, and swamped alike the Erasmian humanists and the pioneers of modern science. These ideological crimes, perpetrated by a self-appointed Elect who regarded themselves as the true Church, to propitiate the wrath of their God, reflect the breakdown of Charles V's

[1]T. H. L. Parker. *John Calvin: a biography*. London, 1975. p. 90.
[2]Born in 1511 in Spain and brought up a Catholic, in 1530 he had attended the Coronation of Charles V as Holy Roman Emperor at Bologna, and been shocked by the pomp of the occasion. In the following year he wrote a book on the Trinity and, when this was ill received, was rash enough to write another. He was a friend of the great physician Vesalius, discovered the function of the lungs in the circulation of the blood and wrote on botany and astrology. He then became physician to the Archbishop of Vienne, and misguidedly sent Calvin his next book on the *Restitution of Christianity*, on perusal of which Calvin swore that if Servetus came to Geneva the heretic would not leave the city alive if he had the power to prevent it. Servetus was fated to make the worst of both worlds: his letters to Calvin were intercepted and he was incarcerated by the Archbishop. He escaped from Vienne and most unwisely made for Geneva where, unable to resist attending one of Calvin's sermons, he was recognized, arrested, tried and burnt, though Calvin had wanted him merely decapitated. Servetus was a Unitarian pantheist devoted to imitating Christ. See E. M. Wilbur. A *History of Unitarianism*. Vol. I *passim*.

attempt to unite a Christendom riven by political and religious strife; they also mark the beginning of far-flung and important Protestant Christian Churches which would predominate in various forms in Northern Europe, most powerfully in North America, and beyond the oceans in other parts of the English-speaking world.

When Charles II of England remarked, after personal experience of it, that Presbyterianism was "no religion for a gentleman", he showed his usual social insight; the Calvinist religion particularly appealed to the townspeople, as originally in republican Geneva. The Calvinist preachers denounced the flamboyant and insolvent way of life of the courtiers and the aristocracy: a rancorous strain of envy and moral disapproval is common among *petit-bourgeois* ideological fanatics, religious and secular, and armed with their self-righteousness, they interfered as eagerly in private life as had the hitherto ubiquitous Catholic clergy. The violent kind of ideological conflicts that Constantine had endeavoured to assuage, and which had early added fury to the wars of Arian and Catholic barbarian converts, now cropped up again, and even undermined the position of the sovereign princes whose growing power was the most obvious political fact of the time. Extremists of both sides, Calvinist and Jesuit, even argued that it was right to kill an heretical prince, and that conscience came before political obligation. The late sixteenth century, like the late nineteenth and our own, became an age of political assassination, and the princes on whom so much depended went in fear of their lives, particularly as security arrangements were often rudimentary. Moreover the appeal to conscience made for radical criticism of the social order itself, and even for republican ideas, incongruous in so hierarchical a society.

Among these radicals the most extreme were the Anabaptists. They had offended many powerful interests: parents for risking the damnation of infants left unbaptized; clergy, Catholic and Protestant, by claiming the power to rebaptize grown ups; and people of property by attempting Christian communism; but they had not been eradicated. Indeed in Münster in Westphalia they were now to have their finest hour. For these redoubtable evangelists had extended their influence from Moravia and the Netherlands into northern Germany, where a recession in the cloth industry had worsened long standing tensions between the aristocratic higher clergy and urban patriciate and the depressed and under-employed citizens who were ripe to find compensation in Millennarian fantasies of the Second Coming of Christ.

The main influence had come from Holland. Jan Mathyszoon of Haarlem, a militant baker, had sent disciples to Münster, who had inspired Jan Bockelszoon—Jan of Leyden, another Dutchman—to establish a "rule of the Saints". By February 1534 the Anabaptists controlled the town council, drove the more prosperous Catholic and Lutheran bourgeois out into the snow, and wrecked the statues, pictures and library of the Cathedral.

The prince-bishop quickly raised an army of mercenaries and besieged the city; whereat Mathyszoon and Jan of Leyden established a reign of terror in their New Jerusalem. The private ownership of money was abolished, and communal dining halls established for requisitioned and rationed food; "there was to be no private property and nobody was to do any more work but simply trust in God."[1] The poor from other cities sensed hope, and tried to find their way to Münster, but most of them were intercepted and executed by the authorities who had now made Anabaptism a capital offence.

In March Mathyszoon was killed leading a sortie, and Jan of Leyden, the twenty-four-year-old bastard of a Dutch village mayor and a Westphalian serf, "endowed with extraordinary good looks and an irresistible eloquence, [who] had from youth upwards revelled in writing, producing and acting plays,"[1] at once took control. He proved a dictator; after running naked through the town in a frenzy, he claimed divine revelations according to which he formed a government. He then—to the horror of Christian Europe—established polygamy, himself setting a hardy example by taking on sixteen wives. Under pain of death, his followers followed suit, often to the disruption of their married households, and "it seems certain that norms of sexual behaviour in the Kingdom of the Saints traversed the whole arc from a rigorous puritanism to sheer promiscuity."

The siege, of course, continued, and Jan of Leyden proved an able and ruthless disciplinarian in the defence. He called himself a "Messiah of the Last Days" (before the Second Coming), claimed "power over all nations on earth" and declared that he would reign over the whole world. He wore a crown, dressed with showy magnificence and was accompanied by a gaudy entourage, including pages holding copies of the Old Testament, of which he had read far too much. His motto was *Gottes Macht ist myn Cracht*. With modern means of mass communication, there is no telling where this Teutonic megalomaniac with his mad eyes might have got.[3]

The bishop, however, had not been idle. He had convened a meeting of the states of the Upper and Lower Rhine at Koblenz and raised an army equipped with siege engines and artillery, while an Imperial Diet at Worms contributed troops. It was decided that Münster be reduced not by assault but by starvation following blockade. In January 1535, when Charles V was preparing his expedition against Tunis, the grim business began, and by the spring the bishop had reduced his flock to cannibalism. The crazed Messiah declared that God would change the cobblestones into bread, but by May he had to allow all who wanted to do so to leave the town. These wretched people "lingered for five long weeks in the no-man's-land before the town walls, begging the mercenaries to kill them, crawling about and eating grass like animals until the bishop removed the survivors".[4] Those in the town were still held fast by the Messiah's grip of terror imposed by his followers, who were deluded to the last that the Millennium would dawn, that Münster would be relieved and that they would all rule the world, and terrorized by the executions carried out in

---

[1]See Norman Cohn. *The Pursuit of the Millennium*. London, 1957. p. 288 for the best account relating the movement to its origins, to the Doctrine of Mystical Anarchism, and to the strict Flagellants of Thuringia and other choice manifestations of popular ardour.
[2]Cohn. *op. cit.* p. 291.
[3]Cohn. See his expression in the engraving by Aldegrever. *op. cit.* p. 304.
[4]Cohn. *op. cit.* p. 304.

person by the Leader himself. In the end the besiegers had to take the city by assault. They massacred the surviving Anabaptists, and Jan of Leyden, after being led about in chains, "like a performing bear", was tortured to death with red hot irons.

III

The spread of heresy north of the Alps had been only one aspect of the intense vigour of the times, and Magellan's epoch-making circumnavigation of the world had also coincided with the spread of High Renaissance humanism north of the Alps. As Magellan had been planning his voyage, Francis I had lured Leonardo da Vinci (1452–1519) to end his days in France. That tremendous genius had been born a Florentine and taught by the Florentine Verocchio; and he had been employed at first mainly as a military engineer by Ludovico Sforza *il Moro*, tyrant of Milan, where in 1497 he had painted his famous but soon dilapidated *Last Supper*. He had also worked for Cesare Borgia and from 1513–16 for Cardinal Giuliano de Medici in Rome, before he took service with Francis I at Amboise. He was a restless and versatile genius, who often left his masterpieces unfinished and is now as celebrated for his sketch books as for the few of his great paintings that have survived, and he was passionately interested in engineering and science. He was a portent of the early modern High Renaissance, and he died just when Luther was setting off an age of neo-medieval religious fanaticism.

Charles V was a great collector of pictures and his principal court painter was Venetian. Born about 1488 at Pieve de Cadore near the Julian Alps, Titian had studied in Venice under Giorgione and Giovanni Bellini, and by 1516 he was official painter to the Venetian Republic. By 1532 his reputation was such that he was commissioned to portray Charles V, whom he painted accompanied by a large hound. Charles soon made him Court painter and a Count of the Empire, and in 1547 Titian painted him in battle armour on horseback from the life after his victory at Mühlberg on the Elbe; finally as a tired but wary and formidable statesman, resting on a terrace that commands a distant and suitably melancholy landscape. In 1538 Titian had also painted Francis I, whose sly and sensual animal magnetism he had known well how to evoke: he also in 1545 painted Pope Paul III (Farnese), the great architect of the Counter-Reformation and of Counter-Reformation Rome; the very embodiment of weary, disillusioned, yet still forceful cunning. So while Leonardo won recognition all over Italy and and in France, the greatest artist of the Venetian High Renaissance won a European reputation; the humanist art that had emanated from Florence had been received in Venice, the most conservative and Byzantine of the Italian states, and was now eagerly competed for by the two greatest monarchs north of the Alps.

The Italians of the Renaissance of the *Trecento* and *Quattrocento* had possessed the immense advantage over the northern peoples that they had had a precise and sophisticated vernacular language;[1] while German, English and even French were still relatively clumsy and uncouth. And if the impact of Italian method on government and administration has been exaggerated, for the Italians were probably no more skilled than the officials of the courts of Burgundy, England or France, or of Lisbon, Seville and Barcelona, the demand for a humanist education for laymen was now widespread in the north, and by the early years of the sixteenth century, with the consolidation of kingship and the cult of the prince, the social pattern in the north was more receptive of the urban Italian culture than it had been when the magnates and gentry had been more rural and military.[2]

In painting the influence was reciprocal. The Italians greatly admired the Flemish Jan van Eyck, described by one Italian as "*nostri saeculi pictorum princeps*"—"the first painter of our age"—and Vasari attributed the discovery of oil as a medium to him.[3] It has indeed been maintained that "the influence in painting was rather from the north to the south."[4] The Germans were certainly showing spontaneous genius by the early sixteenth century, predictably from Nuremberg and Augsburg. Albrecht Dürer (1471-1528) was born at Nuremberg, his father an immigrant from Hungary. Apprenticed as a goldsmith, he early travelled to Basel, Strasbourg, Colmar and the Netherlands; then in 1494-5 he studied in Venice, which he again visited in 1507, and was influenced by Mantegna and Bellini. He was appointed Court painter to the Emperor Maximilian I, whom he brilliantly portrayed,[5] visited Antwerp and attended the coronation of Charles V as King of the Romans at Aachen. But though steeped in Italian and Flemish influences, his style is emphatically German. He was a pioneer water colourist, his elaborately narcissistic self-portrait (in the Prado) shows a delicate sensibility, and he was a superb draughtsman, at his best commanding a fine economy of line. But there is a morbid introspective touch in his massive overwrought allegorical engravings, and he well knew how to discern and express, as in the portrait of Oswald Kroll, the neurotic instability of a haunted Teutonic face.

The other great northern Renaissance German painter, Hans Holbein the younger, came of a family of artists in Augsburg. Born in 1497, he early frequented Konstanz and Basel, and in 1518-19 travelled in Italy, where he saw the work of Mantegna and Leonardo. After settling in Basel, he visited France and Antwerp and in 1526 England, where he stayed in the household of Sir Thomas More. After a brief return to Basel, he became court painter to

[1]As displayed in *Orlando Furioso, the Madness of Roland* (1516) by Ludovico Ariosto, a blend of medieval fantasy and humanist irony. It depicts Roland losing his reason for love of the daughter of the Great Khan of China. The sorcerer Astolfo visits the moon, where the lost wits of lunatics are kept in bottles, to return with Roland's, labelled "*Roland's sanity*". This spirited epic was translated into English in 1591 by Sir John Harington, who also wrote the *Metamorphosis of Ajax*.
[2]See Denys Hay. *The Italian Renaissance in its Historical Background*. second edition. 1977. pp. 185 ff. This book has a particularly good bibliography.
[3]Hay. *op. cit.* p. 188.
[4]*ibidem.*
[5]Most accurately perhaps in his sketch of him. See E. Schilling. *Albrecht Dürer. Drawings and Water Colours*. Trans. E. Winkwort. London, 1949.

Henry VIII, for whom he painted rather too favourable a portrait of Anne of Cleves, so that the monarch was sadly disillusioned when he met the original. Holbein's charming portrait of Georg Gisze (1532) depicts a merchant of the German "steelyard", and Holbein most memorably depicted Henry VIII to the life, as well as the long-suffering Archbishop Warham and Thomas More. Like Dürer, he was a master of realistic detail and set new standards of portraiture in a country long accustomed to the flat and wooden work exemplified in the surviving portraits of Edward IV and Richard III.

IV

When by the mid sixteenth century Francis I, Henry VIII and Charles V, all mighty princes, had passed from the European scene, the widening of geographical horizons and the shift of political and economic power to the Atlantic states and Antwerp was an accomplished fact, from which the Iberian states had so far reaped the greatest benefit; while the originally Florentine Renaissance humanism had been assimilated and re-interpreted by the other major Italian powers, most brilliantly by the Papacy and by Venice. The Italian influence had also spread far beyond the Alps, while the Burgundian–Netherlandish culture had reciprocally influenced the Italians. But the widening of geographical horizons and artistic consciousness had not, as in the early sixteenth century had seemed likely, been accompanied by the success of a rational Christian humanism which might have reformed the Church and kept Christendom united. Erasmian humanism had been swamped by religious fanatics, whose ideological warfare political rulers had exploited, so that, as Kenneth Clark puts it, the Church, "the great civilizer of Europe, was aground"; now, in face of the militant schism of Luther and Calvin, the Catholics, under the leadership of Pope Paul III, with the foundation of the Jesuit Order, and in 1545 at the opening of the Council of Trent, set about their own equally militant "Counter-Reformation", expressed in the architecture and painting of the Age of the Baroque.

XXVIII

Czechs, Magyars, Poles and Turks: Ivan Groznyi

The Central European and now cadet house of the Habsburgs, under the Emperor Ferdinand I, was no longer based on the Germanies, but on Vienna and Prague. After the death of Louis II of Hungary at Mohacs in 1526, both the Hungarian and Bohemian crowns had devolved upon his sister Anne, the Consort of Ferdinand I, whose own sister Mary was now Dowager Queen of Hungary. Since both crowns were elective, they were transferred by coercion, bribery and intrigue to Ferdinand. This inheritance, though greatly diminished in Hungary by Turkish invasion and civil war, confirmed the Austrian Habsburgs as a Danubian and Bohemian rather than a North German power, and set them on their difficult dynastic task of mastering an inheritance of late medieval variety and incoherence. Against the odds, and though they failed to regain control in Northern Germany, they would long succeed in their main objective, even after Napoleon had abolished the old Holy Roman Empire itself, and survive into the nineteenth and even the early twentieth century.

Charles V had planned that after Ferdinand had inherited the Empire, Ferdinand's son, the Archduke Maximilian, would in due course give place to his cousin Philip II, who, true to Habsburg form, would again unite this colossal inheritance. But by 1550 for once family interest—if interest it would be—was sacrificed to personal ambition: Maximilian, it was arranged, not Philip II, would succeed his father to the Empire as Maximilian II, after being crowned as King of Bohemia in his father's lifetime. This solution proved realistic: particularly since the Central European Habsburgs did not share the fanatical purpose of Philip II, but turned out, under their official Catholicism, to be tolerant Erasmian Humanists. Moreover they had great administrative difficulties to contend with, and did not dispose of the centralized and bureaucratic power of the monarchies of the West; indeed, they had to walk warily amid the frightful complications of the Hungarian and Bohemian medieval institutions exploited by the nobility. So, following the Peace of Augsburg and the Treaty of Câteau Cambrésis, the Germanies and Bohemia were long spared the poisonous religious animosities of Western Europe. It was not until 1618 that, under the influence of the Jesuits, Ferdinand of Habsburg, following provocation by the Czechs, launched a Counter-Reformation and provoked the Thirty Years War, when Germany, after a relatively peaceful and prosperous interlude, would get its full share of Machtpolitik, fuelled by fanaticism and prolonged by French and Swedish intervention.

The main concern of the Habsburg emperors was still the continuing threat from the Turks; a responsibility they shared with Philip II, who fought them in the Mediterranean; but the Emperors' immediate problem was how to control their own territories and raise revenue. When in 1526 Ferdinand had been elected King of "the lands of the Crown of St. Wenceslas ... [they] comprised the Czech lands of the Kingdom of Bohemia and the margravates of Moravia, the dozen or so duchies of Polish-German Silesia, the two separate Wendish-German duchies of Upper and Lower Lusatia, and various islands of unassimilated duchies and lordships such as Cheb (Eger), Kladski (Glatz), Loket (Elbogen) and Opara (Troppau)."[1] As Poland was dominated by pani and szlachta—magnates and gentry, so the Bohemians had their pans and šlechta, who controlled the local assemblies and local councils. There was a proliferation of medieval provincial parliaments or diets; as in Moravia, Silesia, Lusatia, as well as in the "unassimilated" lordships. And above them was a snem or "Diet of Bohemia" itself, consisting of delegates from the others. And of course when Ferdinand tried to convene what would now be called a "federal parliament" for all his dominions, the habit of parliamentary representation was not strong enough to induce the Czechs to attend one outside their own country or the Hungarians to come to Bohemia. It was only with the utmost difficulty that he could raise money for the urgently necessary defence against the Turks, and after his election to the Empire, he chose to fix his main capital at Vienna, in the Habsburg territory, not in Hungary or Bohemia.

His son Maximilian II (1564-76) followed his example and also developed his own hobbies; botany, music, and collecting clocks, then novel and fascinating instruments which long appealed to royalty. And his successor Rudolf II (1576-1612), whose long reign covered the renewal of war with the Turks, the wars in the Netherlands and the "crusade" of the Armada and its sequel, proved a tolerant humanist, an art patron and a Maecenas for scientists—as Kepler and Tycho Brahe, the astronomers—and for the astrologers then considered so important. He was indifferent to the dogmas of both Calvinists and Catholics, and set up his court in the old Hradschin palace in Prague, where he revived the cosmopolitan cultural traditions of the Luxembourg emperor Charles IV, arranged his own laboratory (for alchemy as much as primitive science) and even, unfashionably in Central Europe, tolerated the Jews. He patronized the Mannerist painter Sprenger; also, with better judgement, the younger Breugel and the sculptor de Vries; and he gave shelter to Flemish landscape painters who had fled from the wars in the Netherlands. "If Philip II in the Escorial was the patron of unyielding Catholicism throughout Europe, Rudolf II in the Hradschin can be seen as the patron of that secular, ecumenical world of Renaissance humanism which still resisted both Reformation and Counter-Reformation, and which, with the passage of

[1]New Cambridge Modern History. Vol. II. op. cit. pp. 464-5.

time, had been impregnated with magic and tinged with Melancholy."[1] In time
the melancholy so far suffused the Emperor, an eccentric bachelor recluse
unable to control his own unpaid troops who ravaged Bohemia, that by 1612
he had to be deposed by his brother, the Archduke Matthias. But politically
the cosmopolitan grandeur of his Court had not been without effect, and
indeed set an example long followed by the Habsburgs; for, unlike their
Spanish cousins, they had no single national base, and had to create a personal
imperial myth to unite their heterogeneous empire.

In 1606 Rudolf II had come to terms with Sultan Ahmad I of Turkey, now
undermined by a crisis of his own currency, by lack of manpower, indiscipline
in his armies and bad communications in his over-extended empire, and
threatened by renewal of the war with Persia. The Emperor Matthias
(1612–19), King of Hungary by 1608 and of Bohemia by 1611, who had already
failed to pacify the Netherlands after the death of Don Juan of Austria, now
dealt more successfully with a Lutheran/Calvinist revolt in Hungary. But by
1618 the relative peace of Central Europe under the ageing Matthias was
disrupted by a Czech revolt, when the Czechs, following their Bohemian
custom, flung the envoys of their newly-elected King, Ferdinand of Habsburg,
from the high Hradschin Palace onto a dunghill which cushioned their fall,—a
gesture dignified as the "Defenestration of Prague—", and offered the Crown
of Bohemia to the Calvinist Elector Palatine of the Rhine, son-in-law to James
I of England, whom they considered carried more weight than in fact he did,
either through personality or political influence.[2] They thus began the Thirty
Years War (1618–48), a hideous conflict which, although its impact on the
Germanies is not now considered to have been as devastating as once believed,
has left its record in the engravings of Callot's Miseries of War.

II

The difficulties faced by the Habsburgs in asserting their authority and
organizing defence against the Turks were increased by the impact of the
Protestant Schism, which here met very different conditions from those in the
West. Where in Spain, France and England strong centralized monarchies
were already established which had either superseded medieval representative
institutions or, as in England, exploited them, in Central and Eastern Europe
large realms with fluctuating boundaries in Bohemia, Hungary and Poland had
been ruled, by the chances of dynastic inheritance, by princes with shadowy
authority, and the magnates and gentry had developed and dominated the
complicated and fissiparous institutions inherited from medieval times. The
principle cujus regio, ejus religio, was hardly appropriate when it was uncertain
whose the regio was. If religious enthusiasts could expect all or nothing in the

[1]Hugh Trevor-Roper. Princes and Artists: Patronage and Ideology at four Habsburg Courts
1517–1633. London, 1976. p. 101.
[2]See C. V. Wedgwood. The Thirty Years War, London, 1938, still the most lucid
treatment of the immense subject, pp. 78–90.

west; in the east they could expect infiltration and competition. Moreover, while in the west, the big cities had become much more powerful and tended to support the monarch and the central bureaucracy, in Eastern Europe, where monarchical government had been so much weakened, towns had often been backward, commerce much in the hands of socially ostracized Jews, and the peasantry increasingly bound to the soil and legally at the mercy of their masters.

As usual in Bohemia the incompatibility between the Czechs and the Germans conditioned politics, and the Catholic Church had become identified with the magnates and the German settlers. Among the Czechs the soul of Huss went marching on, and a poverty-stricken national Church, so far unrecognized by Rome that the Popes left the archbishopric of Prague vacant from 1431 to 1561, commanded widespread loyalty. The Czechs, indeed, considered that they had realized their own Reformation. Theologically the moderate Hussites remained conservative, though they emphasized the authority of the Bible: the main question which separated these Utraquists from Rome was whether or not the laity ought to have *both* the cup and the consecrated wafer at communion. But this question had not, as so often in the militant sixteenth century, proved a burning one; and although Luther was generally considered to have echoed and revived the "opinions of Boheme", his nationality made many patriotic Czechs wary of rushing to embrace his doctrines.

When King Louis II, King of Bohemia and Hungary, had been slain by the Turks as he fled from a stricken field and the Emperor Ferdinand of Habsburg had been elected his successor in Bohemia, the Czechs had found themselves with a pro-Catholic monarch realistic enough not to attack the Utraquist Church, which was supported by many nobles and gentry who had obtained the old Catholic Church's lands: and over the years it proved impracticable for Ferdinand's government to stop the infiltration of Lutheran ideas, preachers and books among the German settlers within the Bohemian frontiers and in Moravia. The "Bohemian Brethren", puritanical Hussites with radical inclinations, far to the left of the Utraquists, became allies of the Lutherans, and even Anabaptist refugees were tolerated in Moravia for the technological skills they brought from Switzerland and Tyrol. So it turned out that, vaccinated, as it were, first by Huss, then by Luther, even the more radical Czechs long remained impervious to the infection of Calvin; and when after Charles V's victory at Mühlberg in 1547, the Czech rebels who had fought against him were at a disadvantage, Ferdinand I maintained a statesmanlike policy of reconciling Catholics and Utraquists as the best insurance against Protestant extremism. He did, however, in the following year, expel various "Bohemian Brethren", who removed to Poland or remained, protected by their lords, in Moravia; moreover, Ferdinand I had established the Jesuits at Prague and persuaded Pope Pius IV to appoint a Catholic archbishop to the long vacant see: he even induced him to permit both kinds of communion to be administered to the laity. But so well rooted was the Utraquist Church in Czech patriotism that even this concession was not enough, the attempt to reconcile Catholics and Utraquists failed, and under Maximilian II even the

Jesuits were defeated; the Utraquist and, increasingly, Lutheran gentry came to dominate the country. The Counter-Reformation in Bohemia, though discreetly amd moderately conducted, had predictably and utterly failed; nor would Rudolf II be the man to revive it.

In Hungary after the death of Louis II, the election of Ferdinand as King had been contested: a majority of magnates and churchmen had elected John Zápolyai, Voivode of Transylvania, so that civil war had been added to Turkish invasion when the Turks besieged Vienna and permanently occupied Buda. Both archbishops and five bishops had been slain at Mohács, and in the ensuing crises the magnates had laid hands on the revenues of their sees. Ferdinand himself was dependent on the Magyars who controlled the strategic castles. After Mohács there was not much that either Ferdinand or his rival, both politically paralysed by old Hungarian representative institutions, could do to stop the spread of Lutheran doctrines; even the Turks in Buda tolerated Lutherans: after all, unlike the Catholics, they were iconoclasts and so a less pernicious kind of Infidel. Before the deluge of 1526, at the genial and tolerant court of King Vladislas "very well" and at that of Louis II, brother-in-law of Charles V, Erasmian Humanism had been encouraged, and the New Testament translated into Magyar. After 1526 Lutheran pastors were appointed by Protestant magnates and harboured in the mainly German towns, even in Transylvania. They preached salvation by faith, and denounced the doctrines of purgatory. Feeling, perhaps, that they had already had their share of the latter, many Hungarians, Magyars as well as Germans, became Lutheran.

III

In Poland the Habsburgs, fortunately for them, had to accept no regal responsibilities. Sigismund I Jagiello "the Old" (1506–48), roughly a contemporary of Henry VIII, had been succeeded by Sigismund II Augustus (1548–72), the last of the Jagiellon line. The Polish nobility, needing an ineffective monarch, then elected Henri Duc d'Anjou, afterwards Henri III of France and the last of the Valois, who not unnaturally, on the death of his brother Charles IX in 1574, returned rapidly to France to take up his inheritance. By now the need for a warrior king eclipsed even the Polish love of aristocratic anarchy, and the Poles elected Stephen Báthori, Prince of Transylvania (1575–86) who fought the Muscovites with good effect. On his death the Poles elected a Catholic Swedish prince. He was Sigismund III Vasa (1587–1632), son of Johan III Vasa of Sweden and Catherine, sister of Sigismund Augustus of Poland, and in 1594 he was crowned King of Sweden at Uppsala as well, though he failed to maintain his authority and was expelled in Sweden by his uncle Duke Charles, "Crooknose", who became Charles IX, the father of Gustav II Adolph.

The monarchy of the *rzecz pospolita* (which is Polish for *res publica*) was even more restricted by the power of the *pani* and the *szlachta* than were the Habsburgs by the magnates and gentry of Bohemia and Hungary. Among the

Czechs and Magyars medieval institutions had proliferated; in Poland, exploited by the nobility, they had run mad. The Polish *sejm* (parliament) was composed of an upper House of the archbishops, the bishops, the *woiwodes* and the *castellans*, along with nominally royal officials and prelates who were in fact dominated by the magnates; and of a lower House of gentry or *sejmniks*. Both Houses were entirely under the control of the greater or lesser landowners. They were thus able to exempt themselves from the jurisdiction of the Catholic ecclesiastical courts, a move which coincided with the widespread success of Calvin's doctrines in Poland, rather surprisingly considering that Krakow had been a remarkable centre of humanist Renaissance learning. The Polish Catholic Church, like the Polish constitution, had long been exploited by the nobility, who in 1515 had obtained sanction from Leo X for the decree that only those of noble lineage could be appointed to bishoprics, abbacies or the more lucrative lesser offices of the Church; but although, or perhaps because, their kinsmen enjoyed the Church's wealth, the magnates and nobles coveted its lands. Lutheranism was German; but Calvinism was French, and, what was more, subversive of royal authority, so it was Calvinism that appealed to the Polish landowners, and by the 'fifties a Calvinist Church, with all its openings for laymen, had taken root in parts of Poland and Lithuania. Although the official Catholic hierarchy remained, the Italian arch-heretic Fausto Sozzini (Socinius) was harboured in Poland though he had dared to question the fundamental doctrine of the Trinity. This Neo-Arian and his followers were the ancestors of the Socinians and Unitarians of the following century, whose influence would spread to the West.

Lithuania, fully reunited, after the interruption of 1489, to Poland by the Union of Lublin in 1569, which extended similar privileges to those of the Polish aristocracy throughout the already loosely organized Grand Principality, contained large eastern Orthodox populations, and, in spite of the formation of the Uniate Church, they resolutely refused to compromise with the Catholics. The way here also lay open, in these debatable lands, for Protestants of various denominations to infiltrate areas of Eastern Europe. But the conflict with the orthodox Uniates rallied many Poles to the Catholic Church, as did the wars of Stephen Báthori against the Muscovites. The Counter-Reformation, despite the Calvinists, triumphed in Poland.

IV

With the Habsburg emperors handicapped by their constitutional difficulties in Bohemia and Hungary and by the spread of relatively mild religious controversy, it was fortunate for Central Europe that by the mid sixteenth century the Turkish war effort began to wane.

After Mohács the Turks had, indeed, overrun most of Hungary: by 1529 they were besieging Vienna, and by 1541 they had established themselves at Buda, whence they dominated most of central Hungary and cut off western or Habsburg Hungary from Transylvania beyond the Carpathians. But the

Turkish empire, sprawling from the borders of Persia to the middle Danube, proved over-extended; and though the sequel to Mohács nearly crippled the Hungarian monarchy and wrecked the Hungarian Catholic Church, the Turks did not fully follow up their success. Unofficially, guerrilla war continued on the long frontier from the eastern Alps to the Carpathians; but by 1568 a truce was arranged, including considerable "tribute" paid by the Empire to the Sultan.

In 1570 the Turks invaded and captured the strategically important island of Cyprus, where they massacred 20,000 Cypriots and flayed the Cypriot commander alive; but this event was counteracted in 1571 by the resounding Christian victory at Lepanto under Don Juan of Austria and Andrea Doria. For while it had not been followed up late in the year and had little effect on Turkish landpower in Europe, it depressed Turkish morale at sea and led to a truce of exhaustion which in fact marked a turning point in the conflict. On this one occasion that Philip II of Spain induced the Venetians to collaborate and concentrate the full Christian force in the Eastern Mediterranean, 30,000 Turks were killed or wounded, at the cost of 29,000 Christian casualties, and a great number of galley slaves, essential to the Turkish fleet, were liberated.[1]

On land, probably more from a renewed threat from the Persian front than from the consequences of Lepanto—for the Turks had kept and would keep Cyprus—the truce on the Danube frontier was renewed from 1579 to 1583, when under Mahmud III the guerrilla war, mainly one of local sieges, raids and routine devastation, became official again, so that Rudolf II ordered the *Turkenglocke* or "Turk bell" to be sounded at noon throughout the Empire to remind his subjects of the conflict, and the Sultan ordered the Green Banner of the Prophet to be brought to Hungary from Damascus to incite his armies. The war was most intense on the fringes of the Habsburg lands, where Croat, Carinthian and Styrian warbands attacked the Turkish raiding parties and the marcher lands were devastated. The Uskoks of Dalmatia and the Haiduks of the Alföld, like the Tatars and Cossacks of the Polish and Muscovite frontiers, relished this "piracy on land" as much as did the Turks,[2] and it extended from the Adriatic to the Black Sea. Under the Albanian Grand Vizier, Sinān Pasha, anxious to find occupation for restive and unpaid veterans of the Persian wars—the *janissaries* and *Sipahis* had mutinied because of their debased pay— the official war was more vigorously prosecuted by both armies, both living off the country and neither with sufficient cavalry for a decisive break through.

On balance the Christians had the advantage; help came from Germany, Italy and even France; Transylvania, Moldavia and Wallachia, whose cereal crops were so important, rose against the Turks. Michael the Brave of Wallachia drove Sinān Pasha from Bucarest, and only the intervention of the

---

[1] The carnage in this action, fought when the Turkish fleet had been trapped in the Gulf of Lepanto, marked the climax and decline of battles between galleys as fought since Antiquity. By removing the rams of their galleys Don Juan and Andrea Doria lowered the trajectory of their forward-firing guns to devastate the Turkish crews, while the big Venetian galleasses out-gunned the galleys, as Drake's ships in 1587 did the galleys at Cadiz.

[2] See Braudel. *op. cit.* Vol. II. pp. 1196 ff.

Sultan himself, who won the important battle of Mezo-Keresztes in October 1596, turned the tide and enabled the Turks later to counter-attack along the Danube. But war with Persia against Shah Abbas the Great now distracted the Turks, and the peace of Zsitva-Torok registered a stalemate, save for the psychologically important point that the Empire no longer paid tribute to the Sultans, who had hitherto still maintained the arrogant attitude shown by Suleimān the Magnificent to Francis I "King of the Franks", but now condescended to recognize the emperors as equals.

V

In contrast to the form in Hungary and Poland, where the kings were increasingly trammelled by medieval institutions exploited by the magnates and gentry, the Tsars of Muscovy were building up an increasingly autocratic power. Ivan III the Great had refused to pay tribute to the Tatars, and his capture of Smolensk and then of Nizhnyi Novgorod in 1478 had made Moscow much more formidable. While in neighbouring Poland-Lithuania the magnates and gentry had it all their own way, in Muscovy the Tsar brutally knocked them into shape, having inherited Tatarized administrative methods which included confiscation of lands and even mass deportation; though, in Ivan's day, it merely implied transfer, not confiscation of rights, it proved a policy at which the Muscovites became highly efficient. Nor, unlike Charles V, did the "autocrat of the Russias" have trouble with heresy; the rich and long established Orthodox Church was entirely self-sufficient, loyally supported for its resistance to the Tatars and impervious to western ideas of Reformation both in theory and practice. If, save for Italian influence in architecture and the arts at the court of Ivan III, there was no Renaissance in Muscovy, there was no Reformation either.

Under Vasilyi (Basil) III (1505–33) Ivan's work was furthered and consolidated, to become the basis for that of Ivan IV *Groznyi*—the Thunderbolt or Terrible (1547–84). Ivan, like Frederick *Stupor Mundi*, had a horrible childhood, for which he later got his paranoiac revenge. He succeeded as Grand Prince in 1533 at the age of three, and his Lithuanian mother, whose lover was a Prince Obolensky, died when the child was only eight; whereat the Boyars fought over the regency and insulted and bullied the precocious boy, who was kept short of food and clothes. But Ivan, even as a child, had "tortured animals and thrown cats from the roof",[1] and he was more than a match for them. At thirteen he set on his kennel keepers to arrest and murder Andrew Shuisky, the predominant Boyar, and by sixteen in 1547, the year of Henry VIII's death, he had insisted on beng crowned Tsar. He then married Anastasia Romanov, the first of his seven successive wives, and when, following a more than usually devastating fire in Moscow, the people rose against the government and drove him from the city, he soon put down the rebellion so ruthlessly that the rebels were permanently cowed.

[1]Bernard Pares. *A History of Russia*. London, 1937. p. 100.

Having asserted his authority, in 1550, Ivan, aged twenty, summoned the *Zemskii Sobor*, an assembly of the whole land which included representatives of all classes, including the townspeople and some of the free peasants, and with their acquiescence and even support, he improved the law code, the enforcement of the criminal law and the collection of taxes. He then in 1552 launched a massive expedition against Kazan, the strategically placed Tatar fortress at the junction of the Volga and the Kama, and their main stronghold between Moscow and the Urals. That autumn the Muscovites cut its water supply and destroyed its garrison. The sequel to this strategic victory was the annexation of Astrakhan, which extended Muscovite power to the Caspian.

Ivan IV also encouraged trade with the West. In 1553 an English trade mission led by Anthony Jenkinson rounded the North Cape, reached Archangelsk on the White Sea, and was permitted to come to Moscow, whence Jenkins proceeded, on Ivan's behalf as well as his Company's, to Persia. Then in 1559 the first English Ambassador, Thomas Randolf, was received by Ivan in the Kremlin at midnight—an hour when, like Stalin, he liked to do business—and was granted extra-territorial rights for English merchants. The Tsar was eager to obtain expert doctors and technicians from the West through the northern route, since the Baltic one was still blocked off by Swedes, Poles, Lithuanians and Teutonic Knights of the Sword, now a secularized and Protestant state under Albrecht of Hohenzollern, Duke of Prussia.

By now the Tsar had become totally convinced of his divine mission and pathologically suspicious of any resistance by the Boyars, gentry or towns to his autocratic regime.

Ivan had always regarded himself as "born to rule", the "autocrat of a Russian Kingdom" which went back to Vladimir—for he was well-read in Russian chronicles—and to Alexander Nevskii "who won victory over the Godless Germans". "How, pray," he demanded in an acrimonious correspondence with his former ally, Prince Kurbskii, who in 1564 had deserted to the Lithuanians, "can a man be called autocrat if he himself does not govern?"[1] He consistently claimed to be the "Pious Tsar"; "the Ancient Rome" having fallen through heresy, and the second been held by the "Godless" Turks, the Tsar's Russian Rome has now surpassed them both in piety. He insisted that he alone was the "Christian Tsar everywhere and among all Christians". Yet in 1588-9 the English envoy Giles Fletcher was observing "the state and forme of Government is plaine tyrannical".

By 1564 just this kind of rule had been inaugurated. Infuriated by his boyars and officials, Ivan had deserted his people in Moscow and, with his entire family household and bodyguard, disappeared "none knew whither", and "forsaken his realm". With nice psychological timing, he had also commanded that a letter be read to the Muscovites explaining that he had no displeasure with them, only with the magnates and officials who had cheated him during his minority and were still doing so. And the people had reacted as he had

---

[1]*Sourcebook for Russian History*, ed. G. Vernadsky et al. New Haven, 1972. Vol. I. pp. 172-3, q.v. for this revealing and famous correspondence.

foreseen; "Who will deliver us from the onslaught of the foreigner? How shall we be without a shepherd?" They had petitioned that the Metropolitan of All the Russias should intercede.

Ivan had then relented and returned. But he had now established a separate realm, an *oprichnina*, for himself (1564–72); "splitting the country as with an axe", but leaving the rest of the state, the *Zemschenina*, still indirectly under his rule. The *oprichnina* thus comprised an entirely separate and self-sufficient estate, including officials and musketeers (*strel'tsy*) supported by the revenues of over forty towns and of vast estates, often confiscated from owners who were compensated in distant parts of Russia; and "all the *oprichniki* walked and rode in black, with brooms in their quivers".[1] They lived separately, cut off from their families in the *Zemschenina*.

They reached the climax of their terror in November 1570, when Ivan used *oprichnik* troops to punish Novgorod; those guilty were first "scorched", then dragged behind hurdles and thrown into the river, while their wives and children were tied up and flung to drown from a high tower, and soldiers with pitchforks and hooks pushed them under if they surfaced.[2] This year also saw mass executions in public in Moscow following public trials. If by 1573 the *Oprichniki* had become so detested that Ivan abandoned this experiment, the reign of terror had consolidated his absolute power, which was backed by a subservient Church.[3] By a ferocity which earned him his appellation *The Thunderbolt*, Ivan IV had succeeded where the rulers of Central Europe had failed.

In his declining years, Ivan became increasingly paranoiac. In 1570, for sound political reasons, he had executed the two principal *Oprichniki*, instruments of his worst public oppression; but when in 1581 he killed his own son with a sudden blow of a steel-tipped staff, he was gratifying a purely private impulse. He became a dangerous recluse in the Kremlin, muttering of abdication or further vengeance: it is alleged, probably with justice, that, unable to sleep, he used to howl. His own and his country's nightmare ended in 1584 when he was killed by a stroke brought on by sudden rage.

He died having created a "service State", conscripting all classes for military defence or expansion. Indeed, the most permanent internal achievement of Ivan's reign was to create a hierarchy of non-hereditary service fiefs, independent of the old nobility by inheritance, who themselves were also compelled to serve in the higher posts of the Tsar's administration. Unlike most contemporary sovereigns, he won entire control of his magnates and gentry; the *Zemskii Sobor*, which included clergy, boyars and great and lesser merchants, was entirely subservient, though it would apologetically express an opinion—"this is how we see it."[4]

Externally, the attempt to secure a major port on the Baltic in Livonia failed owing to Polish and Scandinavian resistance; but the war on the southern

[1]*Sourcebook for Russian History. op. cit.* p. 143.
[2]*Sourcebook for Russian History. op. cit.* p. 149.
[3]Vehement in forbidding all Christians "to shave or cut their whiskers", for "such is not an Orthodox but a Latin custom".
[4]*Sourcebook for Russian History. op. cit.* p. 147.

fronts which had secured Kazan and Astrakhan had opened the way to the most important expansion.

In 1581 Ermak or Yermak, Ataman of the Cossacks on the Volga and the Don, along with nine lesser chiefs all under a cloud for brigandage, had been allowed to lead an expedition into Western Siberia. It was financed by the great Strogonoff family, marcher lords who had obtained extensive rights of settlement and development from the Tsar, and it was made up of 540 Cossacks, and three hundred Germans and Lithuanians. It was particularly strong in artillery and in arquebusiers—weapons the Tatars greatly feared. "When they shoot from their bows," said the Tatars, "flames burst out and much smoke belches forth with a loud roar . . . and the arrows that emerge cannot be seen . . . they penetrate everything all the way through . . ."

So began the vast and surprisingly swift colonization of Siberia; it covered more ground than the settlement of North America, and although Ermak himself soon perished, drowned when attempting to escape a sudden attack by plunging into the Irtysh, since, ironically, he was wearing the rich coat of mail presented to him by the Tsar, the exploration and settlement, backed and roughly planned by governments, would continue, by 1598 driving out Kuchum, Khan of the Siberian Tatars, by 1607 reaching the Yenesei river, and by 1640 the Pacific Ocean.

The main objective had from the first been furs; even in Ivan IV's time rich sables and fox furs were coming back to Moscow, and substantial import duties beginning to accrue. Thus out of Eastern Europe an equivalent to the western expansion across the ocean to the Americas was launched, in due time decisive for the shifts of world power.

XXIX

The European Crisis of 1588

During the Council of Trent, which continued, intermittently from 1545 until 1563, the year before Ivan IV established his *oprichnina*, the Catholic Church set itself in stricter order and launched a counter-attack against the Protestant schismatics. This massive enterprise, with all its cultural consequences, depended on the Spanish military and naval might which continued to dominate Western Europe. The wealth, which poured in from the Americas, and after 1580 from the Portuguese commercial empire, was spent lavishly on the ideological conflict and brought little benefit to the Spain of Philip II. As Braudel writes, " . . . for the greatest drain on the silver reserves the King himself and Spanish foreign policy in general were responsible. Instead of using this silver at home to set up new and profitable enterprises, as the Fuggers used the silver from their Schwarz mines in Augsburg, the Spanish Habsburgs let themselves be drawn into foreign expenses, already considerable in the time of Charles V and quite extraordinary under Philip II—a thoughtless policy, it has often been said." And if, as Braudel concludes, this burden was "the price of Empire" and Spain could hardly abandon the Netherlands for fear of "bringing the war nearer home",[1] the commitment to war had long been rooted in the dedicated Charles V's idea of himself as "the Standard Bearer of God".

Philip II (1556–98) was not merely dedicated; he was fanatical. This sombre and conscientious bureaucrat, long cast by English historians as an ogre, was in fact an amiable private character; but he had the egotism of almost arbitrary power and the inflexible purpose and disregard for human life of the obsessed; although his monastic white-walled apartments in the Escorial are not, as often supposed, gloomy, but command all the sunshine and a splendid view, the main purpose of the gigantic building was to be a Habsburg Mausoleum and one of his favourite artists was Hieronymus Bosch. On his mother's side Portuguese, he did not inherit the aquiline Habsburg profiles of Maximilian and Charles V, but looked more ordinary, as indeed he was; a laborious routine administrator with an appetite for writing minutes on state papers. He had

[1]Braudel. *op. cit.* Vol. I. pp. 478–9.

been trained and brought up for this sacred task and, far from revolting against his upbringing, spent his laborious life carrying it out—a very appropriate personality in an age which saw the rise of great states and state capitalism.

Pope Paul III (Farnese) (1534-49), who launched the Counter-Reformation, had summoned the Council of Trent in an attempt to pacify Christendom; but, once assembled, the prelates naturally debated dogma rather than Erasmian compromise or Church reform, and, claiming inspiration from the Holy Ghost, they soon became intransigent. The Protestants assembled at Magdeburg, from its foundation a potential rival to Rome; and, though Luther had died in 1546, they were not interested in compromise. Also claiming inspiration from the Holy Ghost, they had plunged into acrimonious theological debate so that "the controversies of these troublesome years create an impression of *rabies theologorum*."[1] They could not even agree with each other: and were totally hostile to reconciliation with Rome. So when in 1551 the adjourned Council was reopened at Bologna, and Protestant representatives, under Imperial pressure, consented to attend, the Council refused even to admit "condemned heretics", and it became clear that the Council was no instrument for reconciliation, but like many Councils and Assemblies before and since, a sounding board for ideological controversy.

The Papacy had by now added two powerful agencies to its Counter-Reformation. In 1542 the Holy Office had been established in Rome, the supreme and centralized tribunal of the Inquisition, recently and most macabrely active in Spain; and in 1540 the Society of Jesus had been first established. This Jesuit Order originally aimed mainly at the propagation of the Catholic Faith in the Far East and the Americas, so redressing the balance of a disunited Christendom, but it soon became dedicated to a systematic political attempt to win back the Protestant realms in Europe.

The Order had been founded by Don Iñigo López de Loyola, St. Ignatius (1491-1556), a Basque gentleman who had been a gallant and worldly soldier until, aged thirty and badly wounded in the leg, he had been forced to introspective contemplation and wide reading, and become converted to complete austerity. He went on pilgrimage to Montserrat in Catalonia, where he exchanged his fine clothes for those of an astonished beggar, and took to months of disciplined meditation by methods recorded in his *Spiritual Exercises*. He then made a pilgrimage to Jerusalem, where he was rejected by the local Franciscans; then, determined to make up for a knightly and limited education, he studied at the University of Paris (1528-35), where he collected six followers. He then went to Rome, where he obtained recognition for his project, and by 1541 the nucleus of his Order was established. After some vicissitudes, it greatly expanded, and by the time of the Founder's demise the Order numbered a thousand, of whom 43 were fully professed in the highest grade. Under its first General, Claudio Acquaviva (1581-1615), it was superbly designed to be active in the world, in a carefully selected hierarchy under a General chosen for life. The founder had entirely rejected any contemplative monastic ideal, and subjected novices to a long and exacting training—

[1]*New Cambridge Modern History*. Vol. II. *op. cit.* p. 184.

"novitiate," "scholasticate" and full "profession". Though the Order was a centralized autocracy, its rulers were instructed to take full account of the personalities and talents of their subordinates, and all took vows of poverty, chastity and total obedience. The Jesuits accepted the new Humanist learning and early concentrated on the education of upper-class boys, at a time when in Germany and France the old system had been much impoverished by the Protestant Schism, so that Jesuit educators and confessors, well groomed in the latest fashions of knowledge and in the ways of Courts, pervaded the lives of the royalty and nobility of Catholic Europe.Where Calvin's pastors bullied and lectured, the Jesuits were suave, amusing, ingratiating and, as missionaries, often heroic. In time their close and sometimes devious involvement in politics made them unpopular, and their cosmopolitan sophistication provoked particular distrust among the patriotic and provincial English, Dutch and Scots. They were foremost in casuistical political theory, and not above recommending the assassination of heretic princes. Moreover, they shared some of the detestation provoked by the Inquisition, who sanctioned torture and the burning of heretics, on occasions politely termed *autos da fé*.

Armed with these new weapons, the Popes of the Counter-Reformation, Paul IV and Pius V, set about extirpating any Lutheran heretics they could find in Italy, and then commissioned Bernini and his followers to complete the impressive transformation and embellishment of Rome. Michelangelo survived to complete the Sistine Chapel with his terrific Last Judgement, and St. Peter's was finished in its full splendour by 1560.

All this impressive counter-attack on the heretics would have been impossible without the backing of Spain, now drawing more bullion from America and, in effect, in military occupation of Italy; though the main battles, ideological and military, would be fought out beyond the Alps, in the religious wars which convulsed France, in the Hispano–Dutch wars in the Netherlands, and in the attempt to invade England that failed when the "Invincible" Armada—the term caught on as a typical Spanish sarcasm after its failure— was defeated in 1588.

II

The dispatch of *La Invincible* was an attempt to win back by force the heretical realm of England after a traditional Habsburg marriage policy had failed, and so retrieve the rapidly deteriorating position of the Catholic Counter-Reformation in the North. For although, at his father's behest, in 1554, Philip II had married Mary Tudor, Queen of England, she had not borne him an heir. The policy had been far seeing and perhaps realistic, though England would have been hard to hold; "there was indeed an imaginative boldness typical of the emperor, coupled with a greater awareness of economic and strategic realities than had characterized some of his previous grand designs. In place of a vast and cumbersome geographical monstrosity that passed for an empire under Charles V, Philip II would rule an empire of three logical units, England and the Netherlands, Spain and Italy, and America".[1]

It was not to be. All failed, as had the marriage of the Infanta Catherine of Aragon to Henry VIII, since their sole surviving offspring proved incapable of producing a male—or any—heir.

How had it come about that the English had broken away from Catholic Christendom? A retrospective glance at the events which caused this revolution will indicate their course. The English during the fourteenth and fifteenth centuries had been best known on the Continent as the plague of France, as the close colleagues of the merchants of the Low Countries in the wool trade, and as the originators of the heresies of Huss. Now in the early sixteenth they were a considerable economic and even naval power. Erasmus had found enough patronage in England to compensate for the climate, and the Court had a Burgundian and even Italianate affluence. Henry VIII (1509–47) had made his nuisance value felt in traditional campaigns in Picardy and Flanders; more effectively, he had founded the English navy and the dockyards and forts on which it was based. Through his marriage to the Infanta Catherine of Aragon, Henry had inherited a pro-Spanish and pro-Imperial policy, and, as already recorded, had obtained the title *Fidei Defensor* by a vigorous attack on Luther.

Then in the Habsburg–Valois conflict that dominated Europe, Henry VIII and Wolsey had fished in tides far too strong for them; the King aiming at the Crown of France, Wolsey at becoming Pope. But on the death of Leo X, Charles V had Adrian VI (of Utrecht) elected (1521–3)—"the schoolmaster of the emperor", as the French King called him; he proved a pious and provincial Pope, disliked in Rome for his guttural pronunciation of Latin,[2] and to whom the "magnificent art of the Renaissance was a closed book. He failed to unite the French and Germans against the Turk or unite the German Catholics against Luther; and died after a brief reign, to be succeeded by Clement VII. Wolsey had never had a chance; and when in 1525, after the victory at Pavia, Henry VIII had thought to invade France, Charles V had proved that he no more wanted his uncle by marriage to displace Francis I than he wanted Wolsey to be Pope. In disgust King and Cardinal had decided to switch to a French alliance.

The decision had coincided with Henry VIII's desire for a male heir, an essential point of his policy. Wolsey's solution was a collusive annulment of the King's marriage and a marriage with a French princess. But here, momentarily, King and Cardinal had diverged, for the King had been determined to marry Anne Boleyn, a court lady of no dynastic consequence and dubious reputation. He always considered himself a Catholic, but in his passionate course he now broke through all obstacles. He risked "wronging" the Habsburg-Spanish royalties "in blood" and honour; he destroyed Wolsey; he made Anne his Queen, and he wrenched the Church of England out of obedience to Rome. With the backing of Parliament he had himself proclaimed

[1]Elliott, *op. cit.* p. 202.
[2]L. F. A. von Pastor, *History of the Popes*, trans. E. Graaf, London 1891, Vol. IX.

"Supreme Head" of the Church of England "under God", brought England over to the side of the Lutherans whose founder he had denounced, and in due course dissolved and plundered the English monasteries, thus creating a social revolution.

In 1529, after the "King's great matter" of the annulment of his marriage had been revoked to Rome, the King's lawyers devised a devastating attack on the English Church. They refurbished a medieval statute of *Praemunire*, originally designed to catch those evading royal jurisdiction where papal "provisions" had conflicted with royal rights, and interpreted it as forbidding the exercise of any foreign jurisdictions within the realm. It applied both to Wolsey and, in general, to the whole Church. Then, with his sure political instinct, Henry summoned a Parliament, and in 1531 got its anti-clerical backing for an attack on the Church and its property, thus giving a lead to the most dynamic, insular and representative interests in the realm. For here as elsewhere, the "Reformation" would have got nowhere without the backing of a powerful Prince. Soon, in full cry, after the attack on the Church under the law of *Praemunire*, the Parliament withdrew payment of Annates[1] to the Pope, and the year after by an Act for Restraint of Appeals withdrew the right of appeal to Rome. By now Cranmer, a subservient don from Cambridge, had been appointed Archbishop of Canterbury and, fortified by his blessing, Henry had married Anne Boleyn in flamboyant style. When at last Clement VII pronounced against the annulment of the King's marriage to Queen Catherine, the Pope had been presented with a *fait accompli* confirmed in 1534 (the year before Charles V led his crusade against Tunis) by Parliament's Act of Supremacy which united the Imperial crown of England with the Headship of the Anglican Church and sanctioned a new and extended interpretation of "Misprision" of treason. Henry was now *Henricus Octavus Dei Gratia Angliae et Franciae Rex, Fidei Defensor et Dominus Hiberniae et in terra Supremum caput Anglicanae Ecclesiae*. As such he now turned savagely on the Catholic opposition, and beheaded Bishop Fisher of Rochester and Sir Thomas More, formerly Lord Chancellor—both men famous in western Christendom. Then, after making a brisk assessment of Church revenues, the King turned on the monasteries, and on mainly trumped up charges of immorality and malversation of funds, dissolved them, although, improvidently for the Crown, he soon sold off their lands, thus creating a powerful "Protestant" interest among the purchasers, whose descendants would prove able to thwart the monarchy. Having by now tired of the temperamental Queen Anne, Henry further blackened his reputation abroad by beheading her for alleged adultery, after she had borne, not a boy, but a daughter, Princess Elizabeth; and Cranmer, having discovered that the King's second marriage had also been null—her sister had been the King's mistress—had married Henry to his third wife, Jane Seymour, by whom in October 1537 he at last had a son. But after the birth of Prince Edward, the Queen died, and none of the Continental powers yet officially recognized this heir.

Such is the blackguardly story of the English "Reformation"; but Henry

[1] Annates were the first year's income on a benefice.

VIII, like the Lutheran princes, had widespread popular support, above all that of Parliament and the magnates of the City, soon reinforced by those of the old aristocracy and the new who bought up the monastic lands, some of which were resold to lesser men, thus creating an even broader interest. But Henry was an elaborately educated and versatile patron of Erasmian learning and diverted large sums to founding or enriching colleges, as Christ Church at Oxford and Trinity at Cambridge, and there was no root and branch eradication of the old structure of the Church, which preserved more of the Catholic organization and ceremonial than the "Reformed" Lutheran or Calvinist Churches on the Continent.

Gross, brutal and tyrannical in its doing, the Henrician Reformation founded the Church of England. And it was founded without civil war; for it commanded the support of the most representative and dynamic of the Tudor English, an insular people, deeply distrustful of foreign influence and united against the foreign attack which Henry VIII's revolution provoked.

For King and Cardinal, playing with European forces beyond their control, now faced a reckoning. After the peace of Créspi which had ostensibly reconciled Charles V and the French, the latter turned their full force on the island in the most dangerous threat of invasion for centuries. It was held off; more by the incompetence of the invaders than by the skill of the English, whose biggest ship, the *Mary Rose*, foundered when turning to get out of harbour because the ports of her lower gundeck had not been closed; but the rash of commitments of Henry VIII's foreign adventures had nearly bankrupted the government, and he left an unstable and encumbered legacy to Edward VI (1547–53), his weakly, intelligent, son. And when under Edward VI Protestant-ism and social change had been driven too hard, there had seemed to Charles .V a good chance that, with the accession of the half Spanish and strongly Catholic Mary (1553–8), his grand dynastic design might be accomplished.

III

The peace of Augsburg, with its Erastian principle "to him the realm, his the religion", had kept the Germanies comparatively quiet, and the usual quarrels among a successful ideological movement had diminished the Lutheran drive. Germany remained divided, with the Protestants entrenched in strategic Bohemia and in the strategic Palatinate, which threatened the Spanish land communication with the Netherlands. Fortunately the Emperor Ferdinand I, the brother and successor of Charles V as Emperor, had been no fanatic, and his son Maximilian II took up the unusual stance of neutrality. Rudolf II, that versatile, talented celibate intellectual of melancholy mind, then virtually abdicted his responsibilities, and, following the ineffective Matthias, it was not until the accession of Ferdinand II that the Empire under Jesuit influence would belatedly be mobilized for the Counter-Reformation.

It was therefore not in Germany, but in the Netherlands and the Channel that the first European crisis of the religious wars was fought out. Antwerp and Amsterdam were the economic power houses of the Spanish Empire, and here, as in England, Protestant beliefs had taken root, originally in Lutheran guise, but soon among a militant minority, as Calvinist. The rule of pale Spanish grandees of gaunt distinction and sombre formality had always been incongruous among the red-faced Hollanders and Flemings depicted by the Breughels, and over the raw and misty harbours reeking of tar and fish at Vlissingen and Veere. Nor had French-Burgundian civilization imposed by the Habsburg court much altered the native boorishness of the more representative Flemings; and under Calvinist influence the iconoclast compatriots of the van Eycks and Memlinc were soon desecrating churches and destroying pictures, statues and stained glass.

Had the Spaniards been more realistic, they would have continued to rule through the native aristocracy, as the fourth Count of Egmont, the popular young cavalry commander who had helped defeat the French at St. Quentin, or William of Orange, later known as the "Silent" (or rather "Slim"—in the sense that Smuts would earn the epithet in South Africa) on whose shoulder Charles V had lent when he came to make his speech of abdication in Brussels. But, like Charles I afterwards towards Scotland, Philip II was determined to impose the new fashion of centralized government in religion as well as administration: with Jesuit assistance, he enforced Tridentine doctrines, backed by the feared and detested Inquisition. In 1564 the relatively mild rule of Cardinal Granvelle and the Regent, Margaret Duchess of Parma, half sister of Philip II, was superseded, a decision which spread popular risings and iconoclasm through most of the Netherlands, so that most of the nobles rallied to the Regent against the populace.

Philip II, however, would have no compromise over religion: the revitalized strength of the Hispanic empire in the Mediterranean, the influx of silver in the Indies fleets—these Philip II was determined to use in the North ... "You may assure his Holiness", he wrote to his ambassador in Rome, "that rather than suffer the slightest thing to prejudice the true religion and the service of God, I would lose all my States, I would lose my life a hundred times over if I could, for I am not and will not be the ruler of heretics."[1]

So in 1566, denuding the Mediterranean of troops, and in spite of Pius V's demands for a crusade against the Turks, Philip ordered the Duke of Alva with his Spanish tercios—pikemen and arquebusiers quartered in Naples and Sicily, the most dreaded troops in Europe—to prepare to move north.

By now Egmont had been driven into opposition, and the more intransigent Dutch Calvinists who called themselves les gueux—"the Sea Beggars", had taken to their ships; Philip II had to shift the main weight of his effort to Flanders. By 1567 the Duke of Alva had arrived in Brussels, and at once began a reign of terror: in the following year Count Egmont[2] and Count Hoorn were beheaded in the market place in Brussels, while Orange, who had escaped to Germany, was outlawed. In 1572-3 the Spanish troops committed atrocities in

[1]Braudel. op. cit. Vol. II. p. 1040. q.v. for the best modern brief account.
[2]Charles V had sent him to England to ask for the hand of Princess Mary for Philip, and made him Stadthouder of Flanders and Artois and a Knight of the Golden Fleece. Even that, to the horror of the aristocracy, did not save him.

Mechlin, besieged Haarlem, and failed to take Alkmaar. Heavy taxation called the "Tenth Penny" was imposed and collected, but the Spanish troops, stranded unpaid on Zeeland, mutinied, like the Germans of Charles V in Rome, while the "Sea Beggars" blockaded the mouth of the Scheldt, thus strangling Antwerp's trade. Finally in 1576 all the troops, in a "Spanish Fury", converged to make an appalling sack of the city.

That settled the business of what had been the Spaniards' greatest commercial and financial power house in Northern Europe, and the "Sea Beggars", who had captured Brill commanding the mouths of the Rhine and the Meuse, and Vlissingen in Zeeland commanding the mouth of the Scheldt, prevented its revival.

Philip II's troops, who by now "consisted of only some 3000 Spanish infantry as against 25,000 Germans and 8000 Walloons",[1] had been unpaid for good reason. By 1575 the King for the second time had gone bankrupt. Forced to a show of conciliation, he therefore sent his half-brother, Charles V's royal bastard, Don Juan of Austria, the glamorous victor of Lepanto against the Turks, as Regent of the Netherlands; an unsuitable choice, for Don Juan was set, unpractically and romantically, on the conquest of England and marriage with Mary Queen of Scots.

In 1576, by the Pacification of Ghent, the Protestant and Catholic Netherlanders combined in common resistance to the Spaniards, but the Calvinist extremists soon so far alienated the Catholics that when in 1578 Alessandro Farnese, prospective Duke of Parma and son of the Regent Margaret, arrived to take over Don Juan's command after his death, many French-speaking Walloon Catholics rallied to Farnese and the army in the Union of Arras. Whereat in 1579 Holland, Zeeland, Utrecht, Gelderland and Gröningen organized the Union of Utrecht, the basis of the modern Netherlands.

This would become a republic, something new. Nowhere else in Europe, save among the Swiss, had such a polity come into being, and here, at the economic hub of Northern Europe with access to the North Sea, the Baltic and the Atlantic, now emerged a republic with vastly greater scope. So, in the "United Provinces" was launched what would be briefly the greatest sea and colonial power in the north, the admired centre of religious toleration and free thought.

But the Spaniards saved the southern provinces. In 1584 William of Orange was shot descending a staircase in Delft; the Spaniards under the able Farnese, now Duke of Parma, regained Flanders and Brabant, and even, in the following year, Antwerp which would become the cultural centre, signified by Rubens's superb paintings, of the Counter-Reformation in the North, though the *Gueux* still held the mouth of the Scheldt. That year the English intervened, when Leicester appeared in the Netherlands and established himself at Utrecht; but he soon failed, and the Dutch had to rely on themselves.

They did so with outstanding success. Maurice, brother of William of Orange, became Stadthouder of Holland, Parma was diverted from his

[1] Elliott. *op. cit.* p. 257. The "Spanish Fury" at Antwerp, like that in Rome in 1527, had been mainly German.

successful campaigns by the impossible demands made on him to collaborate with the Armada of 1588 against England, and the Dutch extended their territory to Breda, Nijmegen and the Lower Rhine. Philip II thereupon shifted the problem onto the shoulders of the Austrian Habsburgs by giving the entire Netherlands as the dowry of his daughter, the Infanta Isabella, on her marriage to the archduke Albrecht of Austria. But neither Austrians nor Spaniards could re-unite the whole country: the Dutch of the United Provinces had immensely profited from the eclipse of Antwerp which had been the making of Amsterdam; now religious and commercial interests combined to strangle Antwerp; and while the United and Protestant Provinces went their own way, the Catholic Austrian/Spanish Netherlands, their ·boundaries extended by the Spanish commander Spinola and dominated by French-speaking minorities even in Flanders and by Walloons in the east, became the nucleus of modern Belgium; and "the power house, and the shop window, of the Counter-Reformation in the Protestant lands";[1] Catholic indeed, but afterwards the scene both of European wars and of internal tensions between speakers of Flemish and French as well as of the masterpieces of Rubens and of "an Indian summer of the Pax Hispanica".[2]

IV

The conflict between the Spaniards and the Dutch, in which the Protestant English had become involved, had presented attractive opportunities to the French in their strategic position commanding communications by land and sea. But France, too, in spite of the continuing strength and cultural prestige of the monarchy, its court centred on the valley of the Loire, was riven by ideological strife, which by 1562 had erupted into open war and culminated in 1572, the year after Lepanto, in the notorious massacre of St. Bartholomew when 4000 Huguenots were killed. As in the Germanies, popular religious fanaticism was exploited by the magnates; as Seignobos wrote, "the great people of that time lived in a world which received hardly any religious instruction and took but little interest in religion. Most of them showed very little zeal in the practice of religion and were indifferent to its doctrines. They took sides for one Church or the other mainly from motives of personal interest, and because the leaders of two opposing parties which were at once religious and political."[3] The atrocities and betrayals which signalize the French Wars of Religion are mainly the fruits of Machiavellian power politics exploiting popular religious zeal.

The French monarchy had emerged by the early sixteenth century as still the strongest in Europe, well able to challenge the Habsburg empire in the

[1]Trevor-Roper. Princes and Artists. p. 142.
[2]op. cit. p. 141.
[3]Charles Seignobos. A History of the French People. Trans. C. A. Phillips. London, 1933. pp. 214–15. He was referring, of course, to the strife had grown up before the Jesuits had become so influential.

futile and sanguinary international European power struggle; it was now, after the death of François I, like the fifteenth-century Lancastrian monarchy in England, fated to temporary but not lasting eclipse, owing mainly to the incompetence of the monarchs concerned. When Henri II died accidentally in a tournament in 1559, he left his widow, the not ill-meaning Catherine de Medici, a daunting task; to preserve the authority of the Crown which passed successively to their offspring François II, Charles IX and Henri III. François, the husband of Mary Queen of Scots, was dead within a year, so that his queen was compelled to take up her incongruous Scottish inheritance, with disastrous results. Charles IX (1560–74), a feeble youth if his portraits do him justice, was a minor, so that Catherine the Queen Mother became Regent, and when Henri III (1574–89) succeeded him, his undoubted flair for intrigue and murder barely saved the monarchy, if he can hardly be dismissed as the mere "degenerate" that his "Italianate" morals led nineteenth-century historians to depict.

The so called "Wars of Religion", which lasted intermittently for over thirty years, began with the massacre of a Huguenot[1] congregation in a barn at Passy in north-eastern France; they were fought by small armies, mainly of cavalry and arquebusiers with insufficient artillery for sieges, and the mainly professional troops were hired Swiss pikemen and Germans. As in the English civil wars, regional interests and loyalties and provincial feeling against the government in Paris much determined campaigns; but the main strength of the Huguenots was in the south-west and west, their principal stronghold La Rochelle; while the main strength of the Catholics was in the north-east and Lorraine. The majority of Parisians, the conservative theologians and even most of the students of the Sorbonne, were Catholic.

The Huguenots were led at first by the Bourbon Prince de Condé, and after his death at the battle of Jarnac in 1569, by Gaspard de Coligny, Comte de Châtillon (1519–72), a veteran of the Italian wars and since 1552 Admiral of France, though he fought entirely on land. After regrouping his army in the south-west, he retrieved the Huguenot position, and in 1570 won recognition for the Huguenots by the Peace of St. Germain, which guaranteed them their strongholds at La Rochelle and Montauban. But the youngest and ultimately most important Huguenot leader was Henri of Navarre, son of Antoine de Bourbon, Duc de Vendôme, and Jeanne d'Albret, Queen of Navarre: he ended the wars of religion as Henri IV and restored the monarchy.

The internal conflict was related to international politics: Coligny tried to involve Charles IX in war against the Spaniards in the Netherlands, while the Catholic Guises of the Holy League attempted to seize Paris and Henri III himself, as part of the grand Spanish-Papal strategy which would reinforce the "enterprise of England" undertaken by the Armada in conjunction with Parma's troops in the Netherlands. When, in 1572, Coligny perished in the Massacre of St. Bartholomew at Paris and, after the defeat of the Armada, the Duke of Guise was assassinated at Blois in December 1588 by the King's

[1]The term Huguenot or Higuenot is a French effort to pronounce the outlandish *"Eidgenossen"* (Confederates), applied originally to the Protestant Cantons of Switzerland.

Gascon guards, two extremists were eliminated; and Henri III, the last of the Valois, had the political sense to collaborate with his dynastic heir and brother-in-law Henri of Navarre, so that they were jointly besieging Paris when Henri III, too, was assassinated by a Catholic fanatic in August 1589. In 1593, after deciding that "Paris was worth a Mass", and after months of negotiations, Henri IV entered the city, fully established as the first Bourbon King of France.

In 1598 (the year of the death of Philip II of Spain) the Huguenot problem would be shelved by the Edict of Nantes, which gave generous terms to the Huguenots and allowed them to control many important cities and strongholds, regardless of the current principle *cujus regio, ejus religio*. Moreover, the wars had not disrupted the potentially absolute monarchy, centred on the King and his Council with its permanent officials, Treasurer-general, Secretaries of State in Paris and tax collectors in the provinces, which had developed from the original structure created in the struggle for survival during the latter part of the Hundred Years War and been consolidated by Louis XI. This royal bureaucracy was still to hand, along with the basically conservative French social hierarchy, now reinforced by the professional *noblesse de robe* and the upper bourgeoisie scrambling for official appointments. The tides of European ideological warfare had washed into France but had not swamped it, and the challenge to the central authority had failed. The tragedy had been due mainly to the dynastic chance that had thrown up three incapable kings in succession, and to the failure of Catherine de Medici to manage a situation beyond her own considerable political finesse.[1]

V

The fate of France and of all Northern Europe would have been very different had Philip II's great "enterprise of England" succeeded. In fact the Armada never had a chance: the entire strategy of so complex a combined operation was then impracticable and the inflexibility of the King's orders tied the commander's hands. Further, the talented Elizabeth I (1558–1603), after a precarious start, had been playing a cautious and skilful hand, and was now well established. The danger of a Scots-French attack, which might have coincided with rebellion in the still strongly Catholic and feudal North of England, had greatly diminished when the follies of Mary Queen of Scots had driven her to take refuge in Elizabeth's power; while in foreign policy the English had long been able to play off the Spaniards against the French. Most important, Elizabeth and her advisers had early made a compromise settlement for the impoverished Anglican Church, whereby much more of the medieval hierarchy had been preserved—as bishops, deans and Cathedral Chapters—than on other Protestant establishments. In this the majority of the clergy and

[1]She was a highly educated and intelligent woman, not a Medici for nothing, and brought Italian standards of cooking to France, where, with far better materials, the French proved apt pupils and created *la cuisine française*.

the people had acquiesced, and it was heartily supported by the magnates, gentry and merchants who had purchased the Church lands. The government, in 1561, had also called in the debased Edwardian and Henrician coinage and issued sound money, and though considerable inflation continued, powerful interests benefited by it. And when, in 1568, after the Spaniards had attacked Hawkins' ships in the Mexican port of San Juan de Ulloa, war with Spain had become open in the Caribbean, Elizabeth had winked an eye at the growing depredations of the English corsairs against the Spanish colonies. These had culminated in 1577–80 in Drake's immensely profitable circumnavigation of the world.

So when in 1586 the Babington plot had been discovered to assassinate the Queen and replace her with Mary Queen of Scots, most of the English were delighted when in the following year Elizabeth I allowed her most dangerous rival, who was hopelessly implicated, to be executed, and the Queen, excommunicated and execrated abroad, became the symbol of an insular Protestant people's defiance; for, like her father, she had an instinctive flair and popular eloquence in a crisis. Thus the danger of internal religious warfare and even the collapse of the Tudor dynasty had been avoided: an English Conciliar government working, without any standing army or major bureaucratic centralization, in alliance with the nobility and gentry in the shires, and until the last years of the reign in harmony with Parliaments when summoned, was able to face the grave threat of 1588 with most of the people behind them.

The threat was particularly alarming, for, as Mattingly points out, there had never been such an oceanic confrontation before. "No naval campaign in previous history, and none afterwards until the advent of the aircraft carrier involved so many fresh and incalculable factors."[1] The conflict opened a new chapter in naval strategy and tactics, and all politically conscious Europe watched the outcome which would decide whether the north-west and the Netherlands would be won back for the Counter-Reformation. Pope Sixtus V proclaimed a crusade; Parma in the Netherlands made laborious preparations for concentrating a polyglot army of Spaniards, Walloons, Germans, Burgundians and Italians on the Belgian coast.

The size of the originally termed "most felicitous" Armada was spectacular: and it was extremely well equipped, carrying over 27,000 men and 2650 guns. The Iberian crews and ships were of course very efficient, and the Duke of Medina Sidonia a dogged and cool-headed commander,[2] so that the English were awed and impressed by the "castle-like" crescent formation they maintained. Not that the Armada ships were larger than the English, a legend

[1]Garrett Mattingly. The Defeat of the Spanish Armada. London, 1959. p. 226. q.v. for the best modern account.
[2]H. A. L. Fisher calls him "a foolish and cowardly landsman" (A History of Europe. London, 1936. p. 606), refers to the "vast galleons" of the Armada, and states that "the whole scheme foundered on the incompetence of the Spanish navy" (p. 607). In fact the English were alarmed by the discipline and seamanship of the Armada, whose Spanish and Portuguese crews and navigators would not long have survived in the Atlantic seas off the iron-bound coast of Portugal had they been "incompetent".

long perpetuated: indeed the English were better gunned and, following the new streamlined design adopted under Hawkins, more manoeuvrable.

Further, Lord Howard of Effingham, and Drake, his Vice Admiral, had reckoned it fatal to adopt the conservative medieval strategy of standing to fight a confused melée in the Channel itself on the old tactics of grapple and board, which the Spaniards wanted them to do, but had preferred first a spoiling attack the year before on the Iberian coast at Cadiz and Cape St. Vincent. Drake had then, as he wrote, destroyed "hoops and pipe staves sixteen or seventeen hundred ton in weight, which cannot be less than 25 or 30 thousand ton if it had been made in cask, ready for liquor, all which I commanded to be consumed into smoke and ashes by fire which will be unto the King no small waste of his provisions ..." For "casks were a prime necessity, not only for stowing water and wine but for salt meat, salt fish, [and] biscuits ..."[1]

And then, when on July 29th 1588 the delayed Armada was reported off the Scilly Isles, the English fleet warped out of Plymouth Sound and stood out to sea, so that as the Armada advanced up Channel the English got to windward of them and held the advantage. The Spaniards kept their grim crescent formation, with both sides uncertain of the next move. For "Fleets like this were a new thing in the world. Nobody had ever seen two such in combat. This was the beginning of a new era in naval warfare, of the long day in which the ships of the line, wooden walled, sail driven and armed with smooth bore cannon would be queen of battle."[2]

In spite of an enormous English expenditure of ammunition, the still all but intact Armada, following instructions, came near its strategic objective when it arrived in Calais Roads. But now the English, never so dangerous as when cornered, improvised. They sent in fireships—thought by the Spaniards to be explosive "hell burners"—crackling with flames and thundering with double shotted guns, against the anchored fleet. Before this weapon—in darkness, as much psychological as practical—the Spaniards panicked, cut their cables, stood out to sea. Only a lucky change of wind prevented total disaster on the long treacherous shoals of the Flemish coast and Zeeland, as the English and Dutch harassed them in the North Sea; and Medina Sidonia in fact did rather well in bringing home as many ships as he managed to do after taking the correct if dangerous decision to return round the north of Scotland and past Ireland.[3]

So, in brief, was fought the first battle of the Channel and North Sea of first rate European consequence; it decided that England and the Dutch (or "United Provinces") would remain independent, and signalled that a first class naval power had arrived on the Atlantic, confirming the largely unofficial war which had long been waged by the Dutch in the East Indies and the English

[1]Mattingly. *op. cit.* p. 117.
[2]*op. cit.* pp. 237–8.
[3]He brought back forty-four ships out of the original sixty-eight, "a beaten shattered fleet, but many an experienced admiral had brought back fewer ships against less formidable odds", and "these ships were saved by the leadership and will power of their commander." (Mattingly. *op. cit.* p. 311).

in the Caribbean and the Americas against the sprawling and vulnerable empires of Portugal and Spain. European rivalries, intensified by the late medieval religious strife which had coincided incongruously with early modern oceanic discoveries, were now to be fought out on the oceans and beyond Europe; and the northern European peoples, hitherto backward compared to the Iberians in oceanic enterprise and colonization, would now make up for lost time, first by raiding and reconnaissance, and then, in the seventeenth century, by settlement.

XXX

The Protestant North

If in the north-west the English and Dutch had defied Philip II, in the north-east Ivan Groznyi, that champion of an Orthodox God, had been blocked from obtaining a port on the Baltic not only by the Poles and Lithuanians, but by a Scandinavian power. Sweden, with a population of little over a million and a quarter and relatively vast territories of forest and lake, including the Duchy of Finland, had always been a predominantly peasant country, and its landowners had never been feudatories nor its peasants serfs. By the Treaty of Kalmar it had been briefly united with Denmark and Norway, but by the mid-fifteenth century during the reign of Erik of Pomerania, great-nephew of Margarethe of Denmark, the Swedes had broken the union: they were still, however, menaced by the Danish mercenary fleets and armies and by the Danish control of the Sound and Kattegat, while the German Hansa city of Lübeck dominated trade with the South, and Poland and Muscovy were potential enemies in the East.

The climax of the Danish attempts to restore the union had occurred in 1520, when Kristian II of Denmark had defeated the Swedes on the ice of Lake Åsunden and perpetrated the notorious "blood bath of Stockholm". Thus provoked, the Swedes, with the backing of Lübeck, had united under a landowner of political genius, in 1523 elected him to the Swedish throne, and finally and officially repudiated the Treaty of Kalmar.

Gustav I Erikson Vasa (1523–60) has affinities with Henry VIII of England, save that where Henry VIII inherited his throne Gustav had to fight every inch for his, and himself had to found his dynasty. This many-sided soldier, statesman and man of business, a major figure of the Northern Renaissance, had nothing to learn from the Italians in the arts of diplomacy or apt violence. Like the first Tudor, he used the new weapon of printed propaganda, as well as his own commanding presence, homely eloquence and genial charm: he won over the towns by promoting trade and ousting the Lübeckers who had backed him, the nobility by encouraging them to join in the plunder of the immensely wealthy Catholic Church, and the peasants—an articulate and well represented interest in Sweden—by lightening the taxes. Moreover he put down rebellion with extreme ferocity.

He thus got away with murder and imposed a Lutheran reformation—since Lutherans would be docile to the centralized monarchy he was building up. Although in 1530 Gustav decreed that one bell in every Church should be melted down for the public revenue, and the peasants of Väster Gotland rose in rebellion—for the bells were notoriously far the best means of dispersing the evil spirits in the air, the religious revolution was consolidated. In 1536 at the Church Assembly at Uppsala presided over by Laurentius Petri, the first Lutheran Archbishop, the break with Rome was confirmed: the previous Archbishop had been allowed to retire to Italy, and by 1540, six years before Luther's death, a Lutheran State Church under the control of the Crown was established. In the following year an authorized Swedish translation of the Bible was printed in Amsterdam; like its English equivalent, it had a salutary effect in the vernacular and it enabled Lutheran doctrines to be more widely understood.

With the nobility reconciled by the plunder of the Church estates, Gustav I Vasa during the 'forties organized a more capable centralized administration; indeed, it was said, that he ran two-thirds of the country "as if it had been his own estate". He improved stock breeding and encouraged colonization into Lapland and Finland; and "no detail escaped his notice, whether it [was] a bailiff's addiction to ale or a peasant's neglect of the land."[1] Moreover, in 1544 he persuaded the Riksdag at Vasteras, near Stockholm, to make the Elective Crown of Sweden hereditary in the Vasa House.

He thus transformed a large and provincially disunited country, hitherto poor and backward save for its potential wealth in iron and copper mines and timber, into a relatively homogeneous realm, strong enough to survive the dissensions of his two sons, and in due course to counter-attack its neighbours— Danes in the West; Poles and Muscovites in the East.

Gustav Vasa had married Catherine of Sachsen–Lauenberg and their son had succeeded him as Erik XIV (1560–68). But by a second marriage he had also raised a larger family, including the eldest, Johan, Duke of Finland, and Duke Karl, known as "Crooknose".

Erik XIV, highly intelligent like all the Vasas, proved a talented, versatile but neurotic and unstable Renaissance prince. He was outstandingly handsome with fine eyes and a sensitive wilful mouth, and, being original and imaginative,[2] he came to disaster. Gustav I had attempted to break the Danish stranglehold on Swedish trade with the West by marrying this fine youth to Elizabeth I of England, and although the English had consistently discouraged the project, in 1559, the year after Elizabeth's accession, Duke Erik himself set out for England with a large and expensive fleet, though, characteristically, when it was dispersed by a storm, he abandoned the enterprise. Elizabeth I and her Council had never been interested and considered Swedes outlandish; but had this handsome, high-strung prince overcome the young Queen's

[1]Carl Ingvar Andersson. *A History of Sweden*. Trans. Carolyn Hannay. London, 1956.
[2]Aware of the possibilities of Lapland, he caused a display of Lapps and reindeer to be arranged for his coronation.

inhibitions, English and Swedish history could have taken a different and probably disastrous turn.

In the event, after his accession, Erik XIV soon plunged into trouble, both at home and abroad. A second generation prince, he lacked the caution and earthy business sense of his originally provincial father, and he involved Sweden in a "Seven Years" war on two fronts; unsuccessful with the Danes, successful with the Muscovites (1563–70); while by overdriving the power of the Crown and its bureaucracy of "new men" he incurred the hatred of the nobility. In 1567 he judicially murdered two of their leaders, Svante and Nils Sture, and, on the verge of madness, himself took part in their execution. He then went out of his mind, and when he recovered his sanity, married Karin Mansdotter, his plebeian mistress, by whom he already had children. He had also in 1563 imprisoned his half-brother, Duke Johan, who, having married Catherine Jagiellonica, sister of Sigismund II August of Poland, was appealing for Polish help. But during the King's madness, the Duke's supporters had him released from Gripsholm castle; and in 1568 Dukes Johan and Karl "Crook-nose", with the backing of the nobility, deposed and imprisoned their half-brother. Nine years later Erik XIV conveniently died.

Johan III (1569–92) succeeded to a throne undermined by these events, and by a long gruelling and, in the East, successful war in which the Swedes had kept the Russians out of Reval and in 1581 recaptured Narva, and the nobles took full advantage of his dependence on them. Like his half-brother, Johan was highly educated and a patron of the arts, particularly of foreign architects whom he brought in to improve and embellish his castles: but he also tried to restore some of the old Catholic ritual. So he provoked the wrath of the Lutherans, already apprehensive since the heir to the throne was the Catholic Sigismund III Vasa, already King of Poland (1587-1632) and Johan's son by Catherine Jagiellonica.

On the death of Johan III, there was thus a crisis. When in 1594 Sigismund III was crowned King of Sweden at Uppsala, Duke Karl "Crooknose", that wicked uncle, saw his chance. Regent on Sigismund's return to Poland, he won widespread Lutheran support against a Jesuit-educated Polish–Lithuanian King. Though not averse to a monarch who was an absentee in Poland, many of the nobility feared Sigismund's absolutism, and the peasants, who were represented in the Riksdag, had now got used to being Lutheran and detested Catholic foreigners. So "Crooknose" became Karl IX (1604–11).

The strategically important war in Livonia and Esthonia still dragged on, and in 1595, the year after Sigismund III's brief accession to the Swedish throne, the Muscovites had been forced to accept the Peace of Teusina, giving the Swedes control of all Esthonia and a favourable readjustment of the sketchy boundaries of Finland, long the scene of persistent Swedish coloniza-tion to the East.

But in the West the war with Denmark had ended in 1570 in a peace of exhaustion, on terms favourable to the Danes. They had captured Älvsborg on the Kattegat, Sweden's only direct link with the West and with the essential supplies of Bay salt; so they exacted a huge ransom, which took four years to pay off, and although this respite enabled the Swedes to follow up their success in the East, Karl IX's invasion of Livonia rallied even the Polish nobility to Sigismund III their king, and in 1605 the Polish cavalry inflicted a severe defeat on the Swedish army at Kirkholm near Riga. But Sigismund III, who was married to a Habsburg princess, had unlimited ambitions, and now became distracted by opportunities in Muscovy. In 1605, after the death of the usurper Boris Godunov, a Polish Pretender had briefly proclaimed himself Tsar and, though the Pole did not last, Sigismund hoped to be Tsar himself, or at least that his son Ladislas might be.

Alarmed at this prospect, the Swedes and Muscovites made a Treaty at Viborg; and the latter, disgusted at the prospect of a Polish Catholic Tsar, even offered the Crown to the Lutheran Swedish Prince Karl Philip, youngest son of Karl IX. And this obviously impracticable project the Swedes exploited to strengthen their hold on the Karelian Isthmus; on Ingria, south of the Neva; and even on Novgorod. They also alarmed the Danes into renewing the Western war, by interfering with Danish trade with Riga and by penetrating into sub-Arctic Lapland, threatening to capture Arkangelsk in the White Sea, and so to develop trade with the West round the North Cape, evading the passage of the Sound.

When in 1611, Karl IX "Crooknose" died, he had succeeded in the long-term Swedish strategic aim of blocking off the Muscovites from the Gulf of Finland and the Baltic, and thwarting one of the most cherished Muscovite ambitions; but he left the legacy of a renewed war with Denmark and heavy commitments in Livonia and even Muscovy to the seventeen-year-old Gustav II Adolf, his heir, whose profile, like that of his own daughter, Christina, showed so complete a resemblance to his father's.

II

In Denmark the disruption of the Treaty of Kalmar by the Swedes had left the realm united with Norway, Iceland and Greenland. Kristian II (1513–23) had tried to create a Renaissance-style monarchy, based on collaboration with the towns and a subordinate clergy; but although he married Isabella of Habsburg, sister of Charles V, he had earlier, as governor of Norway, taken up with a Dutchwoman, Dyveke Villoms, and her mother, Sigbrit. And when Sigbrit got her hands on the shipping tolls of the Sound, essential to the Danish economy, hostility to the King and his entourage became acute. In 1517 Dyveke died, whereat Kristian executed the Castellan of Copenhagen Castle, who, he was convinced, had poisoned her. Now bitterly unpopular with the Rigsraad, Kristian had launched the diversionary attack on Sweden which had led to the "Stockholm blood bath",[1] the Swedish national rising under Gustav Eriksson

[1] It had occurred in the small hours of a November night: two victims were beheaded as heretics and their bodies burnt. "Probably no event in Swedish history, unless it is the death of Karl XII, has been the subject of more prolonged controversy; scarcely an incident on which there is an agreed opinion." Michael Roberts. *The Early Vasas. A History of Sweden 1523–1611*. London, 1968. p. 17.

Vasa, and the expulsion of the Danes. With this failure behind him, Kristian's schemes, backed by the Central European Fuggers and Habsburgs, for developing the trade of the Baltic at the expense of the Hanseatic League, never had much chance, while the nobility were infuriated by the attacks on their privileges. And when in 1523 the Jutlanders formally deposed Kristian in favour of his Oldenburgh uncle, Duke Frederick of Schleswig–Holstein, the King took refuge in the Netherlands.

Frederick I (1523–33) soon became officially Lutheran and, in spite of attempts to restore Kristian II after Frederick's demise, the reign of Frederick's son Kristian III (1534–59), a pro-German Protestant, saw the official establishment of the Lutheran Church, the dissolution of the monasteries and the plunder of the Church lands. Under his successor, Frederick II (1559–88), the Danes enjoyed great prosperity, for the European inflation then setting in meant profits for an agricultural country already depending on exports. In Shakespeare's time the Danes had the reputation of living high and drinking deep; and they did so on the profits of the inflated prices of exported butter, hides and bullocks. They also developed silver mines in Norway, and Frederick II, who took the Seven Years War against Sweden in his stride, built the elaborate northern baroque castle of Elsinore, the supposed scene of "Hamlet".

Kristian IV (1588–1648), who succeeded to the throne as a child, had large military ambitions, and when James VI of Scotland married his sister, Anne of Denmark, he made what seemed a good match. Kristian expanded the Danish fleet, and after a short war with the Swedes (1611–13), in 1625 became involved in the Thirty Years War, But Gustav II Adolf of Sweden proved a better warrior and a better diplomat, and the Danes got little good out of the conflict; nor was his Danish brother-in-law much help to Charles I of England in his wars with Parliament. Kristian IV, however, won much military prestige, though he is best remembered by the palace of Fredericksborg and for importing Dutch architects to rebuild parts of Copenhagen.

III

The now Protestant northern peoples had created a network of trade over the North Sea and the Baltic; and since the Danes, with control of the Sound, held a strategic position, the ties between Scandinavia and the Northern Netherlands, now the United Provinces, were close. After the Union of Utrecht in 1579 and the death of Parma in 1592, the Protestant Dutch had gradually forced the Spaniards to abandon all the territories north of the Rhine and Meuse, and eliminated the threat they had poised against Holland and Zeeland; but neither Maurice of Nassau, son of William of Orange, nor the Genoese captain Spinola, the Spanish Commander-in-Chief, could overrun each other's territories. Henceforward, "though the masses who found themselves suddenly cut adrift from their former spiritual leaders were by no means easily absorbed into the new Church ... and a regular system of spiritual compulsion was needed to turn the North-Netherlanders into a nation of

Calvinists,"[1] the Protestant north and the Catholic south or Spanish Netherlands went their separate ways. In the south the Archduke Albrecht of
Habsburg and the Infanta Isabella, known as the "Archdukes", proved
munificent patrons of the artists of Antwerp, of whom Rubens achieved the
greatest fame, and the Catholic Spanish Netherlands settled into what would
become Belgium; but in the Protestant United Provinces a far more dynamic
society came into being.

Its horizons were oceanic. Already by 1602 the Dutch had formed the
United East India Company with ample capital behind it, and proceeded to
exploit directly the spice trade with the Far East. Dutch sea captains were
soon ousting the Portuguese in Indonesia, and harrying the Spanish trade in
the Caribbean; in Europe in 1609–21 the Spaniards accepted a twelve-year
truce in the Netherlands, and admitted that at least for a time the seven
northern Provinces were lost. They at first found able leaders. The lawyer Jan
van Oldenbarnevelt, pensionary of Rotterdam by 1576 and Advocat of Holland
in 1586, at first worked in harmony with Maurice of Nassau, by 1585
Stadthouder and supreme commander. They negotiated alliances with both
the English and the French, which constituted de facto recognition, but after
the French in 1598 and the English in 1604 had made peace with Spain, strife
broke out in the United Provinces between the peace party led by the civilian
Oldenbarnevelt, and the war party, with many victories behind it under the
soldier Maurice of Nassau, the rift worsened by doctrinal disputes between the
Arminian Calvinists and the Gomarists.

The Arminians were followers of Jacob Harmenson (1560–1609), Professor
of Theology at Leiden, who asserted that others besides the predestinate
Calvinist Elect might attain salvation, since mankind had free will. This
recklessly optimistic doctrine horrified the more rigid Calvinists, who, following Franciscus Gommer (Gomarus), a native of Bruges, and also a professor at
Leiden, suspected Arminius of being pro-Catholic and so pro-Spanish. The
University of Leiden was rent with this controversy, and Gommer retired to
the more provincial setting of Middelburg on Walcheren; but he outlived
Arminius, and in 1618 attended the Synod of Dort where the Gomarists, with
nationalist feeling behind them, succeeded in getting the Arminians officially
condemned. But the Arminian doctrine, which blended better with the
Erasmian tradition that had survived in the Anglican Church and universities,
had much influence in England during the reign of Charles I, when Laud, an
Arminian who believed in free will, became Archbishop of Canterbury.

The truce of 1609–21 was bitterly unpopular with the war party, who
considered it merely gave Spain time to recuperate, and tension became so
acute that in 1618 Oldenbarnevelt was imprisoned, and in 1619, in spite of his
eminent services to the State, executed for alleged high treason.

With the wealth from trade with the Far East behind them, the Dutch had
now become a great maritime power, far outclassing any Scandinavian state;
and what was more, their policy of toleration began to make them the
intellectual leaders of Western Europe. The Venetian republic had hitherto

[1]Peter Geyl. *History of the Low Countries*. London, 1964. pp, 36–7.

been regarded as the model Commonwealth; now it became the fashion to admire the Dutch. Indeed, they deserved it. Amsterdam had become the greatest centre of international banking in Europe; the Dutch, disregarding the censorship prevalent elsewhere, printed the most influential new books; undeterred by lack of stone, limited space, and a misty climate, they built high brick houses with huge windows along the quays of their canals, at once homes of substantial comfort and, with their hoists for merchandise on the top floor, places of business. The Dutch also became pioneers of medicine. They thus created a wealthy civilization which would be the setting of the splendid genius of Rembrandt and be commemorated by the calm interiors of Pieter de Hooch and Vermeer. And they knew how to protect themselves by building ships of the line powerful enough and with sufficient range in 1609 to defeat the Spaniards off Gibraltar. They also designed the best gardens and made the best maps in the world, and introduced improved methods of agriculture, of stock breeding and of draining polders and reclaiming land from the sea, as well as of making the scientific instruments without which even rudimentary experimental science would have been impossible.

So out of a very small area bounded by the inhospitable North Sea and with a raw and damp climate, the Dutch, who spoke a dialect of German which sounded comic to the Germans themselves, as Flemish, an even broader dialect, was despised by the Dutch, and who were most of them descended from peasants and fishermen, created a civilization of wealthy patrician merchants and redoubtable seamen, house-proud and methodical; liable to provincial jealousies and to doctrinal strife, but united in the resistance against an unfriendly environment and an encroaching sea, and hardened in a terrible conflict with the might of Spain.

IV

The other major Protestant maritime and colonial power in the north-west also emerged tempered by conflict with the Spaniards. Modern research on the reign of Elizabeth has shown how divided the English had been and how relatively weak the central government continued to be, resting as it did much more on persuasion than on force, with no standing army and inadequate revenues, and contending with a tradition, still strong in the largely Catholic north, of conspiracy and treason. Henry VIII had shown little foresight in squandering the wealth of the confiscated monastic and church lands on campaigns on the continent, and had lost the chance of founding a really rich monarchy. On the other hand, in a manageable area with well defined frontiers, central administration had long been more effective than in the larger states of the continent, and Elizabeth had inherited and developed the Tudor practice of collaboration between the Crown and Parliament, as well as between the Conciliar government and the nobility and wealthier gentry who controlled the counties. Further, the cloth industry, on which the country had so long depended for its export trade, had proved able to adapt itself to changing times: with the decline of exports to the Low Countries, trade had been developed with the Levant and already in the reign of Edward VI with Muscovy and even Persia. The English, indeed, founded their East India Company in 1600, before the Dutch, and since the Dutch kept them out of Indonesia, they concentrated on India, in the long run a better investment. The English had also become the greatest exporters of coal, and begun to exploit iron deposits and make their own cannon, instead of, like Henry VIII, having to buy them abroad. By the 'seventies root crops were being cultivated for winter keep for the animals, and the magnates and gentry who had bought the church lands were proving more enterprising farmers and sheep masters than the clergy.

The English were thus developing a more solid basis for expansion than the Dutch, though the Dutch were more systematically exploiting their limited resources. And, like the Dutch, they had long taken to the sea and developed oceanic trade. The fate of the Armada had demonstrated that the English ships, streamlined and heavily gunned, were more than a match for those of the Spaniards and the Portuguese, and capable of operating far from base off the coast of the Iberian peninsula itself; while the resounding success of Drake's voyage round the world (1577–80) had announced that a new and major sea power had arrived on the oceans, capable of a world wide strategy.

Immediately, the effect of the defeat of the Spanish Armada was decisive not only for England, but for the continent. Given impracticable orders, Parma had been distracted from his main purpose of overwhelming the Dutch; the murder of the Duke of Guise in the winter of 1588/9 had marked the failure of the Counter-Reformation and of the pro-Spanish party in France, and although the Spaniards managed to exploit the conflict in Ireland in which the English were bogged down during the 'nineties, the Catholic Irish could never evict the English and Scots settlers.

With an officially Protestant Church, using liturgy and Bible in the vernacular, the English were now, like the Scandinavians, doctrinally turning their backs on the cosmopolitan Latin Church represented by the Counter-Reformation. On the other hand, they now assimilated Renaissance culture in a far more creative way, in the most brilliant version achieved by any of the Northern peoples. The contrast between the inept verses of most early or even middle Tudor writers and the superb poetic dramas of Marlowe and Shakespeare is profound. In lyric poetry and in prose the change is just as striking, as the clumsy if pungent English of the time of Henry VIII gives place to the splendid cadences of late Elizabethan and Jacobean writers; as of Raleigh, and Francis Bacon, Viscount of St. Albans, who could express elaborate ideas in a way far beyond the capacity of Sir Thomas More or Skelton. It was an extraordinary flare up, too well known to dwell upon; decisive for the whole English speaking world, then about to come into existence overseas. Moreover with the accession of James VI & I (1603–25), the dynastic union of England and Scotland removed a major weakness of the island towards the continent, and although the new Stuart dynasty proved incapable of managing its English subjects by working in harmony with the politically conscious and politically dominant classes in the realm, Court patronage and the cultural effervescence continued, and the first major colonization of North America was launched.

But the Scots had taken to Calvinism with spontaneous fervour; here the "Reformation" had not been imposed as had Calvinism even in Holland, but fought for with massive popular support. The dynastic union under an Anglican King thus became the immediate cause of the breakdown of the old English Conciliar government of Charles I (1625–49), when the monarch tried to impose Anglican ritual on his Scots subjects. Moreover, the Scots intervened decisively in the subsequent First English Civil War (1642–45) and combined with the English rebels to impose a short-lived Presbyterian Calvinist Church on England. The settlement of Scots Presbyterians in Northern Ireland had also contributed to the outbreak of the Civil Wars, since it provoked a rising among the Catholic Irish which further stretched the resources of the English Crown and set off anti-Catholic and so anti-Court hysteria in England. The English did not, therefore, entirely avoid the blight of "religious" warfare that convulsed the continent, for it was set off in Great Britain by the attempt of the inefficient Caroline government to impose Anglican ritual on the Scots.

In the event, the Church of England, for which Charles I and Laud had both died, was re-established, and though Laudian ritualism was played down, and a strong "Non-Conformist" Dissenting movement continued, the important old Erasmian tradition survived. The Protestantism which had taken over all the north from Lutheran Sweden, Denmark and northern Germany to the Calvinist United Provinces, and was still strong among the Calvinist Huguenots in France, took on a more conservative form in England, though not in Scotland. But only the native Irish, though subjected to an Anglican Church establishment, remained, alone among the northern peoples, ineradicably Catholic under the alien domination.

This major transformation of Northern Christianity, mainly among the North German and Scandinavian peoples most recently converted by the Mediterranean Catholic Church, made early modern Europe differ from Medieval times. It also broke the united front of dogma and interest which had long resisted the most powerful intellectual movement of the seventeenth century; and this was not, for all the fanatical strife of Catholics and Calvinists, religious, but practical, scientific and sometimes even humane. Since the settlement of North America was now being made mainly from the Protestant North, the change of outlook, religious and secular, would prove extremely important for the civilization of the New World.

XXXI

The Recovery of France and the Peace of Westphalia

When Henri IV restored the position of the French monarchy after the wars of religion, he had inherited a potentially powerful realm: under Louis XI the great regions had been brought systematically under control and even the Bretons included; then François I had been strong enough to challenge the Habsburgs for the hegemony of Europe, and although the French conquests in Italy had proved ephemeral, the eastern frontier of France had been better secured. The wars of religion, exploited by great regional magnates—Montmorencys in the west and Normandy, Guises in the east, Bourbons in the south-west—had threatened the fabric of the realm, but Henri IV, after a severe military and diplomatic struggle, had now emerged as a saviour of society and refounded a monarchy claiming sovereign Divine Right.

His son, Louis XIII (1614-43), though of limited abilities and deviant inclinations, grew to realize the danger of irresponsible favourites and factious nobles, and had enough sense of the interest of the realm to support a man he disliked. He gave supreme power to Armand-Jean du Plessis, Cardinal Duc de Richelieu (1585-1642), one of the main architects of the great state, now the prevalent form of European polity. The youngest son of François du Plessis de Richelieu and grandson of a military-minded favourite of Henri III and his aristocratic wife, Richelieu was brought up in comparative poverty, then sent to Paris to be trained at an aristocratic military academy. Henri IV in 1606 made him Bishop of Luçon, one of the poorest bishoprics, and in the following year he was consecrated by the Pope in Rome. He then wisely retired from Court to administer his diocese with alarming efficiency, and then sat in the Estates General of 1614 as a representative of the clergy. The assassination of Henri IV was his opportunity, for all was in confusion; and having won the confidence of Regent Marie de Medici and of her favourite the Maréchal D'Ancre, by 1616 he was a Secretary of State and Ambassador to Spain. He survived the ups and downs of Court intrigue as one of her advisers and in 1621 helped to reconcile her with Louis XIII. Though the Queen Regent turned against him, by 1624 he was the Chief Minister on the King's Council and, despite successive attempts to destroy him, of which the most dangerous failed in 1630 on the "Day of Dupes", after which he was created *Duc et Pair* de France, he remained in supreme power as Louis XIII's principal minister for eighteen years until his death. He died a multi-millionaire, having built the Palais Cardinal in Paris and vastly enlarged and embellished his family mansion and other estates.

As a young bishop he had systematically and coolly prepared himself for power, and even written a Machiavellian memorandum *Instructions to Myself to Bring Me to Court*, a handbook of sound advice, such as "leaving those whom one despises in ignorance of the real feelings they inspire", swallowing insults "in order the better later to avenge them", and "not allowing one's eyes to wander when someone speaks".[1] A great man of action, Richelieu, created a Cardinal in 1622, believed in the God-given sanctity of government, which reflected both God's purpose and the light of Reason. A good Frenchman, he believed in logic: "man being created reasonable, reason ought to be the guide to all his actions, since otherwise he would act against his nature and consequently against Him who is the Author of it." He even states in his *Political Will and Testament*, which, if perhaps not by his own hand, expresses his beliefs, that "it is impossible for a people not to love a Prince when they are sensible that reason is the guide of all his actions."

Armed with these large, lucid and logical assumptions, Richelieu determined to secure the foundations of an "absolute" Monarchy, the apex of a hierarchy of Church, Nobility and Third Estate, with the common people kept under entire control by "just laws" backed by a standing army. A state so organized need fear no attack and could carry war into the enemy country. So, building on the now accepted tradition of paid standing forces of the crown which had originated from the final years of the Hundred Years War, the *Cardinal Duc* achieved a formidable, if relatively superficial, concentration of the power of government against provincial and aristocratic divisiveness: he vastly increased the army, paid for by increased taxation raised by the *taille* and *gabelle*; he also built a great fleet, and he mobilized the clergy to support the claims of the monarch to arbitrary power by Divine Right and to preach "passive obedience". He crushed the Huguenots after the siege and capture of La Rochelle, forcing them to submit to the Peace of Alais in 1629. He made the Royal Council the supreme instrument of executive power and discarded the rival claims of the *Parlement de Paris*; as a Frenchman, aware of their importance, he also mobilized writers and men of learning, he stabilized the French language by founding the *Académie Française* in 1635, and increased the endowment and amenities of the Sorbonne, where he built a splendid church. Moreover, he was aware of oceanic and colonial horizons and encouraged French enterprise in North America and the Caribbean. The factious and belligerent nobility were won over to support the crown by the vast patronage of which the monarch disposed. Their duelling was forcibly discouraged, while a large class of office holders was created, in whose interest it was that an ordered and centralized regime should continue. The whole tone of French civilization had been aristocratic and military since Carolingian and Crusading

[1] Auguste Bailly. *The Cardinal Dictator, a Portrait of Richelieu.* Trans. H. Miles. London, 1936. p. 49.

times, while the grandeur and prestige of the nobility and the Church kept the vast majority of poverty stricken peasants cowed and, save for periodic revolts, docile. The system was in fact inefficient, precarious and corrupt, and the wealth and grandeur of the monarch and the Court existed above a realm where the medieval traditions of aristocratic and civic independence had been deliberately undermined but not crushed, where taxation was concentrated on those who could least afford to pay it and where famine and epidemics among the peasantry were taken for granted. There was a chronic shortage of capital for productive investment, and the French, though encouraged and sometimes subsidized by government, could make little headway against the more effective private enterprise of the Dutch and the English.

But the greatest handicap on the absolute monarchy in France was the necessarily belligerent and expensive foreign policy which went along with Richelieu's internal consolidation. Since the conflict between the Valois kings and the Habsburgs for Italy had shifted in the mid-sixteenth century north of the Alps, the French needed to control the strategic fortresses of Metz, Toul and Verdun and, most urgently, to strengthen their north-eastern frontier with the Spanish Netherlands. They wanted to be poised to strike into Germany, and although their wars of religion had paralysed any forward policy abroad and given opportunities for Spanish Habsburg interference in France, once the monarchy had reasserted itself, the French looked eastwards to undermine the Austrian Habsburg's power in the Germanies and southwards across the Alps and Pyrenees to neutralize the Spanish Habsburgs, first by diplomacy and then by war.

Richelieu's temperament and ambitions were well attuned to this forward policy; and he had already profited by the dynastic marriage of the fourteen-year-old Louis XIII to the Infanta Anna, daughter of Philip III of Spain, for he had become the young Queen's almoner, and ingratiated himself with Louis' sister Elizabeth, who had married the Infante Don Felipe of Spain. Having secured at least a temporary truce on the Pyrenean frontier, Richelieu proceeded in his own words to "exalt the name of the Majesty of France to its due place among foreign powers".

The Valtellina which leads up from Lake Como to central Switzerland, and so gives access to the valley of the Inn, was the most important strategic passage both for the armies of the Spanish Habsburgs and those of the Habsburgs of the Empire. Now that the Spaniards controlled Milan, in 1620, with the consent of Pope Gregory XV, they had seized the occasion of religious strife of Protestants and Catholics in the Grisons Canton of Switzerland to occupy the strategic Valtellina, ostensibly to protect the Catholics there from the Protestant Swiss.

Here was a crisis of European scope, and Richelieu soon showed that he was more of a Frenchman than a prince of the Catholic Church; in 1624 he ordered the French Ambassador to the Grisons to recruit and pay a large Swiss army, backed by 3500 French troops and to clear the Papal garrison out of the strategic area. Further discarding ideological differences, Richelieu made an alliance with the Protestant Dutch and agreed to the marriage of Henriette

Marie of France, sister of Louis XIII, to the Anglican Charles I of England.[1] By neutralizing the Valtellina and by an apparent alliance with the two strongest naval powers in the north-west, Richelieu had enhanced the strategic standing of France. Thus this Christian prelate was foremost in organizing resistance against the Austrian and Spanish Habsburgs who, led by the Emperor Ferdinand II, following the outbreak of the Thirty Years War in 1618, were attempting to restore the power of the cosmopolitan Catholic Church in Europe. For Richelieu, a typical early modern statesman, the interests of the French monarchy transcended those of the Counter-Reformation, and national power politics were more important than the unity of Christendom.

II

The wars in the Germanies, misleadingly known as *Der Dreissigjährige Krieg* or "Thirty Years' War (1618–48)", now played into French hands. Even the name of these complex, concurrent and chronologically untidy conflicts is tendentious. It was originally coined by the then Elector of Bavaria when demanding money from his subjects,[2] to emphasize how long and expensive his share in the wars had been; and layers of Protestant and nationalist propaganda have still to be removed for an objective view.

The origins of the struggle, go back into medieval times, for it spread through the final attempt of the Austrian Habsburg rulers of the already diminished Holy Roman Empire to regain control of the Germanies and even of the Baltic, to restore Catholicism, and all that it socially implied, in the areas taken over by the Protestant Princes, and to impose the Counter-Reformation of which the Jesuits had become the inspiration and the great Baroque artists and architects the propagandists.

When in 1619 Ferdinand von Habsburg of Styria (1519–37) succeeded Matthias to the Empire, he already had a war with Bohemia on his hands, and here again the conflict had medieval origins. For the heretical Czechs had coveted Catholic wealth long before Luther, at the time when Huss and his followers had set off an already ancient Czech-German feud, and the Catholic Church had rewarded Henry Plantagenet, Bishop of Winchester, with a Cardinal's hat for organizing a failed crusade against them. Since the time of Huss and Žiška the Czechs had remained sullenly acquiescent under German Catholic rule, and a *Letter of Majesty* of Rudolf II in 1609, granting them a larger toleration, had not assuaged their resentment. Bohemia had then become a bastion of Calvinism, more intransigent than the Lutheran states.

[1]The conclusion of this match by Buckingham, Charles I's favourite, who arrived in Paris with fantastic pomp, gave rise to a scandal that much delighted the Parisians. Louis XIII's queen, the Infanta Anna of Spain, understandably dissatisfied with her husband, encouraged the advances of the enterprising ambassador, who attempted her virtue in a garden, and even, under the guise of apology, access to her bedroom. Here was a scandal that the King, and Richelieu, could hardly ignore and they purged the Queen's household, the Cardinal thus earning her hatred.
[2]See S. H. Steinberg. *The Thirty Years' War*. London, 1966.

So when in 1618 the Czech Calvinist nobles, in protest against an imperial decree suppressing their constitutionally legitimate Diets, flung the Catholic envoys from a window of the Hradschin Castle at Prague, they expressed a furious Czech nationalism as well as religious fervour; and when Frederick V, the Elector Palatine of the Rhine, son-in-law of James I of England by his marriage to the Princess Elizabeth, was rash enough to accept the Bohemian throne and try to oust Ferdinand, the first phase of the Thirty Years' War had begun. By 1620 at the Battle of the White Hill near Prague, Frederick the "Winter King" had been routed; and along with his queen, who had written that she would rather eat *Sauerkraut* as the wife of a king than dine off gold plate as an Electress, had been driven from the country. The Czechs were handed over to German officials and Catholic clergy, their education pervaded by Jesuits and their economy subordinated to Vienna.

Not only was the strategic bastion of Bohemia itself now commanded by the Empire; Ferdinand II also determined to drive the Calvinist influence out of the Elector Frederick's own strategically important Palatinate, and transferred it to Prince Maximilian of Bavaria, of a Catholic branch of the Wittelsbachs. This combined purpose of reimposing Catholicism and regaining political, economic and strategic control is typical of the entire war, which was far from being the strife of fanatical ideologists once depicted, but a slow laborious struggle to take over the vast apparatus and deep-rooted social and economic influence of the Catholic Church and adapt them to new demands.

The war now entered a second and wider phase, dominated by professional *condottieri* commanding private armies much larger than those of their prototypes in Italy. The Emperor's double strategic success had alerted the Protestant power of Kristian IV of Denmark, who counted on English subsidies never in fact paid, and whose armies penetrated as far as Thuringia; so Ferdinand had to employ the veteran mercenary captain, the Graf von Tilly[1] to defeat him at Lutter, an Imperialist success confirmed when Bethlen Gabor of Transylvania failed in a coordinated attack. Ferdinand thought even more highly of another and more dangerous mercenary captain whom he had already employed in 1617 for a campaign against the Venetians, and it was to Albrecht von Wallenstein,[2] already Governor of Bohemia since 1621, a far more formidable and incalculable professional than Tilly, to whom he confided the campaign against Kristian IV which followed up Tilly's victory. Wallenstein

[1]Originally a Brabantine mercenary named Tserclaes, Johan von Tilly had served in the Netherlands under Farnese, and had already fought for the Emperor Rudolf II against the Turks. As commander of the Bavarian army and Imperial troops, he had won Ferdinand II's confidence by defeating the Elector Palatine at the battle of the White Hill at the beginning of the war, and then capturing the Palatinate.

[2]Originally named Valdstein, he was the son of a minor Czech Protestant squire. Born in 1583, he had visited Italy, turned Catholic, and, in spite of his unprepossessing appearance, married a widow with vast estates in Moravia. He had then been able to raise his own mercenary army for Ferdinand's campaign against Venice. As Governor of Bohemia he had already bought up huge Protestant-owned estates on highly favourable terms; by 1623 he had been created a Prince of the Holy Roman Empire, and by 1624 he was created Duke of Friedland. For the best biography see Golo Mann: *Wallenstein, his Life Narrated*. Trans. C. Kessler. London, 1976.

conquered all continental Denmark, and Ferdinand had to reward him with a great estate at Sagan in Silesia and the hereditary Duchy of Mecklenburg.

The price of Ferdinand's victories had thus been heavy; there were now two over-mighty subjects in the Empire; Tilly, an old-fashioned character with comparatively limited objectives, and Wallenstein, a new kind of tycoon of mercenary warfare who made it pay, and who possessed enormous ambitions. These had now become Baltic and commercial, and he was attempting to share the monopoly of the Baltic trade with Gustav II Adolf of Sweden.

Ferdinand was thus in a dilemma; Wallenstein was far his best commander, with the best army; but Ferdinand's own heir (afterwards Ferdinand III) was determined to get rid of him, and, fearing his ambitions, the major princes of the Empire demanded that he be dismissed.

It was at this crisis for the Emperor that the third phase of the war began which involved the intervention first of Sweden, then of France. In 1629 the Imperial armies had laid siege to the strategically important archiepiscopal and now Lutheran city of Magdeburg on the Elbe, which Ferdinand had assigned to the Archduke Leopold, his second son. Wallenstein having failed to take it, Tilly took over the attack; but the siege dragged on. Already alarmed at the success of Wallenstein against Denmark, the Swedes watched the struggle with growing concern.

Their young King Gustav II Adolf, unlike Kristian IV, was a military genius. Blooded in battle since boyhood against Muscovites, Danes and Poles, he had devised new tactics which, like Napoleon's, restored mobility to war. His cavalry, instead of trotting up to the enemy in column, firing, wheeling about and retreating to reload, charged full tilt at the enemy; and, what was more, the Swedes had mobile light artillery and their infantry had superior fire power. They prided themselves on being descended from the Goths, with the predatory dash of the old Vikings of Kievan Russia, and their nobles were no longer rustic squires but cosmopolitan warriors and diplomats. Their armies moreover were drawn from a sturdy and relatively free peasantry.

Under a commander of genius, who was backed by the far seeing statesman, Axel Oxenstierna, with whom he had collaborated since his accession and before it, the Swedes were poised for great raids into the Germanies with unlimited objectives. And where the Vikings had been heathen, Gustav II Adolf and his armies could proclaim and believe themselves the champions of Protestant Christianity against the Catholic Counter-Reformation, which had already reached out through the claims of the Catholic Sigismund III Vasa of Poland against their own shores. Not without reason Gustav Adolf himself feared the success of the Imperial Catholic armies under Wallenstein, which after the defeat of Kristian IV at Lutter, had overrun Schleswig-Holstein. "As one wave follows another," he told the Swedish Diet in 1627, "so the Popish League comes closer to us ... if they are not powerfully resisted in good time."[1] The Polish Sigismund III was now accused by the Swedish King of "open conspiracy to deprive us of all trade and navigation, and (worst of all) of the sovereign rights we enjoy in the Baltic".

[1]Quoted by Michael Roberts in *Gustavus Adolphus and the Rise of Sweden*. London, 1973.

In 1628 Wallenstein's Imperialist army had besieged the important town of Stralsund opposite the island of Rügen on the Eastern Baltic, which was saved only by a tardy expedition by the Danes. Better placed to provide and provision a garrison, by 1630 the Swedes had taken over the fortified city and harbour, and this commitment, essential to counteract any German or Polish invasion of Sweden, was new: it proved the first springboard for an attack on the Germanies. Further, Richelieu had now brought pressure on the Poles to make the Truce of Regensburg with Sweden, thus releasing Gustav Adolph from war with Sigismund III.

So, in June 1630, Gustav Adolf, at Peenemünde, like William the Conqueror near Hastings, fell on his knees on the beach and, unlike William, prayed to a Protestant God, while "in good heart", as military historians put it, his soldiers came ashore. Meanwhile the Imperial army's siege of Magdeburg had continued, and Gustav Adolf, concerned primarily to consolidate his bridgehead against a major attack by Tilly, reinforced the city by a Swedish garrison.

With the Swedes now so far committed, Richelieu now saw his opportunity; and early 1631 the French signed the Treaty of Bärwalde whereby they agreed to subsidize a major Swedish attack into Germany. One plague was to be let loose there to drive out another and neutralize the Habsurg power. And when Tilly's subordinate, Pappenheim, at last succeeded in storming Magdeburg, sacked and burned most of the town and massacred most of the inhabitants, the atrocity rallied Protestant feeling against the Catholics and committed the Swedes to a war of revenge.

Ferdinand II now seemed more vulnerable: he had been compelled to dismiss Wallenstein, the Elector of Saxony had joined the Swedes, and many German princes, if not openly hostile, were manoeuvring, following medieval precedent, to undermine the Imperial power. Many of the Emperor's troops were in North Italy, campaigning with Spanish help to prevent a French Duke obtaining Mantua. Moreover, the German Protestants had rejected a Swedish protectorate which could have stabilized North Germany, and in September 1631 Gustav Adolf, advancing far into the south, routed an army under Tilly at Breitanfeld near Leipzig in Saxony. He then advanced on Prague, captured Mainz and Wurms and the Rhenish Palatinate, and, pursuing Tilly to the Lech near Augsburg, destroyed his last reserve and hunted him to his death near Ingoldstadt. The Emperor now decided that Wallenstein was indispensable and recalled him to supreme command. The Swedes were manoeuvred out of Bavaria back to Saxony, and in November 1632 at Lützen, west of Leipzig, Gustav Adolf, charging at the head of his Småland cavalry, was cut off, pistolled through the back and, as he lay face downwards, shot through the head.

So ended the brief spectacular incursion of Gustav Adolf into the heart of the Germanies, but not the Swedish grip on the north and the Baltic. Lützen, despite the King's death, had been a Swedish victory, which by 1633 led to the Protestant League of Heilbronn, and by eliminating Gustav Adolf, Wallenstein eliminated himself. No longer indispensable, and vehemently suspected of coveting the crown of his native Bohemia, this multi-millionaire who had all but won the war for the Emperor, and was now in flight towards the Swedes, was murdered in 1634 .by order of Ferdinand II. His own mercenaries had gladly obeyed the imperial command: an Irish butler, always ready for an affray, roused him in his bedroom, an Irish officer kept the door, and an English captain ran him through with a halberd, all the islanders thus living up to Central European standards of political crime.

Deprived of their king, the Swedes were now defeated by the Emperor's son Ferdinand at Nordlingen, between Stuttgart and the Danube, and the Lutheran Elector of Saxony went over to the emperor. Ferdinand II was thus able to retrieve his position. But by the Peace of Prague in 1635, he had to grant freedom of worship to the German Protestants and allow them to keep the estates of the Catholic Church for fifty years. This compromise held until the emperor's own death in 1637, when he was succeeded by the abler and more diplomatic Ferdinand III (1637–57).

After this ideological stalemate, the war might have ended; in fact it continued as a power struggle fomented by the French, determined to keep the Germans in confusion, and by the mercenary commanders and armies who were living off it. Indeed, the conflict extended; for in 1635 the long-expected war broke out between France and Spain, itself still at war with the Dutch, and by the Treaty of Compiègne in the same year a formal alliance was concluded between France and Sweden, to which French subsidies were now more essential since the war no longer paid for itself.

The results of this fourth, final, and dismal phase of the war were that the Germanies fell into further political disintegration, and Spain lapsed into worse political, social and economic decline, while the Swedes, exhausted by the expense and casualties of the campaigns and now ruled by their young queen Christina (1644–54), who was eccentric enough to dislike war, were encumbered by many profitless commitments in Germany.

In the Empire itself, following the comparative failure of the Catholic Counter-Reformation, North Germany, even where divided into many small states, remained mainly Lutheran, and the old principle of *cujus regio, ejus religio* was reaffirmed.

In fact this disunity, so much deplored by German nineteenth-century historians, had many cultural advantages for the Germans and obvious advantages for the rest of Europe. The devastations of the Thirty Years War have also been grossly exaggerated: Fisher declares, for example, that it created "an abysm of barbarism and misery ... It is indeed impossible to exaggerate the miseries which the helpless peasants of the German empire were compelled to endure in these iron times. There was marauding, there was starvation, there was even *cannibalism* ... moral restraints broke down and ceded to *wild bursts of profligacy*."[1] It was and is repeatedly stated that the population of Germany, then an indefinite area for which statistics are not available, was reduced by half.[2]

In fact, like the miniature Wars of the Roses in England, the conflict has

---

[1] H. A. L. Fisher. *A History of Europe. op. cit.* p. 611 (present author's italics).
[2] Even that sober and homespun historian David Ogg described the late seventeenth-century Germans as "a sparse population of survivors trying to cultivate a desert". *Louis XIV.* London, 1933. p. 52.

been over-dramatized. The armies, like those of the English Civil Wars, were not large, ranging from about 18,000 to 12,000 men, and the areas over which they marched and counter-marched were so extensive that, with the best will in the world, they cannot have committed really thorough devastation. Doubtless in the areas fought over, refugees fled before marauders and atrocities were committed; but, with the usual endurance of peasantry, the rural population carried on, while the inflation at the beginning of war which went along with the decline of some of the famous old cities proved, as inflations often do, the opportunity for new men, and the price-rise in foodstuffs benefited the larger landowners and farmers. Further, logistics were far too inefficient for long sustained campaigns, the supposed famines were inflicted only on relatively small areas, and the only authenticated case of cannibalism occurred among the garrison during the siege of Breisach.[1]

Indeed, from the mid-seventeenth century onwards, the accounts of the war have been distorted by propaganda, for Axel Oxenstierna, that shrewd Swede, early persuaded a Pomeranian called P. C. Bogislav to write a history slanted against the Catholic Emperor, and appointed the famous Pufendorf, the Saxon professor of Law at Heidelberg, to a chair at Lund, whence he weighed in heavily on the Swedish side. Further, the Protestant "Great Elector" Frederick William (1640–88) of Brandenburg, who first set the Hohenzollerns on the road to greatness, deliberately had the conflict written up as a struggle of "true German" Protestants against "alien" and Catholic Austrians. The contemporary evidence of Grimmelhausen's autobiographical picaresque novel *Der Abenteuerliche Simplicissimus* (1669),[2] with its vivid and coarse observation of the horrors of the war observed at first hand, early provided a further lurid picture; in due course, eagerly assimilated by Romantic German historians. Above all, by the famous dramatist Schiller, whose *History of the Thirty Years' War* (1791) and *Wallenstein* (1799) had immense impact. Then the Prussian social historian Freytag's widely popular *Pictures of the German Past* attributed the atrocities to invading foreigners, among whom Austrians were included, and further stereotyped the Germans as victims of a uniquely ghastly experience, unfairly disabled from becoming a great power. This point of view was further propagated by Treitschke. In fact the statistics available do not support it, nor does commonsense based on the experience of greater modern wars.

[1]See R. Ergang. *The Myth of the All Destructive Fury of the Thirty Years' War*. Pocono Pines, Pa. 1956.
[2]Translated as *The Life of the Adventurous Simplicissimus* by H. Weissonhorn and L. MacDonald, 1964).
    Jakob Christopher von Grimmelhausen (c. 1621–1676) was born the son of a Lutheran innkeeper at Gelhausen near Hanau, and early orphaned in the sack of his birthplace. He was then kidnapped by Croat mercenaries but rose to become secretary on the Staff of the Commandant of Offenburg in the Imperial army. After the war he earned a living as steward of the Schauenburg estates, then reverted to his father's calling of innkeeper, at Gaisbach. He had by now long turned Catholic and served as an administrator of the estates of the Bishop of Strasbourg. Turned out of this appointment by further upheavals, he died at Reuchen, having somehow managed to turn his experiences into a masterpiece.

It is astounding what humanity can endure, and some Germans were then in fact happily adapting Italian styles of music (as in the compositions of Schütz, who flourished until 1672, and of his pupil Rosenmüller (d. 1684)); the former translating foreign books and writing drama and poetry, and both destined to influence Bach. Even the Habsburgs had time, in their own lands and cities, to commission Italian architects to build baroque palaces and churches; and a wealth of sixteenth- and seventeenth-century architecture has survived in the regions even of supposed devastation by the intermittent campaigns.

Obviously, if thousands of Germans, Czechs, Swedes and Frenchmen, some inspired by religious fanaticism or plain blood lust, and hordes of polyglot mercenaries avid for loot, were even intermittently let loose for thirty years in seventeenth-century conditions, memorable atrocities were committed; but it does not follow, considering the limited weapons of mass destruction available, that large areas of Germany were reduced to "deserts" inhabited by "profligate" cannibals. Ghastly as the wars were, far too many historians have "failed to recognize the distinct perspective from which the contemporary accounts were written".[1]

III

In 1645–48 a Congress was convened at Münster in Westphalia, once notorious for the regime of Jan of Leyden, to end the Thirty Years' War in Central Europe. It marked an agreement to live and let live; the fading out of the historic Catholic idea of a united Christendom imposed by a *pax Hispanica* or by a Holy Roman Emperor based on Vienna, in face of the early modern facts of a balance of power between sovereign states, whose religion, no longer under the political control of the cosmopolitan authority of Rome, was decided by their own governments. The dynastic great state had superseded Papacy and Empire as the final source of power; the congress was the first to reflect the new notion of an *International* Law between sovereign states, as defined by Grotius in his *De Jure Belli ac Pacis* (1625), and the first at which the official language was French, not Latin.

The change was appropriate; the French, as Richelieu had planned, had profited most from the war. The Treaty of Münster or Peace of Westphalia decided that there would be no German *Reich* outside Austrian Habsburg territories for nearly two and a quarter centuries: that the Hohenzollern Elector of Brandenburg obtained large tracts of Pomerania and the reversion of the important archbishopric of Magdeburg; that the authority of the princes of the Empire, for which they had fought since the days of Barbarossa and Frederick II, was formally reasserted against the Emperor, and that the sovereignty of the Diet of the Empire was reaffirmed, while toleration of religion was established in all but the Catholic domains of the Habsburgs themselves.

[1]Steinberg. *op. cit.* p. 92.

With Germany pacified, the foreign powers took their spoils: Sweden obtained part of Pomerania and took Stettin, Bremen and Werden and an immense indemnity. But the greatest gainer from the Peace was France. In Lorraine, Metz, Toul and Verdun now became French possessions and in Alsace the French obtained strategically important Breisach on the Upper Rhine and much other territory. They were thus armed with formal rights for diplomatic and military offensives against Württemburg and Bavaria. Belatedly, also, the United Provinces of the Dutch Republic, following a separate peace with the Empire, now obtained official recognition; the Swiss Confederation, much disliked socially by monarchical aristocratic governments, was also admitted on equal terms as a sovereign power. The essential achievement of the Peace of Westphalia was to accept the *fait accompli* of the sovereign State, and make the best of it.

The Franco-Spanish war dragged on. In 1648 a separate Dutch-Spanish Treaty of Münster was agreed which recognized the fact of the independence of the United Provinces, but it was not until 1659 that the war with France ended with the Treaty of the Pyrenees. It marked the final abandonment of the Imperial aspirations of Spain to impose a *Pax Hispanica,* and it provided for the marriage of Louis XIV to the Infanta Maria Teresa, daughter of Philip IV. The Treaty of the Pyrenees, like the Peace of Westphalia, was a diplomatic victory for France.

IV

When in 1621 Philip IV of Spain had succeeded Philip III, the incompetent regime of the latter's favourite, the Duke of Lerma, had already been superseded and in 1619 an attempt had been made at better administration; but Philip IV, who succeeded to the throne at sixteen, was entirely under the influence of the Andalusian adventurer Gaspar de Guzman, Conde d'Olivares, by 1625 Duque de Sanlucar and so the "Conde-Duque" who, as a *privado* or political favourite, in effect ruled Spain until 1643. Able, forceful, arrogant and unstable, Olivares was not as incapable as Buckingham in England or anything like as formidable as Richelieu in France: but he was determined on the impossible task of both reforming the administration at home and continuing a high Imperial policy abroad. In the Netherlands he had no choice; for the truce concluded in 1609, never well observed, ran out in 1621, and here the Spaniards inherited an impracticable commitment and a wasting war which it paid the Dutch to continue. As Olivares wrote to Philip IV, "Kings cannot achieve heroic actions without money,"[1] and Spain was once more drifting to bankruptcy. The obvious remedy was to spread the burden of armaments from Castile, which no longer obtained the large income in silver from the New World it had disposed of under Philip II, to the other provinces of Spain; a project presented as a "Union of Arms" and officially inaugurated in 1626. In

[1]Cited in Elliott. *op. cit.* p. 322.

the following year the Crown again repudiated its debts, hoping by bankruptcy to gain a fresh start, and in 1628 the currency was devalued by half; then in the next year the Dutch caught the treasure fleet and plundered its entire cargo of American silver, thus creating an immediate shortage of cash.

The Spaniards, whose greatest writer, Cervantes (1547–1616), had published the first part of *Don Quixote de la Mancha* in 1605, remained obstinately convinced that they were a great imperial power; in 1628–31 they committed more men and money to North Italy to keep the French out of Mantua—a move which worsened the relations of Spain and France. In a vain attempt to centralize the administration, the *Conde-Duque* organized an executive Junta to replace the old Council of State, increased the taxes, and, like the government of Charles I, exacted obsolete feudal dues from the aristocracy. But the Catalans, always resentful of the domination of Castile, refused any subsidy; and, when in 1635 the French invaded their territory, they refused to defend it. The Catalans hated the Madrileños more than they did the French: in 1640 they broke into rebellion and murdered their Viceroy.

On the other side of the peninsula, the demands of war had brought the long-standing discontent of the Portuguese since the union of 1580 with Spain to a climax; a situation exploited, like the Catalan revolt, by Richelieu. In December 1640 they assassinated the principal Spanish official in Lisbon and politely escorted the Infanta Margarita, the King's sister sent there as governor, to the frontier.[1]

The two richest provinces of the Iberian peninsula had broken away. The war in the Netherlands and the Rhineland had meanwhile been going from bad to worse: in 1637 the Dutch had recaptured Breda; the fall of Breisach in the following year cut the route from Milan to the Spanish Netherlands, and in 1639 van Tromp, with the connivance of the English, routed a Spanish fleet at the battle of the Downs. Worse still, in 1640 the large Spanish-Portuguese armada sent to recapture Brazil from the Dutch was defeated off Pernambuco and the command of the western South Atlantic and the Caribbean lost. Then, in May 1643, the famous Spanish infantry were defeated at Rocroi on the Flemish frontier by the French, and in the same year the *Conde-Duque* was dismissed and rusticated to his estates, to die two years later after a career of grandiose failure. Such were the consequences for Spain of participating in the last phase of the "Thirty Years' War".

V

If the Counter-Reformation had failed in the now impracticable aim of reuniting Christendom under Church and Empire at the price of a *Pax Hispanica*, it had encouraged superb art, at its climax in painting in the work of Rubens and Velásquez.

[1] The determined fair-haired Princess in a dress of pink and silver, depicted by Velásquez, now in the Prado.

Peter Paul Rubens (1577-1640) had a fantastically successful and versatile career, both as painter and diplomat. An entirely cosmopolitan figure, fluent in six languages, at a time when royal courts were centres of all aspects of culture as well as of politics, he was ennobled by Philip IV of Spain and knighted by Charles I of England.[1] Such was his genius that he assimilated and reinterpreted a European range of influences; the Flemish Mannerism in which he was first trained, the style of the High Renaissance masters, Leonardo, Raphael and Michelangelo, the neo-pagan chiaroscuro of Caravaggio, the brilliance of Tintoretto and Caracci, and the colour and swirl of Titian. All this he summed up and transmuted into his own sumptuous, if occasionally turgid, Flemish idiom, with its plump beauties and cupids and its liberating rush of paint and splendour of colour. Far from being the last painter of a Silver Age Northern Renaissance, his influence inspired later masters of subject pictures, Catholic or pagan, as well as painters of portraits and landscape. Watteau and Fragonard would owe much to him, so would Reynolds and Gainsborough.

And in his own time he strove for an Erasmian peace, painting his *Blessings of Peace* and *Horrors of War* to point the moral—writing of his "Peace", that the grief-stricken woman clothed in black, with torn veil, robbed of all her jewels and other ornaments, was "the unfortunate Europe who for so many years has suffered plunders, outrage and misery".[2]

Rubens's near contemporary, Diego Velásquez (1599-1660), was born at Seville, and early obtained the patronage of Philip IV and Olivares at Madrid. By 1627 he was Court painter and gentleman usher to the King, who liked to watch him painting. He was less caught up than Rubens in religious subjects,[3] and, like him, he was influenced by Caravaggio's chiaroscuro and won his first celebrity by depicting a popular and earthy scene, *Los Borrachos,* or *"The Topers"*. Already heavily influenced by Titian, he painted equestrian portraits

---

[1]He was born at Siegen, Westphalia and brought up in Cologne, but was educated in Antwerp in Erasmian humanism. He then took service with Vincenzo I Gonzaga, Duke of Mantua, under whose patronage he went to Rome and saw the great Renaissance masterpieces. Then in 1603 the Duke sent him to Madrid, where he saw the largest available collection of Titians and painted an equestrian portrait of the Duke of Lerma. In 1609 he returned to Antwerp, married Isabella Brandt, quickly won fame for his paintings in the splendid Jesuit churches then being built, won the friendship of the "archdukes" Albrecht and Isabella, and continued as adviser to Isabella and to the Cardinal Infante Fernando, who succeeded her in 1635. Rubens' fame had now spread to France; in 1622-4 he painted the nuptials of Maria de Medici and Henry IV in the Luxembourg, and in 1625 met the Duke of Buckingham and the English art collector Gerbier in Paris. Philip IV, anxious for peace with England, then sent him as envoy (1628-30) to Charles I, where he laid the foundation of the peace treaty of 1630 between England and Spain, and painted his picture of the *Blessings of Peace*, the apotheosis of James I, completed in 1634. Though proud of his diplomatic achievements, Rubens that year retired to his Chateau de Siegen, married Hélène Fourment aged sixteen, a real Flemish Venus, and concentrated on landscape painting. His last big commission was to illustrate mythological subjects from Ovid for Philip IV.

[2]Trevor-Roper. *Princes and Artists* p. 156—a study in which an historian illuminates art in relation to politics, and to which this brief account is indebted.

[3]These were best depicted by Francisco de Zurbarán (1598-1664), another native of Seville, who brought Spanish realism to bear on the textures and form of the garments of those devoted to religion in a way that anticipates Chardin.

of Philip IV and Olivares. The King sent him twice to Italy where he visited Naples, Rome and Venice, and on his second visit bought pictures by Titian, Tintoretto and Paolo Veronese for his master's collection. He was always a Court painter, appointed Chamberlain to the Palace, and displayed his virtuosity in depicting Court scenes, as in the famous *Las Meninas*, the Maids of Honour, which shows the King and Queen reflected in a mirror at the back. His Spanish realism and gravity forbade him the Flemish exuberance of Rubens, and his portraits, as in that of Pope Innocent X, show a piercing insight into character. Many will prefer his cooler ideal of beauty to that depicted by Rubens, as with luminous colour and masterly design he created a tradition that would come to another climax in Goya.

BOOK V

THE AGE OF THE OCEANS

XXXII

The Early Modern Mind

The sixteenth and early seventeenth centuries in Europe had seen the rise of great centralized states whose power relationships the Peace of Westphalia had attempted to recognize. While not yet able fully to meet their growing responsibilities, they were better organized than the realms of the later Middle Ages, while the conflicts between them, following the usual pattern of power politics in any age, had been made more virulent by popular religious intolerance. Indeed, at first sight, the age seems one of peculiar violence and persecution, a time of singular cruelty and delusion. Yet in the longer perspective it appears very creative; it is now that the most original contribution of Europeans to world history becomes defined, and in their corner of the world the novel idea takes root that man by systematic experiment may find out the secrets of nature and even improve the human condition.

The rise of a scientific outlook and of applied science in the seventeenth century is more original and important than the re-assessment of the Ancient World at the Renaissance, and proved far more decisive for the whole planet. It is, therefore, worth while to stand back briefly from the course of general history and concentrate on the unspectacular but revolutionary ideas of a few men of genius which in early modern times gradually changed the climate of opinion in Western and Central Europe and, incidentally and indirectly, gave Europeans and their descendants a mastery of the world only now being challenged.

In cosmology, the first great pioneer had come from Poland. In 1543, by English reckoning in the declining years of Henry VIII, Nicholas Kopernik—Copernicus[1]—published his De Revolutionibus Orbium Celestium—"On the

---

[1] He was born in 1473, the son of a well to do merchant at the Hanseatic city of Torun on the Vistula, and on the death of his father, he was adopted by his maternal uncle, Lukas Walzenrode, bishop of Ermelund in the neighbourhood of Königsberg. The bishop sent him to study at Bologna where he learnt Greek and astronomy, and in 1500 he visited Rome. Elected in the following year a Canon of Frauenberg (now Frombork), south-west of Königberg, near the gulf of Dantzig, he was soon sent back to Italy to study medicine and law at Bologna and Ferrrara, and when he settled down in Poland he was a qualified physician. He had long felt dissatisfied with the complicated and inaccurate geocentric astronomy devised by Ptolemy, and, knowing Greek, he had

Revolutions of Celestial Spheres", and it made the staggering assertion that the earth and the planets went round the sun. This heliocentric hypothesis also maintained that the earth was spherical and moving; not, as hitherto almost everywhere believed, the fixed centre of a series of overlapping and probably crystalline spheres. The theory had already been put forward and discussed in Rome with the approval of Pope Clement VII, who was anxious to reform the Gregorian Calendar, as a convenient way of computing the motions of the planets, and Copernicus' Protestant colleague, Rhaticus, had published it as the First Narrative in Germany. Naturally Luther became frantic (the Bible had been contradicted) and had him driven out of Nuremberg. But Copernicus' hypothesis took a long time to sink in: it was so outrageous that few contemporaries could comprehend it. Astronomers, however, had great prestige since they could predict the movements of the planets and make astrological calendars, and the planets, it was well known, determined the fates of mankind. As adjuncts to astrology, astronomers were patronized by Kings.

Copernicus had been a Catholic Canon of Frauenberg; Tycho Brahe (1546–1601) was a layman who came of Danish gentry in Knudstrup in Scania. Copernicus, a man of the Polish Renaissance, had studied in Italian universities; but Brahe studied at Copenhagen, Leipzig and Augsburg, and was greatly valued as an astrologer by Frederick II of Denmark. He was wealthy enough to build his own observatory and laboratory; from Uranienborg he catalogued some of the stars; and when in 1577 a comet appeared which, considering the rising political tensions in Europe, clearly boded no good, Brahe demonstrated that it must have come from outer space. Though he did not accept Copernicus' hypothesis that the Earth moved round the Sun, he accepted that the planets did, and he distinguished between the planetary system and the stars, pointing out that the stars were very much further off.

When young Kristian IV, his head full of war and glory, came to the Danish throne, he got rid of Tycho Brahe and even stopped his pension; so in 1599 the astronomer migrated to Prague where he was given a castle and ample funds by the Emperor Rudolf II, always interested in astrology and astronomy. And here, in his declining years, he was joined before his death in 1601 by a German genius, Johannes Kepler.

Kepler (1571–1630) accepted and developed the full heliocentric hypothesis of Copernicus. He had been born in Württemberg, the son of an army officer and his well-born wife, and educated at Tübingen, where in 1588 he took his degree. He became Professor of Mathematics at Graz and well known as a maker of astrological almanacs prognosticating the movements of the planets and stars. He married a rich wife and was then appointed to succeed Tycho Brahe at Prague, where he made horoscopes for Rudolf II. He also did fundamental research on optics and the refraction of light and his Astronomia Nova was published in 1609. The Emperor Matthias continued to support him, and he died at Ratisbon in 1630.

unearthed the heliocentric theory of the early Ionian philosophers. Only a heliocentric hypothesis, he became convinced, fitted the facts, but he did not fully commit himself until the year of his death at Frombork in 1543. Through no fault of his own his book was given a misleading title, since the whole point of his theory was to abolish the concept of celestial spheres.

Kepler disregarded the mounting chorus of commonsense objections—that the earth was plainly far too heavy to go rushing through space; that if it revolved, everything and everybody would fall off, and the oceans would swamp the land. (Probably few candid readers to-day would deny that they would then have agreed with these arguments.) Like Brahe, Kepler insisted that the planets were separated by enormous distances from the stars, and, since he was not a Catholic, he was not inhibited from speculation by Papal authority or terrified by the Inquisition.

The Italian Galileo Galilei (1546–1642) was born at Catholic Pisa. He was the son of a musician, and studied medicine at Pisa University. He then studied geometry and mathematics, but left through poverty without taking a degree. After lecturing at Florence, he returned to Pisa to lecture on Mathematics, but removed in 1592 to be permanent Professor of that subject at Padua, then under the Venetian Republic. Here he did experimental research on the theory of motion, which anticipated aspects of Newton's discoveries on gravity.

By now he had been converted to Copernicus' hypothesis, and when in 1609 telescopes became available, he had one built at Padua in which the curve of the lenses was corrected and the magnifying power was without precedent. In 1610 Galileo published his *Messenger of the Heavens* (*Siderius Nuncius*), and became Mathematician to the Duke of Tuscany. In the following year he visited Rome, where his eloquence brought him a dangerous popularity. The conservative clergy were alarmed, and in 1616 Cardinal Bellarmine warned Galileo that he must only put forward his doctrine as a mathematical hypothesis, not as something proved. Galileo discreetly retired to a villa near Florence, and defended himself against the Jesuits by his *Loggiatore* which he dedicated to Pope Urban VIII. In 1624 he obtained permission from the Pope to compare the Ptolemaic and Copernican theories, on condition that he vindicated the former, and by 1632 he had written his *Dialogo dei Massimi Sistemi, Dialogue of the Principal Systems*. It achieved immediate fame, but it horrified the Pope and the Jesuits. Galileo was prosecuted for heresy and in 1633 tried in Rome. He was convicted; but imprisonment was commuted to house arrest on his property at Arcetri near Florence, where, nine years later, he died.

Galileo was the first astronomer to possess a fairly good telescope of Dutch make, with a power of 32 magnification, efficient enough to prove the Copernican-Kepler hypothesis, and he was a good enough experimenter to be a pioneer of mechanics and physics as well as astronomy. He discovered that the surface of the moon was rough; that the "Milky Way" was composed of stars and that there were "spots" on the sun, which, he maintained, by showing that the sun rotated, proved that Copernicus was right. Galileo took in the traditionally separated "Heavens" and "Earth" at one view, since the laws of mechanics and physics applied everywhere, and so, to the horror of the Church authorities, destroyed the distinction between the two. He was consciously original and called his most mature and hard-hitting work *A Discourse and Mathematical Demonstration of Two New Sciences* (1634). Galileo had been able to prove his hypothesis by observation; and since the main centre for uncensored printing was now in the Protestant United Provinces, it was impossible for the Papacy or the Jesuits to prevent the dissemination of the results of his work.

Another Italian, a Neapolitan, Giordano Bruno, a Dominican Friar, who in 1584 had published dialogues, Del'infinito Universo e Mondi—(On the Infinite Universe and Worlds), had also fully accepted the new cosmology which had followed from discarding overlapping geocentric spheres, and gone on to speculate boldly on the possible consequences, for he believed that the planets and stars were of similar substance to the earth. But he had been laid by the heels in Venice by the Inquisition[1] and, after seven years of imprisonment, burnt in 1601 as a heretic, as indeed, on many counts, he was—if more of a late medieval eccentric than an exponent of early modern ideas.

It is usual to look back upon these pioneers as liberators, emancipating mankind from millennia of errors and superstitions, and, being ourselves accustomed to having the earth and its inhabitants utterly dwarfed by a universe apparently out of scale with terrestrial life and indifferent to the human condition, to take the situation for granted. But for the men of the early seventeenth century, aware of the current revolution in cosmology, the prospect often appeared appalling, as the geocentric and intelligible vanished into a void, and the Great Chain of Being which had long been thought to hold a Divinely ordained cosmos in due order, apparently disintegrated. The age was, therefore, more pessimistic than a superficial hindsight would expect, and the "Ancients" regarded the "Moderns" as subverters rather than as liberators. It was not until Newton apparently explained the universe in terms of a new sort of God-directed rational order that the confidence which inspired the eighteenth and ninteenth centuries, and even gave rise to the novel belief in "progress", would return.

II

Perhaps because it so intimately concerns mankind, no science has been so perverted by misplaced ingenuity as medicine. There had been brief periods of sensible treatment and empirical observation in Ionian Greece and during the Age of the Antonines, but with the decline of Graeco-Roman civilization and the interdict placed by the Christian Churches upon dissection and their acceptance of an ascetic ideal of life (which often, as in the case of Pope Gregory the Great, led to chronic illness), doctors in Western Christendom

[1]Bruno, wayward and original genius, had long been under suspicion for advocating Pelagian doctrines of free will; in 1576 he had absconded from his Neapolitan monastery and, after further brushes with authority, fetched up in Geneva, where he had become a Calvinist. But he had soon quarrelled with the Calvinist divines, and decamped to France, where, having taken a degree at Toulouse, he obtained the patronage of Henry III of France, as an expert in the Renaissance Ars Reminiscendi, the techniques of mnemonics then so popular. In 1583 he was lecturing in Oxford on the immortality of the soul, writing pamphlets on The Expulsion of the Triumphant Beast, and on Heroic Madness, attacking Aristotelian Physics and dedicated to Sir Philip Sidney.

had become benighted. Only in the Muslim world had standards been maintained, and they had been limited by the available apparatus of research. By the sixteenth century in Western Christendom standards of hygiene were worse than they had been in the thirteenth, since the custom, inherited from antiquity, of taking public steam baths had gone out of fashion, condemned by the Church as immoral. Europeans had become used to sanitation and personal hygiene worse than that of the contemporary East. These conditions continued into the seventeenth and even eighteenth centuries, as among the refugee courtiers of Charles I in Oxford during the Civil War, or among the courtiers of Louis XIV at Versailles.

Yet, as the fashion for objective observation set in, a few physicians began to question the dogmas inherited from Antiquity and garbled during the Middle Ages. Andreas Vesalius of Brussels (1514–1564), court physician to Charles V and Philip II—not that he did them much good—founded the modern science of anatomy and greatly contributed to biology. He graduated from Padua in 1537, and, next year, published his *Six Tables of Anatomy* in Venice. In 1543 his *De Humani Corporis Fabrica* appeared in Basel; it was comprehensive, fully illustrated, and relatively accurate (for he corrected various errors of Galen). Vesalius was a good enough Catholic to make the pilgrimage to Jerusalem and died on the way back. He was a Belgian, but the main centres of medical training and research continued to be Italian until, by the mid-seventeenth century, Leiden in the United Provinces gained greater prestige, in part because of the Dutch skill in making microscopes.

The most sought-after appointments were still at the courts of princes; Ambroise Paré (1510–90) was surgeon to successive French Kings, and served in the French armies, where his methods were less painful than those of his contemporaries who cauterized wounds as a matter of routine. The Swiss eccentric, Theophrastus Bombastus von Hohenheim (1490–1541), who came from Canton Schwyz and, not content with his own names, called himself Paracelsus (Super-Celsus) as the superior of that then well-known Roman physician,[1] developed the role of drugs in medicine. This pioneer of rashly applied chemistry also studied the problems of mining and the disabilities of miners in the Tyrol; and being a great showman and something of a charlatan, prefaced his course of lectures in German at Basel University by burning the works of Galen and even of Avicenna. But he soon quarrelled with the authorities at Basel, and settled in Salzburg, where he died under mysterious circumstances, either through an orgy of drink or through being thrown down a "precipice" by his professional rivals. He was an alchemist with wild Neo-Platonic ideas, but he understood the use of mineral salts in hot baths, and sensed the uses of sulphur and mercury. He is not in the main stream of experimental science, but a hit or miss practitioner, handicapped by alchemical theories, who showed remarkable initiative.[2]

[1] Aulus Cornelius Celsus (floruit c. 30 AD) wrote *De Medicina,* republished in Florence in 1478; it had been the first medical treatise in print and very influential during the High Renaissance.
[2] The term "bombast" derives not from his name but from *Bombax* (Latin for "Silk") which was applied to cotton stuffing for dresses, as in "bombazine".

Henry VIII, in medicine as in so much else, was a great patron, and in 1518 founded the College of Physicians of London with Linacre and John Caius, founder of Caius College, Cambridge, as successive presidents, and in 1540 presented the Barber Surgeons of London with their Charter. And an Englishman, William Harvey of Folkestone (1578-1657), who had studied at Caius College and at Padua, in 1628 published *De Motu Cordis,* having discovered by experiment the circulation of the blood; then in 1651 his *Experiments concerning the Generation of Animals,* which made him a pioneer of embryology.

His genius brought him little reward. "I have heard him say", writes Aubrey, "that after his Booke of the Circulation of the Blood came out, that he fell mightily in Practize and 'twas believed by the vulgar that he was crack-brained; and all the Physicians were against his Opinion, and envyed him; many wrote against him. With much to-do at last, in about 20 or 30 years time, it was received in all the Universities in the World." Aubrey calls him "Inventor (finder out) of the circulation of the blood". He was a royalist, and during the battle of Edgehill "the Prince (of Wales) and Duke of York were committed to his care. He told me that he withdrew with them under a hedge and took out his pocket booke and read; but he had not read very long before a Bullet of a Great Gun grazed on the ground near him, which made him remove his station." Charles I made him Warden of Merton College, Oxford, but "the times suffered him not to receive or injoy any benefit by it". Harvey collected material for a book on insects, but his papers and goods were plundered by the Roundheads and "he often said that of all the losses he sustained, no griefe was so crucifying to him as the losse of these papers, which for love or money he could never retrieve or obtaine ... He was wont to say that Man was but a great Mischievous Baboon."[1]

With the transfer of the main centres of medicine to Leiden, research became more precise, since doctors could investigate freely and publicly without fear of persecution by the Catholic Church—the Calvinists, surprisingly, tolerated their research—and the cult of public cleanliness, already apparent from the paintings of Dutch houses and interiors and which still distinguishes Protestant Holland from Catholic Belgium, gave their remedies a better chance.

It was the Dutch Anton van Leeuwenhoek (1632-1723), himself a manufacturer of single-lens microscopes, who first discovered the red corpuscles in the blood, and in 1677 discovered and described spermatozoa. He was elected a Fellow of the English Royal Society, in whose journals his discoveries were published, and he was the first investigator to depict bacteria. He got rid of the prevalent idea that insects were generated "spontaneously" by corrupt matter, whereby James Harrington, the political theorist, had "grown to have a phancy that his Perspiration turned to Flies, and sometimes to Bees".[2] Leeuwenhoek even lovingly depicted the life of the flea, an animal which then so much pervaded human life, but which had not hitherto been thought worth

[1]Aubrey's *Brief Lives.* ed. O. Lawson Dick. London, 1950. pp. 128-132.
[2]Aubrey. *op. cit.* p. 126.

investigation. With his microscope he also revealed the anatomy of ants and, though unaware of the fantastic migrations of eels to and from the Caribbean, proved that they were not, as hitherto supposed, derived from dew. Though he wrote mainly in Dutch, he also revealed the facts of life in Latin, which all learned men could then read, and his ideas were soon widely disseminated.

By the end of the seventeenth century medicine had thus greatly advanced, following Vesalius' empirically verified anatomy, Harvey's discovery of the circulation of the blood and studies in embryology, and the use of the microscope by Leeuwenhoek to show how life was transmitted. It seems hard to believe that Shakespeare, Bacon and Donne, with their superb range and command of language, were ignorant of these things, which had also been a sealed book to all the great figures of the European past here described; but so they all had been.

These men of scientific genius are far more important than the politicians and soldiers whose often mischievous activities have inevitably filled so much space on our canvas; the great Humanist scholars and philosophers who changed the general climate of opinion and set mankind on a new course now also demand consideration.

III

The importance of Erasmus, a Catholic of the Northern Renaissance who had hoped to adapt official Catholicism to the new Humanism, has already been suggested. Though he was swamped by the contending fanatics of the Reformation and the anti-Reformation, whose bawling makes the mid-sixteenth century—also distinguished by the swashbuckling Teutonic vulgarity of its fashions—so gross an age, his influence lived on, through the meticulous scholarship of his editions of the scriptures as well as through his *Colloquies* and *Adages* which went on appealing to a widening public.

Other writers with Erasmian affinities won fame. Juan Luis Vives (1492–1540) of Valencia made his career in the North, studied in Paris and in 1519, under Charles V, became a professor at Louvain. In 1523 he was appointed supervisor to the Princess Mary of England, and came to reside in Corpus Christi College, Oxford. But he fell foul of Henry VIII over the latter's divorce from his Spanish queen, Catharine of Aragon, and was lucky to escape to Bruges where, unmolested, he lived out the rest of his life. Vives was a humanist pioneer of the theory of education, who wrote on the education of boys, a treatise he dedicated, inappropriately, to Catharine of Aragon, on an *Introduction to Wisdome,* and on the *Instruction of a Christian Woman,* as well as on that perennial subject, the *Decay of Learning,* and rather boring Latin Dialogues which were set books for generations of schoolboys. This Spanish humanist was also interested in psychology, and wrote *De Anima et vita libri tres* which discusses not what the "soul" is, but how it affects life. Like most of the best minds of his time, he had abandoned the scholastic attempts at total explanation of the cosmos, and wrote that he "wondered how schoolmen could sleep quietly; they asked such monstrous questions and thought of such terrible matters all day long."

Where Vives applied gentle irony to the schoolmen, François Rabelais, who wrote to entertain and shock, showed them up by parody and rumbustious satire. François Rabelais (c. 1494-1553) was born near Chinon in Touraine, the son of a lawyer who owned substantial property. He became a Franciscan friar, but in 1525 transferred to the Benedictine Order, and was appointed secretary to the Bishop and Abbot of Mailezais, with whom he travelled in southern and western France. In 1528 he joined the Benedictine Abbey of Saint Denis in Paris; then, in 1530, studied medicine at Montpellier; two years later he was lecturing on anatomy at Lyons. In 1532 his first Chronicle of Gargantua appeared, followed by Pantagruel, which was condemned as obscene by the Sorbonne. Rabelais then visited Rome as physician to Jean du Bellay, and obtained a Bull of Absolution from the Pope, which enabled him to become a Canon of St. Maur. In 1537 he was lecturing on Hippocrates at Montpellier. After two more visits to Italy and working as a doctor at Metz, Rabelais in 1551 obtained the living of Meudon. Volumes III and IV of his book were published in 1546 and 1548-52 and he died in Paris.[1] He retained an adolescent intoxication with life, language and learning, and showed in riotous digressions and vast Renaissance erudition just what could by done with the French language. Careless of design and unrepentantly repetitious, Rabelais mocks the pedantry of lawyers ("How the furred law cats lived on corruption"), the hypocrisy of pompous divines, and the drunkenness and lechery of idle monks; also, as well he might in the reign of François I, he indirectly showed up the idiocy of war. By contrast, using the Renaissance convention of Utopia, he depicts the peaceful and convivial freedoms of the Abbey of Thelème, with its motto, "Do what you will". He made a chequered and precarious living as a physician, and coming out of the medieval tradition of ribald French urban satire, spiced and enriched it with exuberant Renaissance Latin, left an oeuvre which has delighted generations of rebels against the respectable.

For the more conventional, discursive vernacular Essays—a "trying out" of a subject—packed with recondite learning, anecdote and comments on life, now became a powerful means of spreading a humanist outlook. They were written by laymen, and where Erasmus, Vives and their friends were Catholics, Montaigne, the founder of this genre, though formally Catholic, was more sceptical—his motto "Que scay je?". Michel de Montaigne (1533-92), owner of the Chateau de Montaigne between Bordeaux and Périgueux, came of a family of merchants and lawyers; on his mother's side he was a Lopez, descended from Spanish converted Jews. He was intensively educated at the Collège de Guyenne at Bordeaux. In 1565 he married, but his only daughter died an

[1]Sir Thomas Urquhart's English translation appeared in 1653, completed by Pierre le Motteux in 1693. The most convenient modern edition is Rabelais, the Lives, Heroic Deeds and Sayings of Gargantua and his son Pantagruel, translated from the French into English by Sir Thomas Urquhart and Peter le Motteux, London 1921. Urquhart, who rendered the spirit of the original and embellished it, was the perfect translator, and a memorable eccentric in his own right.

infant, and in 1570 he resigned his position as *Conseilleur* at the *Parlement* of
Bordeaux and went to live in his Chateau, where he devoted himself to
writing. In 1577 he became involved in the negotiations between Henry of
Navarre and the Catholic party, but refused permanent employment, though
in 1580-81 he travelled in Germany and Italy, and from 1581-85 he was Mayor
of Bordeaux. His *Essais* were published from 1580-88, and as he continually
elaborated them, the definitive edition was posthumously published in 1595.[1]
Montaigne had a more modern outlook; more introspective and self-aware;
more in tune with the world of Pagan Antiquity which it evoked: indeed, the
Antique learning was now so fully assimilated, so much part of the French
culture represented by Montaigne that it had become homely, part of the
furniture of men's minds.

In marked contrast to the theologians of his age, Montaigne was tolerant
and humane, with a touch of Stoical self-sufficiency and detachment. He set
great store by friendship and idealized a slightly older contemporary, Etienne
de la Boëtie, whose early death caused him much misery.

So after many centuries, in the countryside described by Ausonius, a writer
expressed a sensibility and reflectiveness which had not been articulate in
Western Europe since the days of the landowners of the late Roman Empire,
who had enjoyed their leisure among similar vineyards and in the same sort of
climate. The Sieur de Montaigne, to be sure, did not own slaves, so the
ambience was socially different; but he was well enough off to afford to
cultivate his sensibilities, and talented and learned enough to write them
down. He set a fashion which, broadening out through print, permeated and
humanized a civilization still medieval and "Gothick" in fanaticism and
superstition, but which was becoming ripe for change into the humaner
rationalism of the late seventeenth and the eighteenth centuries. Nor is
Montaigne's wisdom irrelevant today. Though his many sententious imitators
would become tedious, he lives still by his versatility, his candour and his sly
humour. *"J'ai naturellement"*, he writes, *"un style comique et privé."*

Other humanists, following the objectivity of Machiavelli, faced the problems of public order, so urgent during the wars of religion in France; Jean
Bodin (1530-96), the son of a tailor of Angers and originally a Carmelite monk,
obtained dispensation from his vows, studied law and lectured at Toulouse,
then entered the household of the Duc d'Alençon, after whose death he retired
to be *Procurateur* at Laon, where he died. In 1576 appeared his *Six Livres de la
République* which won him immediate fame, going into ten editions in his own
lifetime and being widely translated. It proved of lasting importance, for it
made the first definition of *Majestas* or *Sovereignty*; that cardinal concept of
modern government. "Puisque la conservation des Royaumes et empires et de
tous peuples", he writes, "dépend, après Dieu, des bons Princes et sages
Gouverneurs, c'est bien raison ... que chacun les assistera"; for only through
a supreme power can states and individuals be preserved from "licentious

---

[1] The most famous early translation is by Florio. Montaigne also dictated a travel journel
of his journeys to Germany and Italy which remained unpublished until 1774. For a
good English edition see *The Essays of Montaigne*, trans. E. J. Trechman, with
Introduction by J. M. Robertson. 2 vols. Oxford, 1927.

anarchy". It follows that the essential point in politics is to establish *majestas*, an "absolute and perpetual power"; yet no political philosopher has defined it. So this Bodin does, sweeping aside the ideal of Dante's *Monarchia* and providing a charter for the modern great state: "He is sovereign who recognizes nothing greater than himself save only Immortal God" and "God alone can call to account the prince or people who have it."[1]

At a time when France was threatened by anarchy through religious wars and regional divisions, it was to become a basic assumption of early modern politics and to continue, a lethal anachronism reinforced by popular national feeling, into the twentieth century.[2]

Another good humanist faced the facts of international politics and inaugurated the modern concept of International Law. Thirteenth-century medieval Christendom had foundered in the conflict of Papacy and Empire, successive attempts of the Conciliar movement had failed to revive it, and the Reformation and Counter-Reformation had further disrupted Western and Central Europe. Out of the wreckage there had emerged the "sovereign" dynastic great state which Bodin had defined; but with the collapse of the authority of the Holy Roman Empire, there was now not even in theory any final European authority. So Grotius (Hugo van Groot, 1583-1645), historiographer to the Province of Holland and pensionary of Rotterdam, a lawyer of high distinction and author of the *Law of Prizes* (at sea) (1604), who had to escape from Holland in 1619 as a partisan of Oldenbarnevelt's faction which had wanted to continue the Truce with Spain, turned his mind in exile in France to the crucial problem of the relations between sovereign states threatening to become more urgent with the outbreak of the Thirty Years' War. In 1639 he became ambassador to France of Queen Christina of Sweden and he died at Rostock on the Baltic.

In the *Prolegomena* of his *De Jure Belli ac Pacis* (1625) he states the problem succinctly. "None have methodically examined the Law which is common to many nations ... though it is in the interests of mankind that it should be done." So instead of evoking the authority of a transcendental Thomist Cosmic Order, he tries to deduce a new form of Natural Law from the instincts of mankind, and asserts that since men are by instinct sociable and have the gift of speech, they have "a care of maintaining society in a manner conformable to the light of human understanding", and that this concern is "the fountain of Right properly so-called". It follows that, supernatural sanctions apart, the mother of Natural Law is human nature itself, acting, he hastens to add, on instincts implanted by God. This view, which takes an optimistic view of human public behaviour, is followed up by a utilitarian argument. "Amongst all or most states, there might be, and in fact there are, some laws agreed by common consent, which represent the advantage of all in general ... and this

---

[1]"*Princeps vero populusve in quibus maiestas inest rationem rerum gestarum nemini, praeterquam Immortale Deo, reddere coguntur.*" Bodin was also a pioneer of economic theory, who understood the importance of climate on institutions and investigated the causes of sixteenth-century inflation (1574) as well as being a typical antiquarian scholar, who wrote *De la Démonomanie* (1580).
[2]See my *Western Political Thought*. (ed. 1961) pp. 292-295, for Bodin's great importance.

is what is called the Law of Nations; if these laws are observed all will benefit." Without this law there is international anarchy, for "the Moment we recede from Right we can depend on nothing." So essential is this law that even war is justified as a last resort against an aggressor who breaks it. A refugee in France, Grotius casts the French monarch Louis XIII for the role of enforcing this "international" law, and proceeds, citing the immense and fascinating Northern Renaissance erudition of his age, to make his famous treatise highly readable;[1] a work of literature in its own right as he argues from history and precedent the merits of his case. Since the rival powers of sovereign states, not least at sea and in the Far East and the Americas, were creating friction which governments did not want to lead to official war, Grotius' original idea of an International Law regulating the relation of sovereign states for their mutual convenience took on, and became an important aspect of early modern and modern international politics. It did not, of course, achieve Grotius' objective, to control the often irrational power struggles of the great states which paid lip service to it; but it did provide a basis for rules of diplomacy and war other than the elaborate but limited laws of war of the later Middle Ages, which, though cosmopolitan, applied only to the knightly class, and the negotiators of the Treaty of Westphalia were influenced by Grotius' ideas.

IV

Far more revolutionary, the English Lord Chancellor and statesman, Sir Francis Bacon (1561–1626), popularized the idea that knowledge should be applied to the deliberate "betterment of man's estate". He first adumbrated this notion in 1605, in his *Advancement of Learning*, and then in 1620 projected what he termed a *Great Instauration* or *Renewal* based on empirical knowledge, and defined its method in his *Novum Organum* of the same year.

He also used the now traditional Renaissance convention of sketching a Utopia which he called the *New Atlantis* (1627); like More's *Utopia*, it is memorable for applied common sense, with the addition of organized facilities for scientific research. And Bacon had meanwhile been winning many readers by a series of *Essays* in the manner of Montaigne, which appeared intermittently from 1597 to 1625, whereby he discoursed with memorable phrase and pungent wit in a style far more formal and sententious than Montaigne's, which summarized the experience of a seasoned courtier, lawyer and politician. His famous phrases—"What is truth, said jesting Pilate, and would not stay for an answer"—held the attention of a large public and have gone on doing so; they are more oratory than prose and none the less memorable for that.

More importantly, his *Essays* drew attention to his heavyweight books, which are much more original, contributed to a change in outlook not only in England but later in France, and furthered the movement for "enlightened"

[1]See my *Western Political Thought. op. cit.* pp. 245–305 for an introductory account.

improvement so important and so original in the eighteenth century. Following Ockham, Bacon distinguishes between the truths of religion, which do not depend on proof by reason, which the Thomists had claimed to have found, but depend on faith and the truth of scientific inductive method based on experience and experiment. Having marked out a clear field for scientific studies, Bacon, in the manner of his time most fully elaborated in Burton's encyclopaedic *Anatomy of Melancholy* (1621), makes a complicated scheme of learning, in a still medieval style; then pushes out in the *Novum Organum* into an attack on the received opinions—Idols of the Tribe, the Cave, the market place and theatre. This attack reinforces the most important of his works, the *Magna Instauratio* or *Renewal*, which states firmly that man has no business speculating on questions outside his range, but ought, by deductive method, to probe the secrets of nature and so control and exploit it.

Here is a new outlook which in time became realized in a way incredible to previous generations, and which in its benefits and its dangers still dominates the modern world.

The philosophical foundations of this *"Renewal"* were now laid by René Descartes,[1] whose *Discours sur la Méthode* (1637) is one of the decisive books of European thought. Having spent much of his youth "studying the book of the world" in courts and armies, Descartes decided to examine himself. In a famous passage he wrote, "I was then in Germany . . . and as I found no society to interest me, and was besides fortunately undisturbed by any cares or passions, I remained the whole day in seclusion in a room heated by means of a stove with full opportunity to occupy my attention with my own thoughts." Out of this introspection emerged the Cartesian *méthode*, not uninfluenced by the Jesuit discipline in which he had been trained. "First, never to accept anything for true which I did not clearly know to be such; . . . and to comprise nothing in my judgement than what was presented to my mind so clearly and distinctly as to exclude all ground of doubt. Second, to divide each of the difficulties under examination into as many parts as possible, and as might be necessary for an adequate solution, and third, to begin with the objects which were simplest and easiest to know." The simplest and most direct knowledge, he believed, was simply *cogito ergo sum*—"I think therefore I am"—and on that basis he intended to "ascend as it were step by step to the knowledge of the most complex". For this sublimated methodical commonsense, Descartes made high claims; he was convinced that it could lead to knowledge "highly useful to life", and promised, "in room of the speculative philosophy usually taught in the schools to discover a practical means by which we might render ourselves the lords and possessors of nature".

[1]Born in 1596 at La Haye Descartes south of Tours on the Creuse, of a gentry family and educated by the Jesuits at La Flèche in Maine (1604–12), Descartes fought under Prince Maurice of Nassau in the Netherlands, and after the truce between Spain and the United Provinces, under Maximilian of Bavaria on the Danube. He then lived in Holland and followed up the publication of his *Discours* with *Méditations* (1649). Summoned, like Grotius, to Stockholm to the court of Queen Christina of Sweden, he died, as Grotius had died, at Rostock five years earlier, probably of the Baltic climate, in February, 1650.

Descartes' *méthode*, since regarded as inadequate for philosophy, gave just the theoretical sanction needed for the upsurge of scientific investigation then in train, from Galileo's investigation of the universe to Vesalius' examination of anatomy and Harvey's discovery of the circulation of the blood, to Bodin's analysis and definition of sovereignty and Bacon's advocacy of exploiting nature to improve the human condition. And this at a time when, with superior technology, Europeans had taken to distant seas, were making colonies of settlement in the Americas, and were beginning to dominate the ancient civilizations of the East. We are here concerned, as seldom before, with events not simply in European but in World History, which make the history of Europe of even greater significance in an Age of the Oceans.

XXXIII

Dutch and English Mercantilist Empires

The Peace of Westphalia of 1648 had not concluded the war between France and Spain; still less the mounting rivalry of the Atlantic powers for trade and colonies in the Americas and the East. The Dutch had been fighting the Spaniards for eighty years and in doing so become a first class maritime power: the English, with a more substantial base, had been forced into a comparable strategy, and to turn away from their obsession with conquests in France to oceanic trade and even colonization. By the mid-seventeenth century the two northern naval powers with the most far-flung oceanic commerce were the Dutch and then the English, and the focus of oceanic trade had finally shifted from the Mediterranean to the Atlantic.

Such were the facts of northern sea-power; but the Protestant northerners had found their best hunting grounds already occupied by the vast, casual and over-centralized Spanish colonial empire in Central and South America and the Caribbean, and by the Portuguese commercial empire in the Far East. They therefore increased their efforts; the Dutch through the wealthy *Vereenigde Oostindische Compagnie*, mainly in what is now Indonesia, and the British mainly in India and in the Americas. Brought up to face the bitter climate and treacherous currents of the North Sea, the Dutch and English proved as skilled and hardy as the Iberians; by 1619 the Dutch were established at Batavia and by 1623 they had so far superseded the Portuguese in the Eastern Spice Islands that although, after the end of the truce with Spain in 1621, they had a renewed war with the Spaniards on their hands, they staged the sensational "massacre at Amboyna", in the Moluccas, when, after parading their English rivals with every circumstance of degradation before the local inhabitants and subjecting them to "torments of fire and water", they beheaded a generous selection of them and of their Japanese assistants. The rival Western adventurers, uncouth barbarians in Siamese, as in Chinese, eyes, were also competing at Bangkok and Ayuthia, and a few even reached Japan. The Dutch also seized Colombo (1640) and made a settlement in 1652 at the Cape.

But by 1608 the English, who had already reached Persia through Muscovy, had gained a foothold in India at Surat, whence they penetrated to the Court of the Great Moghul Jahangir at Agra, and would later extend their commerce from Madras, then into Bengal and Orissa from the estuary of the Ganges. In West Africa, too, the Dutch and English managed to drive out the Portuguese from their forts and trading posts on the sweltering coast, so important for the slave trade with the sugar plantations in Brazil, and penetrate the Bight of Benin. Far more important, and to the grave concern of Spain, the English began their "plantations" of North America. Newfoundland, with its teeming fisheries, had been first annexed, a move officially recognized after the peace of 1604 with Spain, and by 1617, in competition with the French, Nova Scotia was being settled by Welsh and Scots. But the plantations of Virginia in 1607, in a far better climate, consolidated following the discovery of Bermuda in 1609–10, had proved far more promising, and by 1625 it had been taken over as a Crown Colony.

Then by 1620 the so-called "Pilgrim Fathers" in the Mayflower had fetched up and survived on Cape Cod, "Independent" sectaries ready to face the hazards of the New World for their beliefs; and in 1627–9 a more substantial expedition from East Anglia and Dorset "planted" the Massachusetts Colony— the main foundation, along with the socially contrasting settlement of Virginia, of the English colonies of the Eastern seaboard of North America.

The French, meanwhile, had penetrated deeper into the wilderness. A century earlier, in 1534–6, Jacques Cartier of St. Malo had made his way up the St. Lawrence to the site which would become Montreal, later, moving in behind the English, the French trappers, fur traders and missionaries, on better terms than the Puritan English with the Amerindians, had been founding trading posts in Canada. In 1608 Champlain, who went on to explore the Great Lakes, founded Quebec, a depot for the fur trade, and French settlers, their main base Port Royal, had colonized in Nova Scotia which they called Acadia. Unlike the English governments, Richelieu put state backing behind the "*Company of New France*", and later in the seventeenth century the French explorers, backed by Colbert, were far more enterprising, penetrating down to the Ohio and even by 1682–7 down the whole length of the Mississippi to the Gulf of Mexico. But when French *coureurs des bois* discovered the way overland to Hudson's Bay, the English reaped the benefit, and by 1670 had founded the Hudson's Bay Company with its monopoly of the fur trade.

For the French were naturally reluctant to leave France; and in spite of government encouragement, they were never numerous enough, save around Quebec, for effective permanent plantations. Here the Puritan English and the Cavalier Virginians, with stronger if opposite motives for emigration, supplied a more decisive weight of settlement, along with the practice of oligarchic self-government crucial to the political development of the colonies and so of the United States.

All three northern sea powers, Dutch, English and French, were more interested in the Caribbean. The Portuguese, in their early and extensive plantations in Brazil, had developed the cultivation of sugar by slaves imported from West Africa, and after the opening phase of piracy and plunder, the Northern Europeans annexed most of the islands then, following Portuguese methods, exploited them for sugar. Barbados, which was uninhabited, was annexed by the English in 1625, and the Dutch also broke into Spanish waters to exploit the salt deposits of Araya in Venezuela, which they obtained for nothing except back breaking toil in tropical heat. In 1621, after the war with Spain was renewed, the Dutch West India Company financed much larger naval enterprises, and in 1628 achieved the resounding success of intercepting the homeward bound Spanish treasure fleet with "booty worth fifteen million guilders, enough to pay a dividend of fifteen per cent ... and to finance a campaign of conquest in Northern Brazil".[1] They then gradually took over the carrying trade of the Spanish and Portuguese empires and made Amsterdam its principal market, annexed Curaçao in Venezuela, and by seizing the fine port they named New Amsterdam in "New Netherlands" at the mouth of the Hudson on the North Atlantic, obtained the best harbour for the fur trade out of the North American continent. The Spaniards, preoccupied with the Dutch pioneers of mercantilist imperialism, were unable to deal with the more permanently important English settlement of Virginia or evict the English and French from the best islands in the Caribbean.

Thus on both sides of the world, in the Far East and in the Americas, the Northern Europeans reached out to found their own colonial mercantilist empires, while Spain, her communications increasingly threatened with her vast Central and South American territories which had hitherto pre-empted and dwarfed all other European settlement, now derived dwindling benefit from them, just at a time of declining power and cohesion in the Iberian peninsula itself.

II

In the age of the oceans of which the Iberian states had been the pioneers and which the northern Atlantic powers were now beginning to exploit, the power politics of Europe took on a new dimension. Great sovereign states now competed not only for territory in Europe but for the mercantile and colonial advantages that victory on European battlefields could bring; by the eighteenth century the future of vast tracts of territory in the Americas and the East was settled by treaties between European powers, and campaigns, which at a first glance appear inconclusive and even futile, led to historically decisive results far beyond Europe.

The sixteenth century had witnessed the supremacy of Spain, sustained by the revenues of Spanish America, and by the steady dedicated purpose of Philip II. Court fashions in Western and Central Europe had followed sombre Spanish styles and long continued to do so until the flamboyant style of the Court of Louis XIV set a different tone and French manners and etiquette predominated. The change of fashion reflected the facts of power. As the war with France dragged on, the financial and administrative strain on the

[1]Parry. *op. cit.* p. 188.

government in Madrid proved too much, the regional resentments of Catalans and Portuguese against the centralizing policies of Philip IV and Olivares undermined the political and economic cohesion of the peninsula, and the incompetence of the Habsburg Philip IV gave place to the near imbecility of Carlos II—the Bewitched (1665–1700). The French obsession with "encircle-ment" by the Austrians and Habsburgs under Leopold I (1658–1705), and his cousins of Spain, now gave place to the French obsession with dominating Europe; for it was in France that, following the work of Richelieu, the new sovereign "great state" was first able to exploit, if still clumsily, the potentially richest country in the West.

With a population at most a third of that of France, it did not seem likely that England, for all its invulnerable island base and potential sea power, could become a serious rival to the mighty French monarchy of Louis XIV; indeed, until the brief Republican regime under Oliver Cromwell, the Dutch, not the English, were the predominant naval and commercial power. Although the personal union of Crowns of England and Scotland under James Stuart VI and I had deprived the French of their traditional strategically placed ally in the north, the mounting tension between the Conciliar governments of the early Stuarts and their Parliaments, between the Erasmian Anglicans and the Calvinist Puritans which the Elizabethan settlement of religion had postponed but not resolved, and the growing incompetence and corruption of the administration, worsened by James I's habit of appointing his "favourites" for their looks rather than their abilities—a penchant he shared with the young Louis XIII—combined to make "Great Britain" relatively unimportant in continental politics, if also, to the advantage of the British, to keep the country out of entanglement in the Thirty Years' War.

When in 1625 Henriette-Marie, sister of Louis XIII, was married to Charles I of England, the French, far from securing a valuable alliance, obtained a liability. Apart from Buckingham's inept expedition to relieve the Huguenots in La Rochelle, the apparent prosperity of the personal rule of Charles I during the 'thirties, when at least England, unlike much of the continent, had peace, concealed the growing weakness of the Crown. For the English monarchy, unlike the French, depended on the collaboration of the gentry in the counties whose work as Justices of the Peace was essential to a decentralized govern-ment with no adequate standing army. And Charles I, Scots on his father's side and Danish on his mother's, had none of the Tudor political intuition; a remote, fastidious and politically devious aesthete, he inclined, following his father, to the prevalent French view of monarchy as instituted by Divine Right, and hankered, an incompetent innovator, to impose on his two realms the kind of centralizing policy which Richelieu was imposing on France, and which Strafford, if supported, might have created in England. And when, impelled by an unpolitical sense of high religious duty, Charles attempted to force Anglican ritual on the Calvinist Scots, he stirred up a hornets' nest, nearly bankrupted his regime and put himself at the mercy of his enemies in Parliament.

By 1642 the essentials of their constitutional demands had been conceded: the Tudor-style Conciliar government and its Prerogative Courts of Justice had been dismantled, and the way was clear for a compromise between Crown and Parliament. But the extremists in the Commons and their backers in the Lords now over-reached themselves: they tried to make Charles, in his own words, "but the painted sign of a king" and to abolish the Anglican bishops. In consequence much moderate opinion rallied to the intransigent king; enough to enable him to fight, and at first nearly win, a civil war, amateurish and desultory to continentals, but devastating by English standards, which was decided in 1644 by the intervention of a Scots Presbyterian army at Marston Moor, and concluded in 1645 at Naseby with the utter defeat of the King. In this struggle the real victors, once the Scots had been paid off, were the Independents of the Army, hostile to the Presbyterian oligarchy in Parliament who had begun the war. The King tried to play off Scots, Army and Parliament against each other, until the Scots invaded England and the royalists rose in Essex and Kent in a second civil war; Cromwell routed the Scots at Preston in Lancashire and occupied Edinburgh, and the royalists' risings failed. Whereupon the grandees of the army, afraid that the King would come to terms with the Parliament and disband them, decided that he was too dangerous to live: so they cut their way out, purged parliament, and staged his judicial murder, thus setting a precedent of formal Regicide, not lost on a later generation in France.

In doing so they sealed their own long-term fate, for they outraged the feelings of the majority of the country; but for nearly a decade as "saviours of society" they established a government which put down the radicals and Levellers, and which, unpopular at home, proved efficient and aggressive abroad. First Scotland, then Ireland were subdued; then the internal administration was improved, taxation imposed and regularly collected, far greater than anything demanded by the old regime. An efficient fleet was developed round the nucleus of ships built by Charles I out of the contested rates for "ship money", and an active mercantilist policy, defined by the Navigation Acts of 1650, 1651 and 1657, aimed first against the Dutch, with whom in 1652–4 the English went to war, was pursued in collaboration with the French against Spain and the Spanish American empire (1655–9). In 1655 Jamaica was annexed, and four years later St. Helena taken over, as an essential port of call for ships trading with India and the Far East. With the emergence of such a British Navy under the Republic and the prosecution of a mercantilist policy similar to that to be directed by Colbert in France and long practised by the Dutch, England became a potential rival to the French in India and over the strategic bases on the route to it, as well as in the West Indies and North America. As the Spaniards and the Dutch ceased by the late seventeenth century to be first rate powers, the scene was set for a global rivalry between Great Britain and France which caused another Hundred Years' War to be fought out, from King William III's and the Marlborough wars, through the great struggles for empire in the mid-eighteenth century to the long and conclusive conflict between the British and Revolutionary and Napoleonic France.

In the peaceful years before the Civil Wars Charles I had established the last and highly distinguished late Renaissance court in Northern Europe. He was the greatest art patron and collector of all the English Kings, and he maintained the Tudor tradition of making the Court a centre of patronage for music, architecture, painting, and—to the disgust of his Puritan subjects—for the theatre and the masque. His father's court had been lavish but vulgar; Charles, a fastidious and aloof monarch, reacted against this genial bawdiness and confusion, and, perhaps impressed by the majestic formality of the Spanish court, to which as Prince of Wales he had made his way *incognito*, introduced a more restrained and well ordered regime. But it did not escape the unpopularity inherited from Jacobean times; indeed it became more disliked because considered exotic and pro-Catholic by the more insular and philistine Puritans. There are thus two facets of the vigorous culture of mid-seventeenth-century England; that of the Court and the Anglican High Church that it patronized, and that of the Calvinists and Independents during the Civil Wars and the short-lived British Republic, when a babel of radical ideas were pungently expressed, and when, after the Anglican censorship had been broken and a rift had appeared in the ranks of the propertied classes, a roar of pamphleteering and "unauthorized" preaching broke out. During the Civil Wars and the Republic a native moralizing Puritanism, apparent since the Lollard movement in the late fourteenth century, for the first time briefly captured the seats of power and imposed its sectarian blight upon the British. It was long stereotyped by the "English Sunday" and the Scots Sabbath, and it lived on in the "Nonconformist" conscience.

In contrast, at the exotic northern Renaissance Court, architecture and painting flourished. The influence of Palladio, long prevalent on the Continent, was interpreted in England by a Welsh genius, Inigo Jones (1573–1650), the first British architect of cosmopolitan fame. He had designed masques for Anne of Denmark, consort of James I, and his first major commission was the Palladian Queen's House at Greenwich—its functional plan revolutionary compared to the rambling red brick Tudor palaces; he designed the fine Banqueting House at Whitehall (1622)—still extant, from which, by the irony of fate, Charles I stepped out to his execution. The classical tradition, originally Italian, was thus brought into England—as in the newly built part of Wilton House designed by Webb; and it began to supersede the Elizabethan and Jacobean complexities of Hardwick and Hatfield with their affinities with the northern Danish palaces. The elegant simplicity of the new architecture was paralleled by the lively skill of the Flemish painters patronized by the Court— of whom the most famous was Rubens and the most rewarding was van Dyck, whose knack of making his sitters look distinguished has endowed Charles I, his Queen and his cavaliers, with memorable and perhaps artificial charm. Charles had also been collecting paintings by Raphael, Titian, Caravaggio, Tintoretto and even Dürer, and forming the superb collection which was sold and dispersed by the Republican governments.

The Caroline Court also patronized the spectacular but ephemeral production of masques and encouraged the theatre, still flourishing since the previous reign, when some of Shakespeare's greatest dramas had been produced: it remained for the Puritan regime to close the theatres and abolish the custom of boys acting women's parts, a practice which had particularly infuriated the prurient pamphleteer Prynne, the most hysterically violent of the enemies of the theatre,[1] and a custom finally superseded when the boys, whose acting had been good enough for Shakespeare, were replaced, following French fashion, by the chaste actresses of the reign of Charles II.

The English had now fully assimilated the riches of Renaissance learning. Sir Thomas Browne's *Religio Medici* (1642) is a masterpiece of baroque latinized English, at its most entertaining in the desultory and curious learning of *Pseudodoxia Epidemica*, or *Enquiries into Vulgar and Common Errors.*

John Milton (1608–72), the greatest English epic poet, was also steeped in Renaissance learning, Latin, Greek and Hebrew. His masque, *Comus* (1637), was written in the fashion of the Court, but in spite of his travels in Italy and feeling for Italian civilization, he took the Parliamentarian side in the Civil Wars, hoping to realize a Calvinistic and righteous Commonwealth of the Elect, and by 1652 working himself blind as Latin secretary to the Republican Council of State. His consequent disillusion with politics did not impair, but reinforced, the genius which impelled him to compose *Paradise Lost*, and the mastery of English which has made the epic famous.

Much more down to earth, and profoundly original, Thomas Hobbes (1588–1678) constructed with superb power of phrase a new and secular political theory well suited to the early modern sovereign state. His *Leviathan* (1651), accepting the limitations of mind that followed a nominalist scepticism about metaphysics, attempted to found a practical theory of the state from the current mechanistic physics and psychology. Anxious to preserve the social order, he gave it a novel and utilitarian sanction: natural law was not the metaphysical and transcendental fantasy evoked by the Thomist schoolmen but the law of self-preservation. So actuated, men united to form commonwealths in which religion was subordinated to the state, and in which the state's justification was simply that it protected its citizens. If it failed to do so, it forfeited its authority, just as law was only law if it could be enforced.

This pragmatic view horrified conservative "Ancients" accustomed to doctrines of Divine Right; but it appealed to "Moderns" including even those anxious to strengthen the monarchy in France. Hobbes also took for granted that the natural relationship of states was a "posture of warre". He thus became the ancestor of much modern political theory, both of the internal utilitarian relationship of governments to their peoples and of their brutal external relationships to one another. Most *bien pensant* readers were shocked; but most politicians knew quite well that Hobbes had seen through them.

Hobbes also wrote *Behemoth, or the Long Parliament* (1682), an account of the Civil Wars, which has worn very well in comparison with most subsequent explanations of them.

On a more popular level during the Interregnum a spate of radical pamphlets poured from the press, often illustrated by more or less hideous woodcuts. Popular journalism came into being; and a horde of Levellers, Diggers and Ranters staged what has been interpreted as a rehearsal for the popular revolutions of modern times, championing the claims and rights of the

[1]See my *Charles I: a biography.* London, 1975. pp. 138–9.

"common man"; often in memorable phrases—as the "Levellers" "The poorest hee that is in England hath a life to live as the richest hee", or the Digger slogan that God had "made the earth a common treasury". In fact much more a backwash of medieval heresies than pioneers of modern revolution, these radicals were briskly put down by Cromwell, who, for all his sectarian fanaticism, remained in mind an Elizabethan squire; but they have since been accorded an importance they did not possess in their own time. Like nearly all their contemporaries, they wrote and mouthed memorable English, and their radical traditions would live on in the Puritan colonies in North America to contribute to the American and indirectly to the French revolutions.

With the Restoration of 1660 the English created the social and political structure and the early modern outlook which was fully developed in the eighteenth century into oceanic empire and a brilliant upper class culture. Liberal historians with Puritanical prejudices have dismissed the Restoration as a time of political corruption and mere "profligacy"; but for most contemporaries, immensely relieved to be rid of Cromwell's military government and the cant of the sectaries satirized in Butler's *Hudibras*, it was a time of liberation. Behind the shifting political intrigues of the courtiers, capable professionals developed the administration improved under the Republic: Pepys administered the Admiralty, in 1664 Thomas Mun's posthumous *England's Treasure by Foreign Trade* defined the principles of mercantilist policy, and the much maligned Charles II and James II both systematically encouraged colonization in North America. Sir William Petty, who had made his name and fortune surveying Ireland, became a pioneer economist; Sir Christopher Wren, the greatest English architect, rebuilt St. Paul's after the Great Fire of 1666.

In the field of science John Wilkins, Warden of Wadham College, Oxford, briefly Master of Trinity, Cambridge and finally Bishop of Chester, was the main founder of the Royal Society, that "Colledge for the Promotion of Physical and Mathematical Experiment and Learning", incorporated in 1662.[1] By 1640 he was trying to prove that " 'tis probable our Earth is one of the planets". At Wadham, he was immensely successful, tolerant and hospitable, entertained a circle of remarkable men, including Petty, Wren, and the diarist, John Evelyn, and prevented the Parliamentarian soldiery from damaging the libraries and buildings of the University.

Wilkins became particularly celebrated as a patron of scholars learned in science; John Ray (1627–1705), "the Aristotle of England and the Linnaeus of his Age", won fame as a botanist[2] and, in conjunction with the naturalist

[1]The son of an Oxford goldsmith, he attended Magdalen Hall and became Chaplain to Charles Louis, Prince Palatine of the Rhine, then in exile. In 1638 he published *The Discovery of a World in the Moon, or a Discourse tending to prove that 'tis probable there may be another Habitable World in that Planet* (1638), to which he added *A Discourse concerning the Possibility of a Passage* thither.

[2]Son of a blacksmith near Braintree in Essex, Ray was sent to Cambridge by the local squire. At Trinity (1646) he became expert in Greek, Latin and Hebrew and explored the locality, cataloguing plants. In 1663–6 he travelled widely on the Continent. His friend, Francis Willughby, who died in 1672, left him an annuity which enabled him to continue his vast researches which culminated in 1694 in his *Flora of Europe*.

Francis Willughby of Middleton Hall, as an ornithologist. Elected F.R.S. in 1667, he wrote the *Catalogus Plantarum Angliae* in 1670, *Observations on Plants* in 1673 and in 1691 *The Wisdom of God Manifest in the Works of His Creation*, to which Paley's *Evidences of Christianity* would be indebted.

Another Fellow of the Royal Society was the natural philosopher, the Hon. Robert Boyle (1627–91), a son of the first Earl of Cork, who early managed to enjoy algebra and mental arithmetic at Eton, studied at Geneva and Florence, and by 1669 had devised "new experiments Physico-Mechanical touching the spring and weight of the Air". This versatile experimentalist who "fancied his laboratory an Elysium" invented tests for acidity and alkalinity and the sealed thermometer.

Such are only a few representatives of the ingenuity of Restoration England, which is also memorable for the first great English statesman-historian, Edward Hyde, first Earl of Clarendon, whose *History of the Rebellion* is a masterpiece of narrative, analysis and characterization. This sense of character also appears in the miniature biographies of John Aubrey (1625–97), who can depict eccentricity with a few sympathetic and memorable phrases, while the diaries of Pepys and Evelyn portray at once their authors and their times.

The English transition to an early modern outlook is most strikingly symbolized by the change from the baroque prose and complex poetry of the early and mid-seventeenth century to the plain, lucid and precise prose of Dryden, his hard hitting satire provoked by the frenetic political intrigues and crises of the time. Famous in his day as a prolific dramatist, Dryden has better kept his reputation as a prose writer and satirist, and he points the way towards the pace, lucidity and rapier swift irony of Swift and the Augustan writers of the early eighteenth century.

III

When the eighty years war between the Dutch and the Spaniards was concluded by the Treaty of Münster in 1648, the Dutch Republic had at last gained formal recognition. It was anomalous in a Europe increasingly dominated by the cosmopolitan monarchical and aristocratic French civilization, but it survived as a major power and an intellectual and artistic influence. The United Provinces had fought through to independence in part on French subsidies, since the French interest had been to weaken the hold of Spain on the Spanish Netherlands; but though the Dutch interest pursued by Oldenbarneveldt had become fixed on peace and commerce, the warlike anti-Spanish policy of the Stadthouder Maurice of Nassau had led to Oldenbarneveldt's execution, and, continued by his cousin Frederick William, had been revived by Charles I's son-in-law, Frederick William's son, the young Stadthouder William II (1647–50), who aspired to reconquer the Spanish Netherlands and, ineffectively, to restore the Stuarts in England; a policy consistently thwarted by the States of Holland, "determined to keep in with the winning side".[1] This

[1]P. Geyl. *op. cit.* p. 85.

divergence had nearly led to civil war; but, on the Prince's death, Johan de Witt had reverted to entirely commercial objectives.

The immense sea-borne prosperity of the Dutch had provoked the English governments to the Anglo-Dutch wars of 1652–4 and 1664–7, but the main threat now came from France. By 1668, Louis XIV was determined to overrun the Spanish Netherlands, and Charles II, in French pay, joined the French in again attacking the Dutch at sea, in spite of the Triple Alliance de Witt had organized between the Dutch, the English and the Swedes. It was at this critical juncture that in 1672 William III (1672–1702), son of William II and Mary of England and so grandson of Charles I, became Stadthouder, his position confirmed by the assassination of de Witt and his brother Cornelis, and began his career as the dedicated Protestant opponent of the French in their European and colonial ambitions. His marriage to the Princess Mary, daughter of the Duke of York, afterwards James II, would bring him to the throne of Great Britain where he became the inspiration of the long Anglo-Dutch campaigns which culminated for the British in the victorious Marlborough wars.

Such, in brief outline, were the political fortunes of the United Provinces of the Dutch Republic in the second half of the seventeenth century. They were constantly at war; held together more by a common religion than by political ties, always tenuous; and sustained by accumulated wealth from oceanic commerce, by the fine seamanship of their fleets and by the intelligent objectives of their civilian governments. They achieved a singularly creative civilization, renowned for freedom of thought, toleration in religion, and original and extremely attractive landscape painting.

It may seem strange that a republic of Provinces dominated by a dour Calvinistic religion should have produced such a culture; but in fact "The remarkable development of Dutch civilization which took place in the seventeenth century was almost entirely a phenomenon of the province of Holland. The cultural life of the provinces outside Holland lacked vigour, and it is difficult to point to any independent artistic or literary tradition in any of them. Notable artists and writers were indeed born outside the narrow boundaries of Holland, but it was only here that they could develop their art and find a market for their work."[1] In this overwhelmingly urban culture the "regent" oligarchy of Amsterdam was predominant; Leiden in Holland had far the greatest prestige among the universities, Haarlem became a centre for artists, and the population of Holland in 1622 accounted for nearly half the 1,400,000 inhabitants of the entire Republic. Leiden and Haarlem, moreover, were far ahead of the rest in textile industries, as were Amsterdam and Rotterdam in shipping. The ubiquitous Dutch *fluits*, designed to carry bulk cargoes of grain out of the Baltic or to Spain, were handy to manoeuvre and sturdily built to face the choppy waves of the North Sea or the long heave of the Atlantic. They also imported ample stores of sugar, tobacco and timber for their own shipyards at Zaandam.

[1] J. L. Price. *Culture and Society in the Dutch Republic during the Seventeenth Century.* London, 1974. p. 65.

Moreover, the one objective on which all the Dutch were agreed was to prevent the revival of Antwerp by blockading the mouth of the Scheldt, a policy so important that it prevented any serious attempt to win back the southern provinces or Spanish Netherlands. Since the demand for skilled labour was brisk and the population limited, wages were higher in Holland than in any other part of Europe, so that while the French peasants often appeared to live like animals, the Dutch enjoyed a diffused prosperity. This meant that the Dutch painters, many of whom were of Flemish origin but had branched off from the splendid Netherlandish-Burgundian tradition which had now developed in a more cosmopolitan and fashionable Baroque style in Antwerp and the Spanish Netherlands, made a reliable living out of a new secular middle class market, and evolved an original form of landscape painting which depicted nature and cloudscapes for their own sake, not as mere adjuncts to religious pictures. The middle-class Dutch also demanded their own likenesses in homely settings and genre paintings, while the "regent" oligarchy demanded group pictures, of which the most famous are Rembrandt's *Stael-meesters* or *Syndics* and the superb *Company of Captain Franz Banning Cocq* known misleadingly, since after cleaning the picture shows daylight colours, as the "Night" Watch (1642). In contrast with the artists of the Medieval Church or of the contemporary Counter-Reformation, the Dutch painters, reflecting the early modern thought of their time, painted from nature with accurate observation in the light of common day rather than *sub specie aeternitatis*. And such was their genius that the light remained uncommon; Jacob Ruisdael and Hobbema, for example, have a feeling for nature and the movement of wind and clouds that are unmedieval, and out of their tradition came Constable and Turner. Vermeer, a master of calm interiors with a technique that descends from Jan van Eyck, could also depict a whole range of buildings—and their reflections—in satisfying harmony, as in his view of Delft.

The Dutch artists also loved the now plain white-washed interiors of originally Catholic churches, whose spacious proportions and massive pillars they set off in skilled perspective. Naturally, the Dutch also specialized in seascapes and in paintings of their ships; from battlepieces and great East Indiamen with a huge spread of sail, as in the paintings of the Van de Veldes, to fishing boats putting out off sandy shores into grey-green seas. All these painters, even the vulgar ones who depicted festoons of game fish and fruit for their gourmandizing patrons, stoking up against the Dutch climate, and the junketings in snug taverns, as designed by Steen, had a passion for light in an environment where it was often obscured, or palely reflected from the meres and canals which intersected a countryside so close to the cities that one had only to walk out of them to meet the scent of polders and the flight and sound of duck.

Rembrandt van Rijn is *sui generis* (1607–69), a genius of European stature; but he also sums up and represents the achievement of his country. Rembrandt was born the son of a miller near Leiden. He became in 1624 a pupil of Pieter Lastman at Amsterdam, who painted "historical" pictures, and had visited Italy and been influenced by Tintoretto. Rembrandt early concentrated on biblical and historical subjects and on portraits of his family and their circle. In

1631 he settled in Amsterdam, won great reputation as a portrait painter and, three years later, married Saskia van Uylenburg whose family were well-to-do art dealers. There followed the most prosperous period of his life, when he produced a succession of splendid portraits and groups of the Dutch *haute bourgeoisie* transfigured by the painter's psychological insight and mastery of colour. He continued to depict biblical subjects, but began to paint landscapes and to develop his superb skill in drawing and etching. In 1642, soon after the birth of their son, Titus, Saskia died, and Rembrandt, who had lived lavishly, found himself in financial straits which led in 1656 to bankruptcy. His large house and valuable collections were sold up; but he continued to receive important commissions, and Titus collaborated with Rembrandt's mistress and servant, Hendrickje Stoffels, by whom the painter had a daughter Cornelia, to manage his affairs and shield him from hardship. But though in 1668 Titus died, and in the following year Rembrandt died himself, the great artist was never in penury; he merely became less fashionable and less affluent, and the widespread impression that he died in poverty is false. His art, moreover, continued to develop as his genius dictated, with enhanced freedom and skill.

Rembrandt was steeped in the Bible, not least in the Old Testament, and familiar with the Jews of Amsterdam, and he early followed the demand for historical painting, then considered the highest art; but he also transfigured the ordinary by his brilliant chiaroscuro and depth of colour. His roots are in the same soil as the more representative Dutch painters of lesser genius, who were then unlike any others in Europe. No longer dominated by the Catholic Church, their theologically neutral subjects did not outrage the Calvinist iconoclasts. At a time when the most profound drift of European thought was towards science and humanism, these Dutch painters were realists who loved life. Rembrandt in particular was a liberator, profoundly original. "It is evident from literary documents that Rembrandt's idea of a drawing as an instantaneous reaction to visual inspiration or impulsive expression of inner vision seemed something new and stupendous to his contemporaries ... The new estimation of the drawn sketch as a mode of artistic expression in its own right which begins with Rembrandt, can be noticed in the historical and theoretical writings of his biographer and pupils."[1]

The reputation of the Dutch Republic was even more enhanced for contemporaries by tolerance of original and conflicting beliefs; due more to the failure of the Reformed Calvinist Church to impose its censorship on them than to any amiable humanism. Hence the flourishing state of publishing and printing, particularly in Holland, so that the most important scientific and academic books in Europe were produced there. Unlike the Spaniards, who had driven all the Sephardic Jews they could from their peninsula, the Dutch Republic had accepted them and allowed them to form their synagogues and schools. And when, as towards Spinoza (1632–77) their great philosopher, the Jews proved intolerant to each other, and cursed and expelled him for heresy, the Dutch allowed this man of genius to live near Leiden and there discuss his *Tractatus Politicus* and *Tractatus Theologico-Politicus* with learned Christian

[1]Otto Benesch. *Rembrandt—Selected Drawings*. London, 1947. pp. 7–8.

radicals. As Spinoza was a Pantheist, the scope of Dutch toleration was surprisingly large: but of course he had not much influence on his contemporaries since he thought that religion was a private concern, and that everyone, wherever he might be, should "worship God and mind his own business, which is the duty of a private man", while the state was a utilitarian contrivance, designed, like Hobbes's *Leviathan*, to "remove fear", and with no intrinsic claim on its citizens if it fails to maintain security and promote the quality of life. Spinoza's objective and scientific view of the human condition, summed up in his intention "not to laugh at men or weep over them or hate them but to understand them", is humanist, and it develops the tradition of Montaigne and Bacon with a more scientific bias.

If Spinoza's Pantheism expressed Jewish vision, Joost van der Vondel (1587–1679) was essentially Dutch. He was born in Cologne, where his parents had fled from the Spanish sack of Antwerp, but after 1597 was brought up by them in Amsterdam, where his father, a hatter, became a minor silk merchant. He early dramatized the exodus of the Jews from Egypt as an allegory of the flight of the Dutch from the Spaniards, and in 1625 attacked the murderers of Oldenbarneveldt in *Palemades*. In imitation of Virgil's *Aeneid*, he composed *Sigstrect van Amstel* (1637) on the foundation of Amsterdam, then wrote on *Adam in Exile* and twenty-four plays, mainly on biblical subjects, of which the most famous are the Sophoclean-style tragedies *Jephtha* and *Lucifer*—on a theme comparable to that of Milton's *Paradise Lost*. Besides Sophoclean dramas, he wrote political satires, pastorals and lyric poetry. Of humble origin, Vondel made his living as a clerk in the Amsterdam Bank where he worked until pensioned on full pay at eighty. He made very little money by his voluminous and famous writings.

This versatile and indefatigable genius, brought up a Mennonite nonconformist Protestant, was converted in middle age to the Catholic faith, then bitterly unpopular among his countrymen, and after a laborious self-education in the Bible and Renaissance learning, including Virgil and the dramas of Sophocles, became the greatest playwright in an intractable vernacular, as well as a satirist and lyric poet unsurpassed in Dutch literature.[1]

[1] J. R. P. Mody, *Vondel and Milton, with a translation of Lucifer*. London, 1942.

XXXIV

The Defence of Vienna: Prussia: the Modernizing of Muscovy

While the most Christian French King was conducting his laborious campaigns in Lorraine, Flanders and Franche Comté, the last an Imperial possession, the Emperor Leopold I was contending with a renewed Turkish threat on the Danube. In 1664 he had made the peace of Vasvar with Sultan Muhammad IV, but at the price of admitting de facto Turkish domination of Transylvania; while the Hungarians, under the guise of Calvinism, were asserting their liberties against Vienna, thus providing the Turks with an opening. By 1681 they were in open rebellion, and next year, in spite of overtures from the Emperor, the Turks had seized their chance when they recognized the Hungarian leader, Imre Thokoly, as King of Hungary. In 1683, by English reckoning in the final years of Charles II, the Grand Vizier, Kara Mustafa Pasha, had assembled a huge army at Belgrade, poised to advance on Vienna itself.

The Central European powers were alarmed: the Poles, fallen into more than their usual disorder, who had in 1674 elected Jan Sobieski as King John III. He was a soldier of genius who had already defeated the Turks at Choczim the year before and regained most of Podolia, and he now, under pressure from the Pope, made the Treaty of Warsaw with Leopold I. The Elector of Bavaria also rallied to the Emperor, and Duke Charles of Lorraine, the victim of Louis XIV, took command of an Imperial army which attempted to hold the Turkish advance on the Danube at Raab. But by July 1683 the Turks had enveloped Vienna and the siege began.

They were particularly good at sieges, and with ample and expendable manpower they sapped away at the elaborate modern defences. The technique was now quite different from the battering with heavy guns that had smashed the high wall of Constantinople at a chosen point; it was to mine. The defenders, under the command of Prince Ernst von Starhemberg, held on through early August, when their position looked doubly precarious, for a Turkish-Hungarian force was threatening their communications with the relieving Germans and the Poles. But it was defeated at Stammersdorf by

Charles of Lorraine, and by mid-August a substantial Bavarian and Thuringian army had reached Krems, along with Imperial troops from the Rhine. Most decisively, a Polish army had assembled at Krakow, and by the end of August Jan Sobieski had joined forces with Charles of Lorraine and a massive German army. Advancing rapidly through the Vienna woods, they caught the Turks off guard, and on 12th September, when they were hard pressed by the German infantry attack, Sobieski in person led a charge of Polish cavalry which decided the day. The victory was swiftly followed up and by October the Turks were driven from Esztergom further down the Danube in the heart of Hungary.

The famous event was more a turning point for the Ottoman Empire than for Central Europe. The Turks had long been over-extended, and even had they taken Vienna, they would hardly have been capable of further advance. Its fall would have been a European cultural disaster, but the strategic Turkish threat had long been on the wane.

The economic and social weaknesses of the vast Uthmanli empire had long been evident; it had always remained in principle a nomad encampment exploiting an extraordinary variety of subject peoples and religions, and dependent for controlling its army and administration on the Kullar, or slave household of the Sultan, recruited from the subject peoples. "The regular levy of boys, as long as it lasted, enabled (the rulers) to press into their military and civil service and to assimilate the flower of the male youth of the subject non-Moslem communities. Some of the best talent of the conquered people was sucked and funnelled into the capital, there to be Islamized, Turkized and utilized to the glory and advancement of the Imperial state. Circassians, Greeks, Albanians, Slavs, Italians and even Armenians rose to the highest offices of the Empire . . ."[1] But all remained slaves liable to arbitrary execution or ruin by the Sultan. The defeated Sultan Caliph had followed the old Turkish custom of having Kara Mustafa Pasha beheaded and his head conveyed to the Sublime Porte on a silver dish, and the Grand Vizier was lucky not to have been impaled. Such a regime could not stand the strain and consequent stagnation of defeat, nor face the mounting technological challenge of the west, to which it was no longer superior. The day of the Grand Turk was on the wane; after the Treaty of Karlowitz in 1699, which concluded the war, he began, though still dangerous, to be the Sick Man of Europe, kept alive mainly by the dissensions of his Christian enemies. For the Treaty concluded between Austria, Poland, Venice and the Turks conceded all but a relatively small southern area of Hungary, including Transylvania, to the Habsburgs, the whole of Podolia to the Poles, and the Morea in Greece to the Venetians; in due course Karlorci—as it is in Serb—north-east of Belgrade, would become a main focus of Serb nationalism.

II

While the Austrians, Poles and South Germans had been fighting off the Turks, in Northern Germany the electorate of Brandenburg, which extended

[1]P. K. Hitti. *History of the Arabs*. London, 1960. p. 716.

intermittently and vulnerably from the Vistula to the Rhine, had become a formidable power. It centred on the ancient Mark of Brandenburg, its capital Berlin, and included the Dukedom of Prussia to the east, now independent of Polish suzereignty; the Rhineland Duchies of Cleves and Mark, north of Cologne, and Ravensburg and Minden on the Weser. The Hohenzollern Electors exploited their vulnerable position by exacting regular taxation for the standing army it obviously demanded, while confirming the nobility and the upper bourgeoisie in their traditional privileges. The "Great Elector" Frederick William (1640–88) had been educated at Leiden, and wished to create a maritime and commercial state on Dutch lines; but he never gained Stettin, the coveted port in Western or "Swedish" Pomerania; so he was compelled to concentrate on organizing an army 45,000 strong and a royal bureaucracy to sustain it. In doing so he formed the framework of Brandenburg–Prussia.

The army, mainly recruited from other areas of Central Europe, as well as from peasant levies, was officered by the nobility, whose hard core were the Prussian aristocracy with their great estates, who had inherited the martial and colonizing tradition of Teutonic knights and Baltic barons: while in Poland the gentry had paralysed the Crown, in Brandenburg–Prussia they were its main support. They formed an exclusive caste, forbidden to trade, intensely loyal to their sovereign, and contemptuous of the bourgeoisie and peasants from whose taxes their army was maintained. The Great Elector had mercantilist and maritime ambitions, but, as might be expected from the fierce history of this bleak part of Europe, it was the army which created Brandenburg–Prussia, not the state the army. The officer corps became arrogantly aloof with its own intense *esprit de corps* and exacting concepts of military honour and sacrifice, and the landowners became known as *Junkers* (young masters) from their service as ensigns in the army.

Moreover, these relatively poor landowners were genuinely impervious to the corruption and inefficiency of the self-indulgent aristocrats who monopolized the higher ranks of the French armies. They became dedicated professionals of the new kinds of warfare which had superseded the campaigns of the casual and individualistic mercenaries of the Thirty Years War, and relied on iron discipline and quasi-automatic drill in armies in which the officers were socially segregated from the "other ranks". The main military development occurred in the early eighteenth century; but events round the Baltic had early played into the "Great Elector's" hands. In 1660 under the Treaty of Oliva, whereby under Austrian and Dutch pressure, Poland and Denmark had been emancipated from Swedish rule, Frederick William had acquired the Duchy of Prussia for supporting the Poles; and in 1675, in the Franco–Dutch war which had broken out in 1672, as an ally of the Dutch, he had won a crucial victory over the pro-French Swedes at Fehrbellin. After this success he found his main interest in recruiting gigantic grenadiers for his Potsdam guard. He also developed armament industries less massive but more efficient than those behind the huge Russian armies then being improvised by Peter the Great, promoted Prussian agriculture and forestry, encouraged textile industries, and imported Huguenot settlers who knew how to conduct them.

So, with the decline of Austrian Imperial influence in the north following the Thirty Years War, and the subsequent destruction of Swedish power on the southern shore of the Baltic, Brandenburg–Prussia, radiating from Berlin, had by 1680 already spread its tentacles round Magdeburg on the Elbe, and by 1720 had clinched its hold on Eastern Pomerania, secured in 1648 by absorbing the western (Swedish) part of the country including Stettin on the Oder. This at last gave Brandenburg the major port on the Baltic which the "Great Elector" had desired. Though still separated from East Prussia by a large slice of Poland, the Hohenzollerns had already made Brandenburg–Prussia a major power, poised to take advantage of the perennial political confusion of the Poles, long over-extended by impracticable ambitions in the Ukraine and even in Muscovy.

III

Eastward in Muscovy the death of Ivan Groznyi in 1584 had been followed by a "Time of Troubles" and of Polish and Swedish attack. Feodor Ivanovitch, Ivan's half-imbecile second son, whom his father had thought fit only to be "a bell ringer in a convent", had indeed been crowned Tsar, but his Tsaritza's uncle, Boris Godunov, had got himself made Regent with the resounding titles of Familiar Great Boyar and Viceroy of Kazan and Astrakhan. In part of Tatar origin, this able man had conducted the government without disaster until the death of Tsar Feodor in 1598, when, in spite of the opposition of most of the magnates, the *Zemsky Sobor* had elected him Tsar. But his position was soon challenged by the great Boyars, led by the Romanovs, most of whom in 1601 he had deported to Siberia or the White Sea, where they "were treated with such rigour that only one of them survived".[1] Moreover, following a succession of famines, there had been peasant revolts, and although the worst one led by *Hlopka Kosolap* (Slave Crooked-paw) had been put down, one of the Romanov retainers had organized a more serious threat. In 1591 Tsar Feodor's younger half-brother Dmitri, the son of Ivan Groznyi's last wife, and never legitimized for the succession, had been done to death on his estate at Uglich; now one Yury Otrepyev had claimed to be the murdered prince. In 1604 he had turned up in Krakow, where he had become a Catholic and been betrothed to the daughter of the Voivode of Sandomir. King Sigismund III of Poland had subsidized him to claim his "rights" in Muscovy, which he had invaded that autumn; and though at first defeated, the "false Dmitri' had soon been joined by considerable forces of Cossacks, while the Muscovites had put up only half hearted resistance to a "born Tsarevitch".

Then, in April 1605, Boris Godunov had died: by May the major Boyars had gone over to "Dmitri"; by June Feodor Godunov, Boris's son, had been assassinated and "Dmitri" had entered Moscow and been recognized as Tsar. But "Dmitri" (1604–06) had proved too unconventional for the more conserv-

[1] Bernard Pares. *op. cit.* p. 132.

ative Boyars, and had married his Catholic Polish betrothed. By May 1606, the powerful Boyar, Basil Shuisky, with other armed magnates had broken into the Kremlin, and "Dmitri" had escaped them only by jumping out of a window. Injured by the fall, he had demanded an interview with his supposed mother, the Dowager Tsaritza Martha; but, though she had at first acknowledged him, she had then disowned him; so he had been hacked to pieces on Red Square, his remains burnt, and the ashes fired from a cannon towards Poland.

Muscovy by now had lapsed into further confusion: Basil Shuisky had become Tsar (1606–10) and himself carried the exhumed body of the original Dmitri to be buried beside former Tsars in Moscow, when miracles at his tomb had soon proved that he was authentically dead. But over much of the vast country there had been peasant and Cossack revolts, and the Poles, undaunted, had produced a second "false Dmitri". He had won support from the Zaporoznian and Don Cossacks, in 1608 defeated the Tsar's army on the Volkhov and, with Polish support, marched on Moscow. He had been held off; but in 1609 Sigismund III of Poland himself besieged Smolensk. The second "false Dmitri", to whom the first's Polish widow had transferred herself, had continued his own attack on Moscow, and Basil Shuisky had been forced to abdicate. Rather than admit the second "false Dmitri" and his mob, the Boyars had then invited the Poles into Moscow, and had offered the Crown to Prince Wladyslaw, Sigismund III's son. The Polish king, however, jealous of his own son, had stood out for stiff terms.

Then in December 1610 the second "false Dmitri" had been killed by a Tatar—then a normal hazard of life; and with the last "Dmitri" out of the way, the Russians had reunited and attacked the Poles in the Kremlin, who in revenge had burnt most of the rest of the town. They had then held out until November 1612, when they had been starved into submission.

The victorious Muscovites, who had rallied from all over the country, now decided to elect a Tsar. The choice fell on the surviving Romanov, a great-nephew by marriage of Ivan Groznyi and the son of the Metropolitan Philaret, who had encouraged resistence to the Poles. In February 1613, by English reckoning the year after the death of Henry, Prince of Wales, Michael Romanov, aged sixteen and lately released from being a hostage in the Kremlin, had been elected Tsar, and that July he had been crowned: out of resistance to the Polish occupation and from the confusion of internal strife, a new Muscovite dynasty had been established. It would endure until 1917. Tsar Michael Romanov reigned until 1645, and his son, Tsar Alexis, had been succeeded in 1676 by Feodor, his offspring by his first wife Maria Miloslavsky; but Feodor had died young, and since his younger brother, Ivan, was epileptic and half blind, Alexis' ten-year-old son Peter by Natalia Maryshkina was proclaimed Tsar Peter I (1682–1725). The Miloslavskys then roused the Streltsy guards who proclaimed Ivan joint Tsar as Ivan V, and Ivan's sister Sophia became Regent; it was not until 1696 that Ivan V died and Peter I, assuming sole power, set about the transformation of Muscovy that made him Peter the Great, Emperor of all the Russias.

IV

It is widely imagined that Peter the Great, who so transformed Muscovy, imposed a sudden and unprecedented change; in fact his swift violent methods, like most successful political transformations, were the culmination of tendencies long in train. "The daemonic element in Peter's personality, his violence and cruelty, the unrelenting pace that he set, the magnitude of the ubiquitous burdens that he imposed—these features of his reign have given the impression that Peter broke completely with the past, and that the period of imperial Petrine Russia, which lasted until the October Revolution, was sundered by a broad unbridged chasm from the period of Muscovite Tsardom ... it was not so. The greatness of Peter lies in the fact that to a large extent he gave shape to needs and aspirations growing within Muscovite society of the late seventeenth century."[1] Ivan Groznyi and Boris Godunov had both hired foreign experts from the West, and the all-important conquest of Siberia had been proceeding even through the "Time of Troubles" that had brought a Polish garrison to the Kremlin. Under Michael Romanov the Tsar became utterly dependent on the civil and military gentry of service, who tightened their own grip on their peasantry, who were now more closely bound to the soil and by law hunted down if they escaped. Moreover, by 1646 all landowners had to register their peasants, whose descendants officially inherited their parent's status. Serfdom thus became a state institution, in the interests of Government, while flight was punished by the knout.

This harsh regime seemed necessary for survival. Indeed the new dynasty was fighting for its life. The Poles and Swedes again combined with dissident Muscovites to attack; Prince Wladyslaw combined with the Don Cossacks to assert his claim to be Tsar, and it was not until 1632 that, although the Muscovites had failed to recover Smolensk from the Poles, he admitted Michael Romanov's claim. But the Tsar Michael was still too insecure to profit by the exploit of the Don Cossacks when they captured Azov from the Turks, and in 1642, under pressure from the *Zemsky Sobor*, he had to order them to evacuate their conquest. When in the final phase of the Thirty Years War and of the first Civil War in England his young son Alexis succeeded him (1645–76) he came into a troubled inheritance; taxation was so severe and administration so inefficient and corrupt that in 1648 the people of Moscow rioted and threatened the Tsar himself, and a particularly hated tax collector was assassinated. Down in the Ukraine, in 1667–71, fugitive peasants and other malcontents joined lawless Don Cossacks under a *Hetman*, Stenka Razin. He assembled a fleet on the Caspian, defeated both Muscovite and Persian counter-attacks, and in 1670 advanced up the Volga inciting peasant revolts. But he failed to capture Simbirsk and, defeated and captured by the Tsar's avenging army after one of the most spectacular and in some eyes romantic revolts in Russian history said to have cost a hundred thousand lives, he was sent caged to Moscow and there executed, leaving a halo of legendary prowess

[1]B. H. Sumner. *Peter the Great and the Emergence of Russia*. London, 1950. p. 3. q.v. for a compelling and readable account.

by land and sea, in the eyes of the "shifting underdog world of the Volga and South-Eastern Steppes".[1]

In these circumstances of foreign invasion and regional turmoil, the government had increasingly been compelled to rely on Western engineers, mercenaries, doctors and merchants, mainly Protestant Germans, Dutch, English and Scots. They were disliked but tolerated; particularly for training the army, half of which were "troops of foreign formation", and despite the denunciation of the conservative clergy, who declared that "man was made in the image of God with a beard, not like cats, dogs or monkeys",[2] foreign dress and shaving were being accepted well before Peter the Great made them compulsory.

A youth of powerful physique, great stature and boundless energy, by 1696 Peter I had developed a passion for mechanical devices, ships, carpentry and war. In contrast to Louis XIV, he was bored with court ceremonial, loved to make things with his hands, and by fifteen had a passion for ships and the sea. Impatient of convention, he had a fine flair for essentials and no inhibitions, and since he had, writes Sumner, "a head like a Madeira cask", he enjoyed carousing with boon companions sometimes for days on end; but he was also a natural autocrat who inspired terror. No sooner had he come to full power than in 1697 he set out for the west to learn modern technology for himself, and the Electress Sophia of Hanover who, had Queen Anne died sooner, would have been Queen of England, encountered and described him: "a very tall fine man, with a handsome face and good posture. His mind is very lively and his retorts quick and incisive. But", she added, "with all these great gifts of nature he could well have better manners."[3] The Tsar had long surrounded himself with foreigners, and picked up fluent if inaccurate German; he could write, but his spelling was "wild"; what he most enjoyed was working in shipyards, sailing, and letting off fireworks. He worked first in the East India Company's shipyard at Amsterdam, then, finding the Dutch deficient on theory, at Deptford near London, where he and his entourage "damnified" John Evelyn the diarist's house, Sayes Court, on which, as subtenants of Admiral Benbow, they had been quartered. He then descended on Vienna to learn about fortification.

Peter the Great loved noise; but unlike most royalties of his day, he did not care for hunting, though, when necessary, he did not mind in person executing men. Indeed, he signalized his return to Russia by decapitating 320 of the Streltzy who had rebelled in his absence; according to rumour, even beginning the good work himself and certainly insisting that his principal officials carried it out in turn themselves, inexpert though they might be.[4]

Having learnt about warships from the English and Dutch, and about war on land from the Austrians, the Tsar developed the two royal regiments, the Preobrazhenskii and the Semenovskii; both were trained by foreigners, since "no one in Russia was competent" to do so, and under the command of a French adventurer François Le Fort, who held his own in the Tsar's drinking

[1]Sumner. *op. cit.* p. 9.
[2]Quoted in Sumner. *op. cit.* p. 14.
[3]*A Sourcebook of Russian History*. *op. cit.* Vol. 2. p. 314.
[4]The foreigners declined, saying that such was not the custom in their countries.

bouts into middle age, when the Vodka bottle claimed him. His principal Russian minister was the low-born, almost illiterate, Menshikov, whom he made a Duke, and most of Peter's immediate subordinates, to the disgust of the old Boyar families, came from "the lowest and neediest gentry".

In all Peter's reign there were only two years of peace. In 1695, before his visit to the west, he had recaptured Azov from the Turks, and in the following year in Vienna he had renewed the first Russian alliance with Austria against them. It came to little, since by 1699 the Austrian Emperor was more than satisfied by the Peace of Karlowitz, and preoccupied with the aggressions of Louis XIV; but it marks the acceptance of Russia as a major power by central Europe. Meanwhile, Peter pressed on with his campaign to westernize Muscovy and, symbolically, himself cut off the cherished beards of the great Boyars at Court. By 1701 he decreed that all the upper class except the clergy had to wear European dress, the "upper dress French or Saxon", the "lower dress German": only German saddles were to be used; by 1705 he commanded that all his subjects, save clergy and peasants, were to shave.

These changes, like those of Kemal Ataturk, symbolized a relentless drive to change the whole society. The Russians had always been strong in artillery, and in the course of the reign the Ural iron mines were better exploited, factories built to produce far more guns; printing houses were set up and the first libraries established; sail cloth was manufactured for the fleet, and the equivalent of milestones set up on the roads. The capture of Azov had whetted the Tsar's appetite for an attack on the Black Sea and even Constantinople, and he launched a massive project for building a Russian Black Sea Fleet at Voronezh-on-Don. And behind these projects, economic, social and military, the Tsar had reorganized the bureaucracy, tightened up and increased taxation and strengthened the hold of central and local government on the immense land.

Even Ivan Groznyi had failed to win the "window in the Baltic", and Gustav Adolph had left Sweden the major Baltic power; but Peter was statesman enough to realize that the Baltic was more important than the Black Sea. So in August 1700 the Russians came to terms with the Turks, retaining only Azov and Taganrog, and that year, in alliance with Denmark and Poland, they renewed the war with Sweden, which, known as the Great Northern War, lasted until 1721. It began badly for the Russians, for Charles XII of Sweden was a first rate fighting general, and, crossing the Baltic to Livonia, he caught them in a November snow storm outside Narva and routed them. Fortunately for them, Charles XII turned on Poland, and gave Peter time to reorganize and modernize his armies and develop his armament industry, as well as to counter-attack into Ingria and the Karelian isthmus and on Lake Ladoga; then, by 1704, even to recapture Narva. Moreover, in 1703, the year by western reckoning before Blenheim, the Tsar had founded St. Petersburg— an entirely artificial new capital constructed at appalling cost of serf labour in a marsh on the Neva, whose silt protected the city from the sea. Its architecture was entirely Western, at first baroque and afterwards in rococo style. It was modelled on French, Florentine and Dutch styles; its first principal architect, Domenico Trazzini (floruit 1670), was an Italian-Swiss, and it was coloured to suit the pale sunshine of northern summers and the alternating gloom and sparkle of bitter winters. To protect the new city Peter constructed the fortress of Kronstadt on the mouth of the Neva, while the dreaded island prison fortress of Peter and Paul, *Petropavloskaya*, formed the nucleus of the city. So, in a setting in total contrast to that of Moscow and on the sea, Peter began to construct the window on the west which became his capital and one of the finest cities in Europe.

Charles XII had by now become bogged down in Poland, where Polish resistance was disunited and the Lithuanians were fighting one another, so in 1704 Charles had a puppet King, Stanislas Lesczynski, elected to the throne in place of Augustus of Saxony; having put down Augustus, he determined to deal with Peter, who, he was convinced, would never leave the Poles or the Baltic in peace. Early in 1708 Charles XII therefore invaded Muscovy, his objective Moscow. But in face of the Tsar's devastation of the land before him, he turned south-east into the fertile Ukraine, following intelligence that the Don Cossacks under Bulavin and Mazeppa, *Hetman* of the Ukraine, were in revolt. But Charles had taken a great risk; he now depended on reinforcement by another Swedish army and on a baggage train under Lewenhaupt. The Muscovites intercepted and defeated these reinforcements at Lesnaya, east of the Dnieper, between Smolensk and Kiev, in a battle in which Peter himself took part. And the Ukrainians, much as they detested the Tsar, identified Charles XII with the Poles, whom they hated even more, and Mazeppa's Cossack support waned, so that the Swedes had to winter, substantially without reinforcements, in the Ukraine.

By July 1709 the Muscovites closed in on them; at Poltava in the southern Ukraine, under Peter's command, they surrounded and overwhelmed the invaders. Charles XII, wounded in the foot, managed to escape, along with Mazeppa, into Turkish Moldavia.[1] It was a tremendous Muscovite victory: St. Petersburg was now secure from Swedish attack and Muscovy recognized as a great Baltic power.

The Russians now captured Viborg at the north-western end of the Karelian peninsula and threatened Finland, then in 1710 they took Riga at the mouth of the Dvina in southern Livonia, hitherto an outpost of German trade and influence. At last the window to the west and a port on the Baltic had been fully secured.

Charles XII was now in Constantinople, and the Turks belatedly declared war; so Peter appealed to the Serbs and Montenegrins as co-religionists, thus initiating another regular Russian gambit in the Balkans, not yet pan-Slavist, but at least Christian Orthodox. The Russians advanced across the Pruth into Moldavia, but the Hospodar of Wallachia was, rightly, too much afraid both of the powerful Turkish army on the Danube and of Russian domination to

[1]Ivan Mazeppa had been a page at the Polish Court, and educated in the West. He had been made *Hetman* after betraying the plans of the pro-Turkish Cossacks in the Ukraine to the Muscovites, and had fought against the Tatars. But he had intrigued with the Poles and Swedes and Stanislas Lesczynski to create a Polish-Ukrainian union, before he joined Charles XII. He died in 1709 in Moldavia, and the legend that he was tied to a wild horse or torn to pieces by wild horses is fantasy.

commit himself, and the Russians, outnumbered, suffered crushing defeat. They had again to give up Azov, renounce interference in Poland and allow Charles XII safe conduct back to Sweden. It was Austria, not Russia, which would become the Christian power against the Turks in the Balkans, and even the perennially militant Montenegrins had to withdraw to their fastnesses.

It was easier to overrun Finland. By 1714, thanks to a large fleet of galleys, most of the more accessible areas had been conquered in an amphibious campaign, and off Hangö at the south-western extremity of Finland the Russians had won their first naval victory, mainly with Russian built men-of-war. So Charles XII returned to Sweden to find nearly all her foreign possessions lost, and by 1717 Peter was in Paris, negotiating with the Regent's government to substitute a Franco–Russian alliance for the French alliance with the Swedes. But the Great Northern War dragged on. And when in December 1718 Charles XII was shot through the head in an obscure siege in Norway, it took three more years before in 1721 the Treaty of Nystad ended the long conflict. It left only the wreckage of the once great Swedish power, and the Russians firmly established in control of the Baltic provinces and the Gulf of Finland. In celebration of the victorious peace, Peter changed his title of Tsar of Muscovy to Emperor of all the Russias.

Though preoccupied with the wars and constantly moving about his enormous realm, Peter managed to found the complex and overlapping bureaucracy that dominated Russia for centuries and formed the society depicted by great Russian writers. On 1st January 1700 he started his revolution well by imposing a calendar conformable to that of the rest of Europe, though it followed the "old style". Then in 1710 he imposed a modernized script; he also abolished the medieval Council of the Boyars and appointed a Senate strictly under his own control: in 1708 he divided the country into eight subordinate governments with military and judicial powers, themselves divided into many provinces. Overlapping these civilian jurisdictions, he added in 1722 regimental districts supporting garrisons of conscript troops officered by gentry, no longer employed in the Great Northern War. And at the centre he set "colleges" or ministries, for the Army, Navy, Justice, Education, Mines and Industry. The Church, too, was firmly brought under control and subordinated to his own autocracy through a subservient "Holy Synod". But although he destroyed the separate power of the great Boyars, he maintained the position of the nobility and gentry on the land, strengthened by a law of primogeniture, which, modified by choice of heir, kept estates intact. He needed and used the nobles and gentry for the civil bureaucracy as well as the Army, and in 1722 by a table of ranks made precedence depend on rank in the services, civilian as well as military. He also encouraged the nascent bourgeoisie by granting new liberties to the towns and high rank to successful industrialists. Strictly and overwhelmingly hierarchical, a civil and military bureaucracy was imposed on the vast peasant population, and tied to the estates of the ruling classes, themselves subordinate to the autocracy of the Emperor-Tsar.

So Muscovy was transformed into an absolute monarchy and turned towards

Central and Western Europe, instead of, as under the Tatar domination, to Asia, and a colossal work of adaptation was at least superficially achieved.

Only in one aspect did the great Tsar fail—the succession. By his marriage at seventeen to the beautiful but uncongenial Eudoxia Lopukhin, whom he soon discarded, he had a son Alexis, who proved totally unsuited to carry on his work; incompetent and terrified, he became a focus of conservative resistance. So in 1718, after he had fled for protection to the Austrian Emperor in Tyrol and Italy and been retrieved, Peter had him incarcerated in the *Petropavloskaya* fortress and destroyed. By now the Tsar had married Catherine, a buxom young Lithuanian serving wench, long his mistress, whom in 1724 he crowned Empress of Russia. She proved an admirable wife, but when on Peter's death in the depth of winter in 1725 following a plunge into the icy Neva to rescue sailors drowning by their sinking yacht, she proved inadequate to her appalling responsibilities, and Alexis' son, Peter II (1727–30) died young. Peter's work was only saved by the good sense of Catherine's half-Lithuanian daughter, the Empress Elizabeth (1741–62), and then by the outstanding abilities of the German princess, Catherine II the Great (1762–96).

XXXV

Le Roi Soleil

While the Dutch and English had greatly increased their wealth and power, the French had remained extremely formidable. Richelieu had laid the foundations of an impersonal and absolute regime in France and made it much more powerful abroad; but his success, over-estimated by French nationalist historians, had been limited by medieval and regional liberties and been too much a personal *tour de force*. As Tapié writes, "Ce qui était accompli ne consistait pas en réformes profondes dans la structure sociale et économique de la nation, mais lui était superposé."[1] Hence a violent and dangerous reaction intermittently from 1648 to 53, known as the *Fronde* from the *Frondeurs* or "slingers" who rioted and threw up barricades in Paris and interrupted the take over of power by Mazarin, the designated successor of Richelieu. There had been two *Frondes*: the first, coincident with the crisis in England which led to the judicial murder of Charles I, is known as the *Fronde* of the *Parlement* and of the Parisian insurgents, and was occasioned by grievances over taxation and the withholding of interest on the *rentes* or public debt; the second, the *Fronde* of the Princes, had been a neo-medieval revolt of *les grands*, the high aristocracy, against centralized government as such, which, worsened by soldiers unemployed after the Thirty Years War, had brought France so near anarchy that the politically conscious French propertied classes had rallied to Mazarin and the young Louis XIV. The power of the nobility was finally broken; but Louis XIV never forgot the humiliations the *Frondes* had inflicted on him when still young. "Louis never really trusted Paris again; he never really trusted the *Parlement*, and he never forgot that the greatest misfortune that could come to a king is the loss of his power to govern his kingdom. In his *Mémoires*, in his letters and in his conversation for the rest of his life the fears . and terrors caused by the barricades and rebellion always remained."[2] While, until 1659, the government still had the war with Spain on its hands, the *Parlement*, encouraged by the success of the very different English Parliament, had demanded the restoration of its judicial powers and the dismissal of the

[1]Victor L. Tapié. *La France de Louis XIII et de Richelieu*. Paris, 1953. p. 534.
[2]John B. Wolf. *Louis XIV*. London, 1968. p. 42. This American biography is the best, most thorough and most fairly assessed study of the King.

intendants—the key men of Richelieu's regime in the provinces. Moreover there was endemic peasant discontent and even revolt which continued far into the reign. The nobility, clergy and crown officials were all exempted from the *taille* or land tax, and low official salaries led to ramified corruption and fraudulent accounts. Both Richelieu and Mazarin had been rapacious, and Fouquet, the superintendent of finances, had made a colossal fortune and become a great art patron before being found out. Office went by purchase, and the buyers recouped themselves and provided lavishly for their families. Tax farmers, financiers (*traitants*) and army contractors piled up wealth and unpopularity, while the sale of offices became a main source of government revenue to meet the wars. Sales of office, indeed, created a huge vested interest in supporting the regime, and "it can be argued that the creation of absolute monarchy in France was not so much the result of the power of the crown as its weakness. Henri IV said that he had liquidated the great nobles of the League not so much by the exercise of power as by bribery ... similarly by the device of the annual payments (as the *rentes*) he bought the support of the middle class. Absolute monarchy was therefore in this aspect no more than a gigantic system of bribery of those whom the crown thought it worth while to bribe."[1] In the first *Fronde* the holders of *rentes* and middle-class office holders, normally supporters of the establishment, had turned against the regime, and been backed by the Parisians; but the nobility so much despised them that they had scorned to combine with them, and in the second *Fronde* they were too arrogant and touchy to combine with each other.

Cardinal Mazarin—Giulio Mazzarini, an adventurer of Sicilian origin, born in Abruzzi—had graduated from Papal to French diplomacy in 1639 after being Papal Nuncio in France, and two years later had been made a Cardinal to enhance his prestige in preparing for the Peace of Münster, though in fact he prolonged the Thirty Years War. He had then been installed by Richelieu as *Chef du Conseil de la Reine*, a position greatly enhanced when Anne of Austria, as Queen Dowager, became Regent for the child Louis XIV. An able diplomat and administrator, he had managed to survive the *Frondes*, though three times driven out of France, and remained as principal minister until his death in 1661, when Louis XIV took over in no uncertain terms and imposed his personal rule until 1715. Mazarin, who was fifty-nine when he died, was bitterly disliked because, in the Italian tradition, he had provided well for his relatives; he left immense wealth, a fine collection of pictures and a splendid library. He was vehemently suspected of being the lover of the Queen Regent. During the aftermath of the *Frondes* and of the Peace of Westphalia, the Cardinal consolidated the impersonal centralized government founded by Richelieu and recruited the ablest of Louis XIV's administrators, for whom during *La Grand Siècle* the "Sun King" has since often got the credit.

II

The monarch who from 1661 to 1683 dominated Europe, and from 1683 to

[1]*France: Government and Society.* Ed. J. M. Wallace-Hadrill and J. McManners. London, 1957. Ch. VI: M. Prestwich. The Making of Absolute Monarchy (1559–1683) p. 121.

1715 provoked a resistance so widespread that it frustrated his vast ambitions, was a personality of great force and conventional mind. Half Spanish on his mother's side, he had inherited something of his ancestor Philip II's immense powers of work, and, in contrast to his lazy and frivolous father, conscientiously pursued what he termed his *métier du roi*—the craft of kingship. Devoid of the wit and charm of Henri IV, though he derived from him a vigorous Bourbon temperament which, unlike his cousin Charles II of England, he discreetly directed into regular channels, he took himself with Spanish seriousness, and from his accession to the throne at the age of four and a half became accustomed to be always on parade. He had a steady flair for public relations, and successfully deployed the wealth and splendour of his court for political propaganda, so that he became a tremendous impresario for French political and cultural imperialism. Sustained by an invincible conviction that, like a Byzantine emperor, he was God's representative on earth, with God a "superior power of which the royal power is part", he accepted absolute authority as by Divine Right. The doctrine of "sovereignty", propounded by Bodin as *majestas*, was embodied by Louis XIV, who regarded himself quite simply and literally as responsible to no one but his God. The medieval institutions that had made up the old community of the realm, along with the cosmopolitan temporal authority of the Papacy, were swept aside, and the splendour and formality of the court were mobilized to glorify the entire supremacy of the *Roi Soleil*.

This majestic conception of Kingship was an end in itself: its object the perennial French idea of *la gloire*, military and cultural, so that with her *mission civilisatrice* France, embodied in *Louis le Grand*, could dominate Europe and create a rich mercantilist colonial empire. There was nothing original in these ambitions, which, apart from the desire for colonies, were rooted in French history, and "the political evolution of the French nation under the personal rule of Louis XIV consisted not in any innovations but merely in giving a settled form to those of earlier days. Mazarin left as his legacy to Louis a docile nation, great princes reduced to submission, and a *Parlement* that had been tamed; he further bequeathed an experienced body of officials trained in administration. The absolute monarchy was an accomplished fact ... it was an impersonal government, operating arbitrarily in secret, and having at its disposal a royal prison, the Bastille, in which it could imprison and detain indefinitely without trial anybody who incurred its displeasure."[1] It could censor literature and, though a difficult thing to do in France, try to stifle discussion. In a word, Louis XIV became the embodiment of arbitrary power.

This was exercised through a small *conseil d'état* of bourgeois ministers detested by the high aristocracy, with clearly defined responsibilities, which both promulgated the royal orders, and in its judicial capacity dealt rapidly with law suits between the state and any individual or corporation rash enough to resist it. Policy over justice, police and finance was imposed by *intendants* originally organized by Richelieu, whose jurisdiction cut across the motley

[1]Seignobos. *op. cit.* p. 248.

collection of purchased provincial offices and superseded local jurisdictions, so that authority radiated from Paris. Moreover, although Richelieu and Mazarin had never solved the problem baffling to all seventeenth-century governments, of making revenue match expenditure, under Jean Baptiste Colbert a more systematically mercantilist policy was carried out, designed to heap up wealth within France and develop colonies economically subservient to the home country. Born in Rheims in 1619, the son of a draper, this *petit bourgeois* lawyer had turned to banking and declared that "it is nothing but the abundance of money in a state that makes the difference to its greatness and power." He admired the business methods of the Dutch and was the first professional economist to wield political power; as often is the way of such experts, his theories, though orthodox at the time, were wrong. He instituted tariffs against rival powers and tried to direct the trade of state-backed industries, particularly in luxury goods as silk, tapestries and porcelains; but his state-sponsored companies for export trades and colonization never attracted the necessary private capital: the French preferred to invest in public offices which also brought social status. By 1664 Colbert had ousted Fouquet as superindendent of Finance, and himself became *Contrôleur Général,* as well as Secretary for the Royal Household and the Navy, a position from which he was able to develop a formidable French fleet and mercantile marine. Unable to make radical reforms, he brought some order into the collection of revenue and the keeping of accounts, so that he much increased the revenues and the security behind the *rentes* in an attempt to improve the government's credit. He also promoted the cultivation of cereal crops and flax; improved horse-breeding in Normandy; in effect nationalized many textile factories and saw that they were better run. He attempted, indeed, to get the whole nation to work—a *petit bourgeois* notion, novel at the time. It went down better in France than it would have in England or in Spain.

With apparently more substantial revenues, Louis XIV, unlike his father, whose small armies had to be improvised under unreliable aristocratic commanders, could afford an enormous standing army. The armies of the Thirty Years' War and of the English Civil Wars, as already seen, had been quite small—seldom more than 16,000–20,000 men. Louis le Grand built up an army of over 200,000, by 1680 of nearly 300,000 men. Even here, it was only in scale that his work was original: the Spaniards had organized disciplined infantry, and Gustav Adolf's cavalry could charge home; the Dutch, in face of the Spanish attack, had become expert in the defensive siegecraft that so much determined warfare. And here France produced a master.

Sebastian le Prestre de Vauban (1633–1707), who came of Burgundian gentry, was not the kind of commander whom François I would have admired; he was a military engineer—in English terms a "Sapper"—who specialized in the defence of the vulnerable north-eastern and eastern frontiers, and who abandoned the time-honoured custom of building imposing stone fortifications, as at Loches round its eleventh-century keep, or—as most massively—at Constantinople. He preferred unobtrusive defences sited for cross fire and defended by ditches and oblique earthern counter-scarps which could resist even cannon. Appointed Commissary-General of Fortifications in 1667, he elaborated a systematic doctrine of siege work which dominated the warfare of Louis XIV and even the military genius of Turenne and Condé. In 1703 the King made him a Marshal of France: but he offended by airing his views on the economic value of the banished Huguenots, and on the *taille*, for he urged in his *Projet d'une Dixième Royal* (Project for a Royal Tithe), published in the last year of his life, that it should be made applicable to all subjects, not merely to the peasants. If adopted, it might have saved the *ancien régime*; but his invention of bombardment by ricochet and of the bayonet proved much more popular.

While the French army was greatly enlarged, and much better disciplined, Colbert set about creating a navy fit to face the English or the Dutch. He had dockyards built at Toulon and Brest, and an arsenal at Rochefort; but French social distinctions, rigidly observed, blocked careers made by merit, while, as in the British navy, crews often had to be forcibly enlisted. But the fleets were now more self-sufficient for timber, ropes, tar and canvas—no longer so dependent on trade with the Baltic States—and the design of the ships was excellent. France thus became a great naval and colonial power as well as much more formidable in her traditional field of martial "gloire", a modern and contrived version of the traditional *Gesta Dei per Francos*.

At the centre of this radiating power, with its unsound social and economic base, the French Court took on a new and deliberately pompous aspect, more in the Spanish than the French tradition. Far from doing justice under an oak tree or being proud of having bread, wine and gaiety instead of wealth, Louis XIV deliberately set the example of a stifling and formal grandeur. Detesting Paris since his humiliation during the *Fronde*, he built the colossal new palace at Versailles, to which the nobility were lured, there compelled to dance attendance on the monarch, and so distracted from their traditional occupation of conspiracy. Thus tamed, they eagerly competed for petty ceremonial distinctions, and tolerated a boredom which was quite un-French: as Seignobos remarks, "The Court of Versailles was never gay. Louis XIV may have appeared as the incarnation of the greatness of France, but he never represented the French character."[1] The King's marriage to the Infanta Marie-Thérèse of Spain, for dynastic reasons which did not include love for a pious and boring princess, did nothing to enliven the royal circle, though her gambling losses "were the principal means of support for a sizeable company of the court."[2] Ponderous ceremonial and laborious etiquette followed him even to his tedious wars, to which he was conveyed in an immense coach, and at which he surveyed the battlefields and sieges from a safe distance. His exacting and methodical way of life was not that of a martial aristocrat, rather of a conscientious multi-millionaire dedicated to routine duty.

But his contrived splendour paid off, more than his military conquests. The French language, French luxuries and French manners came to dominate the courts of Europe; the language of diplomacy, no longer Latin, became and remained French; and French cuisine became justly renowned. Originally

[1]*op. cit.* p. 254.
[2]Wolf. *op. cit.* p. 289.

devised in Italy in the households of the princes of the cosmopolitan Church, and brought to France by Catherine de Medici, Italian skills applied to French resources had already created the classic recipes of La Varenne, whose *Cuisinier François* had been published in 1651, and Condé's Chef, Vatel, was sufficiently important to throw temperaments. La Varenne was the first cook to condescend to use mushrooms, asparagus and herbs, and Louis XIV, who was a glutton, was a pioneer at least in consuming salads.[1] The basic French sauces were now invented and imitated, and *bourgeoie* as well as *haute cuisine* became elaborate—not the least of *toutes les gloires de la France*.

III

Well aware of the political importance of the arts, Louis XIV exercised a vast patronage. Ever since Richelieu had founded the Académie Française, and François de Malherbe (d. 1628) had written official verse for Henri IV with its formal phrasing, "improving" upon Ronsard's classical style, French playwrights and authors had become much more conventional. The formal alexandrine verse of Corneille (1606–84) proved well suited for solemn themes of conflicting love and duty, of public obligation and private character, set in Roman history and clearly deployed, which fascinated audiences accustomed to accept *raison d'état* as duty. Jean Racine (1639–99) used the stately alexandrine line more subtly and composed dramas, modelled on Greek tragedy, concerned with intimate passion; as in *Andromaque* and *Britannicus* (which portrayed Nero) and in *Bajazet*; while *Phèdre*, reinterpreting the Greek tale of Phaedra and the virtuous Hippolytus, shows harrowing psychological insight. Never had sonorous French rhetoric been so superbly declaimed, and the neo-classic conventions admired by the monarch and his entourage been given such depth.

More akin to the natural French genius and its medieval urban ancestry, Molière[2] (1622–73), intermittently and capriciously patronized by royalty but

[1] So often, for ceremonial reasons, having to eat alone, the monarch was perhaps better able to concentrate on the pleasures of the table.

[2] Molière was his stage name: his real one, which he understandably disguised, was Jean Baptiste Poquelin. His father was an upholsterer to the King, so he must have had plenty to do, and could afford to send his son to the *Lycée Louis le Grand*. But the boy was determined to go on stage, and by 1644 was calling himself Molière and next year in prison for debt. He emerged as actor and producer, mainly in the south, at Albi, Lyon, Montpellier and Béziers, but it was not until 1658 that he got his big chance. Louis XIV, who had sat through the whole of Corneille's *Nicomède*, was delighted with a short following piece by Molière, whose title speaks for itself, *Le Docteur Amoureux*. The King's brother, Philippe Duc d'Orléans, then took over Moeière and his company, though he failed to pay the promised pension, and in 1660 Molière was granted the right to his father's post as upholsterer to the King, which he presumably farmed out. In 1662, he married Armande Béjart, but the marriage was not a success and only one child survived. In 1665 Louis XIV himself took over Molière's company as the *Troupe du Roi*. In February 1673 Molière was taken ill on the stage and died that night. He was fifty-one.

never part of the establishment, derived plots and stock characters from popular Italianate plays long performed in the provinces, when he was himself long an itinerant actor-manager; it was not until 1659 with *Les Précieuses Ridicules* that he took the Court and Paris by storm by satirizing the perennially tiresome feminine intellectuals of the salons. He followed up this success by *Sganarelle* on the equally perennial French theme of cuckolds, and by *Le Tartuffe* (1664, but not licensed for general performance for five years), which ridiculed religious asceticism and humbug. He then turned to the equally well-worn theme of *Don Juan* which he made a farce, and created the famous cuckold *Georges Dandin*; created *Le Misanthrope*, and reached the climax of his comedies of manners in *Le Bourgeois Gentilhomme*, first performed in the magnificent setting of Chambord, and died acting his own *Le Malade Imaginaire*. He was the greatest of French dramatists. Unlike Shakespeare, who made a fortune and obtained a coat of arms, Molière never got above the struggles of his profession; nor can Louis XIV be credited with more than intermittent patronage; but his comedies, enhanced by music and by ballets, are far more popular and intimately French than the formal splendours of Corneille and Racine, and contributed to the charm of French civilization which proved more lasting than the military *gloire*.

Opera, which had originated in Italy, when Monteverdi's splendid *Orfeo* had been produced in Venice in 1607, was developed, as was ballet, at the court of Louis XIV by the Florentine Lully (1632–87), the King's Master of Music, whose compositions were at once melodious, stately and gay.[1]

French classical architecture, which derived from Rome and Venice, was already flourishing when Richelieu had commissioned Lemercier to design the Church of the Sorbonne, with its restrained and elegant front, not dissimilar to the idiom of Inigo Jones; but François Mansart (1598–1666) was more original and French. The son of a carpenter, he rose by the force of genius, and if "as far as we can judge his character, he was arrogant, obstinate, intolerant, difficult and probably dishonest ... these qualities were only the unattractive reverse of his high feeling for his own calling and his justifiable confidence in his ability as an architect."[2] He exploited the contrast between brick and stone, and is popularly best remembered for his high pitched roofs. The excellent proportions and simplicity of the extension he built for Louis XII's brother, Gaston d'Orléans, at Blois contrast with the clumsy renaissance staircase adjacent to it. For austere elegance in a manner paralleled by the Banqueting House at Whitehall, the early work of Mansart compares with that of Louis le Vau (1612–70), whose most famous surviving Chateau is Vaux le Vicomte, built for Fouquet in 1657–61, where, whether or not one likes the pompous dome, the proportions and balance of the building, set off by Le Nôtre's formal gardens, are extremely satisfying. The estate became the prototype of Ver-

[1]He had risen from being a violinist in the King's orchestra to obtain *lettres de noblesse*, to be one of the *Secrétaires du Roi* and entirely to dominate the musical life of the Court. He used such a large conducting stick with such verve that he wounded his own foot and so, in the conditions of the time, perished.

[2]Anthony Blunt. *Art and Architecture in France 1500–1700* Pelican History of Art. Penguin, Harmondsworth, 1957. p. 202.

sailles for, after Fouquet's disgrace, the King took over his architects and craftsmen and employed them to build his own chateau which was designed to supersede all others. And in 1661 Louis XIV, delighted by the historic paintings of Alexander by Charles Le Brun, made him director of Arts, a dictatorship he exercised until his death in 1690.

Le Vau was the son of a master mason, and less arrogant and exacting than Mansart; in collaboration with Le Brun, he created a team of architects, decorators and landscape gardeners who, by 1669, produced the first version of Versailles in which the small earlier chateau built for Louis XIII was incorporated and which was enlarged by Hardouin Mansart (1646–1708), Mansart's great-nephew, to its present vast proportions, appropriate for the setting of the most dazzling and powerful monarch in Europe, but coarse compared with the elegance of the Habsburg equivalent at Schönbrunn. French architects were now thought as good as Italian; and even Bernini, that genius of the Baroque, summoned from Rome, was turned down in the competition in designs for enlarging the Louvre. The artistic capital of Europe had moved from Rome to Paris.

The greatest French classical artist was Nicholas Poussin (1593–1665). He was born near Les Andelys on the Seine in Normandy and worked first in Rouen and then in Paris; but by 1624 he had settled in Rome, where he found a patron in Cardinal Berberini. Influenced by the Venetian Veronese, he formed his own style, distinct from the Counter-Reformation Baroque, and turned to subjects from pagan mythology. Influenced also by Titian, he achieved a romantic depth of colour, and added his own lyrical power of composition, as in the "Kingdom of Flora" (1631). In 1640 Poussin was lured by Richelieu back to Paris, but, unable to contend with official tasks, returned to Rome for the rest of his life. He can thus hardly be considered part of the French Royal Establishment; but, like Mansart and Le Vau, he obtained his most reliable patrons among the affluent French bourgeoisie, and his pictures display the rational order that appealed to French minds. This austere Cartesian mood makes him more French than Italianate.

A French artist also now excelled in painting landscape. Claude Gellée le Lorrain, or Claude Lorraine (1600–80), was born near Nancy and began life as a pastry cook in Freibourg and in Rome, where, employed by a landscape painter, he turned artist. He then visited Naples and was overwhelmed by the beauty of its surroundings, which formed his style. After briefly revisiting Nancy, he settled in Rome where Pope Urban VIII bought his landscapes, and where he remained for the rest of his life. Though he painted in Italy, Claude had a northern feel for pervasive light, which he found in the Roman Campagna, the Tiber valley and the Sabine hills, as well as in Neapolitan seascapes, all haunted with the memories of Antiquity. Where the Dutch pioneers of landscape had been realistic, Claude brought French classical feeling into it, inspired by Italian light and prospects.

IV

Poussin and Claude are only the greatest of several French painters who contributed more to civilization than did the wars of Louis XIV. But these heavyweight public events, which shifted the balance of power in Europe and beyond the oceans, demand attention. Louis XIV had expanded an army reorganized by Chancellor Michel de Tellier, whose son François de Tellier, Marquis de Louvois, took over as Secretary for War in 1662, and by 1672 had become a Minister of State. He was an arrogant and able administrator who improved logistics and supply, and, in collaboration with Colbert, he attained great influence, the more so as he encouraged the King in ambitions for military *gloire*. Failing war, Louis used diplomatic insults, as against Pope Alexander VII over a French Ambassador's alleged humiliation by the Papal Corsican guards, not perhaps the most urbane of men. He also used money, as when he bought Dunquerque outright from Charles II and subsidized him to negotiate with the Portuguese for marriage with the Infanta Catherine of Braganza, an alliance directed against Spain.

But the potentially dangerous frontier for France was still in the north-east, and here the long-standing conflict between the English and the Dutch played into French hands. It had begun under the English Republic and continued informally after the Restoration of Charles II in 1660, so that in 1664 the English took New Amsterdam in New Netherlands and in due course renamed it New York, and in 1664-7 it broke out into the second Anglo-Dutch war. By treaty Louis XIV was bound to support the Dutch, but though he formally kept his word, he did little to help them; and when in 1665 Philip IV of Spain died leaving the incapable Carlos II his heir, and the succession, should he die childless, to his sister Margaret, wife of the Emperor Leopold of Austria, Louis claimed that by Flemish law the succession ought to go his own queen, Margaret's elder sister, the Infanta Maria Theresa. Then in 1667, in support of this unconvincing and hypothetical claim, he invaded the Spanish Netherlands, and occupied Charleroi and Lille.

This aggression induced the Dutch and English to make peace; then along with Sweden, to form a triple alliance against the French, whereat Louis allowed Condé to overrun Franche Comté up to the Jura and the borders of Switzerland, a move that threatened the Empire and gave him a good bargaining counter. It was promptly used: by the Treaty of Aix-la-Chapelle in 1668 Louis exchanged it with Leopold for the unprepossessing but strategically important area of Charleroi, Douai, Armentières and Lille. He had also extracted a secret treaty from Leopold which partitioned the Spanish Empire if Carlos II died without a male heir. He next exploited a Treaty made with the Duke of Lorraine who, retaining a life interest, had made the French King his heir, and the French had occupied strategically vital Lorraine, which extends from the Ardennes and the Argonne to the Vosges. Concurrently, in 1670 Louis XIV made a secret treaty of Dover with Charles II which detached that wily monarch from the Dutch, engaged him to provide ships against them, and to follow the example of his brother York in declaring himself, at a suitable moment, a convert to Roman Catholicism.

So fortified, in 1672 the *Roi Soleil*, without declaring war, launched an enormous army against the Dutch, themselves divided by conflict between the de Witt and Orange factions. In the crisis, the Dutch murdered the de Witts and rallied round the young Statdhouder, William of Orange, and when that autumn they opened the dykes round Amsterdam, the French were bogged down. The Dutch, moreover, defeated an Anglo-French fleet at the Battle of the Texel, and prevented an enemy landing in the north, so the French had to withdraw from the United Provinces. But not from the war: the Emperor, Spain and the Duke of Lorraine had now turned against the French: the English had made a peace with the Dutch, later signalized by the important dynastic marriage of York's daughter Mary to William of Orange, and Louis struck hard on the eastern frontier, again capturing Franche Comté, and sending Turenne to devastate the Rhenish Palatinate and expel the Emperor's armies from Alsace. The conflict even spread to the Mediterranean, but in Flanders, as usual, became immobilized in siege warfare.

Apparently victorious, but with failing revenues wrung mainly from the peasantry, for fiscal arrangements were still archaic, in 1678 Louis made the Peace of Nijmwegen, when, having already bought off the Dutch by lowering tariffs against them, he obtained Franche Comté, Cambrai, Ypres and Mauberge, but failed to secure a strategically satisfactory frontier in Flanders. But three years later he threw away any credit for moderation by annexing the strategic imperial cities of Colmar and Strasbourg in Alsace, and then in 1684 the town of Luxembourg. He reckoned he had a heaven-sent opportunity, for the Emperor Leopold was engaged in a desperate battle with the Turks. As we have seen, in 1683 Vienna had been saved by the Germans and the Poles led by Jan Sobieski of Poland, but in 1684 by the Treaty of Ratisbon the French king was able to keep Strasbourg and Luxembourg, a decision which signalized a truce between the French and the Emperor and Spain.

On the face of it, Louis XIV now appeared to be master of Europe; in fact he had already overreached himself. He had also in 1685 made a decision which, designed in part to conciliate the Pope for his ambivalent attitude towards the Turks, greatly harmed the economy of France. Since 1598 the Edict of Nantes had given toleration to the Huguenots, whose power of military rebellion had afterwards been crushed by the capture of La Rochelle by Richelieu. But they remained an anomaly in an increasingly centralized State, persecuted by the government who quartered "dragoons" on them with instructions to behave in a brutal and licentious manner. Now, under the pretence that most of them had been converted to Catholicism, Louis XIV declared that the Edict of Nantes had become superfluous and judged "that we can do nothing better than wipe out the memory of the troubles ... that the progress of this false religion has caused in our Kingdom, than revoke the said Edict."[1] The Huguenot pastors who would not conform were exiled, their churches destroyed, their schools closed, their benefactions confiscated. They were even threatened with the atrocious fate of being sent to the galleys should they be caught emigrating. But emigrate they did; to Norwich and Southampton, to London and Bristol, to Holland and Prussia and Denmark, where they contributed their skills to the development of countries hostile to France and a valuable element to the populations.

[1] Cited by Wolf. *op. cit.* p. 394.

Powerful states were now converging against France. In 1686 the Habsburg Emperor made a double alliance: in the north with Sweden and the Hohenzollern Elector of Brandenburg, hitherto the bought ally of France; and in Germany with the Catholic German states. Together with Spain, these powers formed the League of Augsburg. Further, Louis XIV—not the last Frenchman to do so—grossly miscalculated the politics of England. On the accession of James II in 1685, he reckoned on a staunch ally who would carry out all and more than the bought promises of Charles II; but the English political nation threw out the Catholic James II and accepted William of Orange and Mary, the former the most dedicated enemy of the *Grand Monarque*, so that the two greatest sea powers in the north were now also ranged against France. By 1689 the Dutch and the English had allied themselves to the Empire, determined to keep the French within the boundaries recognized by the Treaties of Münster and of the Pyrenees. By overplaying his hand, Louis XIV had ranged all the major powers of Europe against him.

V

The reasons that induced the insular English to accept a Dutch Stadthouder, dedicated entirely to continental politics and devoid even of the Stuart charm that he might have inherited from his grandfather, Charles I, are rooted in the English Civil Wars. Although the Stuarts had been restored, and with them the great landowning aristocrats and the wealthy merchants of the City, a strong "Nonconformist" interest of those who had fought for the "good old" parliamentarian "cause" was still in being, though socially despised; and nearly all classes detested the Catholics, whose hold on the exotic court of Charles I had greatly contributed to its unpopularity. The monarchy, though it still had the initiative, was "mixed", since parliament held the pursestrings, and it was only by concealing his not very ardent religious faith, by taking subsidies from his cousin Louis XIV, and by much political skill that Charles II had managed to enjoy his own again. With the accession of James II, all the old rabid fears of Catholicism, a standing army and a French invasion were swiftly let loose, and although Louis XIV deliberately refrained from interfering in William III's expedition since he thought it would paralyse the country in civil war, the "Glorious Revolution" proved bloodless and William succeeded in his objective, to swing English wealth and naval and military power into line against the French whom he had been resisting in war and diplomacy since 1672.

There was a lamentable sequel in Ireland, where the civil war expected by the French in fact broke out, and the battle of the Boyne, still celebrated in Northern Ireland, led to the permanent exile of James II and the repercussions, still vibrant, of an "Orange" Protestant victory. The Scots, too, remember William III by the massacre of Glencoe; but the English learnt to put up with him, and in 1694 founded the Bank of England. The French had thus landed themselves in the far-flung war of the League of Augsburg or, as the English call it, "King William's War". It lasted from 1690 until 1697, and for the

English it was decided by the resounding naval victory off La Hogue, when, in 1692, a French invasion fleet was defeated and dispersed. For William the war dragged on in the usual dreary and inconclusive campaigns in Flanders, in which he was generally defeated but doggedly survived. Hostilities were concluded by the Peace of Ryswick whereby Louis XIV was compelled to recognize the sovereignty of William and Mary in Great Britain and Ireland, restore Luxembourg and the Palatinate to the Emperor, and Lorraine to its Duke: all that the French kept was Strasbourg. This Treaty was not much to show for the decades of war against the far better organized Dutch and English economies and the man-power of Germany, and a mounting strain on the French financial and social order was caused to a nation hypnotized by the *Roi Soleil*. What was worse, it proved only a breathing space before the more monstrous conflict known as the War of the Spanish Succession.

VI

Poised on what appeared a summit of power, but in fact set for military frustration, the French had won a far-flung and lasting cultural domination. The fear and hatred inspired by the tramp of their armies, the jingle of their showy cavalry and the thunder of their guns showed them apparently the predominant military power in Europe, and the glamour and brilliance of their civilization, manifest in diplomacy, literature and the arts, as well as in its arrogance and affectation, fascinated the royalties and aristocracies even of hostile states. For European culture was still hierarchical and cosmopolitan, and if the mercantile Dutch and the rich squirearchy of England resented what they considered the simian antics of French fashion, their grandchildren in the eighteenth century often succumbed to it.

French influence was obvious in architecture; in England Inigo Jones's palladian influence had been followed up on a great scale by Wren, who took the opportunity presented by the Great Fire of London in 1666 to create a new and still more majestic St. Paul's and many elegant city churches. Wren's St. Paul's, completed in 1709, was vast, without precedent in England, and more in French classical style than Italianate Baroque. Wren, who had early studied architecture in Paris, when Mansart senior and Le Vau were at the height of their powers, and who lived and prospered until he was ninety-one, also created the elegant library at Trinity College, Cambridge and "Tom" Tower at Christ Church, Oxford, somehow harmonious with the late Gothic of the great hall and even with the unfinished cloisters.

Charles II had brought in French fashions and what the French call "gallantry" at the Restoration, and Restoration drama which superseded the Jacobean and Caroline theatres, crippled by the Puritan regime, was a witty and artificial echo of Molière, without his insights. In Holland the aristocratic supporters of William of Orange were culturally French, and developed their cult of gardens and palaces on formal French lines, while in Central Europe even the Habsburgs abandoned Spanish fashions for a Frenchified elegance, often in better taste than the version projected by the *Roi Soleil* himself. And the German princes and aristocrats, even at the relatively uncouth court of the Hohenzollern Elector of Brandenburg, followed French fashions, or, in the south, Viennese fashions derived from France. So docile were the ruling classes to fashion that they took to wigs following the example first set by Louis XIII in about 1624, who had covered his premature baldness with a periwig or *peruke,* and continued by Louis XIV in the 1670s, of wearing a huge *peruke* of human hair to preserve a youthful appearance. Even the young cut off their natural hair, thus disfiguring themselves for the bedroom, and wore "night caps'. These unhygienic and expensive *perukes* reached their most extravagant size during the old age of the *Roi Soleil.* The custom, deriving from the vanity of the French kings, must have made rouged old faces in fact look older, but it made the wig a mark of social status which would long in attenuated form persist, and give the portraits of Western Europeans of that time a distinctive character. So, backed by military fanfare and pomp, the French took over a "civilizing mission" from the Italians, who continued in Rome to cultivate their own exuberant but now provincial Baroque and Rococo, exuberant too in Austria and South Germany. French, not Latin, became the European second language, and in a Europe more than usually disfigured by dynastic wars, a cosmopolitan culture radiated from France even among her most obstinate enemies. Nor did it remain confined to the West or even to Central Europe; it spread to Poland, and to Muscovy under Peter the Great, as Muscovy became Imperial Russia.

XXXVI

The War of the Spanish Succession: Peace of Utrecht

The Peace of Ryswick, which in 1697, the year when the young Tsar Peter had first visited the West, had concluded the War of the League of Augsburg, proved only a truce: another and worse cause of conflict soon erupted. Carlos of Spain, the Bewitched, had long been fading out of life in an agony of delusion and superstition—intermittently convinced that he was already possessed by the devil—and with no direct heir. The great powers, anxious to maintain the peace, had long been negotiating on the future of the vast Spanish inheritance in the Iberian Peninsula, in Italy, the Netherlands, the Americas and the Philippines; and in 1698 William III and his allies had negotiated a partition treaty with the French. It had assigned the bulk of the Spanish Empire to the infant Electoral Prince Joseph Ferdinand of Bavaria, a descendant of Philip IV of Spain, thus preserving the balance of power between the French and the Austrian Empires. Then, even when the child had died, they arranged a second treaty of Partition, whereby the Archduke Charles of Austria, brother of the Archduke Joseph (Emperor as Joseph I (1705–11)) and second son of the Emperor Leopold I, was to have Spain, the Spanish-American colonies and the Spanish Netherlands, while the Grand Dauphin Louis would inherit the Spanish possessions in Italy, including strategic Milan, Naples and Sicily.

But when at last, in the fall of 1700, Carlos II died, he proved naturally to have held to one obsession; to keep his inheritance intact. Passing over other claimants, he had left the entire Spanish inheritance to Philippe Duc d'Anjou, grandson of Louis XIV and Maria Theresa, Infanta of Spain; and he had added that if the inheritance were refused, it should pass intact to the Archduke Charles of Austria. Louis XIV, though anxious to avoid another great war, really had no choice; afraid of "encirclement" from the Netherlands, the Rhineland, Italy and Spain if the Spanish succession passed to the Austrian Habsburgs, he recognized the seventeen-year-old Philippe d'Anjou as Philip V of Spain, an occasion for the Spanish Ambassador's famous remark "There are no more Pyrenees".

The English were horrified; alarmed at the prospect of the disruption of their trade and of a Franco-Spanish colonial domination of the world; the

Dutch shared their alarm and feared a French invasion of the Spanish Netherlands—fears amply justified when the French promptly took over the border fortresses from their Spanish garrisons. William III appointed John Churchill, Earl of Marlborough, as Commander-in-Chief and Ambassador to the United Provinces: Whigs and Tories united to vote supplies for a war, while the Emperor Leopold I and his principal commander, Prince Eugène of Savoy, were already attacking the French in northern Italy in defence of the vital communications over the Alps which linked Spain with the Empire.

Then at the critical moment, in the spring of 1702, William III, whose horse had thrown him after stumbling on a mole-hill—the work of "a little gentleman in black velvet" long the toast of his enemies—died worn out at fifty-two, and Louis XIV infuriated the English when he recognized the Stuart "Pretender", the son of the dying James II, as James III of Great Britain and Ireland. He thus violated the Treaty of Ryswick, and then spread wider alarm by proclaiming that the "will of God" would decide if Philippe and his heirs should be called upon to wear the French as well as the Spanish Crown, despite treaties to the contrary. The Spaniards, moreover, were already transferring commercial privileges accorded to the English and Dutch, including the right of trading African slaves to their colonies, to the French.

So, in 1702, despite anxious attempts to preserve the peace, the gathering momentum of the policies of the great Western powers plunged Europe into the far-flung War of the Spanish Succession (1702–13), coincident with the Great Northern War around the Baltic and in Muscovy. It decided that the British and Dutch maritime empires would survive, and in the words of Marlborough's memorial in Blenheim Park, its outcome "asserted and preserved the liberties of Europe" against the ambitions of Louis XIV.

At the accession of Queen Anne (1702–14) in England, the prospect of doing so did not seem bright. The French were now in alliance with Spain and Spanish America; Bavaria sided with them; and Hungarians and Turks were again menacing the Empire: for the first time in centuries the English had to intervene heavily on the Continent of Europe. And this they did. Marlborough as Captain-General combined military genius with diplomatic skill, and took over William III's role as the "fixed important centre" of a new Grand Alliance. Sustained by the command of the sea already asserted off La Hogue, the English and their Dutch allies could now strike at Spain and dominate the Mediterranean. Backed by more modern methods of finance through the Bank of England and by the unwonted liberality of a Parliament fearful of French invasion and depredations on commerce, Marlborough could organize massive armies for campaigns far better controlled than those of the Thirty Years War. The ring bayonet had just superseded the pike, and the flint lock the matchlock musket; and the flint lock could fire much faster so that infantry deployed in three rank lines could give sustained and steady fire. Moreover, since the days of Gustav Adolf, cavalry had restored mobility to the battlefield and artillery became easier to concentrate at a decisive point. When not bogged down in sieges, early-eighteenth-century warfare could be rapid and give an outstanding commander scope. Indeed, "for almost the first time since the far simpler and smaller conflicts of antiquity it was now possible for armies, not simply at the outset of a battle but throughout its course, to be the instruments of a single controlling will ... hence the appearance of so many outstanding generals ... Eugène of Savoy and John Churchill, Duke of Marlborough, the greatest of them all."[1]

In 1703 the French adopted an ambitious strategy. Their army under Villars, in collaboration with the Elector Duke Max of Bavaria, struck towards Vienna itself, while the Hungarians were to rise in the East, and the French to strike north through the Brenner with their army in Italy. Then in 1704, following this almost Napoleonic plan, Louis XIV sent a great French army under Marshal Tallard into Bavaria. Marlborough, who had out manoeuvred the French on the Meuse and was now a Duke, marched fast from Koblenz with an Anglo-Dutch-Prussian army, and caught and defeated the French in August 1704 at Blenheim near Donauwörth on the Danube. It was a huge and bloody battle in which forty thousand French and Bavarians were killed, wounded, captured or totally routed—something quite out of scale with the battles of the sixteenth century or of the Thirty Years' War. Vienna was saved; Tallard captured, the French driven back to the Rhine, the Bavarians knocked out of the war. Moreover, having previously intercepted the Spanish treasure fleet in Vigo Bay, the British, in collaboration with the Dutch and based on Lisbon, captured Gibraltar, the key to the Western Mediterranean, and to the naval base at Minorca—Port Mahon.

But Louis XIV, determined to remain master of the Netherlands and of his vulnerable north-eastern frontier, now in May 1706 committed another army to counter-attack at Ramillies, between Louvain and Liège. Twenty-five thousand English, Dutch and Danes fought a mainly cavalry battle against roughly the same force of French and routed them. The Allies overran all the Spanish Netherlands, including Brussels and Antwerp, and in the same year, Eugène drove the French from Northern Italy. Further, in 1705 an English expeditionary force under the Earl of Peterborough had been shipped round from Lisbon to Catalonia; Barcelona had been captured and the Archduke Charles, with the support of the Catalans, Aragonese and Valencians, been proclaimed Charles III of Spain. And by 1707, at the height of the successful war, the Act of Union between England and Scotland was ratified.

But the French had not been eradicated from the Netherlands, and in 1708, at Oudenarde on the Scheldt south-west of Ghent, Marlborough and Eugène outmanoeuvred them in flat enclosed, waterlogged country, and opened the prospect of an invasion of France. But Lille, Bruges and Ghent had first to be taken; Marlborough's political influence in England was being undermined, so the war was not concluded. And in Spain, surprisingly, most of the people had rallied to the French Philppe V. To get rid of him, a major campaign would be necessary: and the peace negotiations between Louis XIV and the Allies broke down since Louis refused to send French troops to help dethrone his own nephew. The war continued, now in the conventional rut of sieges, first of Tournai then of Mons. Then the final and most monstrous battle took place. At Malplaquet over a hundred thousand allied troops attacked about ninety

[1]Howard. *op. cit.* p. 62.

thousand French and the combined casualties amounted to thirty-four thousand. It was a battle comparable in scale only to the worst in the Napoleonic campaigns, and it was too much for eighteenth-century governments and public. The Grand Alliance began to falter; Marlborough, his influence diminished by political factions of the English Court, still showed great virtuosity in siegecraft and manoeuvre, but the English, deserting their Allies, made a separate peace. By 1713 all the Allies except the Empire had made the Treaty of Utrecht. The Archduke Charles, since 1711 the Emperor Charles VI, fought on until 1714, when he concluded the Treaty of Rastadt with France. Marlborough, in disgust, went to live among the Germans and the Dutch, and remained on the continent until the accession of George I of Hanover to the British throne.

As often, after brilliant victories, many of the gains of war were muddled away at the conference tables, but the essential objective was achieved. By the Treaty of Utrecht the proposal of a union of the French and Spanish colonial empires was abolished; the British retained Gibraltar and Minorca and the command of the Western Mediterranean, along with the Hudson's Bay territories in Canada, Newfoundland and Nova Scotia, thus strengthening their command of the North Atlantic, while they increased their access to Spanish American markets, not least in exploiting the slave trade. Following the Treaty of Rastadt in 1714 the Austrians displaced the Spaniards in the Netherlands and protected the Dutch from French attack; they also displaced them in most of Italy and remained there until the mid-nineteenth century, thus, along with a more powerful Savoy, blocking any French incursions into the peninsula, while Sicily was assigned first to Savoy, then to Austria. In the light of these adjustments, it was considered safe to leave a Bourbon on the throne of Spain, as the Spaniards now demanded, and the Catalans and Aragonese were handed over to the government of Philippe V in Madrid.

So the British emerged as far the greatest maritime power and displaced the Austrian Habsburgs as the "natural" enemies of France, the incongruous Spanish domination was at last removed from the Low Countries and replaced by a more easy-going Austrian regime, while the Italians exchanged Spanish for Austrian masters.

II

The Spaniards, like previous conquerors, had not found Italy easy to rule. In the Kingdom of Naples and Sicily, the Spanish Viceroys had been forced to contend with revolts in Calabria, Palermo and Naples. In 1647 one Masaniello, a fisherman from Amalfi had raised insurrection in Naples; and when the Spaniards had killed him, the Neapolitans, in medieval fashion, had appealed for help to the French. But a new Spanish viceroy proved equal to the emergency; having induced the Neapolitan leaders to negotiate, he had them all arrested and executed.

Then, during the War of 1672 between Louis XIV and the Dutch, a revolt against the Spaniards in Sicily had been backed by a Dutch fleet under de Ruyter, and in 1707 an Austrian army drove the Spaniards out of Naples and Sicily, which was assigned by the Treaty of Utrecht to the Duke of Savoy, to keep both the French and Spaniards out of the Mediterranean.

Milan, also, was of course assigned to Austria, while Tuscany remained the preserve of a succession of picturesque and variously degenerate Medici Grand Dukes. So the only Italian prince who did well out of the war was the Duke of Savoy, whose dominions were enlarged into a buffer state, in part as a reward for the successful generalship of Prince Eugène. Having obtained Sicily, he exchanged it in 1718 for Sardinia, and after his becoming King of Piedmont and Sardinia, his descendants were destined to rule a United Italy.

The Venetians, on the other hand, once an august and wealthy power and regarded as a model Commonwealth, now fell into decline. In 1669, after an immensely long siege, the Turks had captured Crete and then overrun Dalmatia and the Morea: the main sources of Venetian wealth were gradually extinguished, though not the gaiety of Venetian social life.

The Papacy had been helpless during the Thirty Years' War to control the violence of either side; but in the reigns of Urban VIII (1623-44) and Innocent X (1644-55) Italian Baroque architecture had flourished. Francesco Borromini (1599-1667), born north of Milan, dramatized the Classical Renaissance style and the more emotional aspects of the Counter-Reformation in its decline; while the Neapolitan Giovanni Bernini (1598-1680) surpassed him in creative brilliance and versatile accomplishment, for he was painter and stage-designer as well as architect and sculptor. His immense bronze baldachino above the tomb of St. Peter in Rome enhances even its majestic setting, and his portrait busts are sublimated portrayals of character. He also designed superb fountains, in which tritons and dolphins gambol amid cascading water, and symbolic nymphs frolic with amphibious animals. He could also handle mystical subjects, as the famous ecstasy of St. Teresa—a very physical interpretation—and variously dramatic moments in the lives and deaths of martyrs and saints. But his most superb monument is the vast colonnade that frames the piazza of St. Peter's, and which still adequately contains the crowds at papal ceremonies.

While the royalties, politicians and soldiers were afflicting their peoples with the English Civil Wars, the Thirty Years' War, the Great Northern War and the War of the Spanish Succession, Bernini's splendid genius, under enlightened Papal patronage, was creating works of art for all time. Nor did it matter that, when asked to design the Louvre, he was snubbed by the French: he had already become, as he would remain, a European influence. Bernini's and Borromini's style soon spread north of the Alps, making cultural conquests for Rome where political influence had waned, and, under the patronage of Leopold I, himself a composer, a bibliophile and the founder of the Universities of Osnabrück, Olmütz and Breslau, it inspired South German and Austrian baroque and its brilliant rococo sequel.

Alessandro Scarlatti (1658-1725), like Bernini, came from the south, and founded the new style of opera at Naples, where he was Master of Music to the Spanish Viceroy, though he also composed church music in Rome. He was a pioneer of the kind of music later developed by Haydn and Mozart, so started an august and brilliant pedigree. His son, Domenico Scarlatti (1685–1757), was born in Naples and probably died there; he was the first European virtuoso of the harpsichord of international fame, and became musical director at St. Peter's in Rome, as well as holding appointments in Spain. "Underlying much of the work of the German composers was the international style of the great Italians, in particular of Alessandro Scarlatti. With its mastery of long curving lines, its controlled elaborations, its perfection of detail, it is remarkably close to the architecture of Borromini."[1] Indeed, while the Italians after Utrecht and Rastadt experienced another change of masters as the Austrians took over from the Spaniards, and the Papacy went further into political eclipse, Italian civilization was not much affected. The tradition of the grand tour had now become well established, and many more northerners came to appreciate the culture and the amenities of the south—to return enriched in mind. While in the glare of political and military history the campaigns of Marlborough and Eugène retain their importance, for they changed the balance of oceanic world power and wealth, and while Peter the Great knocked barbarous Muscovy into shape as a mighty Eurasian power, the sources of European civilization in Italy continued their creative and inextinguishable influence.

III

Though the cultural creativeness of Italy continued, the commerce of the Mediterranean ports had long been far surpassed by the oceanic trade of the Atlantic seaboard, long mainly in the hands of the Dutch. Originally based on selling Baltic wheat, timber and cordage, in exchange for Spanish wool and silver, and Mediterranean luxury goods and wine, the Dutch carrying trade had become oceanic, bringing spices from the East Indies and tobacco and sugar from the Spanish and American colonies. As the volume of colonial trade increased, the Dutch, with their small and vulnerable base, itself dependent on imported wheat, could no longer monopolize it; the English and the French won a larger share, and their wars were fought as much for commercial advantage as for continental territory. Since the first Navigation Acts of 1650 and 1651, aiming at "the increase of the shipping and Navigation of the Nation" under the English Republic, a vigorous Mercantilist policy, directed mainly against the Dutch carrying trade, had been pursued by successive English governments, determined to confine trade with their colonies to English shipping. This deliberate commercial imperialism, backed by the monarchy, the great landowners, the great merchants and by a' new class of investors, was now sustained by a larger navy, and the United Kingdom of Great Britain, Scotland and Ireland became the predominant naval and commercial state in Atlantic Europe. The rivalries of the Genoese and the Venetians in the Levant were now paralleled on a greater scale in the North Atlantic and Caribbean. Moreover the English had abandoned the East Indies

[1]Clark. Civilisation. op. cit. p. 224.

to the Dutch, and concentrated on India; in 1661 a revised and extended charter granted by Charles II to the East India Company gave it far greater political powers; to create "a large well-grounded secure English dominion in India". In 1708, at the height of the Marlborough wars, the company could lend a million pounds to the government, and already there were three strategically placed Presidencies, Bombay, Bengal and Madras. With the disintegration of the Mughal Empire after the death of Aurangzebe in 1707, the year, by English reckoning, of the Union of England and Scotland, the company was forced to extend its political commitments to protect its commerce, though it long remained wary of political responsibilities.

On the other side of the world, the English colonization of Barbados and other potentially rich West Indian islands, and the capture of Jamaica in 1655, had laid the foundation of vast fortunes made from sugar, so that the Augustan age was the hey-day both of the first nabobs from India and the earliest millionaires from the Caribbean.

The French, too, had long been determined to surpass the Dutch; the mercantilist Colbert had tried to promote colonial enterprise, and while the French, preoccupied with their own country, never backed their state sponsored companies as did the English and the Dutch, they eagerly competed for the sugar islands of the West Indies which were considered the greatest prize. The English exploited Barbados and Jamaica; but by the Treaty of Utrecht the French held on to Martinique, San Domingo and Guadeloupe, and even secured a half share of prized St. Christopher's—so great was the wealth then produced by sugar plantations worked by slave labour. Moreover the West Indies became strategically essential as bases in the conflict to dominate the Atlantic.

By the early eighteenth century European civilization was therefore bound up with oceanic commerce round the Cape to the East and across the Atlantic in a way inconceivable in classical or medieval times, and, while the Levantine trade remained important, it was dominated by the capital and the shipping of the Atlantic powers. The centre of gravity, as it were, had finally shifted and settled in the North-West, and the most decisive cultural and intellectual influences now emanated from peoples who no longer looked, as in classical and medieval times, to the Mediterranean and its way of life to set standards to be imitated and admired. Powerful as the influence of the old classical education and of Italianate culture, art and music long remained, the "Moderns" now set standards of scale, wealth and far flung enterprise which were their own.

IV

If the main architectural, artistic and musical impulse continued to derive from Italy, along with the pervasive cultural predominance of France, Great Britain now, for the first time, set a political and intellectual example. After the Restoration of 1660, there had followed a time of confused and hectic political intrigue since, although the monarchy was dependent on the Parliament for money, no means had been devised of making the executive responsible to the Parliament. With the accession of the Catholic James II (1685–88), who hankered for a continental style absolutism backed by a standing army, friction had come to a crisis, and the Revolution of 1688 completed what the Revolution of 1642 had begun. The Catholic King was discarded, a Protestant foreigner accepted, and William and Mary displaced James II. The solidarity of the English upper classes had been resoundingly affirmed and a common interest of great landowners and wealthy merchants had in effect taken over the government: in spite of violent political factions, both Tories and Whigs managed to finance the War of the Spanish Succession and reap its essential though not its entire rewards. Now united with Scotland, and with Ireland subdued, Great Britain had become the greatest maritime power, and taken the place of the Habsburgs in Vienna as the most formidable rival of France. From a second rate peripheral power, possessing mainly nuisance value, Great Britain was now one of the great states of Europe, with a growing colonial empire in North America and India, and institutions which it became the fashion to admire.

In France, in particular, where the medieval inheritance had been largely crushed out by a monarch backed by a huge standing army, and where absolutism held sway, without the administrative reforms which might have made it efficient, intelligent people became interested in the achievements of the English, who had adapted their medieval parliaments to modern purposes and retained a monarch without submitting to arbitrary power. They appeared to have combined the method and business acumen of the Dutch with an aristocratic but flexible social order. They had stabilized the cost of living after the Tudor and early Jacobean inflation, while the Anglican Church, having devised a compromise which diminished the influence of both Calvinist and Catholic extremists, was content with merely social discrimination against "Dissenters", the legacy of the Civil Wars. The country was now much more prosperous; mining and iron foundries were beginning to develop heavy industry, and ship building surpassed even that of the Dutch—as witness the young Tsar Peter's visit to England. Moreover, new methods of agriculture and stock breeding had been learnt from the Dutch, new crops acclimatized. Exports were no longer so dependent on the cloth trade, but were flourishing through the re-export of tobacco and sugar from Virginia and the West Indies, and of muslins and calicos from India. While most of the people still lived, as elsewhere, in poverty, the upper classes in England in the reign of Anne were flourishing, and the politically conscious nation, though riven at the top by fierce political faction, was united in maintaining the oligarchic economic and social order which had at last emerged from the Civil Wars of the previous century and their brief Republican sequel. It compared well with the bureaucratized and absolute monarchies of the continent, and had now proved itself well able to stand up to them.

The English constitution and the ideas behind it thus became respected abroad, and the intellectual initiative of seventeenth-century Holland was paralleled in early eighteenth-century Great Britain. The prevalent theory of the Divine Right of Kings, of which Louis XIV had been the embodiment and in which he entirely believed, was undermined by a more commonsensical view of the state, and by writers who considered the *Roi Soleil* not only dangerous but ridiculous.

Hobbes had written to justify the state, not as an expression of a Divine cosmic order, but as a useful contrivance designed for self-preservation—the most fundamental law of nature—and founded it upon a mechanistic view of human psychology. He had pointed out that law was only "positive" law when enforced, and that the state which failed in protecting its subjects' lives and property forfeited their allegiance. Further, instead of evoking religious sanctions for Government, he argued that Churches and Sects should be firmly subordinate to the secular power. Accused of cynical atheism, Hobbes had held no public office and had been discountenanced by the authorities of his day; but his doctrines had long been seeping through and creating a more realistic view of politics.

John Locke (1632-1704), on the other hand, proved publicly and vastly influential, particularly in the North American Colonies as well as on the continent. He came of middle-class Roundhead family in Somerset, and by way of Westminster School and Christ Church, Oxford, entered the great world under the patronage of Anthony Ashley Cooper, Earl of Shaftesbury, the founder of the Whig party, who in 1673 made Locke Secretary to the Board of Trade and Plantations. Though James II drove him into exile in Holland, he returned with William III.[1]

Locke, like Hobbes, held that the state existed not to glorify a ruler by Divine Right, part of a cosmic and authoritarian "Chain of Being", but for the benefit of the "people", by whom he meant the propertied classes and the politically articulate nation. This doctrine, formulated in his *Two Treatises on Civil Government* (1679-81), very well served the turn of the Protestant establishment determined to get rid of James II, and with the success of the Revolution of 1688-9, Locke's writings became extremely important; on government, on religious toleration and on education. Unlike Hobbes, he was not particularly original, drawing from Hooker's medieval, originally Thomist doctrine that Government is responsible to the *Communitas* or Commonwealth as a whole; but what he wrote was highly topical, relevant and idiomatic, justifying the actions of great and successful interests. Like Hobbes, Locke argued that the purpose of society is to get out of the evils of a "state of nature", and to set up and enforce laws which will protect life and property— "the peace, safety and public good of the people"; not of course of the semi-literate labouring masses, but of his own kind. Once this principle was admitted, the whole imposing edifice of absolute monarchy, weighing down society with inequitable taxes and dragooning it by a standing army, ceased to command consent; while Locke declared that "the care of each man's salvation belongs only to himself", and struck at the traditional hierarchy of the Catholic Church, with its monopoly of revealed religion. It was the plain prose of

---

[1] His main intellectual interest was in philosophy, more than in politics, and is expressed in his *Essay Concerning Human Understanding*. See Maurice Cranston. *Locke; a Biography*. London, 1957.

Locke, not Bossuet's baroque eloquence, which would have the greater influence.

And the English had another weapon in their armoury, unobtrusive but deadly; not the stiletto of malicious wit, but the broad humour of commonplace ridicule. Confronted with arbitrary power, the pomp and pretension of the *Grand Monarque*, Locke quietly remarks that "no man in civil society can be exempted from the laws of it", and George Savile, first Marquis of Halifax, the principal architect of the settlement in 1689, describes the French King as "a mistaken creature, swelled with panegyrics and flattered out of his senses, not only an encumbrance but a nuisance to mankind ... an ambitious ape of the Divine greatness ... and with all his pride, no more than a whip in God Almighty's hand, to be thrown into the fire when the world had been sufficiently scourged by it."[1] Here is a new note of confident individuality. Neither Locke nor Halifax is the spokesman of any institution: they write from their own minds. No wonder that across the Channel the elite of the cleverest people in Europe, misgoverned and exploited by an irrational and archaic regime, turned to these robust English writers for political wisdom. And no wonder that this practical, shrewd and independent outlook took on among the predominantly British colonists in North America, where Locke's ideas had even greater and more important influence than they did in Great Britain itself.

In even more important fields Sir Isaac Newton now won world wide influence. He was born in 1642 at Woolsthorpe, near Grantham in Lincoln-shire, the son of Isaac Newton and Hannah Ayscough. He was educated at the Grammar School at Grantham, but at fourteen set to farming by his widowed mother. Through his maternal uncle, a Lincolnshire rector, in 1661 he went up to Trinity College, Cambridge, where, three years later, he was elected a scholar. By 1665–6 he was "in the prime of his age for invention and minded mathematics and philosophy more than at any time since." Having retired to Woolsthorpe to avoid the plague, he there "fell into a speculation on the power of gravity which he considered must extend much further than was usually thought. Why not so high as the moon? Perhaps she is retained in her orbit thereby." Having checked the observation with only a rough estimate of the earth's size, and found that the moon's motion answered "pretty nearly", he then laid aside the subject for twenty years. In 1667 Newton was elected a Fellow of Trinity and in 1669 Lucasian Professor, in which capacity he lectured on optics and deduced from the spectrum that "white light is ever compounded." Elected Fellow of the Royal Society in 1672, he was allowed, though not in Holy Orders, to continue his Fellowship at Trinity by the special intervention of Charles II, then in 1687, the year before the "Glorious Revolution", in his *Philosophiae Naturalis Principia Mathematica* he stated, as he put it, "the system of the world", and "explained the universe on mechanical principles".

Newton's exploit confirmed the change in the climate of opinion long setting

[1] For much political wisdom, still relevant, see *The Complete Works of George Savile, First Marquis of Halifax*. ed. Walter Raleigh. Oxford, 1912.

in from "Ancient" to "Modern" and it cleared away the doubt and bewilderment which had afflicted so much seventeenth-century thought in the backwash of the Ockhamist scepticism which had undermined Thomist certainties. The Universe itself now seemed rational on empirical evidence, and its Creator mechanically minded. The way was open for the triumph of empirical reason, the more so since Locke's philosophy had presented mind as a blank tablet on which impressions could be imposed, so that education could make men reasonable. English commonsense, already successful in politics and commerce, was thus extended, at a time when the language had become particularly pithy and lucid, to explain the world and chart hopeful prospects for its future, and Bacon's empirical method and improving purpose was now reinforced by a cosmic sanction. Having accepted the Cartesian limitations of Mind, philosophy, turning to "Natural Philosophy"—their term for Science—now held out a new hope for mankind that from applied reason there might even come happiness.

After 1688 Newton became Member of Parliament for Cambridge University in the Convention Parliament but, being disqualified by the Statutes of the College, failed to become Provost of King's College, Cambridge. By 1696 he was made Master of the Mint to supervise a reform of the coinage, and gave up his Cambridge appointments, but was elected President of the Royal Society. In 1705, the year after Blenheim, he was knighted, and died at Kensington aged eighty-five in 1727, leaving the then very substantial fortune of £32,000.[1]

Where Locke and Newton left off, the Philosophers of the French Enlightenment and the Founding Fathers of the American Revolution began. Nor was this powerful influence confined to the West: the "Enlightenment" spread to central Europe and Russia, and enlightened even some of the despots themselves. The ambivalent relations between the English and French continued, and while intermittently at war, the two peoples influenced each other. For long the French had predominated, and the Court of Charles II, in effect an outpost of French civilization, had deeply affected the English, not least in language. For the baroque cadences of Milton, Hobbes and Sir Thomas Browne, and the cloudy eloquence of the Cromwellian sectaries, had given place by 1688, in part under Court influence, to the clear hard hitting prose of Jonathan Swift (1667-1745). He now perfected a deadly irony which relied on plain language and ordinary similes for its effect, while the letters and even political pamphlets of the time show English at a climax of lucidity and force. Indeed, brilliantly creative as had been the Elizabethan and Jacobean achievement, the writers of the Augustan age had greater impact abroad, for they were more attuned to the still predominant French civilization, and more intelligible on the continent.

In the late seventeenth century England also produced its greatest musical genius. Henry Purcell (1658-95) had been early influenced by the prevalent

[1]The *Principia* only got printed at the expense and under the supervision of the astronomer Halley, since the Royal Society could not raise the funds. The story that the fall of an apple directed Newton's thoughts to gravitation was popularized by Voltaire, who had it from a daughter of Newton's niece.

fashion for the Florentine Lully's music in France; he composed both for the theatre and as organist at Westminster Abbey and the Chapel Royal. Charles II preferred Italian composers, and Purcell, as "Composer in ordinary to his most sacred Majesty", sought "a just imitation of the most fam'd Italian masters and to bring their seriousness and gravity into vogue". In 1684, when he had published his famous Odes for St. Cecilia's Day and written the music for several of Dryden's operas, it was held that he "joined to the delicacy and beauty of the Italian way the graces and gayety of the French composers", and Dryden declared that "we have at last found an Englishman equal to the best abroad."

Across the whole range of the national life from the Revolution of 1688 and after the Hanoverian settlement at the summit which changed the dynasty without civil war, through the army and navy, finance, commerce and colonization, to science, architecture, literature and music, England—now merged with Scotland as Great Britain—emerged as a formidable power and cultural influence both in Europe and beyond the oceans.

XXXVII

World Conflict and "Enlightenment": Spain and Portugal

When, after reigning seventy-two years, Louis XIV died in 1715, he was succeeded by his great-grandson, aged five, who reigned until 1774. Though the French monarchy had created the model of the new Despotic State, and Paris—if not Versailles—had launched the rationalist "Enlightenment", France itself never had an "Enlightened" despot. Until 1743 Louis XV was too frivolous and lazy to take even intermittent charge; and the Regency of his uncle, Philippe d'Orléans, was followed by the rule of the King's former tutor, the octogenarian Cardinal Fleury, after whose demise government was long conducted mainly through the King's irresponsible *maîtresse-en-titre*, the Marquise de Pompadour.

The Regency saw a reaction against the absolutism and stiff conventions of the previous regime: the Regent himself, though versatile and intelligent, preferred elaborate and deviant debauchery to the conduct of business, which he left to the Abbé Dubois, who became Archbishop of Cambrai. The great nobles were brought back into government, and the bourgeois professional civil servants discarded; but, as Saint-Simon wrote in his *Mémoires*, "L'embarras fut l'ignorance, la légèreté, l'inapplication de cette noblesse, accoutumée à n'être bonne à rien qu'à se faire tuer."[1] The professionals trained under Louis XIV had to be brought back.

The Regent also had to squash the attempt of the *Parlement de Paris*, following the English example, to examine state expenditure and control revenue, and to declare roundly that the *Parlement* "only existed by the sovereign's will", which was "by itself sufficient to make law". Anxious to diminish the enormous debts of the previous regime, he also risked appointing a Scots financier, William Law of Lauriston, as controller-general of Finance. A pioneer of the theory of credit—always a tricky subject—in 1717 Law founded the *Compagnie d'Occident* based on the monopoly of trade with the French colony of Louisiana; two years later it obtained the monopoly of the

---

[1] "The difficulty was the ignorance, frivolity and idleness of this nobility, accustomed to be good for nothing except to get themselves killed."

entire foreign trade of France; then Law himself obtained the right to collect the taxes and issue what was in effect paper money. By 1719 the object of the Regent's operation was disclosed: the *rentes*, representing the bulk of the enormous French national debt, were written off and made payable in the shares of the *Compagnie*, now the *Compagnie des Indes*. But the trade, even of *les Indes*, let alone of Louisiana, was quite inadequate to support this colossal commitment. The consequent crash ruined thousands of investors who had not had the luck or judgement to get out at the top of the market, and apart from a few roads and canals built on credit, the one lasting asset of Law's enterprise remains New Orleans.

The result of these reverses, the failure of the nobility to take its chance of power, the clash with the *Parlement* and the widespread ruin spread by the collapse of Law's speculation, was to restore the old fashioned and cumbersome administration of the previous reign, so that France went forward into the eighteenth century with the archaic institutions of the seventeenth.

Only in foreign policy did the Regency achieve brief success. After the Treaty of Utrecht, in the way of power politics, the two main adversaries in the West, France and England, combined to maintain peace. In 1716 they even concluded an alliance, joined in the year after by the Dutch. Both the Hanoverian and the Regency governments were too precarious to risk further upheavals; the English feared the Jacobites; the French feared the resurgent power of Spain and the claims of Philip V on the French throne; still, until the birth of a Dauphin in 1729, following the marriage of Louis XV to Marie Lesczinska of Poland, without a direct heir.

Already Cardinal Alberoni in Spain was intriguing on behalf of Elizabeth Farnese, the second queen of Philip V, who was anxious for Italian territory for her sons, to upset the settlement of Italy, and the British had to destroy a large Spanish fleet off Cape Passaro in Sicily to postpone a renewed Spanish presence in Italy itself.

But both Sir Robert Walpole (1721–42) and the French Cardinal Fleury (1726–42) remained determined on peace; and when in 1733 Louis XV rashly tried to replace his father-in-law, Stanislaus Lesczinski, on the Polish throne, and oust Augustus III of Saxony, the War of the Polish Succession was contained in Central Europe and fought out mainly in Italy, not in the West. So the Spaniards drove the Austrians from Naples and imposed a dynasty of Spanish Bourbons on the throne of Naples and Sicily—a curious repercussion of Polish politics. Stanislaus was compensated by Lorraine, where the splendid *Place Stanislaus* at Nancy commemorates him, with reversion to his daughter the Queen of France. And when at last the relatively long peace in the West was broken, it collapsed through friction between Great Britain and Spain over smuggling, piracy and the slave trade in the West Indies; indeed, it was only in response to popular outcry that in 1738 Walpole sent Rear-Admiral Nicholas Haddock, who had served under Peterborough at the relief of Barcelona and distinguished himself at Cape Passaro, to blockade Cadiz and Barcelona and capture what treasure ships he could. By 1739 Great Britain and Spain were in a war known to the British as the War of Jenkins' Ear,[1] and the conflict soon merged into the major European War of the Austrian Succession (1740-8) in which the traditional Anglo-French hostilities were renewed. Then, following the inconclusive Treaty of Aix-la-Chapelle in 1748, Europe lapsed into the first global conflict—the Seven Years' War (1756-63).

II

All these wars, conducted between princes when dynastic policies had broken down, were waged by professional armies, dependent on an elaborate and cumbersome apparatus of depots and supply. Save for the Russians, who generally lived off the country, they were kept under rigid discipline without which they might have deserted, and even plunder and sack were conducted by fixed conventions. This formalized slow moving warfare was now often deliberately inconclusive, since soldiers were expensive, winter campaigning was generally impracticable and there were more sieges than battles: though wars were long, they were not so intense as modern mass warfare. But they were important because campaigns fought on the Elbe or near the Rhine determined the future of vast tracts of North America, of rich West Indian islands and of the Indian sub-continent.

During much of this time France was misgoverned by Louis XV. Spoilt and flattered from childhood, furtive through premature exposure to publicity, his boredom relieved only by incessant hunting and successive mistresses, this charming, handsome and treacherous monarch was surrounded by a clique of the highest aristocracy and dominated by the one mistress who lasted because she could amuse him. A beauty of middle class origin, introduced into the court as Madame d'Étoiles, the Marquise de Pompadour controlled appointments and even made policy; under her reign the French addiction to boudoir government reached a damaging climax. Infuriated because Frederick II of Prussia called one of his bitches after her, and flattered because the Empress Maria Theresa pretended to treat her as a confidante by correspondence, this tiresome woman helped to plunge Europe into the war of the Austrian Succession and to prolong the Seven Years' War.

But naturally the causes went deeper. The War of the Austrian Succession followed the traditional and ancient rivalry between the French monarchs and the emperors. Since Vienna had repelled the Turks, Charles VI (1711-40), developing the traditions of Leopold I, had established there a more aristocratic and elegant court culture than had the arrogant Bourbons at Versailles. Indeed, in the Age of "Enlightenment", the "Enlightened Despots" were in Central Europe and briefly in Spain. Conservative and Jesuit ridden, the Austrian court had not the modernity of the Parisian salons; but, as C. A. Macartney writes, "the *Hochbarock* culture of the age ... found at Charles' court expressions surpassed nowhere in Europe for splendour or for delicate and

[1]See Richard Pares. *War and Peace in the West Indies. 1739-63.* Oxford, 1936 for Richard Jenkins and his ear.

curious grace: for that Court was not only the seat of what was already the most august dynasty in Europe, but also a unique meeting point where influences from Germany, Italy, Spain and the Netherlands met and mingled with those of the Danubian peoples to produce results which were not only magnificent but also at once local and universal. The dominant note was the Italian ... but while Italian opera comprised half the repertoire at Vienna's new theatre ... it alternated with broad popular farces in the Viennese dialect. The heart of this life was the Court itself: Charles personally composed an opera, which was performed, his daughters dancing in the ballet."

But Charles VI had no surviving male heir, and his eldest daughter, the Archduchess Maria Theresa, could not succeed either to the Empire or to the entire Habsburg inheritance; so in 1713 the Emperor had tried to guarantee her succession at least to the latter by a Sovereign Imperial Pronouncement or "Pragmatic[1] Sanction", while supporting her husband, Francis Stephen of Lorraine, as a candidate for the Empire. And he had induced a majority of the German Imperial Princes and most of the Great Powers, including France, Great Britain, Prussia and Russia, to recognize the validity of the "Sanction."

In 1740, no sooner was the Emperor dead, than Frederick II of Prussia invaded Silesia, between the Bohemian massif and Poland, the Wittelsbach Elector, Albert of Bavaria, claimed the Empire and threatened Vienna, while the French invaded Bohemia and occupied Prague. But the Hungarians supported Maria Theresa as their hereditary Queen, and the British, who feared for Hanover, and defended the Pragmatic Sanction, in 1743 defeated the French at Dettingen—in the last battle fought in person by a British monarch on the continent.[2] The most important result, in Europe, was that by the Peace of Dresden in 1745 Frederick II secured, and would keep, Silesia; while the failure of the French-backed Jacobite rising in 1745-6 secured the Hanoverians on the British throne, the Russians obtained greater influence in the eastern Baltic and in Poland, and in 1745, Maria Theresa achieved the election of Francis Stephen to the Imperial throne. Outside Europe, the Peace of Aix-la-Chapelle made minor changes in the West Indies, but the destruction of a Spanish fleet by Vernon off Cartagena in 1741 and Anson's circumnavigation of the world (1740-44) proved the prelude to the climax of the first British Empire in the Seven Years' War (1756-63).

This was the most decisive and far-flung conflict. It had been preceded by a "diplomatic revolution" whereby the centuries old Habsburg-French hostility

[1]A legal term which implied that the fact of its being promulgated by supreme Imperial authority gave it binding force.
[2]The political complications of this war are tedious and baffling, even as elucidated by Sir Charles Grant Robertson. "Great Britain, at war with Spain in 1739, was not at war with France until 1744; Spain was at war with Austria, particularly over the Habsburg territories in Italy, in 1741; France was not at war with Austria until 1744; Charles Albert the Elector of Bavaria as such, and not as Emperor, was at war with Austria in 1741; Prussia was twice at war with Austria in 1740 and 1745 but never with any other state; the Dutch were 'neutral' throughout. When the British and French fought each other at Dettingen (1743) they did so as auxiliaries for or against the Pragmatic army defendng Austria from Bavaria." *Chatham and the British Empire*. London, 1946. pp. 33-34.

was turned into an alliance, mainly by Austria for fear of mounting Russian power and through dislike of the mercantile maritime British, and by France through fear of Prussia and personal hatred of Frederick II. From the beginning the war was oceanic: following Hawke's victory in a gale off Quiberon Bay and Boscawen's off Lagos in Portugal, the British were soon masters of the North Atlantic and the Caribbean.

Then, in North America in 1759 James Wolfe and Admiral Saunders, in a combined operation, captured Quebec, a strategic victory completed in the following year by the capture of Montreal. All the vast territories of the interior down to what became Pittsburgh and beyond to Louisiana were lost to the French, and North America became part of the English speaking world. In the East during the War of the Austrian Succession, the British had also early mastered the Indian ocean, and Clive's victory at Arcot (1751) had made them the predominant European power; now in the Seven Years' War, in 1757 they conquered Bengal at Plassey, and in 1760–1 they drove the French from southern India. By the end of the war the East India Company was the paramount power over the entire sub-continent. In the West Indies, too, the British consolidated and extended an already predominant economic and strategic position.

Meanwhile, on the continent of Europe, Frederick II, who had started the conflict by invading Saxony in a "pre-emptive" strike south from Berlin, and whose only support came from massive English subsidies and from Hanover and Brunswick, fought off successive attacks by great French, Austrian, and Russian armies. In 1757 he routed the French under the Prince de Soubise at Rossbach in Saxony;[1] and in the following year he defeated the Austrians at Leuthen in Silesia. But even his military skill failed to prevent 83,000 Russians from overrunning and thoroughly devastating East Prussia, which they occupied until the end of the war; and at Zorndorf in Pomerania in a drawn battle of attrition the Russians inflicted 12,000 casualties on the Prussians for the loss of 20,000 of their own men—a rate of competition which the Prussians could not afford. Then in 1759, a combined Austro-Russian army overwhelmed them. Frederick himself declared "I will not survive it", and next year the Russians raided Berlin.[2]

Then Frederick's luck changed: in January 1762 the Tsaritza Elizabeth died, and was succeeded by her half-daft nephew, Peter III, who, crazed with admiration for Frederick II, and intent on an attack upon the Danes, suddenly called off the war and made an alliance with Prussia. But Peter, Danish on his mother's side, was a Lutheran, and ordered the Orthodox priests to remove the ikons and dress as pastors, as well as putting his guards into uncomfortable Prussian-style uniforms. He had to abdicate, and was soon strangled by his own drunken officers, who, credibly enough, reported to his Tsaritza, afterwards Catherine the Great, "we cannot ourselves remember what we did".

In England, William Pitt, later Earl of Chatham, the first "Great Com-

[1] A victory celebrated by Voltaire in an *Ode to Frederick II*.
[2] "The traditional alarm with which the Germans have later contemplated an advance of Russian hordes upon Germany and Europe may be dated from this time." Pares. *History of Russia. op. cit.* p. 229.

moner", who had appealed over the heads of Parliament to the politically conscious nation as the first prophet of imperialism, had now been brought down by his jealous colleagues, in spite of the brilliant success of the global war he had personally inspired; and the belligerent George II had been succeeded in 1760 by the pacific George III. The French, moreover, had made a "family compact " with Bourbon Spain, thus counteracting successive defeats. So on February 10th 1763 the French and British concluded the Peace of Paris whereby the British secured Canada, Nova Scotia and rights of navigation on the Mississippi throughout the Middle West down to the Gulf, and also acquired the important base of Minorca, as well as Florida, from Spain. They also retained Gibraltar and secured more West Indian islands, but Havana and Manila in the Philippines, both captured by the British Navy, and strategically important bases against the oceanic trade of the Spanish Colonial Empire, were restored to Spain. On the other hand, British paramountcy in India was *de facto* recognized. Thus the French, though stripped of vast potentially rich areas of Empire both in North America and the East, were not, as Pitt had intended, crippled at sea. Great Britain retained enormous gains but not all that Pitt had hoped for.

Frederick II, who signed the Peace of Hubertusburg with Austria, in the same month and year, gave up Saxony but retained Silesia with its textile and metallurgical wealth, both vital to the Prussian economy, reoccupied East Prussia and remained poised, a first rate military power, to take his share of the probable partition of a disintegrating Poland.

III

Although Great Britain and France, the two greatest powers in the West, were intermittently at war through much of the mid-eighteenth century, their intellectual influence combined to promote changes far more momentous and interesting than the diplomacy and campaigns that make the foreground of political history.

Men of genius in both countries had long contributed to this early modern outlook. Descartes had been determined in principle, though hardly in practice, to "arrive at knowledge highly useful to life ... by means of which ... we might render ourselves the lords and possessors of nature"; Francis Bacon had defined the "purpose of the sciences" as the "endowment of human life with new inventions and riches", and to "increase men's happiness and mitigate their sufferings". Erasmian humanism was now to be based on empirical knowledge: Hobbes and Locke had both justified the power of governments, not because it was divine but because it was useful, and if, and only if, it promoted the "security" and protected the property of its subjects, while Newton had apparently explained the universe as the work of a rational and mechanically minded Creator.

It was according to these principles that Europeans and their descendants overseas were to revolutionize science, industry, medicine, technology and war. Both in England and in France the formidable front of the "Ancient" religious establishment had crumbled during the previous century. The English Civil Wars and their aftermath had let loose a flood of sectarian religious controversy in which most of the accepted dogmas had been denied, while the Anglican Church of the Restoration, though bitterly hostile to the "Dissenters", had abandoned Laud's High Church zeal and accepted a tepid "rational" or neo-Platonic religion which led to the Deism of the early eighteenth century. In France, the bitter controversy between the puritan Jansenists and cosmopolitan Jesuits destroyed the united front which a monarchy by divine right demanded; in 1713 the Papal Bull *Unigenitus* had attacked Jansenist doctrines widely accepted by the French Gallican Church, and provoked a clash between the *Ultramontane* Jesuits, obedient only to the Pope, and the majority of French Catholics including the *Parlement*. Thus the hoary old medieval controversy had again disrupted the Church, and quasi-medieval miracles were performed at the tomb of a Jansenist priest. In southern and south-western France, moreover, the authorities continued to persecute the remaining Huguenots with a medieval zeal. And when owing to unwise speculation during the Seven Years War, the Father Superior of the Jesuits in the West Indies went bankrupt, the *Parlement* saddled the Jesuits with his debts; then, after an inquiry into the Jesuit statutes, in 1762 ordered the Society to be abolished in France, a move which had its repercussions elsewhere.

Thus, by the mid-eighteenth century, the French established Church had been undermined not merely among intellectuals, but among the people. And the intellectuals had not been idle. They had launched the rationalist campaign known as the "Enlightenment": and very brilliant it was, including early scientific popularization obliquely or directly reflecting upon Christian dogma.

Pierre Bayle (1647–1706), a French Calvinist Professor of History at Rotterdam, had been converted to Catholicism and then relapsed, thus making the worst of both worlds, and, finally, lapsing into toleration, had devised a new attack, launched in his *Dictionnaire historique et critique* (1697) in which the annotations—sometimes spiced with obscenity—showed up the ostensibly orthodox articles. This technique was afterwards used—without the obscenity—by Diderot, in the vastly influential French *Encyclopédie*. Before that, the *Lettres Persanes* of Montesquieu (1689–1755), published as early as 1721, had depicted a supposed foreigner's astonishment at French society. Then, in *De l'Esprit des Lois*, he followed out Newtonian method, declaring that reason could ascertain the laws of human society, since it was absurd to suppose that a *"fatalité aveugle"* could have produced intelligent beings. And reason showed that laws, which varied according to race and environment, were relative. Like Spinoza, Montesquieu looked at men as they are: he also ranged, with superb French assurance, over the entire panorama of the then known world and became a founder of sociology. He had written an entirely modern book

Then, in 1751–72 Diderot, influenced by Bayle, having satirized the *Ancien Régime* in *Lettres sur les Aveugles*, launched in collaboration with the mathematician d'Alembert, a systematic rationalist attack. In the *Encyclopédie ou Dictionnaire Raisonné des Sciences, des Arts et des Métiers*, they set out, he wrote, to "expound as far as possible the order and connections of human knowledge". He paid tributes to Bacon, Descartes and Locke. Though inspired by a French translation of Ephraim Chambers' Cyclopedia or Universal Dictionary of Arts and Sciences, which, published in England in 1728, had reached a fifth edition by 1746, here on such a scale was an unprecedented enterprise, in seventeen volumes, with three supplements. It at once appealed to the logical and systematic mentality of the French,[1] won an enormous public, and undermined the stabilizing dogmas of the Church more effectively than more direct attacks. Diderot and d'Alembert mobilized the most brilliant writers of the day and gave them a vast public. The Baron d'Holbach, a German from the Palatinate, the Maecenas of this circle and a spirited aristocrat, had a naif confidence in the power of reason in human affairs and discarded religion even as a social necessity. Voltaire (1694–1778), far the most brilliant and influential of these people, was an independent writer of genius, who commanded a European influence umparalleled since that of Erasmus, and embodied the barbed wit and satire of French civilization, constant since medieval times and now enlarged into a cosmopolitan range. He was the putative son of an accountant of Poitivin origin, and owed his first education to the Jesuits of l'École Louis le Grand. He won his first fame as a Regency wit and court poet, and served briefly as secretary of the Embassy at The Hague; but his wit made him enemies, and, being considered too ignoble to fight a duel, he was beaten up by the lackeys of the Chevalier de Rohan. After a spell in the Bastille for libel, from which he emerged calling himself de Voltaire (1726), he spent two years in England, where he became fluent in the language and met Congreve, Swift and Pope. Deeply influenced by English thought and political example, Voltaire returned to France and lived for years with a Mme du Chatelet at the Chateau de Cirey in Champagne. With this secure background, he poured out books, pamphlets and plays, of which the most important were Lettres Philosophiques (1734); Zaïre, a "Tragedy of the Crusades" (1732); and Alzira (1736), a tragedy set in Peru on the fashionable theme of noble savages: he also popularized the scientific discoveries of Newton. Meanwhile he was making a fortune by judicious speculation and indirectly from army contracts; by 1745 he was an Academician. In 1747 appeared Zadig, a satirical tale set in Babylon. In 1750, after the death of Mme du Chatelet, Voltaire accepted Frederick II's invitation to live at his court at Berlin; but these two brilliant individualists could not agree. After the publication of his Siècle de Louis XIV (1751), in 1753 Voltaire left Prussia in rage and settled near Geneva. Still insecure, in 1758 he purchased the estate of Ferney in Switzerland, near the French border, where, in 1759, the year of the publication of Candide, he settled as a wealthy, popular and benevolent Seigneur de village, holding court for celebrities and admirers from all over Europe and pouring out pamphlets, books and plays; most notable his Essai sur les Moeurs (1756), a pioneer survey of world history, followed by his Philosophie

---

[1]The publication was only allowed to proceed because Malesherbes, the chief censor, was secretly in favour of it, and in 1756 the Conseil d'Etat ordered it to be suppressed. D'Alembert resigned, and Diderot became anonymous. But the unpopularity and expulsion of the Jesuits removed the strongest opposition.

de l'Histoire (1756). Voltaire also used his formidable influence to help the dependants of Calas, a Protestant broken on the wheel for alleged blasphemy, and posthumously to vindicate the nineteen-year-old Chevalier de la Barre, beheaded for alleged sacrilege. In 1778 he returned to Paris to supervise the production of his play *Irène*, and was acclaimed and crowned with laurel; but the strain was too much for him and he died of it. Whether or not mistaking red bed-curtains for Hell, he exclaimed *"les flammes déjà"*—"the flames already"—the legend is *ben trovato*. The most attractive representation of Voltaire is the statue by Houdon.

Voltaire was a Deist and a humanitarian, who believed that intelligence, properly harnessed, could improve society; he therefore attacked *l'infame*—his name for the established Catholic Church. But he was no atheist and no radical; he believed that enlightened despots could best promote improvement. He also detested the romantic and confused doctrines of Rousseau, and he was politically on the side of a rational and humane order, based on compassion and common sense. In his most famous and influential book, the satirical novel *Candide, ou l'optimisme traduit de l'Allemande de M. Le Docteur Ralph*, which appeared in 1759, by English reckoning in the "year of victories" during the Seven Years War, he scarifies the imbecilities of war and the fatuities of metaphysical philosophers, caricatured in the immortal Dr Pangloss, and contrasts the human decency of his originally innocent characters with the monstrous crimes of public authority. The lucidity and verve of this short masterpiece have made it one of the classics of European literature; a brilliant show up of the habitual abuse of public power. The book opens quietly with compelling narrative art: "Il y avait en Westphalie, dans le château de M. le Baron de Thunder-ten-Tronckh, un jeune garçon à qui la nature avait donné les moeurs les plus douces. Sa physionomie annonçait son âme ... " It concludes, after depicting a nightmare of human and natural catastrophe, with Candide's disillusionment, and the individualist and Epicurean moral that all one can do is to "cultivate one's garden".

Voltaire's career and outlook would have been inconceivable in medieval times; here is the free play of a rational independent mind, who, unlike the detached Epicurean individualists of Antiquity, felt that something must and could be done to improve society and, unlike them, could appeal to a vast audience through print. Himself part of a brilliant minority culture, Voltaire underestimated the inertia and obtuseness of the mass of mankind and the immense difficulties of political action; but his objective, ironic, and immensely readable description of the acts of public power have consoled many subsequent victims of its imbecilities to endure and resist.

The most original aspect of the "Enlightenment" was the doctrine of progress, since taken for granted. Hitherto history had been thought to be a pattern of cyclic recurrence, and it was still believed to have been very short. It was not until well into the nineteenth century that the date 4004 BC for the Creation of the world was discarded; there was still no conception of the immense antiquity of mankind. But with the victory of the "Moderns" over the "Ancients" clinched by Newton, at least the scientific prestige of the great classical authors had been undermined, and Fontanelle, whose witty *Dialogue* of the Dead had appeared in 1683, and his Digression on the Ancients and Moderns in 1688, could write "we are under an obligation to the ancients for having exhausted almost all the false theories that could be found."[1] And once it was admitted that the latest scientists might be the best, the novel assumption of progress came in. Time was not the enemy, but on our side.

The economist Turgot, inspired by Montesquieu, early drafted Discourses of Universal History (1750), in which, setting aside Bossuet's doctrine of Providence, he sought more mundane principles of explanation, and although the data for such a work were then quite inadequate, his project is representative of a secular and cosmopolitan view of the past than becoming fashionable—a world away, for example, from the blinkered if eloquent History of the World compiled in the Tower by Sir Walter Raleigh. Once accept the view that progress is possible and that the purpose of government is to promote the well-being of all its citizens, and one of the most fundamental assumptions of modern civilization has been made. In time, indeed, it became a dogma.

The new popularization of well charted knowledge, as achieved by Buffon's Histoire Naturelle (1749) found a huge public, and the Swedish Carl von Linnaeus, a doctor in Stockholm, developed the classification of botanical science, in his Systema Naturalis (1735) and his Species Plantarum (1753).

It was indeed through the new scientific academics and their periodicals, following the example of the Royal Society in London, that the most pervasive spread of the Enlightenment occurred; as in Berlin, Stockholm and St. Petersburg; and soon the first universities were founded in Russia in St. Petersburg (1747) and Moscow (1755). Nor were the Italians backward in the sciences; in Giambattista Vico (1668–1744) Naples produced an original genius who invented a new kind of sociology. His Of the Wisdom of the Ancient Italians appeared in 1710, towards the end of the Marlborough wars, and his Scienza Nuova in 1725. This immense work by the Professor of Rhetoric at Naples was practically ignored; but it was to have great influence on Herder, Hegel, Michelet and Marx. For Vico tried to interpret history by getting inside it by intuition—a profoundly original idea in the rationalist eighteenth century—and with a subtler psychological insight than Hobbes, to understand history as the external consequence of the changing mentality of mankind. Of course the vast enterprise failed; but his strategy had adumbrated a new secular philosophy of history, tracing emergent rather than superimposed laws. It had not mattered to him which authority, Austrian or Spanish Bourbon, was misgoverning Naples, or how many mercenary soldiers had been massacred at Malplaquet.

IV

The advent of a French Bourbon king to the throne of Spain had brought an alien cosmopolitan influence to the Iberian peninsula. The French had

[1]Cited in J. B. Bury, The Idea of Progress. London, 1921. p. 104.

managed to construct the most powerful, if not yet a very efficient, model of the Great State which had been emerging since the reign of Philip II, and Philip V (1700–40) now attempted the daunting task of centralizing the government of Spain. But it was more than he or his son Ferdinand VI or his grandson, the amiable and "enlightened" despot Carlos III, could do to alter the ingrained and proud conservatism of the Spaniards. The Habsburg Emperor Charles VI, before his accession to the Empire, had spent many years in Spain, attempting, with Catalonian and allied support, to claim the throne, and the centralizing government at Madrid saw that the Catalans paid the penalty. But the Castilians, exhausted by the wars and bankruptcies of Philip II and weakened by the decline and maladministration of the Spanish-American empire, were in no condition to contend with the perennial problems of an archaic and disunited society, oppressed by a largely parasitic nobility and Church. Carlos III (1759–88),[1] who started his reign badly by being dragged into war against Great Britain through the Bourbon "Family Compact" of 1761, and lost Florida, now attempted an "enlightened" despotism. Determined to bring the Church under his control and following Portuguese precedent, in 1773, he expelled the Jesuits from Spain, well after Louis XV had expelled them from France. He also curbed the power of the Inquisition. He brought with him some of his Neapolitan ministers, took advice from Irish and British economists, and brought the outlook of the "Enlightenment" to Spain which had once assimilated so much Erasmian learning.

Although, during the eighteenth century, Spain lost most of her European empire—Naples and Sicily, Tuscany and Milan, Luxembourg and the Spanish Netherlands as well as Sardinia and Gibraltar—Spanish upper-class culture became more European under Carlos III. Liberal humanitarian ideas became fashionable but did not percolate far among the illiterate majority of the population. Government encouraged the people to re-colonize the often depopulated interior, tried to develop leather, cloth and linen industries and to improve roads and bridges. But the weight of habit and tradition was generally impervious to the propaganda of the economists, and farming proceeded at the pace of the donkey and mule. Only in fruit growing areas, where the Arab tradition was still strong, was there substantial prosperity.

Under royal patronage an elite culture briefly flourished. An *Academia de la Lingua* was founded to standardize the language, on the French model, at Madrid; then an Academy of History, Colleges of Law and Medicine. The famous old medieval universities even turned their attention to modern studies. Biologists and botanists explored and classified in the Spanish American empire.

Pedro Jeronimo Feijóo, a Benedictine monk (1676–1764), reviving the old Spanish Erasmian tradition, had been the first exponent of the Spanish Enlightenment, a many-sided scholar in law, education, science and medicine, whose *Cartas eruditas y curiosas* appeared in 1742–62. Masdeu wrote his *Historia Critica de España y de la Cultura Española*, a work of immense scope.

[1] A son of Philip V by his second wife Elizabeth Farnese, he had been Duke of Parma and King of Naples, so had testing experience. Goya painted him, quizzical and intelligent, and dressed for a shoot. He had a passion for most forms of sport.

Leandro de Moratin, whose father, Nicolas, had won reputation with a poem on the perennially popular subject of a bull fight, wrote sardonic comedies in the manner of Molière as *The Old Man and his Girl* and *The Young Girl's "Yes".*

The great Spanish tradition of baroque architecture was enriched by Neapolitan architects brought in by Carlos III who, as King of Naples, had sponsored the first excavations of Pompeii. In Spain Salcillo (1727-77) was the most influential architect, but it was in Portugal that baroque developed most luxuriantly into rococo, as at Queluz, its pale green and light brown interiors in cool contrast to its pink and white façades.

V

After the successful revolt from Spain backed by France in 1640, João IV (1640-56), the first of the Braganzas, had been crowned King of Portugal. Immensely rich in his own right, he was more concerned with his estates, his music and his libraries than with the desultory war with Spain. Here the Portuguese owed much to their alliance with the British, reaffirmed in 1654 with the Republican regime, and confirmed by 1661 by the marriage of Catherine of Braganza, daughter of João IV, to the restored Charles II. British armaments had sustained the war of liberation, which had culminated in 1665 when the Portuguese, under a German commander Hermann von Schomberg, had defeated the Spaniards at Monte Cicero; and in 1668 King Afonso V (1656-83) had been able to conclude the Treaty of Lisbon which recognized the independence of Portugal.

The British had exacted a heavy price. It was from the Treaty of 1654 that the British economic domination of Portugal derived, English merchants had established extra-territorial rights as if in Asia, and the right to practise their own Protestant religion in a Catholic country. And under the marriage treaty of 1661 they had exacted the promise of a large dowry, the garrisoning of Tangier and the handing over of Bombay, ostensibly to defend it against the Dutch. It had then followed naturally, with the outbreak of the War of the Spanish Succession, that in 1703, when the Archduke Charles of Austria, claiming to be Carlos III of Spain, had landed in Portugal with English backing on his way to Catalonia, that the Methuen Treaty was signed whereby English cloth was admitted to Portugal, and Portuguese wines imported on favourable terms to Great Britain, at the expense of French. In mercantilist terms, this famous Treaty proved more advantageous to the British than to the Portuguese, since, although the British drank "port" as hard as they could, the Portuguese bought more goods from Great Britain and their banks, indebted to London, had to pay for their adverse trade balance in gold from Brazil.

They could do so because in 1694 gold mines had been discovered in the interior of the colony; then Brazilian diamond mines made the Portuguese monarchs and upper classes unwontedly rich during most of the eighteenth century.

So, under João V (1706-50), under a priest-ridden but wealthy absolutism, distinctively delicate baroque and rococo palaces were built, set in the superb gardens which flourished in the Atlantic but sunny climate, and Portugal attained at least a surface prosperity; but during the reign of José (1750-77), in November 1755, catastrophe struck the capital.

The Lisbon earthquake of that year horrified Europe. The conservatives thought it a punishment for sin, the Deists were shaken in their fashionable belief in a benevolent Creator, and rumour greatly exaggerated the numbers of the dead. Fortunately an able minister was for once in charge: Sebastio José de Carvalho e Mello, better known as the Marquis de Pombal (1769), was one of the few of his countrymen with cosmopolitan experience, as ambassador in London and Vienna, and of rational turn of mind; since 1750 Secretary for War and Foreign Affairs, he managed to control the panic and, despite the clergy who proclaimed that the city should be left in ruins as a monument to the Wrath of God, he had Lisbon rebuilt on the rational "grid" plan it still retains, and created the great piazza, facing the Tagus, known to generations of English sailors from its equestrian statue of King José, as "Black Horse Square".

In 1756 Carvalho became principal minister, a position he consolidated after a Jesuit-inspired plot had been discovered to assassinate the King, and in 1759 the Jesuits were expelled from Portugal and the Portuguese Colonies. There followed, in King José's name, nearly two decades of "enlightened" despotism: even the condition of the peasants was improved, and sardine fisheries and silk manufacturing developed. State-controlled companies improved agriculture and vineyards, the trade with Brazil flourished, and even education was modernized. The Portuguese "enlightenment" was more successful than the contemporary one in Spain since the colonial empire was now more productive and conditions more attractive for foreign capital. But Pombal's regime, like other Portuguese authoritarian governments, had meant executions and imprisonment for its enemies, and on the death of King José and the accession of Maria I, Pombal was disgraced and sentenced to retire to his estates south of Coimbra, where in 1782 he died. His monument was Lisbon, rebuilt according to the latest French principles of town planning, but still Iberian with its coloured tiles and wrought iron balconies, and still the capital of a rich South American, if not now of an East Asian, empire.

VI

Such were the political fortunes of the Western Oceanic powers, France, Great Britain, Spain and Portugal, during the culturally most creative period of the eighteenth century, the climax of pre-industrial European civilization. Its legacy in music and the arts is superb. In France, where the Italianate influences of Lully had long predominated and been assimilated, Jean-Philippe Rameau (1683-1764), court musican to Louis XV, developed a Parisian style of opera, wrote pioneer works of musical theory, and first introduced the clarinet into the orchestra. In England the prevalent Italian opera was characteristically parodied in *The Beggars' Opera* (1728) a "Newgate pastoral", the equivalent of Hogarth's pictures of low life, for which the poet Gay wrote the libretto and J. C. Pepusch, a German musician, arranged a mixture of London street tunes and country airs backed by pseudo-formal music which has stood the test of time and even of modern prettification. Thomas Arne, an old Etonian, composed *Rule Britannia,* and set many of Shakespeare's best known lyrics to music. *"God Save the King",* which became popular in answer to the Jacobite rising of 1745, has no one author; but, deriving from folk tunes and hymns and psalm tunes, has caught on ever since.

Of course, the main musical achievement of the age is German, both Protestant and Catholic. Johann Sebastian Bach (1685–1750), born at Eisenach in Thuringia, who became the principal organist at Leipzig, and Georg Friedrich Handel (1685–1759), born at Halle in Saxony, both came from middle-class Protestant backgrounds in entire contrast to the Italian-French Court setting of Lully. Bach led a provincial and happy domestic life, but he had assimilated Italian influence. He owed much to the great Venetian composer Antonio Vivaldi (1675–1742), and his soaring genius was universal, expressing more the intellectual severity of the early seventeenth century than the sophisticated gaieties of the eighteenth. Handel was much more worldly and adventurous; as a youth he visited Rome, and in London, where he made his main career and where he died, he produced many operas on historical and biblical themes in high baroque style. Both these composers, the former content with routine, the latter a venturesome man of the world who made and lost fortunes, went blind in their declining years. They achieved great music by apparently simple means, and both have the splendid confidence of the age of Newton, which saw the universe as the harmonious work of a rational Creator.

By the mid-eighteenth century the Catholic and conservative Habsburg Imperial Court at Vienna was the greatest centre of patronage. The Emperor Charles VI, himself like his father Leopold I a composer, had set high standards, the wealthy Austrian and Hungarian aristocracy retained their own musicians and orchestras, while Prague ever since the reign of Rudolf II had been a centre of culture. Christoph von Gluck, born in 1714, the year after the Peace of Utrecht, a Bavarian under Italian and French influence, produced *Orpheus and Eurydice* in Vienna (1762), and *Iphigenia in Aulis* in Paris. Thus the original Italian impulse set off in Venice by Monteverdi in the seventeenth century—when his splendid *Coronation of Poppaea* had been performed there in 1642—was enriched by Vivaldi in Venice, by Lully and Rameau in Paris, by Bach and Handel in Germany and England, and elaborated by Gluck in Vienna.

It was a kind of music far beyond anything composed in Antiquity or in medieval times, one of the distinctive and original expressions of the confident and rational outlook of late-seventeenth-century and early-eighteenth-century Europe.

In painting the early-eighteenth-century harvest was, also rich. Reacting against the classical formality of Poussin and Bourdon, and the competent but theatrical portraits of Rigaud, Jean-Antoine Watteau (1684–1721) introduced a more delicate and eclectic style. Stylistically a distant descendant of Giorgione, he introduced the *fête champêtre*, and gave Rubens' robust goddesses a much more fragile appearance, sublimating his art into a transient and subtle beauty, as in his *Pilgrimage to Cythère*. He died, consumptive, at thirty-seven; a herald of the rococo style, his work far surpassing similar sublimations of nature that have survived from Antiquity.

More robust, and as typically French, is the work of that successful court painter Francois Boucher (1703–70). He taught Madame de Pompadour engraving, became *premier peintre du Roi,* and made a great deal of money; the delicate sensuality of his *La Petite Morphine*, sprawling on her bed, recalls the pleasures to which the monarch devoted so much of his life. Chardin (1699–1779), also typically French, transfigures another essential side of existence—as in his painting of a sturdy scullery maid about to peel an onion, or, one less essential, of an idle pageboy stacking up a house of cards.

The English, who even in the seventeenth century, when Poussin and Claude and the van de Veldes were creating masterpieces, had to rely mainly on Dutch painters to record royalties and magnates and their women, now began to produce artists of their own. They were realistic like Hogarth or idealizing like Sir Joshua Reynolds, and they excelled at portraits. The best of them, Gainsborough (1727–88), a Suffolk man who made his successful career in Bath and London, was as much at home painting a gorgeous waistcoat or hitting off character as painting a landscape; he never went abroad, and disliked the foreign fashion for great historical "subject" pictures. Reynolds (1723–92), who came from Devon, studied in Rome, Florence and Venice; he became a fashionable figure in London, the knighted President of the Royal Academy, founded in 1768; and though he evoked the ambience of insular patrons with subtle flattery, he was more scholarly and cosmopolitan. For the first time in England native artists had achieved recognition and even affluence.

In Italy the great Venetian tradition of Titian and Paulo Veronese was carried on by Giambattista Tiepolo (1696–1770) who found his widest scope in the rococo palaces of northern Italy and in southern Germany. His largest painting was commissioned for the palace of the Prince-bishop of Würzburg in a setting designed by the German decorator, Neumann, but his most beautiful effects, reminiscent of Watteau, are to be found on the ceilings of Venetian churches and palaces. Invited to Spain by Carlos III, he died in Madrid.

The work of Spanish artists, with their brilliant traditions created by Velázquez, would culminate in Goya (1746–1828), but the first rate monuments of the new Bourbon dynasty are their palaces. Philip V commissioned the *Sitio Real* or Royal Seat at La Granja near Segovia, north-west of Madrid beyond the Guadarramas, with its rococo interiors, the model for many Portuguese palaces, and its magnificent formal gardens designed with their woods and fountains by Ardemans. Here the Spanish style is blended with cosmopolitan influence, seventeenth-century French and Italian, the settings created by gardeners imported from Versailles and Naples, and in this version of an

Italianate Versailles, Philip V and his second wife, Elizabeth Farnese, attempted to retire from the world.

The Spaniards embellished their rococo saloons with porcelain, as at the Palace at Aranjuez, south of Madrid, enlarged and modernized by Carlos III, and in the Royal Palace at Madrid itself, with its grand prospect over formal gardens and staggering wealth of interior decoration. It was built mainly by Italian architects, on the site of the ancient Alcázar, and completed enough for Carlos III to install himself in 1764. It is a riot of chinoiseries and arabesques, of chandeliers, mirrors and tapestries, with a gigantic throne room with a ceiling by Tiepolo.[1] In total contrast to the grand austerity of the Escorial of Philip II, it remains the *Palacio Real de los Borbones* to the Spaniards, who like to put their dynasties in their historical place.

[1] It still contains the finest armoury in Europe, including the armour and trappings used by Charles V at Muhlberg in which Titian painted him.

BOOK VI

INDUSTRIAL CIVILIZATION: DEMOCRACY AND NATIONALISM

XXXVIII

The French Revolution

The Seven Years' War, concluded in 1763 by the Treaty of Paris, had deprived France of most of her colonial empire, but it had not broken the power of her fleets. When, therefore, the British American colonies in 1776 rose in revolt, the French mobilized a formidable European Coalition for a war of revenge, which, incidentally but momentously, set an independent United States on its feet.

After that epoch-making event, the last military and naval effort of the French old régime in fact proved its own undoing, for the American Revolution now set a more urgent example than had the seventeenth-century English one, and the cost of French intervention threatened to bankrupt an already indebted government. Hence an immediate cause of the French Revolution which convulsed the most powerful nation on the continent and gave rise to the monstrous upheavals of the Revolutionary and Napoleonic Wars. And while these tremendous changes were impending in America and Western Europe, in Central and Eastern Europe the Prussians and Austrians were partitioning Poland, and Imperial Russia, which took the rest of it, was becoming a vast Eurasian power, colonizing far into Siberia and Central Asia. In the broad perspective of world history the eighteenth-century Americans and Russians were already creating a shift of power that by the twentieth century would dwarf Europe.

II

That France was ripe for radical change had long been obvious; but historians have now revised the facile explanations current in the nineteenth century. As most revolutions, the French one started among discontented elites and got out of hand; then, passing through a phase of near anarchy and terror, it was brought under control and exploited by a military dictator, who distracted the people from rebellion at home by conquests abroad, spread the ideas of the revolution with his invading armies and bureaucracy more by revulsion than example, and so changed the face not only of France but of much of Europe, either directly or by nationalist reaction. For good and ill the eighteenth-century "public law of Europe", whereby wars were not fought à l'outrance and peace was habitually patched up by a balance of power, was swept aside, and the way opened to the mass conflicts of conscript "peoples in arms" which would culminate, made more frightful by successive industrial and technological revolutions, in the near suicide of European civilization in the two world wars of the twentieth century. It was Napoleon who first set Europe on this disastrous course.

The French Revolution was not made either by starving or prosperous peasants, for the condition of the peasantry greatly varied over the different regions of France. It began at the summit when the clever and incompetent Louis XV was succeeded in 1774 by his grandson, the stupid and incompetent Louis XVI, both of whom inherited the archaic regime still unreformed from the days of Louis XIV.

The nobility, long frustrated since deprived of political powers and responsibilities for which they had now become incapable, tried to erode the "absolute" monarchy; the merchants were discontented since the archaic social order stifled enterprise; the brilliantly articulate writers, as Voltaire and Diderot and their colleagues, had for decades been attacking the privileges of the nobility and of the Church; the lawyers wanted social recognition and the peasants of varying status, on whom fell almost the entire weight of taxation, had to conceal what prosperity they had and grudge every sou of rent they paid to their detested seigneurs, who, unlike most of the English squires, held disdainfully aloof. There was no French equivalent to the unpaid English Justices of the Peace; in a country still overwhelmingly agricultural and dependent on harvests, preposterous internal customs barriers and tolls handicapped commerce, and in spite of successive governments' attempts to encourage manufacturing industry, French investors, obsessed with social status, still preferred to purchase minor office. Only the export trade in wine and luxury goods flourished, and made the fortunes of the great commercial ports, Le Havre, Bordeaux and Marseilles.

In spite of these handicaps, French civilization was becoming richer, but the nobility and the Church weighed heavily on this ill-organised society. There were about a quarter of a million of the noblesse de l'épée in a population of around twenty-six million, and, in contrast to the English convention whereby only the eldest son inherited the title, all the sons of a nobleman did so. Since the great noblesse, forced to attend at a lavish court, were deep in debt, they battened on the King's capricious favours and regarded living on their estates as exile; by contrast, the rustic provincial noblesse in Gascony or Brittany had little but their titles and their pride to distinguish them from their peasants. Right down the official hierarchy, including the army, higher appointments went not by ability but by lineage. Under Louis XIV, bourgeois ministers—a Colbert or a Louvois—had wielded great power; now the highest posts had to be bought or obtained by intrigue through the all-pervading influence of a Marquise de Pompadour, the King's mistress, and confined to those with sufficient quarterings on their coats of arms.

The only alternative career for an aristocrat to a court appointment or a commission in the army was in the Church. It was immensely rich: where the Anglican Church had been impoverished and its prestige diminished by the plunder imposed by Henry VIII and his Parliaments, and shaken by the persecutions under the English Republic, the mainly Gallican French establishment had flourished after the suppression of the Huguenots and, in spite of Jansenist attacks, it remained an integral part of the regime. Here, too, the high appointments were reserved for the *noblesse*; who enjoyed enormous incomes, were generally non-resident, and formed a separate class from the *vicaires* and *curés de village*, who lived in poverty.

Both in Church and state the *noblesse*, whose influence had been curtailed in the seventeenth century, had thus regained much of their power, though they now exploited the realm rather than disrupted it; the wealthy tax farmers, bankers and army contractors still asked nothing better than to marry their sons and daughters into the *noblesse*, and since the days that Molière had portrayed the *Bourgeois Gentilhomme*, the newly rich had hankered to "live nobly".

Yet, in spite of disastrous wars and administrative muddle, the later years of Louis XV had seen an underlying and diffused prosperity as well as fantastic luxury at the Court; Menon's *La Cuisinière Bourgeoise* (1746) had been written for a wide public, and it was now that the classic simple and intelligent French cuisine came in, superseding the baroque plenty favoured by the gluttonous Louis XIV. In 1765 the first *restaurant*, as opposed to the traditional tavern, and accessible to anyone who could pay, opened in Paris.

So articulate and brilliant a society was cynical about itself. The sparkling conversation of the Parisian salons, like the pen of Voltaire, did not spare the institutions which framed and distorted the most civilized *beau monde* in Europe and, smarting with resentment at the arrogant exclusiveness of the *noblesse*, in Church and State, the middle-class urban intellectuals mounted a campaign of ridicule and invective. More insidiously, they now appealed to emotion. The versatile Jean-Jacques Rousseau had contributed an article on music to the *Encyclopédie* as well as one on "Political Economy"; he now turned his devastating power of phrase to politics. "Man is born free", he wrote—quite untruly—in *Du Contrat Social* (1763), "and he is everywhere in chains." Rousseau (1712–78) was descended from French Calvinists who had fled to Geneva, and was Savoyard on his mother's side. His mother died soon after his birth, and his father, Isaac, a watchmaker at Geneva, fled from his creditors to Nyon. The boy was apprenticed to an engraver in Geneva, but in 1728 decamped to Annecy, where he found a protectress in a Mme de Warens, a convert to Catholicism, who sent him to a seminary at Turin, where he, too, became a reluctant convert. Back in Annecy, he soon found he had no vocation for the priesthood, and in 1730 taught music at Lausanne and Neuchâtel. From 1733 he "lived with" Mme de Warens at Chambéry until, in 1742, he set out for Paris intent on success as a musician and playwright. Two years later he travelled to Venice as secretary to the French ambassador, with whom, following his life-long habit of biting the hand that fed, he had a violent quarrel. Back in Paris he cohabited with a serving wench, Thérèse Lavasseur, by whom he had five children, all of whom were consigned to the Foundling's Hospital—in fact the only humane course as their parents could not support them—but he did not marry her until 1768. In 1750 he won an easy celebrity by obtaining a prize for a *Discours sur les Sciences et les Arts,* on a subject set by the Academy of Dijon on "Whether the Progress of Science and the Arts had contributed to corrupt or purify Morals". Shrewdly—perhaps on the advice of Diderot—Rousseau attacked fashionable optimism and said that "progress" had corrupted morals, thereby winning notoriety. After one of his operettas had been performed before Louis XV, Rousseau could not face the interview with the King that could have brought him a pension, and in 1754 retired to Geneva where he reverted to Protestant beliefs.

Here began the spate of books which made him famous: *Julie ou la Nouvelle Héloïse* (1761); *Émile,* on education (1762); *Du Contrat Social* (1763). He attacked both official Christianity and rational enlightenment and thus both infuriated the authorities and quarrelled with Diderot. So he took refuge at Neuchâtel, then under the government of Frederick the Great, whose Scots-Jacobite governor got Rousseau to England, where he was befriended by Hume, with whom he soon quarrelled. But returning to France in 1767, he found powerful aristocratic patrons who assigned him comfortable quarters in the country. He had by now written his exhibitionist *Confessions* and his popular *Rêveries d'un Promeneur Solitaire.* He died at Ermenonville at a refuge provided by the Marquis de Girardin. Unlike Voltaire, Rousseau never kept any money; but like many apparently helpless "Bohemians" of genius, he always found protectors.

With Rousseau, a writer and musician of irresponsible genius irrupted into political and social theory with deplorable results. But if he gave the wrong answers, he raised urgent questions; a naturally centrifugal character, he questioned the basis of society in an apparently lucid but in fact opaque style. He was a natural Bohemian and vagabond, detested the social and political establishment and the coercive power of the state, and hankered for village communities in which individuals could participate and feel fulfilled.

His onslaught on the state, even on rational Enlightenment, proved highly topical in France, and coincided with the nascent "romantic" movement with its cult of emotion, "escape" and the "noble savage". Rousseau broke away from the legalistic contractual theory of the state as defined by Hobbes and Locke, tried to restore the organic relationship between individual and community and to base authority not upon force but upon the emergent "will" of participating "citizens", so that as he paradoxically put it, "in obeying it they obeyed only themselves". He thus created an intoxicating idea which contributed to the myth of modern democracy,[1] witheringly described by

---

[1]Liberal apologists for Rousseau have made much of his two excursions into constitutional theory, both devised for singularly unpromising fields, and never put into effect; *Projet de Constitution pour la Corse* (1764) and *Considérations sur le gouvernement de Pologne,* the latter not even published until 1881. Here he sometimes deviates into commonsense, but the myth of the general will was more representative and influential.

Pareto as "one of the sublimest dogmas of the democratic religion".[1] Though Rousseau never advocated violent revolution, his vague and eloquent ideas contributed to inspire it.

For the *Vicaire Savoyard*, a moralist and Deist emancipated from Christian orthodoxy, appealed to a growing lay public, looking for a prophet. He was one of the first that they found: in the nineteenth century they would find far too many. It is very peculiar that he should have been Swiss.

By the mid-eighteenth century the French *ancien régime* was thus being steadily undermined by the resentment of a spirited people against the archaic and stifling weight of the *noblesse* and the higher clergy, by the sheer incompetence of the administration which imposed inequitable taxation and handicapped internal trade, by the scarifying criticisms of the "Enlightened" intellectuals who demanded humanitarian improvement of the existing regime, and by the heady dogmas of romantics who wanted to transform the social order, and, like the rationalist emancipated intellectuals, attributed to the mass of the people a power of reason and moral choice which from the circumstances of their lives they could hardly possess.

III

When in 1774, aged nineteen, Louis XVI succeeded to the throne of France, he brought mediocre abilities to his monstrous task. "Weak but not actually imbecile", wrote his brother-in-law, the Emperor Joseph II, and subject to "indecision and apathy". He had a passion for hunting and an appetite as gross as that of Louis XIV;[2] and he was dominated by his silly young Habsburg Queen, Marie Antoinette. Bored with the public parade of Versailles, she did not put herself out to entertain the courtiers, so that the Palace ceased to be the brilliant social centre of the *ancien régime*, and the royal family lived among a small clique, while the Queen diverted herself with private theatricals and her artificial farm and dairy. The French soon found a word for her— *L'Autrichienne*.

Meanwhile in North America the mounting friction between the British and their colonists seemed to be playing into French hands. The French early began to supply the Americans with money and arms and, paradoxically, the intensely conservative French Monarchy encouraged a revolution which would in fact promote the kind of society which it loathed. For in North America, across three thousand miles of ocean and in colonial conditions, it was impossible to enforce the authority of any *ancien régime*, even George III's.

[1] See Vilfredo Pareto. *The Mind and Society.* ed. A. Livingston. London, 1935. Vol. III. pp. 1048–50 for a classic dissection of the dogma.
[2] An ordinary menu for breakfast being a fat capon and cutlets, the king remarked "That's not much—tell them to do me some eggs in gravy." He then ate four cutlets, the capon, six eggs and a slice of ham, and drank a bottle and half of champagne—a good start for a day's hunting. Cited by John Lough. *An Introduction to Eighteenth Century France.* London, 1960. p. 197.

Here the Whig tradition as expressed by Locke had been reinforced by more radical ideas, sometimes deriving from the Commonwealth and Protectorate.

Impossible here to depict the varied influences or the environment that built up the American Revolution, which was led by landowners from Virginia, influenced, as were Jefferson and Franklin, by the French Enlightenment, and by wealthy merchants from New England with a strong background of "dissent" against the Anglican Church. Suffice it that in December 1775 the Americans in Massachusetts and Virginia, the two oldest colonies, rose in a War of Independence, in which the British, using conventional European tactics, were defeated in what became a far-flung and often guerilla war, and in which, following the Declaration of Independence in 1776, they lost the Northern colonies when in 1777 Burgoyne surrendered at Saratoga. The defeat tempted the French, who had been heavily subsidizing the Americans, to intervene, and Spain followed suit. The British lost control of the North Atlantic; and when in 1781 Cornwallis surrendered at Yorktown to an American-French army, they lost the South. The French, more interested in the West Indies than in the American Revolution, moved their fleet out of Chesapeake Bay to mop up the more vulnerable British sugar islands; but in 1782 they were defeated in the battle of the Saints, and in 1783, under the Treaty of Versailles, the French retained only five of the less important Antilles, leaving the British in control of their main strategic bases and sugar islands in the Caribbean, but the United States a sovereign power.

France had entered the war already on the verge of bankruptcy. Turgot, an able but tactless administrator appointed in 1774, with a programme of strict economy and of paying off the immense public debts, had been frustrated by the court nobles and the tax farmers, backed by the Queen; and although in 1776 Turgot had succeeded in briefly abolishing the *corvée*, spreading the land tax to the landowners as well as the peasantry, and in destroying the stranglehold of the ancient guilds on industry, he had roused so much opposition from the *Parlement de Paris*, and from the judges, that he had jeopardized his own position. In 1776, the year of the American Declaration of Independence, the King had dismissed him before he had time to make further salutary changes. Louis fell back on a Swiss banker, Jacques Necker, whom he appointed Director of Finance (1777–81). Having to finance the American War, Necker, like any modern government, raised massive loans, thus avoiding immediate heavier taxation, but laying up trouble, if apparently balancing the budget; but by 1781 he decided to get out while the going was good and resigned.

By 1786 the banks were demanding enormous interest on further loans, and there was a substantial deficit; and in the following year the King convened an Assembly of Notables, representing the Princes, the great nobles, and the higher clergy, with a few representatives of the towns, to hear the new Minister, Calonne, put forward proposals to restore solvency. Since he attacked their privileges and declared that without change France was "impossible to govern", the Assembly proved obdurate, and Calonne, too, had to go. "To maintain its social leadership, to survive even, the Crown had to strike at the heart of privilege, at exemptions from taxation. It did so, and evoked an aristocratic reaction with which the Revolution began. Calonne's demand for a universal land tax with no privileged exemptions met with decisive opposition from the Notables and from the *parlements* allied with great nobles of the sword and princes of the blood. The King, left with no alternative, summoned the States General and appealed to the Third Estate against the new Fronde ... it was the Crown which called in a new factor, and left the way open for the bourgeoisie."[1]

IV

On 5th May, 1789, Louis XVI summoned the Estates General to Versailles; three hundred deputies each from *noblesse* and clergy, and six hundred from the Third Estate. But the government gave them no guidance, either for procedure or an agenda. And when the privileged orders predictably refused the Third Estate a single combined assembly, voting by the head, the latter, on 20th June, at a separate meeting improvised in a tennis court (*jeu de paume*), took an oath to transform themselves into a National Assembly and not to disperse before devising a constitution for France.

Technically they had no right to do so; but the King climbed down and ordered the *noblesse* and clergy to join them in a Constituent Assembly, while, with characteristic vacillation, he ordered troops to stand by in camp near Versailles and again dismissed the reinstated Necker in whom the Third Estate still had hopes. Paris, by now in the full heat of summer, seethed with panic, and on 14th July, with the help of disaffected soldiers and their artillery, some of the Parisian populace attacked and wrecked the Bastille,[2] symbol of the old order and of arbitrary imprisonment; an episode still celebrated. The symbolic fortress had been surrendered because the soldiers inside had refused to hold out, and because those guarding the Tuileries had allowed the populace access to arms. Nor were the King's regiments outside the capital any more reliable. The Parisians organized a "National Guard", their own middle-class militia to protect property, and set up a self-governing municipality; most of the principal towns of France went the same way. The King's government could no longer govern.

The Constituent Assembly now made a permanent and thorough administrative revolution. Their arrangements for debate remained chaotic, and the French proved far too individualistic to coalesce in organized parties; but they found it more congenial to compose a *Déclaration des Droits de l'Homme et du Citoyen*. It owed much to the American Declaration of Independence: "*Le but*

---

[1] J. M. Wallace-Hadrill and John McManners (Ed): *The Revolution and its Antecedents in France: Government and Society.* London, 1957. p. 172. q.v. for an admirable analysis in depth.

[2] A fourteenth-century fortress converted by Richelieu into a state prison, by then little used. Only seven inmates, consigned by *lettres de cachet*, were discovered, of whom the better off lived in comfort with their own food and servants and the others fairly well. Voltaire had done time there in 1717–18.

de la Société", it began, hopefully "est le bonheur commun—the aim of society is public happiness": government, it continued, is instituted to guarantee the "natural rights" of mankind; these rights are "equality, liberty, security and property". Further "tous les hommes sont égaux par la nature et devant la Loi— all men are equal by nature and before the law." Then, borrowing a phrase from Rousseau, it declared that the law was "the free and solemn expression of the general will". It went on to declare that all citizens were equally admissible to public office, thus dismissing the privileges of the noblesse and higher clergy, and that everyone had a right to express their ideas through the press "or in any other way", and to worship as they thought fit. The Declaration also firmly asserted (para. 25) that "sovereignty resides in the people, is one and indivisible, subject to no other's authority and inalienable." Finally, it declared, for good measure, that "if government violates the people's rights", the "most sacred and indispensable duty of the people and of each part of the people is insurrection".

Such was the formal manifesto of the French Revolution. It was the work of middle-class lawyers and intellectuals, with a singularly optimistic view of politics; and, far from being a manifesto of radical class war, it was designed to liberate private enterprise and protect property. It showed the way both to careers open to talent and to the tyranny of politicians who claimed to represent the "general will". It brought politics into a new dimension.

Meanwhile, having abolished all hereditary titles, committees of the Constituent Assembly had been hard at work, and they ably transformed the entire administration of France. These lawyers and magistrates were far more practical than the "ideologists" of abstract political theory, and since the Constituent Assembly had refused to create a "Senate" or Upper Chamber, their authority was unchecked. Moreover, they had widespread support in most of the regions of France. Backed by the long-established preponderance of Paris, their passion for system and symmetry was given full rein, and in consultation with regional representatives they replaced the clutter of the ancien régime by "departments" and municipal "communes", the former with geographical, not feudal, names, as Haute Marne, Indre-et-Loire, or Tarn, familiar today. At a stroke the old regional divisions were administratively superseded and in theory all Frenchmen came under the same central authority and the same law. But widespread local autonomy was conceded; even a federal union was envisaged; and, significantly, the franchise still excluded most labourers and all domestic servants, as people "unable to feed themselves". The Constituent Assembly was overwhelmingly made up of professional men and substantial bourgeois, and a stiff property qualification was set for candidates for election.

The perennial grievance over taxation was assuaged by the abolition of the taille and the gabelle; instead "contributions" were levied in accordance with professions and with apparent standards of living, so that the more prosperous French still contrived to appear poor. Free trade was established, a decimal metric system devised, and the Jews were emancipated; but, since the guilds had been swept away, trade unions and strikes were declared illegal. The first and lasting achievements of the Revolution were bourgeois; and they reflected prevalent political opinion and economic theory.

Not so the next phase, which touched off more violent passions. The Constituent Assembly, bent on tidying up a logical and comprehensive administration, nationalized the vast estates of the Church, closed down most of the historic monasteries and abolished the ancient dioceses, some going back to Merovingian times; they also now demanded that the clergy take an oath to a "*Civil Constitution of the Clergy*". After much agony of mind the Pope forbade them to take it, and most of the clergy, though already Gallican, obeyed him. Most of the people had accepted the constitutional changes; but now the Revolution ran into massive opposition, for in conservative areas the "non-juring" clergy were supported by their flocks. As the attack on bishops had rallied support to Charles I, so Louis XVI now attracted more loyalty. And he had a shrewd adviser to hand. Had he taken the advice of the brilliant but unstable Comte de Mirabeau, that renegade aristocrat thrice imprisoned by *lettres de cachet,* who now, as Deputy for Aix-en-Provence, had been trying to create a constitutional monarchy, he would have withdrawn to Rouen in royalist Normandy and waited for a come-back when factions had paralysed the Assembly. But in June 1791 the King, after being denied his usual visit to St. Cloud for his Easter Communion, belatedly decided to escape by a bungled flight to Varennes on the eastern frontier. Instead of making off unobtrusively to the coast, the portly and all-too-recognizable monarch bundled himself and his family into a large and conspicuous coach and trundled to the eastern frontier. He was recognized at midnight by a M. Drouet, a zealous local postmaster, who managed to raise two National Guards who arrested their sovereign. Drouet became a hero of the revolution, rewarded with thirty thousand depreciated francs. The English, politically more perspicacious, had encouraged James II to bolt. So Louis destroyed any credibility he still had, and became a hostage and a scapegoat.

By now the Constituent Assembly, having shown its high principles and lack of sense by decreeing its own Deputies ineligible for re-election, had given place to a Legislative Assembly under the new constitution. The new regime ordered all royalist émigrés to return to France, threatened to deport the non-juring clergy, and, as a desperate expedient, invaded the Austrian Netherlands, hoping, as did the captive king, to rally the country by a war.

The war fever worked the other way. In August 1792, Parisian artisans and radicals, maddened by fear of Austrian invasion, rose against the bourgeois-controlled Paris commune, "purged" it, and attacked the Tuileries. The King and Queen had to take refuge with the Legislative Assembly; the Assembly "suspended" the King, and summoned a National Convention to revise the constitution. They declared France a Republic and imposed a Revolutionary calendar, while the Parisian radicals massacred alleged "counter-revolution-aries" detained in the prisons. The *sans-culottes* in Paris and the provinces who organized such demonstrations were hardly the democrats of popular imagi-nation, but power-hungry politicians. "For there existed, at least in the bureaux, an inner ring of self-taught militants who ... were soon learning how to manipulate an assembly and prepare business from within a *comité*. In time

A History of Europe

they would have become professionals ... considering themselves indispensable to the forward march of the Revolution." They conducted the "bitter
personal struggles" usual among revolutionary militants, and were "most of
them ... loud mouthed, arrogant, intolerant, some of them were impossible
little tyrants, constantly boasting of how they disposed of their power of life
and death, gaily talking of the heads that would fall and taking an obvious
enjoyment in sending shudders down the backs of those they were seeking to
impress or to cow."[1]

Faced with near anarchy in Paris and war on the eastern frontier, with
rampant unemployment and inflation—for the *assignats* or paper money
secured on confiscated lands were rapidly depreciating—the Convention, after
an unexpected major success in September 1792 known as the "Cannonade at
Valmy" against the dreaded Prussians, launched its ragged armies against the
traditional objectives—the Rhine, Savoy and the Austrian Netherlands.
Inspired by the *Marseillaise,* the French were on the march.[2]

Within the Convention a small close-knit set of fanatics, led by Robespierre,
a lawyer from Arras, had obtained power; they were known as the Jacobins
from the club where they thrashed out their policies. Under the stress of war,
they had pushed the Convention further to the "Left"; then, having unearthed
evidence that Louis XVI was in correspondence with the enemy sovereigns, in
January 1793 they sent him to the guillotine, and that October also executed
Marie Antoinette.[3]

This gesture horrified the dynasts and the rest of established Europe; and in
1793 the wealthy and tenacious British, determined not to allow the Austrian
Netherlands to fall into the hands of a hostile power and to assert themselves
against their greatest potential rival in the trade whereby they lived, joined
the Austrians, the Prussians and Spain in a counter-attack which they promoted
by sea-power and subsidies. Revolts fomented by royalists broke out in France
and Toulon went over to the British.

At the price of terror and dictatorship, the French republican government
held the country together. The extremist Jacobins, backed by one of the

[1]Richard Cobb. *The Police and the People: French Popular Protest 1789–1820.* London,
1970. p. 123. This book is essential for an understanding of the French Revolution.
[2]Composed by C. J. Rouget de Lisle, an engineer officer of the army of the Rhine at
Strasbourg, as a marching song for young soldiers, the words and music, sung by the
composer, first came into fame in the expansive ambience of a banquet at Marseilles,
and the song so inspired the volunteers who were marching to Paris that they got there
in time for the attack on the Tuileries. The composer, who was too much of a royalist
to take the oath of Loyalty to the Republic, got little reward for his exploit and survived
into an old age of penury.
[3]This instrument, symbol of atrocity, at first coyly called *le petit Louison,* was in fact
designed, with its oblique and heavily weighted knife, by the good doctor whose name
it bears to cut short pain. A version of it had already been used, as might be expected,
in medieval Germany; in Italy (as a special privilege for noblemen) and, of course, in
Scotland, where it was called with pawky humour "the Maiden". Joseph Ignace
Guillotin was a member of the Constituent Assembly and induced it to decree that all
executions should be mechanized, but it is not clear if he got a percentage *per capita.*
The new method was considered more democratic, as hitherto only the *noblesse* had
been decapitated.

Parisian communes and some of the National Guards, seized power in the Convention by a *coup d'état* and imposed a more centralized government, in effect controlled by a "Committee of Public Safety", elected by the Convention. They sent out representatives to purge the Departments and the armies, and to spread terror throughout France by arrests and executions.

Purged of Girondin moderates, the Committee of Public Safety was dominated by Robespierre, of all the Jacobins the most fanatical, xenophobic and politically astute: he proclaimed a cult of the Supreme Being and the Brotherhood of Mankind and in its name executed many opponents. Regarded as "incorruptible" compared to the other demagogues, he established a brief and sanguinary ascendancy which culminated in June 1794 in the *Law of Suspects,* whereby "moral" proof of guilt made legal evidence superfluous and even the Deputies in the Convention were no longer immune from prosecution. That July (*Thermidor*), none too soon, Robespierre's colleagues had him killed.

According to the record of "official" executions over fourteen months, the terror accounted for seventeen thousand victims. One might think that such an authenticated estimate would be allowed to speak for itself. Yet, such still is the cult of the Revolution that a modern historian can write, "Conservatives have created a lasting image of the terror, dictatorship and hysterical blood lust unchained, though by twentieth-century standards ... its mass killings were *relatively modest*. Revolutionaries, especially in France, have seen it as the first people's republic, the inspiration of all subsequent revolt. For all it was an era not to be measured by *everyday human criteria*";[1] such as, one might add, humanity, the rule of law, or political commonsense.

Meanwhile, the Committee of Public Safety had done its work. Conscript republican armies raised by the *levée en masse* and led by officers often promoted for ability in battle had swarmed to the frontiers, cleared the relatively small and belatedly mobilized professional invading armies out of France and spilled over into Holland, Switzerland and even Italy, where they set up and occupied satellite republics and whence they sent back plunder. As never before, a "People in arms" had been improvised by a powerful central government, and the Republic had defied the formidable First Coalition.

Robespierre had been overthrown by relatively conservative "Thermidorian" Deputies in the Convention impelled by *la grande peur de la bourgeoisie française*, backed by middle-class elements in the Parisian National Guards, and by a widespread reaction into "White Terror" in the provinces; the Convention, now seriously depleted by the Terror, tried to stabilize the country by a new constitution with an "Executive *Directory*" elected by a *corps legislatif* and two *conseils,* the latter drawn from the Convention, who also elected the first batch of five *directeurs.* Inflation, food shortages, epidemics, mounting disorder and discontent continued, in spite of the success of the revolutionary armies abroad. After the atrocities committed under the White Terror over most of France, following those under the Committee of Public

---

[1]E. J. Hobsbawm. *The Age of Revolution. Europe 1789–1848.* London, 1956. p. 68. (Italics mine.) The reader who prefers objectivity and deeper research is referred to Richard Cobb, *op. cit.*

Safety, "the common people were back where they had started: they were in fact much worse off, for they were now faced with a much more efficient and ruthless apparatus of repression than that of the *ancien régime* ... All they had gained was a strange religio-revolutionary mish mash, the Cult of Robespierre, and a lot of good that would do them."[1] Under the corrupt *Directoire,* Napoleon Buonaparte came to power.

V

The French Revolution did not merely transform the administration of France, and show what Frenchmen would do to one another; it altered the assumptions on which the politics of Europe had been conducted. Not since, in a very different and miniature setting, the failure of a democratic experiment in classical Greece, had power been habitually wielded by demagogues through oratory as well as intrigue. Medieval revolutionaries did not last. A new sort of "politician" had now emerged, usually of middle-class origins, who, with a few renegade aristocrats or an occasional proletarian, appealed to a large, if still limited, electorate, and who attained public office by manipulating his colleagues, by oratory and by the press. In theory, and increasingly in practice, the basis of authority and promotion was no longer the King and Court, but the enfranchised "People" and its *"General Will"*.

The change can hardly be explained in Marxist terms of an economically determined class conflict between the feudal *noblesse* and the capitalist *bourgeoisie,* since France had remained so relatively little industrialized that a capitalist class, controlling the means of production, did not yet substantially exist. Indeed France remained predominantly agricultural, and commercial fortunes had been invested in land and public office. Nor were the leaders of the Revolution "socialists", a term not yet current; Adam Smith, whose *Wealth of Nations* (1776) had founded the modern science of "political economy", was their prophet, and as exponents of *laissez faire* they wanted to liberate production from old restraints, and save under stress of war, not to interfere with it.

This optimism about the economy was also applied to politics. The emancipated lawyers and professional men of the *Tiers Etat* had a curious belief, encouraged by the writers of the "Enlightenment", in the goodness and reasonableness of mankind. Robespierre was not cynically professing his Rousseauist ideals to gain power: he was mad enough to believe in them and kill for them.

Even after the Terror and the Counter-Terror, and after Napoleon had tamed and canalized the forces of the Revolution and secured its administrative achievements, a new political optimism survived in the West, and by the end of the nineteenth century, inspired an accepted orthodoxy at least as a façade for the manipulation of power.

[1]Richard Cobb. *op. cit.* p. 210.

In countries where western style "democracy" took on, government became conducted within the framework of a "Constitution" by which the fundamental rights of the citizens were guaranteed under the rule of Law, by elected politicians; no longer by even "enlightened" hereditary monarchs or aristocrats or military dictators. This form of government, at least in form, avoided arbitrary power: it spread over most of Europe and much of the world beyond it, and was something new on such a scale. Hitherto, even in republican city states, authority had generally been oligarchic, and in the republican peasant communities of Switzerland, it had been miniature. Now, contrary to the precedent of almost the entire sweep of European history here surveyed, hierarchy was, at least apparently, abolished and a new method of "self-government" was launched, dependng on competing politicians, more or less organized political factions or "parties" and a wider and wider franchise; finally on "one man (and one woman), one vote".

Defended as a peaceful way of obtaining change by consent, and as guaranteeing liberty by a constitution, and so "the least bad form of government", it has since become so entirely accepted that, whatever the historical and environmental setting, anyone in the western democracies who denies the supremacy of the emergent will of the People, even over the Law, is considered as heretical as a thirteenth-century Albigensian. Emancipated from the *ancien régime,* from the Napoleonic police state and from the Bourbon Restoration, the heirs of the French Revolution in France and outside it would launch an unprecedented enterprise, originally a blend of Anglo-Saxon Constitutionalism with French Enlightenment, and later inspired by more radical ideals of equality and fraternity—the Liberal-Democratic shading into the Social-Democratic experiment.

XXXIX

Central Europe: Imperial Russia

While the French monarchy was declining into bankruptcy and revolution, in central Europe and Russia variously "enlightened" despotisms still prevailed. In the Austrian empire, after the death in 1765 of Francis Stephen of Lorraine, consort of Maria Theresa as the Emperor Francis I, their son, the Emperor Joseph II, ruled conjointly with his mother until 1780, then, until 1790, alone. Highly intelligent and extremely forceful, this "enlightened" monarch endeavoured to impose a centralized bureaucratic despotism on the naturally incoherent Habsburg dominions. But the Imperial claims on Germany were systematically thwarted by Frederick the Great who, in medieval fashion, organized a *Fürstenbund* of the major German princes against the Emperor, and Joseph II had to contend with reconciling the hereditary Austrian Habsburg territories with the Czech Kingdom of Bohemia and the elective Kingdom of Hungary, with its ungovernable Magyar nobles, Calvinist minorities and, on the eastern frontier, its habit of pro-Turkish intrigue. And besides the problems which immediately confronted Vienna, the large Austrian territories in Italy had to be governed and the recalcitrant Austrian Netherlands controlled.

With able and untiring purpose Joseph II set about the daunting task. He centralized government in Vienna and Buda, he promulgated an enlightened and uniform code of law; and though he imposed German as the official language of the Empire,[1] physical torture and arbitrary executions were abolished; an inappropriate but coherent mercantilist economic policy was devised, and in 1781 the abolition of serfdom decreed. Though a devout Catholic, Joseph II insisted that Protestant worship be tolerated, obviously redundant monasteries suppressed, and a Concordat be made with the Pope allowing the Emperor considerable control of the wealthy and architecturally splendid Church establishment. The ideas of the French enlightenment were not merely tolerated; they were encouraged. Where in France Louis XVI was

[1]Except in the Austrian Netherlands, where, it was recognized, most of the people could never be persuaded to speak anything but Flemish.

abdicating his responsibilities, his brother-in-law in Vienna was showing a constructive but headstrong and often much too hopeful initiative.

In foreign policy Joseph II relied on the alliance with France concluded since the "diplomatic revolution" of the mid-eighteenth century, and in 1780, as a make-weight against Prussia, he concluded an alliance with the Empress Catherine the Great of Russia, though he failed to exchange the disaffected Austrian Netherlands for Catholic Bavaria and so strengthen his position in southern Germany.

The Vienna of the widowed Maria Theresa, of Joseph II and of his brother, Leopold II (1790–92), remains illustrious as the setting of the music of Haydn and Mozart, and of a culture more attractive than that of the hectic Parisian *Salons* on the eve of the Revolution or than the tedious formality of Versailles. Joseph Haydn (1732–1809), born at Rohrau in Lower Austria in part of Croatian descent, early entered the service of the great Hungarian Esterházy family, whose vast estates and private orchestra and choir gave him ample scope. Much influenced by Emmanuel Bach, he became the principal creator of the classical symphony and the string quartet, and by 1798 achieved cosmopolitan fame with the performance of *The Creation* at Vienna.

Wolfgang Amadeus Mozart (1756–91), the greatest of all European composers, of the rococo age or any other, after a childhood of brilliant and cosmopolitan promise, found uncongenial employment under the Archbishop of Salzburg, from whose palace he was literally kicked out; he found more understanding if unreliable patronage in the Vienna of Joseph II, where he produced his *Figaro, Don Giovanni* and *The Magic Flute,* and by 1788 composed his three greatest symphonies in the year before the French Revolution. He died in poverty of typhus in 1791, aged thirty-five, before the cannonade of Valmy opened two decades of war, having immortalized much of the best in the old eighteenth-century civilization.

While Joseph II had wisely left the Habsburg claims as Emperors of a Holy German *Reich* in abeyance, the upstart Prussian state, which Frederick II had made into one of the great military powers of Europe, had emerged from the Seven Years' War with wider ambitions. Frederick II, having absorbed Silesia, turned his eyes on Poland, and here, at least, Prussians and Austrians had a common interest.

Since Jan Sobieski's death in 1696, the Poles had fallen on more than usually evil days. Out of eighteen candidates for the throne, Augustus, Elector of Saxony, had been elected as Augustus II, and his son, Augustus III (1733–63), had held his own against a French-backed rival, Stanislaus Lesczezynski, father-in-law to Louis XV; but he had succeeded only through Russian help. The great land-owning families continued to fight one another; then Stanislaus August Poniatowski, a handsome youth related to the predominant Czartoryskis, had established a decisive lead. Sent on a diplomatic mission to St. Petersburg in 1755, he had briskly become the lover of Catherine the Great. After that there had been no stopping him: and in 1764 on the death of Augustus III, he had been elected, with active Russian support, King of Poland, as Stanislaus II.

Naturally some infuriated Polish gentry, known as the Confederates of Bar, and subsidized by the French, had raised rebellion; and the Turks, long concerned at Russsian threats to their frontier, had seized the opportunity to declare war. So Prussia first and then Austria, sinking their differences in common dread of a Russian-dominated Poland, had also seized their chance and moved into accessible parts of Poland. Hence the first partition of the country, consummated with active Russian connivance in 1772. The Prussians had obtained what became Eastern Pomerania, save for the key port of Danzig, and linked up their heartland with East Prussia; the Austrians took over most of south-western Poland up to the Vistula, but not including the historic Polish capital of Krakow, and called the area Galicia; the Russians got the largest share, all Polish territories east of the Dvina and the Dniester.

Liberal nationalist historians have considered these arrangements particularly criminal; but a power vacuum had appeared in a strategically important area. Considering that it was an essential interest for Berlin to link up with East Prussia, and after the successive record of Polish attacks on Muscovy, partition had long been predictable. When Frederick II died in 1786, he had rounded off his conquest of Silesia with neat and characteristic opportunism, and now the Austrians and Russians, to use a modern phrase, had "rectified their frontiers".

II

Only one traditional menace had been spared the Poles. Having long got rid of their more belligerent Vasas, the Swedes had no excuse to intervene. Nor, after the disasters inflicted on them by the adventures of Charles XII, with whom the direct male Vasa dynasty had ended, had they been in a position to do so. Moreover in 1772, just when Poland was being partitioned, their own dashing Gustav III was making a coup d'état.

After the death of Charles XII, the Swedish nobility had revived the old Council of the Realm and curbed the royal power, while the Vasa line had continued only through Charles XII's sister, Ulrica Eleanora. She had been elected Queen in 1719, and her consort, Frederick of Hesse, elected King with limited powers in the following year, had reigned as Frederick I until his death in 1751. The Treaty of Nystadt which had ended the Great Northern War had been most unfavourable to the Swedes, who had given up Livonia, Esthonia, East Karelia and Viborg to Russia, so that they had lost their grip on Finland, essential as a buffer state. Thrown back on themselves, and relieved of a military monarch, they concentrated on their shipping and timber trade with the west, while their oligarchic internal politics centred round the Riksdag, with its four estates, nobles, clergy, bourgeois and peasants.

The pro-French and dynamic party were called the Hats—as liable to be out and about, and their rivals, the pro-English and sometimes pro-Russian Caps, were named from night caps, because so unenterprising. During this phase of party governments in the Riksdag an elaborate kind of constitutionalism had developed, free of the crown; but it proved less successful than the English variety; arguments became so heated that "it was not unknown (in the Fourth or peasant estate) for violent scuffles to break out ... Peace might sometimes be restored for a short time by a resourceful member striking up a hymn, in which the entire assembly would join, only to be at loggerheads again as soon as it was over."[1] From 1739 to 1765 this regime, known as the "Age of Freedom", had been maintained, and the power both of Frederick I (succeeded by his son Adolf Frederick (1751–71)) and of the Council had been further eroded, while the strife of Hats and Caps had intensified.

So in August 1772 the new young monarch, Gustav III (1772–92), with the aid of his guards and a rising in Finland, brought off a bloodless *coup d'état*— just when the Russians and Prussians were preoccupied with the partition of Poland. The *Riksdag* was dissolved, not to meet for six years, and the King set about restoring the supposed Golden Days of Gustav II Adolf. Many reforms were brought in, most of them acclaimed by the populace, though when the King nationalized the distilleries to control the excessive supplies of schnapps, there was naturally much resentment. But in a more temperate realm there was a cultural effervescence—the King himself wrote Frenchified plays and may have seen himself as a character in one of them. He was talented, cosmopolitan, travelled and versatile; a high strung intellectual said to prefer his pages to the ladies of the Court, and determined to become an enlightened despot. In 1779 the Jews were invited to return and did so—always a sign of economic revival.

But in 1788 Gustav III overreached himself in a quest for glory; he declared war on Russia, now again embroiled with the Turks, to regain the territories lost by the Treaty of Nystadt. From this rash act he managed to emerge comparatively unscathed, when in 1790 the Peace of Värälä restored the *status quo*; but the war had severely strained the finances of Sweden, still a predominantly agricultural country with backward methods of farming, and the King, who had promoted the interests of the professional and middle classes, had now incurred the hatred of the nobility. In 1792, with heady news of the French Revolution coming in, a Captain Anckarstrom, backed by a widespread conspiracy, shot the monarch at a masked ball at the opera. Gustav III survived for a fortnight showing much charm and fortitude; but by taking a desperate risk he lost his life. He had been an "enchanter on the throne"; "a fascinating and diverse personality, a strange mixture of infant prodigy, cold-blooded intriguer, high principled hero, and unworldly aesthete".[2] As a contemporary English traveller observed, "The King's vanity was his ruling passion. It betrayed itself in all his words and actions. When he entered the levee, every step, every gesture, every speech was studied ... he prided himself very much upon his eloquence, and indeed with reason."[3] He had at

[1]Andersson. *op. cit.* p. 267
[2]Andersson. *op. cit.* p. 295.
[3]The Rev. John Parkinson. *A Tour of Russia, Siberia and the Crimea, 1792–1794.* ed. with Introduction by William Collier. London, 1971. p. 9. Parkinson, a Fellow of Magdalen College, Oxford, accompanied Edward Wilbraham-Bootle on an unusual Grand Tour, travelled to St. Petersburg through Sweden, and left a singularly illuminating record of his experience, strangely little known, but comparable to Burnaby's account of the American colonies before the War of Independence and as interesting.

once, writes Andersson, romanticised the past, and "thrown open the gates to the burgesses and peasants, the social classes of the nineteenth century".

III

While enlightened despots were ruling the Habsburg empire and Sweden and a military genius Prussia, and the Revolution was brewing in France, in Russia the work of Peter the Great was being given new impetus by a determined and dissolute German princess. Sophia Augusta of Anhalt Zerbst, renamed Ekaterina in 1745 on her Orthodox marriage to the Grand Duke Peter, nephew of the Tsaritza Elizabeth, now became known to history as Catherine II the Great (1762–96).

This able woman had long detested and despised her husband; on the death of Elizabeth, she organised a *coup d'état* in collaboration with her lover Grigori Orlov and usurped the throne. An "Enlightened" despot influenced by Montesquieu and the penal reformer Beccaria, Catherine ruled Russia with great energy, and, although the obstacles to internal modernization proved almost insuperable, she greatly expanded the boundaries of her empire. Nor did she allow the successive lovers whom she entertained and discarded to deflect the policies on which she set her mind.[1]

Catherine accepted and tried to exploit the entire autocracy of the Tsars. "The Sovereign", she wrote at the height of her power, "is absolute. For there is no other authority but that which centres on his single person, that can act with a vigour proportionate to the extent of such a vast Dominion. The extent of the Dominion requires an absolute Power to be vested in that Person who rules over it."[2]

Though well aware of the evils of serfdom, Catherine had to conciliate the nobility and connive at the further degradation of their serfs. While the condition of the numerous state peasants, who suffered an impersonal oppression, was improved, the serfs on the vast estates of the nobility and gentry became the chattels of their masters; they could no longer even petition the Monarch against their owners, and were liable to be sold, banished, or gambled away. Indeed, their condition was often no better than that of the negro slaves

---

[1] Estimates for those *en titre* vary between twelve (A. Polovtsov, *The Favourites of Catherine the Great*. London, 1940) and twenty-one (G. Soloveytchik, *Potemkin*. London, 1938. New edition, 1949). She called them her "pupils" (*élèves*) and had them examined by her doctor before they entered into their functions, generally after she had dined at 1 p.m., when she would spare two hours for the current favourite; only one perished *"en sa place"*. Those discarded were generally treated with generosity and some, as Orlov and Potemkin, attained great wealth and power.

[2] *The Instruction to the Commissioners for Composing a New Code of Laws*. This discursive and comprehensive document, mainly the work of the Empress's own hand and promulgated in 1785, shows the influence of the French Enlightenment, particularly in its faith in education as the supreme long term remedy. There is a large section lifted entirely from Montesquieu and Beccaria. See *Documents of Catherine the Great*. ed. W. F. Reddaway. London, 1931.

in the American south, and the immense inert mass of serfdom made Catherine's attempt to create a free economy as advocated by Adam Smith quite impracticable. Moreover, though she attempted to encourage responsible self-government in the towns, there were still too few middle-class people capable of carrying it on. Even the nobility, having no feudal roots, and not following any exact primogeniture, were ultimately dependent on the sovereign, and their privileges never brought full independence. Peter I had "introduced the concept of the active, creative, goal directed state",[1] but even by Catherine's day it still lacked effective administrators. It was thus impracticable either to administer the enormous multi-national empire efficiently from the summit, or to decentralize it; and in spite of the Empress's spirited intentions, it proved impossible to achieve responsible government by consent. Only on the frontier was there liberty, and at first too much of it. The Cossack hosts of the steppe had a different tradition from that of the forest-bound Muscovites, and long fought against assimilation, until they were converted into the crack light cavalry of the Imperial army, and also later into the regime's mobile police.

In 1768 Catherine felt secure enough to resume the Russian conquest of the Black Sea steppes, and during her reign she took over the entire Black Sea coast from the Dniester eastward to the Kuban, including the Crimea. The first war against Turkey was prosecuted to a running and flattering commentary by Voltaire to the Empress, "*Je me crois né dans les anciens temps héroïques, quand je vois vos armées au delà du Caucase, etc.*"[2] A Russian fleet was dispatched by way of Minorca to the Aegean; in 1770 it defeated the Turks off Chios in Chesme Bay, and if it failed to capture the Dardanelles—its strategic objective—its appearance in the Atlantic and Mediterranean was the first manifestation of Russian sea power in the West.[3] On land Catherine's godson, Rumyantsev, whose temperament had proved too violent for diplomacy,[4] and who had won great reputation in the Seven Years' War, took Jassy in Moldavia, and in 1770 defeated a vast Turkish army at Kagul; Panin took Azov and Taganrog, and Dolgoruky Euphatoria and Kerch in the Crimea. The young Suvorov, most brilliant of Russian generals, routed another Turkish army in a night attack at Kozludji on the Danube, and in 1774 the war was concluded by the Peace of Küchük Kaynarji. The Russians acquired Azov and access to the Black Sea along territories which extended from the Dnieper to the Bug and which formed the strategic hinterland of Crimea, now declared independent of the Turks. They also obtained a "protectorate" over the Christians in Moldavia on the Danube which would later be extended over all

---

[1]R. Autey and D. Obolensky. *An Introduction to Russian History*. London, 1976. p. 121.
[2]See Reddaway. *Documents. op. cit.* for a vastly entertaining correspondence, in which the *vieillard* or *ermite des Alpes* deploys all his insinuating charm and wit, and the Empress replies in kind.
[3]One frigate, passing Constantinople, entered the Black Sea; the Sultan having sent a skiff to warn the captain of the currents and rocks of the Bosphorus.
[4]He had been recalled from the Russian embassy in Berlin for "refusal to study, nightly brawls, smashing furniture, throwing his clothes out of the window" in protest at having been rejected for the army. These tactics having succeeded, he developed into the "best trained military theorist in the Russian armies". Bernard Pares. *op. cit.* p. 262.

Christians in the Ottoman Empire. Catherine's first Turkish war had obtained all the objectives of Peter the Great and much more.

As already recorded, in 1772 this war had occasioned the first partition of Poland following Turkish exploitation of Polish discontent. But in 1773, when the armies were committed to the Turkish war, Catherine's government had to face the greatest peasant/Cossack revolt in Russian history. Yemelyah Ivanovich Pugachev, its leader, was the son of a small-holding Cossack farmer on the Don; he had fought in the Prussian and Turkish wars and then been invalided out of active service, but not, as he had petitioned, discharged. He had then taken up with the sect of Old Believers, who wished to restore the Orthodox religion as before the innovations of the seventeenth-century Patriarch Nikon. He first raised revolt among the Cossacks of Yaitsk on the Yaik river (now the Ural) which flows from the Urals to the Caspian, and was joined by the conscript workers of the Ural metallurgical industries, as well as by the Bashkirs of the area between the Kazan and the Yaik and by the Churash Tartars of the Middle Volga. His rising was doubly dangerous: a serf revolt and a colonial war.

In the traditional way, he claimed to be the murdered Tsar Peter III Fedorovitch; incited his followers to murder the landowners, which they did; and declared that he would "make the Empress a nun". He was illiterate ("*Il ne sait ni lire ni écrire*," wrote Catherine II) but he was resourceful and tough.[1] He told his original Cossacks, " 'I grant you the rivers from the mountains to the sea, and the land and pastures, and pay and money and lead and powder and food' . . . He would love and reward the Yaik Host as did the Tsars of old and give them fishing rights, land, hay fields, and all the fruits thereof." In 1774 he captured Kazan, crossed the Volga, and threatened to advance on Moscow, proclaiming land for the peasants, restoration of the Old Believers' ritual and vengeance on the "malefactor" gentry. Many landowners and their entire families were massacred, and it took months before the rebels, 30,000 strong with many guns, were hunted down and rounded up by the regular army.

The revolt was ferociously suppressed, and after hair-raising adventures and escapes, Pugachev, pursued by Suvorov, fresh from his exploits against the Turks and moving sixty miles a day, was betrayed by his own followers and handed over to the authorities; then, transported to Moscow in an iron cage, on 10th January 1775, in bitter cold, publicly beheaded and quartered. "The executioners entertained the huge crowd with a truly splendid show . . . the executions began shortly after eleven; it was evening by the time they were finished."[2]

Catherine decreed that the very names of the places concerned should be blotted out and the whole harrowing episode "buried in everlasting oblivion and deep silence". The Yaik river became the Ural, and the victorious war with the Ottoman Empire went on. Voltaire wrote to say that he understood

[1]See Pushkin's *The Captain's Daughter* for a rather romantic account of him. In *The Queen of Spades and Other Stories*. Trans. R. Edmonds. Penguin, Harmondsworth. 1962.
[2]Philip Longworth. *The Cossacks*. q.v. for a detailed account of the revolt. London, 1969. pp. 221–2.

that "Le Marquis de Pugetschef ne savait donc plus écrire que Gengïs Kan ou Tamerlan, ... je crois que votre Majesté, qui sait lire et écrire, va reprendre la bel ouvrage de sa législation."[1] But Catherine, by nature realistic, had shed many illusions: in 1783 she decreed that all the Ukrainian peasants be bound to the soil.

The Peace of Küchük-Kaynarji had not satisfied Russian ambitions. Potemkin, the fifth of Catherine's lovers and the one whose political influence proved most lasting, was appointed Governor of the Ukraine; then, commissioned to build a Black Sea fleet, in 1783 he annexed the Crimea and built an arsenal at Kherson and a harbour at Sevastopol. He overreached himself in developing the Ukraine; but when in 1787—two years before the French Revolution—Catherine II made a triumphant journey through the south, he did not, as legend had it, erect bogus villages for her satisfaction. And when, that year, the Turks declared war, Suvorov in December 1788 stormed their stronghold at Ochakov. In spite of Gustav III's attack, concluded by the Peace of Värälä, the Russians, in conjunction with the Austrians, had also continued the war on the Danube, while the Black Sea fleet threatened Constantinople itself, and by the end of 1791 the Peace of Jassy reaffirmed all the gains of Küchük-Kaynarji, and ceded Ochakov to Russia.

The way was now clear for the second partition of Poland. With the Turks subdued and the Austrians preoccupied with their war with revolutionary France, there was nothing to stop the further division of the country in connivance with Prussia. After the Prussians had occupied Krakow and laid siege to Warsaw in 1794 the ubiquitous Suvorov had stormed Pragá, outside Warsaw; the consequent and hopeless rebellion led by Thaddeus Kosciuszko, a veteran of the American War of Independence, was soon put down. Kosciuszko (1746-1817) came of minor gentry and entered the Corps of Cadets in Warsaw, whence Stanislas Poniatowski had sent him to France to study fortifications and painting (1764-74). Employed as a tutor, he tried to elope with his employer's daughter, and was beaten up by the servants. He then tried his fortune in America, where he fought at Saratoga, designed the original fort at West Point and became a brigadier. Returning to Poland with much prestige, he won high promotion in the Polish army, and in 1793 visited Paris, where he was acclaimed by the Republic, but obtained no substantial help. In 1794 he raised an army in Krakow, but it was defeated first by the Prussians, then by the Russians. After a successful defence of Warsaw, the Polish army was overwhelmed by the Russians under Suvorov, and Kosciuszko wounded and imprisoned in the Petropavlovskaya fortress in St. Petersburg. Released by Paul I, he reached London as a refugee in 1797, then migrated to Paris, where he refused to collaborate with Napoleon. He died at Solothurn in Switzerland in 1817, and was buried in the Cathedral at Krakow, a hero of Polish resistance. By the autumn of 1795 the third partition of Poland was completed. The Prussians obtained Warsaw, the Austrians Krakow, and the Russians all Kurland and Lithuania. The very name of Poland was erased.

Such was the expansion of Russia under Catherine the Great. The

[1]Reddaway. *op. cit.* p. 204.

domination of the Eastern Baltic secured; Poland obliterated; the southern steppes and the Crimea occupied; a large grain trade developed out of Odessa; a Russian fleet on the Black Sea. The Empress had failed to eradicate serfdom, and even enhanced the power of the landowners over the peasantry, so that the internal problems of her multinational empire had been increased, but the status of Russia as a great Eurasian power had been enormously enhanced. The army, as in many underdeveloped countries with a weak middle class, was the most modern, relatively efficient and rational aspect of the state, and would prove its staying power in the Napoleonic wars.

An immense colonial empire was also being acquired in Asia. In the Caucasus by 1783 the Russians had established a protectorate over Georgia, though they had hardly subdued the mountainous country; and by the end of Catherine's reign they were fighting the Persians in Dagestan and Azerbaydzhan. Even more important, the colonization of Siberia, begun under Ivan Groznyi, had proceeded apace. Here serfdom did not take root, and in frontier conditions, as in the North American west, there were no local gentry. Though the Government of deliberate policy forced colonization, the distances were too enormous for the heavy footed bureaucracy to keep up with it, and unwonted liberty and initiative perforce allowed.

Many colonists settled along the Ob and the Yenisei in Central Siberia north of the Altai Mountains and Lake Baikal; other settlers penetated to the far east on the Amur and worked down the coast opposite Japan, where in the nineteenth century the Russians would found Vladivostok. The riparian settlements in Central Siberia, like the original Viking settlements in Kievan Russia, were consolidated by strategically placed forts and trading posts. They early brought in a wealth of furs, and in Catherine's day, silver was being mined by the state by conscript labour; and regular tribute was exacted from the native tribes, who were left to practise their Buddhist or Shamanistic cults. Such was the foundation of the swift and comprehensive development of the immense area, to be achieved with the coming of the railways in the nineteenth century.

IV

The capital of this imperial power which, for all its internal administrative limitations and economic stagnation, was now of world consequence, was architecturally splendid. Its architecture was still derivative from the West, Russian only in size: the French-trained Italian Bartolomeo Rastrelli had been appointed principal architect by the Tsarina Elizabeth in 1741: he was a master of rococo, and the Peterhof and much of the Royal Palace at Tsarkoeselo (now Pushkin) near St. Petersburg (1754–62), completed in the year of Catherine's accession, with its vivid blue expanses set off by white borders and its elegant and elaborate pavilions, including a sham Gothic "ruin", are his work. He also built St. Andrew's Cathedral at Kiev and the convent at Smolney. In the later decades of the century Russian metropolitan architecture followed the austerer neo-Palladian and neo-Grecian styles then fashionable in the West. Giacomo Quarenghi, the Italian neo-classical architect, summoned to Russia in 1780, built much of the Hermitage and many royal and private palaces; while in 1776 the French sculptor, E. M. Falconet, began his famous equestrian statue of Peter the Great.

After his glimpse of Sweden, the traveller Parkinson described the glittering luxury of the entertainments of St. Petersburg. "They manufacture larger mirrors at St. Petersburg than anywhere else in Europe."[1] He stresses the lavish food and drink, melons from the south, caviare from Astrakhan; the lively orchestral music at the dinners and receptions; the ubiquitous dancing; and the variety of uniforms and decorations in the huge crowded rooms. He remarks on the constant vivacity and aplomb of the Empress, and on her pleasure in playing billiards. During the cold months she particularly enjoyed her winter garden, with its exotic plants and tropical birds.

Catherine was also a keen collector of pictures; already her galleries contained such masterpieces as the *Bacchus* by Rubens, Rembrandt's *Return of the Prodigal Son,* and many paintings by Raphael, Poussin, Van Dyck, Mengs, Wouverman and other famous artists.

But all this lavish splendour and entertainment was combined with lapses into confusion and squalor; the English complained that even in the grandest houses, there were no "necessary conveniences and the stench was sometimes intolerable".

Russian writers were still, under Catherine II, entirely Westernized and, if they criticized the regime, they were promptly sent to Siberia. N. V. Lomonsov (1711–65) deliberately imitated French and English models, and wrote verse in the style of Boileau and Pope. He also devised the first Russian grammar and, consigning old Church Slavonic to religious purposes, developed an easier style for general writing, important for later literature.

N. M. Karamzin wrote the first novel in Russian—incongruously in the manner of Richardson's *Pamela*; and in 1790 A. N. Radishchev, influenced by Sterne, wrote his *Journey from Petersburg to Moscow.* Since he implicitly criticized serfdom, the Empress packed him off to Siberia, thus inaugurating a lasting Russian custom for dealing with dissident writers.

V

So, while the United States had already emerged as a sovereign republic and extra-European power, and the French *ancien régime* was soon to collapse, in Central Europe and in Russia despotic regimes still flourished.

Just when the Poles had at last begun to set their political house in better order, three military despots moved in on them, and in the final partition, crushed their ancient Kingdom out. The Habsburgs had taken on a new lease of life by abandoning their imperial claims on Germany and concentrating on

[1]Parkinson. *op. cit.* p. 46

a dynastic Empire, which sprawled from Bohemia far down into Italy; while Imperial Russia, at last dominating the eastern Baltic and having absorbed Lithuania and the Ukraine, had thrust down to the Black Sea, seized the Crimea, and sent her fleets to the Aegean. What was more, standing now at the foothills of the Caucasus, Russia was expanding towards Central Asia and had already, by her enormous, if sparse, colonization of Siberia, reached across the whole breadth of northern Asia to the Pacific and even Alaska; not, like the Central European states a merely European power, but a Eurasian extra-European Empire, comparable in potential only to North America.

XL

The First Industrial Revolution: Napoleon

While the United States had won independence and was poised for expansion over the vast North American Continent and the Russians were laying the foundation of a Eurasian empire, the British had been pioneering a new dimension of industrial power. After the loss of all their North American colonies save Canada, they had regained control of the North Atlantic and the Caribbean, confirmed their paramountcy in India, and begun the settlement of south-eastern Australia. So when the French revolutionary government in 1793 took on Great Britain over admitting British exports to the continent, and the control of the Netherlands and the mouth of the Scheldt, they were challenging a much more formidable European and colonial power than had the government of Louis XV in the Seven Years War; and when Napoleon, having tamed the Revolution and diverted it to unite the continent under an Empire on a scale unheard of since the days of Charlemagne, fought both the extra-European might of Russia and the Oceanic power of Great Britain, he also faced the economic might of the first Industrial Revolution.

This new great industry was of world wide, not merely of European, import; it transformed the situation of mankind, and in its successive stages has since dragged the whole planet into swift economic and social changes to which mentality and institutions have singularly failed to adapt themselves.

This process, often weird and horrific to conservatives, had humble and banal beginnings; but it gradually transformed modern Europe and the United States from the agricultural and commercial civilization hitherto surveyed. It had originated in the dismal north; in smoky towns of northern and Midland England and Scotland; the prosperous agricultural south which then mainly controlled government had not been much aware of it: Jane Austen's representative characters are not interested in it, or in the kind of people who were creating it.

It would be tedious here again to traverse the well-known stages of its early development, from the mechanizing of textile factories by water-power to the development of heavy industry based on a vast output of iron through blast furnaces fuelled by the contiguous British coal-mines, and the application of steam to create mobile power on railroads. The British had been no more

enterprising in technology than the French, but pre-revolutionary France had
been no place for initiative, and the relatively free social order in England and
Scotland, the absence of internal tariffs or a pervasive bureaucracy, and the
background of relatively prosperous agriculture and of massive commercial
wealth, gave islanders long immune from invasion an early and decisive
opportunity.

   The first Industrial Revolution could only, indeed, have taken place with a
productive agriculture and a rising population behind it—at once the source of
the labour and of the mass purchasing power on which the transformation was
sustained. The long accepted picture that the process was a disaster for an
already near famine-stricken rural populace, herded into the alien environment
of industrial towns, is not borne out by the facts: between the mid-eighteenth
century and the first quarter of the twentieth the agricultural areas of England
doubled their population, and the notorious hardships of the Regency and
early Victorian countryside were due more to war-time inflation and post-war
depression than to the Industrial Revolution itself.

   It had been created by cotton operatives and by independent inventors,
sometimes by gentry of academic background, as Cartwright, incongruously a
professor of poetry at Oxford. Few of them profited by their ingenuity: the big
profits went to the entrepreneurs; as Sir Richard Arkwright, the first cotton
magnate to make a huge fortune, or Sir John Roebuck who exploited blast
furnaces and made a fortune out of carronades—the guns used in the
Napoleonic wars from the Carron Ironworks in Scotland. And it was at the
Carron works that in 1769 James Watt had first built a steam engine, patented
as a "fire engine" or "fire pump" since this device had first been used to drain
mines.

   By the late eighteenth century the new and still rudimentary if formidable
inventions were transforming the British economy. The textile industries of
Lancashire imported vast quantities of raw cotton from the East, the West
Indies and the Southern states of North America, where in 1793 Eli Whitney
had invented the cotton gin; and the cheap British textiles found eager buyers
on the continent, already, before Napoleon's blockade, dependent on them.
Then the Revolutionary and Napoleonic wars led to a huge demand for
armaments, naval guns, field artillery and small arms; one invention led to
another. So long as their Navy dominated the oceans, the British could largely
monopolize the markets of the Americas and the East, and the agricultural
British economy began to shift over to becoming a top-heavy workshop of the
world, supporting a growing population dependent upon exports for a livelihood. It would become the centre of a world-wide free trading industrial and
commercial empire which would reach its climax in the 'fifties and 'sixties of
the nineteenth century.

   If the colossal wealth and productivity of the early Industrial Revolution
brought the British victorious out of the long war with France, their political
establishment, unlike the French *ancien régime*, had managed to retain the
support of the majority of the politically conscious nation and could rely upon
a redoubtable insular morale. The English Revolution, which had failed so
dismally in the seventeenth century, never recurred in the eighteenth or

nineteenth: in spite of sporadic radical protest, the society proved too homogeneous and too adaptable, and in war too self-confident.

This solidarity derived from a political history contrasting with that of France and of Central and Eastern Europe. Here, in a common prosperity, Crown and Parliament had come to a compromise, for the settlement of 1688–9 had reflected the realities of power. After the faction-fighting under Anne, Sir Robert Walpole had bought time for the Hanoverian monarchy to settle in, and Parliament had come to represent the predominant interests in the politically conscious nation. The great landowners and merchants, like the country gentry who managed the counties as Justices of the Peace, were collectively far more influential than the monarch, and the notorious ineffi-ciency of an archaic and inadequate administration at least prevented the abuses of centralized bureaucracy which were paralysing France and oppress-ing the Austrian and Russian empires. Moreover, the mass of the people had at least the illusion, in spite of a very restricted and ancient franchise, of participating in electing parliaments, and in the mid-eighteenth century William Pitt the Elder, afterwards Earl of Chatham, had appealed over the heads of the establishment to a new sort of "public" opinion. Censorship, so oppressive on most of the continent, was light and ineffective, and the press had long been influential. Yet the King was still supposed to govern, and George III had to descend into the political arena to make do with the shifting cliques in Parliament out of which governments had to be formed. Hence the mediocre statesmanship and administration that lost the American colonies, but which allowed within the privileged political nation a wide range of liberty, criticism and protest. The sustained and versatile brilliance of the oligarchic Great Britain of Gibbon and Dr. Johnson, of Hume and Burke, is hard to beat; an *ancien régime* which, for all its privilege and archaic laws and a shrill radical opposition, still commanded the support of most of the people. The radical protest came mainly from "Non-conformists" excluded from the advantages of the Anglican Church, and from rationalistic philosophers of whom Jeremy Bentham (1748–1832) proved in the long run the most influential through his "Utilitarian" political philosophy of "improvement". But, in contrast to the situation in France, there was little widespread hatred of the regime or virulent class warfare. The problem of making the government responsible to the classes who in fact held power had been solved without revolution, and while the living standards of at least half the nation were still elementary, there was not the sort of peasant degradation widespread in France or the serfdom still extant in Prussia and prevalent in Russia.

In 1783 George III appointed William Pitt, aged twenty-three, and son of the Earl of Chatham, as Prime Minister of a Tory government which lasted until 1801, thus ending the long preponderance of various Whig coalitions. This regime was popular in the City; and, mainly concerned to promote commerce at home and abroad, it began to abolish the more indefensible sinecures in the administration. By the India Act of 1784 the power of the Governor-General over the East India Company and over its army was increased, and in 1791 a Canada Act divided the colony into English and French speaking provinces; a palliative at first successful, but afterwards disruptive. The British still refused to maintain the large standing armies usual on the continent; but, in spite of muddled administration which provoked mutinies, they kept up a large and powerful fleet.

It was thus a formidable and tenacious adversary, disposing of massive and novel industrial resources, strong insular patriotism and solidarity, and far-flung extra-European sea power, with which in 1793 the French Revolutionary government entered into a great conflict that would last, with two brief intervals, until 1815.

II

In January 1793, following the execution of Louis XVI, the Republican French government, after the British had insisted on their withdrawing their troops from the former Austrian Netherlands which had revolted from Austria in 1789, declared war against Great Britain and Holland. It was a new kind of war, now termed "ideological" and called by Pitt, more elegantly, one of "armed opinions"; but most of the Whig opposition, counted on by the French, supported Pitt's decision. Projects for modernizing the franchise and reforming the administration were set aside, and the British, battened down for the hurricane, settled with only intermittent radical protest into a long regime of Tory governments, determined to prevent social radicalism at home and French domination of the Continent and thereby of the oceans.

Confronted with a coalition of Prussia, Austria, Holland, Great Britain and Spain, the French under the Committee of Public Safety fought back, and in December 1793 thanks to the initiative of a Captain Bonaparte, recaptured Toulon from the British and the royalists. Then, in October 14th (*Vendémiaire*) 1795, the "Thermidorian" Directorate established after the fall of Robespierre was saved by General Bonaparte by a "whiff" of caseshot, fired to kill, when insurgents attacked the Tuileries, so they promoted their political General and saviour to command the army of the Interior. Soon, aged twenty-six, he was promoted Commander-in.Chief of a predatory French "Army of Italy".

Outflanking the Alps by way of the Italian Riviera, Bonaparte defeated the Austrians near Turin and the Piedmontese at Mondovi. The Lombard plain was now open to the French: by the spring of 1795 they had captured Milan; a ragged and potentially dangerous army had been satisfied; immense plunder was dispatched to France, and the French occupied Bologna and even Florence. Next year, Austrian reinforcements sent over the Brenner were routed at Rivoli near Lake Garda, and in 1797 on his own authority, Napoleon Bonaparte, advancing on Vienna through Villach and Klagenfurt, concluded the Peace of Leoben with the Austrians, confirmed that October by the Peace of Campo Formio, which recognized the French "liberation" of much of Italy and of the entire Austrian Netherlands. A Cisalpine Republic was created in North Italy, a Ligurian one round Genoa; and the Pope was compelled to relinquish Bologna: in compensation the Austrians obtained the historic republic of Venice, its ancient liberties at last extinguished.

Back in France, the stage was now set for a conflict of political generals as the civilian power of the Directorate declined, while the cession of the Austrian Netherlands to the French—an old French objective, indirectly achieved by the Italian campaign—meant that Great Britain remained implacable. Appointed to command the Army of England, Napoleon decided not to strike at Ireland, where a French expeditionary force had already failed, but at Egypt; and then, somehow, at the British in India. Hence, in May 1798, evading the British Mediterranean Fleet, Napoleon's well-found expedition, having occupied Malta *en route* and sent the Knights packing, descended on the archaic if picturesque Egyptian Mamlūk regime, helpless before European fire power. At the battle of the Pyramids, the Mamlūk host was destroyed, and the French swiftly occupied Cairo. But the British were on their track: on 1st August 1798, nine days after the battle of the Pyramids, Nelson destroyed the French fleet at Abuquir Bay. Napoleon thus achieved three historic French ambitions, surpassing Charles VIII and François I by the conquest of most of Italy and the Southern Netherlands, and St. Louis by the conquest of Egypt; but found himself cut off from Europe. So, after a spoiling attack on the Turks in Palestine, foiled at Akko, Napoleon, having roundly defeated a Turkish land attack at Abuquir, cut his loss and returned by a swift frigate to France and Paris, the centre of power. The *élan* of the French Revolution had thus been exploited by a Corsican adventurer whose campaigns could compare in range and speed with those of Julius Caesar, and whose ambitions were similar to those of the military magnates of the Roman Empire, but backed by fire power and man power unheard of in Antiquity.

He returned to find the Directorate, who were trying to discredit him, in desperate straits. After the battle of the Nile a Second Coalition had been formed against the Republic. The British had been joined by the Turks, by the Kingdom of Naples and Sicily and, early in 1799, the crazy Tsar Paul (1796–1801) of Russia, who had succeeded Catherine the Great and hankered to become Grand Master of the Knights of Malta, had brought Russia back into the war against the French, while the Austrians had followed suit. An Austro-Russian army under the redoubtable Suvorov had crossed the Alps and seized Milan, and was thought to threaten southern France. It was the deepest Russian penetration so far made of the West;[1] and an Anglo-Russian expedition had landed in Holland; soon evicted, it had greatly alarmed the French. Much worse, French finances were now breaking down; their *assignats*—paper money—had become almost worthless and been repudiated, and government bonds were little better, there was a huge deficit on the budget; indeed the

---

[1]Suvorov was created Prince Italiiski and Generalissimo; but, ordered by Tsar Paul to withdraw his armies across the Alps in spite of the onset of winter, he needed all his famed tactical skill to extricate his army over the Gotthard, in spite of the defeat of his subordinate commander Rimski-Korsakov at Zurich. Tsar Paul refused to receive him, and in 1800 he died in disgrace in St. Petersburg, not long before the Tsar himself was murdered by survivors of Catherine's regime, with at least the tacit connivance of the young Tsarevitch Alexander.

social order was disintegrating and various political generals were waiting in the wings to make a *coup d'état*. It might be Jacobin or Royalist.

Napoleon, with his usual luck and nice timing, was the first to bring one off: on 18th *Brumaire* (9th November) 1799, he and his backers dissolved the impracticable structure of the Directory, and established a *Consulate* (1799–1804). The Corsican adventurer and political general had become First Consul, and in December 1800 the new order was endorsed in a plebiscite by a huge majority. It was an ostensibly civilian dictatorship, but with military backing.

It was still precarious; and in June 1800 the First Consul, in command of a new army of Italy, brought off a bold stroke. After crossing the Alps by the St. Bernard pass from Martigny, he descended "like a thunderbolt" on the unsuspecting Austrians who had just taken Genoa, and routed them after a hard battle at Marengo. Napoleon returned to Paris, his authority confirmed; and after another Austrian defeat on the Danube, in February 1801 he secured all and more of the gains of Campo Formio by the Treaty of Lunéville. Then, conveniently, Tsar Paul, infuriated because the British had occupied Malta, pulled out of the Second Coalition, and organized an armed neutrality of the Baltic powers against the British. And although Nelson had soon made it a disarmed neutrality by destroying most of the Danish fleet at Copenhagen, and, that spring, Paul had perished in a palace revolution, Napoleon in March 1802 obtained the Peace (or truce) of Amiens with Great Britain. He had presented France with a victorious peace; he now turned, as a civilian statesman, to create an internal one.

III

Detested by both Jacobins and Royalists, who both tried to assassinate him, the First Consul now represented the predominant interests in France, anxious to return to financial stability and social order, yet keep their gains won by the Revolution in a more open social order and particularly in confiscated Church and émigré estates. So Napoleon, as First Consul, embarked on his most creative and permanent achievement which survived the brief grandeur of his European Empire. For Napoleon was the last of the Enlightened Despots, as well as the first of the charismatic modern dictators, who started the mass warfare which culminated in the near suicide of Europe. As Markham writes, "Whereas the political institutions of the First Empire proved ephemeral, its legal and administrative institutions proved to be permanent. The Council of State, the Prefects, the Codes, the Legion of Honour, the Bank of France all remind us that the Consulate is one of the most important and formative periods of the development of France."[1] As Napoleon remarked, he embodied the Revolution and he had ended it.

First he censored the vitriolic Parisian press; then he and his subordinates rationalized the administration, the law, the finances of France, and regularized

[1]Wallace-Hadrill and McManners. *op. cit.* p. 188.

the relations of Church and State. He restored the old *Conseil d'État* and nominated its members, and, retaining the revolutionary *départements*, appointed salaried prefects to control them, in effect successors of the *Intendants* of the old regime. Taxation was now regularly collected, education centralized, and a rational and modern code of laws devised. As the *Code Civil* (1804), renamed the *Code Napoléon* three years later, it was to last, and to form the model of other modernized codes in other states, a landmark in the history of Europe and the world. Always alert in "public relations", in 1802 Napoleon had devised the Legion of Honour, which included civilians, and of which the higher grades, unlike those of more time-honoured orders, were pensionable. Though himself an agnostic, Napoleon regarded religion as essential since without it society could not hold together, so he set about making a *concordat* with Pius VII, the newly elected and pro-French Pope, instructing his diplomats to "treat the Pope as if he had 200,000 men".[1] The synthetic state religions of the heady days of the Revolution were abandoned, Napoleon remarking that Rousseau had been a "madman", and the Roman Catholic faith was recognized as that "of the majority of Frenchmen"; while by paying modest salaries to the clergy the Government signalled that the Church lands would never be restored. Napoleon was to nominate all new bishops, but the Pope could consecrate them. One rift in the establishment had been at least diminished, and Napoleon had "restored the altars" on the best conditions he could. Moreover, the French upper classes, having had their lesson, came to think, like the First Consul, that Catholicism was a social necessity, and eighteenth-century-style scepticism became unfashionable.

As First Consul, now appointed by plebiscite for life, Napoleon, in spite of heavy censorship and secret police, had won great popularity in France as the guarantor of the economic interests created by the Revolution. Had he taken Talleyrand's advice and come to an understanding with Great Britain jointly to "develop" the world, and remained within the boundaries his armies had won for France, he might have come to terms as an "Enlightened Despot" with the other dynasties of Europe and established his own. But Napoleon, though he had showed himself a statesman, was a soldier and an adventurer: he could not renounce the excitement of war. Moreover, he had to employ his vast armies and keep them fed and occupied outside France and, though a product of the Enlightenment, he was also a romantic. He intended to revive the shadowy Empire of Charlemagne.

IV

The French armies, too, having tasted plunder and *gloire*, and representing a disrupted social order open to enterprise both in business and conquest, were set on further adventure. They found in Napoleon just the leader for their mood; at once a saviour of a bourgeois society anxious to conserve property,

[1]Wallace-Hadrill and McManners. *op. cit.* p. 199. Napoleon was thus thinking in similar terms to Stalin, who remarked "How many divisions has the Pope?"

and a victorious general whose armies had plundered Italy, secured the coal and iron resources of the Austrian Netherlands, and provided employment for many revolutionary sans-culottes now in danger in France. With his flair for publicity, Napoleon had even managed to gain credit for the Egyptian fiasco.

He now launched into a fantastic attempt to create a European empire on a scale unknown since the days of Charlemagne. And he very nearly succeeded; for in the crisis of 1793, by the law of 23rd August of that year, the French had imposed universal military service until the invading counter-revolutionary armies had been expelled from France, and under this law a steady stream of conscripts would be drafted into Napoleon's armies. Already by 1794 there had been a million men under arms, and Carnot had tried to organize the entire national economy for war, in the armaments industries, textiles and agriculture. With such huge forces at his disposal, Napoleon applied late-eighteenth-century ideas already current in the old army, as expressed in Guibert's *Essai Général de Tactique* (1772), and exploited the new mobile field artillery, developed by 1777 by Gribeauval, along lines adumbrated by du Teil's *"Usage de l'artillerie nouvelle dans la guerre de campagne"*: indeed, France had produced "seven thousand cannon in 1793", so that "Napoleon was the first commander who was in a position to use artillery fire lavishly."[1] He also adapted his armies to mass warfare on an unheard of scale: creating independent *divisions* moving on a parallel lines across country or manoeuvring freely to envelop the enemy before the main attack, and using his superior numbers to attack in column. With such vast numbers, it was impossible to maintain the old elaborate apparatus of supply; and the French armies lived off the country or off depots captured in their rapid advance. Equally essential for this warfare of rapid attack and manoeuvre, the morale of the troops was sustained by the fierce patriotism of a "nation in arms" and by the personal magnetism of Napoleon, strongest among the Imperial Guard, which he expanded into a crack force of all arms, held in reserve for the decisive blow. "These units would not have fought as well as they did. . ." or "for so long as they did, if they had not been organized in the first instance by a fanatically totalitarian régime and then led by the greatest military genius the world had seen since Alexander the Great."[2]

Thus the "Enlightened" intellectuals who had encouraged the Revolution to promote the brotherhood of man, in fact contributed to more ferocious warfare, since the peoples were corralled into the existing structure of eighteenth-century dynastic sovereign states, whose warlike policies now became more dynamic because of their enthusiasm. In the immediate event, also, the notion that the French armies of occupation were long inspired by ideals of the brotherhood of man is a sentimental illusion. After they had realized that the "liberated" peoples were not rushing to arms to collaborate with their conquerors, they abandoned any cosmopolitan ideas and soon

[1] F. M. H. Markham. *Napoleon.* London, 1963. p. 21. Hobsbawm, idealizing the Revolution, writes that "French military superiority was due to a simple hierarchy of military courage ... never backed by an armaments industry faintly adequate to its nominal needs." *op. cit.* p. 73. Markham, like Cobb, supplies the facts.
[2] Howard. *op. cit.* p. 80.

"former commanders of peoples' armies (were) once more lording it over the peasantry. This time, however, it was not a matter of Parisians or Bourbonnais making themselves felt at the expense of Briards, Lyonnais, Foréziens or Dauphinois, but of Frenchmen making life hell for Flemings, Piedmontese, Catalans and Rhinelanders. They became closed in even more on themselves, ignorant of the language, complaining of the food, contemptuous of the dirt and of the 'superstition' of their administrés, acquiring a colonialist mentality."[1] They also dug themselves into subordinate administration of the conquered territories and remained there, often sans-culottes embusqués, until the fall of Napoleon. The French cleared the ground of ancient institutions, but the nationalism they provoked was far more one of reaction than imitation. For those at the receiving end, the empire of the new Charlemagne was an exploitation.

V

In 1803 Napoleon plunged Europe and much of the world into a decade of turmoil and transformation. The Peace of Amiens had proved only a truce: the French, having bought back Louisiana from Spain, had reverted to their former colonial ambitions in North America and the Caribbean, and were excluding British goods from large areas of Europe and from their colonial possessions. Moreover, they annexed Piedmont and Elba and were infiltrating Switzerland: while they continued to occupy the Austrian Netherlands and Holland. So the British held on to Malta, in May 1803 renewed the war, and contrived a Third Coalition. They also connived at plots to assassinate the First Consul, who in revenge kidnapped the nearest available Bourbon—the harmless Duc D'Enghien—and had him shot. Having thus, by Corsican methods, made any reconciliation with the Bourbons for his own regime and its supporters impossible, in May 1804 Napoleon founded his own dynasty by proclaiming himself, after a plebiscite, "Emperor of the French". What was more, he meant to be Emperor of Europe, bringing "Enlightened Despotism", modern administration by French officials and the paraphernalia of Revolution to the rest of the continent, the preliminary to a world empire overseas.

Hence a decade of far-flung and sensational campaigns conducted by armies far larger than those of early modern times, often over territories of Central and Eastern Europe unknown to the warring magnates of the Roman Empire and disregarded by the most ambitious Medieval Western Kings. Napoleon determined first to deal with the British, the wealthiest and most tenacious of his enemies. An ambitious and impracticable strategy was devised: the entire French Atlantic fleet from Brest, Rochefort and Ferrol was to make for the West Indies, there to concentrate with the French Mediterranean fleet from Toulon. The British, reacting to this threat, would denude the defences of the

[1]Cobb. op. cit. p. 162.

Channel, and Villeneuve, returning to Europe, would secure the Straits for the few hours Napoleon needed to invade England with an enormous army assembled at Boulogne. But the French had misread their opponents' psychology and underestimated their professional skill. Only Nelson with the Mediterranean Fleet pursued the French across the Atlantic; the English Channel fleet refused the bait and continued to patrol the western approaches, and when Villeneuve failed even to return to a French base and took refuge at Cadiz, the entire French strategy had collapsed. When in October 1805 he emerged with a Franco-Spanish fleet, Nelson at Trafalgar turned what had been a vast British strategic defensive success into a conclusive victory which gave the British command of the oceans for more than a century.

Turning his back on the hazardous project of invasion, Napoleon had already directed his armies into Central Europe, determined to defeat the Third Coalition in detail. First he defeated the Austrians at Ulm and occupied Vienna; then, in December 1805, turning on the Russians and Austrians, he routed them at Austerlitz in Moravia, east of Brno—the Russians *"non seulement battues mais détruites"*. They were thrown out of Central Europe and the Austrians forced to the Peace of Pressburg, abandoning even Tyrol and Vorarlberg, historic Habsburg lands, as well as Venetia, Dalmatia and all Italy. Terrified of Napoleon's armies, the Prussians, in return for Hanover, made the Peace of Schönbrunn, giving up Neuchâtel and Anspach, and acquiescing in a "Confederation of the Rhine" which replaced the historic Holy Roman Empire which Napoleon abolished. When, too late, in 1806, in continuing alliance with the British, King Frederick William III declared war, he was totally defeated that autumn by Napoleon at Jena near Weimar. The French occupied Berlin; Napoleon made his Headquarters at Sans Souci, the palace of Frederick the Great; Prussia was deprived of half its territory. In November 1806 Napoleon issued the "Berlin Decrees" boycotting British goods.

The French now controlled the Low Countries, the southern shores of the Baltic, most of Central Europe, Italy and Dalmatia; the heart of the continent, but not its peripheries—Russia and the Iberian Peninsula. And the British, in control of the oceans, monopolizing oceanic trade and subsidizing their allies, remained intransigent. Moreover, with Austria and Prussia crippled, the Russians had invaded Prussian Poland and East Prussia, and early in 1807 Napoleon had to fight a terrible drawn battle against them at Eylau near Königsberg; but that summer, at Friedland on the Alle, he utterly defeated them, concluding the campaign in the marches of North-Eastern Europe and forcing the Emperor Alexander I to sue for an armistice. There was now not much left of the Third Coalition on the continent. Napoleon now tried to ruin the British by economic warfare; and in so doing he overreached himself in the Iberian Peninsula and in Russia.

In June 1807, on a raft in mid-stream on the Nieman near Tilsit, north-east of Königsberg, a curious summit meeting was arranged: for an hour and three quarters Napoleon and Tsar Alexander I conferred alone, while "along opposite banks men who had fought at Friedland ... watched the strange meeting place of their sovereigns rising and falling on the gleaming waters."[1] The Tsar emerged "dazed and subdued" but somehow "exalted"; and Napoleon thought him "quite a handsome and good young Emperor".

For the Tsar had conceded the main point; to intensify the *blocus continental*; and next year the Russians annexed -Finland, while resuming their war against the Turks. The briefly liberated and perennially dissatisfied Poles were assigned a "Grand Duchy" of Warsaw, while Jerome Bonaparte became King of Westphalia, to look after Bremen, Hamburg and Rostock and overawe the Danes. The British replied by capturing the Danish fleet and bombarding Copenhagen.

At the other end of Europe the Portuguese, with ancient economic ties with England, had long been more than casual in enforcing the blockade; soon after Tilsit, Napoleon was planning to coerce them, and in so doing, get a grip on Spain and perhaps the Spanish Colonial Empire. Napoleon thus risked giving the British an opening, and encouraged by the difficulties of the French in Spain, in March 1809 the Austrians declared war. Vienna had to be occupied all over again, and once more from Schönbrunn Napoleon issued his Decrees. As successor of Charlemagne he incorporated the Papal States into his empire and ordered the Pope, who had excommunicated him, to be deported from Rome. Then at Wagram, he routed an Austrian army attempting to relieve Vienna. By a second Peace of Schönbrunn the Austrians lost even Salzburg and part of Galicia. Then, in 1810, Napoleon determined to legitimize his Empire, and after he had divorced Josephine, the Habsburgs were forced to allow the young Archduchess Marie Louise to become Empress of the French. In the following year she bore Napoleon a son, the King of Rome, and the Corsican dynasty seemed more secure, firmly at the summit of a European empire sustained by a cosmopolitan nobility of service and exploiting a continent for *la Grande Nation*.

But beneath this splendid quasi-eighteenth-century façade, the foundations were crumbling. Launched by a nation in arms, the Empire had provoked the conquered peoples into a novel national resistance, which reinforced the determination of the old dynasts for revenge. And the British were still in the war. The *blocus continental* had to be intensified; but by the end of 1810 Alexander I, under pressure from his subjects, decreed that Russian ports could trade freely with neutrals carrying British and Colonial goods. At once Riga was flooded with imports and the continental system defied. It was a defiance Napoleon could not permit. So, in 1811, in spite of bad news from Spain, he mobilized over half a million men, the greatest European army so far concentrated, not to invade Russia, but to bring the Russians to a battle even more decisive than Friedland, preferably near Vilna in Lithuania.

In the summer of 1812 the Russians were saved not by deliberately luring the invaders deep into their country, but by their own inefficiency. Unable to

[1]Alan Palmer. *Alexander I. Tsar of War and Peace*. London, 1974. pp. 135-6. The Tsar afterwards wrote to his sister, the Grand Duchess Catherine, "Just imagine my spending days with Bonaparte, talking for hours quite alone with him." To which she replied, "While I live I shall not get used to the idea of your spending your days with Bonaparte ... It seems like a bad joke and impossible." p. 139.

mobilize their manpower and at first without even unified command, they were forced to retreat to Borodino, only seventy miles from Moscow, where they inflicted appalling casualties on the *Grande Armée* but failed to defend the capital. The invaders found an apparently deserted city; soon, by intent, set on fire. But Napoleon lingered there too long, in the unrealistic hope that the Tsar at St. Petersburg would negotiate, while Kutuzov's Russians lulled the French by a show of fraternization. By mid-October, with more news of defeat in Spain and of unrest in Paris, Napoleon ordered a retreat.

Begun in dust and heat, the monstrous invasion ended in awful cold. Forced to return along the route through Smolensk already devastated by the invasion, harried by Cossacks and by the infuriated peasantry, the cosmopolitan and dilapidated horde perished in thousands. By the end of November the really perishing cold had struck; and at the Berezina, a tributary of the Dnieper, with the Russians already at Minsk beyond the western bank, Napoleon extricated only a remnant of his original expedition.

After this feat, he abandoned them, and with only two companions made for Dresden, then for Paris, where he arrived by 18th December. He had no alternative; only by holding France and the natural frontiers could he negotiate from any credible strength. But first he tried to defend his Empire. By the Spring of 1813 Napoleon had concentrated another great army at Mainz, and at Lützen and at Bautzen near Dresden, again routed the Russians; in defence, said the Emperor, of "European Civilization". But Wellington in northern Spain defeated the French at Vittoria, and extruded Napoleon's brother, the "intruding" King Joseph, while the Austrians were demanding the return of Northern Italy and Illyria and the dissolution of the Confederation of the Rhine, as well as most of Poland. By August the former French Marshal Bernadotte, now with Napoleon's backing the accepted heir to Sweden, had come out against him; and by the autumn of 1813 at Leipzig, with 160,000 against 300,000 men, Napoleon was overwhelmed by Austrian and Prussian armies in a battle lasting three days. The ephemeral Napoleonic Empire had been destroyed.

The Confederation of the Rhine collapsed; Holland revolted; Murat, whom Napoleon had made King of Naples, changed sides. By 1814 Napoleon's best chance was to defend the "natural frontiers" of France, in the hope that the Austrians and Prussians, in fear of Russia and dislike of the British, would accept his dynasty in a general settlement of Europe. But the British were already in south-western France, the Prussians and Russians on the Marne and the Austrians on the Seine. In a brilliant defensive campaign Napoleon held them off; but as the allies converged on Paris, he was forced by his marshals to abdicate. On 24th April, 1814, Louis XVIII, brother of Louis XVI, returned. On the inept suggestion of the Tsar Alexander, Napoleon was assigned the principality of Elba, eighteen miles long and twelve miles wide, and far too near the mainland of Europe.

VI

The Allies assembled in Vienna to settle a war-torn Continent and its dependencies, and their momentous decisions determined the international politics of the first half of the nineteenth century. The brief and sensational interruption termed the Hundred Days, when Napoleon returned to power in France and nearly won the battle of Waterloo, made colourful but relatively unimportant history. After 1815, the great powers, including France, managed to stabilize Europe.

But after the French Revolution and the Napoleonic Empire, Western and much of Central Europe had profoundly changed: the collapse of the *ancien régime* had led to atrocious terror and counter-terror in France, but the exploitation of the Empire had brought a feverish prosperity to the Imperial elites and their dependants, and created a more dynamic and varied society. The relatively austere official art and architecture of the Empire succeeded the parvenu excesses of the Jacobin regime, and, disregarding the perennial plight of the poor, the French celebrated the rehabilitation of a bourgeois social order by the unprecedented feats of gastronomy of the age of Carême[1] and Brillat Savarin. The more formal aspects of eighteenth-century dress and comportment gave way to the more casual fashions of the incipient "romantic" age, and powdered wigs to the tousled hair styles of Napoleon's marshals and their imitators. It now seems extraordinary that the sceptical, ruthless and realistic Napoleon greatly admired the bogus romances of "Ossian", but he had led his armies and their following into adventures as fantastic and far-flung as any celebrated in romance. He had compassed the deaths of millions, but he had glamorized war, particularly to civilians, and he had deliberately created a Napoleonic "legend" at St. Helena.

No great contemporary French epic celebrated his victories: a heavy censorship weighed on France, but the Breton aristocrat Chateaubriand (1768–1848), who took refuge in America and England, then became a diplomat under the Empire and briefly Foreign Minister after the Restoration, is memorable for his *Mémoires d'Outretombe*; and his romantic sense of history and place influenced nineteenth-century French historians. Madame de Stäel, an irrepressible cosmopolitan figure, daughter of Necker the financier, turned to Germany for inspiration, and her romantic *De L'Allemagne* (1810) made the country appear something more than a place to be fought over.

Indeed, it heralded a new phase in European intellectual history. For the first time, the Germans began to be admired in the West, and the greatest of all German writers, Johann Wolfgang von Goethe (1749–1852), now won a deserved reputation. This many-sided genius, unlike most contemporary German romantics, always remained cosmopolitan; he was grounded in Classical scholarship, yet, influenced by Herder's romantic feeling for the German past, and by Shakespeare, whom the French intellectuals considered "formless", he early showed astonishing range. Nor was he paralysed by the Germanic introspection which inspired him to write *The Sufferings of Werther* (1774).

[1] An example of the "Career open to Talent", he began as an illiterate cook-boy and became the most celebrated chef in Europe, employed by Talleyrand, Alexander I and the Prince Regent, but unhappy outside France. Probably the greatest cook of all time (1783–1833).

He soon won celebrity. Coming of prosperous burgher stock at Frankfurt-am-Main he found wider horizons at the universities of Leipzig and Strasbourg. In 1775 he became principal administrator to Duke Karl August of Saxe-Weimar, a position which did not interfere with his creative genius. His Italian journey of 1786 produced a classic of travel; present at the "cannonade of Valmy", he wrote a vivid *Campaign in France*. He wrote *Roman Elegies, Egmont* and *Iphigenia in Tauris*; in 1795 *Wilhelm Meister's Lehrijahre* (Apprenticeship), and in 1808 appeared the first part of *Faust*, its sequel published in 1827. Goethe's introspective autobiography *Dichtung und Wahrheit* (Poetry and Truth) reveals how he combined the "Enlightenment" with intuition. He was the last cosmopolitan Renaissance universal man, standing out above the swirl of revolution and battle, one of the most Olympian minds of European civilization.

The other German of genius who remained cosmopolitan was Immanuel Kant, who tried to create a quasi-Platonic world of permanent morality above the flux of phenomena by the exercise of will, and who reacted to the Revolution and Napoleonic Wars by writing a treatise on *Zum ewigen Frieden*—On Perpetual Peace.

Most of the other Germans reacted into mild or strident nationalism. Herder (1744–1803), a Prussian taught and befriended by Kant, wrote on *The Philosophy of the History of Mankind*. He understood, like Chateaubriand, the importance of the geographical setting of the past and created the idea of a *Volk-nation*; Fichte became a prophet of German nationalism. Other antiquarian romantics wrote up German history in prose and lyric verse; Schiller, a friend of Goethe's, dramatized the Thirty Years War. The poet Arnim and the dramatist Kleist wrote of *consecrated daggers* and *cohort stormers*, rousing young Germans against the French occupation. Germany became a land of a new kind of lay-prophet, who took over the leadership of a failing Church as the hungry sheep looked up to new "authorities" to be fed.[1] This phenomenon distinguished the nineteenth century from any other since Antiquity, often with disastrous results.

In England the two most characteristic streams of thought, practical and unimaginative and romantic and historicist, were expressed respectively in Bentham and Burke. The former, who founded the pragmatic "Utilitarian" movement, subjected all institutions to a "felific calculus" which indicated whether or not they promoted "the greatest happiness of the greatest number". He attained world wide influence and inspired systematic "improvement"; a new idea peculiar to Europe. Burke, an eloquent Irishman, had much in common with the German romantics, having a brilliant sense of society composed of successive generations, but much more sense than they had of the limits and difficulties of political action. He is one of the great political theorists, emphasising the trusteeship of government and the need for government by consent, views which he pressed in vain upon the administrators who lost the North American colonies.

[1]See my *Politics and Opinion in the Nineteenth Century*. London, 1954. Paperback, 1963. Chapter I.

Impossible here to do justice to the immense cultural riches of this tumultuous and creative time. Ludwig van Beethoven (1770–1827) combined an eighteenth-century form with a tumult of romantic melody which often shocked his contemporaries but which posterity has passionately acclaimed. His violent and superb genius embodies the force and novelty of his time and adapts the tradition of Haydn and Mozart to a new and dynamic world.

And of all the painters Goya (1746–1828), who came of peasant stock in Aragon, seems best to depict the stress and struggle of his age. He developed from painting elegant diversions, as *La Cometa* (the kite), through devastating portraits of the half-imbecile Spanish Bourbon royalties evicted by Napoleon, in which their scintillating costume shows up the vacuity of their expressions, to the terrible *Disasters of War*, including the appalling *Los fusilamentos de la Moncloa*, and culminating in the *Witches Sabbath*, with the Devil, silhouetted and dominant, confronting a submissive crowd. Here is one of the greatest artists of Europe, and one who reminds posterity of the price of the Revolutionary and Napoleonic Wars, so ominous for the future.

XLI

The Congress of Vienna and its Consequences

The statesmen who assembled at Vienna in 1814 to rehabilitate Europe have been much maligned; but they were more successful than the peace-makers of Versailles and Potsdam after the First and Second World Wars. The revolutionary and Napoleonic upheavals had shaken the cosmopolitan fabric of dynastic sovereign states and by example and repulsion provoked a new "nationalism"; but the dynasts and their ministers held to the principles of dynastic legitimacy as the only way they knew of restoring peace in Europe; and, in the absence of any supreme European authority, they tried to re-establish a "balance of power" which would in the general interest achieve what they termed "tranquillity". They intended to establish a collective authority of the great powers, or pragmatic "Concert of Europe"—"an agreement", as Pitt put it, "to do something, not an orchestra".[1]

In contrast to the politicians who made the Peace of Versailles, they did not therefore severely "punish" the vanquished French; but, recognizing the inevitable status of France as a great power, brought it back after the Bourbon Restoration into the European power balance, so that Great Britain and Austria even joined diplomatically with France to resist the aggrandizement of Russia and Prussia in Eastern Europe. The atrocities of the Revolution at home and the exploitation of the Napoleonic empire abroad had naturally given Jacobin principles a bad name, and after the spectacle of the French "people in arms" the participants in the Congress of Vienna can hardly be blamed for regarding the idea of national popular sovereignty with distaste. Talleyrand and Metternich were indeed both good Europeans, in that they sought to preserve the continent from further disruption, and Castlereagh did not deserve the abuse heaped on him by Byron, and, with less excuse, by "liberal" historians. In fact the so-called "reactionaries" of Vienna contrived a settlement that kept Europe free of major wars from 1815 to 1854, when the British and French fought the Russians in the Crimea to shore up the crumbling Turkish empire and keep the Russians out of the Levant; and it did not entirely collapse until the Germans destroyed the balance of power in the

[1] quoted by E. L. Woodward in *Prelude to Modern Europe*. London, 1972. p. 55.

Franco-Prussian War of 1870-1. But the concept of a "balance of power", an idea derived from eighteenth-century mechanistic science,[1] was inadequate for an age in which, with the removal of Napoleon, the only man who had tamed the Revolution, the revolutionary tides had resumed their deflected course, and in which the Industrial Revolution was beginning to transform not only Great Britain but the continent. The principle of "legitimism" was not enough to control those areas of Europe flooded with "liberal" and "radical" ideas in which more of the people, hitherto peasants and craftsmen, were becoming rootless urban factory "hands" at the mercy of entrepreneurs pioneering new methods of production. The original "bourgeois" revolution had favoured property and *laissez faire*; but, as the clearer sighted conservatives understood, the obvious next step, following the abolition of political and social privilege, would be an attack on property. And in fact Saint-Simon, who advocated the rule of bankers and technocrats, and Robert Owen, who advocated co-operatives, would be succeeded by Proudhon, who claimed that "property is theft", and by Marx and Engels, the prophets of Communism.

The Revolution, originally political, was thus now seeping into the economic order, itself in process of dynamic change. With the social and economic foundations shifting beneath it, it is remarkable how long the restored "legitimate" order managed to last.

II

The French economy, crippled in the early years of the Revolution, had again come near famine in 1812; but it had managed to survive the taxation and conscription of the Napoleonic wars and the frustration of the *blocus continental*, since it had remained, with its primitive methods of farming, mainly agricultural in a country naturally rich. The French had exploited the Napoleonic empire, but they were not dependent on it; and for all the Imperial cult of martial glory, the majority of their small-holding peasants and careful *bourgeoisie* preferred peace to military adventures. The restored Bourbons might be ill-received by the veterans of the Imperial Guard, who, infuriated by the abolition of the tricolour, ground their teeth and glared at Louis XVIII when they had to present arms, but a more representative reaction to the disappearance of Napoleon had been, as he had himself prophesied, a heartfelt *"Ouf"*.

Louis XVIII (1814-24), Comte de Provence and brother of Louis XVI, was not without shrewdness and wit; a constitutional monarchy on the English model was set up, with a *Conseil des Ministres* appointed by the King, an hereditary Chamber of Peers and a Chamber of Deputies for the Departments, elected from a very limited franchise. Nationalized estates were not resumed by the *émigrés*, and the officials of the empire were assimilated into the new

[1]See E. L. Woodward. *Three Studies in European Conservatism* Metternich: Guizot; the Catholic Church in the Nineteenth Century. London (second edition), 1963. pp. 38. ff, far the best study of Metternich's "principles" in theory and action.

establishment. The administrative and centralizing changes made by the Revolution, along with internal free trade and theoretical equality before a uniform law, remained intact.

But this quasi-constitutional monarchy failed to overcome the hatreds created by the Jacobin terror and the "white" reaction; indeed those who had gone over to Napoleon during the Hundred Days were particularly detested by the Royalists. Ancient social prejudices survived, particularly in the provinces; the aristocracy, converted to the social uses of religion, reverted to Catholic piety, and the religious Orders returned. The now prevalent *bourgeoisie*, on the other hand, remained anti-clerical and sent their sons to lay schools; they were not yet mobile in their recreations, and mainly cultivated the pleasures of gastronomy and good wine. This stabilizing influence percolated down to the more prosperous artisans and *vignerons*; once out of penury, the *gens du peuple*, unlike the British masses, knew good food when they got it.

Charles X (1824–30), Comte d'Artois, like James II of England, was an elderly rake and would-be autocrat of strong religious principles and no political sense. He assigned a huge sum for compensation for the *émigrés'* confiscated lands, disbanded the Parisian national guard, and appointed Prince Jules de Polignac, who came of an illustrious and ancient family and who had been created a Roman Prince by the Pope, as his principal minister.

By July 1830 this ultra-royalist and ultramontane Catholic had tampered with the electroral law and tried to censor the press. Paris broke into revolt; Charles X abdicated and proceeded with a large military escort to Cherbourg, whence he fled to Britain, where he was accommodated in Holyrood House in Edinburgh, then betook himself to Prague.

So began the '*bourgeois*' constitutional monarchy of Louis Philippe, Duc d'Orléans (1830–48), son of Philippe Égalité who had accepted the revolution and perished in it.[1] After fierce fighting for three days he was inaugurated as King of the French; and he kept France out of military adventures during a period of apparent, though resented, middle-class prosperity. His position as Saviour of Society was early strengthened by risings of the populace of Paris and Lyons, and although the "legitimists" never accepted the "Orléanist" branch of the Bourbons, and the Austrian and Russian royalists looked down on them, he chose able ministers in Thiers and Guizot.

But the economic recessions of the 'forties undermined his regime, which came under fire from new "socialist" attacks on property much more radical than the mainly legalistic and laissez-faire ideas of 1789. The King refused to adapt to even a moderate extension of the restricted franchise: he was further alarmed by the threatened defection of the National Guard, still strangely out

[1]The new King had been a member of the Jacobin Club and fought with distinction at Valmy; but in 1793 had gone over to the Austrians and taken refuge in Switzerland. In 1797 he went to the United States for two years, then to England. After the Restoration he regained his immense family estates and greatly profited by the indemnity under Charles X. His sense of public relations was clumsy, and historians never tire of citing his habit of promenading with a rolled-up umbrella—a precaution somehow considered ridiculous and which still did Neville Chamberlain's reputation no good. Today he would be considered a model of royal walkabout "mateyness".

of control in so sophisticated a country, and by a spate of republican speeches delivered at the political banquets then so popular in Paris. He lost his nerve and made off to Honfleur, whence, like Charles X, he sailed for the tolerant or indifferent shores of England.

So in February 1848 France inaugurated the brief Second Republic, with a National Assembly which proved conservative. The country was belatedly suffering the impact of the Industrial Revolution, and a misguided Corsican journalist, Louis Blanc, persuaded the provisional government to set up *ateliers sociaux* in Paris and a few major cities, to be supplemented by public libraries, mainly of revolutionary literature, in which state-aided unemployed craftsmen would be educated. These measures proving irrelevant, since their products were little in demand, the craftsmen were set to work digging a railway embankment and finally disbanded.

The Parisian radicals and socialists now broke into armed insurrection, which the government ordered the army to suppress, and after severe casualties on both sides, the revolt was put down. The *bourgeoisie* had won; but at the cost of popular support, and the way was open for a political adventurer, long waiting in the wings. Louis Napoleon, nephew of the great Emperor, stepped forward as another Saviour of Society, and stood for the new office of President of the Second Republic, elected by universal suffrage. To the astonishment and disgust of the established politicians, he was elected with a huge majority, the rural masses in France having heard of the name Bonaparte. He was confronted with a single Chamber or National Assembly, also elected by universal suffrage, and heavily conservative, which soon set about restricting the franchise and thwarting his relatively liberal policies. But in December 1851, a *coup d'état* brought Louis Napoleon to power. As Markham writes, "In the vacuum of power caused by the flight of Louis Philippe the social revolution, strong in the Paris clubs and working class, made its first bid for power in Europe; in doing so it killed the Second Republic and opened the way for the Second Empire."[1]

III

While the French failed to work the virus of the original revolution and its Terror and Counter-Terror out of their politics, the British were thrusting ahead as the pioneers of the first Industrial Revolution and painfully adapting their eighteenth-century style of government to contemporary facts. The Battle of the Nile had regained their control of the Mediterranean and in 1801 they had captured the Cape of Good Hope and Ceylon from the Dutch, forced by Bonaparte into the war. Strategically reinforced, the British could now confirm and consolidate their *raj* in India and with it control of the East. But the perennial problem of Ireland had been worsened by token French landings, and the Catholic Irish had risen in rebellion: Pitt's remedy in 1801 had been to

[1] *The French Revolution.* In the *Concise Encyclopaedia of World History.* (ed. J. Bowle). London, 1958. p. 325.

unite Ireland with Great Britain under an Imperial Parliament at Westminster. But since George III, true to his coronation oath, refused to give the Catholic Irish the vote, only Protestant Irish were elected, a situation not remedied until 1829; so the grievances of the Catholic majority in Ireland were unassuaged. The horror inspired by the crimes of the Jacobins and by the "White Terror", along with the alarm provoked by the belligerence of the Republic and of the First Consul, had taken some of the wind out of the sails of the English radicals, and had rallied most of the country behind Pitt's government, while the collapse of the Truce of Amiens had led to the return of Pitt to office after the brief ministry of the appeasing Addington. After Pitt's death, worn out at forty-six, Tory cabinets continued to conduct the war at sea and as it developed in the Iberian Peninsula, and when in 1810 George III finally went insane, they continued to govern under the Prince Regent (1811–20) and then after he had become George IV (1820–30).

But the victorious outcome of the long war in 1815 was followed by economic recession and bitter social discontent. The liberal foreign policies of Canning, a new kind of Tory with a wider popular appeal, were not paralleled after his death in 1827 by an extension of the franchise at home; radical agitation for the "Reform" of the eighteenth-century franchise and administration became dangerously bottled up. In 1820 conspirators meeting in Cato Street and plotting to murder the entire cabinet had been headed off only just in time. But there was to be no English Revolution in the nineteenth century. By 1824 Trade Unions, forbidden in France, were legalized; the political agitation, rick burnings and riots were provoked mainly by the protective tariffs that kept up the price of bread, by the stringent game laws against poaching, by the indiscriminate savagery of the old penal laws and by inadequate and corrupt Poor Relief. The old Nonconformist resentment at the "established" Church of England also combined with Benthamite ideas of "improvement" to whip up radical political anger.

The accession of Louis Philippe in the "bourgeois" revolution of 1830 may have influenced British opinion, and, fanned by a free press of limited circulation, the demand for "Reform" became so overwhelming that in 1832, after an election that even under the old franchise had given the Whigs a big majority, a Reform Bill was brought in. When the Lords rejected it, the ministry resigned, and William IV (1830–7) asked the Duke of Wellington to form a government; it too resigned after a week; so the King summoned the Whig leader, Lord Grey, and agreed to create enough peers to swamp the opposition in the Lords. Wellington, though strongly against the Bill as leading to an attack on property (which in the long run it did), withdrew his party's opposition to it in the Lords, and it became law. Thus, after a potentially revolutionary crisis had been allowed to develop, King, Lords and Commons combined in a pragmatic English way to adapt the constitution to majority public opinion. It can be imagined what a political "General" of Wellington's prestige could, and probably would, have done in France. Unbeaten in battle, the Iron Duke understood when in politics to give ground.

The famous Reform Bill began an age of bourgeois supremacy, but not for some time. It had in fact conceded only a very limited extension of the franchise, and the kind of people elected were generally much the same as before. The Whigs were socially grander than the Tories, and Grey himself, the son of the first Earl Grey, brought up at Fallodon and educated at Eton and King's College, Cambridge, was no "enthusiast"; indeed, by the time he became Prime Minister he had "outlived the power of feeling or inspiring enthusiasm; but it was perhaps fortunate that at a moment of such popular excitement the ministry was led by so cold a man."[1] And when Lord Melbourne succeeded him, that amiable, casual and disdainful character was not the man for radical measures either. A massive change had in fact occurred; but the English, hypocritical as usual, hushed it up. The social order was still dominated by the great landed aristocracy, most of them established since Tudor and Stuart times, and by the new plutocrats of the Industrial Revolution now being assimilated into the landowning interest.

With the first Industrial Revolution in full tide, government belatedly tackled the immense problems created by the spread of great industrial towns. Lighting, police, sanitation, conditions in factories, were all dealt with; local government rationalized, the Poor Law reformed, if dehumanized. During the early 'thirties the economy was relatively prosperous and popular discontent diminished;[2] but when in 1837, the year of the accession of Queen Victoria, a recession set in, a militant "Chartist" movement demanded universal male suffrage, secret ballots and payment for M.P.s—demands all now long conceded. But it was not and could not be geared to the nascent trade unions who were set on more limited and parochial objectives; and when in 1841 a Tory government under Sir Robert Peel came to power, Peel began to take over where the reformers of 1832-4 had left off. Peel himself (1788-1850) was the grandson of a self-made calico printer from Blackburn, Lancashire, and his mother's family were cotton manufacturers in Bury in that county. He did well at Harrow, and at Christ Church, Oxford, got a double first in Classics and Mathematics, then at twenty-one entered the House of Commons for the rotten borough of Tipperary, purchased by his father, the first baronet. By 1812 he had graduated to being MP for Chippenham, Wiltshire. His career illustrates exactly how the "new men" of the time were assimilated. Thus in a pragmatical way, the two main British political parties came to share similar objectives; and when representing powerful advocates of "Free Trade", the manufacturers Cobden and Bright denounced the protective Corn Laws as taxing "the food of the people", the Tory Peel took the plunge, on the immediate occasion of an appalling famine in Ireland, of abolishing them, against the interests of the landowners and large farmers, who had prospered during the Napoleonic wars. This decision, made in 1846, more than the

[1] *Dictionary of National Biography.*
[2] The Grand National Consolidated Trade Union of 1834 was inspired more by the "Utopian" socialist Robert Owen than by revolutionary ideas; and the heroes of Trade Union history did not die on "barricades" but were labourers from Tolpuddle in Dorset, transported to Australia in that year for administering local trade union oaths. They were retrieved after two years, following a press campaign which dubbed them "martyrs", and the name has stuck. But they were not "martyrs" by continental standards, and were careful not to exploit their brief celebrity; all but one shrewdly preferred to leave Dorset and make a fresh start as small-holders in Essex.

passing of the Reform Bill, marked the shift of political power to the Midland and Northern *bourgeoisie*, then towards the urban working classes, and away from the agricultural and commercial conservative interests that under both Whigs and Tories had hitherto ruled Great Britain. Peel and Wellington had recognized accomplished facts; coal and iron were now more important than home grown wheat, and the railways, far the most extensive and elaborate in Europe, were transforming an increasingly urban society, bringing a new uniform and shallow metropolitan culture to swamp the millennial rural way of life. By the end of the century, after the coming of refrigerated steamships, the near ruin of agriculture would be the price of the "free trade" which brought cheap food for the factory "hands" of great industry. Already, by 1848, the year of revolution on the continent, Great Britain, for good and ill, was becoming the "workshop of the world", a position maintained for over twenty years of mid-Victorian affluence.

No barricades had been improvised; even the monarchy, amply discredited by the antics of the sons of George III, had righted itself under Victoria and Albert; and the British found themselves, despite official reluctance, landed with a second British Empire, even more extensive than the first.

For they were now responsible for Canada and India, for Australasia, South Africa, Ceylon and Singapore, linked by the strategic bases and islands which secured the Oceanic *Pax Britannica*. And the island base, defended at immense cost from the full might of Napoleon's empire, repaid the reward of a sound investment in a war fought for survival and economic world domination, while the ancient constitution had proved adaptable to changing times.

IV

The Grand Alliance against Napoleonic France, held together by the Treaty of Chaumont of March 1814 had ended the war against Napoleon by the First Treaty of Paris in that May; and in June 1815 the Treaty of Vienna had dealt with the redistribution of the Napoleonic Empire. After the failure of Napoleon's final adventure at Waterloo, a Second Treaty of Paris, imposing an indemnity and an army of occupation on France, had been concluded. The "Hundred Days" had further renewed the fragile alliance of the Great Powers, and the short lived Holy Alliance devised by Alexander I and the Quadruple Alliance of September and November 1815 had both been agreed upon.

Under these arrangements an important change was effected in the strategically vital Netherlands. The Austrian Netherlands, Catholic and Spanish since the rise of the Dutch Republic, then transferred to Austria, were now relinquished by Austria to form part of a buffer state in conjunction with Holland and Luxembourg, and the Protestant Dutch were compensated for the distasteful union by the return of their rich Indonesian colonies, which the British could have had for the taking.

Naturally the Union did not last: memories of doctrinal and economic conflict went too deep. In August 1830, following the July revolution in Paris, the French-speaking Catholic Belgians, understandably exasperated at having to use Dutch as the sole official language, rose in revolt in Brussels; there were riots, quelled in blood. A Dutch army was evicted by the French, but Belgium was not absorbed into France: Talleyrand and Palmerston found a way out by assigning the throne of an independent Belgium to Leopold of Saxe-Coburg, uncle of Queen Victoria. The country was "neutralized" and in 1839 its neutrality guaranteed by the great powers; an arrangement which led in 1914 to the British entering the First World War, and which did not prevent tensions between French-speaking Walloons and Flemings, who spoke a coarse kind of Dutch, which have troubled Belgian politics ever since.

On the south-western flank of France, the Spaniards soon reverted to their own inward-looking politics, mainly determined by the traditional regional antipathies towards central government. In 1814 Fernando VII, released from captivity in France, had regained his throne; but his inept policies led in 1820 to a mutiny in an army assembled at Cadiz to put down the revolt of the Spanish-American colonies, and the King became the captive of a military *junta*. In 1810 a Cortes had set itself up in Cadiz in which "Liberals"—the Spaniards had invented the term—had predominated under an ineffective constitution; and in 1823, with the encouragement of the Tsar Alexander I and against the protests of the British, who left the "Holy Alliance", a large French army moved into Spain and "liberated" Cadiz, with a view to intervention in South America. This threat of intervention, which in part caused President Monroe to declare the Monroe Doctrine of that year deterring European intervention in the Americas, was headed off, mainly by the British Tory statesman Canning, determined to protect the independence of the Spanish American colonies and British commercial interests bound up with it. In 1828 Fernando VII, long without a direct heir, married Maria Christina, a Bourbon of Naples and Sicily; in 1830 she bore him a daughter, Isabella, who succeeded him in 1833. Maria Christina acted as Regent; but this unexpected outcome led to civil war, for Fernando's autocratic brother, Don Carlos, the equivalent in Spain to Charles X in France, backed by the most conservative and regionally conscious elements in Spain, tried to depose Isabella and her mother.

In Portugal the aftermath of the Napoleonic wars was predictably confused. The Portuguese under British pressure had acquiesced in the campaign against the slave trade, and in 1817, in return, won recognition of their colonies in Africa; but they lost their hold on the far more important colony of Brazil. João VI, the son of Maria I, who had been driven finally insane by the news of the French Revolution, was a refugee in Brazil and reluctant to return to Portugal, and General Sir William Beresford, Conde de Trancoso and afterwards Viscount Beresford,[1] who had reorganized the Portuguese armies, met with increasing resistance from the "liberal" Portuguese, who refused to pay for the British army. Beresford crossed to Rio de Janeiro to obtain support

[1] One of the most picturesque figures of the age, this Irishman had fought at Toulon, in Corsica, the West Indies, India, Egypt, Capetown and Buenos Aires. In 1807 he was made Commander-in-Chief, Madeira, on behalf of the King of Portugal and in 1809 reorganized the Portuguese army against the French and was highly regarded by Wellington. See *Dictionary of National Biography* for his fascinating career.

from the King; but in 1820 the Portuguese refused to allow him to land at Lisbon. And when in 1821 João VI at last himself returned, he assigned Brazil to his eldest son Pedro, who in the following year became Emperor of an independent country. In the general Braganza interest, João VI acknowledged the position of Pedro, who, on João's death in 1826, also became Pedro IV of Portugal, only to resign his rights there to his daughter, the child Maria de Gloria. Pedro's brother Miguel, a rigid conservative, was appointed Regent, but his attacks on the liberal constitutionalists induced Pedro to make a comeback, and from 1831–4 a "War of the Two Brothers" afflicted the country, concluded only when Miguel was driven out, and Maria de Gloria (1834–53) came to the throne.

Thus in Portugal as in Spain, the restoration of the Braganzas, like that of the Bourbons, touched off a conflict of regional rivalries, of clericalism and anti-clericalism and of liberal ideas from France with Iberian conservatism, that greatly impeded the economic and social recovery of both countries after the incursion and eviction of the French. Where the sequel to the Napoleonic Wars in Italy contributed to the *Risorgimento*, the Iberians preferred to revert to their traditional and internecine strife.

V

Such in broad outline was the course of the main political events in Western Europe during the decades that followed the fall of Napoleon and the settlement made at Vienna, which also saw the very gradual impact of the first Industrial Revolution spread over the continent. But among the men of talent and enterprise who found new scope in the general upheaval were many who did not devote their abilities to politics, and who created in the spheres of science, medicine and the arts one of the most original and important eras of European history. The brilliant amateurs of the Enlightenment had pioneered in many fields: now middle-class experts began to professionalize knowledge. Moreover, the Romantic Movement in Germany was in full spate, while the poetry of Byron, which won European fame, explored new depths of feeling and brisk satire.

During the historically brief period between being oppressed by the aristocracy and undermined by the "People", the professional classes, emancipated from the censorship of the Church and no longer side-tracked into idleness in monasteries, showed an epoch-making creativeness. The scientific outlook defined by Bacon and Descartes and designed to make man the master of nature had brilliantly if superficially flourished in the eighteenth century; the ground then charted was now systematically explored, in France with encouragement from government, in Great Britain by private initiative. The *École Normale Supérieure* and the *École Polytechnique* had been permanently established under the Consulate, both productive of brilliant elites; the British Association for the Advancement of Science was founded in 1831, the year when the *Proceedings of the Royal Society* were first circulated. Nonconformist

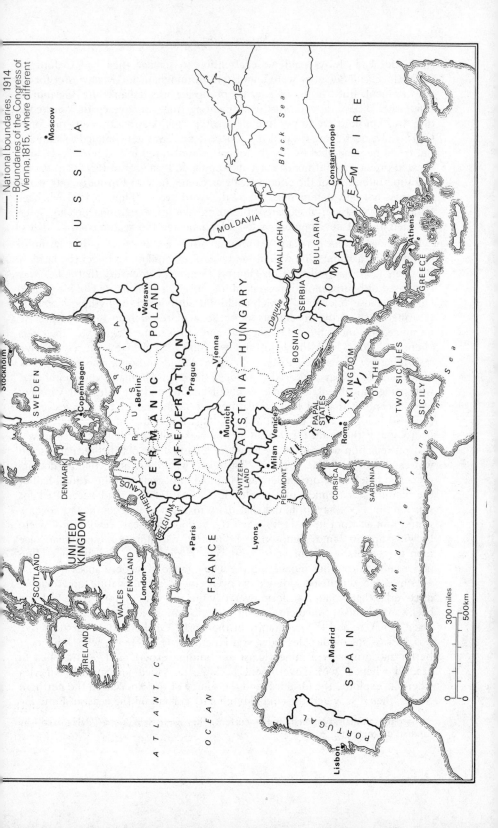

National boundaries, 1914
Boundaries of the Congress of
Vienna, 1815, where different

RUSSIA

•Moscow

Black Sea

Constantinople

OTTOMAN EMPIRE

MOLDAVIA

WALLACHIA

Danube

SERBIA

BULGARIA

BOSNIA

GREECE

Athens•

SWEDEN

Stockholm

Copenhagen•

POLAND

Warsaw•

Berlin•

GERMANIC CONFEDERATION

Prague•

Vienna•

AUSTRIA—HUNGARY

DENMARK

Munich•

SWITZER-LAND

Milan•

Venice•

PIEDMONT

PAPAL STATES

Rome•

(KINGDOM OF THE TWO SICILIES)

ITALY

CORSICA

SARDINIA

SICILY

Mediterranean Sea

NETHERLANDS

BELGIUM

UNITED KINGDOM

SCOTLAND

IRELAND

WALES

ENGLAND

London•

Paris•

FRANCE

Lyons•

ATLANTIC

OCEAN

SPAIN

Madrid•

PORTUGAL

Lisbon•

300 miles
500 km

0

academies had always paid more attention to science than had Oxford or Cambridge, and Societies were founded in Birmingham and Manchester for its advancement. But the crucial advance of physics was Italian. Luigi Galvani of Bologna (1737–98), at the price of tormenting frogs, discovered the "current" or passage of negative to positive electricity;[1] then Alessandro Volta of Como (1745–1827) next demonstrated that "electric fire" was not confined to animals, but could be generated by inorganic matter and stored in "batteries", whence it could provide a continuous current. Appointed Professor of Physics at Pavia, and superintendent of the Scuola Reale at Como, he won European and world celebrity, lastingly commemorated by the word "volt". Then in 1831 Michael Faraday (1791–1867) discovered the principles of electro-magnetism, later destined for vast development in the telephone and the mass-media.

In chemistry, the Parisian Antoine Lavoisier, a pioneer of better farming, better public accounts and weights and measures, guillotined under the Jacobin terror in 1794, had followed up Henry Cavendish's discovery that water was composed of hydrogen and oxygen, in his *Traité élémentaire de Chimie* (1789). He listed those "elements" which could not be reduced to anything less, thus creating much of the vocabulary of subsequent research in terms of precise formulae. In medicine, the ancient and misleading dogma of the four "humours" long held the field, and was only dispelled by the cumulative researches of German scientists, as Johannes Muller of Bonn, whose *Handbook of Human Physiology* appeared in 1833–40; his pupil Hermann von Helmholtz, who made fundamental discoveries about hearing and eyesight; and Virchow who, accepting that all living creatures are composed of cells, investigated their pathology. The Englishman Sir Charles Bell had investigated the neurology of the brain (1811); but it was not until Pasteur (1822–95) proved that putrefaction was caused by living bacteria that the old theory that disease was caused by invisible chemical "particles" was discredited, though doctors remained helpless before cholera and typhoid until well into the second half of the century. Dr. Jenner, of Berkeley in Gloucestershire, had vaccinated for smallpox in 1798, having found that dairy maids who had contracted cowpox were immune from it. In 1847, when the various political "revolutions" were brewing up, Sir James Simpson of Edinburgh did more for the human race than the generally mischievous politicians by performing the first operation under chloroform, thus pioneering the whole range of modern anaesthetics.

While the scientists and doctors were investigating nature and making discoveries that would transform everyday life and vastly improve the hitherto backward science of medicine, other men of genius were investigating man's place in nature and the geography of the world. Of these the most attractive was a Prussian, Baron Alexander von Humboldt (1769–1859), who, born near Berlin and originally a minerologist and mining expert, in 1796 travelled to Madrid whence, with government backing, he sailed for Spanish America where he explored the Orinoco, and the source of the Amazon in the northern Andes, then discovered the cold "Humboldt" current off the coast of Peru. He

[1]When the animals twitched in the current, they were said to be "galvanized" by "animal magnetism".

thus became the greatest pioneer of physical geography, climatology and tropical botany. He ascended Mount Chimborazo, nearly 19,000 feet high, and he illustrated the records of his travels. Having attained European celebrity, he also travelled across the whole of Siberia to the border of China, returning through Central Asia, and from 1845 to his death, aged ninety, he wrote the five volumes of his *Kosmos*, a survey of the entire range of geophysical, geographical and botanical knowledge. He was the founder of the modern sciences of physical and plant geography[1].

Research had also been demonstrating the vast antiquity of mankind. By 1825 Jacques Boucher de Perthes, director of Customs at Abbeville, had discovered pear-shaped flint implements chipped to a point in the gravel beds of the Somme, which in 1838 he claimed, proved the existence of mankind long before the accepted Christian date for the Creation of 4004 BC; and these discoveries were to be paralleled by those of the Cornish antiquary William Pengelly, who in 1846 found much better made flint implements in juxta-position with the bones of rhinoceros and cave bear in Kent's cavern near Torquay. This evidence lay, as it were, waiting to be interpreted in the light of Darwin's theory of Evolution as developed in his epoch making *Origin of Species by Means of Natural Selection* (1859).

More recent pre-history was also now pioneered in Scandinavia, where after 1841 Frederik, Crown Prince of Denmark, had promoted the excavations of Jens Worsaae into the numerous tumuli in that country, and where Christian Thomsen, head of the Museum in Copenhagen, in 1836 first divided pre-history into ages of Stone, Bronze and Iron.

With the emergence of a large literate public with greater purchasing power, many writers reaped a rich harvest and a cosmopolitan fame. Sir Walter Scott (1771–1832) invented the historical novel, exact in "period" detail, if not in psychological insight, and became a European influence: Jane Austen (1775–1818), with more subtle insight untouched by the Romantic Movement, and with far less contemporary fame, could depict the nuances of character in the turn of a phrase. William Wordsworth (1770–1850), who managed to create a substitute for religion out of the cult of scenery, relate introspection to nature, and transform ordinary experience into sublimity, was the greatest English Romantic poet, if Lord Byron (1788–1824) was far the most famous on the continent, where the eccentricity of an English milord of reckless genius was better appreciated than it was at home.

But the most popular medium had now become the novel, depicting a whole panorama of society. Henri Beyle—Stendhal—(1783–1842) had served in the armies of Napoleon and describes in a lapidary style, comparable to the neo-classical painting of David, the conflict between the cold realism of the careerists of his age and their romantic passions. Unlike Chateaubriand, who tried to rehabilitate the Church by romanticizing its grandeur, Stendhal, in *Le Rouge et Le Noir*, remains strongly anti-clerical, though his hero is an outsider in the aristocratic circles which his charm and ability enable him apparently to

[1]See Douglas Botting. *Humboldt and the Cosmos*. London, 1973. for a well illustrated general account.

enter. Stendhal's *La Chartreuse de Parme* satirized romantic views of the Italians, and he is a master of lucid irony. Benjamin Constant (1767-1830), a French-Swiss from Lausanne, whose novel *Adolphe* (1806) shows remarkable psychological insight, was a cosmopolitan advocate of liberty, whose *On the Spirit of Conquest and Usurpation and their effects on European civilization* (1813) attacked Napoleon's empire, and whose *De la Réligion considérée dans sa source, ses formes et ses développements* (1824-31) concludes that true religion, as opposed to institutional religion, is a form of "freedom".

Honoré de Balzac (1799-1850) was far more representative of the dynamic, tumultuous times; a voracious bourgeois genius who revelled in all the aspects of the "human comedy" he brilliantly depicted. Nothing really disgusted him: he slapped it all down with the robust power of narrative one would expect from someone of his gross physique, and, like Dickens, he was not above caricature in the interest of a good read. He glorified the self-made bankers who Saint-Simon had hoped would take over a technocratic society, and rightly depicted them as interested in more intimate human passions than in government. His main interests were metropolitan, but he could hit off the tensions of provincial towns and remote villages. His own hectic life and relatively premature end read like one of his own novels.

Charles Dickens (1812-70), as befitted an Englishman of his day, had more moral purpose. He depicted and caricatured his urban middle-class world as it faced the Industrial Revolution, writing it up to make it interesting to his middle-class readers, who liked what was familiar with an added spice of humour and melodrama. His *Pickwick Papers* (1836-7) at once caught on; a picaresque tale of the adventures of variously and emphatically labelled characters, developed into a panorama of English life. *Nicholas Nickleby* (1838-9) created the horrible character of the schoolmaster Squeers and the nightmare of Dotheboys Hall, and *Oliver Twist* (1837-9) attacked the workhouses imposed by the Poor Law; then *The Old Curiosity Shop* (1841) with its unbridled sentimentality about Little Nell, won Dickens even more readers, in America as well as at home. With astonishing fecundity, and with the wolf never far from the door, he went on pouring out fiction through the 'forties and 'fifties, which culminated in *Great Expectations* and *Our Mutual Friend* (1864-5), and he satirized the intense snobbery of the mid-Victorians. The sheer creative power of Dickens, his delight in the quirks of character and his streak of vulgarity, made him just the man for the time, and his narrative power won him a cosmopolitan readership, not least in Russia.

By contrast Thackeray (1811-63) is detached and ironical; an anatomist of the cruelty of the social order and the heartlessness and folly of those who try to exploit it; *Vanity Fair* (1847-8) describes the arts of those who live by their wits in all their successful hypocrisy: like Dickens he was a Victorian moralist, but with an indirect attack. So great was the success and prestige of both these novelists that they were read by an otherwise philistine public, and were still staple fare in otherwise semi-literate households into the early twentieth century.

In the arts, architecture remained decently neo-classical, as it had become under the French Empire and the English Regency; indeed, in Western

Europe, as in North America, domestic architecture remained satisfying and convenient. It was not until well into the mid-century that the appalling effects of the Industrial Revolution combined with the Gothick revival to create lobster-gothic pseudo-baronial monstrosities, many of them still extant and even admired.

In painting, on the other hand, the Romantic movement combined with a revolt against urban ugliness to produce outstanding work. The pictures of David (1746–1825), Napoleon's official artist, are technically almost flawless, neo-classical and influenced by the High Renaissance and by Poussin; but he became the propagandist, first of the Revolution, as in the theatrical and over-estimated *Oath of the Horatii* (1785) and the *Oath of the Tennis Court*; then, most famously, in his romantic version of Napoleon on a prancing horse and wearing a swirling cloak, crossing a slippery rock during his passage of the Alps. Other "subject pictures" include Napoleon's coronation. David's Gascon pupil Ingres (1780–1867), a genius for line and contour, painted the technically splendid *Napoleon Enthroned* became popular for his neo-medieval subject pictures after the Restoration and under Charles X, and is much respected by later artists for his drawing.

Where Ingres is identified with the conservative "reaction", Eugène Delacroix (1798–1863), probably the illegitimate offspring of Talleyrand, was a whole hearted romantic, whose first picture to win acclaim was one of Virgil and Dante in Hell (1822). Two years later, following the Greek rising against the Turks, he painted his overrated *Massacre of Scios*, famous for its original contrasts in colour. Then in 1830 he painted his melodramatic *Liberty guiding the People*, symbolized by a liberal revolutionary in a top hat and a boy flourishing two pistols across a barricade encumbered with the dead. They all make excellent targets.

The contemporary English painters chose subjects of more lasting interest; and for the first time since Anglo-Saxon days had a powerful influence on the continent.

J. M. W. Turner (1775–1851), a self-educated genius, expressed the romantic cult of nature, building up since the mid-eighteenth century and articulate in the early Wordsworth, with a new swirl and range of composition and colour; one of the great painters of Europe, who took his subjects from Venice and the Alps as well as from the mists of the Thames estuary, and tramped on foot over the most beautiful areas of France, Switzerland and Italy.

John Constable (1776–1837), the son of a miller in Suffolk, who had grown up to the sound of water wheel and sluice, painted the meadows, elms and willows of his native countryside with a new attention to cloudscape, to the wind, rain and intermittent sunshine of England. Like Turner, though in a less dramatic way, he brought back colour into landscape, long dimmed by eighteenth-century conventions into drabness, and he reinterpreted the great seventeenth-century Flemish traditions of landscape painting. Thus two great English painters won continental fame, at a time when English water colourists, as Cotman, de Wint and David Cox, were the best in Europe.

XLII

Liberal Nationalism and the Reaction

While in the West sovereign nation states had emerged from dynastic realms whose boundaries had long been established, in Central Europe the Germans still had no centralized dynastic realm to develop; in 1806 the ancient Holy Roman Empire with its patchwork of principalities and cities had been swept away by Napoleon, leaving, after the collapse of his own ephemeral empire, two great powers round which the Germans might coalesce; Lutheran Prussia, with its grip on the Middle Rhine; and the polyglot Habsburg empire, a purely dynastic Catholic state based on the Danube and its hinterland and, directly and indirectly, extending over most of Italy.

The Prussian state, cut back by Napoleon, had emerged all the tougher for the pruning, with its military tradition enhanced by strident bourgeois nationalism, its archaic administration modernized and its limited territories relatively compact. The Austrian Empire—no longer Holy or Roman—depended on playing off various and vocal nationalities—Czechs, Hungarians, Croats and Italians—against each other, and on an elaborate and Germanic bureaucracy whose mills ground slowly but not ineffectively. Both were military and conservative; Prussia a state built round an army by the Hohenzollerns; Austria the embodiment of an august and ancient dynasty, its prestige enhanced by the wealth and social, military and cultural glamour of Vienna, the imperial capital.

In 1815 the Treaty of Vienna, as well as rehabilitating and guaranteeing the Swiss Confederation and assigning Norway to Sweden as a reward for Bernadotte's desertion of Napoleon, had created a Germanic Confederation of which the Austrian Emperor was President, containing thirty-nine States of varying size, still in theory autonomous, and represented by a Diet at Frankfurt. Though determined to prevent a "Jacobin" or Liberal Germany, both Prussia and Austria were resolved that neither of them should dominate a united German *Reich*. This loose federation therefore lasted until 1866, when the Austro-Prussian War won Prussian hegemony.

Still free of the doubtful blessing of a centralized Reich and army, the Germans developed various civilian anti-French patriotic movements, as that of Jahn in Berlin, who "wore a grey unbleached shirt open at the neck, with the shirt collar lying over the collar of the jacket (and) no waistcoat"[1]—a daring get up at the time—and who built an open air gymnasium and took his pupils tramping through the woods, singing marching songs. A neo-classical romantic Hellenism coloured these expeditions, spiced with a cult of *Deutschheit*. At Jena, in Thuringia, under the rule of Karl August of Saxe-Weimar, where in 1816 the Grand Duke had convened a freely elected parliament, the students had a romantic cult of Shakespeare, Dante and, of course, Goethe; they formed a *Burschenschaft* designed to promote a Liberal Germany following the eviction of the French, whose defeat at Leipzig was annually celebrated. This academic fervour had been dangerously surpassed by the battle songs of Arndt and Kleist, who wrote of "cohort stormers" and evoked the barbarian ancestors of the Germans who had "overcome the Romans". The philosophers in Protestant Germany also took a hand, in the long run far more harmful. Following on Herder's cult of the *Volk* and its past, Georg Wilhelm Hegel (1770–1831) had been appointed in 1816 Professor of Philosophy at Berlin. His *Fundamentals of the Philosophy of Right* appeared in 1821 and his *The Philosophy of History* (lectures 1822–31)[2] after his death. Hegel regarded history as a "dynamic process in which successive stages of consciousness and political organization came to fruition"; a more exciting vision than the grand but static concepts of Thomism or the banal outlook of Bentham. The individual, he maintained, is reconciled with society in this "becoming": he also claimed to understand by "speculative intuition" the entire course of world history and the "laws" by which it was determined. This insight informed him that history was culminating in the Germanic peoples, at the moment the favourites of the conductor in the Hegelian cosmic symphony. A substitute and pretentious religion was thus provided for the many German intellectuals susceptible to this sort of appeal; later translated into Marxist "dialectical materialism", it was to become fundamental to the Marxist claim to have created a Science of History. In Hegel's time it merely contributed to German nationalism building up in the Germanic Confederation, which had been strengthened by a *Zollverein* (Customs union) for North Germany in 1819–34.

The revolution of 1848 in Paris brought the long postponed crisis of liberalism and nationalism in Germany to a head. Revolution broke out in Vienna, and after street fighting in Berlin, Frederick William IV had to announce a constitution, and even to promise to merge Prussia into a Federal German Reich. By now the liberal nationalists in the Germanic Federal Diet at Frankfurt were demanding a *Vorparliament* or preliminary National Assembly for all Germany; but when they met in May 1848, at Frankfurt, the *Vorparliament*, composed almost entirely of lawyers, administrators and fifty all-too-articulate professors, proved mainly concerned with attacking the other nationalists in Bohemia, Poland and Schleswig, and with building a pan-German fleet without having the means to pay for it. It was not until March 1849 that the Frankfurt politicians got around to offering the Crown of a United Germany (without Austria) to the Prussian King, who by then had

[1]R. B. Mowat. *The Romantic Age. Europe in the Early Nineteenth Century*. London, 1937. pp. 96–7.
[2]Trans. J. Sibree. London, 1857.

gone back on his enforced promises, dissolved his own equally unpractical Prussian assembly, and now refused the offer as not coming from the German Princes.

By now, too, the situation had entirely changed in the Austrian Empire. In the spring of 1848 a Constituent Assembly in Vienna had emancipated the peasants, but its restricted franchise proved unpopular; and in October a radical rising, in which the Minister of War was literally hung from a lamp post, had driven the court to Olmütz in Moravia. Here in December Prince Felix von Schwarzenberg, an able soldier and diplomat, had forced the Emperor Ferdinand IV to abdicate in favour of his apparently promising eighteen-year-old nephew, the Archduke Franz Joseph, who reigned until 1916. He had then called in his brother-in-law, Field Marshal Windischgratz, to crush the revolution in besieged Vienna, and collaborate with Croatian troops to put down the revolt in Hungary. The Hungarians, led by Kossuth,[1] put up a spirited resistance, and were only crushed with the help of a Russian army and after major atrocities committed by General Haynau, known to British Liberals as "General Hyena". The Hungarians would remain under martial law for eight years.

Schwarzenberg, who died in 1852, had little time to impose his centralized Germanic bureaucracy on the various parts of the Empire, and failed in his ambition to bring it as the dominant partner into the German Confederation. The Prussians, themselves thwarted, frustrated him; and the other Germans did not wish to be amalgamated with Czechs, Hungarians and Croats. The amiable Viennese, the stubborn Czechs, the belligerent Magyars and Croats, were thus caught up in the swirl of nationalist and radical violence emanating from Paris in 1848; and those Germans who had been enjoying a period of cultural creativeness and political peace after the eviction of the French found their hopes of a United Germany under a liberal constitutional regime frustrated—not that it would have remained liberal, given the manifest incompetence of the Frankfurt Assembly and the ineradicable militarism of both Habsburgs and Hohenzollerns.

II

The Empire, now of Austria-Hungary, had to play Germans against Czechs and Croats against Hungarians; in Italy it faced even more ancient antipathies. Moreover, the satellite republics of Napoleon's Empire had given at least

[1]Louis Kossuth (1802–94) came of minor Hungarian gentry and trained as a lawyer. He then turned to estate management but in 1830 discovered his flair for journalism. He became a nationalist agitator and in 1840 editor of *Pesti Hirlop*. Then in 1848 he emerged as a brilliant orator and a Minister of Finance in the Hungarian revolutionary government. He refused the subsidies due to the Imperial government and hindered the dispatch of troops to fight Carlo Alberto of Sardinia-Piedmont and to put down the Milanese and Venetian revolts. He led the resistance to the Russians and the Croats, but was driven into Turkish territory, whence he escaped and fled, via England, to the United States. He died an exile in Milan.

middle-class Italians a taste for modernity, while the Kingdom of Sardinia-Piedmont, left intact by Napoleon and now incorporating Genoa, had a historic belligerent tradition, deriving from its command of the great and lesser St. Bernard passes and from the ancient French Duchy of Savoy. Italy was so deeply divided by geography and history, and the economic and social contrast between the relatively prosperous North and the poverty-stricken and mostly arid South, that the prospect of union was remote and could obviously come about only by French intervention. But the Vienna settlement had extended Austrian responsibilities; the resentment they provoked, and the ancient Italian hatred for the Germans, going back to Barbarossa and the feuds of Papal Guelfs and Imperialist Ghibellines, had been mounting up, fanned by the conspiratorial *Carbonari*, originally improvised in the Abruzzi against the French.

The Italian *Risorgimento*, which culminated in 1870 in a united Italy, was not the spontaneous revolution of a whole people depicted by liberal historians: it derived from the romantic nationalism of intellectuals and the devious manoeuvres of interested politicians, while the mass of the illiterate peasantry or semi-literate workmen remained preoccupied with their own traditional concerns. Nor was it a purely Italian achievement; like the independence of Greece, it was finally brought about by the intervention of the Western Powers.

The *Risorgimento* thus divided into roughly three phases: the first, conducted by the Italians themselves and almost entirely ineffectual, began in 1820 and continued through the revolutionary year 1830 to the election of the supposedly liberal Pope Pius IX in 1846. The second phase, launched by Carlo Alberto, King of Sardinia-Piedmont in 1848, was concluded by the victory of the Austrians in 1849 and the destruction of the short-lived Roman Republic by a French army, dispatched to restore the Pope, no longer the hoped for figurehead for a liberal united Italy.

Finally, in 1859–60, Italian unity was achieved in the only way it could be, by a massive intervention by the French, who drove the Austrians out of Lombardy, while Garibaldi, with the connivance of the British Navy, overthrew the Bourbon regime in Sicily and in Naples, and was then compelled to hand over his conquests to Vittorio Emmanuele II, King of Sardinia and Piedmont, who became King of a united Italy with its capital at Florence. Even then, the full unification of Italy depended, not on the Italians, but on events north of the Alps. In 1866, following the Austro-Prussian War, the Austrians abandoned Venice; and in 1870, after the defeat of the French in the Franco-Prussian War, Rome, at last free of its French garrison, could become the capital of an Italian State.

Naturally the most archaic and inefficient regime in Italy had provoked the first revolt. In the Kingdom of the "Two Sicilies" there were no modern roads and only primitive agriculture: Naples, far the largest town in the South, had been living off the patronage of the gaudy and corrupt Court of the restored Bourbon monarch, Ferdinand II. In 1820 a revolt had broken out in Palermo, put down by Austrian troops. In the same year, in the relatively prosperous kingdom of Sardinia-Piedmont, an attempted revolution against King Charles-

Felix had met the same fate. The Italians were far too much divided by political and tariff barriers and inter-civic rivalries to organize a widespread and co-ordinated revolt.

It followed that the Paris revolution of 1830 had only mild repercussions, athough in 1831 the accession of Carlo Alberto to the throne of Sardinia-Piedmont raised the hopes of Mazzini, the prophet of romantic nationalism, already campaigning and conspiring for a United Italy.[1] In 1831 he founded *La Giovine Italia* which mobilized "intellectuals", students and professional men frustrated by Austrian rule, but it had little appeal to the Catholic and mainly illiterate peasantry and labourers. Nor were the amateur cloak and dagger conspiracies he inspired effective.

But Mazzini was a portent for Europe and the world. Giuseppe Mazzini (1805-72) was born the son of the Professor of Anatomy at the University of Genoa. In 1827 he joined the Carbonari and in 1830 he was imprisoned at Savona after the revolution of that year. He then migrated to Marseilles, where, in hiding, he edited *La Giovine Italia*. Having moved to Geneva, he conspired to launch a revolution in Savoy, and in 1837 he took refuge in London, where he was befriended by Carlyle and began to make his name as a journalist. Back in Milan during the Revolution of 1848, he travelled to Rome after the defeat of the Piedmontese armies, and there acted as *Triumvir* during the siege of the city by the French. He then again became a refugee in Switzerland and London, and refused to support Cavour's version of a united Italian kingdom or to accept a seat in the Italian Parliament. He continued to conspire even against this regime, and died in hiding at Pisa. Mazzini was an entirely one-sided intellectual; fanatically devoted to his ideas expressed in the spate of writing to which he devoted his life and which fill the forty volumes of the *Scritti editi ed inediti di Giuseppe Mazzini*.[2]

He was hardly a success either as conspirator or statesman, and spent most of his life as a refugee. Yet as a writer he had enormous influence, far beyond Italy. He was the prophet of the liberal-democratic Nationalism which was to hypnotize the modern world. He devised a cult of Humanity and Progress which has proved a substitute for transcendental religion, and propagated a mystical belief in the virtues of "the people", who, once liberated, he was misguidedly convinced, would "accept genius and virtue as their guides" and live together in brotherly concord.

This gospel did not make much impression on the peasants and workmen of the time, but it did convert the many middle-class intellectuals who created influential public opinion. It encouraged the cult of "self-determination" and of "one man, one vote"; and it was the direct inspiration of the unpractical ideas embodied in the League of Nations after the First World War. Mazzini intended to create a Humanitarian religion; he succeeded in launching

[1] Alessandro Manzoni's *I Promessi Sposi* (1823-7), ostensibly about Spanish rule in seventeenth-century Italy, had political implications which won it immense fame all over Italy.
[2] For an introductory account see my *Politics and Opinion in the Nineteenth Century. op. cit.* Chapter VIII, *Humanitarian Nationalism.*

Nationalism, one of the most irrational, powerful and pervasive dogmas of the modern world.

The hopes of Mazzini and the Liberal Nationalist revolutionaries were prematurely aroused by the election of a new Pope. In 1846 the supposedly "liberal" Giovanni Mastai-Ferretti began his long Pontificate as Pius IX (1846–78). His election at first roused the revolutionaries to extravagant expectations, but the Pope could not afford to fall out with Austria—the most powerful Catholic monarchy in Europe—and his "liberal" posture soon became untenable. When in March 1848 Carlo Alberto of Sardinia-Piedmont rashly declared war on Austria, the prospect of a federated Italy under a Liberal Pope advocated by Gioberti's *The Moral and Civil Primacy of the Italians* (1843) vanished at once. The Pope, after all, had an oecumenical dominion which dwarfed Italy.

The revolutionaries turned bitterly against *Pio Nono*, and murdered his moderate minister, Rossi. They set up a "Roman Republic", with Mazzini as its dominant *triumvir*, and the Pope fled to Gaeta in Neapolitan territory. But the "Roman Republic" was doomed: the campaign of Carlo Alberto in the north was swiftly defeated, and with it the one slender hopes of success. The rising of the Milanese had compelled Radetsky, the Austrian commander, to retreat on the famous "quadrilateral" of Verona, Mantua, Peschiera and Legnano, which ensured his communications over the Brenner, for what they were worth since Vienna was in revolution; but the Piedmontese army had proved inefficient, not least in communications and supply, and unpopular with the Milanese. Soon the better disciplined Austrians and Magyars, who held the Italians in contempt, made short work of them in July 1848 at Custozza. The Austrians pressed on to Milan, which surrendered early in August; Carlo Alberto was forced to sign an armistice and even when he broke it in the spring of 1849, he was again roundly defeated at Novara, abdicated in favour of his son Vittorio Emmanuele II, and fled to Portugal. Only in Venice, Manin, a Jewish lawyer that March had become president of a Venetian republic after a revolt which had evicted the Austrians but he had succumbed after a siege and a token bombardment in the autumn of 1849.

So the "Roman Republic" was naturally short lived. Under a triumvirate headed by Mazzini, and defended by the "romantic" hero Garibaldi, it was put down in June 1849 by a French expeditionary force dispatched by Louis Napoleon, now President of the Second French Republic, anxious to further his ambition to be Emperor of the French by restoring the Pope and so attracting the French Catholic vote.

But the siege of Rome had a major propaganda success, and liberal historians have amply celebrated it. "The defence was conducted by Garibaldi. This great blond leader of irregular troops, who hated priests, worshipped liberty and had returned from a wild life in South America to help make his beloved Italy a free republic, now with his following of shaggy red-shirts burst into the very heart and centre of the Italian drama."[1]Though Rome hardly needed

[1]Fisher. *op. cit.* p. 917. Political shirts, shaggy or neat, now have less appeal.

political advertisement, the memory of the siege contributed to Rome, not Florence, finally becoming the capital of a united Italy.

Meanwhile, the restored Pio Nono, disillusioned with Liberalism, presided over a conservative regime in the Papal States. Spreading across Italy from sea to sea, it became a barrier to further projects of Italian unity. The Papal government forbade the construction of railroads and elaborated its police and censorship;[1] it would last until 1870 when an Italian national government took over the Papal States, whilst recognizing the sovereignty of a subsidized but intransigent Pope over the Vatican and its immediate surroundings. This conservative stance won much popular support, for the Romans had long lived off the Papacy and the pilgrims, and the ancient ritual of festivals and Saints Days gave psychological satisfaction to people to whom the new frothy cult of Humanity and Nationalism propagated by Mazzini was unintelligible.

The Risorgimento, writes a modern authority whose work has superseded that of Trevelyan and Fisher, was "a civil war between the old and new ruling classes, the peasants were neutral except insofar as their own perennial social war became accidentally involved." "The wars and rising of the risorgimento," he adds, "had little effect on ordinary people."[2] The fever of nationalism propagated by Mazzini was confined to a minority of the educated classes: true to their realistic traditions, most Italians trimmed their sails to exploit any changes of regime, and the redistribution of local offices and business which they implied, while local rivalries, descending from times of civic independence, were prosecuted under new slogans. As for the peasants, it mattered little to them if a regime of corrupt priests was exchanged for one of corrupt politicians and rapacious businessmen, as one "elite" ousted another. The sentimental view of the Risorgimento long accepted has now given place to a more realistic appraisal consonant with Italian history.

III

In the opening of Eothen the young Kinglake vividly describes the contrast between Christian and Turkish Europe, emphasized by the strict Austrian quarantine against the plague, as he crossed the Sava from Semlin to Belgrade, still in Ottoman territory. The "hyper-Turk-looking fellows" who received him, Turks of the old "once victorious race" in gaudy but dilapidated dress, their thick sashes stuffed with pistols and yataghans, with their long drooping

[1] G. M. Trevelyan, in his brilliantly written and thoroughly biased account of the Risorgimento, eloquently denounces the restored Papal regime, but shows no impartial comprehension of the motives of the Oecumenical Papacy; he admits but finds it hard to explain the continuing loyalty of the conservative peasantry to the Pope or the importance of the festivals of the Church in their lives. All is slanted towards what he terms the "redemption" of Italy—by her "children": Mussolini turned out to be the main "Redeemer".

[2] Denis Mack Smith. Italy, A Modern History. London, 1959. This is far the best survey, and may be supplemented on a less academic level by Luigi Barzini. The Italians. London, 1964.

moustachios, ample folds of once white turbans lowering over their piercing eyes, had "an air of gloomy pride, and that appearance of trying to be disdainful under difficulties which one almost always sees in those of the Ottoman people who live and remember old times".[1]

Turkish Europe had not yet become part of the nineteenth century. In the Balkans the peoples subject to the Turks thought more in terms of religious differences than of nationality, and it was only among the Greeks, where there was a widespread educated class and a widespread *diaspora* throughout most of the Turkish empire—not least in Istanbul and the Balkans—that romantic nationalism flourished: the other Balkan peoples still thought mainly in terms of heroic brigandage, celebrated by bards and led by warrior chiefs, whose aim was to set up a local power, if necessary paying nominal allegiance to the Sultan. The earliest brigand hero had appeared in Serbia, when Kara Djordje (Black George) had risen against the Turks in 1804-7.[2] His army defeated the Turks at Ivankovac and Misar and captured Belgrade. Then, on belated Russian intervention, his followers proclaimed him "supreme leader of the Serbs". But in 1812, following the Peace of Bucharest between Russia and Turkey, the Turks turned their full force on Serbia, and by 1813 Kara Djordje was driven from the country into Austria, while every Turk was officially allowed to kill any male Serb over fifteen in a fortnight's orgy of slaughter. After a sojourn in Russia, he got back to Serbia, since 1815 again in revolt under another peasant leader, Miloš Obrenovich, who, jealous of a rival, had him assassinated in his sleep and sent his head to the Sultan. This episode, as the reader will recognize, smacks more of medieval Balkan history than of high-minded nineteenth-century nationalism. It also secured Miloš Obrenovich I (1814-39) as hereditary ruler of an autonomous principality under Turkish suzerainty, though the Turks kept a garrison in Belgrade. This regime was backed by Russia and recognized in 1829 after the Russo-Turkish War of 1828-9 by the Treaty of Adrianople. The British, too, supported Miloš, as they would later support Tito; for they hoped to create a buffer against the Russians. So Miloš made the best of both worlds. But Miloš, temperamentally as much a brigand as Kara Djordje, was unable to manage a formal constitution or even council, and by 1839 was forced to abdicate. His son, Milan, having died within a month, he was succeeded by Michael Obrenovich III, a younger brother, under whom a Regency was established. It did not last long; by 1842 the young prince was driven out into Austria.

It was now the turn of the pro-Western Alexander Karadjordjevič, who managed to last until deposed in 1858, when a Miloš Obrenovich was restored. So plot and counterplot created constant tension; but the Serbs, riven with

[1]A. W. Kinglake. *Eothen, or Traces of Travel brought Home from the East* (1844).
[2]Djordje Petrovich (1763–1817), the son of peasant parents and called Black because of his appearance, started life herding pigs. Having killed some Turks, he fled to Austria, when he became a forester and killed game; he then fought for the Austrians against the Turks. Returning to Serbia, he made a fortune in the cattle trade, and was elected leader of the rising of 1804. He was the founder of the modern Serbian dynasty, for his son, Alexander, became the first Prince of Serbia.

internal feuds, could count one blessing—freedom from intermittent massacre by the Turks.

IV

The Greek War of Independence (1821–30) gained far wider support than had the Serbs, and succeeded mainly through the intervention of the Russians and the Western powers. The Phanariot Greeks of Istanbul were a wealthy and far-flung community, and the Greek Orthodox Patriarch commanded the obedience of his co-religionists in the Balkans and in Moldavia and Wallachia. There were Greek merchants in Vienna, and the *Philiké Hetairiá* (Friendly Companionship), the secret society which largely inspired the rising against the Turks, had been founded in Odessa. The Greek Orthodox clergy had always been identified with resistance to the Muslims, while there was as tough a tradition of banditry among the *klephtai* in the mountains as anywhere in the Balkans, and among the small Westernized middle class the cults of Byzantium and Hellas had survived.

Moreover, the resistance had begun as early as 1770, when, under the stimulus of Catherine the Great's wars with the Turks, the Greeks of the Peloponnese had risen in a revolt, savagely put down; then Ali Pasha of Jannina had rebelled against his Turkish masters and set up an independent principality in Epirus. Indeed, the revolt of this wily old ruffian in 1821 engaged the main Turkish army and set off the Greek War. It was at first desultory and ill-contrived; the thirty-six-year-old Lord Byron, who had landed on the British controlled Ionian island of Cephalonia in 1823, and did not arrive at the squalid and unhealthy town of Missolonghi until January 1824, found a riff-raff of rapacious and even mutinous partisans, incapable of the attack on Lepanto which he had planned. Even his "page", the sixteen-year-old Loukas Chalandrit-sanos, proved unrewarding; and by April, his end hastened by incompetent physicians, Byron died of the acute malaria endemic in the local marshes. Yet the death of this European celebrity advertised and enhanced the cause of Greece, already enthusiastically supported by western Philhellenes conscious of their debt to classical Hellas.

But it was not until the battle off Navarino in October 1827, when the British, French and Russian fleets blew the obsolete Turkish navy out of the water, that the Greeks were strong enough to think of establishing a government and that the Corfiote Giovanni Capo d'Istrias[1] was elected its President. Nor did he last long. Establishing himself at Nauplion where the small building which housed the early Greek Parliament still survives, and

[1]Count Giovanni Capo d'Istrias (1776–1831) had been born in Corfu when it was still under the Venetians and educated at Padua. He became second Secretary of State to Tsar Alexander I and from 1822–27 retired to Geneva, feeling as a Greek patriot unable any longer to serve in Russia.

relying on British help from General Sir Richard Church[1] and Lord Cochrane, both of whom regarded him as too pro-Russian, he set about creating a solvent and relatively efficient administration; but in October 1831 he met with no better reward than had Kara Djordje in Serbia, for he was assassinated by members of the Mavromikhalis (Black Michael) clan for giving appointments to Corfiote and Phanariot Greeks. Church, however, though he had failed in 1827 to relieve the Acropolis from the besieging Turks, had managed with his Suliotes to free Akarnania and Aetolia in Western Greece and drive the Turks out of Lepanto and Missolonghi. He did far more than Byron had been fated to do in liberating Greece.

In the Morea, meanwhile, Kolokotronis, a native of Messenia, who had earlier served under Church, had heavily defeated a Turkish-Egyptian army in 1822, and after the murder of Capo d'Istrias, tried to form his own government backed by what would now be termed guerrillas. All this activity in the field had been supported by the voluminous writings, scholarly and propagandist, of the veteran Adamanlios Korais (d. 1833). Born in Smyrna, he had lived in Paris where he had promoted the Philhellenic cause both by raising money and by his collections and translations from the ancient authors of Hellas, including a translation of Herodotus into modern Greek. He compiled the first dictionary of that language, and remains a founding father of modern Greek culture.

The sequel to Navarino had been the Russo-Turkish War of 1828–29, which had further distracted an already crippled Turkey from reprisals on the Greeks. The British sent their Mediterranean fleet to Alexandria, the Russians advanced on Adrianople, and the French occupied the Morea. Then, in 1832, the Whig government in London, anxious to forestall the Russians, called a conference which established an independent Kingdom of Greece. The Crown of "Hellas" was offered to Leopold of Saxe-Coburg, who, after acceptance, shrewdly declined it and afterwards settled for the humdrum but wealthy monarchy of the Belgians; so another German, the boy-prince Otto of Bavaria, was installed, fortified by a substantial loan to Greece from the protecting powers. Since Otto was only eleven, there had to be a Regency, which presided over the fierce faction-fighting of the Greeks.

At first all seemed promising: in 1834 the capital was moved from the cramped little harbour of Nauplion to Athens, where in 1837 a University of Athens was founded, housed in elegant neo-classical style. But the mainly Bavarian regime found it hard to control the country, still swarming with armed bands, and although in 1835 Otto came of age, his heavy-handed bureaucrats provoked so much resentment that in 1843 a mild revolution in

[1]Church (1784–1873) had run away from his Irish-Yorkshire parents and from school to enlist in the Army, had served in the Corsican Rangers under Sir Hudson Lowe, Napoleon's gaoler, and gallantly defended Capri against Murat, then King of Naples. He had then helped to capture Zante, Cephalonia and Ithaca, and in 1809 formed a regiment of Suliote Greeks under their own chieftains. As a Major General in the service of the restored Bourbons, he had also put down brigands in Apulia, and was promoted Commander-in-Chief in Sicily, an appointment terminated by the rising of 1820. When the Greek war broke out he was invited back by his Suliotes and elected Generalissimo of Greece. Already knighted in England, he continued to live in Greece, where he died full of honour at a great age.

Athens toppled the government. Otto granted a Constitution, complete with upper and lower houses of Parliament, which served its turn, until in 1863 a *coup d'état* by a clique of politicians deposed him. The monarchy then made a fresh start under a Danish prince, the seventeen-year-old second son of the King of Denmark, who became George I; king this time not of "Hellas" but of "The Hellenes".

So a compromise between the Russians and the Western powers determined that Greece should not become a Russian satellite, an independent Greece was created, and the medieval Western influence, as under the French and Catalan feudatories and Venice, reasserted in nineteenth-century terms, making the new Kingdom a barrier to both Russian and Turkish power in the Balkans and the Levant. And once the Greeks had a state, the other Balkan peoples, Serbs, Bulgars, Roumanians, became all the more determined to assert themselves against all comers

V

In July 1839 a singularly perceptive traveller arrived at Travemünde *en route* for St. Petersburg by sea. The Marquis de Custine, who was going to Russia "in search of arguments against representative government . . . returned from Russia a partisan of constitutions". The German innkeeper at Travemünde had given him a preliminary warning, based on the expressions of Russians leaving their country and going back; the former were "like horses turned out to pasture"; those returning had a "worried look".[1] And this was natural, for the Russia of Nicholas I had become a police state. The early liberal tendencies of Alexander I had evaporated well before his death from malaria in the Crimea in 1825, and he had been succeeded by his much younger brother Nicholas I (1825–55), a far more formidable man. He had immense and sombre personal dignity, as displayed during the cholera epidemic in St. Petersburg in 1831 when a frantic mob were attacking the hospitals. He drove slowly into the midst of them and then ordered them to their knees. "Come nearer," he said, "I am afraid of no one. Cross yourselves and ask pardon from God." The kneeling crowd obeyed him. Nicholas had also given the order to fire cannon when a palace revolution, designed to replace him by his brother the Archduke Constantine, had been quelled. The ringleaders of this *Decembrist* coup had been hanged and others exiled to Siberia.

After this grim start, Nicholas I had to deal with the repercussions of the July Revolution of 1830 which had reached Russian Poland, now a separate Kingdom under the Tsar. That November the Poles in Warsaw assassinated a Russian general whom they mistook for the Archduke Constantine, who had escaped from the city. A Polish Diet, deluded by hopes of French backing, then formally deposed the Tsar. Nicholas ordered his armies to move in and

---

[1]Marquis de Custine. *La Russie en 1839*. Ed. P. P. Kohler as *Journey for our Time*. London, 1953. This famous account is comparable on its level to Alexis de Tocqueville's classic *De la Démocratie en Amérique*.

by 1832 he had crushed the insurrection, abolished the Diet, and closed the University of Warsaw. Russian institutions and education were imposed and the Catholic clergy persecuted. In the year of the Reform Bill in England even the nationalistic poems of Mickiewicz[1] were banned and a censorship clamped down. Many highly articulate Poles fled and remained abroad; among them Chopin, who having won brilliant success in Warsaw in 1830, had already left for Vienna; but who now, instead of returning to Poland, settled in Paris.

The Polish rising had brought the King of Prussia, the Emperor of Austria and the Tsar together in a common interest to put it down, and Nicholas, who inherited Alexander I's great position abroad, now became the principal pillar of military autocracy in Eastern and, indeed, Central Europe. The Holy Alliance had long broken down when the British had opposed Russian intervention in South America, and President Monroe had declared his Doctrine that the Americans should be free of outside imperialism; now Russian influence became more active in Central Europe, while the full force of a police state and censorship was deployed in Russia itself. Thus the Revolution of 1848-9 had brought down the weight of Russian military might on Hungary, and it had been in part under Russian pressure that Frederick William IV had refused the Crown of a Liberal German *Reich*.

When Custine visited St. Petersburg, Nicholas I had fully established his despotic power, and the visitor was impressed by the Tsar's appearance in the Imperial box at the opera. "When he approched the front of his loge accompanied by the Tsarina, and followed by their family and court, the entire audience rose. The Tsar, in dress uniform of bright red, was particularly handsome ... it enhanced both the nobility of his features and his height." In an intimate talk with Custine, he declared that despotism was "in keeping with the character of the nation, that distances were the scourge of Russia, and that he considered constitutional monarchy degrading".[2]

This sombre regime of repression and censorship did not prevent the first brilliant efflorescence of Russian literature. Alexsandr Sergeivich Pushkin (1799-1837) was the greatest genius.[3] He was the greatest Russian poet and

---

[1]Adam Mickiewicz (1798-1858) had early won fame by poems published in 1822 and 1823, and been deported to Russia for his nationalism, where he had plotted with the *Decembrists*. In 1826 he wrote his *Crimean Sonnets* and made friends with Pushkin. By 1829 he had managed to get to Rome, whence he moved to Dresden and Paris, where he wrote *The Books of the Polish Nation and of its Pilgrimage* (1832), and *Pan Tadeusz* (1834). He became Professor of Slavonic Literature at the *Collège de France*, and died in Constantinople during the Crimean War. His nationalist ideas are Mazzinian and romantic; he was the greatest of modern Polish poets in his own right, both in lyric and epic poetry.

[2]Custine. *op. cit.* pp. 93-94. For a vivid description of St. Petersburg see pp. 48-64, and of Moscow pp. 103, 185-215.

[3]He was born in Moscow of an aristocratic boyar family, and had Abyssinian descent through his mother, grand-daughter of Abram Hannibal, Peter the Great's *protégé*. He was brought up to French literature and also to the folk tales of the Russian peasantry, and in 1817 became a diplomat in the Russian Foreign Office. In 1820 he published an epic, *Ruslan and Ludmila*—about Kievan Russia. He also became involved in Liberal politics, and in 1820 was exiled to Ekaterinoslav, whence he visited the northern Caucasus and Odessa. His Byronic *The Prisoner of the Caucasus* reflects his exile. In 1823 Pushkin began *Eugene Onegin*, which he finished only in 1831, a panoramic novel

playwright and writer of short stories, most famous for his poetic drama *Boris Godunóv* and his romantic verse novel *Eugene Onegin*. He had a Shakespearean sympathy for the predicaments of his characters and wrote superb love lyrics with an undertone of melancholy. Pushkin more than anyone else was the creator of the literary language of Russia, in verse and prose, and his work has become world famous. Lermontov (1814–41) had an even shorter life, and like Pushkin, he was killed in a senseless duel; not before he had created that typical Russian character, the introspective and futile Pechorin *in A Hero of our Time*, and written poems expressing *taedium vitae*. "Life," he wrote, "if you look around attentively and dispassionately, is such an empty and stupid joke."

Thus the Romantic movement produced not so much imitators as a distinctly Russian reaction among a few brilliant writers who combined foreign horizons with a feel for the folk tales and the ironic resignation and apathy of the illiterate peasants who formed the vast majority of the population.

By the mid-century, too, the Russian novel appears in full maturity in Gogol's *Dead Souls*, who depicted Russian characters with a Dickensian eye, and showed up the inept pomposity of officials in *The Inspector General*. But the greatest days of the Russian novel belong to the latter part of the century.

The greatest Russian composers also flourished in the middle and late nineteenth century, but Mikhail Glinka (1804–57) belongs to the romantic age. The son of a landowner near Smolensk, he entered the bureaucracy but, invalided out, he went to Italy, where the operas of Bellini and Donizetti were then being acclaimed. He also studied in Berlin and, returning to Russia, became its first nationalist composer with his opera *A Life for the Tsar* (1836) on the theme of the Polish invasion of the early seventeenth century. He also set Pushkin's *Ruslan and Ludmila* to music. Glinka applied Western technique to Russian folk songs and to Polish dances, and used Asian melodies from the steppe; he was the first Russian to draw on the native musical resources of the country, and the forerunner of the most characteristically Russian composers.

VI

The Romantic Age or Age of Revolution was still cosmopolitan and European. The nobility and the upper *bourgeoisie* were still in control, and the majority of the population, even in the West, were still illiterate. The world of the

in verse written about St. Petersburg and Moscow. In 1824 he was relegated to his mother's estate near Pskov, in the north-west, at the request of the governor of Odessa. Here, just before the *Decembrist* rising, he wrote *Boris Godunóv* (1824–5). It is a quasi-Shakespearean tragedy based on chronicles. Nicholas I recalled Pushkin to St. Petersburg and, when he complained of the censorship, offered to censor his works himself, an exacting privilege. At St. Petersburg Pushkin wrote the short story, *The Negro of Peter the Great* and the famous poem, *The Bronze Horseman* about the Tsar's statue. In 1831 he married and was given a court appointment, which he disliked, but was not allowed to resign, and he was killed in a framed-up duel by his own brother-in-law, a French émigré officer in the Guards.

mass market, the mass electorate and the popular press had not yet arrived, and "public opinion" was reflected and created by newspapers, periodicals and books with relatively small circulation. Moreover, the Industrial Revolution and its railroads took a long time to spread from Great Britain over the continent, and in the 'thirties well-to-do travellers, such as Ruskin's parents, still toured France, Switzerland and Italy in a self-sufficient travelling carriage complete with courier and postillion. Even by 1850, though the British, Prussian, and Belgian systems were well developed, there were no railroads from Paris to Dijon and Marseilles, hardly any in Italy and none in the Iberian peninsula. In Russia the only railroad was from St. Petersburg to Moscow. Though in England over twenty per cent of the population was concentrated in big industrial towns, in France and Italy only ten per cent were urbanized, and in central Europe, Poland, European Russia, Spain and Portugal, less than five per cent. The heaviest price for such "progress" would be paid by the British.

In this predominantly agricultural Europe, with travel not much swifter than in late Roman times, a leisured public formed an eager audience for music, the most cosmopolitan of the arts. It was now greatly flourishing in Europe, as the superb late-eighteenth-century tradition, at its unsurpassed climax in Mozart, and developed with romantic innovations by Beethoven, was popularized mainly by central European composers, often inspired by the folk music of their peoples and the ambience of their landscape. No civilization in the world has ever produced such great music as Europe in the late eighteenth century and in the nineteenth, and European and American civilization is still largely living off the capital then created. Franz Schubert (1797–1828) lived his short life in Vienna; trained in the Royal choir school, he composed in the tradition of Haydn and Mozart and is most celebrated for his songs. Robert Schumann (1820–56) came from Zwickau in Saxony, and died in the Rhineland at Bonn. His father was a bookseller and an admirer of the English romantics; an enthusiasm which his son extended to the Germans, Hoffmann and Richter. Incongruously put to learn law, he insisted on becoming a composer and married Clara Wieck, herself a brilliant pianist. He settled in Leipzig where he founded a musical paper, but his many-sided activities ended in madness, attempted suicide and death in an asylum.

Another romantic of great spirit but sometimes over-sentimental feeling was Felix Mendelssohn (1809–47). He was born in Hamburg, the son of an affluent Jewish banker, and developed his precocious talent in Berlin. He early visited England, and after being a Director of Music at Düsseldorf, he founded the Conservatoire at Leipzig.

In France the most striking Romantic composer was Hector Berlioz (1803–69). Born near Grenoble the son of a doctor, he moved to Paris to study medicine, which he abandoned for music. He soon got to know Chopin and Liszt, Delacroix and Balzac. He is the most flamboyant and violent of all the romantic composers and demands large orchestras, much percussion and big choirs: he is the musical equivalent of Delacroix in painting. Chopin (1810–49) was a more elegant romantic, essentially a pianist of changing moods. The son of a Polish schoolmaster and French mother, he translated all the fire, panache and melancholy of his father's country into music which has retained enormous appeal.

Another great pianist, who long outlived Chopin into the mid and late 19th century, was the Hungarian Franz Liszt (1811–86). The fire and splendour of his playing and his compositions are as much Magyar as Chopin's are Polish, and he spans the age of the Esterházys who had launched Haydn and who launched him, to that of Wagner at Bayreuth. His most formative years were spent in the "Romantic" Paris of the 'thirties, among the fraternity of writers and artists of that creative time. Entirely cosmopolitan and everywhere feted, he lived in Paris, Rome and in Budapest and also travelled widely. He was the inventor of the symphonic poem, and his brilliant spirited work is still immensely popular.

Meanwhile the Italians, impervious to or excited by political upheavals, had greatly contributed to romantic music, particularly to Opera. Vincenzo Bellini (1801–35), a friend of Chopin, was a Sicilian, born in Catania, who died young in Paris after brief success. Gaetano Donizetti (1797–1848) lived and died in Bergamo; he was a prolific composer of operas whose melodies have outlasted the romantic age into less melodious times.

Gioacchino Rossini (1792–1868) was the most popular musical celebrity in his day. Born in Pesaro, where his father was town trumpeter, he was brought up to the stage by his mother in Bologna, where he particularly studied the work of Mozart. He became director of the principal theatre at Naples, where in 1816 he produced the *Barber of Seville*. A more nationalist piece, *William Tell*, brought him immense popular fame. But the greatest romantic Italian composer was Giuseppe Verdi (1813–1901); and, though he lived into the twentieth century, the events of 1830–1 when Mazzini founded *La Giovine Italia* coincided with his adolescence, and his genius remained romantic and melodramatic in the style of that time, as in the first version of *Macbeth* written in 1847 on the eve of the year of Revolutions. Though the climax of his achievement belongs to the later nineteenth century, his idiom and passion are rooted in the 'thirties, and one of his greatest compositions, the Manzoni *Requiem* was composed for the nationalist author of the *I Promessi Sposi*. Quintessentially Italian, Verdi was a powerful prophet of the *Risorgimento*, as well as a genius of cosmopolitan range.

XLIII

Cultural Climax and Political Disruption

The second half of the nineteenth century saw a cultural climax but mounting political disruption of Western European civilization; it was a superbly creative time in which modern science fully came into its own, and, following the epoch-making work of Darwin, placed mankind in a new biological and environmental context; in literature, music and the arts it was as creative as the Romantic Age, and following the far-flung explorations and massive settlement of Europeans in other continents, their influence and that of their descendants became briefly paramount in world history. Economic expansion was fantastic, as, after the first Industrial Revolution, rail transport and steamships had their full impact and a new Technological Revolution based on oil and electricity began to get under way. Mankind, following Western initiative, was caught up in an unprecedented rush of inventions and of great industry which was creating a world-wide, interdependent economy, and exploiting anything exploitable anywhere.

The minorities who benefited from this exploitation and their dependants enjoyed a hectic cosmopolitan prosperity which began to eclipse the relatively modest affluence of the professional and managerial classes, in their hey-day in the West during the 'fifties and 'sixties; while the rift between the skilled artisans with bourgeois objectives and the proletarian unskilled workers defused the threat of radical revolution poised in the "hungry 'forties". The condition of the urban poor remained deplorable until well into the twentieth century; but the plutocracy, the professional classes, the rentiers and the more enterprising artisans were full of confidence; currencies were stable, travel unimpeded, inheritance secure. In the West there got about a general belief in "progress".

But this mighty liberal bourgeois civilization was flawed by inherited defects. Where in the West, as in North America, liberal ideas were being adapted to the new mass civilization that applied science and technology were bringing into being, in Central and Eastern Europe archaic military regimes persisted and maintained an arbitrary power. And what was more, the idea of a Concert of Europe, or even of a Balance of Power, became eroded; the brute fact of the national sovereign state commanding conscript "peoples in arms" had ousted the relatively responsible concept of "legitimacy"; and the "right to self-determination", based on Mazzini's Utopian visions of a "sisterhood" of amicable nation states, had become a substitute for political thought. For far from being a pacific influence, the mass of the people, co-opted by extended franchise or plebiscite, proved more belligerent than the old ruling classes, who had a common interest in limiting wars or avoiding them. Incited by an increasingly "popular" press, the peoples even urged governments to war. Add to this the waning of the influence of the old idea of Christian Europe, having its roots in the Roman Empire and still strong even in medieval times, and also the rise of a perversion of Darwin's doctrine of the survival of the fittest misapplied to the competition between nation states, and the darkening of the political prospects of Europe and of the world becomes intelligible.

Such are the themes of European history predominant in the second half of the nineteenth century: the wealth, power, scientific and cultural efflorescence of a dynamic society, and, underneath the whirl and rush of its machinery, the sounds of approaching doom; faint at first, but mounting as the *Realpolitik* and competing armaments of sovereign and centralized nation states, acknowledging no superior in heaven or on earth, begin to threaten the diverse and brilliant cultural achievement of the continent. It is not for nothing that the most original and all too representative music of the age was written by Wagner, and that one of his most famous compositions was *The Twilight of the Gods*.

II

In Waterloo Place in London stands the first really hideous modern British war memorial: it commemorates the breaking of the European peace which had lasted from 1815 until 1854, when France and Great Britain fought Russia in the Crimea. There they stand, iron men in greatcoats, beards and bearskins, with bayonets fixed, before the first of the modern cenotaphs to the dead.

The civilian British who, under a succession of Whig-Liberal governments and free trade, had been piling up immense prosperity, and the French, whose relatively Liberal empire under Napoleon III had enjoyed massive economic expansion, had both gone to war with the Russia of Nicholas I. The British had long been alarmed at the prospect of the collapse of the Ottoman Empire and the expansion of Russian power into the Balkans, the Levant and Central Asia, which they considered a threat to their communications with India; while Napoleon III, an adventurer who needed the glamour of military success, was following traditional French policy in the Levant, this time by shoring up the decadent regime of the Sultan Abd-al-Majid I. The Western powers, having thwarted Russian expansion into the Balkans by helping to create independent Christian states in Serbia and in Greece, now feared Russian political and commercial expansion within Asia Minor and Persia, and, above all, a Russian threat to Constantinople and the Straits. Fortunately, the Prussians and Austrians wisely remained neutral, so that the antagonists could only get at each other in the Crimea; thus avoiding a European conflagration. In the event, although the conflict showed up the incompetence of the British High Command and the appalling organization of the British army, unchanged since Waterloo, the Russians were so badly mauled that after Alexander II (1855–81) had succeeded Nicholas I, they postponed further ambitions to the south. By the Treaty of Paris of 1856, Russia lost her monopoly of the Black Sea, conceded in 1840 by the Treaty of London, and renounced her claims on Moldavia and Wallachia and the estuary of the Danube, while Alexander II turned to deal with the urgent and overdue emancipation of the Russian serfs, begun in 1861. And since large armies had been immobilized guarding the Western frontiers and an Austrian ultimatum had forced the Russians to accept the Anglo-French terms of peace, the remnant of the Holy Alliance formed in 1814 and hitherto persisting between Prussia, Austria and Russia was further attenuated.

A hitherto unimportant buffer state, created in 1815 between France and Austria in North-Western Italy, profited by the Crimean War. Count Camillo Cavour, the Savoyard-Piedmontese architect of United Italy, had dispatched 15,000 Italians to fight on the Anglo-French side in the Crimea, and thus secured for Piedmont representation at the Peace Conference. Cavour, once described as "a cross between Sir Robert Peel and Machiavelli",[1] had been modernizing Piedmont ever since the failure of Carlo Alberto in 1848–9, developing strategic railroads and even getting Rothschild money and influence behind his projects for irrigation. Now carrying more weight in international politics, he had intrigued with Napoleon III, in return for ceding Savoy and Nice to France, to obtain military backing in a war to evict the Austrians from North Italy.

So in 1859 the second and relatively minor war of the mid-nineteenth century was decided through French intervention—the only practicable way— at the bloody battles of Magenta and Solferino. An independent Italian Kingdom under the House of Savoy came into being, extended, at first against Cavour's intention, over the south, when Garibaldi and the Thousand, sailing from Genoa in a fantastic exploit, took over first Sicily and then Naples.[2] For Cavour promptly invaded the Papal states, ostensibly to save the Pope from the republican anti-clerical Garibaldi, and compelled Garibaldi to resign Naples and Sicily to Vittorio Emmanuele II. Save for Rome, still occupied by

---

[1] Mack Smith. *op. cit.* p. 23.
[2] Wearing "the outfit which he wore for the rest of his life ... loose grey trousers of a sailor cut, a plain red shirt, no longer worn like a workman's blouse as in '49, but tucked in at the waist, and adorned with a breast pocket and watchchain, a coloured silk handkerchief knotted around his neck, and over his shoulders a great American puncio or grey cloak ... a black felt hat completed the figure." G. M. Trevelyan. *Garibaldi and the Thousand.* London, 1909. pp. 203–4.
The expedition proceeded from Genoa by two paddle steamers, the *Piedmonte* and *Lombardo*; but, having neglected to lay in adequate food and water, had to put in at Talamone on the Tuscan coast. By 11th May 1860, they made Marsala in western Sicily and, striking north-east through the high interior, defeated the Neapolitan troops at Calatafimi, then stormed Palermo by a tactical ruse. "*Questa Spedizione*", wrote one of them, "è così poetica.'

the French, and Venetia, occupied by the Austrians since Napoleon III had pulled prematurely out of the war, a United Italy had been made by the cunning realism of Cavour, more French than Italian in mind and language, and by the South-American-style republican exploit of Garibaldi and his following, mainly of ardent middle-class adolescents and older hardened adventurers.

North of the Alps, meanwhile, that other Machiavellian, Otto von Bismarck, a statesman of Churchillian eccentricity and force, was improvising the unification of north Germany under Prussia. Contrary to much received opinion, Bismarck's wars were less cold-bloodedly planned than Cavour's; he was in fact an opportunist of genius, who exploited crises as they arose. On his father's side a Junker aristocrat, he came through his mother's family from a professional and intellectual background, and in spite of his public posture as a fire-eating soldier, remained essentially a civilian diplomat and politician waiting on the tides of fate. These had carried him in 1852, by the chance of a colleague's illness, to be Prussian delegate to the Diet of the restored and Austrian-dominated German Confederation; and it had been then that, as he put it, he had "conceived the idea of withdrawing Germany from Austrian control, at least that part of Germany united by its spirit, its religion, its character and its interests to the destinies of Prussia—Northern Germany".[1] Now, in 1863, as Minister-President of Prussia, Bismarck saw his chance, when with the death of Frederik VII of Denmark, "the question of Schleswig and Holstein was opened; and Bismarck stumbled, without knowing it, through the door that led to victory."[2] Hence the third decisive European war of the mid-century which led to the Prussianizing of Germany north of the Main and to the fateful Franco-Prussian War of 1870–71.

The Schleswig-Holstein question is one of daunting and tedious complexity; in essentials, it provoked a clash between German and Danish nationalism through the breakdown on the death of Frederik VII (1848–63) of a peculiar dynastic arrangement, supposedly guaranteed under the Treaty of London of 1852 by Great Britain, France and Russia, none of whom could now intervene.[3]

For the new King of Denmark, Kristian IX (1863–1906) had incorporated Schleswig into the Danish state; but since he had inherited his crown by female descent, his cousin Frederik of Augustenburg, insisting that under the ancient Salic Law of the Franks the King could not inherit the Duchies, had claimed them himself. He had thus won the ardent support of the nationalists of the German Confederation; but Bismarck, who had his eye on Kiel and the Duchies for Prussia, out-trumped their hand by bringing in Austria, ostensibly to prevent a violation of the Treaty of London, since technically Kristian IX

[1]A. J. P. Taylor. *Bismarck. The Man and the Statesman.* London, 1955. p. 34.
[2]Taylor. *op. cit.* p. 69.
[3]Holstein was almost entirely German and a member of the German Confederation; Schleswig, north of it, predominantly Danish. Both had rebelled against Denmark in 1848, although by the Treaty of London the ancient personal union with the Kings of Denmark had been affirmed. The Prince of Wales had just married Princess Alexandra of Denmark—the "Sea-King's daughter from over the sea"—but the British could not get at the Prussian land power; Napoleon III was preoccupied with his disastrous adventure in Mexico, and the Russians with again crushing the Poles after their rising in 1863.

had exceeded his rights. In February 1864, Prussian and Austrian armies acting for the German Confederation occupied Holstein and Schleswig and crossed the Danish frontier; but although an armistice was arranged, the Danes, who detested all Germans, refused to abandon their claims on the Duchies. Whereupon war broke out again, until in August 1864 the Danes were forced to surrender both Duchies to Austria and Prussia jointly.

Possession was nine-tenths of the law; but the victors soon fell out. Moreover—a far more serious rift—the Prussians refused to admit Austria to the Confederate *Zollverein*, due for renewal in 1865. Despite the Treaty of Gastein of August 1865, which amicably divided the administration of the Duchies, Bismarck now made an alliance with the Italians, who promised to attack Austrian Venetia if the Prussians attacked Austria within three months; by mid-June 1866, the Prussian armies, concentrated by strategic railroads, had advanced into Bohemia, and on 3rd July, armed with "needle guns" (rifle-barrelled breech-loaders which could be fired lying down), they had routed the Austrians at Königgrätz (Sadova).

After the war had been concluded by the Peace of Prague, Prussia was supreme in north Germany, and took over Schleswig as well as Holstein, while Austria had to renounce all political claims over predominantly Catholic south Germany, and surrender Venetia to the Italians.

The main losers in this game had been the French. Bismarck had upset the balance of power in Central Europe by undermining Austria. It was not only Austria that had been diminished: France was no longer the strongest power on the continent.

The Prussians now organized a new North German Federation whose armies were controlled by the Prussian King, with a federal council of princes, their decisions nominally subject to a federal parliament elected by universal suffrage. Bismarck became Federal Chancellor, and in this capacity even more powerful than as Minister–President of Prussia.

The main power in Germany was now in the North, the Southern German princes were still autonomous but unimportant; and politically and economically Austria now faced east towards the Danubian lands and the Balkans. Bismarck was apparently content; "we have done enough", he said, "for our generation."[1]

In 1867 the Austrian Empire, excluded from North Germany and Italy, was reorganized as a Dual Monarchy of Austria-Hungary, at once *Kaiserlich* and *Königlich*; while Bismarck set himself to consolidate and modernize north Germany, where the Industrial Revolution was now in full swing in the Ruhr and where oceanic as well as Baltic commerce was booming from Hamburg. Economic supremacy in Europe was already Germany's for the taking.

[1]He settled down to enjoy the estate at Varzin in Pomerania which he had bought with the large capital sum voted to him by the Prussian Parliament after the victorious war, and to realize his proclaimed intention of drinking 5000 bottles of champagne in the course of his life—this apart from other wines, beer, brandy and cigars, of which he would smoke a dozen a day. He also lived up to his good German remark, "The essential thing is to eat well." "He lived at Varzin a patriarchal life, patronizing his peasants and even occasionally beating them." Taylor. *op. cit.* p. 113.

After the excitements of the Austro-Prussian War, however, the South German states were restive over their military commitments to Prussia, and the Liberals in the Federal Parliament, reluctant to continue to finance the Federal army, had provided for it only until 1871. So a new stimulus was needed. In July 1870 it was discovered. A crisis arose over the monarchy in Spain, where Queen Isabella's deplorable reign had ended in her abdication and exile; and where Bismarck, to offset a threat of Franco-Austrian alliance, had put forward Prince Leopold of Hohenzollern as a Liberal Catholic candidate for the Spanish throne. He could not have done anything better calculated to set off an hysterical reaction in France; here was a threat of "encirclement" from the South.

The French government, anxious to retrieve its waning prestige, made the most of the crisis, confident that the rest of Germany would not support a purely dynastic Hohenzollern venture; and Leopold himself wished to evade a commitment of which William I of Prussia disapproved. So Leopold withdrew his candidacy, and the French won a "diplomatic" victory. They then overplayed their hand. Napoleon III, determined to "humiliate" Prussia, demanded that under threat of war William I "apologize" for Leopold's candidature and promise that it would never be renewed. To these demands, presented at Ems, the King civilly reiterated that the candidature had been withdrawn and implied that the incident was closed. Not so Bismarck. Determined not to let the French off the hook, he edited the telegram sent him by the King from Ems and so described the transaction that the King appeared to have been "insulted" by the French, who, in their madness, declared war.

If Bismarck had not deliberately planned the war, he had pounced on the opportunity to provoke it, and it served its turn to create a Prussianized *German Reich*. It also led indirectly to the catastrophes of the twentieth century.

Contrary to the best military opinion, which expected the French to be in Berlin within three months, the Germans, with greater manpower better mobilized and armed with new steel breech-loading Krupp artillery, outflanked and rounded up the French; within weeks the Emperor Napoleon III and 80,000 men had surrendered at Sedan, and Bazaine, with the other French army, was besieged at Metz. In January 1871, in the Hall of Mirrors at Versailles, William I of Prussia was proclaimed Emperor of a second German *Reich*. The German liberals and the South German Kings and Princes had been swept into a united Germany by the victorious war and would be kept there.

With the defeat of its armies, the French Second Empire collapsed; on 4th September 1870 a radical Republican government of "National Defence" was established in Paris. It held out in a bitter winter against the German siege until 26th January 1871, when the starving city surrendered.[1]

In February a National Assembly, elected to make peace, met at Bordeaux

---

[1] Not before Gambetta had escaped in a balloon to improvise a gallant but ineffective resistance on the Loire.

and appointed the veteran Thiers head of a provisional government. But when they submitted to the loss of Alsace and Lorraine and agreed to pay an indemnity, the radical Parisian government which controlled the city's National Guard repudiated the decision. They set up a *Commune* in the fashion of 1793 and defied the provisional government, now established at Versailles.

Civil war followed national defeat, as the Parisian *fédérés* of the National Guard and the half starved proletariat were put down, after mutual atrocities and reprisals, by regular troops to the tune of 17,000 casualties. The last attempts of the Parisian radicals to impose their will on France, where the majority supported a socially conservative, if republican, regime, had been crushed.

By the Treaty of Frankfurt (May 1871) the Germans left the French to it: they annexed the French speaking provinces of Alsace and Lorraine, the cities of Metz and Strasbourg, and imposed a moderate indemnity. They had defeated the supposedly greatest military state in the West.

Such was the succession of wars that in two decades shattered the hard-won peace achieved by the Congress of Vienna, and destroyed the remnant of the Concert of Europe and even of the Balance of Power. They had launched a United Italy, with its capital, after 1870, in Rome; and, after the defeat first of Austria and then of France, left a Prussianized German *Reich* far the strongest military and economic power on the continent.

III

After the resounding proclamation of the second German *Reich*, Bismarck, now a Prince, Imperial Chancellor and still Minister-President of Prussia, considered Germany a satiated power. The Empire had been offered to a reluctant William I by the German princes—Bavaria, Saxony, Württemberg, Baden, Hesse—who had been bribed and persuaded to join it, and the frontiers of the *Reich* had been fixed at the borders of Austria and Hungary.

Bismarck, who had to manage a clumsy kind of government with National Liberal support in the *Reichstag*, now modernized and centralized the *Reich*. A common currency was established, and a common code of civil and commercial law with a High Court of Justice at Leipzig. The standards of the efficient Prussian bureaucracy were gradually imposed on all Germany, and, following the rise of the more radical Social Democratic party, Bismarck took the wind out of their sails by creating the foundation of the first Welfare State—long before the Liberals in England set about doing so before the 1914–18 war. Contributory pensions and insurance against sickness and old age were invented, and while other countries allowed the Industrial Revolution to wreak havoc in mushroom industrial towns, the Germans became enthusiasts for town planning. The administrators could count on the docility of a people who would accept that so much was *verboten*. This stability was agreeable to the increasingly wealthy and powerful industrialists and commercial magnates, and, contrary to deep-rooted anti-semitic traditions, Jews, if they were rich enough, were now tolerated.

The Universities, already long the sponsors of massive and thorough scholarship, produced the best, if not often the most readable research in Europe, and their variety and cheapness encouraged a vigorous student life, while German elementary and secondary education was considered a model of methodical efficiency. It had already produced the N.C.O.s and railway clerks who had handled the conscript armies with such effect in the Franco-Prussian war.

The Catholics in the South and the Rhineland had indeed put up a *Kulturkampf* against the Lutheran North, fought out mainly over the schools; but Bismarck's political tactics overcame even these wily and powerful enemies. Yet there was one essential aspect of the German Empire that remained strongly traditional. The army's prestige was such that it retained all the arrogance of the old Prussian traditions and was fawned on by a populace who were still *siegesgetrunken* ("drunk with victory"). Moreover in 1878 Bismarck even broke with the National Liberals by imposing permanent direct taxes on the *Reich* to finance the army without the periodical consent of the *Reichstag*, so that the fundamental principle of civilian control over the payment of the armed forces was set aside. And when in 1878 a misguided assassin tried to kill the venerable William I, Bismarck used the opportunity to dissolve the *Reichstag* and discredit both the Social Democrats and the Liberals. By 1879, in violation of Liberal free trade, he even introduced protection for agriculture and for great industry. Thus the immense expansion and prosperity of the *Reich*, originally founded on free trade, continued by leaps and bounds even through recession. Between 1871 and 1914 the population increased from 41 million to over 65 million, the production of wheat and cereal crops doubled, the output of coal increased eight times and the production of steel from a third of a million to fourteen million tons.[1] German shipping companies out of Hamburg and Bremen were now competing with the British, and German chemical and electrical industries surpassing them. The Germans were already looking out for colonies, and under pressure of public opinion, Bismarck, otherwise extremely cautious, helped to set off the European "scramble" for tropical Africa in the 'eighties.

In Europe German policy remained very wary; as it had to be, considering the virulent and lasting hatred the loss of Alsace and Lorraine had roused among the French, the difficulty of remaining on good terms with both Austria-Hungary and the Russians, and the growing reluctance of Great Britain towards continental alliances. Since Germany wanted time to consolidate herself and her gains, her interest was to maintain peace.

Then in 1875 the Russians went to war once more with Turkey over the Turkish treatment of the Balkan Slavs. The Bulgars in the Sanjak of Philipopolis, who had joined a revolt of Bosnia and Herzegovina against the Turks, had been massacred by Circassian and Tatar *bashi bazouks* by order of the Sultan; fifteen thousand had been destroyed. The news roused Gladstone

[1]Woodward, *op. cit.* p. 126.

to violent denunciations, and the Bulgars became, incongruously, the heroes of Liberal England. They also gave the Russians an excuse to renew their war on Turkey, get within striking distance of Constantinople, and by the Treaty of San Stephano to force the Turks to recognize a satellite kingdom of Bulgaria under the twenty-two-year-old Prince Alexander of Battenberg (briskly expelled by the Bulgars in 1886).

The British, determined to uphold Turkey, threatened to renew the Crimean War; so Bismarck in 1878 convened the Congress of Berlin, acting, as he claimed, in collaboration with Disraeli, as an "honest broker". The Russians had to back down, and the satellite Bulgaria was diminished, though Bosnia and Herzegovina were assigned to be administered by Austria–Hungary. Bismarck then entered into a defensive alliance against Russia with Austria–Hungary, with the aim of detaching the Dual Monarchy from the Western Powers; a policy that would lead to disaster in 1914, since it involved Germany in the perennially unstable fortunes of the Austro–Hungarian monarchy in the Balkans, and diminished the small stock of goodwill still remaining at St. Petersburg from Prussian friendly neutrality during the Crimean War. No one, not even Bismarck, could long maintain peace in Europe, given the barbaric relationships of the Great Powers, now worsened by colonial rivalries; and when William II became Emperor of Germany and in 1890 discarded Bismarck, within a quarter of a century the momentum of competing powers had led to the First World War.

IV

In 1870 the Germans had invaded France with 1,200,000 conscripts, twice the number Napoleon had taken into Russia, and far the largest force hitherto mobilized in the history of Europe. Conscription had now become the rule among all the great Powers; only the British, who held aloof from continental alliances, maintained a small professional army and a large army in India recruited from the more martial peoples of the sub-continent.

During the 'fifties and 'sixties Great Britain, still the predominant naval power, had attained a peak of prosperity, while the Royal Navy policed and charted the oceans and protected by skill and bluff the most far-flung empire in the world. Steam having superseded sail, oceanic trade vastly increased, while communications were fantastically speeded up by the electric telegraph and the cable. Massive cosmopolitan free trade added to the prosperity of north-western Europe, while heavy industry developed in north-eastern France, in Belgium and the northern Rhineland, on a scale comparable to and sometimes surpassing that in Great Britain.

The British unwritten constitution proved well adapted to social and political change, and when the Conservatives came back to office in 1867, they extended the franchise of 1832 to household suffrage, thus nearly doubling the electorate from just over one million to nearly two. Then in 1868–74

Gladstone's first Liberal government came to power and modernized most administrative aspects of British public life.

Meanwhile, during the 'fifties and 'sixties British scientists transformed the accepted view of Man's place in Nature. Charles Robert Darwin (1809–82) was the son of a Shrewsbury doctor and grandson of Erasmus Darwin, doctor, philosopher and poet, author of *Loves of the Plants* (1789); his maternal grandfather was Josiah Wedgwood, the potter. Darwin casually attended Shrewsbury School where he found the classical curriculum irrelevant; then, after briefly studying medicine at Edinburgh, went up to Christ's College, Cambridge, intending to take Holy Orders. Here his main interests were social, shooting in the fenland and riding at Newmarket; but Professor Henslow, the botanist, interested him in science and procured his appointment as a naturalist to *HMS Beagle*. In 1839 Darwin married his cousin, Emma Wedgwood, and three years later settled at Downe near Westerham, in Kent. Here, on an independent income, he lived in secluded routine, suffering from an undefined illness probably contracted on his travels, but constantly at work. And when in 1858 the naturalist A. R. Wallace sent him a paper from Malaya, setting out a theory of evolution similar to his own sketched in 1844, he arranged for both papers to be read at the Linnaean Society. So stimulated, he enlarged his own paper into the *Origin of Species*.

Enriched, like von Humboldt, whose writings had inspired him, by world travel to South America, Australia and South Africa (1831–6) and disciplined by long research, in 1859 Darwin published his epoch-making *Origin of the Species*. The idea of evolution, already misleadingly defined by J. B. Lamarck (1744–1829), a French pupil of Buffon, was now given empirical backing, for Darwin proved that all species, including mankind, had evolved through the interplay of heredity and environment over millions of years. Mankind was no "special and recent creation" distinct from the other animals, but had evolved through "natural selection" like other manifestations of life. This theory challenged the Judaeo–Christian orthodoxy then prevalent, and Darwin was misrepresented as believing that mankind was descended from apes; but in 1871 he followed up the *Origin* by the *Descent of Man*, thus further undermining traditional mythology.

Darwin had altered the entire climate of opinion throughout the educated world, and although Mendel and de Vries have since further investigated the process of "natural selection," in essentials his work has not been superseded. Thus Great Britain, which had produced William of Ockham, Bacon, Newton, Hume and Bentham, now produced a biologist who in his own modest words, by his "love of science, patience in reflecting over any subject, industry in observing and collecting facts, and a fair share of invention as well as common sense" transformed the outlook of modern mankind.

In 1846–50, another young biologist, Thomas Henry Huxley, had voyaged in *HMS Rattlesnake* to Australia. With his own way to make and a greater appetite for public controversy than Darwin, Huxley championed the theory of evolution, and coined the term "agnostic" for those who had "lost their faith". He was a master of lucid prose and eloquence, a "scientific humanist"; who roundly declared that Science was "organized common sense".

In support of Darwin and Huxley, evidence had long been coming in from French, British and German archaeologists to prove the immense antiquity of Man, and relegate the Biblical Creation Story to the sphere of Myth; an intellectual revolution comparable to that created by Copernicus, Kepler and Galileo pervaded educated Europe, and made the mid-and late-nineteenth century quite different from any previous age.

The most representative and influential English political theorist was John Stuart Mill, whose *Essay on Liberty*, appearing in 1859, the same year as the *Origin*, stressed the vital importance of creative minorities for civilization, championed the emancipation of women, and warned against the tyranny of mass public opinion. His arguments for a pluralistic society within a flexible and constitutional rule of law are still highly relevant.

With the waning of clerical influence, an eager educated public made secular prophets out of the more eloquent writers. Macaulay, who glorified the Whig Revolution of 1688, became the most popular historian; Carlyle, with his Germanic cult of "heroes", lapsed Calvinist flair for denunciation and contorted rhetoric, scarified the predominant Whig-Liberal *laissez faire* optimism; Ruskin, an eloquent aesthete, attacked mid-century complacency with extraordinary effect, while Matthew Arnold in *Culture and Anarchy* (1865) made a memorable onslaught on the mid-Victorian "barbarian" aristocracy and the "Philistine" middle class. Trollope, in *Barchester Towers* (1857), wrote much more amiable satire, extended in many other works to politics.

V

The power of Louis Napoleon had rested on the army, on the police and upon an unobtrusive but effective control of the press; the regime had been supported by the peasants, the propertied classes and the clergy, so that the republican opposition in the towns had been contained. Moreover the contrived glitter of a Court modelled on that of the First Empire gave the Second one style and glamour. Napoleon III's dubious foreign policies, undertaken mainly to conciliate the army, had obtained Savoy and Nice for France, but having connived at the destruction of Austrian power in Germany and upset what was left of a balance of power in Central Europe, in due course he had to face a Prussianized Germany alone. Beside that cardinal error, his adventure in Mexico was a relatively minor mistake. By 1863 Napoleon III had so far "liberalized" the Empire that he had allowed a free press, legalized trade unions and by 1869 had in effect conceded a form of parliamentary government with ministers chosen from the shifting cliques of French politics, who managed to obtain a majority among the deputies of the *Corps Législatif*.

But the main strength of the Empire had been in the surge of capitalist economic enterprise, industrial, commercial and speculative, that it encouraged. As iron and steel works, mines and factories developed, more of the people became urban; though in contrast to England, France did not ruin its tenacious peasantry. Railroads were extensively developed and much of the ancient Paris of cobbled streets and twisting alleys, so well suited to barricades, swept away by the broad boulevards and open squares designed by Haussmann, while the white glare of gas light, so characteristic of the Second Empire, made for safety as well as entertainment. Paris remained the cosmopolitan centre of European luxury and fashion, and it was only military defeat that led to the regime's collapse.

The protean and redoubtable Victor Hugo (1802–85) had won immense fame in France; of Lorrainian and Breton origin, he wrote the melodrama *Hernani* which occasioned memorable riots against the government in 1830, and, in the following year, he wrote *Notre Dame de Paris* about medieval life; forced in 1851 by Louis Napoleon to take refuge in Brussels, then in Jersey, in 1862 he publicized *Les Misérables*, an epic of the Parisian poor. He poured out poetry and drama, not least *La Légende des Siècles*, *La Fin de Satan*, and, simply and comprehensively, *Dieu*; he lived to a great age and was interred in the Panthéon. In contrast to this overwhelming romantic, a realistic movement set in, of which Flaubert (1821–80) became the most famous exemplar: his *Madame Bovary* (1857) anatomized with hatred Norman provincial life, while in *Salammbo* he escaped into alembicated Carthaginian antiquity. Alfred de Vigny (1797–1863) remains a moving romantic poet when he evokes the countryside; but the younger poets now turned to more meticulous techniques and all-too-urban introspection; as in Baudelaire's *Les Fleurs du Mal* (1857), contemporary in publication with Trollope's *Barchester Towers*.

Such are only the outstanding writers of a creative epoch, distinguished even more by scientific discovery. The French, with their anti-clerical tradition, took less time than the English, swaddled by the Anglican Church, to accept the *Positivism* which new knowledge seemed to demand. Auguste Comte, a disciple of Saint-Simon, tried to create a new "scientific", "Positivist", religion, complete with secular saints and calendar; but the construction failed to take on. Much more usefully, Louis Pasteur (1822–95), the micro-biologist, the son of a tanner in the Jura, and a pupil at the *Ecole Normale Supérieure*, discovered that putrefaction was caused by pathogenic micro-organisms in the air, and could be controlled by the right amount of heat: he vastly improved French brewing and viticulture, controlled anthrax in cattle, and saved the French silkworm industry. He is commemorated by the *Institut Pasteur* (1888).

In Germany the creation of the Second *Reich* did not prevent formidable achievements in science and culture—memorably original in Wagner's music. Even more pervasive and powerful than Wagner's creations, another German emanation influenced political theory and practice. In 1848 Karl Marx and Friedrich Engels launched the *Communist Manifesto*, followed up in 1859 by Marx's *A Contribution to the Critique of Political Economy*, and in 1867 by his *Das Kapital*, rounded off in 1878 by Engels' *Anti-Dühring*. Karl Heinrich Marx (1818–83) was the son of a Jewish lawyer, who had, fortunately for his son's impact on political warfare, abandoned Judaism and changed his name from Levi; his mother was an Hungarian Jewess. After studying at Bonn and Berlin, he joined the *Rheinische Zeitung*, of which in 1842 he became the editor. In 1843 he married Jenny von Westphalen and next year moved out of Prussian territory to Paris, where he met Engels. In 1848 he returned to Cologne, expecting the Revolution to succeed in Germany; but he soon took refuge again in Paris and by 1849 in England, where, rescued from penury by Engels, he spent the rest of his dedicated and laborious life. He died in the same year as Wagner.[1] His colleague, Friedrich Engels (1820–95), was the son of a north Rhineland capitalist with a branch of his cotton-spinning business in Manchester, where, horrified at the condition of the local operatives, Friedrich wrote *The Condition of the Working Class in England in 1845*. After the failure of the 1848 revolution in Germany, he settled in Manchester, until in 1869 he sold out his interest in the business and concentrated on revolutionary writing in collaboration with Marx. It was solely due to his industry that the two posthumous volumes of Marx's *Das Kapital* ever appeared.[2]

The mid-nineteenth-century works of Marx and Engels are typical of their age, when vast total explanations were expected, and writers on politics and society attempted to provide them. Engels declared that Marx had "discovered" the "laws of motion", of "history as the evolution of humanity", and that "just as Darwin had discovered the laws of evolution in organic nature, so Marx discovered the law of evolution in human history."

Heirs to the eighteenth-century "enlightenment", Marx and Engels believed in "Progress", and, influenced by Hegel, discerned a "dialectic" in history whereby successive stages of civilization superseded one another; but when Hegel thought in terms of states, Marx thought in terms of classes. Having thus "turned Hegel the right way up", he saw history as determined by successive stages of production according to economic "laws" adapted from the classical English economists, and regarded successive stages of culture as projections or "ideologies" conditioned by the ownership of the means of production. As the *bürgerlich* stage had superseded the feudal, so, inevitably, *bürgerlich* capitalism produced its own "grave diggers" in the *proletariat*, who, driven to revolution by poverty and led by a class conscious élite, would make the revolutionary leap through dictatorship into the classless society created when the means of production were owned by the mass of the people.

This programme, presented as inevitable because following "scientifically" ascertained "laws" of history, was to lead through a politically improbable withering away of the dictatorship of the revolution to the kind of fraternal Utopia envisaged by the Socialists of the Romantic age, but with a new mid-nineteenth-century "scientific" sanction. At a time when the waning of Christian beliefs had left people looking to secular prophets, Marx's gospel, which revived in secular form the prophetic Hebraic belief in the just vindication of an oppressed but chosen people, this time the proletariat, had powerful appeal. Directed originally at the Germans, it naturally found its most ardent disciples among Russian intellectuals, avid for Western ideas, who

[1]See Isaiah Berlin. *Karl Marx, his Life and Environment*. Oxford, 1948, still the best introduction, and F. Mehring. *Karl Marx*, trans. E. Fitzgerald. London, 1936.
[2]See G. Meyer. *A Life of Engels*. Trans. Gilbert and Helen Highet. Ed. R. H. S. Crossman. London, 1936. A more worldly and genial character than Marx, he proved an excellent and uncompetitive collaborator.

used this tremendous myth of political warfare in due course for its stated purpose—to change the world.

In orthodox historical scholarship the Germans were now acknowledged masters. Leopold von Ranke (1795–1886) inherited the range and Olympian confidence of Goethe. Of Thuringian Lutheran origin, and appointed a professor at Berlin in 1865, he set new standards of research on sources, determined to find out "what actually happened." Having escaped the influence of Hegel, he took a calmer view of the past, but also tackled gigantic subjects, as the History of the Latin and Teutonic Nations, or The Roman Papacy; Church and State. His main interest being the rise of the modern state, he wrote the histories of Prussia, France and England, mainly in the sixteenth and seventeenth centuries, and finally embarked upon an unfinished World History, in fact confined to medieval Europe. Such was his flair for essentials and power of research, design and narrative, that this masterly Christian Humanist became the greatest historian of his day. He makes even the brilliant Macaulay look provincial.

Another German scholar, Theodore Mommsen (1817–1903), shows a comparable range. Born in Schleswig and educated at Kiel, he early travelled in Italy, and after the publication of his History of Rome (1854–56) became Professor of Roman History at Berlin. Although he was a Liberal, he excessively admired Julius Caesar; but he had a flair, based on profound research, for bringing the past to life. Like von Ranke, he had range; and he combined social and legal grasp with detailed classical scholarship.

Another great German achievement was musical. Richard Wagner (1813–83) created new forms of music-drama while flooding melodies brought the romantic impulse expressed by the later Beethoven to a colossal climax. As conductor at Dresden, he wrote Tannhäuser and Lohengrin; but, sought by the police for taking part in the revolutions of 1848, he fled to Switzerland, where he began the immense Der Ring des Nibelungen. In 1859, that memorable year, again back in Germany, he composed Tristan und Isolde. He was then rescued from penury and frustration by the eighteen-year-old Ludwig II of Bavaria, who invited him to Munich and enabled him to complete the Meistersinger in 1867. The King also financed the Wagner Festival Theatre at Bayreuth, before he became insane and was drowned. In 1881 Wagner composed Parsifal and two years later died in Venice.

Whatever reservations lovers of Monteverdi, Vivaldi, Haydn and Mozart have about Wagner's music-drama, his sheer creative power was overwhelming; he was certainly the most appropriate composer for the German dominated Europe of his maturity.

VI

Early in 1855 Alexander II became Tsar of Russia during the Crimean War. The Russians had long been in a dilemma; whether to come to terms with the moribund but tenacious Ottoman empire and shore it up, or to attempt the risks and responsibilities of taking over Constantinople. The conquest and exploitation of the steppes and the coasts of the Black Sea had made the control of the straits much more important, since, by the mid-century, the massive grain trade from South Russia had become a more vital interest. As for the British, their trade with Turkey was now more lucrative than that with Russia.

Alexander had been negotiating for peace even before the siege of Sebastopol, which, counting the losses of the relieving army, cost the Russians over a quarter of a million men; and by March 1856, against the will of the British, a peace was patched up. The Black Sea was declared to be neutral, and not even Russian warships or naval bases were allowed there. The whole navigation of the Danube down to the sea was placed under a commission appointed by the Great Powers, and the Russians relinquished the section of Bessarabia between the Dniester and the Dvina to the Turks, who continued to hold Moldavia and Wallachia, merged in 1866 by intervention of the major powers in the new Kingdom of Roumania, under Prince Charles of Hohenzollern, brother of the Hohenzollern candidate for the throne of Spain.

The setback to Russian expansion towards the mouth of the Danube and domination of the Black Sea had been severe; but the near breakdown of the internal administration of the war had been more serious. The Western allies had moved troops by sea to the Crimea more quickly than the Russians, devoid of railroads south of Moscow, had been able to move their armies to the south, while inefficiency and corruption had surpassed even hitherto accepted standards. And although in the Baltic the allied attack had failed, the Peace Treaty exacted that the Russian forts on the strategic Åland islands between Sweden and Finland should be dismantled, and Sweden was "guaranteed" by the allies against Russian aggression.

Having accepted a highly disadvantageous peace, Alexander II, though by conviction conservative, turned perforce to radical change inside Russia. It had long been apparent that serfdom was a dead weight on the social and economic life of the country, and in March 1861 the Tsar began a social and administrative revolution by emancipating the gentry-owned serfs. "The emancipation of the Serfs", writes Sumner, ". . . was the first of the great reforms under which Alexander II began the transformation of Russia into a modern state. It meant the beginning of an economic, social and psychological revolution, especially in the solid Russian regions that were the heart of serfdom."[1] Here about fifty million out of sixty million Russians were serfs; just over twenty million belonged to the landlords, just under twenty million were state peasants, and the other ten million were of varying conditions. The state peasants and those of intermediate standing were separately freed; but the gentry's serfs naturally presented a more intractable problem which took years to unravel. Though emancipated from the landowners, they were, in their own interests, left under the control of their village communities, still responsible for taxes and passports. The gentry retained about half the land concerned, which was divided up by state-appointed Arbitrators of the Peace,

[1]Sumner. *op. cit.* p. 135.

while the government paid immediate compensation to the landowners in state bonds which it was supposed to recoup over forty-nine years from the peasant communities.

Naturally these elaborate arrangements led to friction and disappointment; the value of the state bonds diminished; the peasants, though personally free, often complained that the gentry got the best land, while the power of the village elders over individuals was enhanced. Moreover with the abolition of serfdom, the old infra-structure of government itself seemed undermined. Hitherto the enormous country had somehow been kept under control by an autocrat working through the gentry: now a whole new system had to be improvised, and, among the intelligentsia, to be discussed. Hence a ferment of debate and a passion for change which might lead anywhere; to greater personal freedom, perhaps, more probably to more bureaucracy and collectivism. Herzen, the vociferous champion of liberal ideals, soon became disillusioned; the emancipation, he declared, had not been enough. There was endless discussion in the universities.[1]

Alexander II continued doggedly to modernize the administration. In 1866 he founded a State Bank and ordered the Ministry of Finance to declare public budgets; in 1863 he restored the academic freedom of the Universities, though student organizations were still forbidden. Then in the following year he established elected District and Provincial Zemstva to deal with local communications, hospitals, and schools. Trial by jury was also imported, judges made more independent and adequately paid; while the old and confused jurisdictions of the nobility and gentry were swept away. Only the censorship remained, and it remained outside the law, while the central government, of course, remained in control of the army and the police, but conscription for the army was modified, not on a basis of class, but of relative education.

These reforms, daring in Russia, did not satisfy the intelligentsia, who had uncritically assimilated a hotch potch of extremist Western ideas, and who were infuriated by the unpredictable censorship. The police remained pervasive, but underground pamphlets evaded them. The radical intellectuals felt guilt towards the peasantry, and even wanted to overturn society for their benefit, if necessary by violence; not that the peasants were grateful. Bakunin, who had been exiled to Siberia, but had managed to escape, now wrote propaganda for anarchy, objecting to the state as such. Stenka Razin and Pugachev were now written up as heroes of peasant revolt, and intellectual narodniki (men of the people) orated to mulish and suspicious peasants, who sometimes handed over the urban strangers to the police. A campaign of systematic terrorism was countered by systematic repression. Political prisoners and exiles escaped abroad and from the security of Geneva or Lausanne fulminated against the government in smuggled subversive literature: a "nihilist" shot the Chief of Police in Moscow in daylight in the street.

The government, meanwhile, promoted Russian south-eastern expansion, and despite the famous resistance of Shamil Khan, the Caucasian mountain tribes were conquered and Samarkand was annexed. But these advances in

[1] See Isaiah Berlin. Russian Thinkers. Ed. H. Hardy and A. Taylor. London, 1978.

Asia, paralleled by consolidation in Siberia, hardly offset the Russian diplomatic defeat in 1878 at the Congress of Berlin and the consequent collapse of the *Dreikaiserbund* of Prussia, Austria and Russia. Moreover the Tsar had long been in mounting personal peril. In 1866 a student had shot at him and missed; in 1873 another anarchist had got in five shots at him but somehow missed him again; now in 1880 a revolutionary workman dynamited the Imperial dining room in the Winter Palace and the Tsar was saved only because his guest, Prince Alexander of Battenberg, had the luck to be late. But the anarchists were determined to get their Tsar, who was now, in fact, working on further reforms. In the afternoon of 13th March 1881, Alexander was being driven back to the Winter Palace in St. Petersburg when a nihilist threw a bomb at his carriage, but threw wide, wounding some Cossacks of the escort. Instead of ordering the coachman to drive on at speed, the Tsar, true to his training, descended from the carriage for a word with the Cossack wounded. Whereupon, so bad was the security, a second nihilist appeared and killed the Tsar (and himself) with a better directed bomb. Such was the reward of the emancipator of the serfs.

VII

The political hopes and frustrations of the long political and social upheaval during the emancipation formed the setting of the work of the greatest novelists in Europe, as Russian genius in this field came fully into its own. Fedor Mikhailovich Dostoievsky was born in 1821 and died in 1881, the year of the assassination of Alexander II. He was a creator of the modern psychological novel, and himself lived through the sort of experiences he describes. The son of an army doctor, murdered in retirement by his own serfs, Dostoievsky was born in Moscow and entered the army as an engineer at St. Petersburg. He read widely in Western literature and in 1844 resigned his commission to write. His first book *Poor Folk* (1845) won immediate acclaim and the friendship of Belinsky and other more radical "Utopians". Imprisoned in 1849 for subversion, Dostoievsky was sentenced to death and the preliminaries of execution were even carried out before he was reprieved and sent in chains in mid-winter to hard labour in Siberia, followed by service in the ranks of the army. Returning to St. Petersburg, after an unhappy marriage, he developed epilepsy, and began to write his books, whose titles speak for themselves: *Crime and Punishment* (1866); *The Idiot* (1866) *The Devils; The Possessed;* and *The Brothers Karamazov* (1880). In 1867 he married his secretary who got him out of debt, and in his declining years they lived much at Ems in Germany with their children. Starting his career as a radical revolutionary, who at once squandered his paternal inheritance, Dostoievsky was a gambler and epileptic who touched and described the depths of degradation: he ended as a conservative mystic, convinced of Russia's "mission" to master and lead mankind. Wild and contrasting political opinions accompanied his psychological insight: like Nietzsche, he was "dynamite".

Most Western readers probably find I. S. Turgenev (1818-83) more congenial; though in Fathers and Sons he depicts the conflict between the conservative gentry and the "nihilist" and atheist intellectuals of the mid-century. With his flair for describing scenery and the subtle and sympathetic insight into the peasants and old-fashioned gentry, as in A Sportsman's Sketches, Turgenev is less obviously demanding than the frenetic Dostoievsky.

Count Leo Tolstoi (1828-1910) was the greatest novelist who has ever written, with a Shakespearean range and sympathy; he faces the questions posed by Dostoievsky, but has all and more than Turgenev's understanding of character and power to create it. Count Leo Nikolaevich Tolstoi came of the highest Russian nobility. His parents having died during his childhood, he early inherited the large estate of Yasnaya Polyana, a hundred miles south of Moscow, and, after a brief attendance at the University of Kazan, plunged into the social life of Moscow and St. Petersburg. In 1852 he joined the army and fought in the Caucasus, and in 1854 at the siege of Sebastopol. The years 1857-61 he spent mainly in travel in Western and Central Europe and in developing his interest in educating the Russian peasantry. In 1862 he married Sonya Bers, by whom he had thirteen children, and settled down on his estates, where he wrote War and Peace and Anna Karenina.[1] But by 1879 he gave up worldly interests and pleasures—including tobacco and strong drink, became a vegetarian and dressed like a peasant in hand-made clothes. He transferred his estate to his family and made his home the centre of a cult of Christian anarchism. The resulting friction with his wife and family ended in tragedy, for in his eighties he secretly left home, accompanied by his doctor and youngest daughter, to die of pneumonia in the horrible setting of a railway junction. War and Peace (1863-9), written following the emancipation of the serfs and its sequel, though set in the Napoleonic wars, owes much to Tolstoi's own experience of the ill-conducted Crimean War: it is a tremendous and life enhancing masterpiece. Anna Karenina (1873-76) is more pessimistic; a study of how personal passion which defies the hypocritical conventions of high society leads to destruction. Both these books, like Dostoievsky's, belong to the tense decades of the reign of Alexander II, and both were written during Tolstoi's happy married life at Yasnaya Polyana. He later became absorbed in the Christian anarchism of his later years; for Tolstoi was convinced that only by changing men's hearts through pacific Christianity could the evil power of governments, driving humanity to destruction, be undermined; and, indeed the course of European history during his long life provided ample evidence that some radical cure was needed.

[1]Tolstoi wrote many short stories and sketches, of which the most memorable are The Cossacks (1863), Sebastopol, Kolstomer (a satire presenting a noble horse's view of mankind), The Devil (1889), The Kreutzer Sonata (1891) and Resurrection (1879).

XLIV

The Neutral States

Ironically, some of the most predatory peoples in European history, the Spaniards, the Swiss, the Dutch and the Scandinavians, kept out of the monstrous confrontations of the "Great Powers". Though the Portuguese, to protect their African empire, again committed themselves to the old British alliance, the Spaniards, who had long been engaged in internecine political strife and in 1898 had lost their Caribbean and Philippine colonies to the United States, managed to remain neutral. After the expulsion of Isabella II in 1868, the first Spanish republic had been established, but the ancient regional divisions of the country made it hard to govern, and in 1875 the military and clerical conservatives brought back the seventeen-year-old Bourbon monarch, Alfonso XII. Under this regime the franchise was limited and the power of the crown and the army increased; the Liberal opposition were driven into Marxism or anarchy, and hatred on both sides increased. On the death of the young but tubercular king in 1885, he was succeeded by Alfonso XIII, his posthumous son by his Habsburg wife. Under her Regency, attempts were made to Liberalize the government; but elections were rigged, newly enfranchised Spaniards could not be bothered to vote, and the army retained so much autonomy that Liberal democracy could hardly thrive. Moreover, by the early 'nineties the administration was verging on bankruptcy, and to distract public attention and give employment to the army, the government in 1894 embarked on war in Morocco against the tribesmen of the Rif, as well as on a "forward policy" in the Rio de Oro in the south. They also became involved in a nationalist rebellion in Cuba, supported by the United States. When in 1897 the Prime Minister, Canoves, was assassinated by an anarchist, Spain faced a major colonial crisis.

It soon came to war. Early in 1898 the American battleship, *Maine*, was blown up in the harbour at Havana and the United States demanded that Spain evacuate Cuba. The Spaniards refused. In a short campaign the Americans destroyed the Spanish fleet at Manila in the Philippines, and sank their fleet in the West Indies off Cuba. By the Treaty of Paris of 1898 the Spaniards handed over Cuba and Puerto Rico to the United States (neither of them exactly an asset), while the Americans just bought the Philippines outright. An American Imperialism had ousted a European one—an unexpected sequel to Columbus's exploit—and the Spaniards now had to concentrate on Morocco.

Spain itself remained poor and ridden by regional and class conflict; socialists, anarcho-syndicalists and plain anarchists attacked the establishment; the army, top heavy with officers and supported by Alfonso XIII, played their own hand. In 1910, following a rising in Barcelona, martial law was imposed on the entire country. The same year, Liberal government came in under José Canelejas, but met with tenacious opposition from the Church. In due course, in 1912, he went the way of Canoves, assassinated by an anarchist. Alfonso XIII, now married to Princess Victoria Eugenie of Battenberg, an occasion when their subjects had tried to blow them both up, proved a lightweight monarch, unable to control or even assuage the political hatreds of his people. Only in 1914 would the Spaniards find common ground, when all contending parties wanted to keep out of the First World War and maintain their hold on Morocco and the Canary Islands. Indirectly the war would restore their faltering economy.

The Portuguese managed better to retain their colonial empire, at least in Africa. But the loss of Brazil, in 1821, with its gold and diamond mines, had crippled their own economy, and the late nineteenth century saw a decline into economic stagnation and dependence on foreign loans. The brief reign of Pedro V (1853–61), who died of typhoid, and that of Louis (1861–89) saw the failure of Liberal reforms, and ill-equipped peasants and fishermen had to support a largely parasitic nobility and Church. The Portuguese were reduced to considering whether to pledge or sell outright Goa, and even Madeira; an idea vetoed in 1847 by Palmerston, who refused in the high mid-Victorian way to take advantage of the predicament of an ancient ally.

The Germans, avid for colonies, had no such scruples about Angola or the strategically important Azores; and when the "scramble for Africa" set in, the Portuguese tried to create a more defensible colony extending from Angola to Mozambique. The ambitions of Cecil Rhodes clashed with these designs; the Portuguese had prior claims, but the British occupied Matabeleland, and Rhodes was backed by the British government who dispatched British warships to Lourenço Marques, and in 1890 forced the Portuguese to sign the Convention of London. Unpopular as this arrangement was in Lisbon, and rejected by the Cortes as giving advantage to Rhodes' Chartered Company, the Portuguese were more afraid of German designs on Angola and, following the appointment of the Marquéz de Soveral as Ambassador in London, an Anglo-Portuguese Declaration renewed the old Anglo-Portuguese alliance, with a guarantee by Great Britain to defend the Portuguese colonies from attack.

Meanwhile in Portugal such was the hatred against the conservative clerical regime that in 1908 Carlos I, who had succeeded Luis in 1889, was assassinated along with the Crown Prince Luis Felipe, and Manoel II, the King's brother, after a two year reign, was driven to take refuge in Gibraltar and then in England. A republic was proclaimed which, in the hope of preserving and perhaps extending its African empire, would enter the war of 1914–18 on the side of the Allies.

II

In Central Europe, in the still eye of the mounting storm, the Swiss who in late medieval and early modern times had provided the most efficient mercenaries in Europe and proved their prowess against Habsburgs and Burgundians in defence, maintained the independence originally recognized in 1648 by the Peace of Westphalia but briefly eclipsed when the revolutionary French had over-run the country, proclaimed an "Helvetian Republic" and conscripted Swiss levies into the invasion of Russia. With the defeat of the French, the nineteen cantons had been joined by Neuchâtel, Geneva and the Valais, and in 1815, by the Treaty of Vienna, the whole Confederation had been declared neutral. A Diet at Zurich had created a Federal Parliament, while Bern, Lucerne and Zurich had been acknowledged as the leading cities; and the Swiss textile industry, early established owing to ample water power, was rehabilitated after the recession caused by the Napoleonic *blocus continental*. An oligarchy of the wealthy burghers of the main towns remained predominant.

Following the French revolution of 1830–1, tension had increased between burghers and peasantry; but the main cause of conflict, constant in Switzerland since the days of Zwingli, was still religion. This, combined with economic and social tensions, led to war between the liberal Protestant cities, Bern, Zurich and Geneva, and the conservative and Catholic cantons led by Lucerne, which had formed a *Sonderbund* comprising the most ancient core of Switzerland, Uri, Schwyz and Unterwalden, along with Fribourg and Zug. After the miniature battles of Mainskastel and Gisliken in 1847, Lucerne was captured by the relatively liberal forces of General Dufour, and in 1848, when the Great Powers were preoccupied with their own revolutions, the Swiss sensibly devised a Federal Constitution in which all parties acquiesced. Bern became the capital and seat of the Federal Council; Lausanne the seat of the Federal Courts of Justice; and a legislature was set up of a Council of Cantons and a National Federal Council. A Confédération Helvétique now dealt with foreign affairs, imposed universal military service, and guaranteed freedom of the press and of religion, save to Jesuits and Jews. The "Swiss franc" was accepted as a common currency, posts became the responsibility of the Confederation, Zurich was designated as the principal centre for the development of technology, and the Swiss were prohibited from serving as mercenaries abroad.

These arrangements, modernized in 1874, became the framework of a singular prosperity. The country, with its limited agricultural resources, considerably depended on imported food, but the immense reserves of water power were now exploited for electricity, and railways were built through and over immense obstacles. The skill and method, hitherto proved in war, were diverted to the development of modern light precision industries, and in the second half of the century a new cult of mountains—hitherto regarded as "horrid"—and of "mountaineering", led to the rise of what would become a massive and efficiently organized hotel and tourist industry. Neat paddle steamers plied from Geneva along the green waters of Lac Léman to Lausanne and Vevey, and in the Castle of Chillon the great two-handed swords and hooked halberds hung unused within a once formidable stronghold built to command the valley of the Upper Rhone.

Firmly entrenched in a neutrality which suited the interests of both the Germans and the French, in 1874 the Swiss further centralized their defence forces and democratized their constitution, made more flexible by referenda when "initiated" by sufficient votes. And already by 1864 the Genevan Swiss Jean Henri Dunant (1828–1910), who had written his *Mémoire de Solferino*, brought about the first Geneva Convention which founded the International Red Cross to mitigate the sufferings of those wounded in war. This revolutionary idea had struck him when in 1859 he had witnessed the carnage at the battle of Solferino and he had improvised help at Castiglione for the casualties for whom neither side had prepared. Dunant, who went bankrupt through his single-minded pursuit of his aims, which led to a worldwide orgnization under the *Comité Internationale de la Croix Rouge*, spent most of his life in poverty, though compensated in old age by a Nobel Peace prize. Most historians have paid him little attention, preferring to unravel the details of the power politics and warfare whose results he tried to assuage. The world-wide Red Cross and Red Crescent organizations also came to deal with prisoners of war and displaced persons, and with promoting health and welfare in times of peace.

Other, if lesser, peaceful contributions made by the nineteenth-century Swiss are in fiction and scholarship. *Der Schweizeriche Robinson* (1812–27) (The Swiss Family Robinson) by J. D. Weiss early won a huge public, and for the more academically minded, Jacob Burkhardt's *The Civilization of the Renaissance in Italy* (1860), and the works of his pupil, the art historian H. Wolfflin, won cosmopolitan fame.

Thus the Swiss, though still divided by religion and language, slightly more than half being Protestant and most of the others Catholic, and speaking French, German, Italian and Romansh, managed to unite in a republican Confederation well able to defend itself, and in spite of limited resources maintained a prosperous, well-organized oasis of civilization in a waste of mounting European tension and conflict.

III

The other neutral state that provided a base for another organization to assuage international conflict at the "Peace Palace", seat of the International Court of Justice at the Hague, had a history of much more far-flung, indeed of imperialist, enterprise. The Dutch, with their tradition of sixteenth- and seventeenth-century resistance and of sea-borne empire, had retained their traditional pride and most of the wealth of their old supremacy. In spite of the French occupation and the short-lived monarchy of Louis Bonaparte, they had emerged from the Napoleonic wars with most of their rich Eastern Colonial empire restored, and had never taken to the forced union with the predominantly Catholic Belgians to make a buffer state in which the capital city yearly alternated between Brussels and the Hague. So when, in 1830, the Belgians had broken away, the Dutch had parted with them without regret, and continued to exploit their colonial possessions, impelled by hard times at home and by their efficient merchant navy. Under the Treaty of London of 1839, which guaranteed the neutrality of Belgium, the Dutch under William I ((1813–40) went their own way. The Prussian outrages against Denmark had passed them by, and the Germans had not needed to violate their neutrality during the short conclusive Franco-Prussian War, in which the French armies had rushed briskly to destruction and captivity.

Under William II (1840–49) the more Liberal constitution of 1848 was established, under which the powers of the legislature were increased and ministers made more regularly responsible to a parliament. Politics were still much conditioned by religious conflicts, if compromise between Calvinists and Catholics were often worked out, as in France, over denominational schools. After a succession of predominantly free-trading Liberal governments, in 1887 the franchise was extended to double the electorate, and in the 'seventies trade unions became more important in a country now modernized by railways and more efficient canals.

With the death of William III (1849–90), the male line of the House of Orange Nassau became extinct, and his daughter Wilhelmina succeeded to the throne at the age of ten. By now the colossal development of German heavy industry in the Ruhr and the expansion of maritime commerce had brought a revived prosperity to the major Dutch ports, and modern methods of agriculture and land reclamation had greatly improved the yield of a limited agricultural area; the Dutch economy became part of the great concentration of modern industry which included Great Britain, Belgium, north-eastern France and the Lower Rhine. The Dutch, whose Eastern colonial trade was also flourishing, became prosperous enough to lay the foundations of a welfare state. They also maintained a now traditional neutrality, and when surprisingly in 1899 it occurred to Tsar Nicholas II to convene an International Peace Conference, it was held at the Hague. Since inevitably it accepted war as an unavoidable institution, it did not achieve much; but a "Hague Convention" following the principles of Grotius and the Geneva example of 1864 tried to regulate war at sea, and another to codify the conduct of war on land. The conference also set up a permanent Court of Arbitration at the Hague for the pacific settlement of international disputes.

In 1907 the first Hague Conference was followed up, when, at the instigation of President Theodore Roosevelt of the United States, the Tsar convened another which extended the procedures of 1899 to define the rights and obligations of neutral powers in time of war, and, quaintly, restricted the "discharge of projectiles from balloons". For obvious reasons the next session of the conference, planned for 1915, never took place.

Though no longer a Great Power, the kingdom of the Netherlands
maintained a very distinctive and confident way of life. On a basis of efficient
agriculture, oceanic commerce and colonial exploitation, the country developed
modern light industries rather than the heavy industry most characteristic of
the mid-nineteenth century, and its cities were not swamped by megalopolitan
development. The fine architecture of Amsterdam and the Hague retained its
character, and the polders, extended by reclamation from the sea, still
harboured duck and teal that flighted at sunset across enormous skyscapes.
The neatly kept Dutch villages, set in trim flowery gardens, contrasted with
the slatternly style of Belgian farms, which followed the French fashion of
concealing prosperity from the tax-collector, and Dutch art galleries, as the
Rijksmuseum and the Mauritzhuis, were as fine as any in Europe, while the
tough fishermen who wrested a living from the bitter North Sea maintained a
tradition of seamanship which went back to the days of de Reuter and van
Tromp.

IV

Eastward along the coast of the North Sea past Friesland and its islands and
the mouth of the Elbe, Denmark, following the defeat of 1864, was no longer
a Great Power either. Once the centre of a Scandinavian maritime empire,
guarding the Sound commanding the entrance to the Baltic, and a major
military power in Northern Germany, the Danes, who had been forced to
back Napoleon, had in 1814 lost Norway to Sweden and Heligoland to Great
Britain. Though they still held Iceland, they had no important colonies.
Impoverished after the Napoleonic wars, they had been ruled under Frederik
VI (1808–39) and Kristian VIII (1839–48) under a strictly conservative regime;
but in 1849 Frederik VII, whose accession had coincided with the revolutions
in France and Germany, had inaugurated a limited monarchy with Liberal
representative government under a constitution. This vigorous, eccentric and
benevolent monarch, after a convivial and rebellious youth, had already
travelled widely, and proved a staunch patron of archaeology, one of the most
original Danish nineteenth-century achievements.

The Danes had long been making the most of their agriculture, the Royal
Agricultural Society of Denmark having been founded in 1769. Stimulated by
the competition of grain imports from North America, they set about
developing livestock farming and the export of bacon and butter. Peasant
leasehold farms were converted by government into freehold, and during the
'eighties dairy Co-operatives were organized among the small-holding farmers.
Where in England the peasantry had been ruined by the Industrial Revolution,
and in Russia the legacy of serfdom had left confusion and resentment, in
Denmark the small farmers had been given security and brought into a modern
organization by consent. Hence, between 1875 and 1914, a mounting prosperity, while, since there was little coal save in Jutland, a belated Industrial
Revolution was mainly confined to bettering agricultural methods, improving

communication by ferry and railway, and in due course, motor transport, to salting fish and to brewing beer.

The monuments of sixteenth- and seventeenth-century grandeur survived as in the elaborate castle of Elsinore, and since peat was abundant, the splendid beech forests of Denmark still swept down to the sandy shores of a startlingly blue Baltic; while Copenhagen, with its elegant copper-sheathed spires and shipping moored near the heart of the city, retained the character of a traditional centre of commerce and fisheries, with a touch of gaiety and style not always found in the north.

And during the nineteenth century three Danish writers won European fame. Hans Christian Andersen (1805–75), the uncouth offspring of a shoemaker of Odense on Funen, survived his youthful struggles in Copenhagen to deploy his original genius in his *Tales for Children* (1835–47), soon translated over most of the world. Sören Kierkegaard (1813–55) is claimed by modern "existentialists" as their founder. The son of a wool merchant from West Jutland, in 1830 he attended Copenhagen University and, though never a clergyman, spent his life writing theology. His most influential work, *Either, Or* appeared in 1843: he particularly detested Hegel's claim to understand the "inner go of things" by "speculative intuition", a claim which, not without reason, he considered arrogant. He devised various pseudonyms for himself, of which the most intriguing is *Hilarius Bogbinder*. Much more respected in established theological circles, Bishop Grundtvig (1783–1872) headed a Lutheran revival mixed with a cult of Northern mythology. He translated the works of both Saxo Grammaticus and Snorri Sturluson and even *Beowulf* (1820), thus giving inspiration to Scandinavian and Anglo-Saxon scholars. He also promoted *Volk* High Schools for less advanced pupils, which took root in Denmark and outside it.

But the most important nineteenth-century Danish contribution to European knowledge was the foundation of modern prehistory. King Frederik VII is best known to conventional historians as the monarch whose death occasioned the Schleswig–Holstein crisis of 1863; he is much more memorable for his continued patronage of Jens Worsaae, the greatest archaeological genius of the mid-nineteenth century.

Worsaae had been obsessed with archaeology from his boyhood in Jutland. Rescued from penury, he became a pioneer of excavation; he wrote the *Prehistory of Denmark* which won him a European reputation, and invitations to London and Scotland. Afterwards Inspector of Ancient Monuments, he became the first official pre-historian, and after the accession of Frederik VII, Curator of the Royal Collections with residence in the palace. King and antiquary would conduct excavations together, the latter only slightly impeded by a Court uniform and by the Danish lunches "washed down" by champagne which the monarch liked to consume when on a dig. Combining archaeology with business, King Frederik died of a "chill" when rehabilitating the ancient Viking *Dannevirke* against the perennial threat from the Germans. Worsaae's technique of systematic excavation would be taken up and scientifically developed in England by General Pitt-Rivers.

V

Far the largest and long the most military of the Scandinavian states, Sweden in relation to its relatively small population had the greatest potential resources, which included a wealth of iron in the north with access to the sea through Narvik, since until 1905 Norway remained united with Sweden, and it possessed an even greater wealth of timber. Although the Swedes possessed no coal or oil, they had a potential abundance of water power from their innumerable and stratified lakes.

Though the Crimean War and the Allied expedition to the Baltic had given the Swedes under Oscar I (1844–59) the chance of an attack on the traditional Russian enemy, they had wisely refused it, and concentrated on the internal opportunities and problems of a belated Industrial Revolution now developing in the country. Under Charles XV (1859–82) the *bourgeoisie* tried to consolidate themselves against the old nobility, and in 1867 the old Riksdag of four estates was abolished for a Parliament in which the peasant farmers in fact predominated. An Agrarian party now opposed both the bureaucracy and the new industrialists, and advocated protection for agriculture. Meanwhile the timber industry was expanding and the iron mines were developed; rolling mills adopted the Bessemer process and produced steel. In the 'seventies, Swedish matches captured a world-wide market. But the increasing population was still over 70% agricultural, and as it had long been doing from central Europe, massive emigration set in to North America. In the 'eighties, the Swedish trade unions, in face of the hardships created by swiftly developing industry, began to turn Socialist, and a new *Social Democrat* interest found a leader in Hjalmar Branting. Various Protestant sects, often subsidized by Swedes in North America, hived off from the official Lutheran Church, and since owing to the traditional and understandable Swedish desire to keep warm in the cold and darkness of near sub-arctic winters, heavy drinking had long been an old Swedish custom, politically powerful Temperance Societies began to advocate measures of "Prohibition". Industry, and now agriculture, prospered, but many Swedes were bored: some took to far-flung exploration, as Amundsen, who reached the Antarctic Pole before Captain Scott and survived, or made their fortunes in Russian oil and armaments, as the Nobel family, founders of the Nobel Prizes; others emigrated to Brazil; some became hard-drinking and hard-swearing sea captains. Others penetrated to the Belgian Congo or Abyssinia.

The nineteenth-century Swedish writer who won European fame was August Strindberg, a pioneer of "naturalistic" drama which swept the stage like a north-east wind. Prosecuted for blasphemy and long ignored by the Swedish Academy, this alarming genius, with blazing eyes under a high forehead and a mane of hair, looked the part. He was the son of a steamship agent and of a former waitress, and he failed to adjust to conventional middle-class society and satirized it. His *Roda Rummet* (*Red Room*) in 1879 first won him success, and his autobiography *Tjanstekvinnan's Son* (*Son of a Servant*), which contributed to the modern fashion for uninhibited confession, extended it. He had also turned to drama, and during the 'eighties wrote *The Father*, *Miss Julie*, *Creditors* and the *People of Hemso*. Three times married and divorced, he spent much time out of Sweden, but returned to Stockholm in 1899; here, pouring out plays, mostly tragic and satirical with a spice of Nordic introspection, he remained until his death in 1912, discountenanced by the Swedish establishment he had satirized, but a world famous celebrity.

The Norwegians, united with Sweden in 1814, possessed the slenderest natural resources of the three Scandinavian states, until, towards the end of the nineteenth century, they could exploit their tremendous potential of water power for electricity, the greatest *per capita* in the world. The uneasy relationship with Sweden was peacefully resolved, but not until 1905 when, after the Norwegian *Storting* had unilaterally dissolved the union, a decision overwhelmingly endorsed by plebiscite, Oscar II of Sweden had resigned the Norwegian crown. It was assumed by Prince Charles of Denmark, who changed his name to Haakon and, married to Princess Maud of England, forged closer dynastic links with Great Britain.

One of the most sparsely populated countries in Europe for its size, with vast areas of forest and mountain, Norway concentrated more on livestock and dairy farming than on agriculture; but it possessed a very large fishing fleet and merchant navy; moreover, with the development of electric power, light industries began to flourish. Education, free and compulsory since 1860 and untrammeled by the sectarian feuds that had handicapped it in Great Britain and France, early contributed to a moderate trade union movement and ensured that universal male suffrage (1898) led to a responsible democracy that would lead to a model welfare state.

Culturally, however, the country remained provincial; and the Norwegian genius who made the greatest impact on Europe spent most of his life abroad. Henrik Ibsen (1828–1906), the creator of a realistic prose drama, was the son of a proprietor of saw mills at Skien in Westfold. When his father went bankrupt, Ibsen suffered the social and economic privations of lower-middle-class life, so he learnt the material for his tense domestic dramas the hard way. Having failed his examination at Christiania (now Oslo) he scraped a living and gained experience as a producer at Bergen, and by 1857 became a theatre director in Christiania. In contrast to Strindberg, he was well-treated by his country's cultural authorities, and in 1864 given a state grant to visit Rome. He then lived abroad on further grants for twenty-seven years. He became an international celebrity, and his poetic drama *Brand* was written in Rome in 1866; *Peer Gynt* the following year in Dresden. In 1873 he attempted a major theme in *Emperor and Galilean* about Julian the Apostate, but reverted to provincial social drama in *Pillars of Society*, *A Doll's House* and *Ghosts*. After a long sojourn at Munich and Tyrol, where he wrote *Hedda Gabler* and *The Master Builder*, Ibsen at length returned to Norway in 1891 and remained there till his death seven years later.

His most poetic and famous creation *Peer Gynt* had incidental music by another Norwegian who won world fame. Edvard Hagerup Grieg (1843–1907), who had a strain of Scots descent, was a native of Bergen whose main romantic inspiration came from Norwegian scenery and folk music. He studied at

Leipzig, won the admiring friendship of Liszt and, generously treated by the Norwegian government, visited Rome. But he soon returned to his own country where he lived for the rest of his life in sight of the sea. The unique quality of his music expressed the peace and majesty of Norwegian fjords and forests.

XLV

Technological Revolution and Political Eclipse

The late nineteenth century saw the chequered climax of a brilliant civilization and the beginnings of a technological revolution, exploiting steel, electricity, chemicals, rubber and oil; in spite of a phase of economic recession in their own areas, Europeans, whose emigrants had so massively contributed to transatlantic development, made vast investments in the Americas, in the East and, following the discovery of the richest diamond and gold mines in the world, in South Africa.

In 1885 K. F. Benz devised the first "internal combustion" engine, deriving its power from petrol vapour electrically ignited in a small cylinder, and "automobiles" began to revolutionize transport; in 1903 the Americans Wilbur and Orville Wright made the earliest powered flight in a primitive bi-plane, the first step in the conquest of the air. In 1905 Edison made the first "moving" picture; in 1906 Blériot flew the Channel, and in 1908 Henry Ford started to mass-produce cheap motor cars. These discoveries would transform the tempo and outlook of human life everywhere, and render existing international politics dangerously ill-adapted to an environment radically altered by applied science.

This powerful but precarious civilization also suffered an internal challenge, as the quasi-scientific doctrines of Marx and Engels defined in the *Communist Manifesto* of 1848 and in *Das Kapital* in 1867 gained a wider following for an attack on private property, and a systematic "class war" was promoted by the first Socialist International that met in London in 1864. Bismarck's "welfare" legislation in Germany and the reforms of Liberal governments from Gladstone to Asquith in Great Britain took some of the sting out of this conflict; but the Marxists were waiting their opportunity when, following its built-in liability to war, the old order collapsed in Russia and Central Europe.

On the surface this mighty phase of European economy and civilization, with its flourishing extrapolations in the Americas, Australasia and South Africa, and its enormous colonial Empires in the East and Africa, looked destined long to dominate the earth; but it had achieved no European political order. Whereas the Roman Empire in practice, and China and medieval Christendom in theory, had felt co-terminous with civilization itself, late-nineteenth-century Europeans had abandoned the Concert of Europe which had followed the Napoleonic wars, and were now unable to work even the inferior alternative of a "balance of power". The twentieth century, which opened with so much cultural and technological promise, would regress into mechanized barbarism, into an age of mass slaughter and political assassination, more ferocious than the seventeenth and technologically far more proficient in slaughter than the fifth century AD. Nationalism, originally a myth of freedom and fraternity, contributed to this carnage. The Liberal idealist Mazzini, typical product of the romantic age and of Rousseau's cult of "the People", had tried to found a "Religion of Humanity" in terms of the "self-determination" of emancipated nation states. Once established within their "natural boundaries" he had foolishly hoped that they would form a "sisterhood" in peaceful harmony, each contributing their particular gifts. And this sentimental vision, which made the old dynastic legitimism seem formal and heartless, now blended all too easily with the romantic Hegelian cult of dynamic *Volk-nations* successively aspiring to dominate a cosmic process.

By the late nineteenth century these popularized delusions had been reinforced by a false interpretation of Darwin's biological principle of the "survival of the fittest", now mis-applied to sovereign states, so that nationalism became no longer the inspiration of revolutionary idealists but the creed of the exponents of *Realpolitik* who, caught up in the momentum of the system and by its *idées reçues*, controlled the sovereign *Great Powers* that, after a series of international crises, lurched into the war of 1914–18. "It is a chastening experience", writes Albertini, the greatest authority on this process, "to read the diplomatic documents of the time: all are biased, all incomplete", for not only is the historian chastened by an unprecedented "flood of diplomatic documents" but by the fact, that as the German historian Lutz declares, "all the powers in 1914 put their own interests, true or supposed, before the peace of the world". Europe thus became the centre of a planetary political earthquake and in due course became superseded in the scale of power by the United States and the Eurasian Soviet Union.

Liberal democratic public opinion, though not the statesmen forced to conduct foreign policy, remained oddly unaware of the terrible facts of international life. The Liberal political theorist, T. H. Green, so much the inspiration of the Campbell-Bannerman and Asquith governments in Great Britain, declared that "the military system of Europe is no necessary incident of the relations between independent States"; it was "a legacy of feudalism" which would "disappear" as more states attained representative Liberal governments; they would even, he hopefully believed, "arrive at a passionless impartiality in dealing with one another".[1]

The cosmopolitan Catholic, Lord Acton, was wiser than this academic heir of English Nonconformity. The current world of sovereign nation states, with its cult of unbridled state power, he pointed out, was only "a narrow and disedifying section of history", and the current theory of nationality was

[1]See my *Politics and Opinion in the Nineteenth Century. op. cit.* p. 289. for this aspect of Green's *Lectures on the Principles of Political Obligation.* Ed. Nettleship. London, 1883.

"retrograde". It did not aim "either at liberty or prosperity, both of which it sacrificed to the imperative necessity of making the nation the mould and measure of the state. Its course [would] be marked with material as well as moral ruin." From a more cosmic point of view, Nietzsche was even more accurate: "Do we not feel the breath of empty space? Has it not become colder? God is dead. God remains dead. And we have killed him." "There will be wars", he predicted, "such as never have happened on earth." The outstanding material and intellectual achievements of mid- and late-nineteenth-century Western and Central Europe and the new brilliant Russian contribution in literature and music were thus constricted, distorted and imperilled by the barbaric framework of Hobbesian Great States, so that after 1871 international politics became nothing more interesting than a "struggle for mastery" among these panoplied Leviathans.[1] "*Une lourde et permanente menace pèse sur cette civilization qui perfectionne activement les techniques de mort au même temps que celles de vie.*"[2]

II

Certain milestones stand out on this road to ruin and demand attention before the main economic, scientific and cultural aspects of the time are summarized. The "Great Powers" of Europe now controlled their subjects far more effectively than had any governments before: administration, communications, a network of major and petty bureaucrats now held them in far greater subjection than had the great dynastic states of the seventeenth and eighteenth centuries. Conscription on the continent of Europe provided enormous armies and, as the Industrial Revolution really took off on the continent, massive armaments were provided for them, while problems of logistics which had baffled previous commanders were solved by strategic railroads. The German victory of 1870-71 had shown what could be done, although the uniforms and parade manoeuvres of the monstrous armies still kept a Napoleonic glitter and glamour, and war was still widely considered a romantic adventure. In fact the Industrial Revolution was turning it into a competition of technology—a fact most obvious in the naval armaments race of the late nineteenth and early twentieth centuries.

With this competition of mass conscript armies and of steam and oil powered *Ironclads* and *Dreadnoughts* piling up, the Great Powers played their potentially deadly game of diplomatic blackmail; the "satiated" powers to keep what they had, the "hungry" powers to gain territory, economic advantage or just "prestige". Even sound historians personify these entities, for some reason as feminine: when Russia is "rebuffed" over "her" ambitions in the Balkans, "she" is "humiliated": France is obsessed with "her" grievances over Morocco, and Italy over "her" "unredeemed" territories in the Eastern Alps. These

[1]A. J. P. Taylor. *The Struggle for Mastery in Europe 1848-1918*. London, 1954.
[2]R. Schnerb. *Le XIX Siècle. Histoire Général des Civilizations*, ed. M. Crouzet. tome vi. Paris, 1957. p. 258.

monstrous personifications had no life of their own; they are projections of the ambitions and frustrations of small cliques of political and military leaders who may or may not have been representative of their peoples, most of whom were ignorant of and indifferent to the arcane manoeuvres of "foreign policy", unless some "crisis" was blown up by the politicians and popular press into an occasion of passion.

Caught in the tide of events, the best that the most perspicacious statesmen would do was to fend off and resolve the crises that the system, or lack of it, produced, and the diplomatic history of the half century that preceded the catastrophe of 1914–18 is a record of these occasions.

III

The Third Republic in France, as officially and finally constituted in 1875, managed to patch up the damage of the Franco-Prussian War, consolidate a prosperous if often old-fashioned and always mainly agricultural economy and give further scope to many entrepreneurs who had founded their fortunes under the Second Empire. The urban artisans were backward in organizing themselves; the *Confédération Général du Travail* was not established until 1895 and the right to strike not until 1903. Among an individualist people, there was little "welfare" legislation. Apart from the perennial conflict between clericals and anti-clericals, aggravated by the question of denominational teaching in state schools, and from a novel anti-semitism, in part provoked by a Jewish immigration from Central Europe and culminating in the notorious Dreyfus case (1894–1906), the chronic instability of French politics, due to the multiplicity of political parties, did not lead to more than occasional and dramatic scandals, unearthed by a virulent and witty press. Nor, apart from the comic figure of General Boulanger, who on the aftermath of the Franco-Prussian War, had postured about Paris advocating a war of revenge and finally committed suicide in Belgium at or on the tomb of his mistress, did political generals challenge the authority of shifting coalitions of political cliques. Whatever the antics of the politicians, the administrative framework of France remained intact; and apart from ambitions which occasionally provoked clashes of far-flung colonial policy, France, with a falling population and no longer the strongest power on the continent, looked for reinsurance rather than conquests.

The Germans, on the other hand, united in the Second *Reich*, and with their population rapidly rising, had embarked on a massive drive for industrial supremacy, which was already putting them ahead even of the British and which was assisted after 1879 by Bismarck's new policy of protective tariffs. But when in 1890 Wilhelm II forced Bismarck into retirement, the political weakness of the *Reich* became apparent. The *Reichstag* had no adequate control of the executive, or of the monarch, or of the army; now the army, big business and the Court launched into adventures high-lighted by the histrionics of the temperamental young Emperor.

After the assassination of Alexander II, the Russians under Alexander III had reverted to autocratic repression, and still had no equivalent of an elected national parliament. An inefficient police state clamped down even on the discussion of political change, and revolutionaries challenged the regime by terrorism. They were executed, as was Lenin's brother in 1887; exiled, like Lenin, to Siberia; and driven, like Lenin, to live in penury abroad. And it was in London in 1903, at a Russian Social Democratic party congress, that Lenin imposed his idea of a dedicated close-knit party elite of the *majority* faction— termed *Bolsheviks* as against the *Menshevik minority*.

The Russian internal *impasse* did not inhibit the Tsar's governments from an active policy abroad. Having been saddled with the government of Poland, Alexander II had been confronted in 1865 with yet another Polish insurrection; as usual, it had been crushed. Under Alexander III a systematic campaign was carried out to stamp out Polish culture, so that in 1890 the students in Warsaw University could not even be taught in their own language. Five years later, the Russians, who had annexed Finland in 1809, imposed conscription on the Finns in spite of the resistance of the Finnish parliament.

Poland and Finland, both originally states bordering on Russia, had long been subject to the Tsars: in the Balkans there was less reason for Russian advance. The Congress of Berlin in 1878 had tried to confine Russian interests to the lands of the Lower Danube, the Dobruja, and the Balkan hinterland of the Black Sea, while assigning control of Bosnia-Herzegovina in the west to Austria. But the tangled and perennial vendettas of Serbs, Croats, Montenegrins and Bulgars were bound to involve their patrons, and a Serb-Austrian conflict could involve Russia.

The Austrian Empire or Dual Monarchy, organized in 1867, had always been a ramshackle expedient. As Albert Sorel wrote, "*quand la Turquie aura quitté le lit de l'homme malade, c'est l'Autriche qui viendra la remplacer*". Already hardly viable, this incongruously constituted Empire containing Germans, Magyars and Slavs was impelled through fear of Russia to take on even more exacting responsibilities. Of these the most fateful had been the administration of Bosnia and Herzegovina—its capital Sarajevo. This mountainous country lies inland from the Adriatic coast with its ancient Venetian harbours of Trogir and Split (Spalato), site of Diocletian's palace and retirement, and commands the approach through Mostar to historic Dubrovnik (Ragusa), captured for the Venetians by the Fourth Crusade. It also bordered on the still Turkish Sanjak of Novi Bazaar,[1] separating Serbia and Montenegro, through which it was thought a strategic railway could be built linking up at Skopje with the Vardar valley and Salonika.[2]

Italy, prematurely united considering the great discrepancies between north and south and the traditional particularism of its ancient cities, but launched with such high romantic hopes by Mazzini and Garibaldi and with such cold cunning by Cavour, added to the tensions of Great Power politics. Following

[1]Not to be confused with Novi Bazaar in eastern Bulgaria, south of Silistria and of the Dobruja.
[2]An impracticable project since the Turkish railway guage was wider than the Austrian, and the cost would have been prohibitive through the mountainous country.

opportunist policies, the Italians in 1883 joined in a Triple Alliance with Germany and Austria-Hungary, renewed in 1887 and again in 1901, when the *Reich* Chancellor von Bülow remarked that Italy "would have to choose between matrimony and concubinage". But successive governments, anxious for "prestige", overtaxed the country for armaments and in 1894 launched an incompetent attack on Abyssinia which soon came to particularly humiliating and painful disaster at Adowa. Coming so late to the "scramble for Africa", the Italians then turned their eyes on Tripoli, still under the suzerainty of the Turks, and remained alert to any advantage that a conflict of the Great Powers might throw in their way.

IV

In the interlocking crises that led up to the First World War, the British were compelled to abandon their policy of isolation. In 1897-1900 the Germans launched a twenty-year programme of building a High Seas Fleet, aimed to challenge British supremacy. Already concerned at a potential Franco-Russian threat following the alliance of those powers in 1893, confirmed in 1899, the British in 1902 concluded an alliance with the Japanese, now the strongest naval power in the Far East. Then in 1903-4 they made an *entente* with France, still the ally of Russia. This radical strategic change of course was contrived diplomatically by the British monarch; indeed, though his part has been played down, "in general the chief credit for the Anglo-French entente belongs to the will and tenacity of Edward VII."[1]

The *entente* which settled questions long outstanding in the Far East, in Egypt and Morocco, increased the German fear of *Einkreisung*; and indeed it greatly strengthened the British hand. The British had in fact been out-building the new German fleet; and "at the beginning of 1905, they had forty-four battleships, the French had twelve, the Germans sixteen. The Russians did not count".[2]

The Germans replied by singularly inept diplomacy. In April 1905 von Bülow persuaded a reluctant Wilhelm II to land from a warship in Tangier,[3] "to safeguard German interests in Morocco", force the collapse of the French government which had made the *entente*, and so "knock the dagger from the hand of Edward VII". The French government, in the way of French governments, indeed collapsed; and the Kaiser followed up his amateur diplomacy by taking to his yacht and visiting Tsar Nicholas II—now in the throes of defeat by the Japanese. At Bjorko, he lured the Tsar into a Treaty

---

[1]Luigi Albertini. *The Origins of the War*. Trans. I. M. Massey. London, 1952. Vol. I. p. 146. Met at the railway station by shouts of "Vive les Boers" and "Vive Fashoda", Edward VII with imperturbable bonhomie turned his official visit to France into a resounding popular success.

[2]Taylor. *op. cit.* p. 425.

[3]Where he wrote "he had ridden between Spanish anarchists" and in spite of the impediment of his withered arm, had "mounted a strange horse, thus being within an inch of a fatal fall or the death blow of an assassin". (Albertini. *op. cit.* Vol. I. p. 161.)

which could break the Russian alliance with France, and which was in fact never ratified by the Russian government. Nor did the conference convened on German initiative at Algeciras opposite Gibraltar, to destroy the French hold on Morocco and so the standing of France as a Great Power, turn out as the Germans had hoped: alarm at such diplomacy became more widespread.

Following these clumsy German manoeuvres by which, as Edward VII put it, the Kaiser had "got himself so much talked about", in 1907 the British came to an alliance with Russia, long regarded as their main enemy in Asia. Already in February 1906 Sir Edward Grey, the Foreign Secretary, had written, "an *entente* between Russia, France and ourselves would be absolutely secure".[1] If it is necessary to check Germany, it could then be done." Alarmed by the German project of making a Berlin to Baghdad railway, the Russians were now ready to share "spheres of influence" with the British in Persia: the British, now secure in Cyprus and Egypt, were even ready to let Russian warships pass the Straits. The Russians also accepted that Afghanistan—long the scene of Kipling's "Great Game" of espionage and counter-espionage— should be accounted a "buffer state" to India. The alliance, concluded in August 1907, was mainly a settlement over Asia; but, given the Russian commitment to France, it could have profound implications in Europe.

Moreover by 1906 the British had stepped up the naval race in armaments. They launched the *Dreadnought*, a battleship so heavily gunned and armoured that it outclassed any ship in their own or anyone else's fleet. The Germans responded by projecting *Dreadnoughts* for themselves, and by 1908 the armaments industries of both powers were committed to the expensive competition. Such was now the tense position in Northern Europe.

V

The other main area of tension, from which the final catastrophe would derive, was in the South-East. Here in 1903 distrust between Austria-Hungary and the southern Slavs had been increased when the incompetently pro-Austrian King Alexander Obrenovič II of Serbia, and his Queen Draga, had been cut down in their own palace by nationalist pro-Russian officers of the "Black Hand", who had replaced him by the elderly Peter Kara Djorgevič. Though relatively liberal, Peter's regime was a Pro-Russian focus of Serb nationalism, hostile to Vienna and Budapest. The Dual Monarchy was already hard put to contain Austrians, Magyars and Czechs, and Magyar–Serb hatred had prevented the Serbs being brought into a comprehensive federation.

Now tension worsened. Under the Treaty of Berlin of 1878 Austria-Hungary had taken over the administration of Bosnia and Herzegovina; and when in 1906 Count Aehrenthal became foreign minister, he conspired with the Russian minister Izvolsky to arrange the passage of Russian warships out of the Black Sea in return for a blind eye if Austria-Hungary annexed Bosnia-

[1]Taylor. *op. cit.* p. 442.

Herzegovina outright. And this in 1908 the Dual Monarchy did. The Russians, disappointed, through French and British opposition, of their side of the deal, were confronted, when they demanded compensation, by Wilhelm II, who announced characteristically that he stood by his Austrian allies "in shining armour". The Russians had to back down; the Serbs to accept the *fait accompli*.

The Germans had now shown the risks they were ready to take, and further alienated both the Russians and the British. The naval armaments race went on, then in 1911 the Moroccan question again flared up. Anxious to create a protectorate over the whole country, the French occupied Fez, whereat the Germans sent a warship, the *Panther*, to Agadir on the Moroccan Atlantic coast, ostensibly to protect German subjects. Whereat the Liberal Lloyd George, of all people, now Chancellor of the Exchequer and concerned for Gibraltar, warned all concerned that Great Britain would "not be treated as of no account where her interests were vitally affected". The Royal Navy took up action stations: plans were laid, for the first time, for an expeditionary force to be sent to France. On the German side, Admiral von Tirpitz was allowed to build three *Dreadnoughts* a year instead of two; more conscripts were called up for the German army, and public opinion in Great Britain, Germany and France became more belligerent. The British now commissioned "super *Dreadnoughts*": then in September 1911 the Italians, smarting to "revenge" their humiliation at Adowa, went to war with Turkey, attacked Tripoli, and threatened to attack the Dardanelles. This adventure united Serbs, Montenegrins, Bulgars and Greeks to take their opportunity, and in 1912 they almost drove the Turks out of Europe, ending a centuries-old Turkish occupation. And when in 1913 the Turks renewed the war, they lost even Adrianople, and, accepting the mediation of the Great Powers, retained only a strip of territory bordering on Constantinople and along the European side of the Straits.

True to form, the Serbs and Bulgars then fought each other over Albania and Macedonia, and the Bulgars were defeated by an alliance of Greeks, Roumanians and Serbs. The Turks recaptured Adrianople, but the Serbs had become the most successfully militant people in the Balkans.

The Government of Austria-Hungary, always apprehensive of Serbian influence on the Slav minorities in Hungary and Transylvania, now decided that as the potential "Piedmont of the South Slavs" the Serbs must be broken before they became more dangerous; so they obtained German consent to provoke a war with Serbia.

On 28th June, 1914, the anniversary of the battle of Kossovo and the National Day of Serbia, the Archduke Franz-Ferdinand, the heir to the Austro-Hungarian thrones, paid an official visit to Sarajevo, the capital of Bosnia-Herzegovina. There, at the second attempt he was assassinated. A bomb had bounced off the open hood of his motor, and it was only on the return journey, when his car was almost immobilized backing out of the wrong street, that he and his wife were shot at close range by a Bosnian Serb.

The Emperor Franz Joseph wrote at once to the Kaiser. "Serbia must be eliminated as a political factor in the Balkans." And the Kaiser agreed. By 23rd July an ultimatum was sent to the Serbs from Vienna. Though they accepted most of its stiff demands, on 28th July Austria-Hungary declared war. They wanted to dominate a broken Serbia and a pro-German Bulgaria up to the Black Sea.

Already alarmed at German penetration of Turkey, where, in the interests of the Berlin-Baghdad railway, General Liman von Sanders was installed at Constantinople reorganizing the Turkish army, the Russians found the Austrian declaration of war intolerable. On 30th July they ordered general mobilization. It was the decisive step. On the following day both Germany and Austria-Hungary set their own swifter mobilizations in train. And when the French, committed to Russia, refused to give a guarantee of neutrality, the Germans on 3rd August declared war on France; then, following the Schlieffen plan, they at once invaded Belgium, and after the violation of Belgian neutrality, guaranteed by the Great Powers since 1839, on 4th August the British went to war with Germany.

Thus, at successive signals, the five Great Powers, like the heavy steam trains of the time, pulled out onto their predestined collision courses, long implicit in the alliances of the sovereign states into which Europe had become divided. Once too often the risks, averted only by skilful if frantic diplomacy, had been taken, and the gamblers in power politics had dragged down a brilliant civilization into mankind's first experience of industrialized total war and into the degradation of its sequel—the near suicide of Europe.

VI

Neither the governments, the High Commands, nor the peoples knew what they were in for. It was generally assumed that a prolonged war was financially impossible and that the conflict, like the Franco-Prussian War, would be swiftly concluded.

In fact the Industrial and Technological Revolutions had given warfare a totally new dimension. From 1914 to 1918 millions perished in a slogging match of mechanized slaughter before, with American aid, the Western Powers emerged victorious, but with their economic and social order irretrievably shaken. First in Russia, then in Italy, Germany and the Austro-Hungarian empire, the political and social order inherited from the nineteenth century collapsed, and the ruins were taken over by Communist and Fascist dictatorships, primitive forms of government reminiscent of the rough and ready expedients of the late Roman empire, but more irresponsible and endowed by modern technology with more comprehensive powers of regimentation, propaganda and destruction.

Nor was the tragedy even then worked out. After little more than twenty years armistice which the Western allies in the absence of the United States were too feeble to enforce, a second bout of European conflict broke out and engulfed the world. It was implicit in the blunders of the peace conference, conducted without a proper time table or even systematic agenda, by politicians who thought in terms of their own slogans with an eye on their own electorates. No agreements on essentials had been made in advance, and it was naïvely believed that the principle of "self-determination" and the creation of small sovereign states in Central Europe would bring peace to areas long riven by political hatreds and demoralized by war and its aftermath. Most of the Western politicians were ignorant of the local facts and incapable of understanding the economic implications of their decisions, so that impracticable "reparations" were imposed on Germany, out of whose economic ruin the sinister spectre of Hitler emerged. The statesmen of the Congress of Vienna had been too realistic to ruin France.

The supposed political *Diktat* of Versailles was politically not so devastating as the one the Germans had planned to impose on Great Britain and France; but the "reparations" were so impossible that a still united Germany was ruined, yet left politically strong enough to launch a war of revenge.

After this second conflict, decided mainly, after the victory of the Royal Air Force in the Battle of Britain, and of the Royal Navy in the Battle of the Atlantic, by the colossal Eurasian power of the Soviet Union, and the massive intervention of the United States, Europe suffered eclipse and an unprecedented degree of partition. Dragged along by an unheard of expansion of technology, itself enough to dislocate any human society, Europe has since witnessed a revolt of the masses and a revolution of rising expectations, while superseded as the centre of world power, deprived of its colonies, its eastern half overrun by the Soviet Union and the West surviving mainly under the protection of American power.

Yet this political eclipse has had a surprising sequel—the belated but rapid and fairly successful attempt to create the economic basis of a united Western Europe. To avoid the fate of the warring city states of Hellas or Renaissance Italy, the still autonomous Western Europeans have been driven to put their house at least in better economic order. The foundations of an economic union, already made desirable by a common culture, manageable area and shared technology, have been laid by the Treaty of Rome. In spite of strong nationalist feelings, the common threat from Eurasia has brought about the beginnings of closer political ties.

Such, along with the abdication from colonial empires, are the outstanding changes in the development of Europe since the Second World War: all are overshadowed by the global arms race between the super powers which, extending far beyond Europe, is conducted in terms of outer space, of intercontinental ballistic missiles and worse.

Hitherto wars have been carried on without the total destruction of the civilizations involved, and the civilizations themselves, though based on the labour of masses of peasantry, have been necessarily confined to minorities. Today the governments of the super powers and of some of the lesser ones, their authority vastly increased by two world wars, have the power to obliterate each other's populations, although in social democracies they are hard put to govern against the tide of popular demands which may imply economic and social collapse. In authoritarian states the demands have so far been contained at the sacrifice of liberty.

Such has been the sequel to the launching of the Industrial and Technological Revolutions, of democracy and nationalism, when war, in a world of advanced technology and an international political system of sub-Merovingian barbarity writ large, became even more atrocious, culminating in the use of atomic bombs and extending into the current armaments race.

It is not within the design of an historical survey here to recount the tormented history of our immediate times. "Current affairs" cannot become "history" until at least half a century has elapsed, documents have become available and hindsight cleared men's minds. But, looking back over the hard-won achievements of European civilization here surveyed, one is left pondering whether the still archaic political and social institutions of Europe and mankind can adapt themselves to the radical change in environment which modern science and technology have wrought. We are left with the hope that the Truce of Terror so far imposed by modern weapons will buy time for a change in ideas and institutions which may create a political and social order compatible with the awesome powers of modern science.

INDEX